# Bulletproof SSL and TLS

Ivan Ristić

# Bulletproof SSL and TLS

by Ivan Ristić

Copyright © 2014 Feisty Duck Limited. All rights reserved.

Published in August 2014.

ISBN: 978-1-907117-04-6

**Feisty Duck Limited**
*www.feistyduck.com*
*contact@feistyduck.com*

**Address:**

6 Acantha Court
Montpelier Road
London W5 2QP
United Kingdom

**Production editor:** Jelena Girić-Ristić

**Copyeditor:** Melinda Rankin

All rights reserved. No part of this publication may be reproduced, stored in a retrieval system, or transmitted, in any form or by any means, without the prior permission in writing of the publisher.

The author and publisher have taken care in preparation of this book, but make no expressed or implied warranty of any kind and assume no responsibility for errors or omissions. No liability is assumed for incidental or consequential damages in connection with or arising out of the use of the information or programs contained herein.

# Table of Contents

# Preface

You are about to undertake a journey into the mysterious world of cryptography. I've just completed mine—writing this book—and it's been an amazing experience. Although I'd been a user of SSL since its beginnings, I developed a deep interest in it around 2004, when I started to work on my first book, *Apache Security*. About five years later, in 2009, I was looking for something new to do; I decided to spend more time on SSL, and I've been focusing on it ever since. The result is this book.

My main reason to go back to SSL was the thought that I could improve things. I saw an important technology hampered by a lack of tools and documentation. Cryptography is a fascinating subject: it's a field in which when you know more, you actually know less. Or, in other words, the more you know, the more you discover how much you don't know. I can't count how many times I've had the experience of reaching a new level of understanding of a complex topic only to have yet another layer of complexity open up to me; that's what makes the subject amazing.

I spent about two years writing this book. At first, I thought I'd be able to spread the effort so that I wouldn't have to dedicate my life to it, but that wouldn't work. At some point, I realized that things are changing so quickly that I constantly need to go back and rewrite the "finished" chapters. Towards the end, about six months ago, I started to spend every spare moment writing to keep up.

I wrote this book to save you time. I spent the large part of the last five years learning everything I could about SSL/TLS and PKI, and I knew that only a few can afford to do the same. I thought that if I put the most important parts of what I know into a book others might be able to achieve a similar level of understanding in a fraction of the time—and here we are.

This book has the word "bulletproof" in the title, but that doesn't mean that TLS is unbreakable. It does mean that if you follow the advice from this book you'll be able to get the most out of TLS and deploy it as securely as anyone else in the world. It's not always going to be easy—especially with web applications—but if you persist, you'll have better security than 99.99% of servers out there. In fact, even with little effort, you can actually have better security than 99% of the servers on the Internet.

Broadly speaking, there are two paths you can take to read this book. One is to take it easy and start from the beginning. If you have time, this is going to be the more enjoyable approach. But if you want answers quickly, jump straight to chapters 8 and 9. They're going to tell you everything you need to know about deploying secure servers while achieving good performance. After that, use chapters 1 through 7 as a reference and chapters 10 through 16 for practical advice as needed.

## Scope and Audience

This book exists to document everything you need to know about SSL/TLS and PKI for practical, daily work. I aimed for just the right mix of theory, protocol detail, vulnerability and weakness information, and deployment advice to help you get your job done.

As I was writing the book, I imagined representatives of three diverse groups looking over my shoulder and asking me questions:

**System administrators**

Always pressed for time and forced to deal with an ever-increasing number of security issues on their systems, system administrators need reliable advice about TLS so that they can deal with its configuration quickly and efficiently. Turning to the Web for information on this subject is counterproductive, because there's so much incorrect and obsolete documentation out there.

**Developers**

Although SSL initially promised to provide security transparently for any TCP-based protocol, in reality developers play a significant part in ensuring that applications remain secure. This is particularly true for web applications, which evolved around SSL and TLS and incorporated features that can subvert them. In theory, you "just enable encryption"; in practice, you enable encryption but also pay attention to a dozen or so issues, ranging from small to big, that can break your security. In this book, I made a special effort to document every single one of those issues.

**Managers**

Last but not least, I wrote the book for managers who, even though not necessarily involved with the implementation, still have to understand what's going on and make decisions. The security space is getting increasingly complicated, so understanding the attacks and threats is often a job in itself. Often, there isn't any one way to deal with the situation, and the best way often depends on the context.

Overall, you will find very good coverage of HTTP and web applications here but little to no mention of other protocols. This is largely because HTTP is unique in the way it uses encryption, powered by browsers, which have become the most popular application-delivery platform we've ever had. With that power come many problems, which is why there is so much space dedicated to HTTP.

But don't let that deceive you; if you take away the HTTP chapters, the remaining content (about two-thirds of the book) provides generic advice that can be applied to any protocol that uses TLS. The OpenSSL, Java, and Microsoft chapters provide protocol-generic information for their respective platforms.

That said, if you're looking for configuration examples for products other than web servers you won't find them in this book. The main reason is that—unlike with web servers, for which the market is largely split among a few major platforms—there are a great many products of other types. It was quite a challenge to keep the web server advice up-to-date, being faced with nearly constant changes. I wouldn't be able to handle a larger scope. Therefore, my intent is to start providing additional configuration examples online and hope to provide the initial spark for a community to form to keep the advice up-to-date.

# Contents

This book has 16 chapters, which can be grouped into several parts. The parts build on one another to provide a complete picture, starting with theory and ending with practical advice.

The first part, chapters 1 through 3, is the foundation of the book and discusses cryptography, SSL, TLS, and PKI:

- Chapter 1, *SSL, TLS, and Cryptography*, begins with an introduction to SSL and TLS and discusses where these secure protocols fit in the Internet infrastructure. The remainder of the chapter provides an introduction to cryptography and discusses the classic threat model of the active network attacker.

- Chapter 2, *Protocol*, discusses the details of the TLS protocol. I cover TLS 1.2, which is the most recent version. Information about earlier protocol revisions is provided where appropriate. An overview of the protocol evolution from SSL 3 onwards is included at the end for reference.

- Chapter 3, *Public-Key Infrastructure*, is an introduction to Internet PKI, which is the predominant trust model used on the Internet today. The focus is on the standards and organizations as well as governance, ecosystem weaknesses and possible future improvements.

The second part, chapters 4 through 7, details the various problems with trust infrastructure, our security protocols, and their implementations in libraries and programs:

- Chapter 4, *Attacks against PKI*, deals with attacks on the trust ecosystem. It covers all the major CA compromises, detailing the weaknesses, attacks, and consequences. This chapter gives a thorough historical perspective on the security of the PKI ecosystem, which is important for understanding its evolution.

- Chapter 5, *HTTP and Browser Issues*, is all about the relationship between HTTP and TLS, the problems arising from the organic growth of the Web, and the messy interactions between different pieces of the web ecosystem.

- Chapter 6, *Implementation Issues*, deals with issues arising from design and programming mistakes related to random number generation, certificate validation, and other key TLS and PKI functionality. In addition, it discusses voluntary protocol downgrade and truncation attacks and also covers Heartbleed.

- Chapter 7, *Protocol Attacks*, is the longest chapter in the book. It covers all the major protocol flaws discovered in recent years: insecure renegotiation, BEAST, CRIME, Lucky 13, RC4, TIME and BREACH, and Triple Handshake Attack. A brief discussion of Bullrun and its impact on the security of TLS is also included.

The third part, chapters 8 through 10, provides comprehensive advice about deploying TLS in a secure and efficient fashion:

- Chapter 8, *Deployment*, is the map for the entire book and provides step-by-step instructions on how to deploy secure and well-performing TLS servers and web applications.

- Chapter 9, *Performance Optimization*, focuses on the speed of TLS, going into great detail about various performance improvement techniques for those who want to squeeze every bit of speed out of their servers.

- Chapter 10, *HSTS, CSP, and Pinning*, covers some advanced topics that strengthen web applications, such as HTTP Strict Transport Security and Content Security Policy. It also covers pinning, which is an effective way of reducing the large attack surface imposed by our current PKI model.

The fourth and final part consists of chapters 11 through 16, which give practical advice about how to use and configure TLS on major deployment platforms and web servers and how to use OpenSSL to probe server configuration:

- Chapter 11, *OpenSSL Cookbook*, describes the most frequently used OpenSSL functionality, with a focus on installation, configuration, and key and certificate management. The last section in this chapter provides instructions on how to construct and manage a private certification authority.

- Chapter 12, *Testing with OpenSSL*, continues with OpenSSL and explains how to use its command-line tools to test server configuration. Even though it's often much easier to use an automated tool for testing, OpenSSL remains the tool you turn to when you want to be sure about what's going on.

- Chapter 13, *Configuring Apache*, discusses the TLS configuration of the popular Apache httpd web server. This is the first in a series of chapters that provide practical advice to match the theory from the earlier chapters. Each chapter is dedicated to one major technology segment.

- Chapter 14, *Configuring Java and Tomcat*, covers Java (versions 7 and 8) and the Tomcat web server. In addition to configuration information, this chapter includes advice about securing web applications.

- Chapter 15, *Configuring Microsoft Windows and IIS*, discusses the deployment of TLS on the Microsoft Windows platform and the Internet Information Server. This chapter also gives advice about the use of TLS in web applications running under ASP.NET.

- Chapter 16, *Configuring Nginx*, discusses the Nginx web server, covering the features of the recent stable versions as well as some glimpses into the improvements in the development branch.

# SSL versus TLS

It is unfortunate that we have two names for essentially the same protocol. In my experience, most people are familiar with the name SSL and use it in the context of transport layer encryption. Some people, usually those who spend more time with the protocols, use or try to make themselves use the correct name, whichever is right in the given context. It's probably a lost cause. Despite that, I tried to do the same. It was a bit cumbersome at times, but I think I managed it by (1) avoiding either name where possible, (2) mentioning both where advice applies to all versions, and (3) using TLS in all other cases. You probably won't notice, and that's fine.

# SSL Labs

SSL Labs (*www.ssllabs.com*) is a research project I started in 2009 to focus on the practical aspects of SSL/TLS and PKI. I joined Qualys in 2010, taking the project with me. Initially, my main duties were elsewhere, but, as of 2014, SSL Labs has my full attention.

The project largely came out of my realization that the lack of good documentation and tools is a large part of why TLS servers are generally badly configured. (Poor default settings being the other major reason.) Without visibility—I thought—we can't begin to work to solve the problem. Over the years, SSL Labs expanded into four key projects:

**Server test**

The main feature of SSL Labs is the server test, which enables site visitors to check the configuration of any public web server. The test includes dozens of important checks not available elsewhere and gives a comprehensive view of server configuration. The grading system is easy to understand and helps those who are not security experts differentiate between small and big issues. One of the most useful parts of the test is the handshake simulator, which predicts negotiated protocols and cipher suites with about 40 of the most widely used programs and devices. This feature effectively takes out the guesswork out of TLS configuration. In my opinion, it's indispensable.

**Client test**

As a fairly recent addition, the client test is not as well known, but it's nevertheless very useful. Its primary purpose is to help us understand client capabilities across a large number of devices. The results obtained in the tests are used to power the handshake simulator in the server test.

**Best practices**

*SSL/TLS Deployment Best Practices* is a concise and reasonably comprehensive guide that gives definitive advice on TLS server configuration. It's a short document (about 11 pages) that can be absorbed in a small amount of time and used as a server test companion.

**SSL Pulse**

Finally, SSL Pulse is designed to monitor the entire ecosystem and keep us informed about how we're doing as a whole. It started in 2012 by focusing on a core group of TLS-enabled sites selected from Alexa's top 1 million web sites. Since then, SSL Pulse has been providing a monthly snapshot of key ecosystem statistics.

There are also several other smaller projects; you can find out more about them on the SSL Labs web site.

# Online Resources

This book doesn't have an online companion (although you can think of SSL Labs as one), but it does have an online file repository that contains the files referenced in the text. The repository is available at *github.com/ivanr/bulletproof-tls*. In time, I hope to expand this repository to include other useful content that will complement the book.

To be notified of events and news as they happen, follow @ivanristic on Twitter. TLS is all I do these days, and I try to highlight everything that's relevant. There's hardly any noise. In addition, my Twitter account is where I will mention improvements to the book as they happen.

My blog is available at *blog.ivanristic.com*. This is where I'll react to important ecosystem news and discoveries, announce SSL Labs improvements, and publish my research.

If you bought this book in digital form, then you can always log back into your account on the Feisty Duck web site and download the most recent release. A purchase includes unlimited access to the updates of the same edition. Unless you modified your email subscription settings, you'll get an email about book updates whenever there's something sufficiently interesting, but I generally try to keep the numbers of emails to a minimum (and never use the list for any other purpose).

# Feedback

I am fortunate that I can update this book whenever I want to. It's not a coincidence; I made it that way. If I make a change today, it will be available to you tomorrow, after an automated daily build takes place. It's a tad more difficult to update paper books, but, with print on demand, we're able to publish a revision every quarter or so.

Therefore, unlike with many other books that might never see a new edition, your feedback matters. If you find an error, it will be fixed in a few days. The same is true for minor improvements, such as language changes or clarifications. If one of the platforms changes in some way or there's a new development, I can cover it. My aim with this book is to keep it up-to-date for as long as there's interest in it.

Please write to me at ivanr@webkreator.com.

# About the Author

In this section, I get to write about myself in third person; this is my "official" biography:

> *Ivan Ristić is a security researcher, engineer, and author, known especially for his contributions to the web application firewall field and development of ModSecurity, an open source web application firewall, and for his SSL/TLS and PKI research, tools, and guides published on the SSL Labs web site.*

> *He is the author of two books,* Apache Security *and* ModSecurity Handbook, *which he publishes via Feisty Duck, his own platform for continuous writing and publishing. Ivan is an active participant in the security community, and you'll often find him speaking at security conferences such as Black Hat, RSA, OWASP AppSec, and others. He's currently Director of Application Security Research at Qualys.*

I should probably also mention *OpenSSL Cookbook*, which is a short and free ebook that combines Chapter 12 from this book and the *SSL/TLS Deployment Best Practices guide* in one package.

# Acknowledgments

Although I wrote all of the words in this book, I am not the sole author. My words build on an incredible wealth of information about cryptography and computer security scattered among books, standards documents, research papers, conference talks, and blog posts—and even tweets. There's easily hundreds of people whose work made this book what it is. Without them, this book wouldn't exist.

Over the years, I have been fortunate to correspond about computer security with many people who have enriched my own knowledge of this subject. Many of them lent me a hand by reviewing parts of the manuscript. I am grateful for their help. It's been particularly comforting to have the key parts of the book reviewed by those who either designed the standards or broke them and by those who wrote the programs I talk about.

Kenny Paterson was tremendously helpful with his thorough review of the protocol attacks chapter, which is easily the longest and the most complicated part of the book. I suspect he gave me the same treatment his students get, and my writing is much better because of it. It took me an entire week to update the chapter in response to Kenny's comments.

Benne de Weger reviewed the chapters about cryptography and the PKI attacks. Nasko Oskov reviewed the key chapters about the protocol and Microsoft's implementation. Rick Andrews and his colleagues from Symantec helped with the chapters on PKI attacks and browser issues, as did Adam Langley. Marc Stevens wrote to me about PKI attacks and especially about chosen-prefix attacks against MD5 and SHA1. Nadhem AlFardan, Thai Duong, and Juliano Rizzo reviewed the protocol attacks chapter and were very helpful answering my questions about their work. Ilya Grigorik's review of the performance chapter was thorough and his comments very useful. Jakob Schlyter reviewed the chapter about advanced topics (HSTS and CSP), with a special focus on DANE. Rick Bowen and Jeff Trawick reviewed the Apache chapter; Jeff even fixed some things in Apache related to TLS and made me work harder to keep up with the changes. Xuelei Fan and Erik Costlow from Oracle reviewed the Java chapter, as did Mark Thomas, William Sargent, and Jim Manico. Andrei Popov and Ryan Hurst reviewed the Microsoft chapter. Maxim Dounin was always quick to respond to my questions about Nginx and reviewed the chapter on it.

Vincent Bernat's microbenchmarking tool was very useful to write the performance chapter.

Also, a big thanks to my readers who responded to the early versions of this book: Pascal Cuoq, Joost van Dijk, Daniël van Eeden, Brian Howson, Brian King, Colm MacCárthaigh, Pascal Messerli, and Christian Sage.

My special thanks goes to my copyeditor, Melinda Rankin, who was always quick to respond with her edits and adapted to my DocBook-based workflow. I'd be amiss not to mention my employer, Qualys, for supporting my writing and my work on SSL Labs.

# 1 SSL, TLS, and Cryptography

We live in an increasingly connected world. During the last decade of the 20th century the Internet rose to popularity and forever changed how we live our lives. Today we rely on our phones and computers to communicate, buy goods, pay bills, travel, work, and so on. Many of us, with *always-on* devices in our pockets, don't connect to the Internet, we *are* the Internet. There are already more phones than people. The number of smart phones is measured in billions and increases at a fast pace. In the meantime, plans are under way to connect all sorts of devices to the same network. Clearly, we're just getting started.

All the devices connected to the Internet have one thing in common—they rely on the protocols called SSL (*Secure Socket Layer*) and TLS (*Transport Layer Security*) to protect the information in transit.

## Transport Layer Security

When the Internet was originally designed, little thought was given to security. As a result, the core communication protocols are inherently insecure and rely on the honest behavior of all involved parties. That might have worked back in the day, when the Internet consisted of a small number of nodes—mostly universities—but falls apart completely today when everyone is online.

SSL and TLS are cryptographic protocols designed to provide secure communication over insecure infrastructure. What this means is that, if these protocols are properly deployed, you can open a communication channel to an arbitrary service on the Internet, be reasonably sure that you're talking to the correct server, and exchange information safe in knowing that your data won't fall into someone else's hands and that it will be received intact. These protocols protect the communication link or *transport layer*, which is where the name TLS comes from.

Security is not the only goal of TLS. It actually has four main goals, listed here in the order of priority:

**Cryptographic security**

This is the main issue: enable secure communication between any two parties who wish to exchange information.

**Interoperability**

Independent programmers should be able to develop programs and libraries that are able to communicate with one another using common cryptographic parameters.

**Extensibility**

As you will soon see, TLS is effectively a framework for the development and deployment of actual cryptographic protocols. Its important goal is to be independent of the actual cryptographic primitives used, allowing migration from one primitive to another without needing to create new protocols.

**Efficiency**

The final goal is to achieve all of the previous goals at an acceptable performance cost, reducing costly cryptographic operations down to the minimum and providing a session caching scheme to avoid them on subsequent connections.


# Networking Layers

At its core, the Internet is built on top of IP and TCP protocols, which are used to package data into small packets for transport. As these packets travel thousands of miles across the world, they cross many computer systems (called *hops*) in many countries. Because the core protocols don't provide any security by themselves, anyone with access to the communication links can gain full access to the data as well as change the traffic without detection.

IP and TCP aren't the only vulnerable protocols. There's a range of other protocols that are used for *routing*—helping computers find other computers on the network. DNS and BGP are two such protocols. They, too, are insecure and can be hijacked in a variety of ways. If that happens, a connection intended for one computer might be answered by the attacker instead.

When encryption is deployed, the attacker might be able to gain access to the encrypted data, but she wouldn't be able to decrypt it or modify it. To prevent impersonation attacks, SSL and TLS rely on another important technology called PKI (*public-key infrastructure*), which ensures that the traffic is sent to the correct recipient.

To understand where SSL and TLS fit, we're going to take a look at the *Open Systems Interconnection* (OSI) model, which is a conceptual model that can be used to discuss network communication. In short, all functionality is mapped into seven layers. The bottom layer is the closest to the physical communication link; subsequent layers build on top of one another and provide higher levels of abstraction. At the top is the application layer, which carries application data.

> **Note**
>
> It's not always possible to neatly organize real-life protocols into the OSI model. For example, SPDY and HTTP/2 could go into the session layer because they deal with connection management, but they operate after encryption. Layers from five onwards are often fuzzy.

Table 1.1. OSI model layers

| # | OSI Layer | Description | Example protocols |
|---|---|---|---|
| 7 | Application | Application data | HTTP, SMTP, IMAP |
| 6 | Presentation | Data representation, conversion, encryption | SSL/TLS |
| 5 | Session | Management of multiple connections | - |
| 4 | Transport | Reliable delivery of packets and streams | TCP, UDP |
| 3 | Network | Routing and delivery of datagrams between network nodes | IP, IPSec |
| 2 | Data link | Reliable local data connection (LAN) | Ethernet |
| 1 | Physical | Direct physical data connection (cables) | CAT5 |

Arranging communication in this way provides clean separation of concerns; protocols don't need to worry about the functionality implemented by lower layers. Further, protocols at different layers can be added and removed; a protocol at a lower layer can be used for many protocols from higher levels.

SSL and TLS are a great example of how this principle works in practice. They sit above TCP but below higher-level protocols such as HTTP. When encryption is not necessary, we can remove TLS from our model, but that doesn't affect the higher-level protocols, which continue to work directly with TCP. When you do want encryption, you can use it to encrypt HTTP, but also any other TCP protocol, for example SMTP, IMAP and so on.

# Protocol History

SSL protocol was developed at Netscape, back when Netscape Navigator ruled the Internet.[1] The first version of the protocol never saw the light of day, but the next—version 2—was released in November 1994. The first deployment was in Netscape Navigator 1.1, which was released in March 1995.

Developed with little to no consultation with security experts outside Netscape, SSL 2 ended up being a poor protocol with serious weaknesses. This forced Netscape to work on SSL 3, which was released in late 1995. Despite sharing the name with earlier protocol versions, SSL 3 was a brand new protocol design that established the design we know today.

---

[1] For a much more detailed history of the early years of the SSL protocol, I recommend Eric Rescorla's book *SSL and TLS: Designing and Building Secure Systems* (Addison-Wesley, 2001), pages 47–51.

In May 1996, the TLS working group was formed to migrate SSL from Netscape to IETF.[2] The process was painfully slow because of the political fights between Microsoft and Netscape, a consequence of the larger fight to dominate the Web. TLS 1.0 was finally released in January 1999, as RFC 2246. The new protocol was different from SSL 3 only in some minor details, but that was enough for the two revisions to be incompatible. The name was changed to please Microsoft.[3]

The next version, TLS 1.1, wasn't released until April 2006 and contained essentially only security fixes. However, a major change to the protocol was incorporation of *TLS extensions*, which were released a couple of years earlier, in June 2003.

TLS 1.2 was released in August 2008. It added support for authenticated encryption and generally removed all hard-coded security primitives from the specification, making the protocol fully flexible.

The next protocol version, which is currently in development, is shaping to be a major revision aimed at simplifying the design, removing many of the weaker and less desirable features, and improving performance. You can follow the discussions on the TLS working group mailing list.[4]

# Cryptography

*Cryptography* is the science and art of secure communication. Although we associate encryption with the modern age, we've actually been using cryptography for thousands of years. The first mention of a *scytale*, an encryption tool, dates to the seventh century BC.[5] Cryptography as we know it today was largely born in the twentieth century and for military use. Now it's part of our everyday lives.

When cryptography is correctly deployed, it addresses the three core requirements of security: keeping secrets (*confidentiality*), verifying identities (*authenticity*), and ensuring safe transport (*integrity*).

In the rest of this chapter, I will discuss the basic building blocks of cryptography, with the goal of showing where additional security comes from. I will also discuss how cryptography is commonly attacked. Cryptography is a very diverse field and has a strong basis in mathematics, but I will keep my overview at a high level, with the aim of giving you a foundation that will enable you to follow the discussion in the rest of the text. Elsewhere in the book, where the topic demands, I will discuss some parts of cryptography in more detail.

---

[2] TLS Working Group [fsty.uk/b1] (IETF, retrieved 23 June 2014)

[3] Security Standards and Name Changes in the Browser Wars [fsty.uk/b2] (Tim Dierks, 23 May 2014)

[4] TLS working group mailing list archives [fsty.uk/b3] (IETF, retrieved 19 July 2014)

[5] Scytale [fsty.uk/b4] (Wikipedia, retrieved 5 June 2014)

---

**Note**

If you want to spend more time learning about cryptography, there's plenty of good literature available. My favorite book on this topic is *Understanding Cryptography*, written by Christof Paar and Jan Pelzl and published by Springer in 2010.

# Building Blocks

At the lowest level, cryptography relies on various *cryptographic primitives*. Each primitive is designed with a particular useful functionality in mind. For example, we might use one primitive for encryption and another for integrity checking. The primitives alone are not very useful, but we can combine them into *schemes* and *protocols* to provide robust security.

## Who Are Alice and Bob?

*Alice* and *Bob* are names commonly used for convenience when discussing cryptography.[6] They make the otherwise often dry subject matter more interesting. Ron Rivest is credited for the first use of these names in the 1977 paper that introduced the RSA cryptosystem.[7] Since then, a number of other names have entered cryptographic literature. In this chapter, I use the name *Eve* for an attacker with an eavesdropping ability and *Mallory* for an active attacker who can interfere with network traffic.

## Symmetric Encryption

*Symmetric encryption* (or *private-key cryptography*) is a method for obfuscation that enables secure transport of data over insecure communication channels. To communicate securely, Alice and Bob first agree on the encryption algorithm and a secret key. Later on, when Alice wants to send some data to Bob, she uses the secret key to encrypt the data. Bob uses the same key to decrypt it. Eve, who has access to the communication channel and can see the encrypted data, doesn't have the key and thus can't access the original data. Alice and Bob can continue to communicate securely for as long as they keep the secret key safe.

---

[6] Alice and Bob [fsty.uk/b5] (Wikipedia, retrieved 5 June 2014)

[7] Security's inseparable couple [fsty.uk/b6] (Network World, 2005)

Figure 1.1. Symmetric encryption

> **Note**
>
> Three terms are commonly used when discussing encryption: *plaintext* is the data in its original form, *cipher* is the algorithm used for encryption, and *ciphertext* is the data after encryption.

Symmetric encryption goes back thousands of years. For example, to encrypt with a *substitution cipher*, you replace each letter in the alphabet with some other letter; to decrypt, you reverse the process. In this case, there is no key; the security depends on keeping the method itself secure. That was the case with most early ciphers. Over time, we adopted a different approach, following the observation of a nineteenth-century cryptographer named *Auguste Kerckhoffs*:[8]

> *A cryptosystem should be secure even if the attacker knows everything about the system, except the secret key.*

Although it might seem strange at first, Kerckhoffs's principle—as it has come to be known—makes sense if you consider the following:

- For an encryption algorithm to be useful, it must be shared with others. As the number of people with access to the algorithm increases, the likelihood that the algorithm will fall into the enemy's hands increases too.

- A single algorithm without a key is very inconvenient to use in large groups; everyone can decrypt everyone's communication.

- It's very difficult to design good encryption algorithms. The more exposure and scrutiny an algorithm gets, the more secure it can be. Cryptographers recommend a conservative approach when adopting new algorithms; it usually takes years of breaking attempts until a cipher is considered secure.

---

[8] la cryptographie militaire [fsty.uk/b7] (Fabien Petitcolas, retrieved 1 June 2014)

Chapter 1: SSL, TLS, and Cryptography

A good encryption algorithm is one that produces seemingly random ciphertext, which can't be analyzed by the attacker to reveal any information about plaintext. For example, the substitution cipher is not a good algorithm, because the attacker could determine the frequency of each letter of ciphertext and compare it with the frequency of the letters in the English language. Because some letters appear more often than others, the attacker could use his observations to recover the plaintext. If a cipher is good, the only option for the attacker should be to try all possible decryption keys, otherwise known as an *exhaustive key search*.

At this point, the security of ciphertext depends entirely on the key. If the key is selected from a large *keyspace* and the breaking encryption requires iterating through a prohibitively large number of possible keys, then we say that a cipher is *computationally secure*.

> **Note**
>
> The common way to measure encryption strength is via key length; the assumption is that keys are essentially random, which means that the keyspace is defined by the number of bits in a key. As an example, a 128-bit key (which is considered very secure) is one of 340 billion billion billlion billion possible combinations.

Ciphers can be divided into two groups: stream and block ciphers.

## Stream Ciphers

Conceptually, *stream ciphers* operate in a way that matches how we tend to imagine encryption. You feed one byte of plaintext to the encryption algorithm, and out comes one byte of ciphertext. The reverse happens at the other end. The process is repeated for as long as there is data to process.

At its core, a stream cipher produces an infinite stream of seemingly random data called a *keystream*. To perform encryption, one byte of keystream is combined with one byte of plaintext using the XOR logical operation. Because XOR is reversible, to decrypt you perform XOR of ciphertext with the same keystream byte. This process is illustrated in Figure 1.2, "RC4 encryption".

Figure 1.2. RC4 encryption

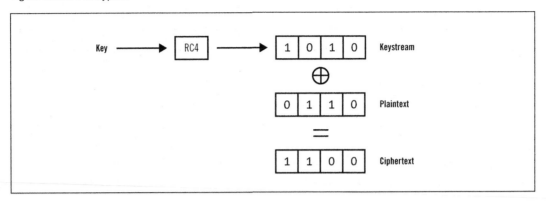

An encryption process is considered secure if the attacker can't predict which keystream bytes are at which positions. For this reason, it is vital that stream ciphers are never used with the same key more than once. This is because, in practice, attackers know or can predict plaintext at certain locations (think of HTTP requests being encrypted; things such as request method, protocol version, and header names are the same across many requests). When you know the plaintext and can observe the corresponding ciphertext, you uncover parts of the keystream. You can use that information to uncover the same parts of future ciphertexts if the same key is used. To work around this problem, stream algorithms are used with one-time keys derived from long-term keys.

RC4 is the best-known stream cipher.[9] It became popular due to its speed and simplicity, but it's no longer considered secure. I discuss its weaknesses at some length in the section called "RC4 Weaknesses". Other modern and secure stream ciphers are promoted by the *ECRYPT Stream Cipher Project.*[10]

## Block Ciphers

*Block ciphers* encrypt entire blocks of data at a time; modern block ciphers tend to use a block size of 128 bits (16 bytes). A block cipher is a transformation function: it takes some input and produces seemingly random output from it. For every possible input combination, there is exactly one output, as long as the key stays the same. A key property of block ciphers is that a small variation in input (e.g., a change of one bit anywhere) produces a large variation (e.g., most bits in the output change).

On their own, block ciphers are not very useful because of several limitations. First, you can only use them to encrypt data lengths equal to the size of the encryption block. To use a block cipher in practice, you need a scheme to handle data of arbitrary length and data that

---

[9] RC4 [fsty.uk/b8] (Wikipedia, retrieved 1 June 2014)

[10] eSTREAM: the ECRYPT Stream Cipher Project [fsty.uk/b9] (European Network of Excellence in Cryptology II, retrieved 1 June 2014)

Chapter 1: SSL, TLS, and Cryptography

is not the exact multiple of the block size. Another problem is that block ciphers are *deterministic*; they always produce the same output for the same input. This property opens up a number of attacks and needs to be dealt with.

In practice, block ciphers are used via encryption schemes called *block cipher modes*, which smooth over the limitations and sometimes add authentication to the mix. Block ciphers can also be used as the basis for other cryptographic primitives, such as hash functions, message authentication codes, pseudorandom generators, and even stream ciphers.

The world's most popular block cipher is AES (short for *Advanced Encryption Standard*), which is available in strengths of 128, 192, and 256 bits.[11]

## Padding

One of the challenges with block ciphers is figuring out how to handle encryption of data lengths smaller than the encryption block size. For example, 128-bit AES requires 16 bytes of input data and produces the same amount as output. This is fine if you have all of your data in 16-byte blocks, but what do you do when you have less than that? One approach is to append some extra data to the end of your plaintext. This extra data is known as *padding*.

The padding can't consist of just any random data. It must follow some format that allows the receiver to see the padding for what it is and know exactly how many bytes to discard. In TLS, the last byte of an encryption block contains padding length, which indicates how many bytes of padding (excluding the padding length byte) there are. All padding bytes are set to the same value as the padding length byte. This approach enables the receiver to check that the padding is correct.

Figure 1.3. Example of TLS padding

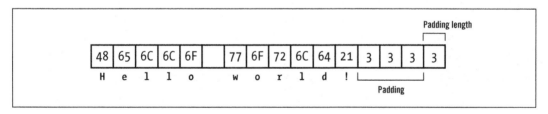

To discard the padding after decryption, the receiver examines the last byte in the data block and removes it. After that, he removes the indicated number of bytes while checking that they all have the same value.

## Hash Functions

A *hash function* is an algorithm that converts input of arbitrary length into fixed-size output. The result of a hash function is often called simply a *hash*. Hash functions are common-

---

[11] Advanced Encryption Standard [fsty.uk/b10] (Wikipedia, retrieved 1 June 2014)

ly used in programming, but not all hash functions are suitable for use in cryptography. *Cryptographic hash functions* are hash functions that have several additional properties:

**Preimage resistance**

> Given a hash, it's computationally unfeasible to find or construct a message that produces it.

**Second preimage resistance**

> Given a message and its hash, it's computationally unfeasible to find a different message with the same hash.

**Collision resistance**

> It's computationally unfeasible to find two messages that have the same hash.

Hash functions are most commonly used as a compact way to represent and compare large amounts of data. For example, rather than compare two files directly (which might be difficult, for example, if they are stored in different parts of the world), you can compare their hashes. Hash functions are often called *fingerprints*, *message digests*, or simply *digests*.

The most commonly used hash function today is SHA1, which has output of 160 bits. Because SHA1 is considered weak, upgrading to its stronger variant, SHA256, is recommended. Unlike with ciphers, the strength of a hash function doesn't equal the hash length. Because of the *birthday paradox* (a well-known problem in probability theory),[12] the strength of a hash function is at most one half of the hash length.

## Message Authentication Codes

A hash function could be used to verify data integrity, but only if the hash of the data is transported separately from the data itself. Otherwise, an attacker could modify both the message and the hash, easily avoiding detection. A *message authentication code* (MAC) or a *keyed-hash* is a cryptographic function that extends hashing with authentication. Only those in possession of the *hashing key* can produce a valid MAC.

MACs are commonly used in combination with encryption. Even though Eve can't decrypt ciphertext, she can modify it in transit if there is no MAC; *encryption provides confidentiality but not integrity*. If Eve is smart about how she's modifying ciphertext, she could trick Bob into accepting a forged message as authentic. When a MAC is sent along with ciphertext, Bob (who shares the hashing key with Alice) can be sure that the message has not been tampered with.

Any hash function can be used as the basis for a MAC using a construction known as HMAC (short for *hash-based message authentication code*).[13] In essence, HMAC works by interleaving the hashing key with the message in a secure way.

---

[12] Birthday problem [fsty.uk/b11] (Wikipedia, retrieved 6 June 2014)

[13] RFC 2104: HMAC: Keyed-Hashing for Message Authentication [fsty.uk/b12] (Krawczyk et al., February 1997)

## Block Cipher Modes

*Block cipher modes* are cryptographic schemes designed to extend block ciphers to encrypt data of arbitrary length. All block cipher modes support confidentiality, but some combine it with authentication. Some modes transform block ciphers to produce stream ciphers.

There are many output modes, and they are usually referred to by their acronyms: ECB, CBC, CFB, OFB, CTR, GCM, and so forth. (Don't worry about what the acronyms stand for.) I will cover only ECB and CBC here: ECB as an example of how not to design a block cipher mode and CBC because it's still the main mode in SSL and TLS. GCM is a relatively new addition to TLS, available starting with version 1.2; it provides confidentiality and integrity, and it's currently the best mode available.

### Electronic Codebook Mode

*Electronic Codebook* (ECB) mode is the simplest possible block cipher mode. It supports only data lengths that are the exact multiples of the block size; if you have data of different length, then you need to apply padding beforehand. To perform encryption, you split the data into chunks that match the block size and encrypt each block individually.

The simplicity of ECB is its downside. Because block ciphers are deterministic (i.e., they always produce the same result when the input is the same), so is ECB. This has serious consequences: (1) patterns in ciphertext will appear that match patterns in plaintext; (2) the attacker can detect when a message is repeated; and (3) an attacker who can observe ciphertext and submit arbitrary plaintext for encryption (commonly possible with HTTP and in many other situations) can, given enough attempts, *guess* the plaintext. This is what the BEAST attack against TLS was about; I discuss it in the section called "BEAST" in Chapter 7.

### Cipher Block Chaining Mode

*Cipher Block Chaining* (CBC) mode is the next step up from ECB. To address the deterministic nature of ECB, CBC introduces the concept of the *initialization vector* (IV), which makes output different every time, even when input is the same.

Figure 1.4. RC4 encryption

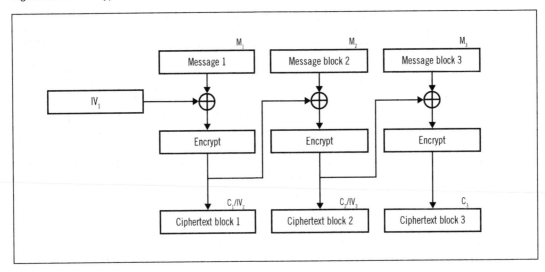

The process starts by generating a random (and thus unpredictable) IV, which is the same length as the encryption block size. Before encryption, the first block of plaintext is combined with the IV using XOR. This masks the plaintext and ensures that the ciphertext is always different. For the next encryption block, the ciphertext of the previous block is used as the IV, and so forth. As a result, all of the individual encryption operations are part of the same *chain*, which is where the mode name comes from. Crucially, the IV is transmitted on the wire to the receiving party, who needs it to perform decryption successfully.

## Asymmetric Encryption

Symmetric encryption does a great job at handling large amounts of data at great speeds, but it leaves a lot to be desired as soon as the number of parties involved increases:

- Members of the same group must share the same key. The more people join a group, the more exposed the group becomes to the key compromise.

- For better security, you could use a different key for every two people, but this approach doesn't scale. Although three people need only three keys, ten people would need 45 ($9 + 8 + \ldots + 1$) keys. A thousand people would need 499,550 keys!

- Symmetric encryption can't be used on unattended systems to secure data. Because the process can be reversed by using the same key, a compromise of such a system leads to the compromise of all data stored in the system.

*Asymmetric encryption* (also known as *public-key cryptography*) is a different approach to encryption that uses two keys instead of one. One of the keys is *private*; the other is *public*. As the names suggest, one of these keys is intended to be private, and the other is intended to be shared with everyone. There's a special mathematical relationship between these keys that enables some useful features. If you encrypt data using someone's public key, only their corresponding private key can decrypt it. On the other hand, if data is encrypted with the private key anyone can use the public key to unlock the message. The latter operation doesn't provide confidentiality, but it does function as a digital signature.

Figure 1.5. Asymmetric encryption

Asymmetric encryption makes secure communication in large groups much easier. Assuming that you can securely share your public key widely (a job for PKI, which I discuss in Chapter 3, *Public-Key Infrastructure*), anyone can send you a message that only you can read. If they also sign that message using their private key, you know exactly whom it is from.

Despite its interesting properties, public-key cryptography is rather slow and unsuitable for use with large quantities of data. For this reason, it's usually deployed for authentication and negotiation of private keys, which are then used for fast symmetric encryption.

*RSA* (named from the initials of Ron Rivest, Adi Shamir, and Leonard Adleman) is by far the most popular asymmetric encryption method deployed today.[14] The recommended strength for RSA today is 2,048 bits, which is equivalent to about 112 symmetric bits. I'll discuss the strength of cryptography in more detail later in this chapter.

## Digital Signatures

A *digital signature* is a cryptographic scheme that makes it possible to verify the authenticity of a digital message or document. The MAC, which I described earlier, is a type of digital signature; it can be used to verify authenticity provided that the secret hashing key is securely exchanged ahead of time. Although this type of verification is very useful, it's limited because it still relies on a private secret key.

---

[14] RSA [fsty.uk/b13] (Wikipedia, retrieved 2 June 2014)

Digital signatures similar to the real-life handwritten ones are possible with the help of public-key cryptography; we can exploit its asymmetric nature to devise an algorithm that allows a message signed by a private key to be verified with the corresponding public key.

The exact approach depends on the selected public-key cryptosystem. For example, RSA can be used for encryption and decryption. If something is encrypted with a private RSA key, only the corresponding public key can decrypt it. We can use this property for digital signing if we combine it with hash functions:

1. Calculate a hash of the document you wish to sign; no matter the size of the input document, the output will always be fixed, for example, 256 bits for SHA256.

2. Encode the resulting hash and some additional metadata. For example, the receiver will need to know the hashing algorithm you used before she can process the signature.

3. Encrypt the encoded hash using the private key; the result will be the signature, which you can append to the document as proof of authenticity.

To verify the signature, the receiver takes the document and calculates the hash independently using the same algorithm. Then, she uses your public key to decrypt the message and recover the hash, confirm that the correct algorithms were used, and compare with the decrypted hash with the one she calculated. The strength of this signature scheme depends on the individual strengths of the encryption, hashing, and encoding components.

> **Note**
>
> Not all digital signature algorithms function in the same way as RSA. In fact, RSA is an exception, because it can be used for both encryption and digital signing. Other popular public key algorithms, such as DSA and ECDSA, can't be used for encryption and rely on different approaches for signing.

## Random Number Generation

In cryptography, all security depends on the quality of random number generation. You've already seen in this chapter that security relies on known encryption algorithms and secret keys. Those keys are simply very long random numbers.

The problem with random numbers is that computers tend to be very predictable. They follow instructions to the letter. If you tell them to generate a random number, they probably won't do a very good job.[15] This is because truly random numbers can be obtained only by observing certain physical processes. In absence of that, computers focus on collecting small

---

[15] Some newer processors have built-in random number generators that are suitable for use in cryptography. There are also specialized external devices (e.g., in the form of USB sticks) that can be added to feed additional entropy to the operating system.

amounts of *entropy*. This usually means monitoring keystrokes and mouse movement and the interaction with various peripheral devices, such as hard disks.

Entropy collected in this way is a type of *true random number generator* (TRNG), but the approach is not reliable enough to use directly. For example, you might need to generate a 4,096-bit key, but the system might have only a couple of hundreds of bits of entropy available. If there are no reliable external events to collect enough entropy, the system might stall.

For this reason, in practice we rely on *pseudorandom number generators* (PRNGs), which use small amounts of true random data to get them going. This process is known as *seeding*. From the seed, PRNGs produce unlimited amounts of pseudorandom data on demand. General-purpose PRNGs are often used in programming, but they are not appropriate for cryptography, even if their output is statistically seemingly random. *Cryptographic pseudorandom number generators* (CPRNGs) are PRNGs that are also unpredictable. This attribute is crucial for security; an adversary mustn't be able to reverse-engineer a CPRNGs internal state by observing its output.

# Protocols

Cryptographic primitives such as encryption and hashing algorithms are seldom useful by themselves. We combine them into *schemes* and *protocols* so that we can satisfy complex security requirements. To illustrate how we might do that, let's consider a simplistic cryptographic protocol that allows Alice and Bob to communicate securely. We'll aim for all three main requirements: confidentiality, integrity, and authentication.

Let's assume that our protocol allows exchange of an arbitrary number of messages. Because symmetric encryption is very good at encrypting bulk data, we might select our favorite algorithm to use for this purpose, say, AES. With AES, Alice and Bob can exchange secure messages, and Mallory won't be able to recover the contents. But that's not quite enough, because Mallory can do other things, for example, modify the messages without being detected. To fix this problem, we can calculate a MAC of each message using a hashing key known only to Alice and Bob. When we send a message, we send along the MAC as well.

Now, Mallory can't modify the messages any longer. However, she could still drop or replay arbitrary messages. To deal with this, we extend our protocol to assign a sequence number to each message; crucially, we make the sequences part of the MAC calculation. If we see a gap in the sequence numbers, then we know that there's a message missing. If we see a sequence number duplicate, we detect a replay attack. For best results, we should also use a special message to mark the end of the conversation. Without such a message, Mallory would be able to end (truncate) the conversation undetected.

With all of these measures in place, the best Mallory can do is prevent Alice and Bob from talking to one another. There's nothing we can do about that.

So far, so good, but we're still missing a big piece: how are Alice and Bob going to negotiate the two needed keys (one for encryption and the other for integrity validation) in the presence of Mallory? We can solve this problem by adding two additional steps to the protocol.

First, we use public-key cryptography to authenticate each party at the beginning of the conversation. For example, Alice could generate a random number and ask Bob to sign it to prove that it's really him. Bob could ask Alice to do the same.

With authentication out of the way, we can use a *key-exchange scheme* to negotiate encryption keys securely. For example, Alice could generate all the keys and send them to Bob by encrypting them with his public key; this is how the RSA key exchange works. Alternatively, we could have also used a protocol known as *Diffie-Hellman* (DH) key exchange for this purpose. The latter is slower, but it has better security properties.

In the end, we ended up with a protocol that (1) starts with a handshake phase that includes authentication and key exchange, (2) follows with the data exchange phase with confidentiality and integrity, and (3) ends with a shutdown sequence. At a high level, our protocol is similar to the work done by SSL and TLS.

## Attacking Cryptography

Complex systems can usually be attacked in a variety of ways, and cryptography is no exception. First, you can attack the cryptographic primitives themselves. If a key is small, the adversary can use brute force to recover it. Such attacks usually require a lot of processing power as well as time. It's easier (for the attacker) if the used primitive has known vulnerabilities, in which case he can use analytic attacks to achieve the goal faster.

Cryptographic primitives are generally very well understood, because they are relatively straightforward and do only one thing. Schemes are often easier to attack because they introduce additional complexity. In some cases, even cryptographers argue about the right way to perform certain operations. But both are relatively safe compared to protocols, which tend to introduce far more complexity and have a much larger attack surface.

Then, there are attacks against protocol *implementation*; in other words, exploitation of software bugs. For example, most cryptographic libraries are written in low-level languages such as C (and even assembly, for performance reasons), which make it very easy to introduce catastrophic programming errors. Even in the absence of bugs, sometimes great skill is needed to implement the primitives, schemes, and protocols in such a way that they can't be abused. For example, naïve implementations of certain algorithms can be exploited in *timing attacks*, in which the attacker breaks encryption by observing how long certain operations take.

It is also common that programmers with little experience in cryptography nevertheless attempt to implement—and even design—cryptographic protocols and schemes, with predictably insecure results.

For this reason, it is often said that cryptography is bypassed, not attacked. What this means is that the primitives are solid, but the rest of the software ecosystem isn't. Further, the keys are an attractive target: why spend months to brute-force a key when it might be much easier to break into a server to obtain it? Many cryptographic failures can be prevented by following simple rules such as these: (1) use well-established protocols and never design your own schemes; (2) use high-level libraries and never write code that deals with cryptography directly; and (3) use well-established primitives with sufficiently strong key sizes.

## Measuring Strength

We measure the strength of cryptography using the number of operations that need to be performed to break a particular primitive, presented as *bits* of security. Deploying with strong key sizes is the easiest thing to get right, and the rules are simple: 128 bits of security ($2^{128}$ operations) is sufficient for most deployments; use 256 bits if you need very long-term security or a big safety margin.

> **Note**
>
> The strength of symmetric cryptographic operations increases exponentially as more bits are added. This means that increasing key size by one bit makes it twice as strong.

In practice, the situation is somewhat more complicated, because not all operations are equivalent in terms of security. As a result, different bit values are used for symmetric operations, asymmetric operations, elliptic curve cryptography, and so on. You can use the information in Table 1.2, "Security levels and equivalent strength in bits, adapted from ECRYPT2 (2012)" to convert from one size to another.

Table 1.2. Security levels and equivalent strength in bits, adapted from ECRYPT2 (2012)

| # | Protection | Sym-metric | Asym-metric | DH | Elliptic Curve | Hash |
|---|-----------|-----------|------------|------|---------------|------|
| 1 | Attacks in real time by individuals | 32 | - | - | - | - |
| 2 | Very short-term protection against small organizations | 64 | 816 | 816 | 128 | 128 |
| 3 | Short-term protection against medium organizations | 72 | 1,008 | 1,008 | 144 | 144 |
| 4 | Very short-term protection against agencies | 80 | 1,248 | 1,248 | 160 | 160 |
| 5 | Short-term protection (10 years) | 96 | 1,776 | 1,776 | 192 | 192 |
| 6 | Medium-term protection (20 years) | 112 | 2,432 | 2,432 | 224 | 224 |
| 7 | Long-term protection (30 years) | 128 | 3,248 | 3,248 | 256 | 256 |
| 8 | Long-term protection and increased defense from quantum computers | 256 | 15,424 | 15,424 | 512 | 512 |

The data, which I adapted from a 2012 report on key and algorithm strength,[16] shows rough mappings from bits of one type to bits of another, but it also defines strength in relation to attacker capabilities and time. Although we tend to discuss whether an asset is secure (assuming *now*), in reality security is a function of time. The strength of encryption changes, because as time goes by computers get faster and cheaper. Security is also a function of resources. A key of a small size might be impossible for an individual to break, but doing so could be within the reach of an agency. For this reason, when discussing security it's more useful to ask questions such as "secure against whom?" and "secure for how long?"

> **Note**
>
> The strength of cryptography can't be measured accurately, which is why you will find many different recommendations. Most of them are very similar, with small differences. In my experience, ENISA (the *European Union Agency for Network and Information Security*) provides useful high-level documents that offer clear guidance[17] at various levels.[18] To view and compare other recommendations, visit *key-length.com*.[19]

Although the previous table provides a lot of useful information, you might find it difficult to use because the values don't correspond to commonly used key sizes. In practice, you'll find the following table more useful to convert from one set of bits to another:[20]

Table 1.3. Encryption strength mapping for commonly used key sizes

| Symmetric | RSA / DSA / DH | Elliptic curve crypto | Hash |
|-----------|----------------|-----------------------|------|
| 80 | 1,024 | 160 | 160 |
| 112 | 2,048 | 224 | 224 |
| 128 | 3,072 | 256 | 256 |
| 256 | 15,360 | 512 | 512 |

# Man-in-the-Middle Attack

Most attacks against transport-layer security come in the form of a *man-in-the-middle* (MITM) attack. What this means is that in addition to the two parties involved in a conversation there is a malicious party. If the attacker is just listening in on the conversation, we're talking about a *passive network attack*. If the attacker is actively modifying the traffic or influencing the conversation in some other way, we're talking about an *active network attack*.

---

[16] ECRYPT2 Yearly Report on Algorithms and Keysizes [fsty.uk/b14] (European Network of Excellence for Cryptology II, 30 September 2012)

[17] Algorithms, Key Sizes and Parameters Report [fsty.uk/b15] (ENISA, 29 October 2013)

[18] Recommended cryptographic measures - Securing personal data [fsty.uk/b16] (ENISA, 4 November 2013)

[19] BlueKrypt: Cryptographic Key Length Recommendation [fsty.uk/b17] (BlueKrypt, retrieved 4 June 2014)

[20] NIST Special Publication 800-57: Recommendation for Key Management – Part 1: General, Revision 3 [fsty.uk/b18] (NIST, July 2012)

Figure 1.6. Conceptual SSL/TLS threat model

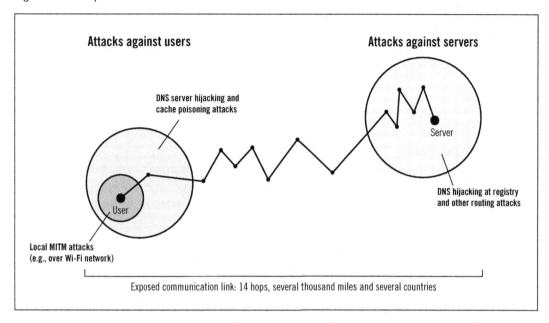

## Gaining Access

In many cases, attacks require proximity to the victim or the server or access to the communication infrastructure. Whoever has access to the cables and intermediary communication nodes (e.g., routers) can see the packets as they travel across the wire and interfere with them. Access can be obtained by tapping the cables,[21] in collaboration with telecoms,[22] or by hacking the equipment.[23]

Conceptually, the easiest way to execute a MITM attack is by joining a network and rerouting the victims' traffic through a malicious node. Wireless networks without authentication, which so many people use these days, are particularly vulnerable, because anyone can join.

Other ways to attack include interfering with the routing infrastructure for domain name resolution, IP address routing, and so on.

### ARP spoofing

*Address Resolution Protocol* (ARP) is used on local networks to associate network MAC addresses[24] with IP addresses. An attacker with access to the network can claim any IP address and effectively reroute traffic.

---

[21] The Creepy, Long-Standing Practice of Undersea Cable Tapping [fsty.uk/b19] (The Atlantic, 16 July 2013)

[22] New Details About NSA's Collaborative Relationships With America's Biggest Telecom Companies From Snowden Docs [fsty.uk/b20] (Washington Post, 30 August 2013)

[23] Photos of an NSA "upgrade" factory show Cisco router getting implant [fsty.uk/b21] (Ars Technica, 14 May 2014)

[24] In this case, MAC stands for *media access control*. It's a unique identifier assigned to networking cards during manufacture.

---

**WPAD hijacking**

*Web Proxy Auto-Discovery Protocol* (WPAD) is used by browsers to automatically retrieve HTTP proxy configuration. WPAD uses several methods, including DHCP
and DNS. To attack WPAD, an attacker starts a proxy on the local network and an-
nounces it to the local clients who look for it.

**DNS hijacking**

By hijacking a domain name with the registrar or changing the DNS configuration,
an attacker can hijack all traffic intended for that domain name.

**DNS cache poisoning**

*DNS cache poisoning* is a type of attack that exploits weaknesses in caching DNS servers and enables the attacker to inject invalid domain name information into the
cache. After a successful attack, all users of the affected DNS server will be given invalid information.

**BGP route hijacking**

*Border Gateway Protocol* (BGP) is a routing protocol used by the core internet routers
to discover where exactly IP address blocks are located. If an invalid route is accepted
by one or more routers, all traffic for a particular IP address block can be redirected
elsewhere, that is, to the attacker.

## Passive Attacks

Passive attacks are most useful against unencrypted traffic. During 2013, it became apparent
that government agencies around the world routinely monitor and store large amounts of
internet traffic. For example, it is alleged that GCHQ, the British spy agency, records all UK
internet traffic and keeps it for three days.[25] Your email messages, photos, internet chats,
and other data could be sitting in a database somewhere, waiting to be cross-referenced and
correlated for whatever purpose. If bulk traffic is handled like this, it's reasonable to expect
that specific traffic is stored for much longer and perhaps indefinitely. In response to this
and similar discoveries, the IETF declared that "pervasive monitoring is an attack" and
should be defended against by using encryption whenever possible.[26]

Even against encrypted traffic, passive attacks can be useful as an element in the overall
strategy. For example, you could store captured encrypted traffic until such a time when you
can break the encryption. Just because some things are difficult to do today doesn't mean
that they'll be difficult ten years from now, as computers get more powerful and cheaper and
as weaknesses in cryptographic primitives are discovered.

To make things worse, computer systems often contain a critical configuration weakness
that allows for retroactive decryption of recorded traffic. The most common key-exchange

---

[25] GCHQ taps fibre-optic cables for secret access to world's communications [fsty.uk/b22] (The Guardian, 21 June 2013)

[26] RFC 7258: Pervasive Monitoring Is an Attack [fsty.uk/b23] (S. Farrell and H. Tschofenig, May 2014)

---

mechanism in TLS is based on the RSA algorithm; on the systems that use this approach, the RSA key used for the key exchange can also be used to decrypt all previous conversations. Other key-exchange mechanisms don't suffer from this problem and are said to support *forward secrecy*. Unfortunately, most stay with the RSA algorithm. For example, Lavabit, the encrypted email service famously used by Edward Snowden, didn't support forward secrecy. Using a court order, the FBI compelled Lavabit to disclose their encryption key.[27] With the key in their possession, the FBI could decrypt any recorded traffic (if they had any, of course).

Passive attacks work very well, because there is still so much unencrypted traffic and because when collecting in bulk the process can be fully automated. As an illustration, in July 2014 only 58% of email arriving to Gmail was encrypted.[28]

## Active Attacks

When someone talks about MITM attacks, they most commonly refer to active network attacks in which Mallory interferes with the traffic in some way. Traditionally, MITM attacks target authentication to trick Alice into thinking she's talking to Bob. If the attack is successful, Mallory receives messages from Alice and forwards them to Bob. The messages are encrypted when Alice sends them, but that's not a problem, because she's sending them to Mallory, who can decrypt them using the keys she negotiated with Alice.

When it comes to TLS, the ideal case for Mallory is when she can present a certificate that Alice will accept as valid. In that case, the attack is seamless and almost impossible to detect. [29] A valid certificate could be obtained by playing the public key infrastructure ecosystem. There have been many such attacks over the years; in Chapter 4, *Attacks against PKI* I document the ones that are publicly known. A certificate that *seems* valid could be constructed if there are bugs in the validation code that could be exploited. Historically, this is an area in which bugs are common. I discuss several examples in Chapter 6, *Implementation Issues*. Finally, if everything else fails, Mallory could present an invalid certificate and hope that Alice overrides the certificate warning. This happened in Syria a couple of years ago.[30]

The rise of browsers as a powerful application-delivery platform created additional attack vectors that can be exploited in active network attacks. In this case, authentication is not attacked, but the victims' browsers are instrumented by the attacker to submit specially crafted requests that are used to subvert encryption. These attack vectors have been exploited in recent years to attack TLS in novel ways; you can find more information about them in Chapter 7, *Protocol Attacks*.

---

[27] Lavabit [fsty.uk/b24] (Wikipedia, retrieved 4 June 2014)

[28] Transparency Report: Email encryption in transit [fsty.uk/b25] (Google Gmail, retrieved 27 July 2014)

[29] Unless you're very, very paranoid, and keep track of all the certificates previously encountered. There are some browser add-ons that do this (e.g., Certificate Patrol for Firefox).

[30] A Syrian Man-In-The-Middle Attack against Facebook [fsty.uk/b26] (The Electronic Frontier Foundation, 5 May 2011)

Active attacks can be very powerful, but they're more difficult to scale. Whereas passive attacks only need to make copies of observed packets (which is a simple operation), active attacks require much more processing and effort to track individual connections. As a result, they require much more software and hardware. Rerouting large amounts of traffic is difficult to do without being noticed. Similarly, fraudulent certificates are difficult to use successfully for large-scale attacks because there are so many individuals and organizations who are keeping track of certificates used by various web sites. The approach with the best chance of success is exploitation of implementation bugs that can be used to bypass authentication, but such bugs, devastating as they are, are relatively rare.

For these reasons, active attacks are most likely to be used against individual, high-value targets. Such attacks can't be automated, which means that they require extra work, cost a lot, and are thus more difficult to justify.

There are some indications that the NSA deployed extensive infrastructure that enables them to attack almost arbitrary computers on the Internet, under the program called *QuantumInsert*.[31]

This program, which is a variation on the MITM theme, doesn't appear to target encryption; instead, it's used to deliver browser exploits against selected individuals. By placing special packet-injection nodes at important points in the communication infrastructure, the NSA is able to respond to connection requests faster than the real servers and redirect some traffic to the exploitation servers instead.

---

[31] Attacking Tor: How the NSA Targets Users' Online Anonymity [fsty.uk/b27] (Bruce Schneier, 4 October 2013)

# 2 Protocol

TLS is a cryptographic protocol designed to secure a conversation that consists of an arbitrary number of messages between two parties. In this chapter, I discuss the most recent protocol version—TLS 1.2—with a brief mention of earlier protocol versions where appropriate.

My goal is to give you a high-level overview that will enable you to understand what's going on without being distracted by implementation details. Wherever possible, I use message content examples, rather than definitions, which can sometimes be dry. The definitions use the syntax that's essentially the same as in the TLS specification, albeit with some minor simplifications. For more information on the syntax and the complete protocol reference, start with RFC 5246, which is where TLS 1.2 lives.[1] However, this document doesn't tell the whole story. There are also many other relevant RFCs, which I reference throughout this chapter.

The best way to learn about TLS is to observe real-life traffic. My favorite approach is to use the network-capture tool Wireshark, which comes with a TLS protocol parser: point your favorite browser at a secure web site, tell Wireshark to monitor the connection (it's best to restrict the capture to just one hostname and port 443), and observe the protocol messages.

After you're reasonably happy with your understanding of TLS (don't try too hard to learn it all; it's very hard to understand every feature, because there are so many of them), you'll be free to roam the various RFCs and even lurk on the key mailing lists. My two favorite places are the TLS working group document page,[2] where you can find the list of key documents and new proposals, and the TLS working group mailing list,[3] where you can follow the discussions about the future direction of TLS.

---

[1] RFC 5246: The Transport Layer Security Protocol Version 1.2 [fsty.uk/b28] (T. Dierks and E. Rescorla, August 2008)

[2] TLS working group documents [fsty.uk/b29] (IETF, retrieved 19 July 2014)

[3] TLS working group mailing list archives [fsty.uk/b3] (IETF, retrieved 19 July 2014)

# Record Protocol

At a high level, TLS is implemented via the *record protocol*, which is in charge of transporting—and optionally encrypting—all lower-level messages exchanged over a connection. Each *TLS record* starts with a short header, which contains information about the record content type (or subprotocol), protocol version, and length. Message data follows the header.

Figure 2.1. TLS record

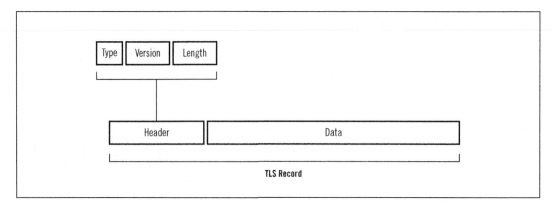

More formally, the TLS record fields are defined as follows:

```
struct {
    uint8 major;
    uint8 minor;
} ProtocolVersion;

enum {
    change_cipher_spec (20),
    alert (21),
    handshake (22),
    application_data (23)
} ContentType;

struct {
    ContentType type;
    ProtocolVersion version;
    uint16 length; /* Maximum length is 2^14 (16,384) bytes. */
    opaque fragment[TLSPlaintext.length];
} TLSPlaintext;
```

In addition to the visible fields, each TLS record is also assigned a unique 64-bit sequence number, which is not sent over the wire. Each side has its own sequence number and keeps track of the number of records sent by the other side. These values are used as part of the defense against replay attacks. You'll see how that works later on.

The record protocol is a useful protocol abstraction that takes care of several important, high-level aspects of the communication.

**Message transport**

    The record protocol transports opaque data buffers submitted to it by other protocol layers. If a buffer is longer than the record length limit (16,384 bytes), the record protocol fragments it into smaller chunks. The opposite is also possible; smaller buffers belonging to the same subprotocol can be combined in a single record.

**Encryption and integrity validation**

    Initially, on a brand new connection, messages are transported without any protection. (Technically, the `TLS_NULL_WITH_NULL_NULL` cipher suite is used.) This is necessary so that the first negotiation can take place. However, once the handshake is complete, the record layer starts to apply encryption and integrity validation according to the negotiated connection parameters.[4]

**Compression**

    Transparent compression of data prior to encryption sounds nice in theory, but it was never very common in practice, mainly because everyone was already compressing their outbound traffic at the HTTP level. This feature suffered a fatal blow in 2012, when the CRIME attack exposed it as insecure.[5] It's now no longer used.

**Extensibility**

    The record protocol takes care of data transport and encryption, but delegates all other features to subprotocols. This approach makes TLS extensible, because new subprotocols can be added easily. With encryption handled by the record protocol, all subprotocols are automatically protected using the negotiated connection parameters.

The main TLS specification defines four core subprotocols: *handshake protocol*, *change cipher spec protocol*, *application data protocol*, and *alert protocol*.

# Handshake Protocol

The handshake is the most elaborate part of the TLS protocol, during which the sides negotiate connection parameters and perform authentication. This phase usually requires six to ten messages, depending on which features are used. There can be many variations in the

---

[4] In most cases, this means that further traffic is encrypted and its integrity validated. But there's a small number of suites that don't use encryption; they use integrity validation only.

[5] I discuss the CRIME attack and various other compression-related weaknesses in the section called "Compression Side Channel Attacks " in Chapter 7.

exchange, depending on the configuration and supported protocol extensions. In practice, we see three common flows: (1) full handshake with server authentication, (2) abbreviated handshake that resumes an earlier session, and (3) handshake with client and server authentication.

Handshake protocol messages start with a header that carries the message type (one byte) and length (three bytes). The remainder of the message depends on the message type:

```
struct {
    HandshakeType msg_type;
    uint24 length;
    HandshakeMessage message;
} Handshake;
```

# Full Handshake

Every TLS connection begins with a handshake. If the client hasn't previously established a session with the server, the two sides will execute a *full handshake* in order to negotiate a *TLS session*. During this handshake, the client and the server will perform four main activities:

1. Exchange capabilities and agree on desired connection parameters.

2. Validate the presented certificate(s) or authenticate using other means.

3. Agree on a shared *master secret* that will be used to protect the session.

4. Verify that the handshake messages haven't been modified by a third party.

> ## Note
>
> In practice, steps 2 and 3 are part of a single step called *key exchange* (or, more generally, *key establishment*). I prefer to keep them separate in order to emphasize that the security of the protocol depends on correct authentication, which effectively sits outside TLS. Without authentication, an active network attacker can interject herself into the conversation and pose as the other side.

In this section, I discuss the most commonly seen TLS handshake, one between a client that's not authenticated and a server that is. The subsequent sections handle alternative protocol flows: client authentication and session resumption.

Figure 2.2. Full handshake with server authentication

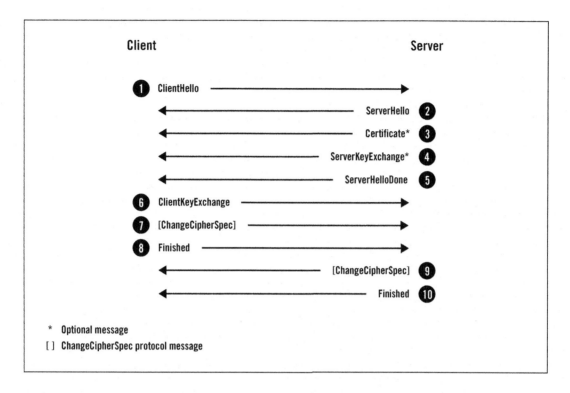

1. Client begins a new handshake and submits its capabilities to the server.

2. Server selects connection parameters.

3. Server sends its certificate chain (only server authentication is required).

4. Depending on the selected key exchange, the server sends additional information required to generate the master secret.

5. Server indicates completion of its side of the negotiation.

6. Client sends additional information required to generate the master secret.

7. Client switches to encryption and informs the server.

8. Client sends a MAC of the handshake messages it sent and received.

9. Server switches to encryption and informs the client.

10. Server sends a MAC of the handshake messages it received and sent.

At this point—assuming there were no errors—the connection is established and the parties can begin to send application data. Now let's look at the handshake messages in more detail.

## ClientHello

The ClientHello message is always the first message sent in a new handshake. It's used to communicate client capabilities and preferences to the server. Clients send this message at the beginning of a new connection, when they wish to renegotiate, or in response to a server's renegotiation request (indicated by a HelloRequest message).

In the following example, you can see what a ClientHello message could look like. I reduced the amount of information presented for the sake of brevity, but all of the key elements are included.

```
Handshake protocol: ClientHello
    Version: TLS 1.2
    Random
        Client time: May 22, 2030 02:43:46 GMT
        Random bytes: b76b0e61829557eb4c611adfd2d36eb232dc1332fe29802e321ee871
    Session ID: (empty)
    Cipher Suites
        Suite: TLS_ECDHE_RSA_WITH_AES_128_GCM_SHA256
        Suite: TLS_DHE_RSA_WITH_AES_128_GCM_SHA256
        Suite: TLS_RSA_WITH_AES_128_GCM_SHA256
        Suite: TLS_ECDHE_RSA_WITH_AES_128_CBC_SHA
        Suite: TLS_DHE_RSA_WITH_AES_128_CBC_SHA
        Suite: TLS_RSA_WITH_AES_128_CBC_SHA
        Suite: TLS_RSA_WITH_3DES_EDE_CBC_SHA
        Suite: TLS_RSA_WITH_RC4_128_SHA
    Compression methods
        Method: null
    Extensions
        Extension: server_name
            Hostname: www.feistyduck.com
        Extension: renegotiation_info
        Extension: elliptic_curves
            Named curve: secp256r1
            Named curve: secp384r1
        Extension: signature_algorithms
            Algorithm: sha1/rsa
            Algorithm: sha256/rsa
            Algorithm: sha1/ecdsa
            Algorithm: sha256/ecdsa
```

As you can see, the structure of this message is easy to understand, with most data fields easy to understand from the names alone.

### Protocol version

Protocol version indicates the best protocol version the client supports.

### Random

The random field contains 32 bytes of data. Of those, 28 bytes are randomly generated. The remaining four bytes carry additional information influenced by the client's clock. Client time is not actually relevant for the protocol, and the specification is clear on this ("Clocks are not required to be set correctly by the basic TLS protocol, higher-level or application protocols may define additional requirements."); the field was included as a defense against weak random number generators, after just such a critical failure was discovered in Netscape Navigator in 1994.[6] Although this field used to contain the actual time, there are fears that client time could be used for large-scale browser fingerprinting.[7] As a result, some browsers add random clock skew to their time (as you can see in the example) or simply send four random bytes instead.

Both client and server contribute random data during the handshake. The randomness makes each handshake unique and plays a key role in authentication by preventing replay attacks and verifying the integrity of the initial data exchange.

### Session ID

On the first connection, the session ID field is empty, indicating that the client doesn't wish to resume an existing section. On subsequent connections, the ID field can contain the session's unique identifier, enabling the server to locate the correct session state in its cache. The session ID typically contains 32 bytes of randomly generated data and isn't valuable in itself.

### Cipher suites

The cipher suite block is a list of all cipher suites supported by the client in order of preference.

### Compression

Clients can submit one or more supported compression methods. The default compression method `null` indicates no compression.

### Extensions

The extension block contains an arbitrary number of extensions that carry additional data. I discuss the most commonly seen extensions later in this chapter.

## ServerHello

The purpose of the `ServerHello` message is for the server to communicate the selected connection parameters back to the client. This message is similar in structure to `ClientHello` but contains only one option per field:

---

[6] For more information about this problem, refer to the section called "Netscape Navigator (1994)" in Chapter 6.

[7] Deprecating gmt_unix_time in TLS [fsty.uk/b30] (N. Mathewson and B. Laurie, December 2013)

---

```
Handshake protocol: ServerHello
    Version: TLS 1.2
    Random
        Server time: Mar 10, 2059 02:35:57 GMT
        Random bytes: 8469b09b480c1978182ce1b59290487609f41132312ca22aacaf5012
    Session ID: 4cae75c91cf5adf55f93c9fb5dd36d19903b1182029af3d527b7a42ef1c32c80
    Cipher Suite: TLS_ECDHE_RSA_WITH_AES_128_GCM_SHA256
    Compression method: null
    Extensions
        Extension: server_name
        Extension: renegotiation_info
```

The server isn't required to support the same best version supported by the client. If it doesn't, it offers some other protocol version in the hope that the client will accept it.

## Certificate

The Certificate message is typically used to carry the server's X.509 certificate chain. Certificates are provided one after another, in ASN.1 DER encoding. The main certificate must be sent first, with all of the intermediary certificates following in the correct order. The root can and should be omitted, because it serves no purpose in this context.

The server must ensure that it sends a certificate appropriate for the selected cipher suite. For example, the public key algorithm must match that used in the suite. In addition, some key exchange mechanisms depend upon certain data being embedded in the certificate, and the certificates must be signed with algorithms supported by the client. All of this implies that the server could be configured with multiple certificates (each with a potentially different chain).

This Certificate message is optional, because not all suites use authentication and because there are some authentication methods that don't require certificates. Furthermore, although the default is to use X.509 certificates other forms of identification can be carried in this message; some suites rely on PGP keys.[8]

## ServerKeyExchange

The purpose of the ServerKeyExchange message is to carry additional data needed for key exchange. Its contents vary and depend on the negotiated cipher suite. In some cases, the server is not required to send anything, which means that the ServerKeyExchange message is not sent at all.

---

[8] RFC 5081: Using OpenPGP Keys for TLS Authentication [fsty.uk/b31] (N. Mavrogiannopoulos, November 2007)

## ServerHelloDone

ServerHelloDone is a signal that the server has sent all intended handshake messages. After this, the server waits for further messages from the client.

## ClientKeyExchange

The ClientKeyExchange message carries the client's contribution to the key exchange. It's a mandatory message whose contents depend on the negotiated cipher suite.

## ChangeCipherSpec

The ChangeCipherSpec message is a signal that the sending side obtained enough information to obtain all connection parameters, generated the appropriate encryption keys, and is switching to encryption. Client and server both send this message when the time is right.

> ### Note
>
> ChangeCipherSpec is not a handshake message. Rather, it's implemented as the only message in its own subprotocol. One consequence of this decision is that this message is not part of the handshake integrity validation mechanism. This makes TLS more difficult to implement correctly; in June 2014 OpenSSL disclosed that it had been incorrectly handling ChangeCipherSpec messages, leaving it open to active network attacks.[9]
>
> The same problem exists with all other subprotocols. An active network attacker can send unauthenticated alert messages during the first handshake and, by exploiting the buffering mechanism, even subvert genuine alerts sent after encryption commences.[10] To avoid more serious problems, application data protocol and heartbeat messages aren't allowed before the first handshake is complete; it's not unusual to see implementations violate these restrictions.

## Finished

The Finished message is the signal that the handshake is complete. Its contents are encrypted, which allows both sides to securely exchange the data required to verify the integrity of the entire handshake.

This message carries the verify_data field, which is a hash of all handshake messages as each side saw them mixed in with the newly negotiated master secret. This is done via a *pseudorandom function* (PRF), which is designed to produce an arbitrary amount of pseudorandom data. I describe the PRF later in this chapter. The Hash function is the same as in

---

[9] You'll find more information about this flaw in the section called "Library and Platform Validation Failures" in Chapter 6.

[10] The Alert attack [fsty.uk/b32] (miTLS, February 2012)

---

the PRF unless the negotiated suite specifies a different algorithm. The calculations are the same in both cases, although each side uses a different label: "client finished" for the client and "server finished" for the server:

```
verify_data = PRF(master_secret, finished_label, Hash(handshake_messages))
```

Because the Finished messages are encrypted and their integrity guaranteed by the negotiated MAC algorithm, an active network attacker can't change the handshake messages and then forge the correct verify_data values.

The attacker could also try to find a set of forged handshake messages that have exactly the same verify_data values as the genuine messages. That's not an easy attack in itself, but because the hashes are mixed in with the master secret (which the attacker doesn't know) she can't even attempt that approach.

In TLS 1.2, the Finished message is 12 bytes (96 bits) long by default, but cipher suites are allowed to use larger sizes. Earlier protocol versions also use a fixed length of 12 bytes, except for SSL 3, which uses 36 bytes.

## Client Authentication

Although authentication of either side is optional, server authentication is almost universally required. If the server selects a suite that isn't anonymous, it's required to follow up with its certificate chain in the Certificate message.

In contrast, the server requests client authentication by sending a CertificateRequest message that lists acceptable client certificates. In response, the client sends the certificate in its own Certificate message (in the same format used by the server for its certificates) and then proves possession of the corresponding private key with a CertificateVerify message.

Figure 2.3. Full handshake, during which both client and server are authenticated

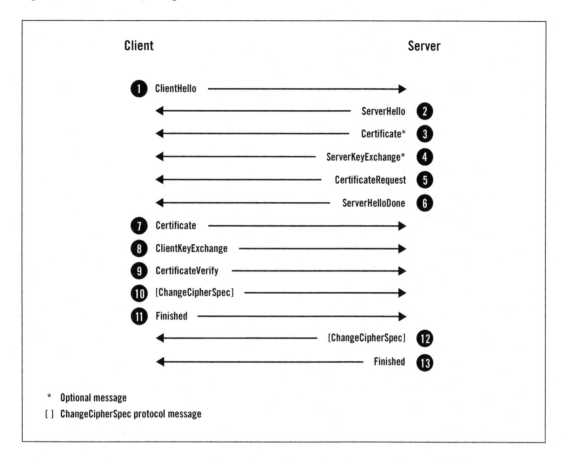

Only an authenticated server is allowed to request client authentication. For this reason, this option is known as *mutual authentication*.

## CertificateRequest

With the CertificateRequest message, the server requests client authentication and communicates acceptable certificate public key and signature algorithms to the client. Optionally, it can also send its list of acceptable issuing certification authorities, indicated by using their distinguished names:

```
struct {
    ClientCertificateType certificate_types;
    SignatureAndHashAlgorithm supported_signature_algorithms;
    DistinguishedName certificate_authorities;
} CertificateRequest;
```

## CertificateVerify

The client uses the `CertificateVerify` message to prove the possession of the private key corresponding to the public key in the previously sent client certificate. This message contains a signature of all the handshake messages exchanged until this point:

```
struct {
    Signature handshake_messages_signature;
} CertificateVerify;
```

# Session Resumption

The full handshake is an elaborate protocol that requires many handshake messages and two network round-trips before the client can start sending application data. In addition, the cryptographic operations carried out during the handshake often require intensive CPU processing. Authentication, usually in the form of client and server certificate validation (and revocation checking), requires even more effort. Much of this overhead can be avoided with an abbreviated handshake.

The original *session resumption* mechanism is based on both the client and the server keeping session security parameters for a period of time after a fully negotiated connection is terminated. A server that wishes to use session resumption assigns it a unique identifier called the *session ID*. The server then sends the session ID back to the client in the `ServerHello` message. (You can see this in the example in the previous section.)

A client that wishes to resume an earlier session submits the appropriate session ID in its `ClientHello`. If the server is willing to resume that session, it returns the same session ID in the `ServerHello`, generates a new set of keys using the previously negotiated master secret, switches to encryption, and sends its `Finished` message. The client, when it sees that the session is being resumed, does the same. The result is a short handshake that requires only one network round-trip.

Figure 2.4. Abbreviated handshake—used to resume an already established session

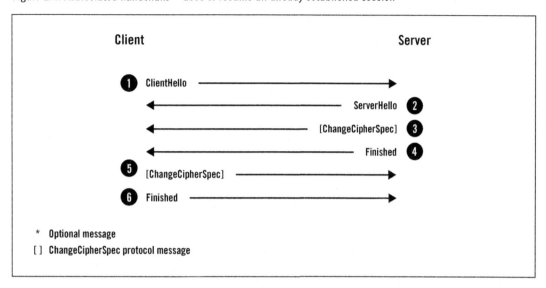

The alternative to server-side session caching and resumption is to use *session tickets*, introduced by RFC 4507 in 2006 and subsequently updated by RFC 5077 in 2008. In this case, all state is kept by the client (the mechanism is similar to HTTP cookies), but the message flow is otherwise the same.

# Key Exchange

The key exchange is easily the most interesting part of the handshake. In TLS, the security of the session depends on a 48-byte shared key called the *master secret*. The goal of key exchange is to generate another value, the *premaster secret*, which is the value from which the master secret is constructed.

TLS supports many key exchange algorithms in order to support various certificate types, public key algorithms, and key establishment protocols. Some are defined in the main TLS protocol specification, but many more are defined elsewhere. You can see the most commonly used algorithms in the following table.

Table 2.1. Overview of the most commonly used key exchange algorithms

| Key Exchange | Description |
|---|---|
| dh_anon | Diffie-Hellman (DH) key exchange without authentication |
| dhe_rsa | Ephemeral DH key exchange with RSA authentication |
| ecdh_anon | Ephemeral Elliptic Curve DH (ECDH) key exchange without authentication (RFC 4492) |
| ecdhe_rsa | Ephemeral ECDH key exchange with RSA authentication (RFC 4492) |
| ecdhe_ecdsa | Ephemeral ECDH key exchange with ECDSA authentication (RFC 4492) |
| krb5 | Kerberos key exchange (RFC 2712) |
| rsa | RSA key exchange and authentication |
| psk | Pre-Shared Key (PSK) key exchange and authentication (RFC 4279) |
| dhe_psk | DH key exchange with PSK authentication (RFC 4279) |
| rsa_psk | PSK key exchange and RSA authentication (RFC 4279) |
| srp | Secure Remote Protocol (SRP) key exchange and authentication (RFC 5054) |

Which key exchange is used depends on the negotiated suite. Once the suite is known, both sides know which algorithm to follow. In practice, there are four main key exchange algorithms:

**RSA**

RSA is effectively the standard key exchange algorithm. It's universally supported but suffers from one serious problem: its design allows a passive attacker to decrypt all encrypted data, provided she has access to the server's private key. Because of this, the RSA key exchange is being slowly replaced with other algorithms, those that support *forward secrecy*. The RSA key exchange is a *key transport* algorithm; the client generates the premaster secret and transports it to the server, encrypted with the server's public key.

**DHE_RSA**

*Ephemeral Diffie-Hellman* (DHE) key exchange is a well-established algorithm. It's liked because it provides forward secrecy but disliked because it's slow. DHE is a *key agreement* algorithm; the negotiating parties both contribute to the process and agree on a common key. In TLS, DHE is commonly used with RSA authentication.

**ECDHE_RSA and ECDHE_ECDSA**

*Ephemeral elliptic curve Diffie-Hellman* (ECDHE) key exchange is based on elliptic curve cryptography, which is relatively new. It's liked because it's fast *and* provides forward secrecy. It's well supported only by modern clients. ECDHE is a key agreement algorithm conceptually similar to DHE. In TLS, ECDHE can be used with either RSA or ECDSA authentication.

No matter which key exchange is used, the server has the opportunity to speak first by sending its ServerKeyExchange message:

```
struct {
    select (KeyExchangeAlgorithm) {
        case dh_anon:
            ServerDHParams        params;
        case dhe_rsa:
            ServerDHParams        params;
            Signature             params_signature;
        case ecdh_anon:
            ServerECDHParams      params;
        case ecdhe_rsa:
        case ecdhe_ecdsa:
            ServerECDHParams      params;
            Signature             params_signature;
        case rsa:
        case dh_rsa:
            /* no message */
    };
} ServerKeyExchange;
```

As you can see in the message definition, there are several algorithms for which there is nothing for the server to send. This will be the case when all the required information is already available elsewhere. Otherwise, the server sends its key exchange parameters. Crucially, the server also sends a signature of the parameters, which is used for authentication. Using the signature, the client is able to verify that it's talking to the party that holds the private key corresponding to the public key from the certificate.

The ClientKeyExchange message is always required; the client uses it to sends its key exchange parameters:

```
struct {
    select (KeyExchangeAlgorithm) {
        case rsa:
            EncryptedPreMasterSecret;
        case dhe_dss:
        case dhe_rsa:
        case dh_dss:
        case dh_rsa:
        case dh_anon:
            ClientDiffieHellmanPublic;
        case ecdhe:
            ClientECDiffieHellmanPublic;
    } exchange_keys;
} ClientKeyExchange;
```

# RSA Key Exchange

The RSA key exchange is quite straightforward; the client generates a premaster secret (a 46-byte random number), encrypts it with the server's public key, and sends it in the ClientKeyExchange message. To obtain the premaster secret, the server only needs to decrypt the message. TLS uses the RSAES-PKCS1-v1_5 encryption scheme, which is defined in RFC 3447.[11]

> **Note**
>
> The RSA key exchange can operate in this way because the RSA algorithm can be used for encryption and digital signing. Other popular key types, such as DSA (DSS) and ECDSA, can be used only for signing.

The simplicity of the RSA key exchange is also its principal weakness. The premaster secret is encrypted with the server's public key, which usually remains in use for several years. Anyone with access to the corresponding private key can recover the premaster secret and construct the same master secret, compromising session security.

The attack doesn't have to happen in real time. A powerful adversary could establish a long-term operation to record all encrypted traffic and wait patiently until she obtains the key. For example, advances in computer power could make it possible to brute-force the key. Alternatively, the key could be obtained using legal powers, coercion, bribery, or by breaking into a server that uses it. After the key compromise, it's possible to decrypt all previously recorded traffic.

Other main key exchange mechanisms used in TLS don't suffer from this problem and are said to support forward secrecy. When they are used, each connection uses an independent master secret. A compromised server key could be used to impersonate the server but couldn't be used to retroactively decrypt any traffic.

# Diffie-Hellman Key Exchange

The *Diffie-Hellman* (DH) key exchange is a key agreement protocol that allows two parties to establish a shared secret over an insecure communication channel.[12]

> **Note**
>
> The shared secret negotiated in this way is safe from passive attacks, but an active attacker could hijack the communication channel and pretend to be the other party. This is why the DH key exchange is commonly used with authentication.

---

[11] RFC 3447: RSA Cryptography Specifications Version 2.1 [fsty.uk/b33] (Jonsson and Kaliski, February 2003)

[12] Diffie–Hellman key exchange [fsty.uk/b34] (Wikipedia, retrieved 18 June 2014)

---

Without going into the details of the algorithm, the trick is to use a mathematical function that's easy to calculate in one direction but very difficult to reverse, even when some of the aspects of the exchange are known. The best analogy is that of color mixing: if you have two colors, you can easily mix them to get a third color, but it's very difficult to determine the *exact* color shades that contributed to the mix.[13]

The DH key exchange requires six parameters; two (dh_p and dh_g) are called *domain parameters* and are selected by the server. During the negotiation, the client and server each generate two additional parameters. Each side sends one of its parameters (dh_Ys and dh_Yc) to the other end, and, with some calculation, they arrive at the shared key.

*Ephemeral Diffie-Hellman* (DHE) key exchange takes place when none of the parameters are reused. In contrast, there are some DH key exchange approaches in which some of the parameters are static and embedded in the server and client certificates. In this case, the result of the key exchange is always the same shared key, which means that there is no forward secrecy.

TLS supports static DH key exchanges, but they're not used. When a DHE suite is negotiated, the server sends all of its parameters in the ServerDHParams block:

```
struct {
    opaque dh_p;
    opaque dh_g;
    opaque dh_Ys;
} ServerDHParams;
```

The client, in response, sends its public parameter (dh_Yc):

```
struct {
    select (PublicValueEncoding) {
        case implicit:
            /* empty; used when the client's public
                parameter is embedded in its certificate */
        case explicit:
            opaque dh_Yc;
    } dh_public;
} ClientDiffieHellmanPublic;
```

There are some practical problems with the DH exchange as it's currently used:

**DH parameter security**

The security of the DH key exchange depends on the quality of the domain parameters. A server could send weak or insecure parameters and compromise the security of the session. This issue was highlighted in the *Triple Handshake Attack* research paper, which covered weak DH parameters used as one of the attack vectors.[14]

[13] Public Key Cryptography: Diffie-Hellman Key Exchange [fsty.uk/b35] (YouTube, retrieved 26 June 2014)

### DH parameter negotiation

TLS doesn't provide facilities for the client to communicate the strength of DH parameters it's willing to use. For example, some clients might want to avoid using weak parameters, or alternately, they might not be able to support stronger parameters. Because of this, a server that chooses a DHE suite can effectively only "hope" that the DH parameters will be acceptable to the client.

Historically speaking, DH parameters have been largely ignored and their security neglected. Many libraries and servers use weak DH parameters by default and often don't provide a means to change their strength in configuration. For this reason, it's not uncommon to see servers using weak 1,024-bit parameters and insecure 768- and even 512-bit parameters. More recently, some platforms have started using strong (2,048 bits and higher) parameters.

These problems could be addressed by standardizing a set of domain parameters of varying strengths and extending TLS to enable clients to communicate their preferences.[15]

## Elliptic Curve Diffie-Hellman Key Exchange

The ephemeral *elliptic curve Diffie-Hellman* (ECDH) key exchange is conceptually similar to DH, but it uses a different mathematical foundation at the core. As the name implies, ECDHE is based on elliptic curve (EC) cryptography.

An ECDH key exchange takes place over a specific elliptic curve, which is for the server to define. The curve takes the role of domain parameters in DH. In theory, static ECDH key exchange is supported, but in practice only the ephemeral variant (ECDHE) is used.

The server starts the key exchange by submitting its selected elliptic curve and public parameter (EC point):

```
struct {
    ECParameters curve_params;
    ECPoint public;
} ServerECDHParams;
```

The server can specify an arbitrary (explicit) curve for the key exchange, but this facility is not used in TLS. Instead, the server will specify a *named curve*, which is a reference to one of the possible predefined parameters:

```
struct {
    ECCurveType curve_type;
    select (curve_type) {
        case explicit_prime:
```

---

[14] For more information on the Triple Handshake Attack, head to the section called "Triple Handshake Attack" in Chapter 7.

[15] Negotiated Discrete Log Diffie-Hellman Ephemeral Parameters for TLS [fsty.uk/b36] (D. Gillmor, April 2014)

```
            /* omitted for clarity */
        case explicit_char2:
            /* omitted for clarity */
        case named_curve:
            NamedCurve namedcurve;
    };
} ECParameters;
```

The client then submits its own public parameter. After that, the calculations take place to arrive at the premaster secret:

```
struct {
    select (PublicValueEncoding) {
        case implicit:
            /* empty */
        case explicit:
            ECPoint ecdh_Yc;
    } ecdh_public;
} ClientECDiffieHellmanPublic;
```

The use of predefined parameters, along with the elliptic_curve extension that clients can use to submit supported curves, enables the server to select a curve that both sides support. You'll find more information on the available named curves later in the section called "Elliptic Curve Capabilities".

# Authentication

In TLS, authentication is tightly coupled with key exchange in order to avoid repetition of costly cryptographic operations. In most cases, the basis for authentication will be public key cryptography (most commonly RSA, but sometimes ECDSA) supported by certificates. Once the certificate is validated, the client has a known public key to work with. After that, it's down to the particular key exchange method to use the public key in some way to authenticate the other side.

During the RSA key exchange, the client generates a random value as the premaster secret and sends it encrypted with the server's public key. The server, which is in possession of the corresponding private key, decrypts the message to obtain the premaster secret. The authentication is implicit: it is assumed that only the server in possession of the corresponding private key can retrieve the premaster secret, construct the correct session keys, and produce the correct Finished message.

During the DHE and ECDHE exchanges, the server contributes to the key exchange with its parameters. The parameters are signed with its private key. The client, which is in possession of the corresponding public key (obtained from the validated certificate), can verify that the parameters genuinely arrived from the intended server.

**Note**

Server parameters are signed concatenated with client and server random data that are unique to the handshake. Thus, although the signature is sent in the clear it's only valid for the current handshake, which means that the attacker can't reuse it.

# Encryption

TLS can encrypt data in a variety of ways, using ciphers such 3DES, AES, ARIA, CAMEL-LIA, RC4, and SEED. AES is by far the most popular cipher. Three types of encryption are supported: *stream*, *block*, and *authenticated* encryption. In TLS, integrity validation is part of the encryption process; it's handled either explicitly at the protocol level or implicitly by the negotiated cipher.

## Stream Encryption

When a stream cipher is used, encryption consists of two steps. In the first step, a MAC of the record sequence number, header, and plaintext is calculated. The inclusion of the header in the MAC ensures that the unencrypted data in the header can't be tampered with. The inclusion of the sequence number in the MAC ensures that the messages can't be replayed. In the second step, the plaintext and the MAC are encrypted to form ciphertext.

Figure 2.5. Stream encryption

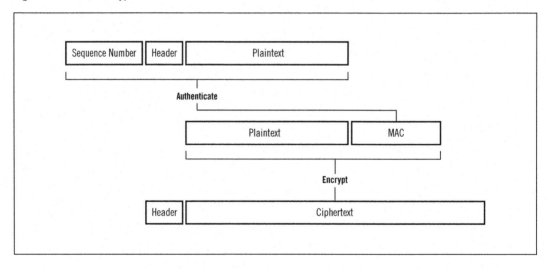

---

**Note**

A suite that uses integrity validation but no encryption is implemented in the same way as encryption using a stream cipher. The plaintext is simply copied to the TLS record, but the MAC is calculated as described here.

# Block Encryption

When block ciphers are used, encryption is somewhat more involved, because it's necessary to work around the properties of block encryption. The following steps are required:

1. Calculate a MAC of the sequence number, header, and plaintext.

2. Construct padding to ensure that the length of data prior to encryption is a multiple of the cipher block size (usually 16 bytes).

3. Generate an unpredictable *initialization vector* (IV) of the same length as the cipher block size. The IV is used to ensure that the encryption is not deterministic.

4. Use the CBC block mode to encrypt plaintext, MAC, and padding.

5. Send the IV and ciphertext together.

Figure 2.6. Block encryption

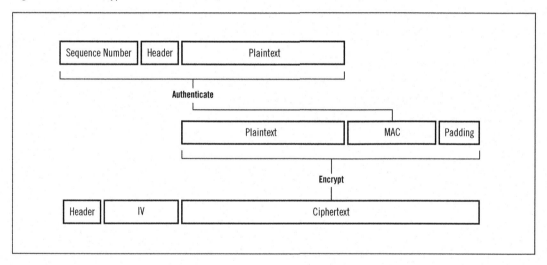

**Note**

You'll find further information on the CBC block mode, padding, and initialization vectors in the section called "Building Blocks" in Chapter 1.

This process is known as *MAC-then-encrypt*, and it has been a source of many problems. In TLS 1.1 and newer versions, each record includes an explicit IV. TLS 1.0 and older versions use implicit IVs (the encrypted block from the previous TLS record is used as the IV for the next), but that approach was found to be insecure in 2011.[16]

The other problem is that the MAC calculation doesn't include padding, leaving an opportunity for an active network attacker to attempt *padding oracle attacks*, which were also successfully demonstrated against TLS.[17] The issue here is that the protocol specifies a block encryption approach that's difficult to implement securely in practice. As far as we know, current implementations are not obviously vulnerable at the moment, but this is a weak spot that leaves many uneasy.

A proposal for a different arrangement called *encrypt-then-MAC* has recently been submitted for publication.[18] In this alternative approach, plaintext and padding are first encrypted and then fed to the MAC algorithm. This ensures that the active network attacker can't manipulate any of the encrypted data.

## Authenticated Encryption

Authenticated ciphers combine encryption and integrity validation in one algorithm. Their full name is *authenticated encryption with associated data* (AEAD). On the surface, they appear to be a cross between stream ciphers and block ciphers. They don't use padding[19] and initialization vectors, but they do use a special value called *nonce*, which must be unique. TLS supports GCM and CCM authenticated ciphers, but only the former are currently used in practice. The process is somewhat simpler than with block ciphers:

1. Generate a unique 64-bit nonce.

2. Encrypt plaintext with the authenticated encryption algorithm; at the same time feed it the sequence number and record header for it to take into account as additional data for purposes of integrity validation.

3. Send the nonce and ciphertext together.

---

[16] This problem was first revealed in the so-called BEAST attack, which I discuss in the section called "BEAST" in Chapter 7.

[17] I discuss padding oracle attacks in the section called "Padding Oracle Attacks" in Chapter 7.

[18] Encrypt-then-MAC for TLS and DTLS [fsty.uk/b37] (Peter Gutmann, 6 June 2014)

[19] Actually, they might use padding, but if they do, it's an implementation detail that's not exposed to the TLS protocol.

Figure 2.7. Authenticated encryption

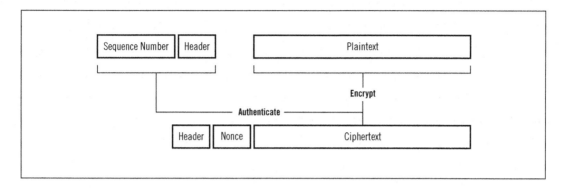

Authenticated encryption is currently favored as the best encryption mode available in TLS, because it avoids the issues inherent with the MAC-then-encrypt approach.

# Renegotiation

Most TLS connections start with a handshake, proceed to exchange application data, and shutdown the conversation at the end. When *renegotiation* is requested, a new handshake takes place to agree on new connection security parameters. There are several cases in which this feature might be useful:

**Client certificates**

Client certificates are not used often, but some sites use them because they provide two-factor authentication. There are two ways to deploy client certificates. You can require them for all connections to a site, but this approach is not very friendly to those who don't (yet) have a certificate; without a successful connection, you can't send them any information and instructions. Handling error conditions is equally impossible. For this reason, many operators prefer to allow connections to the root of the web site without a certificate and designate a subsection in which a client certificate is required. When a user attempts to navigate to the subsection, the server issues a request to renegotiate and then requests a client certificate.

**Information hiding**

Such a two-step approach to enabling client certificates has an additional advantage: the second handshake is encrypted, which means that a passive attacker can't monitor the negotiation and, crucially, can't observe the client certificates. This addresses a potentially significant privacy issue, because client certificates usually contain identifying information. For example, the Tor protocol can use renegotiation in this way.[20]

---

[20] Tor Protocol Specification [fsty.uk/b38] (Dingledine and Mathewson, retrieved 30 June 2014)

**Change of encryption strength**

Back in the day, when web site encryption was brand new (and very CPU intensive) it was common to see sites split their encryption configuration into two levels. You would use weaker encryption by default but require strong encryption in certain areas.[21] As with client certificates, this feature is implemented via renegotiation. When you attempt to cross into the more secure subsection of the web site, the server requests stronger security.

In addition, there are two situations in which renegotiation is required by the protocol, although neither is likely to occur in practice:

**Server-Gated Crypto**

Back in the 1990s, when the United States did not allow export of strong cryptography, a feature called *Server-Gated Crypto* (SGC) was used to enable US vendors to ship strong cryptography worldwide but enable it only for selected (mostly financial) US web sites. Browsers would use weak cryptography by default, upgrading to strong cryptography after encountering a special certificate. This upgrade was entirely client controlled, and it was implemented via renegotiation. Only a few selected CAs were allowed to issue the special certificates. Cryptography export restrictions were relaxed in 2000, making SGC obsolete.

**TLS record counter overflow**

Internally, TLS packages data into records. Each record is assigned a unique sequence number, which grows over time as records are exchanged. The protocol mandates renegotiation if the record identifier is close to overflowing. However, because this counter is a large, 64-bit number, overflows are unlikely.

The protocol allows the client to request renegotiation at any time simply by sending a new ClientHello message, exactly as when starting a brand-new connection. This is known as *client-initiated renegotiation*.

If the server wishes to renegotiate, it sends a HelloRequest protocol message to the client; that's a signal to the client to stop sending application data and initiate a new handshake. This is known as *server-initiated renegotiation*.

Renegotiation, as originally designed, is insecure and can be abused by an active network attacker in many ways. The weakness was discovered in 2009[22] and corrected with the introduction of the renegotiation_info extension, which I discuss later in this chapter.

---

[21] This thinking is flawed; your encryption is either sufficiently secure or it isn't. If your adversaries can break the weaker configuration, they can take full control of the victim's browser. With that, they can trick the victim into revealing all of their secrets (e.g., passwords).

[22] For more information, head to the section called "Insecure Renegotiation" in Chapter 7.

# Application Data Protocol

Application data protocol carries application messages, which are just buffers of data as far as TLS is concerned. These messages are packaged, fragmented, and encrypted by the record layer, using the current connection security parameters.

# Alert Protocol

*Alerts* are intended to use a simple notification mechanism to inform the other side in the communication of exceptional circumstances. They're generally used for error messages, with the exception of close_notify, which is used during connection shutdown. Alerts are very simple and contain only two fields:

```
struct {
    AlertLevel level;
    AlertDescription description;
} Alert;
```

The AlertLevel field carries the alert severity, which can be either warning or fatal. The AlertDescription is simply an alert code; for better or worse, there are no facilities to convey arbitrary information, for example, an actual error message.

Fatal messages result in an immediate termination of the current connection and invalidation of the session (ongoing connections of the same session may continue, but the session can no longer be resumed). The side sending a warning notification doesn't terminate the connection, but the receiving side is free to react to the warning by sending a fatal alert of its own.

# Connection Closure

*Closure alerts* are used to shutdown a TLS connection in an orderly fashion. Once one side decides that it wants to close the connection, it sends a close_notify alert. The other side, upon receiving the alert, discards any pending writes and sends a close_notify alert of its own. If any messages arrive after the alerts, they are ignored.

This simple shutdown protocol is necessary in order to avoid truncation attacks, in which an active network attacker interrupts a conversation midway and blocks all further messages. Without the shutdown protocol, the two sides can't determine if they are under attack or if the conversation is genuinely over.

> **Note**
>
> Although the protocol itself is not vulnerable to truncation attacks, there are many *implementations* that are, because violations of the connection shutdown protocol

are widespread. I discuss this problem at length in the section called "Truncation Attacks" in Chapter 6.

# Cryptographic Operations

This section contains a brief discussion of several important aspects of the protocol: the pseudorandom function, master secret construction, and the generation of connection keys.

## Pseudorandom Function

In TLS, a *pseudorandom function* (PRF) is used to generate arbitrary amounts of pseudorandom data. The PRF takes a secret, a seed, and a unique label. From TLS 1.2 onwards, all cipher suites are required to explicitly specify their PRF. All TLS 1.2 suites use a PRF based on HMAC and SHA256; the same PRF is used with older suites when they are negotiated with TLS 1.2.

TLS 1.2 defines a PRF based on a data expansion function P_hash, which uses HMAC and any hash function:

```
P_hash(secret, seed) = HMAC_hash(secret, A(1) + seed) +
                       HMAC_hash(secret, A(2) + seed) +
                       HMAC_hash(secret, A(3) + seed) + ...
```

The A(i) function is defined as follows:

```
A(1) = HMAC_hash(secret, seed)
A(2) = HMAC_hash(secret, A(1))
...
A(i) = HMAC_hash(secret, A(i-1))
```

The PRF is a wrapper around P_hash that combines the label with the seed:

```
PRF(secret, label, seed) = P_hash(secret, label + seed)
```

The introduction of a seed and a label allows the same secret to be reused in different contexts to produce different outputs (because the label and the seed are different).

## Master Secret

As you saw earlier, the output from the key exchange process is the premaster secret. This value is further processed, using the PRF, to produce a 48-byte (384-bit) master secret:

```
master_secret = PRF(pre_master_secret, "master secret",
                    ClientHello.random + ServerHello.random)
```

The processing occurs because the premaster secret might differ in size depending on the key exchange method used. Also, because the client and server random fields are used as the seed, the master secret is also effectively random[23] and bound to the negotiated handshake.

> **Note**
>
> The binding between the master secret and the handshake has been shown to be insufficient because it relies only on the exchanged random values. An attacker can observe and replicate these values to create multiple sessions that share the same master key. This weakness has been exploited by the Triple Handshake Attack mentioned earlier.[14]

## Key Generation

The key material needed for a connection is generated in a single PRF invocation based on the master secret and seeded with the client and server random values:

```
key_block = PRF(SecurityParameters.master_secret,
                "key expansion",
                SecurityParameters.server_random +
                SecurityParameters.client_random)
```

The key block, which varies in size depending on the negotiated parameters, is divided into up to six keys: two MAC keys, two encryption keys, and two initialization vectors (only when needed; stream ciphers don't use IV). AEAD suites don't use MAC keys. Different keys are used for different operations, which is recommended to prevent unforeseen interactions between cryptographic primitives when the key is shared. Also, because the client and the server have their own sets of keys, a message produced by one can't be interpreted to have been produced by the other. This design decision makes the protocol more robust.

> **Note**
>
> When resuming a session, the same session master key is used during the key block generation. However, the PRF is seeded with the client and server random values from the *current* handshake. Because these random values are different in every handshake, the keys are also different every time.

## Cipher Suites

As you have seen, TLS allows for a great deal of flexibility in implementing the desired security properties. It's effectively a framework for creating actual cryptographic protocols. Al-

---

[23] Although the most commonly used key exchange mechanisms generate a different premaster secret every time, there are some mechanisms that rely on long-term keys and thus reuse the same premaster secret. Randomization is essential to ensure that the keys are not repeated.

though previous versions hardcoded some cryptographic primitives into the protocol, TLS 1.2 is fully configurable. A *cipher suite* is a selection of cryptographic primitives and other parameters that define exactly how security will be implemented. A suite is defined roughly by the following attributes:

- Authentication method
- Key exchange method
- Encryption algorithm
- Encryption key size
- Cipher mode (when applicable)
- MAC algorithm (when applicable)
- PRF (TLS 1.2 only—depends on the protocol otherwise)
- Hash function used for the Finished message (TLS 1.2)
- Length of the verify_data structure (TLS 1.2)

Cipher suite names tend to be long and descriptive and pretty consistent: they are made from the names of the key exchange method, authentication method, cipher definition, and optional MAC or PRF algorithm.[24]

Figure 2.8. Cipher suite name construction

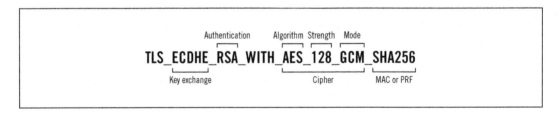

Although a suite name is not sufficient to convey all security parameters, the most important ones are easy to deduce. The information on the remaining parameters can be found in the RFC that carries the suite definition. You can see the security properties of a few selected suites in the following table. At the time of writing, there are more than 300 official cipher suites, which is too many to list here. For the complete list, head to the official TLS page over at IANA.[25]

---

[24] TLS suites use the TLS_ prefix, SSL 3 suites use the SSL_ prefix, and SSL 2 suites use the SSL_CK_ prefix. In all cases, the approach to naming is roughly the same. However, not all vendors use the standard suite names. OpenSSL and GnuTLS use different names. Microsoft largely uses the standard names but sometimes extends them with suffixes that are used to indicate the strength of the ECDHE key exchange.
[25] TLS Parameters [fsty.uk/b39] (IANA, retrieved 30 June 2014)

Table 2.2. Examples of cipher suite names and their security properties

| Cipher Suite Name | Auth | KX | Cipher | MAC | PRF |
|---|---|---|---|---|---|
| TLS_ECDHE_RSA_WITH_AES_128_GCM_SHA256 | RSA | ECDHE | AES-128-GCM | - | SHA256 |
| TLS_ECDHE_ECDSA_WITH_AES_256_GCM_SHA384 | ECDSA | ECDHE | AES-256-GCM | - | SHA384 |
| TLS_DHE_RSA_WITH_3DES_EDE_CBC_SHA | RSA | DHE | 3DES-EDE-CBC | SHA | Protocol |
| TLS_RSA_WITH_AES_128_CBC_SHA | RSA | RSA | AES-128-CBC | SHA | Protocol |
| TLS_ECDHE_ECDSA_WITH_AES_128_CCM | ECDSA | ECDHE | AES-128-CCM | - | SHA256 |

With the introduction of TLS 1.2—which allows for additional custom parameters (e.g., PRF)—and authenticated suites, some level of understanding of the implementation is required to fully decode cipher suite names:

- Authenticated suites combine authentication and encryption in the cipher, which means that integrity validation need not be performed at the TLS level. GCM suites use the last segment to indicate the PRF instead of the MAC algorithm. CCM suites omit this last segment completely.

- TLS 1.2 is the only protocol that allows suites to define their PRFs. This means that for the suites defined before TLS 1.2 the negotiated protocol version dictates the PRF. For example, the TLS_RSA_WITH_AES_128_CBC_SHA suite uses a PRF based on HMAC-SHA256 when negotiated with TLS 1.2 but a PRF based on a HMAC-MD5/HMAC-SHA combination when used with TLS 1.0. On the other hand, SHA384 GCM suites (which can be used only with TLS 1.2 and newer) will always use HMAC-SHA384 for the PRF.

> **Note**
>
> Cipher suite names use a shorthand notation to indicate the MAC algorithm that specifies only the hashing function. This often leads to confusion when the hashing functions have weaknesses. For example, although SHA is known to be weak to chosen-prefix attacks, it's not weak in the way it's used in TLS, which is in an HMAC construction. There are no significant known attacks against HMAC-SHA.

Cipher suites don't have full control over their security parameters. Crucially, they only specify the required authentication and key exchange algorithms, but they don't have control over their exact parameters (e.g., key and parameter strength).

> **Note**
>
> Cipher suites can be used only with the specific authentication mechanism they are intended for. For example, suites with ECDSA in the name require ECDSA keys. A server that has a single RSA key will not show support for any of the ECDSA suites.

When it comes to authentication, the strength typically depends on the certificate or, more specifically, on the certificate's key length and the signature algorithm. The strength of the RSA key exchange also depends on the certificate. DHE and ECDHE key exchanges can be configured with varying strengths, and this is usually done at the server level. Some servers expose this configuration to end users, but others don't. I discuss these aspects in more detail in Chapter 8, *Deployment* and in the following technology-specific chapters.

# Extensions

*TLS extensions* are a general-purpose extension mechanism that's used to add functionality to the TLS protocol without changing the protocol itself. They first appeared in 2003 as a separate specification (RFC 3456) but have since been added to TLS 1.2.

Extensions are added in the form of an extension block that's placed at the end of ClientHello and ServerHello messages:

```
Extension extensions;
```

The block consists of a desired number of extensions placed one after another. Each extension begins with a two-byte extension type (unique identifier) and is followed by the extension data:

```
struct {
    ExtensionType extension_type;
    opaque extension_data;
} Extension;
```

It's up to each extension specification to determine the extension format and the desired behavior. In practice, extensions are used to signal support for some new functionality (thus changing the protocol) and to carry additional data needed during the handshake. Since their introduction, they have become the main vehicle for protocol evolution.

In this section, I will discuss the most commonly seen TLS extensions. Because IANA keeps track of extension types, the official list of extensions can be obtained from their web site.[26]

---

[26] TLS Extensions [fsty.uk/b40] (IANA, retrieved 30 June 2014)

Table 2.3. A selection of commonly seen TLS extensions

| Type | Name | Description |
|---|---|---|
| 0 | server_name | Contains the intended secure virtual host for the connection |
| 5 | status_request | Indicates support for OCSP stapling |
| 13 (0x0d) | signature_algorithms | Contains supported signature algorithm/hash function pairs |
| 15 (0x0f) | heartbeat | Indicates support for the Heartbeat protocol |
| 16 (0x10) | application_layer_protocol _negotiation | Contains supported application-layer protocols that the client is willing to negotiate |
| 18 (0x12) | signed_certificate_timesta mp | Used by servers to submit the proof that the certificate has shared with the public; part of Certificate Transparency |
| 21 (0x15) | padding | Used as a workaround for certain bugs in the F5 load balancers[a] |
| 35 (0x23) | session_ticket | Indicates support for stateless session resumption |
| 13172 (0x3374) | next_protocol_negotiation | Indicates support for Next Protocol Negotiation |
| 65281 (0xff01) | renegotiation_info | Indicates support for secure renegotiation |

[a] A TLS padding extension [fsty.uk/b41] (Internet-Draft, A. Langley, January 2014)

# Application Layer Protocol Negotiation

*Application-Layer Protocol Negotiation* (ALPN) is a protocol extension that enables the negotiation of different application-layer protocols over a TLS connection.[27] With ALPN, a server on port 443 could offer HTTP 1.0 by default but allow the negotiation of other protocols, such as SPDY or HTTP 2.0.

A client that supports ALPN uses the application_layer_protocol_negotiation extension to submit a list of supported application-layer protocols to the server. A compliant server decides on the protocol and uses the same extension to inform the client of its decision.

ALPN provides the same primary functionality as its older relative, NPN (discussed later on in this section), but they differ in secondary properties. Whereas NPN prefers to hide protocol decisions behind encryption, ALPN carries them in plaintext, allowing intermediary devices to inspect them and route traffic based on the observed information.

# Certificate Transparency

*Certificate Transparency*[28] is a proposal to improve Internet PKI by keeping a record of all public server certificates. The basic idea is that the CAs will submit every certificate to a public *log server*, and in return they will receive a proof of submission called *Signed Certificate Timestamp* (SCT), which they can they relay to end users. There are several options for

---

[27] RFC 7301: TLS Application-Layer Protocol Negotiation Extension [fsty.uk/b42] (Friedl et al., July 2014)

[28] Certificate Transparency [fsty.uk/b43] (Google, retrieved 30 June 2014)

the transport of the SCT, and one of them is the new TLS extension called signed_certificate_timestamp.

## Elliptic Curve Capabilities

RFC 4492 specifies two extensions that are used to communicate client EC capabilities during the handshake. The elliptic_curves extension is used in ClientHello to list supported named curves, allowing the server to select one that's supported by both sides.

```
struct {
    NamedCurve elliptic_curve_list
} EllipticCurveList;
```

The main curves are specified in RFC 4492[29] based on the parameters defined by standard bodies, such as NIST:[30]

```
enum {
    sect163k1 (1), sect163r1 (2), sect163r2 (3),
    sect193r1 (4), sect193r2 (5), sect233k1 (6),
    sect233r1 (7), sect239k1 (8), sect283k1 (9),
    sect283r1 (10), sect409k1 (11), sect409r1 (12),
    sect571k1 (13), sect571r1 (14), secp160k1 (15),
    secp160r1 (16), secp160r2 (17), secp192k1 (18),
    secp192r1 (19), secp224k1 (20), secp224r1 (21),
    secp256k1 (22), secp256r1 (23), secp384r1 (24),
    secp521r1 (25),
    reserved (0xFE00..0xFEFF),
    arbitrary_explicit_prime_curves(0xFF01),
    arbitrary_explicit_char2_curves(0xFF02)
} NamedCurve;
```

Brainpool curves were defined later, in RFC 7072.[31] At the time of writing, there are efforts to standardize additional curves, for example, Curve25519.[32] You can find the relevant document on the TLS working group document page.

At this time, there is wide support only for two NIST curves: secp256r1 and secp384r1. There is also virtually no support for arbitrary curves.[33]

---

[29] RFC 4492: ECC Cipher Suites for TLS [fsty.uk/b44] (S. Blake-Wilson et al., May 2006)

[30] FIPS 186-3: Digital Signature Standard [fsty.uk/b45] (NIST, June 2009)

[31] RFC 7072: ECC Brainpool Curves for TLS [fsty.uk/b46] (J. Merkle and M. Lochter, October 2013)

[32] A state-of-the-art Diffie-Hellman function [fsty.uk/b47] (D. J. Bernstein, retrieved 30 June 2014)

[33] The generation of good, arbitrary elliptic curves is a complex and error-prone task that most developers choose to avoid. In addition, named curves can be optimized to run much faster.

## NIST Elliptic Curves

NIST's elliptic curves are sometimes considered suspicious, because there is no explanation of how the parameters were selected.[34] Especially after the Dual EC DRBG backdoor came to light, anything that cannot be explained has been seen by some as suspicious. The fear is that those named curves have weaknesses that are known to the designers but not to the general public. As a result, there are efforts to extend TLS with support for other curves.

The second defined extension is ec_point_formats, which is intended for use with arbitrary curves to enable compression of curve parameters. The theory is that in a constrained environment it's worth saving the bandwidth required to transport curve parameters. However, not only are the potential savings small (e.g., about 64 bytes for a 256-bit curve), but also no one uses arbitrary curves anyway.

# Heartbeat

*Heartbeat*[35] is a protocol extension that adds support for keep-alive functionality (checking that the other party in the conversation is still available) and *path maximum transmission unit* (PMTU)[36] discovery to TLS and DTLS. Although TLS is commonly used over TCP, which does have keep-alive functionality already, Heartbeat is targeted at DTLS, which is deployed over unreliable protocols, such as UDP.

> **Note**
>
> Some have suggested that zero-length TLS records, which are explicitly allowed by the protocol, could be used for the keep-alive functionality. In practice, attempts to mitigate the BEAST attack showed that many applications can't tolerate records without any data. In any case, zero-length TLS records wouldn't help with PMTU discovery, which needs payloads of varying sizes.

Initially, support for Hearbeat is advertised by both the client and the server via the heartbeat extension. During the negotiation, parties give each other permission to send heartbeat requests with the HeartbeatMode parameter:

```
struct {
    HeartbeatMode mode;
```

---

[34] SafeCurves: choosing safe curves for elliptic-curve cryptography [fsty.uk/b48] (D. J. Bernstein, retrieved 21 May 2014)

[35] RFC 6520: TLS and DTLS Heartbeat Extension [fsty.uk/b49] (R. Seggelmann et al., February 2012)

[36] *Maximum transmission unit* (MTU) is the size of the largest data unit that can be sent whole. When two sides communicate directly, they can exchange their MTUs. However, when communication goes over many hops it is sometimes necessary to discover the effective path MTU by sending progressively larger packets.

```
    } HeartbeatExtension;

    enum {
        peer_allowed_to_send (1),
        peer_not_allowed_to_send (2)
    } HeartbeatMode;
```

Heartbeat is implemented as a TLS subprotocol, which means that heartbeat messages can be interleaved with application data and even other protocol messages. According to the RFC, heartbeat messages are allowed only once the handshake completes, but in practice OpenSSL allows them as soon as TLS extensions are exchanged.

It is not clear if Heartbeat is used in practice. However, it's supported by OpenSSL and enabled by default. GnuTLS also implements it. Virtually no one knew what Heartbeat was until April 2014, when it was discovered that the OpenSSL implementation suffered from a fatal flaw that allowed the extraction of sensitive data from the server's process memory. The attack that exploits this vulnerability, called *Heartbleed*, was arguably the worst thing to happen to TLS. You can read more about it in the section called "Heartbleed" in Chapter 6.

## Next Protocol Negotiation

When Google set out to design SPDY,[37] a protocol intended to improve on HTTP, it needed a reliable protocol negotiation mechanism that would work with strict firewalls and in the presence of faulty proxies. Because SPDY was intended to always use TLS anyway, they decided to extend TLS with application-layer protocol negotiation. The result was *Next Protocol Negotiation* (NPN).

> **Note**
>
> If you research NPN, you might come across many different specification versions. Some of those versions were produced for the TLS working group during the standardization discussions. An older version of the specification is used in production.[38]

A SPDY-enabled client submits a TLS handshake that incorporates an empty `next_protocol_negotiation` extension, but only if it also includes a `server_name` extension to indicate the desired hostname. In return, a compliant server responds with the `next_protocol_negotiation` extension, but one that contains a list of the supported application-layer protocols.

The client indicates the desired application-layer protocol by using a new handshake message called `NextProtocol`:

---

[37] SPDY [fsty.uk/b50] (Wikipedia, retrieved 12 June 2014)

[38] Google Technical Note: TLS Next Protocol Negotiation Extension [fsty.uk/b51] (Adam Langley, May 2012)

```
struct {
  opaque selected_protocol;
  opaque padding;
} NextProtocol;
```

In order to hide the client's choice from passive attackers, this message is submitted encrypted, which means that the client must send it after the ChangeCipherSpec message but before Finished. This is a deviation from the standard handshake message flow. The desired protocol name can be selected from the list provided by the server, but the client is also free to submit a protocol that is not advertised. The padding is used to hide the true length of the extension so that the adversary can't guess the selected protocol by looking at the size of the encrypted message.

NPN was submitted to the TLS working group for standardization[39] but, despite wide support in production (e.g., Chrome, Firefox, and OpenSSL), failed to win acceptance. The introduction of a new handshake message, which changes the usual handshake flow, was deemed disruptive and more complex than necessary. There were also concerns that the inability of intermediary devices to see what protocol is being negotiated might be problematic in practice. In the end, the group adopted the competing ALPN proposal.[40] Google currently supports both ALPN and NPN, but will switch to supporting only ALPN after 2014.[41]

# Secure Renegotiation

The renegotiation_info extension improves TLS with verification that renegotiation is being carried out between the same two parties that negotiated the previous handshake.

Initially (during the first handshake on a connection), this extension is used by both parties to inform each other that they support secure renegotiation; for this, they simply send the extension without any data. To secure SSL 3, which doesn't support extensions, clients can instead use a special signaling suite, TLS_EMPTY_RENEGOTIATION_INFO_SCSV (0xff).

On subsequent handshakes, the extension is used to submit proof of knowledge of the previous handshake. Clients send the verify_data value from their previous Finished message. Servers send two values: first the client's verify_data and then their own. The attacker couldn't have obtained these values, because the Finished message is always encrypted.

# Server Name Indication

*Server Name Indication* (SNI), implemented using the server_name extension,[42] provides a mechanism for a client to specify the name of the server it wishes to connect to. In other

---

[39] Next Protocol Negotiation 03 [fsty.uk/b52] (Adam Langley, 24 April 2012)

[40] Some missing context (was: Confirming consensus for ALPN) [fsty.uk/b53] (Yoav Nir, 15 March 2013)

[41] NPN and ALPN [fsty.uk/b54] (Adam Langley, 20 March 2013)

words, this extension provides support for *virtual secure servers*, giving servers enough information to look for a matching certificate among the available virtual secure hosts. Without this mechanism, only one certificate can be deployed per IP address.[43] Because SNI was a late addition to TLS (2006), there are still many older products (e.g., Windows XP and some early Android versions) that don't support it. For this reason, virtual secure hosting is still not practical for public sites that want to reach a large audience.

## Session Tickets

*Session tickets* introduce a new session resumption mechanism that doesn't require any server-side storage.[44] The idea is that the server could take all of its session information (state), encrypt it, and send it back to the client in the form of a *ticket*. On subsequent connections, the client submits the ticket back to the server; the server checks the ticket integrity, decrypts the contents, and uses the information in it to resume the session. This approach potentially makes it easier to scale web server clusters, which would otherwise need to synchronize session state among the nodes.

> ### Warning
>
> Session tickets break the TLS security model. They expose session state on the wire encrypted with a ticket key. Depending on the implementation, the ticket key might be weaker than the cipher used for the connection. For example, OpenSSL uses 128-bit AES keys for this purpose. Also, the *same ticket key* is reused across many sessions. This is similar to the situation with the RSA key exchange and breaks forward secrecy; if the ticket key is compromised it can be used to decrypt full connection data. For this reason, if session tickets are used, the ticket keys must be rotated frequently.

The client indicates support for this resumption mechanism with an empty session_ticket extension. If it wishes to resume an earlier session, then it should instead place the ticket in the extension. A compliant server that wishes to issue a new ticket includes an empty session_ticket extension in its ServerHello. It then waits for the client's Finished message, verifies it, and sends back the ticket in the NewSessionTicket handshake message. If the server wishes to resume an earlier session, then it responds with an abbreviated handshake, as with standard resumption.

---

[42] RFC 6066: TLS Extensions: Extension Definitions [fsty.uk/b55] (D. Eastlake 3rd, January 2011)

[43] Although HTTP has the facility to send host information via the Host request header, this is sent at the application protocol layer, which can be communicated to the server only after a successful TLS handshake.

[44] RFC 5077: TLS Session Resumption without Server-Side State [fsty.uk/b56] (Salowey et al., January 2008)

---

Chapter 2: Protocol

**Note**

When a server decides to use session tickets for session resumption, it sends back
an empty session ID field (in its ServerHello message). At this point, the session
does not have a unique identifier. However, the ticket specification allows the *client*
to select and submit a session ID (in its ClientHello) in a subsequent handshake
that uses the ticket. A server that accepts the ticket must also respond with the
same session ID. This is why the session ID appears in the TLS web server logs
even when session tickets are used as the session-resumption mechanism.

# Signature Algorithms

The signature_algorithms extension, which is defined in TLS 1.2, enables clients to communicate support for various signature and hash algorithms. The TLS specification lists
RSA, DSA, and ECDSA signature algorithms and MD5, SHA1, SHA224, SHA256, SHA384,
and SHA512 hash functions. By using the signature_algorithm extension, clients submit
the *signature–hash* algorithm pairs they support.

This extension is optional; if it's not present, the server infers the supported signature algorithms from the client's offered cipher suites (e.g., RSA suites indicate support for RSA signatures, ECDSA suites indicate support for ECDSA, and so on) and assumes support for
SHA1.

# OCSP Stapling

The status_request extension[42] is used by clients to indicate support for *OCSP stapling*,
which is a feature that a server can use to send fresh certificate revocation information to
the client. (I discuss revocation at length in the section called "Certificate Revocation" in
Chapter 5.) A server that supports stapling returns an empty status_request extension in
its ServerHello and provides an OCSP response (in DER format) in the CertificateStatus
handshake message immediately after the Certificate message.

OCSP stapling supports only one OCSP response and can be used to check the revocation
status of the server certificate only. This limitation is addressed by RFC 6961,[45] which adds
support for multiple OCSP responses (and uses the status_request_v2 extension to indicate
support for it). However, at this time, this improved version is not well supported in either
client or server software.

---

[45] RFC 6961: TLS Multiple Certificate Status Request Extension [fsty.uk/b57] (Y. Pettersen, June 2013)

---

# Protocol Limitations

In addition to unintentional weaknesses, which I will discuss at length in subsequent chapters, TLS is known to currently have several limitations influenced by its positioning in the OSI layer and certain design decisions:

- Encryption protects the contents of a TCP connection, but the metadata of TCP and all other lower layers remains in plaintext. Thus, a passive observer can determine the IP addresses of the source and the destination. Information leakage of this type isn't the fault of TLS but a limitation inherent in our current layered networking model.

- At the TLS layer, too, a lot of the information is exposed as plaintext. The first handshake is never encrypted, allowing the passive observer to (1) learn about client capabilities and use them for fingerprinting, (2) examine the SNI information to determine the intended virtual host, (3) examine the host's certificate, and, when client certificates are used, (4) potentially obtain enough information to identify the user. There are workarounds to avoid these issues, but they're not used by mainstream implementations.

- After encryption is activated, some protocol information remains in the clear: the observer can see the subprotocol and length of each message. Depending on the protocol, the length might reveal useful clues about the underlying communication. For example, there have been several studies that have tried to infer what resources are being accessed over HTTP based on the indicated request and response sizes. Without length hiding, it's not possible to safely use compression before encryption (a common practice today).

The leakage of network-layer metadata can be solved only at those levels. The other limitations could be fixed, and, indeed, there are proposals and discussions about addressing them. You'll learn more about these problems later in the book.

# Differences between Protocol Versions

This section describes the major differences between various SSL and TLS protocol versions. There haven't been many changes to the core protocol since SSL 3. TLS 1.0 made limited changes only to justify a different name, and TLS 1.1 was primarily released to fix a few security problems. TLS 1.2 introduced authenticated encryption, cleaned up the hashing, and otherwise made the protocol free of any hardcoded primitives.

## SSL 3

SSL 3 was released in late 1995. Starting from scratch to address the many weaknesses of the previous protocol version, SSL 3 established the design that still remains in the latest versions of the TLS. If you want to gain a better understanding of what SSL 3 changed and why, I recommend the protocol analysis paper by Wagner and Schneier.[46]

# TLS 1.0

TLS 1.0 was released in January 1999. It includes the following changes from SSL 3:

- This is the first version to specify a PRF based on the standard HMAC and implemented as a combination (XOR) of HMAC-MD5 and HMAC-SHA.

- Master secret generation now uses the PRF instead of a custom construction.

- The `verify_data` value is now based on the PRF instead of a custom construction.

- Integrity validation (MAC) uses the official HMAC. SSL 3 used an earlier, obsolete HMAC version.

- FORTEZZA[47] suites were removed.

As a practical matter, the result of the protocol cleanup was that TLS 1.0 was given FIPS approval, allowing its use by US government agencies.

If you want to study TLS 1.0 and earlier protocol versions, I recommend Eric Rescorla's book *SSL and TLS: Designing and Building Secure Systems*, published by Addison-Wesley in 2001. I have found this book to be invaluable for understanding the reasoning behind certain decisions as well as to follow the evolution of the designs.

# TLS 1.1

TLS 1.1 was released in April 2006. It includes the following major changes from TLS 1.0:

- CBC encryption now uses explicit IVs that are included in every TLS record. This addresses the predictable IV weakness, which was later exploited in the BEAST attack.

- Implementations are now required to use the `bad_record_mac` alert in response to padding problems to defend against padding attacks. The `decryption_failed` alert is deprecated.

- This version includes TLS extensions (RFC 3546) by reference.

# TLS 1.2

TLS 1.2 was released in August 2008. It includes the following major changes from TLS 1.1:

---

[46] Analysis of the SSL 3.0 protocol [fsty.uk/b58] (David Wagner and Bruce Schneier, Proceedings of the Second USENIX Workshop on Electronic Commerce, 1996)

[47] Fortezza [fsty.uk/b59] (Wikipedia, retrieved 30 June 2014)

---

- Support for authenticated encryption was added.

- Support for HMAC-SHA256 cipher suites was added.

- IDEA and DES cipher suites were removed.

- TLS extensions were incorporated in the main protocol specification, although most actual extensions remain documented elsewhere.

- A new extension, signature_algorithms, can be used by clients to communicate what hash and signature algorithms they are willing to accept.

- The MD5/SHA1 combination used in the PRF was replaced with SHA256 for the TLS 1.2 suites and all earlier suites when negotiated with this protocol version.

- Cipher suites are now allowed to specify their own PRFs.

- The MD5/SHA1 combination used for digital signatures was replaced with a single hash. By default, SHA256 is used, but cipher suites can specify their own. Before, the signature hash algorithm was mandated by the protocol; now the hash function is part of the signature structure, and implementations can choose the best algorithm.

- The length of the verify_data element in the Finished message can now be explicitly specified by cipher suites.

# 3 Public-Key Infrastructure

Thanks to public-key cryptography, we are able to communicate safely with people whose public keys we have, but there's a number of other problems that remain unsolved. For example, how can we communicate with people we've never met? How do we store public keys and revoke them? Most importantly, how do we do that at world scale, with millions of servers and billions of people and devices? It's a tall order, but it's what *public-key infrastructure* (PKI) was created to solve.

## Internet PKI

For most people, PKI is about the public-key infrastructure as used on the Internet. However, the real meaning of PKI is much wider, because it had originally been developed for other uses. Thus, it's more accurate to talk about *Internet PKI*, the term that was introduced by the PKIX working group that adapted PKI for use on the Internet. Another term that's recently been used is *Web PKI*, in which the focus is on how browsers consume and validate certificates. In this book, I'll generally use the name PKI to refer to Internet PKI, except maybe in a few cases in which the distinction is important.

The goal of PKI is to enable secure communication among parties who have never met before. The model we use today relies on trusted third parties called *certification authorities* (CAs; sometimes also called *certificate authorities*) to issue certificates that we unreservedly trust.

Figure 3.1. Internet PKI certificate lifecycle

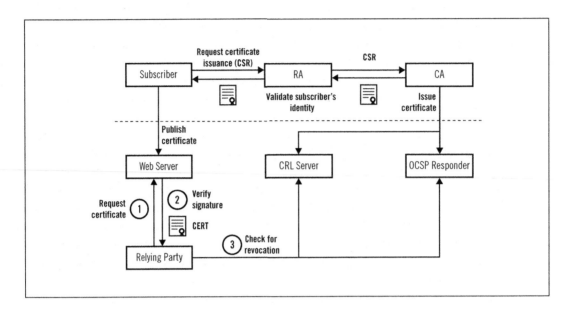

### Subscriber

The *subscriber* (or *end entity*) is the party that wishes to provide secure services, which require a certificate.

### Registration authority

The *registration authority* (RA) carries out certain management functions related to certificate issuance. For example, an RA might perform the necessary identity validation before requesting a CA to issue a certificate. In some cases, RAs are also called *local registration authorities* (LRAs), for example, when a CA wants to establish a branch that is close to its users (such as one in a different country). In practice, many CAs also perform RA duties.

### Certification authority

The *certification authority* (CA) is a party we trust to issue certificates that confirm subscriber identities. They are also required to provide up-to-date revocation information online so that relying parties can verify that certificates are still valid.

### Relying party

The *relying party* is the certificate consumer. Technically, these are web browsers, other programs, and operating systems that perform certificate validation. They do this by operating *root trust stores* that contain the ultimately trusted certificates (*trust anchors*) of some CAs. In a wider sense, relying parties are end users who depend on certificates for secure communication on the Internet.

## What Is Trust?

Discussions about PKI usually use words such as *identity*, *authority*, and *trust*. Because they rarely mean what we think they mean, these words often cause confusion and create a mismatch between our expectations and what exists in real life.

With most certificates, we get only limited assurances that we're talking to the right server. Only EV certificates provide a binding with an offline identity, but that doesn't mean much for security, which depends on too many other factors.

In PKI, *trust* is used only in a very technical sense of the word; it means that a certificate can be validated by a CA we have in the trust store. But it doesn't mean that we *trust* the subscriber for anything. Think about this: millions of people visit Amazon's web sites every day and make purchases, even though the homepage opens without encryption. Why do we do that? Ultimately, because they earned our (real) trust.

# Standards

Internet PKI has its roots in X.509, an international standard for public-key infrastructure that was originally designed to support X.500, a standard for electronic directory services. X.500 never took off, but X.509 was adapted for use on the Internet by the PKIX working group.[1]

From the charter:

> The PKIX Working Group was established in the fall of 1995 with the goal of developing Internet standards to support X.509-based Public Key Infrastructures (PKIs). Initially PKIX pursued this goal by profiling X.509 standards developed by the CCITT (later the ITU-T). Later, PKIX initiated the development of standards that are not profiles of ITU-T work, but rather are independent initiatives designed to address X.509-based PKI needs in the Internet. Over time this latter category of work has become the major focus of PKIX work, i.e., most PKIX-generated RFCs are no longer profiles of ITU-T X.509 documents.

The main document produced by the PKIX working group is RFC 5280, which documents the certificate format and trust path building as well as the format of *Certificate Revocation Lists* (CRLs).[2] The PKIX working group concluded in October 2013.

---

[1] PKIX Working Group [fsty.uk/b60] (IETF, retrieved 16 July 2014)

[2] RFC 5280: Internet X.509 Public Key Infrastructure Certificate and CRL Profile [fsty.uk/b61] (Cooper et al., May 2008)

> **Note**
>
> As is usually the case on the Internet, the reality rarely reflects standards. This is in part because standards are often vague and don't fulfill real-life needs. It's impossible to predict how technologies evolve over time, which is why implementations often take matters into their hands. In addition, major products and libraries often make mistakes and effectively restrict how technologies can be used in practice. You will find many such examples in this book.

*CA/Browser Forum* (or *CAB Forum*) is a voluntary group of CAs, browser vendors, and other interested parties whose goal is to establish and enforce standards for certificate issuance and processing.[3] CA/Browser Forum was initially created to define standards for issuance of *extended validation* (EV) certificates, which first came out in 2007.[4] Although initially a rather loose group of CAs, CAB Forum changed their focus and restructured in 2012.[5] The same year, they released *Baseline Requirements for the Issuance and Management of Publicly-Trusted Certificates*, or *Baseline Requirements* for short.[6]

Although CAB Forum lists only about 40 CAs as members, Baseline Requirements effectively apply to all CAs; the document is incorporated into the WebTrust audit program for CAs[7] and explicitly required by some root store operators (e.g., Mozilla).

Also relevant is IETF's *Web PKI working group*, which was formed in September 2012 to describe how PKI really works the Web.[8] This group is expected to document the Web PKI trust model and revocation practices and the usage of various fields and extensions in certificates, CRLs, and OCSP responses.

# Certificates

A certificate is a digital document that contains a public key, some information about the entity associated with it, and a digital signature from the certificate issuer. In other words, it's a shell that allows us to exchange, store, and use public keys. With that, certificates become the basic building block of PKI.

---

[3] CA/Browser Forum [fsty.uk/b62] (retrieved 16 July 2014)

[4] EV SSL Certificate Guidelines [fsty.uk/b63] (CA/Browser Forum, retrieved 16 July 2014)

[5] The change of focus came from the realization that there were many burning security questions that were not being addressed. During 2011, there were several small and big CA failures, and the general feeling was that the PKI ecosystem was terribly insecure. Some even questioned the ecosystem's survival. With Baseline Requirements, CAB Forum addressed many of these issues.

[6] Baseline Requirements [fsty.uk/b64] (CA/Browser Forum, retrieved 13 July 2014)

[7] WebTrust Program for Certification Authorities [fsty.uk/b65] (WebTrust, retrieved 25 May 2014)

[8] Web PKI OPS [fsty.uk/b66] (IETF, retrieved 25 May 2014)

## ASN.1, BER, DER, and PEM

*Abstract Syntax Notation One* (ASN.1) is a set of rules that support definition, transport, and exchange of complex data structures and objects. ASN.1 was designed to support network communication between diverse platforms in a way that's independent of machine architecture and implementation language. ASN.1 is a standard originally defined in 1988 in X.208; it was last updated in 2008 in the X.680 series of documents.

ASN.1 defines data in an abstract way; separate standards exist to specify how data is encoded. *Basic Encoding Rules* (BER) is the first such standard. X.509 relies on *Distinguished Encoding Rules* (DER), which are a subset of BER that allow only one way to encode ASN.1 values. This is critical for use in cryptography, especially digital signatures. PEM (short for *Privacy-Enhanced Mail*, which has no meaning in this context) is an ASCII encoding of DER using Base64 encoding. ASN.1 is complicated, but, unless you're a developer dealing with cryptography, you probably won't have to work with it directly.

Most certificates are supplied in PEM format (because it's easy to email, copy, and paste), but you might sometimes encounter DER, too. If you need to convert from one format to another, use the OpenSSL x509 command. I'll talk more about that later in the book.

If you're curious about what ASN.1 looks like, download any certificate and use the online ASN.1 decoder to see the ASN.1 structure.[9]

# Certificate Fields

A certificate consists of fields and—in version 3—a set of extensions. On the surface, the structure is flat and linear, although some fields contain other structures.

**Version**

There are three certificate versions: 1, 2, and 3, encoded as values 0, 1, and 2. Version 1 supports only basic fields; version 2 adds unique identifiers (two additional fields); and version 3 adds extensions. Most certificates are in v3 format.

**Serial Number**

Initially, serial numbers were specified as positive integers that uniquely identify a certificate issued by a given CA. Additional requirements were added later as a second layer of defense from chosen prefix attacks against certificate signatures (find out more in the next chapter, in the section called "RapidSSL Rogue CA Certificate "); serial numbers are now required to be nonsequential (unpredictable) and contain at least 20 bits of entropy.

---

[9] ASN.1 JavaScript decoder [fsty.uk/b67] (Lapo Luchini, retrieved 24 May 2014)

---

**Signature Algorithm**

> This field specifies the algorithm used for the certificate signature. It's placed here, inside the certificate, so that it can be protected by the signature.

**Issuer**

> The *Issuer* field contains the *distinguished name* (DN) of the certificate issuer. It's a complex field that can contain many components depending on the represented entity. This, for example, is the DN used for one of VeriSign's root certificates: `/C=US/ O=VeriSign, Inc./OU=Class 3 Public Primary Certification Authority`; it contains three components, one each for country, organization, and organization unit.

**Validity**

> The certificate validity period is the time interval during which the certificate is valid. It's represented with two values: the starting date and the ending date.

**Subject**

> The subject is the distinguished name of the entity associated with the public key for which the certificate is issued. Self-signed certificates have the same DN in their *Subject* and *Issuer* fields. Initially, the *common name* (CN) component of the DN was used for server hostnames (e.g., `/CN=www.example.com` would be used for a certificate valid for *www.example.com*). Unfortunately, that caused some confusion about how to issue certificates that are valid for multiple hostnames. Today, the *Subject* field is deprecated in favor of the *Subject Alternative Name* extension.

**Public key**

> This field contains the public key, represented by the *Subject Public-Key Info* structure (essentially algorithm ID, optional parameters, and then the public key itself). Public-key algorithms are specified in RFC 3279.[10]

> **Note**
>
> Two additional certificate fields were added in version 2: *Issuer Unique ID* and *Subject Unique ID*. They were later deprecated in version 3 in favor of the *Authority Key Identifier* and *Subject Key Identifier* extensions.

## Certificate Extensions

Certificate extensions were introduced in version 3 in order to add flexibility to the previously rigid certificate format. Each extension consists of a unique object identifier (OID), criticality indicator, and value, which is an ASN.1 structure. An extension marked as critical must be understood and successfully processed; otherwise the entire certificate must be rejected.

---

[10] RFC 3279: Algorithms and Identifiers for the Internet X.509 PKI and CRL Profile [fsty.uk/b68] (Polk et al., April 2002)

---

### Subject Alternative Name

Traditionally, the *Subject* certificate field (more specifically, only its CN component) is used to create a binding between an identity and a public key. In practice, that approach is not flexible enough; it supports only hostnames and does not specify how multiple identities are handled. The *Subject Alternative Name* extension replaces the *Subject* field; it supports bindings to multiple identities specified by a DNS name, IP address, or URI.

### Name Constraints

The *Name Constraints* extension can be used to constrain the identities for which a CA can issue certificates. Identity namespaces can be explicitly excluded or permitted. This is a very useful feature that could, for example, allow an organization to obtain a subordinate CA that can issue certificates only for the company-owned domain names. With the namespaces constrained, such a CA certificate poses no danger to the entire ecosystem (i.e., a CA can't issue certificates for arbitrary sites).

RFC 5280 requires this extension to be marked as critical, but noncritical name constraints are used in practice and explicitly allowed by Baseline Requirements. This is due to the fact that some products do not understand the *Name Constraints* extension and reject certificates that contain it if it's marked critical.

### Basic Constraints

The *Basic Constraints* extension is used to indicate a CA certificate and, via the *path length constraint* field, control the depth of the subordinate CA certificate path (i.e., whether the CA certificate can issue further nested CA certificates and how deep). In theory, all CA certificates must include this extension; in practice, some root certificates issued as version 1 certificates are still used despite the fact that they contain no extensions.

### Key Usage

This extension defines the possible uses of the key contained in the certificate. There is a fixed number of uses, any of which can be set on a particular certificate. For example, a CA certificate could have the *Certificate Signer* and *CRL Signer* bits set.

### Extended Key Usage

For more flexibility in determining or restricting public key usage, this extension allows arbitrary additional purposes to be specified, indicated by their OIDs. For example, end-entity certificates typically carry the `id-kp-serverAuth` and `id-kp-clientAuth` OIDs; code signing certificates use the `id-kp-codeSigning` OID, and so on.

Although RFC 5280 indicates that *Extended Key Usage* (EKU) should be used only on end-entity certificates, in practice this extension is used on intermediate CA certificates to constrain the usage of the certificates issued from them.[11] Baseline Require-

---

ments, in particular, require the use of EKU constraints for an intermediate certificate to be considered technically constrained using name constraints.

**Certificate Policies**

This extension contains a list of one or more policies. A policy consists of an OID and an optional qualifier. When present, the qualifier usually contains the URI at which the full text of the policy can be obtained. Baseline Requirements establish that an end-entity certificate must always include at least one policy to indicate the terms under which the certificate was issued. The extension can be optionally used to indicate certificate validation type.

**CRL Distribution Points**

This extension is used to determine the location of the *Certificate Revocation List* (CRL) information, usually provided as an LDAP or HTTP URI. According to Baseline Requirements, a certificate must provide either CRL or OCSP revocation information.

**Authority Information Access**

The *Authority Information Access* extension indicates how to access certain additional information and services provided by the issuing CA. One such piece of information is the location of the OCSP responder, provided as an HTTP URI. Relying parties can use the responder to check for revocation information in real time. In addition, some certificates also include the URI at which the issuing certificate can be found. That information is very useful for reconstruction of an incomplete certificate chain.

**Subject Key Identifier**

This extension contains a unique value that can be used to identify certificates that contain a particular public key. It is recommended that the identifier be constructed from the public key itself (e.g., by hashing). All CA certificates must include this extension and use the same identifier in the *Authority Key Identifier* extension of all issued certificates.

**Authority Key Identifier**

The content of this extension uniquely identifies the key that signed the certificate. It can be used during certificate path building to identify the parent certificate.

RFC 5280 defines several other extensions that are rarely used; they are *Delta CRL Distribution Point*, *Inhibit anyPolicy*, *Issuer Alternative Name*, *Policy Constraints*, *Policy Mappings*, *Subject Directory Attributes*, and *Subject Information Access*.

---

[11] Bug 725451: Support enforcing nested EKU constraints, do so by default [fsty.uk/b69] (Bugzilla@Mozilla, reported 8 February 2014)

# Certificate Chains

In the majority of cases, an end-entity certificate alone is insufficient for a successful validation. In practice, each server must provide a *chain of certificates* that leads to a trusted root. Certificate chains are used for security, technical, and administrative reasons.

Figure 3.2. Certificate structure

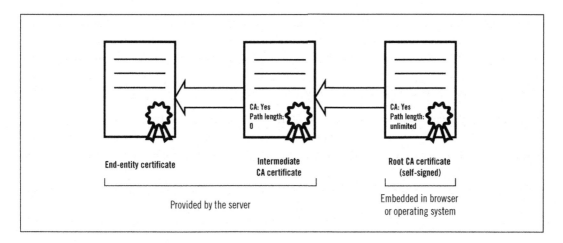

### Keeping the root safe

The root CA key is of great importance not only to the organization that owns it but also to the entire ecosystem. First, it has great financial value. Older, widely distributed keys are effectively irreplaceable, because many root stores are not being updated any more. Second, if the key is compromised it can be used to issue fraudulent certificates for any domain name. If compromised, the key would have to be revoked, bringing down all the sites that depend on it.

Although there are still some CAs that issue end-entity certificates directly from their roots, this practice is seen as too dangerous. Baseline Requirements require that the root key is used only by issuing a direct command (i.e., automation is not allowed), implying that the root must be kept offline. Issuing subscriber certificates directly from the root is not allowed, although there is a loophole for legacy systems that are still in use.

### Cross-certification

Cross-certification is the only way for new CAs to start operating today. Because it's impossible to distribute young root keys widely and quickly, they must get their root key signed by some other well-established CA. Over time, as old devices fade away, the new CA key will eventually become useful on its own.

**Compartmentalization**

> By splitting its operation across many subordinate CA certificates, a CA can spread the risk of exposure. For example, different subordinate CAs could be used for different certificate classes, or for different business units. Unlike roots, subordinate CAs are typically placed online and used in automated systems.

**Delegation**

> In some cases, a CA might want to issue a subordinate CA to another organization that is not affiliated with it. For example, a large company might want to issue their own certificates for the domain names they control. (That is often cheaper than running a private CA and ensuring that the root certificate is distributed to all devices.) Sometimes, organizations might want to have full control, in which case the subordinate CA might be technically constrained to certain namespaces. In other cases, the CA remains in control over the certificates issued from the subordinate CA.

A server can provide only one certificate chain, but, in practice, there can be many valid trust paths. For example, in the case of cross-certification, one trust path will lead to the main CA's root and another to the alternative root. CAs sometimes issue multiple certificates for the same keys. For example, the major signing algorithm used today is SHA1, but, for security reasons, everyone is moving to SHA256. The CA can reuse the same key but issue a new certificate. If the relying party happens to have both such certificates, then they will form two different trust paths.

Path building generally complicates things a lot and leads to various problems. Servers are expected to provide complete and valid certificate chains, but that often doesn't happen due to human error and various usability issues (e.g., having to configure the server certificate in one place and the rest of the chain in another). According to SSL Pulse, there are about 5.9% of servers with incomplete certificate chains.[12]

On the other side, path building and validation is a cause of many security issues in client software. This is not surprising, given vague, incomplete, and competing standards. Historically, many validation libraries had failed with simple tasks, such as validating that the issuing certificate belongs to a CA. The most commonly used libraries today are battle tested and secure only because they patched the worst problems, not because they were secure from the start. For many examples, refer to the section called "Certificate Validation Flaws" in Chapter 6.

# Relying Parties

For relying parties to be able to validate subscriber certificates, they must keep a collection of root CA certificates they trust. In most cases, each operating system provides a root store

---

[12] SSL Pulse [fsty.uk/b70] (SSL Labs, retrieved July 2014)

in order to bootstrap trust. Virtually all application developers reuse the root stores of the underlying operating systems. The only exception to this is Mozilla, who maintain their own root store for consistent operation across a number of platforms.

**Apple**

Apple operates a root certificate program that is used on the iOS and OS X platforms. [13] To be considered for inclusion, a CA must pass an audit and demonstrate that it provides broad business value to Apple's customers.

**Chrome**

Chrome relies on the store provided by the operating system and on Mozilla's store (via their networking library, NSS) when deployed on Linux. However, they have some additional policies that they apply themselves when the underlying facilities are not adequate.[14] For illustration: (1) there's a blacklist of roots they won't trust; (2) an explicit lists of CAs who can issue EV certificates; and (3) a special requirement that, starting in February 2015, EV certificates must implement *Certificate Transparency*.

**Microsoft**

Microsoft operates a root certificate program that is used on the Windows desktop, server, and mobile phone platforms.[15] Broadly, inclusion requires a yearly audit and a demonstration of business value to the Microsoft user base.

**Mozilla**

Mozilla operates a largely transparent root certificate program,[16] which they use for their products. Their root store is often used as the basis for the root stores of various Linux distributions. Heated discussions about policy decisions often take place on the `mozilla.dev.tech.crypto` list and on Mozilla's bug tracking system.

All root certificate programs require CAs to undergo independent audits designed for certification authorities. For DV and OV certificates, one of the following audits is usually requested:

- WebTrust for Certificate Authorities[17]

- ETSI TS 101 456

- ETSI TS 102 042

- ISO 21188:2006

WebTrust operates the only audit program available for issuance of EV certificates.

---

[13] Apple Root Certificate Program [fsty.uk/b71] (Apple, retrieved 25 May 2014)

[14] Root Certificate Policy [fsty.uk/b72] (Chrome Security, retrieved 25 May 2014)

[15] Introduction to The Microsoft Root Certificate Program [fsty.uk/b73] (Microsoft, retrieved 25 May 2014)

[16] Mozilla CA Certificate Policy [fsty.uk/b74] (Mozilla, retrieved 25 May 2014)

[17] Principles and Criteria for Certification Authorities 2.0 [fsty.uk/b65] (WebTrust, retrieved 25 May 2014)

# Certification Authorities

*Certification authorities* (CAs) are the most important part of the current internet trust model. They can issue a certificate for any domain name, which means that anything they say goes. At the surface, it sounds like easy money, provided you can get your roots into a wide range of devices. But what exactly do you have to do to become a public CA?

1. Build out a competent CA organization:

   a. Establish strong expertise in PKI and CA operations.

   b. Design a robust, secure, and compartmentalized network to enable business operations yet protect the highly sensitive root and subordinate keys.

   c. Support the certificate lifecycle workflow.

   d. Comply with Baseline Requirements.

   e. Comply with EV SSL Certificate Guidelines.

   f. Provide a global CRL and OCSP infrastructure.

2. Comply with local laws; depending on the jurisdiction, this might mean obtaining a license.

3. Pass the audits required by the root programs.

4. Place your roots into a wide range of root programs.

5. Cross-certify your roots to bootstrap the operations.

For a long time, selling certificates was a relatively easy job for those who got in early. These days, there is much less money to be made selling DV certificates, given that their price has been driven down by strong competition. Furthermore, if support for DNSSEC and DANE becomes widespread it will mark the end of DV certificates. As a result, CAs are moving to the smaller but potentially more lucrative market for EV certificates and related services.

# Certificate Lifecycle

Certificate lifecycle begins when a subscriber prepares a *Certificate Signing Request* (CSR) and submits it to the CA of their choice. The main purpose of the CSR is to carry the relevant public key as well as demonstrate ownership of the corresponding private key (using a signature). CSRs are designed to carry additional metadata, but not all of it is used in practice. CAs will often override the CSR values and use other sources for the information they embed in certificates.

The CA then follows the validation procedure, using a different steps depending on the type of certificate requested:

### Domain validation

*Domain validated* (DV) certificates are issued based on proof of control over a domain name. In most cases, that means sending a confirmation email to one of the approved email addresses. If the recipient approves (i.e., follows the link in the email), then the certificate is issued. If confirmation via email is not possible, then any other means of communication (e.g., phone or snail mail) and practical demonstration of control are allowed. A similar procedure is followed when issuing certificates for IP addresses.

### Organization validation

*Organization validated* (OV) certificates require identity and authenticity verification. It wasn't until Baseline Requirements were adopted that the procedures for OV certificates were standardized. As a result, there was (and still is) a lot of inconsistency in how OV certificates were issued and how the relevant information was encoded in the certificate.

### Extended validation

*Extended validation* (EV) certificates were introduced to address the lack of consistency in OV certificates, so it's no surprise that the validation procedures are extensively documented, leaving little room for inconsistencies.

Issuance of DV certificates is fully automated and can be very quick. The duration depends largely on how fast the confirmation email is answered. On the other end of the spectrum, validation of EV certificates can take days or even weeks.

### Note

When fraudulent certificate requests are submitted, attackers usually go after high-profile domain names. For this reason, CAs tend to maintain a list of such high-risk names and refuse to issue them without manual confirmation. This practice is required by Baseline Requirements.

After successful validation, the CA issues the certificate. In addition to the certificate itself, the CA will provide all of the intermediary certificates required to chain to their root. They also usually provide configuration instructions for major platforms.

The subscriber can now use the certificate in production, where it will hopefully stay until it expires. If the corresponding private key is compromised, the certificate is revoked. The procedure in this case is similar to that used for certificate issuance. There is often talk about certificate *reissuance*, but there is no such thing, technically speaking. After a certificate is revoked, an entirely new certificate is issued to replace it.

# Revocation

Certificates are revoked when the associated public keys are compromised or no longer needed. In both cases, there is a risk of misuse. The revocation protocols and procedures are designed to ensure certificate freshness and otherwise communicate revocation to relying parties. There are two standards for certificate revocation:

### Certificate Revocation List

A *Certificate Revocation List* (CRL) is a list of all serial numbers belonging to revoked certificates that have not yet expired. CAs maintain one or more such lists. Every certificate should contain the location of the corresponding CRL in the *CRL Distribution Points* certificate extension. The main problem with CRLs is that they tend to be large, making real-time lookups slow.

### Online Certificate Status Protocol

*Online Certificate Status Protocol* (OCSP) allows relying parties to obtain the revocation status of a single certificate. OCSP servers are known as *OCSP responders*. The location of the CA's OCSP responder is encoded in the *Authority Information Access* certificate extension. OCSP allows for real-time lookups and addresses the main CRL deficiency, but it doesn't solve all revocation problems: the use of OCSP responders leads to performance and privacy issues and introduces a new point of failure. Some of these issues can be addressed with a technique called *OCSP stapling*, which allows each server to embed an OCSP response directly into the TLS handshake.

# Weaknesses

Observed from a strict security perspective, Internet PKI suffers from many weaknesses, some big and some small; I will outline both kinds in this section. However, before we move to the problems, we must establish the context. In 1995, when the secure Web was just taking off, the Internet was a much different place and much less important than it is now. Then, we needed encryption so that we could deploy ecommerce and start making money. Today, we have ecommerce, and it's working well—but we want much more. For some groups, encryption is genuinely a matter of life and death.

But what we have today is a system that does what it was originally designed to do: provide enough security for ecommerce operations. In a wider sense, the system provides us with what I like to call *commercial security*. It's a sort of security that can be achieved with relatively little money, makes web sites go fast, tolerates insecure practices, and does not annoy users too much. The system is controlled by CAs, commercial entities in pursuit of profit, and browser vendors, who are primarily interested in increasing their market share. Neither group has strong security as priority, but they are not necessarily to blame—at least not entirely. They won't give us security until we, the end users, start to demand it from them.

CAs, in particular, just can't win. There are hundreds of CAs who issue millions of certificates every year and generally make the world go around. Error rates are very small. Certainly, the security is not as good as it could be, but the whole thing works. Despite that, there's a strong resentment from many because they have to pay for certificates. Most don't want to pay. Those who do pay want to pay as little as possible; at the same time, they demand flawless security.

In truth, anyone looking for real security (for whatever meaning of that word) is ultimately not going to get it from an ecosystem that's—for better or worse—afraid to break things for security. That said, problems are being fixed, as you will see later on. Now onto the flaws.

### Permission of domain owners not required for certificate issuance

The biggest problem we have is conceptual: any CA can issue a certificate for any domain name without obtaining permission. The key issue here is that there are no technical measures in place to protect us from CA omissions and security lapses. This might not have seemed like a big problem early on, when only a few CAs existed, but it's a huge issue today now that there are hundreds. It's been said many times: the security of the entire PKI system today is as good as the weakest link, and we have many potentially weak links. All CAs are required to undergo audits, but the quality of those audits is uncertain. For example, DigiNotar, the Dutch CA whose security was completely compromised in 2011, had been audited.

Then, there is the question of whether CAs themselves can be trusted to do their jobs well and for the public benefit; who are those hundreds of organizations that we allow to issue certificates with little supervision? The fear that they might put their commercial interests above our security needs is sometimes justified. For example, in 2012 Trustwave admitted to issuing a subordinate certificate that would be used for traffic inspection, forging certificates for any web site on the fly.[18] Although Trustwave is the only CA to publicly admit to issuing such certificates, there were rumors that such behavior was not uncommon.

Many fear that governments abuse the system to allow themselves to forge certificates for arbitrary domain names. Can we really be sure that some of the CAs are not just fronts for government operations? And, even if they are not, can we be sure that they can't be compelled to do whatever their governments tell them to? We can't. The only unknown is the extent to which governments will interfere with the operation of commercial CAs.

### No trust agility

Another conceptual problem is lack of trust agility. Relying parties operate root stores that contain a number of CA certificates. A CA is thus either trusted or not; there isn't any middle ground. In theory, a relying party can remove a CA from the store. In

---

[18] Clarifying The Trustwave CA Policy Update [fsty.uk/b75] (Trustwave, 4 February 2012)

practice, that can happen only in cases of gross incompetence or security compromise, or if a CA is small. Once a CA issues a sufficiently large number of certificates, they effectively become too big to fail.

Some slaps on the wrist are still possible. For example, in the past we had relying parties revoke EV privileges from some CAs who showed incompetence. Another idea (never attempted) is to punish a misbehaving CA by revoking trust in future certificates, allowing the existing ones to stay in place.

**Weak domain validation**

DV certificates are issued based on domain name ownership information retrieved via the insecure WHOIS protocol. Furthermore, the interaction is most commonly carried out using email, which in itself can be insecure. It's easy to obtain a fraudulent DV certificate if a domain name is hijacked or if access to the key mailbox is obtained. It's also possible to attack the implementation of the validation process at the CA by intercepting network traffic at their end.

**Revocation does not work**

It is generally seen that revocation does not work. We saw several CA failures in 2011, and, in every case, relying parties had to issue patches or use their proprietary blacklisting channels to reliably revoke the compromised certificates.

There are two reasons why that was necessary. First, there's a delay in propagating revocation information to each system. Baseline Requirements allow CRL and OCSP information to stay valid for up to 10 days (12 months for intermediate certificates). This means that it takes at least 10 days for the revocation information to fully propagate. The second problem is the *soft-fail* policy implemented in all current browsers; they will attempt to obtain revocation information but ignore all failures. An active network attacker can easily suppress OCSP requests, for example, allowing him to use a fraudulent certificate indefinitely.

Because of this, Chrome developers decided to stop checking for revocation except for EV certificates. For important certificates (e.g., intermediate CAs), they rely on a proprietary revocation channel (CRLSets) that's based on CRL information. A possible solution to this problem is the adoption of so-called *must-staple certificates*, which can be used only in combination with a fresh OCSP response.[19] You'll find more thorough coverage of this topic in the section called "Certificate Revocation" in Chapter 5.

**Certificate warnings defeat the purpose of encryption**

Possibly the biggest failure of Internet PKI (or Web PKI, to be more accurate) is a lax approach to certificate validation. Many libraries and applications skip validation al-

---

[19] X.509v3 Extension: OCSP Stapling Required [fsty.uk/b76] (P. Hallam-Baker, October 2012)

together. Browsers check certificates, but, when an invalid certificate is encountered, they present their users with warnings that can be bypassed. According to some studies, from 30% to 70% of users click through these warnings, which completely defeats the purpose of encryption. Recently, a new standard called *HTTP Strict Transport Security* was developed to instruct compliant browsers to replace warnings with errors, disallowing bypass.

# Root Key Compromise

One of the best ways to attack PKI is to go after the root certificates directly. For government agencies, one approach might be to simply request the private keys from the CAs in their countries. If that's seen as possibly controversial and dangerous, anyone with a modest budget (say, a million dollars or so) could start a brand new CA and get their roots embedded in trust stores everywhere. They might or might not feel the need to run a proper CA as a cover; there are many roots that have never been seen issuing end-entity certificates.

This approach to attacking Internet PKI would have been safe for many years, but at some point a couple of years ago people started paying attention to the functioning ecosystem. Browser plug-ins for certificate tracking were built; they alert users whenever a new certificate is encountered. Google implemented public key pinning in Chrome, now a very popular browser. The Electronic Frontier Foundation extended its browser plug-in HTTPS Everywhere to monitor root certificate usage.[20]

A far less messy approach (both then and now) would be to simply break the existing root or intermediate certificates. If you have access to the key belonging to an intermediate certificate, you can issue arbitrary certificates. For best results (the smallest chance of being discovered), fraudulent certificates should be issued from the same CA as the genuine ones. Many sites, especially the big ones, operate multiple certificates at the same time. If the issuing CA is the same, how are you going to differentiate a fraudulent certificate from a genuine one?

In 2003 (more than ten years ago!), Shamir and Tromer estimated that a $10 million purpose-built machine could break a 1,024-bit key in about a year (plus $20 million for the initial design and development).[21] For state agencies, that's very cheap, considering the possibilities that rogue certificates open. These agencies routinely spend billions of dollars on various projects of interest. More recently, in 2013, Tromer reduced the estimate to only $1 million.[22]

In that light, it's reasonable to assume that all 1,024-bit keys of relevance are already broken by multiple government agencies from countries around the world.

---

[20] HTTPS Everywhere [fsty.uk/b77] (The Electronic Frontier Foundation, retrieved 3 July 2014)

[21] On the Cost of Factoring RSA-1024 [fsty.uk/b78] (Shamir and Tromer, 2003)

[22] Facebook's outmoded Web crypto opens door to NSA spying [fsty.uk/b79] (CNET, 28 June 2013)

---

> **Note**
>
> For intermediate certificates, another attack vector is the weak SHA1 signatures. At best, SHA1 provides only 80 bits of security against collision attacks and 160 bits against preimage attacks. Intermediate certificates are easier to target because, unlike root certificates, they are not highly visible.

In some cases, it might also be reasonable to expect that end-entity certificates have been targeted. For example, Google transitioned away from 1,024-bit certificates only in 2013.[23]

Given the small cost of breaking weak certificates, it's surprising that we still have weak *root* certificates in use. Mozilla planned to remove such certificates by the end of 2013,[24] but they faced delays because of potential breakage. To follow their progress, watch bug #881553.[25]

# Ecosystem Measurements

Before 2010, little was publicly known about the state of the PKI ecosystem. In 2010, the era of active scanning and monitoring of the PKI ecosystem began. At Black Hat USA in July that year, I published a survey of about 120 million domain names, with an analysis of the observed certificates and the security of the TLS servers.[26] Just a couple of days later, at DEFCON, the Electronic Frontier Foundation (EFF) announced *SSL Observatory*, a survey of the entire IPv4 address space.[27] Their focus was on certificates, but their most important contribution was making all their data available to the public, sparking the imagination of many and leading to other scanning efforts. The EFF later announced *Distributed SSL Observatory*,[28] an effort to collect certificate chains observed by their browser add-on HTTP Everywhere, but they haven't published any reports as of yet.

In 2011, Holz et al. published a proper study using a combination of a third-party scan of the entire IPv4 space, their own scanning of secure servers in the Alexa top one million list, and passive monitoring of traffic on their research network.[29] They, too, published their data sets.

In April 2012, SSL Labs started a project called *SSL Pulse*, which performs monthly scans of about 150,000 of the most popular secure sites obtained by crawling the Alexa top one million list.[30]

---

[23] Google certificates upgrade in progress [fsty.uk/b80] (Google Developers Blog, 30 July 2013)

[24] Dates for Phasing out MD5-based signatures and 1024-bit moduli [fsty.uk/b81] (MozillaWiki, retrieved 3 July 2014)

[25] Bug #881553: Remove or turn off trust bits for 1024-bit root certs after December 31, 2013 [fsty.uk/b82] (Bugzilla@Mozilla, reported 10 June 2013)

[26] Internet SSL Survey 2010 is here! [fsty.uk/b83] (Ivan Ristić, 29 July 2010)

[27] The EFF SSL Observatory [fsty.uk/b84] (Electronic Frontier Foundation, retrieved 26 May 2014)

[28] HTTPS Everywhere & the Decentralized SSL Observatory [fsty.uk/b85] (Peter Eckersley, 29 February 2012)

[29] The SSL Landscape - A Thorough Analysis of the X.509 PKI Using Active and Passive Measurements [fsty.uk/b86] (Holz et al., Internet Measurement Conference, November 2011)

---

Chapter 3: Public-Key Infrastructure

Also in 2012, the International Computer Science Institute (ICSI) announced their *ICSI Certificate Notary* project, which monitors live network traffic of 10 partner organizations.[31] Their reports are of particular interest, because they show real-life certificates and encryption parameters. They also maintain a visualization of the entire PKI ecosystem and the relationships among CAs in their *Tree of Trust*.[32]

The most comprehensive study to come out so far was published in 2013 by Durumeric et al., who performed 110 Internet-wide scans over a period of 14 months.[33] To carry out their project, they developed a specialized tool called ZMap, which is now open source. All of their data is available online.[34] If raw data is what you're after, Rapid7 publishes data from their monthly certificate scans on the same web site.[35]

None of the surveys uncovered any fatal flaws, but they provided great visibility into the PKI ecosystem and highlighted a number of important problems. For example, the public was generally unaware that CAs regularly issue certificates for private IP addresses (that anyone can use on their internal networks) and domain names that are not fully qualified (e.g., *localhost*, *mail*, *intranet*, and such). After several years, not only is large-scale scanning the norm, but there are also efforts such as *Certificate Transparency* (discussed in the next section) that rely on the availability of all public certificates. In February 2014, Microsoft announced that they are extending the telemetry collected by Internet Explorer 11 to include certificate data.[36] They intend to use the information to quickly detect attacks against the users of this browser.

That same month, Delignat-Lavaud et al. published an evaluation of adherence to the CAB Forum guidelines over time.[37] The results show very good adherence for EV certificates, which always had the benefit of strict requirements, as well as improvements after the introduction of Baseline Requirements.

---

[30] SSL Pulse [fsty.uk/b70] (SSL Labs, retrieved 19 July 2014)

[31] The ICSI Certificate Notary [fsty.uk/b87] (ICSI, retrieved 19 July 2014)

[32] The ICSI SSL Notary: CA Certificates [fsty.uk/b88] (ICSI, retrieved 26 May 2014)

[33] Analysis of the HTTPS Certificate Ecosystem [fsty.uk/b89] (Durumeric et al., Internet Measurement Conference, October 2013)

[34] University of Michigan · HTTPS Ecosystem Scans [fsty.uk/b90] (Internet-Wide Scan Data Repository, retrieved 26 May 2014)

[35] Rapid7 · SSL Certificates [fsty.uk/b91] (Internet-Wide Scan Data Repository, retrieved 26 May 2014)

[36] A novel method in IE11 for dealing with fraudulent digital certificates [fsty.uk/b92] (Windows PKI Blog, 21 February 2014)

[37] Web PKI: Closing the Gap between Guidelines and Practices [fsty.uk/b93] (Delignat-Lavaud et al., NDSS, February 2014)

---

## What Do We Know about Internet PKI?

Certification authorities issue millions of certificates every year. According to the last available information, there are about four million active certificates. There are many more internal and self-signed certificates, but no one can reliably measure how many, because they tend to be used on internal networks.

It's not clear how many CAs there are exactly. There are slightly over 100 common roots (across major root stores), but many CAs use more than one root. There are more than a thousand subordinate CA certificates, but they are often used for administrative reasons; it's not clear how many organizations there are with the power to issue certificates directly. We do know that the top 10 roots control over 90% of the market. The big company names are Symantec, GoDaddy, Comodo, GlobalSign, DigiCert, StartCom, and Entrust.

# Improvements

Over the years, we have seen many proposals to improve the state of PKI. Most of them came out in 2011, after several CA security compromises made us feel that the Internet was falling apart. I am going to discuss the proposals here, but I won't go into much detail, as most are still works in development. The others have made little progress since they were announced. The only exceptions are pinning and DANE; these techniques are (almost) practical, which is why I discuss them in more detail in Chapter 10, *HSTS, CSP, and Pinning*.

### Perspectives

*Perspectives*[38] was the first project to introduce the concept of independent notaries to assist with TLS authentication. Rather than make a decision about certification authenticity alone, clients consult *trusted notaries*. Accessing the same server from different vantage points can defeat attacks that take place close to the client. Notaries can also keep track of a server over a period of time to defeat more advanced attacks. Perspectives launched in 2008 and continues to operate.

### Convergence

*Convergence*[39] is a conceptual fork of Perspectives with some aspects of the implementation improved. To improve privacy, requests to notaries are proxied through several servers so that the notary that knows the identity of the client does not know the contents of the request. To improve performance, site certificates are cached for extended periods of time. Convergence had momentum when it launched in 2011, but it hasn't seen any activity since 2013. The most likely problem is that browsers don't offer adequate APIs to support plugins that want to make trust decisions.

---

[38] Perspectives Project [fsty.uk/b94] (retrieved 27 May 2014)
[39] Convergence [fsty.uk/b95] (retrieved 27 May 2014)

## Public key pinning

*Public key pinning* addresses the biggest PKI weakness of the current ecosystem, which is the fact that any CA can issue a certificate for any domain name without the owner's permission. With pinning, site owners can select (*pin*) one or more CAs that they trust, effectively carving our their own isolated trust ecosystem, which is much smaller than the global one. Public key pinning is currently possible via Chrome's proprietary mechanism. A standard called *Public Key Pinning for HTTP* is in development.

## DANE

DNSSEC is a new set of protocols that extend DNS with integrity checking. With this, a domain name can be associated with a set of keys that are used to sign the corresponding DNS zone. DANE is a bridge between DNSSEC and TLS authentication. Although DANE can be used for pinning, its more interesting ability is completely bypassing public CAs; if you trust the DNS, you can use it for TLS authentication.

## Sovereign Keys

The *Sovereign Keys* proposal[40] extends the existing security infrastructure (either CAs or DNSSEC) with additional security guarantees. The main idea is that a domain name can be claimed using a *sovereign key*, which is recorded in publicly verifiable logs. Once a name is claimed, its certificates can be valid only if they are signed by the sovereign key. On the negative side, there seem to be no provisions to recover from the loss of a sovereign key, which makes this proposal very risky. Sovereign Keys was announced in 2011, but it hasn't progressed past the idea stage.

## MECAI

*MECAI* (which stands for *Mutually Endorsing CA Infrastructure*)[41] is a variation of the notary concept in which the CAs run the infrastructure. Servers do all the hard work and obtain freshness vouchers to deliver to clients. The fact that most of the process happens behind the scenes improves privacy and performance. MECAI was first published in 2011, but it hasn't progressed past the idea stage.

## Certificate Transparency

*Certificate Transparency* (CT)[42] is a framework for auditing and monitoring public certificates. CAs submit each certificate they issue to a public *certificate log* and obtain a cryptographic proof of submission. Anyone can monitor new certificates as they are issued; for example, domain owners can watch for certificates issued for their domain names. The idea is that once this mechanism is in place fraudulent certificates can be quickly detected. The proof, which can be delivered to clients in a variety of ways (ideally within the certificate itself), can be used to confirm that a certificate had been

---

[40] The Sovereign Keys Project [fsty.uk/b96] (The EFF, retrieved 27 May 2014)

[41] Mutually Endorsing CA Infrastructure version 2 [fsty.uk/b97] (Kai Engert, 24 February 2012)

[42] Certificate Transparency [fsty.uk/b98] (Google, retrieved 27 May 2014)

made public. Chrome developers intend to require CT for all certificates, first starting with EV certificates in February 2015.[43]

## TACK

TACK (which stands for *Trust Assurances for Certificate Keys*)[44] is a pinning variant that pins to a server-provided signing key. The introduction of a long-term signing key means more work but has the benefit of being independent from the CA infrastructure. This proposal is different from all others in that it works for any protocol protected by TLS, not just HTTP. TACK came out in 2012. The authors provided proof-of-concept implementations for some popular platforms, but, as of this writing, there is no official support in any client.

Do any of these proposals stand a chance at being implemented? In 2011, when most of these proposals came out, there was generally a strong momentum to change things. Since then, the momentum has been replaced with the realization that we're dealing with a very difficult problem. It's easy to design a system that works most of the time, but it's the edge cases where most ideas fail.

The proposals based on notaries face issues with browser APIs just to get off the ground. They aim to solve the problem of local attacks but have too many caveats. By depending on multiple external systems for trust, they make decision making difficult (e.g., what if there is a disagreement among notaries or rogue elements are introduced to the system?) and introduce various problems related to performance, availability, and running costs. Large web sites often deploy many certificates for the same name, especially when observed from different geographic locations. This practice leads to false positives; a view from any one notary might not be the only correct one.

The pinning proposals show a lot of promise. With pinning, site owners choose whom to trust and remove the huge attack surface inherent in the current system. Google had pinning deployed in 2011; it's how the compromise of the DigiNotar CA came to light. Their proprietary pinning mechanism has since detected several other failures. The hope is that in the near future pinning will be easily accessible to everyone via a standardized mechanism.

DANE is the only proposal that can substantially change how we approach trust, but its success depends on having DNSSEC supported by either operating systems or browsers. Browser vendors haven't shown much enthusiasm so far, but the operating system vendors might, eventually. For low-risk properties, DANE is a great solution and can completely displace DV certificates. On the other hand, for high-risk properties the centralization of trust in the DNS is potentially problematic; the key issue is the unavoidable influences of various governments. There is little support for DANE at the moment, but it's likely that there will be more over time as DNSSEC continues to be deployed.

---

[43] Extended Validation in Chrome [fsty.uk/b99] (Ben Laurie, 19 March 2014)
[44] TACK [fsty.uk/b100] (retrieved 27 May 2014)

Given Google's leverage, it's likely that CT will take off, although it might take a few years before it's deployed widely enough to achieve its full effect.

Overall, there are two directions that we appear to be taking in parallel that lead to a multitier system with varying levels of security. The first direction is to improve the existing system. Mozilla, for example, used its root program as leverage to put pressure on CAs to get their affairs in order. In fact, CAs were under a lot of pressure from everyone, which resulted in the reorganization of the CA/Browser Forum and Baseline Requirements in 2012. Increased monitoring and auditing activities since 2010 helped uncover many smaller issues (now largely being addressed) and generally kept the system in check. Eventually, CT might achieve full transparency of public trust with a repository of all public certificates.

The second direction is all about enabling high-risk web sites to elect into more security. After all, perhaps the biggest practical problem with Internet PKI is that we expect one system to work for everyone. In reality, there is a large number of properties that want easy security (low cost, low effort) and a small number of properties that want strong security and is prepared to work on it. New technologies, such as pinning, HTTP Strict Transport Security, Content Security Policy, and mandatory OCSP stapling, can make that possible.

# 4 Attacks against PKI

There's an inherent flaw in how *Public Key Infrastructure* (PKI) operates today: any CA is able to issue certificates for any name without having to seek approval from the domain name owner. It seems incredible that this system, which has been in use for about 20 years now, essentially relies on everyone—hundreds of entities and thousands of people—doing the right thing.

There are several attack vectors that could be exploited. In many cases, it's the validation process that's the target. If you can convince a CA that you are the legitimate owner of a domain name, they will issue you a certificate. In other cases, the target is the security of the CAs themselves; if a CA is compromised the attacker can generate certificates for any web site. And in some cases it has come to light that certain CAs issued subordinate certificates that were then used to issue certificates representing web sites at large.

This chapter documents the most interesting incidents and attacks against PKI, starting with the first widely reported incident from 2001 and ending with the last major one at the end of 2013.

## VeriSign Microsoft Code-Signing Certificate

In January 2001, VeriSign got tricked into issuing two code-signing certificates to someone claiming to represent Microsoft. To pull off something like that, the attacker needed to establish a false identity, convince one or more people at VeriSign that the request was authentic, and pay the certificate fees of about $400 per certificate. In other words, it required deep knowledge of the system, skill, and determination. The problem was uncovered several weeks later, during a routine audit. The public found out about the incident in late March, after Microsoft put mitigation measures in place.

The certificates were considered to represent a great danger to the users of all Windows operating systems. Because there was no connection to anyone at Microsoft, the certificates would not be seen as inherently trusted, and the code signed by them would not run without a warning. However, because they were issued under the name "Microsoft Corporation," it was reasonable to believe that most people would approve the code installation. In Microsoft's own words:[1]

> *Programs signed using these certificates would not be able to run automatically or bypass any normal security restrictions. However, the warning dialogue that appears before such programs could run would claim that they had been digitally signed by Microsoft. Clearly, this would be a significant aid in persuading a user to run the program.*

Back in those days, Microsoft was relying heavily on automated code installation in their browser (using the technology known as ActiveX), so there was a significant danger to anyone running Internet Explorer. Netscape users were safe.

Upon discovering the mistake, VeriSign promptly revoked the certificates, but that was not enough to protect the users, because the fraudulent certificates had not included any revocation information. Because of that, in late March 2001, Microsoft was forced to release an emergency software update to explicitly blacklist the offending certificates and explain to users how to spot them.[2] This apparently caused a lively debate about the implementation of certificate revocation in Microsoft Windows.[3] One of Microsoft's Knowledge Base articles posted at the time also provided instructions for how to remove a trusted certification authority from one's system.[4]

# Thawte login.live.com

In the summer of 2008, security researcher Mike Zusman played Thawte's certificate validation process to obtain a certificate for *login.live.com*, which was (and still is) Microsoft's single sign-on authentication hub, used by millions.

Mike exploited two facts: first, that Thawte uses email for domain name authentication and second, that Microsoft allows anyone to register @live.com email addresses. The most obvious email aliases (e.g., hostmaster or webmaster) were either reserved or already registered, but as it happened Thawte allowed a particularly wide range of aliases for confirmation purposes. One of the email addresses Thawte accepted for authentication was sslcertificates@live.com, and that one was available for registration. As soon as Mike obtained access to this email address, obtaining a certificate was trivial.

---

[1] Erroneous VeriSign-Issued Digital Certificates Pose Spoofing Hazard [fsty.uk/b101] (Microsoft Security Bulletin MS01-017, 22 March 2001)

[2] How to Recognize Erroneously Issued VeriSign Code-Signing Certificates [fsty.uk/b102] (Microsoft, retrieved 3 July 2014)

[3] Microsoft, VeriSign, and Certificate Revocation [fsty.uk/b103] (Gregory L. Guerin, 20 April 2001)

[4] How to Remove a Root Certificate from the Trusted Root Store [fsty.uk/b104] (Microsoft, retrieved 3 July 2014)

Although Mike disclosed the problem in August of 2008,[5] he revealed the name of the exploited CA only later in the year.[6] Exploit details were revealed the following year, in his DEFCON 17 talk[9].

## StartCom Breach (2008)

On December 19, 2008, Mike Zusman managed to bypass StartCom's domain name validation by exploiting a flaw in StartCom's web site.[7] The flaw in the web application that controlled certificate issuance allowed him to obtain validation for any domain name. (StartCom operates a two-step process: in the first step you prove that you have control over a domain name, and in the second you request a certificate.) Using his discovery, Mike requested and obtained two certificates for domain names he had no authorization for.

His attack was detected very quickly, but only because he proceeded to obtain authorization and request certificates for *paypal.com* and *verisign.com*. As it turned out, StartCom had a secondary control mechanism in the form of a blacklist of high-profile web sites. This defense-in-depth measure flagged Mike's activity and caused all fraudulently issued certificates to be revoked within minutes.

StartCom published a detailed report documenting the attack and events that took place.[8] Mike discussed the events in more detail at his DEFCON 17 talk.[9]

## CertStar (Comodo) Mozilla Certificate

Only a couple of days after Mike Zusman's attack on StartCom, their CTO and COO Eddy Nigg discovered a similar problem with another CA.[10] Following a trail left by some email spam that was trying to mislead him into "renewing" his certificates with another company, [11] Eddy Nigg came across CertStar, a Comodo partner based in Denmark who would happily issue certificates without performing *any* domain name validation. Eddy first obtained a certificate for *startcom.org* and then for *mozilla.org*. Unsurprisingly, a fraudulent certificate for Mozilla's high-profile domain name made a big splash in the press and prompted a lively discussion on the `mozilla.dev.tech.crypto` mailing list.[12]

---

[5] DNS vuln + SSL cert = FAIL [fsty.uk/b105] (Intrepidus Group's blog, 30 July 2008)

[6] Mike's Thawte tweet [fsty.uk/b106] (31 December 2008)

[7] Nobody is perfect [fsty.uk/b107] (Mike Zusman, 1 January 2009)

[8] Full Disclosure [fsty.uk/b108] (Eddy Nigg, 3 January 2009)

[9] Criminal charges are not pursued: Hacking PKI (Mike Zusman, DEFCON 17, 31 July 2009): slides [fsty.uk/b109] and video [fsty.uk/b110].

[10] (Un)trusted Certificates [fsty.uk/b111] (Eddy Nigg, 23 December 2008)

[11] SSL Certificate for Mozilla.com Issued Without Validation [fsty.uk/b112] (SSL Shopper, 23 December 2008)

[12] Unbelievable! [fsty.uk/b113] (mozilla.dev.tech.crypto, 22 December 2008)

After verifying all 111 certificates issued by CertStar, Comodo revoked 11 (on top of the two ordered by Eddy Nigg) for which it could not verify authenticity and said that there was no reason to suspect that any of them actually were fraudulent.[13]

## RapidSSL Rogue CA Certificate

In 2008, a group of researchers led by Alex Sotirov and Marc Stevens carried out a spectacular proof-of-concept attack against Internet PKI in which they managed to obtain a rogue CA certificate that could be used to sign a certificate for any web site in the world.[14]

To fully appreciate this attack, you need to understand the long history of attacks against MD5, shown in the sidebar ahead. You will find that this final blow was the last one in a long line of improving attacks, which started at some point after MD5 had been broken in 2004. In other words, a result of a persistent and sustained effort.

After releasing their work on colliding certificates for different identities in 2006, Marc Stevens and other researchers from his team continued to improve the chosen-prefix collision technique in 2007. They were able to freely generate colliding certificates in a simulation with their own (private) certification authority in an environment they fully controlled. In real life, however, there were several constraints that were preventing exploitation.

---

[13] Re: Unbelievable! [fsty.uk/b114](Robin Alden, 25 December 2008)

[14] MD5 considered harmful today [fsty.uk/b115] (Sotirov et al., 30 December 2008)

## MD5 and PKI Attacks Timeline

- **1991**: Ronald Rivest designs MD5 as a replacement for MD4.

- **1991–1996**: MD5 becomes very popular and is deployed in a wide range of applications. In the meantime, early signs of weaknesses in MD5[15] lead researchers to start recommending that new applications use other, more secure hash functions.[16]

- **2004**: Wang et al. demonstrate a full collision.[17] MD5 is now considered properly broken, but the attacks are not yet sophisticated enough to use in practice.

- **2005**: Lenstra, Wang, and de Weger demonstrate a practical collision,[18] showing two different certificates with the same MD5 hash and thus the same signature. The two certificates differ in the RSA key space, but the remaining information (i.e., the certificate identity) is the same.

- **2006**: Stevens, Lenstra, and de Weger present a new technique,[19] initially called *target collision* but later renamed to *chosen prefix collision*, which allows for creation of two certificates that have the same MD5 hash but different identities. MD5 is now fully broken, with meaningful attacks practical.

- **2008**: Despite the fact that MD5 has been considered weak for more than a decade and the fact that a meaningful attack was demonstrated in 2006, some certification authorities are still using it to sign new certificates. A group of researchers led by Sotirov and Stevens use an MD5 collision to carry out an attack against PKI and obtain a "rogue" CA certificate, which they can use to generate a valid certificate for any web site.[20]

- **2012**: A very sophisticated malware nicknamed *Flame* (also known as *Flamer* or *Skywiper*) is discovered infecting networks in the Middle East.[21] The malware, which is thought to be government sponsored, is later discovered to have used an MD5 collision against a Microsoft CA certificate in order to carry out attacks against the Windows Update code-signing mechanism. After analyzing the evidence, Marc Stevens concludes that the attack had been carried out using a previously unknown attack variant.[22] No one knows how long Flame had been operating, but it is thought that it was active for anywhere from two to five years.

---

[15] Collisions for the compression function of MD5 [fsty.uk/b116] (B. den Boer and A. Bosselaers, *Advances in Cryptology*, 1993)

[16] Cryptanalysis of MD5 Compress [fsty.uk/b117] (H. Dobbertin, May 1996)

[17] Collisions for hash functions MD4, MD5, HAVAL-128, and RIPEMD [fsty.uk/b511] (Wang et al., 2004)

[18] Colliding X.509 Certificates based on MD5-collisions [fsty.uk/b118] (Lenstra, Wang, de Weger, 1 March 2005)

[19] Colliding X.509 Certificates for Different Identities [fsty.uk/b119] (Stevens, Lenstra, de Weger, 23 October 2006)

[20] MD5 considered harmful today [fsty.uk/b115] (Sotirov et al., 30 December 2008)

[21] What is Flame? [fsty.uk/b120] (Kaspersky Lab)

[22] CWI cryptanalyst discovers new cryptographic attack variant in Flame spy malware [fsty.uk/b121] (CWI, 7 June 2012)

---

## Chosen-Prefix Collision Attack

The goal of the attacker is to create two documents with the same MD5 signature. Most digital signature techniques sign hashes of data (instead of the data directly). If you can construct two documents that both have the same MD5 hash, then a signature for one is also valid for the other. All you now need to do is send one of the two documents (the innocent one) to a trust authority for signing and subsequently copy over the signature to the second document (the forgery).

When it comes to certificates, there's another problem: you can't just send your own certificate to a CA to sign. Instead, you send them some information (e.g., domain name and your public key), and *they* generate the certificate. This is a significant constraint, but it can be overcome.

A collision attack can be carried out using two specially constructed collision blocks that manipulate the hashing algorithm, with the goal of bringing it to the same state for two different inputs. Taking into account both inputs (one in the innocent document and the other in the forgery), the collision blocks undo the differences as far as the hashing algorithm is concerned. This means two things: (1) you must know the prefix of the innocent document in advance—this is where the name *chosen-prefix* comes from—and (2) you must be able to put one of the collision blocks into it.

In practice, it's not possible to put the collision blocks right at the end, which is why the resulting files must also have identical suffixes. In other words, once you get the collision right, you don't want any differences in the files to make the hash different again.

## Construction of Colliding Certificates

To use the chosen-prefix technique in real life requires that we carry out the attack under constraints imposed by the structure of the document we wish to forge and the constraints imposed by the process in which the document is created and digitally signed.

In the context of digital signatures, those constraints are as follows:

1. Certificates are created by certification authorities, using the information submitted in a CSR.

2. The overall structure of a certificate is determined by the X.509 v3 specification. The attacker cannot influence the structure but *can* predict it.

3. Some information that ends up in the certificate is copied over from the CSR. The attacker fully controls that part. Crucially, a certificate will always have a public key that is copied verbatim from the CSR. The key is "random" by design, which means that a specially crafted random-looking collision block won't raise any alarms.

4. Some further information will be added to the certificate by the certification authority. The attacker may be able to influence some parts (e.g., the certificate expiration time), but in general, the best they can do here is predict what the content will be.

From this information, it's clear that the collision prefix will include all the certificate fields that appear before the public key (which is where the collision block will be stored). Because the contents of the collision block depends on the prefix, the entire prefix must be known before the collision data can be created and subsequently sent to the certification authority. Looking at the certificate fields in the prefix, most of them are either known (e.g., the issuer information can be obtained from another certificate issued by the same CA) or provided by the attacker in the CSR (e.g., common name). However, there are two fields controlled by the CA and not known in the advance: the certificate serial number and the expiration date. For the time being, we'll assume that the attacker will be able to predict the contents of these two fields; later, we'll examine how that can be achieved.

We also have to figure out what to do with the part that comes after the public key (the suffix). As it turns out, this part consists of several X.509 extensions, all of them known in advance. With proper alignment (MD5 operates on blocks of data), the suffix is simply the same in both certificates.

Thus, the attack process is as follows:

1. Determine what the prefix of the real certificate will look like and determine what some of the CSR fields need to be.

2. Construct a desired prefix for the rogue certificate.

3. Determine the suffix.

4. Construct collision blocks using the data from the previous three steps.

5. Build a CSR and submit it to the certification authority.

6. Build a rogue certificate by combining the rogue prefix, the second collision block, the suffix, and the signature taken from the real certificate.

> ### Note
>
> The second collision block and the suffix must be part of the forged certificate for the attack to work, but they must be hidden in some way so as not to create problems when the certificate is used. In the RapidSSL attack, the so-called *tumor* was placed into an unimportant X.509 v3 comment extension, which is ignored during processing. Someone knowledgeable would be able to spot the anomaly, but virtually no one examines certificates at this level.

# Predicting the Prefix

Now let's go back to discuss how the researchers managed to predict the contents of the two fields (expiration time and serial number) that changed with every certificate. As it turns out, it was a combination of luck and "help" from the CA. Here's how it played out:

- RapidSSL's certificate-issuance process was fully automated, and it always took exactly six seconds from the time a CSR was submitted until the certificate was generated. This meant that it was possible to reliably predict the certificate expiration time down to a second, which was sufficient.

- Rather than randomize the serial number (which is considered best practice), RapidSSL's serial number had been a simple counter incremented by one for every new certificate. This meant that if you obtained two certificates in quick succession you could predict the serial number of the second certificate.

There were six CAs issuing MD5-signed certificates at the time, but it was these two facts about RapidSSL and lack of any other prevention measures[23] that eventually made everything click. However, a big complication was the fact that when using the team's special computing cluster consisting of 200 PlayStation 3 consoles they needed about a day to generate one collision. Thus, they not only had to choose the exact moment in time during which to submit a CSR but also predict the serial number that would be assigned to the certificate.

---

[23] PKI is obviously a tricky business to be in, which is why in cryptography there are all sorts of best practices and defense-in-depth measures designed to kick in when everything else fails. A certificate designed to sign other certificates incorporates a special X.509 v3 extension called *Basic Constraints*, with the CA bit set to true. This extension also has a parameter called pathlen, which can be used to restrict the depth of subsequent CA certificates. If the pathlen parameter in RapidSSL's CA certificate had been set to zero (which means that no further subordinate CA certificates are allowed), the rogue CA certificate would have been useless.

# Figure 4.1. Comparison of the real (left) and collided RapidSSL certificates (right) [Source: Benne de Weger]

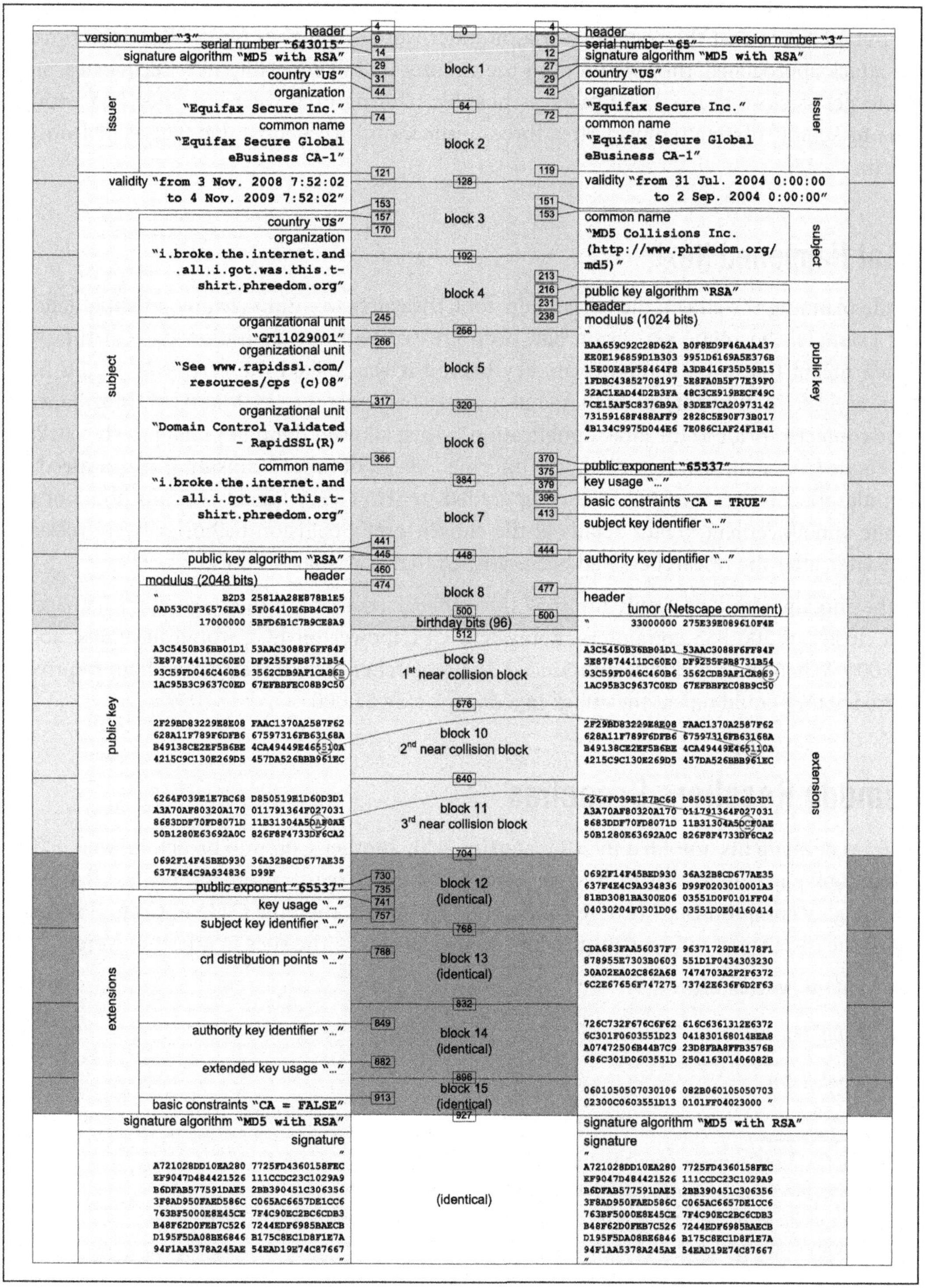

**Left certificate:**

header
version number "3"   serial number "643015"
signature algorithm "MD5 with RSA"

issuer:
country "US"
organization "Equifax Secure Inc."
common name "Equifax Secure Global eBusiness CA-1"

validity "from 3 Nov. 2008 7:52:02 to 4 Nov. 2009 7:52:02"

subject:
country "US"
organization "i.broke.the.internet.and .all.i.got.was.this.t- shirt.phreedom.org"
organizational unit "GT11029001"
organizational unit "See www.rapidssl.com/ resources/cps (c)08"
organizational unit "Domain Control Validated – RapidSSL(R)"
common name "i.broke.the.internet.and .all.i.got.was.this.t- shirt.phreedom.org"

public key:
public key algorithm "RSA"
header
modulus (2048 bits)
"
        B2D3 2581AA28E878B1E5
0AD53C0F36576EA9 5F06410E6BB4CB07
17000000 5BFD6B1C7B9CE8A9

A3C5450B36BB01D1 53AAC3088F6FF84F
3E87874411DC60E0 DF9255F9B8731B54
93C59FD046C460B6 3562CDB9AF1CA86B
1AC95B3C9637C0ED 67EFBBFEC08B9C50

2F29BD83229E8E08 FAAC1370A2587F62
628A11F789F6DFB6 67597316FB63168A
B49138CE2EF5B6BE 4CA49449E465510A
4215C9C130E269D5 457DA526BBB961EC

6264F039E1E7BC68 D850519E1D60D3D1
A3A70AF80320A170 011791364F027031
8683DDF70FD8071D 11B31304A5D0F0AE
50B1280E63692A0C 826F8F4733DF6CA2

0692F14F45BED930 36A32B8CD677AE35
637F4E4C9A934836 D99F

public exponent "65537"

extensions:
key usage "…"
subject key identifier "…"
crl distribution points "…"
authority key identifier "…"
extended key usage "…"
basic constraints "CA = FALSE"

signature algorithm "MD5 with RSA"
signature
"
A721028DD10EA280 7725FD4360158FEC
EF9047D484421526 111CCDC23C1029A9
B6DFAB577591DAE5 2BB390451C306356
3F8AD950FAED586C C065AC6657DE1CC6
763BF5000E8E45CE 7F4C90EC2BC6CDB3
B48F62D0FEB7C526 7244EDF6985BAECB
D195F5DA08BE6846 B175C8EC1D8F1E7A
94F1AA5378A245AE 54EAD19E74C87667

**Center (blocks):**

| Left offsets | Block | Right offsets |
|---|---|---|
| 4 / 9 / 14 / 29 / 31 / 44 / 74 | block 1 | 0 |
| | block 2 (64) | 4 / 9 / 12 / 27 / 29 / 42 / 72 |
| 121 / 153 / 157 / 170 | block 3 (128) | 119 / 151 / 153 |
| | block 4 (192) | |
| 245 / 266 | block 5 (256) | 213 / 216 / 231 / 238 |
| 317 | block 6 (320) | |
| 366 | block 7 (384) | 370 / 375 / 379 / 396 / 413 |
| 441 / 445 / 460 / 474 | block 8 (448) | 444 / 477 |
| | birthday bits (96) (500) | 500 |
| (512) | block 9 — 1st near collision block | |
| (576) | block 10 — 2nd near collision block | |
| (640) | block 11 — 3rd near collision block | |
| (704) | block 12 (identical) | |
| 730 / 735 / 741 / 757 | | |
| (768) | block 13 (identical) | |
| 788 | | |
| (832) | block 14 (identical) | |
| 849 / 882 | | |
| (896) | block 15 (identical) | |
| 913 / 927 | (identical) | |

**Right certificate:**

header
serial number "65"   version number "3"
signature algorithm "MD5 with RSA"

issuer:
country "US"
organization "Equifax Secure Inc."
common name "Equifax Secure Global eBusiness CA-1"

validity "from 31 Jul. 2004 0:00:00 to 2 Sep. 2004 0:00:00"

subject:
common name "MD5 Collisions Inc. (http://www.phreedom.org/ md5)"

public key:
public key algorithm "RSA"
header
modulus (1024 bits)
"
BAA659C92C28D62A B0F8ED9F46A4A437
EE0E196859D1B303 9951D61E9A5E376B
15E00E4BF58464F8 A3DB416F35D59B15
1FDBC43852706197 58EFAD85F77E39F0
32AC1EAD44D2B3FA 48C3C8919EECF49C
7CE15AF5C8376B9A 93DEE7CA20973142
73159168F488AFF9 2828C5E90F73B017
4B134C9975D044E6 7E086C1AF24F1B41
"

public exponent "65537"
key usage "…"
basic constraints "CA = TRUE"
subject key identifier "…"
authority key identifier "…"

header
tumor (Netscape comment)
"  33000000 275E39E089610F4E

A3C5450B36BB01D1 53AAC3088F6FF94F
3E87874411DC60E0 DF9255F9B8731B54
93C59FD046C460B6 3562CDB9AF1CA869
1AC95B3C9637C0ED 67EFBBFEC08B9C50

2F29BD83229E8E08 FAAC1370A2587F62
628A11F789F6DFB6 67597316FB63168A
B49138CE2EF5B6BE 4CA49449E465110A
4215C9C130E269D5 457DA526BBB961EC

6264F039E1E7BC68 D850519E1D60D3D1
A3A70AF80320A170 011791364F027031
8683DDF70FD8071D 11B31304A5DCF0AE
50B1280E63692A0C 826F8F4733DF6CA2

0692F14F45BED930 36A32B8CD677AE35
637F4E4C9A934836 D99F0203010001A3
81BD3081BA300E06 03551D0F0101FF04
04030204F0301D06 03551D0E04160414

CDA683FAA56037F7 96371729DE4178F1
878955E7303B0603 551D1F0434303230
30A02EA02C862A68 7474703A2F2F6372
6C2E67656F747275 73742E636F6D2F63

726C732F676C6F62 616C6361312E6372
6C301F0603551D23 04183016801 4BEA8
A07472506B44B7C9 23D8FBA8FFB3576B
686C301D0603551D 250416301406082B

0601050507030106 082B060105050703
02300C0603551D13 0101FF04023000 "

signature algorithm "MD5 with RSA"
signature
"
A721028DD10EA280 7725FD4360158FEC
EF9047D484421526 111CCDC23C1029A9
B6DFAB577591DAE5 2BB390451C306356
3F8AD950FAED586C C065AC6657DE1CC6
763BF5000E8E45CE 7F4C90EC2BC6CDB3
B48F62D0FEB7C526 7244EDF6985BAECB
D195F5DA08BE6846 B175C8EC1D8F1E7A
94F1AA5378A245AE 54EAD19E74C87667

Their approach was to carry out the attack on Sunday evenings, during the CA's least busy period. They would obtain the value of the serial number counter on a Friday and aim to submit a CSR so that the resulting serial number would be higher by 1,000. As the time of the attack approached, they would push the counter up by requesting new certificates, aiming to get as close to the 1,000 mark as possible. During each weekend, they had enough time to submit three attempts. After three unsuccessful weekends, they succeeded on the fourth.

## What Happened Next

While planning the attack, the researchers took measures to minimize any potential fallout. For example, the rogue certificate had been created with an expiration date in the past, which meant that even if the private key behind it was leaked the certificate would have been useless. The key parties in charge of browser trust stores (e.g., Microsoft, Mozilla, etc.) were contacted prior to the attack publication, which allowed them to preemptively blacklist the rogue CA certificate. RapidSSL was informed ahead of time,[24] causing them to speed up the migration process to SHA1. They upgraded to SHA1 very quickly, within hours of the public announcement.[25] Full details of the chosen-prefix collision technique were released only later, after the researchers had been satisfied that it was safe to do so.

In the end, the attack cost only the $657 in certificate costs,[26] but the researchers had access to a cluster of 200 PS3 computers. Equivalent CPU power on EC2 would have cost about $20,000. When the attack was announced, the researchers estimated that with an improved approach they could repeat the attack in a day for only $2,000.

## Comodo Resellers Breaches

A series of incidents unfolded in 2011, starting with another Comodo breach in March. The attack took place on March 15th, when one of Comodo's registration authorities (RAs) was "thoroughly compromised" (in the words of Robin Alden, then the CTO of Comodo), leading to the issuance of nine certificates for seven web sites.[27] The sites in question were:

- *addons.mozilla.org*

- *global trustee*

- *google.com*

---

[24] Verisign and responsible disclosure [fsty.uk/b122] (Alexander Sotirov, 6 January 2009)

[25] This morning's MD5 attack - resolved [fsty.uk/b123] (Tim Callan, 30 December 2008)

[26] Even though they requested a large number of certificates, most of them were reissued, which RapidSSL allowed for free.

[27] Comodo Report of Incident [fsty.uk/b124] (Comodo, 22 March 2011)

---

- *login.live.com*
- *login.skype.com*
- *login.yahoo.com*
- *mail.google.com*

Clearly, with exception of the "global trustee" certificate whose purpose is unclear, all the certificates were for key internet web sites that hundreds of millions of users visit every day. Fortunately, the attack was detected very quickly and all the fraudulent certificates revoked within hours. It wasn't even clear if all of these certificates were retrieved by the attacker. Comodo saw only the Yahoo certificate hit their OCSP responder (and only twice) and none of the other certificates.[28]

The next day, Comodo started to inform various other relevant parties, and the patching process began.[29] Although Comodo didn't disclose the identity of the compromised RA, it was later alleged by the attacker that it was an Italian company, Instant SSL. The attacks were disclosed to the public on March 22nd by Comodo, Mozilla, Microsoft, and others.

An interesting fact is that some people learned about the attacks several days earlier from clues in the Chrome source code (which is publicly available). Jacob Appelbaum wrote about his discovery on the Tor blog.[30]

Comodo went on to disclose two further reseller compromises on March 26th, although one of them later turned out to be a false report. The other report was genuine but didn't result in any fraudulent certificates being issued. Apparently, the security measures introduced after the March 15th incident were effective and prevented the attacker from issuing further certificates.[31]

Also on March 26th, the attacker himself started to communicate with the public,[32] and that's when we learned about ComodoHacker (the name he chose for himself), which later turned out to be a much bigger story, spanning months of activity, many CAs, and many incidents. You can read more about him in the sidebar later in this chapter.

In May, Comodo was again in the news because one of their resellers, ComodoBR, was found to have an SQL injection vulnerability on their web site.[33] The attacker used the vulnerability to retrieve private customer data (including certificate signing requests), but there were no other PKI-related consequences.

---

[28] Strictly speaking, this is not an entirely reliable indicator of certificate use, because an active man-in-the-middle attacker can suppress all OCSP traffic from the victim.

[29] Bug 642395: Deal with bogus certs issued by Comodo partner [fsty.uk/b125] (Bugzilla@Mozilla, reported 17 March 2011)

[30] Detecting Certificate Authority compromises and web browser collusion [fsty.uk/b126] (Jacob Appelbaum, 22 March 2011)

[31] RE: Web Browsers and Comodo Announce A Successful Certificate Authority Attack, Perhaps From Iran [fsty.uk/b127] (Robin Alden, 29 March 2011)

[32] A message from Comodo Hacker [fsty.uk/b128] (ComodoHacker, 26 March 2011)

[33] New hack on Comodo reseller exposes private data [fsty.uk/b129] (The Register, 24 May 2011)

In the end, this series of incidents exposed how operating a large network of partners on a trust basis alone is entirely unfeasible, especially in a complex ecosystem such as PKI. Comodo claimed that after the 2008 incident only 9% of their partners were left with the ability to fully control certificate issuing, but that was clearly still too many. After the first incident, no resellers were left able to issue certificates without further validation from Comodo (and, according to Comodo, that action prevented further incidents just a couple of days later).

More importantly, these incidents showed how Comodo (and possibly other CAs) had not been maintaining a realistic threat model. This was acknowledged by Robin Alden in a post on `mozilla.dev.security.policy` (emphasis mine):

> *We were dealing with the threat model that the RA could be Underperforming [sic] with, or trying to avoid doing, their validation duty (neither of which were the case for this RA),* **but what we had not done was adequately consider the new (to us) threat model of the RA being the subject of a targeted attack and entirely compromised.**

## StartCom Breach (2011)

In the summer of 2011, StartCom was again targeted, supposedly by the same person who had previously attacked Comodo.[34] Because of the incident, which took place on June 15th, StartCom stopped issuing new certificates for about a week. The following message appeared on their web site:

> *Due to an attack on our systems and a security breach that occurred at the 15th of June, issuance of digital certificates and related services has been suspended. Our services will remain offline until further notice. Subscribers and holders of valid certificates are not affected in any form. Visitors to web sites and other parties relying on valid certificates are not affected. We apologize for the temporary inconvenience and thank you for your understanding.*

Apparently, no fraudulent certificates were issued and the attacker—who might have gained access to some sensitive data and come very close to the company's precious root key[35]—did not cause any significant long-term damage. The company never followed up with an official report about the incident, acknowledging the incident only via a post on Eddy Nigg's blog.[36]

---

[34] Another status update message [fsty.uk/b130] (ComodoHacker, 6 September 2011)

[35] Response to some comments [fsty.uk/b131] (ComodoHacker, 7 September 2011)

[36] Cyber War [fsty.uk/b132] (Eddy Nigg, 9 September 2011)

# DigiNotar

DigiNotar was a Dutch CA that was in business of issuing certificates to the general public as well as handling the PKI aspects of the Dutch e-government program PKIoverheid (*overheid* means government in Dutch). In 2011, DigiNotar became the first CA to be completely compromised, with fraudulent certificates used in real, and possibly very serious, man-in-the-middle attacks. Needless to say, DigiNotar's root certificates were all revoked and the company went out of business, declaring voluntary bankruptcy in September 2011.

## Public Discovery

The incident came to light on August 27th, when an Iranian Gmail user reported intermittent problems when accessing his email account.[37] According to the testimony, there were daily "downtime" periods of 30 to 60 minutes, during which access was impossible due to an unusual certificate warning message. As it turned out, the user used Google Chrome for access, and at that time Google already had public key pinning embedded in it. The downtime described by the user was caused by a man-in-the-middle attack that Chrome detected and prevented.

In the days that followed, we learned that the reported problem was actually part of a very large attack on a scale previously unheard of, affecting an estimated 300,000 IP addresses. Virtually all of the IP addresses were in Iran. The intercepting certificates were all issued by DigiNotar. But how was that possible?

## Fall of a Certification Authority

Faced with a huge security incident that affected its digital infrastructure, the Dutch government immediately took control of DigiNotar and hired an external security consultancy, Fox-IT, to investigate. Fox-IT published their initial report[38] one week later, on September 5th. Here is the most relevant part of the report:

> The most critical servers contain malicious software that can normally be detected by anti-virus software. The separation of critical components was not functioning or was not in place. We have strong indications that the CA-servers, although physically very securely placed in a tempest proof environment, were accessible over the network from the management LAN.
>
> The network has been severely breached. All CA servers were members of one Windows domain, which made it possible to access them all using one ob-

---

[37] Is This MITM Attack to Gmail's SSL ? [fsty.uk/b133] (alibo, 27 August 2011)
[38] DigiNotar public report version 1 [fsty.uk/b134] (Fox-IT, 5 September 2011)

*tained user/password combination. The password was not very strong and could easily be brute-forced.*

*The software installed on the public web servers was outdated and not patched.*

*No antivirus protection was present on the investigated servers.*

*An intrusion prevention system is operational. It is not clear at the moment why it didn't block some of the outside web server attacks. No secure central network logging is in place.*

The full report was released one year later, in August 2012; at 100 pages, it provides the most detailed report of a CA breach ever seen.[39] From the report, we learned that the initial attack occurred on June 17th, when a public-facing web server running a vulnerable content-management application was breached. From there, it took the attacker until July 1st to break into the most secure network segment, where the root material was placed. This network segment was not connected to the Internet directly, but the attacker was able to tunnel into it from less important systems.

The first batch of 128 rogue certificates were issued on July 10th, roughly a week from when the attacker first had access to the CA servers themselves. Several other batches followed, arriving at a total of at least 531 certificates for 53 unique common names. Due to the scale of the breach, the actual number of rogue certificates is not known; the logs were tampered with, and many of the certificates later discovered in the wild could not be found in the appropriate databases.

As you can see in the following table, the list of names used for the certificates consists largely of high-profile web sites, certification authorities, and government agencies.

---

[39] Black Tulip Update [fsty.uk/b135] (Dutch government, 13 August 2012)

---

Table 4.1. Common names used in rogue certificates issued by the DigiNotar attacker

| | | |
|---|---|---|
| *.*.com | *.*.org | *.10million.org (2) |
| *.android.com | *.aol.com | *.azadegi.com (2) |
| *.balatarin.com (3) | *.comodo.com (3) | *.digicert.com (2) |
| *.globalsign.com (7) | *.google.com (26) | *.JanamFadayeRahbar.com |
| *.logmein.com | *.microsoft.com (3) | *.mossad.gov.il (2) |
| *.mozilla.org | *.RamzShekaneBozorg.com | *.SahebeDonyayeDigital.com |
| *.skype.com (22) | *.startssl.com | *.thawte.com (6) |
| *.torproject.org (14) | *.walla.co.il (2) | *.windowsupdate.com (3) |
| *.wordpress.com (14) | addons.mozilla.org (17) | azadegi.com (16) |
| Comodo Root CA (20) | CyberTrust Root CA (20) | DigiCert Root CA (21) |
| Equifax Root CA (40) | friends.walla.co.il (8) | GlobalSign Root CA (20) |
| login.live.com (17) | login.yahoo.com (19) | my.screenname.aol.com |
| secure.logmein.com (17) | Thawte Root CA (45) | twitter.com (18) |
| VeriSign Root CA (21) | wordpress.com (12) | www.10million.org (8) |
| www.balatarin.com (16) | www.cia.gov (25) | www.cybertrust.com |
| www.Equifax.com | www.facebook.com (14) | www.globalsign.com |
| www.google.com (12) | www.hamdami.com | www.mossad.gov.il (5) |
| www.sis.gov.uk (10) | www.update.microsoft.com (4) | |

Some of the certificates were not intended for well-known web sites but were used to carry various messages instead. The phrases in the following table were seen in various places in the certificates.

Table 4.2. Messages seen embedded in the rogue certificates (it's not clear if the translations are accurate)

| Original message | Translation |
|---|---|
| Daneshmande Bi nazir | Peerless scientist |
| Hameye Ramzaro Mishkanam | Will break all cyphers |
| Janam Fadaye Rahbar | I will sacrifice my life for my leader |
| Ramz Shekane Bozorg | Great cryptanalyst |
| Sahebe Donyaye | Possessor of the world (God) |
| Sare Toro Ham Mishkanam | I will break Tor too |
| Sarbaze Gomnam | Unknown soldier |

It also transpired that DigiNotar had discovered the intrusion on July 19th and, with the help of an outside consultancy (not Fox-IT), cleaned up their systems by the end of July. Unfortunately, the damage had already been done. Presumably under the impression that the incident had been contained, DigiNotar quietly revoked a small number of fraudulent certificates (the ones they knew about), and—recklessly—failed to inform anyone.

## Man-in-the-Middle Attacks

Given the scale of the compromise, it is doubtful that a prompt disclosure would have saved DigiNotar, but it would have definitely stopped the attackers from using the rogue certificates. We know this because the rogue certificates were generated with OCSP information embedded, and the investigators were able to track the certificate deployment by examining the logs of DigiNotar's OCSP responder.[40]

Initially, after the certificates were generated the logs showed few requests: most likely a result of testing by the attacker. The first signs of mass deployment were starting to show on August 4th, with continuous increases in volume until August 29th, which was the day on which browsers revoked the DigiNotar root certification and killed all rogue certificates. We know from attacked users that the attack was not constant but occurred in bursts. Perhaps there was a reason for such behavior, such as limitations of the attack method (DNS cache poisoning was mentioned as the likely approach[41] used) or simply an inability to cope with a large amount of traffic at any one time.

Figure 4.2. DigiNotar OCSP activity in August 2011 [Source: Fox-IT]

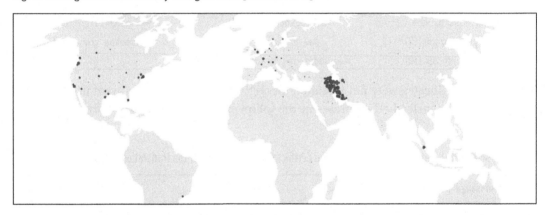

Besides, the attackers were likely only interested in collecting Gmail passwords, and—assuming their capacity was limited—once they saw a password from one IP address they could move on to intercept another. With a password cache, they could abuse the accounts at their leisure (people rarely change their passwords) by connecting to Gmail directly.

---

[40] When a TLS client encounters a certificate that contains OCSP information, it contacts the designated OCSP server to determine if the certificate has been revoked. This method of tracking is not foolproof, because the MITM attacker can suppress all traffic to the OCSP server. Browsers tend to fail quietly when they encounter OCSP communication failures.

[41] DNS cache poisoning is an attack against DNS infrastructure in which the attacker exploits weaknesses in the DNS protocol as well as some implementations. Using clever tricks along with packet flooding, it might be possible to trick a caching DNS server into delegating domain name decisions from the actual owner to the attacker. If that happens, the attacker determines what IP addresses are returned for domain names in the attacking space. A successful attack will impact all users connecting to the caching DNS server. During the DigiNotar MITM attacks in Iran, some users reported that changing their DNS configuration from their ISP's servers to other servers (e.g., Google's) stopped the attacks.

Chapter 4: Attacks against PKI

All in all, the rogue Google certificate saw exactly 654,313 OCSP requests from 298,140 unique IP addresses. About 95% of those were within Iran, with the remaining IP addresses identified as the Tor exit nodes, proxies, and virtual private networks from around the world.

## ComodoHacker Claims Responsibility

ComodoHacker claimed responsibility for the DigiNotar breach, posting from his Pastebin account on September 5th.[42] He followed up with three further posts, as well as the calc.exe binary signed with one of the certificates, thus offering definitive proof that he was involved in the incident. The posts contain some details about the attacks, which match the information in the official report (which was released to the public only much later).

> How I got access to 6 layer network behind internet servers of DigiNotar, how I found passwords, how I got SYSTEM privilage [sic] in fully patched and up-to-date system, how I bypassed their nCipher NetHSM, their hardware keys, their RSA certificate manager, their 6th layer internal "CERT NETWORK" which have no ANY connection to internet, how I got full remote desktop connection when there was firewalls that blocked all ports except 80 and 443 and doesn't allow Reverse or direct VNC connections, more and more and more...

It's not clear if ComodoHacker was actually involved with the attacks in Iran, however. Although he was happy to claim responsibility for the CA hacks, ComodoHacker distanced himself from the MITM attacks. His second DigiNotar post contained the following sentence:

> I'm single person, do not AGAIN try to make an ARMY out of me in Iran. If someone in Iran used certs I have generated, I'm not one who should explain.

In a subsequent post, he repeated that statement:

> [...] I'm the only hacker, just I have shared some certs with some people in Iran, that's all... Hacker is single, just know it

---

[42] Striking Back... [fsty.uk/b136] (ComodoHacker, 5 September 2011)

## Who Is ComodoHacker?

ComodoHacker made his public appearance in 2011 and left a mark on the PKI with a string of attacks against several certification authorities. The first batch of attacks came in March 2011, when several Comodo partners were breached. Rogue certificates were issued but also quickly discovered, which prevented their exploitation.

StartCom appears to have been attacked in June, and the attacker appears to have had some success, but, according to both parties, no fraudulent certificates were issued. StartCom stopped issuing certificates but never provided any substantial details about the incident.

Then there was the DigiNotar attack, which resulted in a full compromise of the DigiNotar certification authority and shook up the entire PKI ecosystem.

After being mentioned as a successful target in one of ComodoHacker's messages, GlobalSign felt it prudent to halt certificate issuance for a period time and investigate. They subsequently found that their public-facing web server, which is not part of the CA infrastructure, had been breached.[43] The only casualty was the private key for the *www.globalsign.com* domain name.

Immediately after the Comodo incidents, the hacker started communicating with the public via the ComodoHacker account on Pastebin[44] and left 10 messages in total. After the DigiNotar incident, he also had a brief period during which he was posting on Twitter, under the *ich sun* name and *ichsunx2* handle[45]. Although he appeared to have initially enjoyed the attention and even gave interviews, his last communication was via Twitter in September 2011.

# DigiCert Sdn. Bhd.

In November 2011, a Malaysian certification authority, DigiCert Sdn. Bhd., was found to be issuing dangerously weak certificates. This company, which is not related to the better known and US-based DigiCert, Inc., was operating as an intermediate certification authority on a contract with Entrust and, before that, CyberTrust (Verizon). Twenty-two certificates were found to be not only weak but lacking in other critical aspects:

**Weak 512-bit keys**
A key that is only 512 bits long can be relatively easily refactored using only brute force.[46] With the key in hand, a malicious party can impersonate the victim web site without triggering certificate warnings.

---

[43] September 2011 Security Incident Report [fsty.uk/b137] (GlobalSign, 13 December 2011)

[44] fsty.uk/b138

[45] fsty.uk/b139

[46] But not brute force in the sense that all possible numbers are tried. It's more efficient to use one of the integer factorization methods, for example, the *general number field sieve* (GNFS).

---

### Missing usage restrictions

Certificates are expected to carry usage restrictions in the *Extended Key Usage* (EKU) extension. Even though DigiCert Sdn. Bhd. had been contractually restricted to issuing only web site certificates, because some of their certificates were missing the usage restrictions they could be used for any purpose: for example, code signing.

### Missing revocation information

None of the 22 certificates contained revocation information. This meant that after the invalid certificates were discovered there was no way to reliably revoke them.

As it turned out, the problem was discovered only after one of the public keys was found to have been broken by brute force and used to sign malware.[47] After finding out about the problem, Entrust revoked the intermediate certificate[48] and informed the browser vendors. Within a week, both Entrust and CyberTrust revoked their respective intermediate certificates, Mozilla informed the public via a post on their blog,[49] and browser vendors released updates to explicitly blacklist the intermediate certificates and the known weak server certificates. In the aftermath, DigiCert, Inc. was left having to explain the name confusion to their customers.[50]

# Flame

In May, security researchers began analyzing a new strand of malware that was making rounds chiefly in the Middle East. The malware in question, called *Flame*[21] (also known as *Flamer* or *Skywiper*), turned out to be the most advanced yet: over 20 MB in size, over 20 attack modules (the usual malware stuff, such as network sniffing, microphone activation, file retrieval, and so on), and built using components such as a lightweight relational database (SQLite) and a scripting language (Lua). It was all done in such a way that it remained undetected for a very long time (which meant low or undetectable failures; it was clearly not an average software development job).

Overall, Flame was discovered on about 1,000 systems in what seemed to be very targeted attacks. Iranian CERT issued a press release about Flame in May 2012. [51] Soon thereafter, the creators of the Flame malware issued a suicide command, with the intention that all instances would delete themselves. Still, many instances of the malware and several instances of the command and control servers were captured and analyzed.[52]

---

[47] Bug #698753: Entrust SubCA: 512-bit key issuance and other CPS violations; malware in the wild [fsty.uk/b140] (Bugzilla@Mozilla, 1 November 2011)

[48] Entrust Bulletin on Certificates Issued with Weak 512-bit RSA Keys by Digicert Malaysia [fsty.uk/b141] (Entrust, retrieved 3 July 2014)

[49] Revoking Trust in DigiCert Sdn. Bhd Intermediate Certificate Authority [fsty.uk/b142] (Mozilla Security Blog, 3 November 2011)

[50] DigiCert, Inc. Of No Relation to Recent "Digi" Insecure Certificates [fsty.uk/b143] (DigiCert, Inc., 1 November 2011)

[51] Identification of a New Targeted Cyber-Attack [fsty.uk/b144] (MAHER, 28 May 2012)

[52] Flame / Skywiper / Flamer reports [fsty.uk/b145] (CrySyS Lab, 31 May 2012)

---

Figure 4.3. Flame activity [Source: Kaspersky Lab]

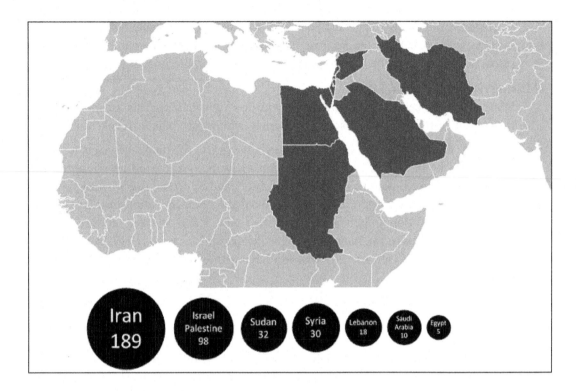

## Flame against Windows Update

What happened next stunned everyone. It transpired that one of the functions of the Flame malware was an attack against the Windows Update mechanism, which could be used to propagate to any Windows installations on the local network. The surprising part was the fact that Flame used a cryptographic attack to achieve it.[53] On top of that, the specific cryptographic technique wasn't previously known.

Once on a local network, subverting Windows Update turned out to be simple. Internet Explorer supports *Web Proxy Autodiscovery* (WPAD), which is a protocol that programs can use to find HTTP proxies on the local network.[54] An adversary with access to the local network can advertise as a proxy and gain access to the victim's HTTP(S) traffic. Flame did exactly this and included a simple web server that posed as a Windows Update server to advertise available "updates" laced with malicious code.[55]

---

[53] Analyzing the MD5 collision in Flame [fsty.uk/b146] (Alex Sotirov, 11 June 2012)

[54] Web Proxy Autodiscovery Protocol [fsty.uk/b147] (Wikipedia, retrieved 3 July 2014)

[55] Snack Attack: Analyzing Flame's Replication Pattern [fsty.uk/b148] (Alexander Gostev, 7 June 2012)

Windows Update does not appear to use TLS (a simple test on my desktop showed all update traffic in plaintext), but Microsoft does use code signing for their updates, which means that no one should be able to create binaries that would be accepted as originating from Microsoft. The twist in the story was that Flame was somehow able to sign all its binaries as Microsoft.

## Flame against Windows Terminal Services

When Microsoft started talking about the weaknesses attacked by Flame, a story of deep incompetence unfolded. In order to operate Terminal Services licensing, upon activation each Terminal Server installation would receive a special subordinate CA certificate. The sub-CA would then be used to create end-user licenses. Microsoft made several critical errors when designing this system:

1. The main Terminal Services CA certificate (which was used to issue subordinate CAs allocated to individual customers) was issued from the same trusted root as the Windows Update CA.

2. The parent Terminal Services CA was allowed to be used for licensing and—for some unexplained reason—code signing.

3. Subordinate CA certificates had no usage restrictions, which meant that they inherited the restrictions of the parent certificate.

What this meant was that every single Terminal Server customer was given an unrestricted subordinate CA certificate they could use to sign Windows Update binaries, *with no hacking required.*

Fortunately for Microsoft, such certificates could "only" be used against Windows XP machines. The subordinate CA certificates contained a proprietary X.509 extension called Hydra, and it was marked critical.[56]

The Windows XP code for certificate checking ignores critical extensions, but Windows Vista (released worldwide on 30 January 2007) and subsequent Windows versions understand critical extensions and handle them properly. This meant that the Flame authors had to find a way to obtain a certificate without the Hydra extension.

## Flame against MD5

The other critical mistake made by Microsoft when designing the Terminal Server licensing scheme was using MD5 signatures for the certificates. The other errors (discussed in the

---

[56] In PKI, when an extension is marked critical certificate chain validation can be successful only if the client (performing the validation) understands the extension. Otherwise, validation fails. The idea behind this feature is that a critical extension might contain some information of which understanding is required for robust validation.

previous section) were relatively subtle and required a good understanding of PKI to detect, but at the time that Microsoft's system was designed MD5 was widely known to be insecure. There had been a very effective demonstration of the insecurity of MD5 in 2008, with the generation of the rogue CA certificate in the RapidSSL attack. To put it into perspective, Microsoft wouldn't even allow MD5 certificates in their own root certificate program at that time, but they were used for Terminal Server licensing.

If you've read the earlier section describing the RapidSSL attack and the generation of a rogue CA certificate, you probably know what happened next: Flame used a chosen-prefix collision attack against MD5 in order to generate a rogue CA certificate. The attack was conceptually the same as the RapidSSL attack described earlier. Here's what we know:

1. Insecure MD5 signatures were used, which opened up the system to cryptographic attacks.

2. Certificate issuance was automated and the timing controlled by the attacker. All fields except certificate validity and certificate serial number were known in advance.

3. Certificate validity was predictable, requiring second precision.

4. Serial numbers were not serial as in the RapidSSL case, but they were predictable (number of milliseconds since boot, followed by two fixed bytes, followed by a serial certificate number) and required millisecond precision.

The millisecond precision required probably made the task much more difficult and required a good network connection in order to minimize jitter. Access to a high-powered computing cluster would have sped up collision search and improved accuracy. We do not know how many attempts were needed (perhaps Microsoft knows, if they're keeping good records of the licensing activity), but the attackers were obviously successful in the end.

Marc Stevens, the principal force behind the previously published chosen-prefix collision attack technique, analyzed the rogue certificate and determined that:[57]

> Flame used a chosen-prefix collision attack. [...] Flame used a birthday search followed by 4 near-collision blocks to obtain a collision.
>
> These collision bits were hidden inside the RSA modulus in the original cert and inside the issuerUniqueID field in the evil cert. Using my forensic tool I was able to retrieve the near-collision blocks of the original cert (that is not available and might never be) and the chaining value before the first near-collision block. Using this information I was able to reconstruct the 4 differential paths. These differential paths clearly show that a new variant chosen-prefix collision attack was used as well as a new differential path construction algorithm that are not in the literature.

---

[57] Microsoft Sub-CA used in malware signing [fsty.uk/b149] (Marc Stevens, 12 June 2012)

Whoever designed Flame and carried out the attacks against Microsoft obviously had at their disposal serious hardware, a capable team of developers, and access to world-class cryptographers.

---

### Counter Cryptanalysis

Collision attacks against hash functions used for signatures are a real danger. Even though MD5 troubles are largely behind us, SHA1, which is still very widely used, is also known to be weak. In an ideal world, we would have stopped using it by now. In reality, it will stay in use for a couple more years, because we have to deal with a massive ecosystem and huge inertia.

In response to this problem, Marc Stevens invented *counter-cryptanalysis*,[58] a system of looking for traces of successful collision attacks in certificates, as described in the abstract of the research paper:

> *We introduce counter-cryptanalysis as a new paradigm for strengthening weak cryptographic primitives against cryptanalytic attacks. Redesigning a weak primitive to more strongly resist cryptanalytic techniques will unavoidably break backwards compatibility. Instead, counter-cryptanalysis exploits unavoidable anomalies introduced by cryptanalytic attacks to detect and block cryptanalytic attacks while maintaining full backwards compatibility.*

---

# TURKTRUST

In December 2012, Google uncovered another serious PKI problem thanks to the public key pinning mechanism supported by the Chrome browser. Pinning is a mechanism that allows user agents to check that only authorized CAs are issuing certificates for specific web sites. Chrome ships with a small, hardcoded list of sites, but they are some of the most visible sites in the world.[59]

In December 2012, when a Chrome user encountered a certificate that did not match with the hardcoded built-in list their browser communicated the entire offending certificate chain back to Google. With access to the chain, they were able to link the rogue certificate to TURKTRUST, a Turkish certification authority.[60]

The invalid subordinate certificates were promptly revoked by all parties. TURKTRUST published a detailed report only a couple of days later and continued to provide regular updates.[61] We learned that a mistake had been made in August 2011 at TURKTRUST during a

---

[58] Counter-cryptanalysis [fsty.uk/b150] (Marc Stevens, CRYPTO 2013)

[59] I discuss public key pinning in the section called "Pinning " in Chapter 10.

[60] Enhancing digital certificate security [fsty.uk/b151] (Google Online Security Blog, 3 January 2013)

[61] Public Announcements [fsty.uk/b152] (TURKTRUST, 7 January 2013)

transition between two system installations, causing two certificates issued on that day to be marked as CA certificates. The mistake remained undetected for about 15 months, during which time the certificates were used as humble server certificates.

At some point in December 2012, a firewall with MITM capabilities was installed at EGO, one of the two organizations in possession of a misissued subordinate CA certificate. A contractor imported the certificate into the firewall, which started to perform its MITM function by generating fake web site certificates on demand. In the process, a clone of one of Google's certificates was made and used and subsequently detected by Chrome.

It's not clear if the contractor knew that the certificate in question was a CA certificate. If you're troubleshooting a MITM device and you are not familiar with PKI, importing any valid certificate you have sitting around seems like a thing that you might try.

The browser root store operators accepted TURKTRUST's position that the incident was the result of an administrative error. There was no evidence of attack against the CA; fake certificates were not seen outside EGO's own network. Mozilla asked TURKTRUST to undergo an out-of-order audit, and Google and Opera decided to stop recognizing TURKTRUST's EV certificates.

# ANSSI

In December 2013, Google announced that Chrome was revoking trust in a subordinate CA certificate issued by ANSSI (*Agence nationale de la sécurité des systèmes d'information*), a French network and information security agency. A few days later, the trust in the parent ANSSI certification authority was restricted to allow only certificates issued for the domain names corresponding to French territories (.fr being the main such top-level domain name). [62]

The reason for the revocation was the discovery that the subordinate CA certificate had been used in a transparent interception (man-in-the-middle) device running on the agency's network. As a result, certificates for various domain names were generated, some of which belonged to Google. Once again, Chrome's pinning of Google's certificate detected a misuse of the PKI.

Mozilla[63] and Microsoft[64] also disabled the offending CA certificate. The agency issued a brief statement blaming human error for the problem. There's been no evidence that the inappropriate certificate was used anywhere outside the network of the French Treasury.[65]

As is usually the case, a discussion followed on `mozilla.dev.security.policy`.[66]

---

[62] Further improving digital certificate security [fsty.uk/b153] (Google Online Security Blog, 7 December 2013 )

[63] Revoking Trust in one ANSSI Certificate [fsty.uk/b154] (Mozilla Security blog, 9 December 2013)

[64] Improperly Issued Digital Certificates Could Allow Spoofing [fsty.uk/b155] (Microsoft Security Advisory 2916652, 9 December 2013)

[65] Revocation of an IGC/A branch [fsty.uk/b156] (ANSSI, 7 December 2013)

In addition to more details of the incident being provided, various other problems with how ANSSI used the CA certificate were uncovered. For example, many of their certificates did not include any revocation information. Unusual activity was detected on their CRLs, with thousands of certificates suddenly appearing on previously empty lists. It's not clear if and how the incident concluded. According to their own admission, ANSSI will be unable to comply with Baseline Requirements until at least December 2015, which is two years after Mozilla's deadline.

---

[66] Revoking Trust in one ANSSI Certificate [fsty.uk/b157] (mozilla.dev.security.policy, 9 December 2013)

# 5 HTTP and Browser Issues

In this chapter, we focus on the relationship between TLS and HTTP. TLS was designed to secure TCP connections, but there is so much more going on in today's browsers. In many cases, the problems that arise come from the browser vendors' struggle to deal with legacy web sites; they're afraid to "break" the Web.

## Sidejacking

*Sidejacking* is a special case of web application session hijacking in which session tokens[1] are retrieved from an unencrypted traffic stream. This type of attack is very easy to perform on a wireless or local network. In the case of a web site that does not use encryption, all the attacker needs to do is observe the unencrypted traffic and extract the session token from it. If a site uses encryption only partially, two types of mistakes are possible:

**Session leakage by design**

Some sites use encryption to protect account passwords but revert to plaintext as soon as authentication is complete. This approach does result in a slight improvement of security, but such sites effectively only end up replacing leakage of one type of credentials (passwords) with the leakage of another type (session tokens). Session tokens are indeed somewhat less valuable because they are valid only for a limited period of time (assuming session management is correctly implemented), but they are much easier to capture and almost as easy to abuse by a motivated attacker.

**Session leakage by mistake**

Even when you try very hard to use encryption on an entire site, it is easy to make a mistake and leave one or more resources to be retrieved over plaintext. Even when the main page is protected, a single plaintext resource retrieved from the same do-

---

[1] In web applications, as soon as a user connects to a web site a new *session* is created. Each session is assigned a secret token (also known as a *session ID*), which is used to identify ownership. If the attacker finds out the token of an authenticated session, she can gain full access to the web site under the identity of the victim.

main name will cause session leakage.[2] This is known as a *mixed content* problem, and I discuss it in detail later in this chapter.

Figure 5.1. Wireshark network capture showing a session cookie in the clear

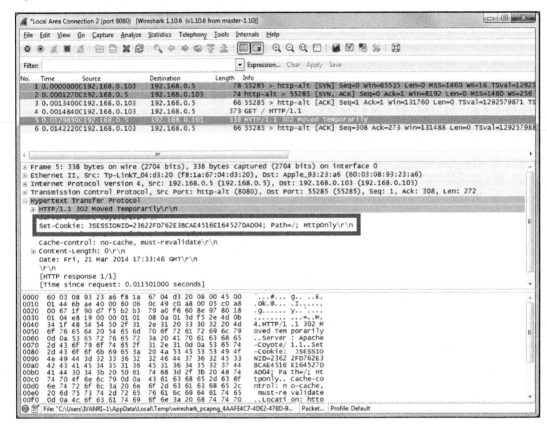

Sidejacking works well against any type of session token transport, because the attacker has full access to the communication between a user and the target web site. Thus, this attack can be used to obtain not only session tokens placed in cookies (the most common transport mechanism) but also those placed in URLs (request path or parameters). Once a session token is obtained, the attacker can reuse the captured value to communicate directly with the web site and assume the identity of the victim.

In the security community, sidejacking became better known in August 2007, when Robert Graham and David Maynor discussed it at Black Hat USA and released the accompanying Ferret and Hermit tools[3] that automate the attack.

---

[2] This is because session tokens are typically transported using cookies, which are sent on every request to the web site. As you will see later in this chapter, cookies *can* be secured, but most sites don't do so consistently.

[3] SideJacking with Hamster [fsty.uk/b158] (Robert Graham, 5 August 2007)

A couple of years later, a Firefox add-on called Firesheep,[4] written by Eric Butler, made a much bigger splash because it made sidejacking trivially easy to carry out. Firesheep become very widely known and even caused several high-profile web sites to switch to full encryption. Firesheep was quickly followed by a detection tool called BlackSheep[5] and a counterattack tool called FireShepard.[6] In addition, a tool called Idiocy[7] was released to automatically post warnings to compromised accounts.

Firesheep is now only of historic interest. For a more recent tool of this type, consider CookieCadger,[8] a passive tool for HTTP auditing developed by Matthew Sullivan.

# Cookie Stealing

Sidejacking, in the form discussed in the previous section, cannot be used against web sites that use encryption consistently, with 100% coverage. In such cases, the session tokens are always hidden behind a layer of encryption. You may think that such complete implementation of TLS also means that sidejacking is not possible, but that's not the case. A common mistake made by programmers is to forget to secure their cookies for use with encryption. When this happens, an attacker can use a clever technique called *cookie stealing* to obtain the session tokens after all.

By default, cookies work across both insecure and secure transports on ports 80 and 443. When you deploy TLS on a web site, you are also expected to mark all cookies as secure, letting the browsers know how to handle them. If you don't do this, at the first glance it may not appear that a vulnerability exists, because your users are always fully protected. But this "works" only because browsers are not submitting any requests to plaintext port 80. If you can find a way to get them to do this, the cookies will be revealed.

Conceptually, the attack is simple: the attacker is an active *man in the middle* (MITM) observing your complete Internet traffic. He cannot attack the encrypted traffic to the target web site, but he can wait for you to submit an unencrypted HTTP request to *any* other web site. At that point, he steps in, hijacks the insecure connection, and responds to one of your plaintext HTTP requests by redirecting your browsers to the target web site on port 80. Because any site can issue a redirection to any other site, your browser happily follows.

The end result is a plaintext connection to the target web site, which includes all nonsecure cookies in your browser's possession. Against a typical web application that doesn't mark cookies secure, the attacker now has the user's session tokens and can proceed to hijack the session.

---

[4] Firesheep announcement [fsty.uk/b159] (Eric Butler, 24 October 2010)

[5] BlackSheep [fsty.uk/b160] (Zscaler, retrieved 15 July 2014)

[6] FireShepard [fsty.uk/b161] (Gunnar Atli Sigurdsson, retrieved 15 July 2014)

[7] Idiocy [fsty.uk/b162] (Jonty Wareing, retrieved 15 July 2014)

[8] CookieCadger [fsty.uk/b163] (Matthew Sullivan, retrieved 15 July 2014)

The attack works even if the target web site is not actually responding on port 80. Because the attacker is in the middle, he can impersonate any plaintext server on any port, and thus the attack still works.

Another approach that could be used by the attacker is to redirect the user to the same hostname and port 443 (which will be open) but force plaintext with *http://www.example.com: 443*. Even though this request fails because the browser is attempting to speak plaintext HTTP on an encrypted port, the attempted request contains all the insecure cookies and thus all the information the attacker wants to obtain.

Figure 5.2. Man-in-the-middle attacker stealing unsecured cookies

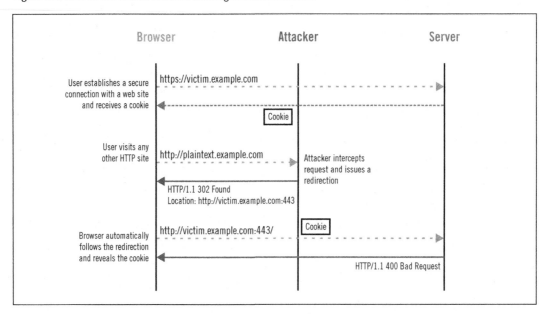

Mike Perry was the first to bring up this problem in public, shortly after sidejacking itself was publicized. But his email to the Bugtraq mailing list[9] went largely unnoticed. He persisted with a talk[10] at DEFCON 16 the following year as well as a proof-of-concept tool called CookieMonster.[11]

# Cookie Manipulation

Cookie manipulation attacks are employed in situations in which the attacker can't access the existing cookies because they are properly secured. By exploiting the weaknesses in the

---

[9] Active Gmail "Sidejacking" - https is NOT ENOUGH [fsty.uk/b164] (Mike Perry, 5 August 2007)

[10] HTTPS Cookie Stealing [fsty.uk/b165] (Mike Perry, 4 August 2008)

[11] CookieMonster [fsty.uk/b166] (Mike Perry, retrieved 15 July 2014)

cookie specification, he is able to inject new cookies and overwrite and delete existing application cookies. The main message in this section is that the integrity of an application's cookies can't always be guaranteed, even when the application is fully encrypted.

# Understanding HTTP Cookies

HTTP cookies are an extension mechanism designed to enable client-side persistence of small amounts of data. For each cookie they wish to create, servers specify a name and value pair along with some metadata to describe the scope and lifetime. Cookies are created using the Set-Cookie HTTP response header:

```
Set-Cookie: SID=31d4d96e407aad42; Domain=www.example.com; Path=/; Secure; HttpOnly
Set-Cookie: lang=en-US; Expires=Wed, 09 Jun 2021 10:18:14 GMT
```

User agents store cookies in so-called *cookie jars*. On every HTTP transaction, they look into their jars for applicable cookies and submit all of them using the Cookie HTTP request header:

```
Cookie: SID=31d4d96e407aad42; lang=en-US
```

From their initial creation, cookies had been very poorly specified and remained so for a very long time. As a result, implementations are inconsistent and contain loopholes. As you will see in this chapter, many of the loopholes can be exploited for attacks. Proper documentation became available only in 2011, in RFC 6265.[12]

From the security point of view, the problem with cookies is twofold: (1) they were poorly designed to begin with, allowing behavior that encourages security weaknesses, and (2) they are not in sync with the main security mechanism browsers use today, the *same-origin policy* (SOP).

**Loose hostname scoping**

Cookies are designed for sharing among all hostnames of a particular domain name as well as across protocols and ports. A cookie destined for *example.com* will work on all subdomains (e.g., *www.example.com* and *secure.example.com*). Similarly, a hostname such as *blog.example.com* emits cookies only for *blog.example.com* by default (when the Domain parameter is not specified) but can also explicitly expand the scope to the parent *example.com*. As a result, a rogue server is able to inject cookies into other sites and applications installed on hostnames that are sharing the same top-level domain name. I'll call them *related hostnames* or *related sites*.

This loose approach to scoping is in contrast with SOP rules, which generally define a security context with an exact match of protocol, hostname, and port. Deploying a

---

[12] RFC 6265: HTTP State Management Mechanism [fsty.uk/b167] (A. Barth, April 2011)

secure web site is much more difficult, because cookies can be set from any related hostname, substantially increasing the attack surface.

**Servers do not see metadata**

Servers receive only cookie names and values, but not any other information. Crucially, they don't know which hostname the cookies came from. If this information were available, servers would be able to reject cookies that they themselves didn't issue.

**Lack of integrity of security cookies**

The fact that cookies work seamlessly across both HTTP and HTTPS protocols is a major worry. Although you can use the secure attribute to denote a cookie that is allowed to be submitted only over an encryption channel, insecure and secure cookies are stored within the same namespace. What's even worse, the security flag is not part of the cookie identity; if the cookie name, domain, and path match, then an insecure cookie will overwrite a previously set secure one.

In a nutshell, the major flaw of HTTP cookies is that their integrity is not guaranteed. In the remainder of this section, I focus on the security implications of the cookie design on TLS; for wider coverage of the topic, including coverage of various application security issues, I recommend Michal Zalewski's book *The Tangled Web*, published by No Starch Press in 2011.

# Cookie Manipulation Attacks

There are three types of cookie manipulation attacks. Two of them can result in the creation of new cookies and so fall under *cookie injection*. The third one allows cookies to be deleted. As is customary in application security, the attacks bear somewhat unusual and dramatic names.

Various researchers have rediscovered these problems over the years, giving them different names. Although I prefer cookie injection, because it accurately describes what is going on, other names you might come across are *cross-site cooking*,[13] *cookie fixation, cookie forcing*,[14] and *cookie tossing*.[15]

# Cookie Eviction

*Cookie eviction* is an attack on the browser's cookie store. If for some reason the attacker does not like the cookies that are in the browser's store, he might attempt to exploit the fact that cookie stores limit individual cookie size, the number of cookies per domain name, and the combined cookie size. By submitting a large number of dummy cookies, the attacker

---

[13] Cross-Site Cooking [fsty.uk/b168] (Michal Zalewski, 29 January 2006)

[14] Cookie forcing [fsty.uk/b169] (Chris Evans, 24 November 2008)

[15] New Ways I'm Going to Hack Your Web App [fsty.uk/b170] (Lundeen et al., August 2011)

eventually causes the browser to purge all the real cookies, leaving only the forced ones in the store.

Some browsers—for example, Internet Explorer—are known for keeping only a small number of cookies. Firefox and Chrome limit the overall size of the cookies to several hundred kilobytes. All browsers limit the number of cookies per domain name, usually to several dozen. Individual cookie size limit is usually around 4,096 bytes. Thus, a cookie eviction attack might require the use of multiple domain names to fully overflow a jar.

## Direct Cookie Injection

When performing direct cookie injection, the attacker is faced with a site that uses secure cookies. Because of that, he is not able to read the cookies (without breaking encryption), but he can create new cookies or overwrite the existing ones. This attack exploits the fact that insecure and secure cookies live in the same namespace.[16]

The attack is conceptually similar to the one used for cookie stealing in the previous section: the attacker intercepts any plaintext HTTP transaction initiated by the victim and uses it to force a plaintext HTTP request to the target web site. He then intercepts that request and replies with an HTTP response that includes arbitrary cookies. The attack could be as simple as:

```
Set-Cookie: JSESSIONID=06D10C8B946311BEE81037A5493574D2
```

In practice, for the overwriting to work, the forced cookie's name, domain, and path must match that of the original. The attacker must observe what metadata values are used by the target web site and replicate them in the attack. For example, the session cookies issued by Tomcat always have the path set to the web site root:

```
Set-Cookie: JSESSIONID=06D10C8B946311BEE81037A5493574D2; Path=/
```

## Cookie Injection From Related Hostnames

When direct cookie injection is not possible (i.e., it's not possible to impersonate the target web site), the attacker might attack the fact that cookies are shared among related hostnames. If the attacker can compromise some other site on a related hostname, he might be able to inject a cookie from there.[17]

For example, you might be running a strongly secured *www.example.com* but also have a blogging site, installed at *blog.example.com* and hosted by a third-party with lesser focus on security. If the attacker can find a *cross-site scripting* (XSS) vulnerability in the blogging ap-

---

[16] Multiple Browser Cookie Injection Vulnerabilities [fsty.uk/b171] (Paul Johnston and Richard Moore, 15 September 2004)

[17] Hacking Github with Webkit [fsty.uk/b172] (Egor Homakov, 8 March 2013)

plication, he will be able to manipulate the cookies of the main application. The attack is the same as in the previous section: the victim is forced to submit an HTTP request to the vulnerable site, where arbitrary cookies can be set.

> ### Note
>
> Of course, any situation in which there are sites run by separate entities or departments should be a cause for caution. Not only are the members of the other groups a potential weak link, but they can be threats themselves.

If the victim does not already hold any cookies from the target web site, the attacker is in luck. Whatever cookies he sets will be used by the victim. Assuming XSS, attacking is as simple as executing the following code (from a page on *blog.example.com*):

```
document.cookie = 'JSESSIONID=FORCED_ID; domain=example.com';
```

Notice how the attacker must use the `domain` attribute to expand the scope of the cookie from the default *blog.example.com* to *example.com*, which will then be valid for the intended target, *www.example.com*.

## Getting the First Cookie

More often than not, the victim will already hold some genuine cookies. If the attacker injects another cookie with the same name (as in the previous example), the browser will accept both cookies and send them with every request to the target web site:

```
Cookie: JSESSIONID=REAL_ID; JSESSIONID=FORCED_ID
```

This happens because the browser sees these two values as separate cookies; their name, domain, and path attributes do not match exactly. But although the attacker has successfully injected a cookie, the attack cannot proceed; when there are multiple cookies with the same name only the first one is "seen" by web applications.

From here, the attacker can attempt to evict all genuine cookies from the store by using a large amount of dummy cookies. That might work, but it's tricky to pull off.

Alternatively, he may try to tweak cookie metadata to push the forced cookie into the first position. One such trick is to use the `path` attribute,[18] which exploits the fact that browsers submit more specific cookies first:

```
document.cookie = 'JSESSIONID=SECOND_FORCED_ID; domain=example.com; path=/admin';
```

Assuming the browser is accessing a URL at or below */admin/*, it will submit the cookies in the following order:

---

[18] Understanding Cookie Security [fsty.uk/b173] (Alex kuza55, 22 February 2008)

```
Cookie: JSESSIONID=SECOND_FORCED_ID; JSESSIONID=REAL_ID; JSESSIONID=FORCED_ID
```

If there are multiple sections that need to be targeted, the attacker can issue multiple cookies, one for each path. But there's still one situation in which forcing a cookie from a related hostname might overwrite the original cookie: when the target web site explicitly sets the cookie domain to the root hostname (e.g., *example.com*).

## Overwriting Cookies Using Related Hostnames

Overwriting a cookie from a related hostname does not always work because most sites set cookies without explicitly specifying the domain. These cookies are marked as *host-only*. When injecting from a related domain name, you have to specify a domain, which means that such a cookie will never match the original one even if the hostnames are the same.

There is another reason overwriting a cookie from a related hostname sometimes fails: you are not allowed to issue cookies for a sibling hostname. From *blog.example.com*, you can issue a cookie for *example.com* and *www.blog.example.com* but not for *www.example.com*.

This brings me to two cases in which overwriting is possible:

- For sites that explicitly "upgrade" the cookie domain to their root (e.g., *example.com*). I tested this case using Firefox 28, but most other browsers should follow the same behavior.

- For Internet Explorer (tested with version 11), which does not make a distinction between explicitly and implicitly set domains. However, because the names still have to match, this attack will work only against sites that issue cookies from the root (e.g., *example.com*).

## Overwriting Cookies Using Fake Related Hostnames

There is one more case in which the attacker will be able to overwrite the original cookie value: the web site is explicitly setting the cookie domain, but it does not have to be the root (as in the previous case).

That's because the MITM attacker can choose which related hostnames he attacks. The core of the Internet runs on unauthenticated DNS, which means that the attacker can take control of the DNS and make up arbitrary hostnames. For example, if he needs to attack *www.example.com*, he can make up a subdomain, say, *www.www.example.com*. From *that* name, he can then issue a cookie for *www.example.com*.

# Impact

Anecdotally, many web sites are designed under the assumption that the attacker can't discover or influence what's in the cookies. Because that's not true, things can break, but exactly how will depend on the particular application. For example:

**XSS**
> If developers don't expect cookies to change, they might use them in insecure ways. For example, they might output them to HTML directly, in which case a compromise can lead to a XSS vulnerability.

**CSRF defense bypass**
> Some web site designs rely on *cross-site request forgery* (CSRF) defenses, which require that a token placed in the page parameters matches that in the cookie. Being able to force a particular cookie value onto a client defeats this approach.

**Application state change**
> Developers quite often treat cookies as secure storage resistant to tampering. It might happen that there is some part of the application that relies on a cookie value for decision making. If the cookie can be manipulated, so can the application. For example, there might be a cookie named `admin` set to `1` if the user is an administrator. Clearly, users can always manipulate their own cookies and thus attack the application, so this is not necessarily a TLS issue. However, it can still be an attack vector used by a MITM attacker. The proposed mitigation techniques (discussed later in this section) defend against all attacks of this type.

**Session fixation**
> *Session fixation* is a reverse session hijacking attack. Rather than obtaining the victim's session ID, the attacker connects to the target web site to obtain a session ID of his own and tricks the victim into adopting it. This attack is not as powerful as session hijacking, but it could have serious consequences depending on the features of the target site.

# Mitigation

Cookie manipulation attacks can generally be addressed with appropriate mitigation steps that focus on preventing the attacker from forging cookies and checking that received cookies are genuine:

**Deploy HTTP Strict Transport Security with subdomain coverage**
> *HTTP Strict Transport Security* (HSTS)[19] is a relatively new standard that enforces encryption on the hostname for which it is enabled. Optionally, it can enforce en-

---

[19] RFC 6797: HTTP Strict Transport Security [fsty.uk/b174] (Hodges et al., November 2012)

cryption on all subdomains. With this approach, a MITM attacker cannot inject any cookies using DNS trickery without breaking encryption.

HSTS significantly reduces the attack surface, but it is not foolproof. First, it's not supported by all browsers. Second, it does not handle cases in which genuine (encrypted) related sites are compromised or run by different, untrusted entities. I discuss HSTS at length in the section called "HTTP Strict Transport Security" in Chapter 10.

**Validate cookie integrity**

The best defense against cookie injection is integrity validation: ensuring that the cookie you received from a client originated from your web site. This can be achieved by using a *Hash-based Message Authentication Code* (better known by its acronym, HMAC).[20]

Cookies that don't need to be accessed from JavaScript can be encrypted for additional protection.

It is critical that the integrity validation scheme is designed in such a way that cookies issued to one user are not valid for another. Otherwise, the attacker could obtain a valid cookie from a web site (using his own account) and inject it into the victim's account.

Cookie integrity validation and encryption schemes can't help secure session cookies, which are effectively a time-limited password-replacement mechanism. Channel ID is an effort to address this problem by creating a cryptographic binding between a browser and a site at the TLS level.[21] This approach, known as *channel binding*, effectively creates a session that could be used to replace HTTP sessions. In practice, it's more likely that the existing cookie-based mechanisms would be kept, but tied to the provably-secure channel as a defense against session hijacking.

# SSL Stripping

*SSL stripping* (or, more accurately, *HTTPS stripping*) attacks exploit the fact that most users begin their browsing session on a plaintext portion of a web site or type addresses without explicitly specifying the *https://* prefix (browsers try plaintext access first). Because the plaintext traffic of these users is fully visible and vulnerable, it can be modified at will by an active network attacker.

For example, if a web site normally contains a link to the secure server, the attacker can rewrite the content to replace the secure link with a plaintext one. Without a secure link to click on, the victim is forever prevented from entering the secure area. In the meantime, the

---

[20] RFC 2014: HMAC: Keyed-Hashing for Message Authentication [fsty.uk/b12] (Krawczyk et al., February 1997)

[21] TLS Channel IDs [fsty.uk/b175] (Internet-Draft, D. Balfanz and R. Hamilton, expired 31 December 2013)

attacker is responding to those plaintext links by proxying the genuine web site content (possibly obtained over TLS). At this point, the attacker can not only observe sensitive information but can also modify the requests and responses at will.

Figure 5.3. Man-in-the-middle attack variations

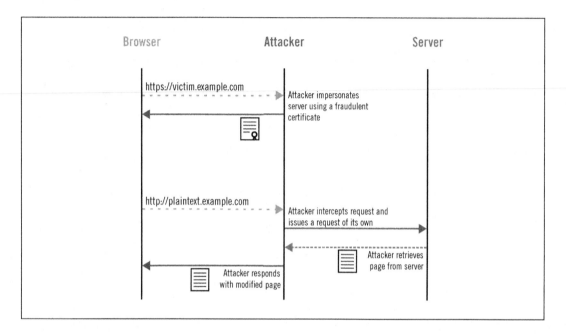

HTTPS stripping attacks rely on the fact that most users can not tell the difference between insecure and secure browsing. Faced with a user who can spot the difference, the attacker can attempt a tricky alternative and redirect the user to a secure web site that's under the attacker's full control but the name of which is very similar to that of the target web site. Common tricks include very long addresses that contain the entire target address within (e.g., *https://victim.com.example.com*) or addresses that differ from the real ones only by one character or that use similar Unicode characters.

Behind the scenes, the attacker may or may not actually be using a secure connection to the target web site, but that's little consolation for the attacked user, because the attacker can not only observe the supposedly secure content but can also modify it at will.

From the attacker's point of view, the best aspects of HTTPS stripping attacks are the fact that they can be easily automated and that easy-to-use tools are widely available. For example, two well-known tools are sslstrip[22] and SSLsplit.[23]

---

[22] sslstrip [fsty.uk/b176] (Moxie Marlinspike, 15 May 2011)

[23] SSLsplit - transparent and scalable SSL/TLS interception [fsty.uk/b177] (Daniel Roethlisberger, 28 January 2014)

# MITM Certificates

HTTPS stripping will probably work against most users (assuming incorrectly secured sites), but there will be situations when it fails. Some users do notice the difference between secure and insecure sites and even actively check for the padlock or (rarely) the green glow of EV certificates. Some users also bookmark secure sites, going straight to the secure area from their first request.

The man in the middle is still able to redirect all traffic to go through him, but exploitation requires much more effort. Here are some possible alternative attack methods:

**Exploitation of validation flaws**
> The security of TLS depends on the client correctly validating the credentials presented to it. If the validation is not implemented correctly, it might be possible to use a special invalid certificate or a certificate chain that can't be distinguished from a valid one. This type of attack is not likely to be very common these days, because validation flaws were widely publicized in 2009 and the expectation is that they are fixed by now. I discuss validation flaws later in this chapter.

**Rogue certificates**
> *Rogue certificates* are fraudulent CA certificates that are accepted by clients as genuine. They are difficult to obtain, but they are still a possibility. For example, one such certificate was forged in an attack on RapidSSL in 2008. You can read more about it in the section called "RapidSSL Rogue CA Certificate " in Chapter 4 . Another possibility is that a powerful attacker can find an existing weak CA certificate (such as 1,024-bit ones, which are still trusted by some browsers at the time of writing), and brute-force the private key. It is estimated that such attacks cost only about $1 million.[24]

> With a rogue certificate in hand, the attacker will be invisible to everyone except the most paranoid users. Combined with the fact that the MITM can interfere with OCSP revocation checks and that most browsers ignore OCSP failures, if the attacker can maintain full control over a victim's Internet connection over an extended period of time it might also be effectively impossible to revoke a rogue certificate.

**Self-signed certificates**
> If everything else fails, the attacker may try the least sophisticated approach, which is to present the victim with a self-signed certificate that has most fields copied from the real one. Such a certificate is bound to generate a warning, but users are generally known to click through such warnings. More about that in the next section.

A very well-known tool for this category of MITM attacks is `sslsniff`.[25]

---

[24] Facebook's outmoded Web crypto opens door to NSA spying [fsty.uk/b178] (CNET, 28 June 2013)

[25] sslsniff [fsty.uk/b179] (Moxie Marlinspike, 25 July 2011)

# Certificate Warnings

For proper security, cryptography needs authentication. If you can't tell that you're talking to the right party, then all bets are off. Someone could be hijacking the communication channel to impersonate your intended recipient, and you wouldn't be able to tell. It's a situation similar to picking up the phone and talking to someone on the other end without knowing if they are who they claim they are.

In the context of TLS, we use certificates for authentication. (TLS supports other authentication methods, but they are rarely used.) When you connect to a server, you have a particular hostname in mind, and the expectation is that the server will present a certificate that proves that they have the right to handle traffic for that hostname.

If you receive an invalid certificate, the right thing to do is to abandon the connection attempt. Unfortunately, browsers don't do that. Because the Web is full of invalid certificates, it's almost guaranteed that none of the invalid certificates you encounter will be a result of an attack. Faced with this problem, browser vendors decided a long time ago not to enforce TLS connection security, instead pushing the problem down to their users in the form of *certificate warnings*.

Which brings me to one of the ugliest truths about TLS: its sole purpose is to protect you from man-in-the-middle attacks, but when the attack comes all you will get is a certificate warning from your browser. Then it will be down to *you* to determine if you are under attack.

Figure 5.4. Examples of certificate warnings in current browsers

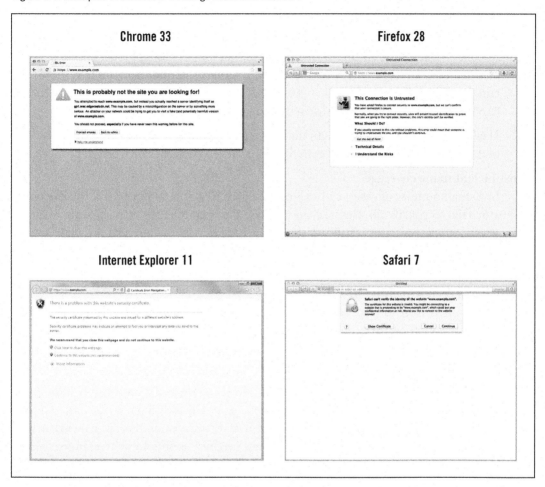

## Why So Many Invalid Certificates?

There's plenty of anecdotal evidence about the prevalence of invalid certificates. It's hard to actually find someone who has not been exposed to them. Here are some of the root causes:

### Misconfigured virtual hosting

Today, most web sites run only on port 80 and don't use encryption. A common configuration mistake is to put such plaintext sites on the same IP address as some other site that uses encryption on port 443. As a result, users who attempt to access the plaintext sites via a *https* prefix end up in the wrong place; the certificate they get doesn't match the intended name.

Part of the problem is that, at the technical level, we don't have a mechanism for web sites to state if they support encryption. In that light, the correct way to host plaintext sites is to put them on an IP address on which port 443 is closed.

In 2010, I scanned about 119 million domain names, searching for secure sites.[26] The lists included all .com, .net, and .org domain names. I found 22.65 million (19%) secure sites hosted on roughly two million IP addresses. However, only about 720,000 (0.6%) sites had certificates whose names matched the intended hostname.

Having a certificate with the right name is a good start, but not enough. Roughly 30% of the name-matched certificates in the 2010 survey could not be trusted.

### Insufficient name coverage

In a small number of cases, certificates are purchased and deployed, but the site operator fails to specify all required hostnames. For example, if you're hosting a site at *www.example.com*, the certificate should include that name but also the plain *example.com*. If you have other domain names pointing to your web site, the certificates should include them, too.

### Self-signed certificates and private CAs

The main reason for trust failure is that certificates are not appropriate for public consumption; they are either self-signed or issued by a private CA. When it comes to members of the public, such certificates can't be distinguished from certificates used in MITM attacks. In my survey, about 48% of the trust failures fell into this category.

Why are people using these certificates, then? There are many reasons, including: (1) purchasing, configuring, and renewing certificates is additional work and requires continuous effort; (2) up until a few years ago, certificates used to be expensive; and (3) some people believe that publicly trusted certificates should be free and refuse to buy them. However, the simple truth is that only publicly trusted certificates are appropriate for public web sites. We don't have an alternative at this time.

### Certificates used by appliances

These days, most appliances have web-based administrative user interfaces and require secure communication. When these devices are manufactured, the hostname and IP address they will use is not known, which means that the manufacturers cannot install valid certificates onto them. In theory, end users could install valid certificates themselves, but many of these appliances are seldom used and are hardly worth the effort. In addition, many of the user interfaces do not allow user-provided certificates to be used.

---

[26] Internet SSL Survey 2010 is here! [fsty.uk/b83] (Ivan Ristić, 29 July 2010)

### Expired certificates

The other substantial reason for invalid certificates is expiration. In my survey, 57% of the failures fell into this category. In many cases, site owners forget to renew their certificates. Or, they give up on having valid certificates altogether but don't take the old ones down.

### Misconfiguration

Another frequent problem is misconfiguration. For a certificate to be trusted, each user agent is required to establish a chain of trust from the server certificate to a trusted root. Servers are actually required to provide the entire chain, minus the trusted root. But according to SSL Pulse, about 6% of the servers in their data set has an incomplete chain.[27] In some cases, browsers will be able to work around that, but often they won't.

When it comes to user experiences, one study from 2013 looked at about 3.9 billion public TLS connections and found that 1.54% of them resulted in certificate warnings.[28] But that's only on the public Internet, where sites generally try to avoid warnings. In certain environments (e.g., intranets and internal applications), you might be expected to click through certificate warnings every single day as you're accessing web applications required for your work.

## Effectiveness of Certificate Warnings

The world would be much better without certificate warnings, but the truth is that browser vendors are balancing on a fine line between improving security and keeping their users happy. In 2008, I made a halfhearted attempt to convince Mozilla to hide the ability to add exceptions for invalid certificates in Firefox, in order to make it very difficult to bypass certificate warnings. Unsurprisingly, my bug submission was rejected.[29] Their response (in the form of a link to an earlier blog post),[30] was that they had tried, but the push-back from their users had been too strong. This is a reflection of a wider problem of misaligned priorities; browser vendors want increased market share, but increasing security usually has the opposite effect. As a result, browser vendors implement as much security as they can while trying to keep their most vocal users reasonably happy. Very occasionally, users complain about certificate warnings that come from genuine MITM attacks, and that reminds everyone what these warnings are for.[31] Perhaps the biggest problem with MITM attacks is that users are not aware of them (after all, certificate warnings are a "normal" part of life) and do not report them.

---

[27] SSL Pulse [fsty.uk/b70] (SSL Labs, July 2014)

[28] Here's My Cert, So Trust Me, Maybe? Understanding TLS Errors on the Web [fsty.uk/b180] (Akhawe et al., WWW Conference, 2013)

[29] Bug 431827: Exceptions for invalid SSL certificates are too easy to add [fsty.uk/b181] (Bugzilla@Mozilla, reported 2 May 2008)

[30] TODO: Break Internet [fsty.uk/b182] (Johnathan Nightingale, 11 October 2007)

[31] Bug 460374: All certificates show not trusted - get error code (MITM in-the-wild) [fsty.uk/b183] (Bugzilla@Mozilla, reported 16 October 2008)

Still, the fact remains that the harder you make it for your users to override certificate warnings, the better security you provide. Today, major browsers generally rely on so-called *interstitial* or *interruptive warnings*, which take over the entire browser content window. The old-style dialog warnings (still used by Safari) are seen as ineffective; they look the same as all other dialogs we get from our machines all the time. Most browsers allow users to click through the warnings. When only one click is required to get around the obstacle, the harsh language is all that stands between you and the web site. As it turns out, lots of people decide to go on.

Early studies of certificate warning effectiveness reported high click-through rates. But they largely relied on controlled environments (research labs), which was considered unreliable by some:[32]

> *Furthermore, our analysis also raised concerns about the limitations of laboratory studies for usable security research on human behaviors when ecological validity is important. [...] The observed reluctance of security concerned people to take part in our study raises concerns about the ability of such studies to accurately and reliably draw conclusions about security practices and user behavior of the general population.*

In the meantime, browser vendors started to use *telemetry* to monitor the usage of their products. That allowed for observation of users' behavior in their own environments, providing more accurate results. It turned out that Firefox had the best implementation, with only 33% of their users proceeding to the sites with invalid certificates. As a comparison, about 70% of Chrome users clicked through.[33] A later study reduced the click-through rate of Chrome users to 56% by mimicking the design used by Firefox.[34]

## Click-Through Warnings versus Exceptions

The success of invalid certificate handling by Firefox could also be explained by the fact that it's the only browser that doesn't use click-through warnings. Instead, it makes you go through a multistep process to create a *certificate exception*, after which the certificate is considered as good as trusted, even on subsequent visits. It is conceivable that each step in the process convinces a number of users to give up and heed the warning.

The argument against exceptions is that you are making the use of self-signed certificates easier. This is certainly true, but that's not necessarily a bad thing. Self-signed certificates are

---

[32] On the Challenges in Usable Security Lab Studies: Lessons Learned from Replicating a Study on SSL Warnings [fsty.uk/b184] (Sotirakopoulos et al., Symposium on Usable Privacy and Security, 2011)

[33] Alice in Warningland: A Large-Scale Field Study of Browser Security Warning Effectiveness [fsty.uk/b185] (Akhawe and Felt; USENIX Security, 2013)

[34] Experimenting At Scale With Google Chrome's SSL Warning [fsty.uk/b186] (Felt at al., ACM CHI Conference on Human Factors in Computing Systems, 2014)

not inherently unsafe if used by people who know what they are. For example, I have an ADSL router in my house that I access over TLS. I am definitely not going to get a valid certificate for it, but I don't need to click through a certificate warning every time I access it. Further, exceptions are created on a per-certificate basis. This means that if someone attacks me a certificate warning will show again. This approach to security is known as *trust on first use*, and is successfully deployed for the SSH protocol on millions of servers worldwide. Another name for this approach is *key continuity management*.

Certificate exceptions are useful only for individual use and for small groups of technical users who know to create exceptions only when it's safe to do so. It's crucial that exceptions are created only when the users are not under attack. In my example, I know that the certificate on my ADSL router is not going to change by itself; seeing a warning would be highly unusual.

## Mitigation

If you care about the security of your web site, you are probably going to be very worried about your users clicking through a genuine MITM attack. After all, you're going through all the trouble of using valid certificates, configuring your servers, and otherwise making sure everything is fine on your end for their protection.

Clearly, there's little you can do about the entire ecosystem, but you can protect your sites by supporting HSTS, which is a signal to the supporting browsers to adjust their behavior and adopt a stricter security posture when it comes to encryption. One of the features of HSTS is the suppression of certificate warnings. If there is an issue with the certificate on an HSTS site, all failures are fatal and cannot be overridden. With that, you are back in control of your own security.

## Security Indicators

Security indicators are user interface elements that relay additional information about security of the current page. They typically say one of four things:

- "This page uses SSL"
- "We know what legal entity operates this web site"
- "This page uses an invalid certificate"
- "Parts of this page are not encrypted"

With exception of extended certificates, which link legal entities to web sites, the other indicators exist largely because web site encryption is optional and because browsers have lax treatment of security. In a world in which the Web was 100% encrypted and there were no certificate warnings and no mixed content, you'd care only about the presence of EV certificates.

Figure 5.5. Examples of security indicators in current browsers

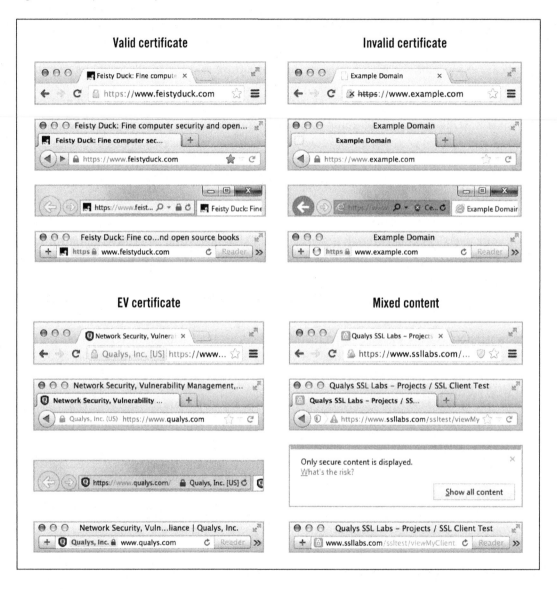

The biggest problem with security indicators is that most users don't pay attention to them and possibly don't even notice them. We know this from several studies that focused on security indicators. One study used eye tracking and determined that many users spend little time looking at browser chrome, focusing on the content instead.[35] In the same study, none of the participants noticed the EV indicators; those that did paid no attention to them. This confirms results of another study, whose authors arrived at the same conclusion.[36]

Perhaps one of the contributing factors to the confusion is the lack of consistency, both among different browsers and in different versions of the same browser. User interface guidelines exist,[37] but they are not specific enough. One must wonder why the major browser vendors can't get together to agree on a unified approach.

I remember how in the early days of SSL there was a huge push to educate browser users about the meaning of the padlock ("If you see a padlock, you're safe."). A couple of years later, browser vendors started playing with the user interface. In some cases (e.g., Firefox), there were changes made with every new release.

At the same time, web sites started to use the padlock on their web pages, further diluting the message. Thus we went from having the padlock mean one specific thing (encryption is present) to using it as a generic security indicator. In many cases, its presence is meaningless. For example, there are many sites that prominently feature a padlock but use no encryption.

Today, the only consistency, and only in the broad sense, is the use of green color for EV certificates. It's still respected by all major browsers.

When it comes to mobile platforms, the situation seems to be worse. Due to much smaller screen sizes, browser vendors are trying to remove virtually all user interface elements, affecting security indicators in particular. With many mobile browsers, even security experts have a hard time distinguishing secure sites from insecure ones.[38]

This has led some researchers to conclude that mobile users are three times more vulnerable to phishing attacks.[39] In addition, the security of mobile (nonbrowser) applications in general is difficult to assess. Although all applications should use secure protocols for backend communication, we don't know if that's actually happening, because they provide no indications. And, even if they did, who is to say that they're not just displaying an image of a padlock without any security at all?

---

[35] Exploring User Reactions to New Browser Cues for Extended Validation Certificates [fsty.uk/b187] (Sobey at al., ESORICS, 2008)

[36] An Evaluation of Extended Validation and Picture-in-Picture Phishing Attacks [fsty.uk/b188] (Jackson et al., Proceedings of Usable Security, 2007)

[37] Web Security Context: User Interface Guidelines [fsty.uk/b189] (W3C Recommendation, 12 August 2010)

[38] Measuring SSL Indicators on Mobile Browsers: Extended Life, or End of the Road? [fsty.uk/b190] (Amrutkar et al., Information Security Conference, 2012)

[39] Mobile Users Three Times More Vulnerable to Phishing Attacks [fsty.uk/b191] (Mickey Boodaei, 4 January 2011)

---

# Mixed Content

The TLS protocol concerns itself with a single connection and focuses only on keeping the data secure at the network level. This separation of concerns works well for simpler protocols, for example, SMTP. However, some protocols (e.g., FTP and HTTP) have multiple connections associated with the same security context (e.g., web browsing session). TLS doesn't provide any guidance for such situations; it's up to user agent developers to provide a secure implementation.

When it comes to HTTPS, you'd struggle to find a page that uses only a single connection. On virtually all sites, HTML markup, images, style sheets, JavaScript, and other page resources arrive not only over multiple connections but possibly from multiple servers and sites spread across the entire Internet. For a page to be properly encrypted, it's necessary that all the content is retrieved over HTTPS. In practice, that's very often not the case, leading to *mixed content* security problems.

> **Note**
>
> This section covers only same-page mixed content, but the same problem exists at the web site level. Web sites that mix plaintext and secure pages are prone to development errors (e.g., use of insecure cookies or sensitive content available without encryption) and SSL stripping attacks.

# Root Causes

To understand why mixed content issues are so pervasive, we have to go back to the origins of the Web and consider the breakneck pace of progress. The focus has always been on getting things done and overcoming the limits imposed by costs, technology, and security.

**Performance**
In the early days of SSL, its performance on the Web was pretty poor compared to the performance of plaintext HTTP. Today, servers tend to have fast processors and plenty of RAM, and we're still concerned about the speed of cryptographic operators. Back in the day, the only way to obtain good SSL performance was to use specialized hardware accelerators, which were terribly expensive. Virtually no one uses those anymore.

Because of the performance problems, everyone tried to stay away from SSL as much as possible. There was no concept of providing 100% encryption coverage for web sites. You might even argue that such an approach was justifiable and that the choice was mostly between some security and no security at all.

Today, performance is still a concern, but it's largely about latency. Because of the additional round trips required to establish a secure connection, there's a slight delay when accessing a secure web site.

**Mashups**

At some point, the Web really took off, and the concept of *mashups* was born. Web sites no longer provided all of the content themselves. Instead, they mixed and matched content from various sites and focused on the user experience, hiding away content origin. In some cases, the content was freely available. In others, mashups operated via commercial deals.

A special case of a mashup is the use of third-party code for web site analytics, made extremely popular by Google when it gave its analytics service away for free. According to some estimates, Google Analytics is used on about 50% of the Web.[40]

Mashups are, generally, a nightmare for security. They're mostly implemented by incorporating some JavaScript code from a third-party web site. Unfortunately, although this approach to site building reduces costs dramatically, it also gives the third-party web sites almost full control over all the sites that rely on them. It also creates a problem for web site users: with so many entities involved on the same site, it becomes difficult to understand what entities they're communicating with and where their data is stored.

In the context of encryption, the main issue is that in many cases third-party content and services are not available via a secure server. Sometimes, secure access is available but costs more. As a result, people simply resorted to including insecure (plaintext) content from their "secure" web sites.

To illustrate this problem, consider that Google's ad platform, AdSense, added support for secure delivery only in September 2013.[41]

**Infrastructure costs**

As competition among web sites grew, it became impossible to deliver a web site from a single geographic location and remain competitive. *Content delivery networks* (CDNs) rose in popularity to deliver content to visitors at the best possible performance. The idea is that by spreading a number of servers across the globe, site visitors can always talk to the fastest one.

The problem with CDNs is that they are intended to serve huge amounts of (usually static) data files for many customers. Encryption not only increases CPU and RAM requirements but also might affect caching and adds the burden of certificate and key management.

---

[40] Usage statistics and market share of Google Analytics for websites [fsty.uk/b192] (W3Techs, 15 July 2014)

[41] Use AdSense on your HTTPS sites [fsty.uk/b193] (Sandor Sas, 16 September 2013)

On top of that, there's the issue of IP addresses. For plaintext HTTP, for which virtual web site hosting is widely supported, IP addresses don't matter. This makes large-scale hosting and distribution easy. Virtual hosting of secure web sites is a different matter altogether; it's still not feasible for public web sites. This means that suddenly you need to track the mapping of web sites to IP addresses and thus servers. You have to split your infrastructure into groups, which leads to a much more complicated architecture and increased overheads.

Plus, there's a worldwide shortage of IPv4 addresses. Some companies try to work around this problem by using shared certificates for unrelated sites, but that's still a significant complication.

The bottom line is that secure CDNs are possible, but they cost much more.

Because of all this history, browsers generally did little to provide encryption integrity at a page level. Mixed content issues were allowed and became deeply ingrained in the development culture.

## Impact

The impact of mixed content issues depends on the nature of the resource that is not being secured. Over the years, two terms emerged: *mixed passive content* (or *mixed display*) for resources that are lower risk, for example, images, and *mixed active content* (or *mixed scripting*) for higher-risk content, such as HTML markup and JavaScript.

Mixed active content is the really dangerous category. A single unprotected inclusion of a JavaScript file can be hijacked by an active attacker and used to obtain full control over the page and perform arbitrary actions on that web site using the victim's identity. The same can be said for other dangerous resource types, such as HTML markup (included via frames), style sheets, Flash and Java applications, and so on.

Mixed passive content is not as dangerous, but it still violates the integrity of the page. In the least dangerous case, the attacker could mess with the victim by sending him messages embedded in images. This could lead to phishing. It's also possible to inject exploits into images, targeting browsers' image processing code. Finally, some browsers are known to use *content sniffing* and might actually process an image as a script; in that case the attacker is also able to take control over the page.

In addition, any unencrypted resource delivered from the same hostname as the main page will expose the site's session cookies over the communication link without encryption. As I discussed earlier in this chapter, cookies that are not properly secured can be retrieved by an active attacker, but with mixed content they can be retrieved by a passive attacker, too.

# Browser Treatment

Initially, mixed content was allowed by all browsers. The vendors expected web site designers and programmers to understand the potential security issues and make the right decisions. Over time, this attitude changed and the vendors started to become more interested in this problem and to restrict what was allowed.

Today, most browsers tend to implement a compromise between breakage and security: mixed passive content is allowed, and mixed active content is not. The only catch is that not all browsers agree with what constitutes active content.

**Android browser**

Mixed content is allowed without any restrictions.

**Chrome**

Chrome changed its handling of mixed active content in version 14,[42] but considered the job done only with version 21.[43]

Chrome (currently in version 36) allows passive mixed content and blocks active mixed content but allows insecure XMLHttpRequest connections. By version 38, Chrome will block all mixed active content.[44]

**Firefox**

Firefox has a long history of being able to detect and warn about mixed content but, due to internal implementation issues, not being able to block it. The bug for this issue remained open for about 12 years.[45] With version 23, Firefox finally started to block all mixed active content.[46]

**Internet Explorer**

Internet Explorer had issues with blocking mixed content from at least Internet Explorer 5 (1999). It would detect a combination of encrypted and plaintext resources in a page and ask the user to decide how to proceed. Microsoft almost switched to blocking insecure content by default (with notification), and even deployed that behavior in IE 7 beta,[47] but backed down due to user pressure. They made the change later, in IE 9.[48] At that time, they also started allowing insecure images by default.

---

[42] Trying to end mixed scripting vulnerabilities [fsty.uk/b194] (Google Online Security blog, 16 June 2011)

[43] Ending mixed scripting vulnerabilities [fsty.uk/b195] (Google Online Security blog, 3 August 2012)

[44] PSA: Tightening Blink's mixed content behavior [fsty.uk/b196] (Mike West, 30 June 2014)

[45] Bug 62178: Implement mechanism to prevent sending insecure requests from a secure context [fsty.uk/b197] (Bugzilla@Mozilla, reported 6 December 2000)

[46] Mixed Content Blocking Enabled in Firefox 23! [fsty.uk/b198] (Tanvi Vyas, 10 April 2013)

[47] SSL, TLS and a Little ActiveX: How IE7 Strikes a Balance Between Security and Compatibility [fsty.uk/b199] (Rob Franco, 18 October 2006)

[48] Internet Explorer 9 Security Part 4: Protecting Consumers from Malicious Mixed Content [fsty.uk/b200] (Eric Lawrence, 23 June 2011)

---

**Safari**

Safari currently does not block any mixed content, making it stand out compared to other major browsers. In fact, there was recently even a regression in how the issue is handled. In Safari 6 on OS X, there was a checkbox that allowed users to enable mixed content blocking. In version 7, which shipped with OS X 10.9, the checkbox is now gone.

The following table shows the details of mixed content handling in major browsers today.

Table 5.1. Mixed content handling in major browsers; "yes" means mixed content is allowed (July 2014)

|                     | Images | CSS | Scripts | XHR | WebSockets | Frames |
|---------------------|--------|-----|---------|-----|------------|--------|
| Andriod Browser 4.4.x | Yes    | Yes | Yes     | Yes | Yes        | Yes    |
| Chrome 36           | Yes    | No  | No      | Yes | No         | No     |
| Firefox 30          | Yes    | No  | No      | No  | No         | No     |
| Internet Explorer 11 | Yes    | No  | No      | No  | No         | No     |
| Safari 7            | Yes    | Yes | Yes     | Yes | Yes        | Yes    |

If you're curious about the behavior of your favorite browser, SSL Labs provides a test for user agents and covers mixed content issues.[49]

> **Note**
>
> Mixed content vulnerabilities can be very deep. In most modern browsers, there are many ways in which insecure HTTP requests can originate from secure pages. For example, it is likely that browser plugins can make whatever requests they want irrespective of the encryption status of the host page. This is especially true for plug-ins such as Flash and Java, which are platforms in their own right. There's now a W3C effort to standardize browser handling of mixed content, which should help get a consistent behavior across all products.[50]

# Prevalence of Mixed Content

Anecdotally, mixed content is very common. At Qualys, we investigated this problem in 2011 along with several other application-level issues that result in full breakage of encryption in web applications.[51] We analyzed the homepages of about 250,000 secure web sites from the Alexa top-one-million list and determined that 22.41% of them used insecure content. If images are excluded, the number falls to 18.71%.

---

[49] SSL/TLS Capabilities of Your Browser [fsty.uk/b201] (SSL Labs, retrieved 15 July 2014)

[50] W3C: Mixed Content [fsty.uk/b202] (Mike West, retrieved 15 July 2014)

[51] A study of what really breaks SSL [fsty.uk/b203] (Michael Small and Ivan Ristić, May 2011)

A more detailed study of 18,526 sites extracted from Alexa's top 100,000 took place in 2013.[52] For each site, up to 200 secure pages were analyzed, for a total of 481,656 pages. You can see the results in the following table.

Table 5.2. Mixed content in 481,656 secure pages from Alexa's top 100,000 sites [Source: Chen et al., 2013]

|            | # Inclusions | % remote | # Files | # Webpages | % Websites |
|------------|--------------|----------|---------|------------|------------|
| Image      | 406,932      | 38%      | 138,959 | 45,417     | 30%        |
| iframe     | 25,362       | 90%      | 15,227  | 15,419     | 14%        |
| CSS        | 35,957       | 44%      | 6,680   | 15,911     | 12%        |
| JavaScript | 150,179      | 72%      | 29,952  | 45,059     | 26%        |
| Flash      | 1,721        | 62%      | 638     | 1,474      | 2%         |
| Total      | 620,151      | 47%      | 191,456 | 74,946     | 43%        |

> **Note**
>
> Even when all third-party links are encrypted, the fact remains that using active content from other web sites essentially gives those sites full control. Too many sites today include random widgets without thinking through the security implications.[53]

# Mitigation

The good news is that despite browsers' lax attitude to mixed content issues you are in full control of this problem. If you implement your sites correctly, you won't be vulnerable. Of course, that's easier said than done, especially with large development teams.

There are two technologies that can help you minimize and, possibly, eliminate mixed content issues, even when it comes to incorrectly implemented applications:

**HTTP Strict Transport Security**
    HSTS is a mechanism that enforces secure resource retrieval, even in the face of user mistakes (such as attempting to access your web site on port 80) and implementation errors (such as when your developers place an insecure link on a secure page). HSTS is one of the best things that happened to TLS recently, but it works only on the hostnames you control.

---

[52] A Dangerous Mix: Large-scale analysis of mixed-content websites [fsty.uk/b204] (Chen et al., Information Security Conference, 2013)

[53] You Are What You Include: Large-scale Evaluation of Remote JavaScript Inclusions [fsty.uk/b205] (Nikiforakis et al., Computer and Communications Security, 2012)

---

**Content security policy**
> To block insecure resource retrieval from third-party web sites, use *Content Security Policy* (CSP). This security feature allows blocking of insecure resources. It also has many other useful features for application security issues.

HSTS and CSP are both declarative measures, which means that they can be added at a web server level without having to change applications. In a way, you can think of them as safety nets, because they can enforce security even for incorrectly implemented web sites.

For example, a very frequent problem on secure web sites comes from the fact that many of them implement automatic redirection from port 80 to port 443. That makes sense, because if some user does arrive to your plaintext web site you want to send him to the right (secure) place. However, because redirection is automatic it is often invisible; a plaintext link for an image will be redirected to a secure one, and the browser will retrieve it without anyone noticing. Anyone except the attacker, maybe. For this reason, consider always redirecting to the same entry point on the secure web site. If you do this, any mistakes in referencing resources will be detected and corrected in the development phase.

Of course, sites that deploy HSTS cannot be exploited, because browsers automatically convert insecure links to secure ones. That said, you can't rely on all browsers supporting HSTS (yet), so it's best to try to minimize such mistakes.

# Extended Validation Certificates

*Extended validation* (EV) certificates are a special class of certificates that establish a link between a domain name and the legal entity behind it. (Individuals can't get EV certificates.) In the early days of SSL, all certificates required strict verification, similar to how EV certificates are issued today. Certificate price wars led to the wide adoption of *domain-validated* (DV) certificates, which rely on cheap email validation. That was possible because there were no formal regulations of the certificate validation procedures. EV certificates were defined in 2007 by the CA/Browser Forum.[54]

EV certificates offer two chief advantages: (1) the identity of the domain owner is known and encoded in the certificate and (2) the manual verification process makes certificate forgery more difficult. As far as I am aware, there's never been a fraudulent EV certificate.

On the other hand, it's questionable if those advantages translate into any practical benefits, at least when the general user population is concerned. As we've seen in earlier sections in this chapter, users rarely notice security indicators, even the prominent ones used for EV certificates. For this reason, end users are going to miss the link to the domain name owner. Further, fraudulent DV certificates can be used to attack EV sites. The only way to prevent these attacks is for end users to understand what EV certificates mean, remember that a site

---

[54] EV SSL Certificate Guidelines [fsty.uk/b63](CA/Browser Forum, retrieved 15 July 2014)

uses them, notice the absence of the appropriate security indicators, and decide not to proceed. This seems unlikely, given the percentage of users who proceed to a web site even after shown a scary certificate warning.

Still, it's possible that the treatment of EV certificates will improve in the future. For example, user agents might add features to allow site operators to always require EV certificates on their web sites, similar to how today you can use HTTP Strict Transport Security to always require encryption.

Another problem is that EV certificates are detected and indicated on the page level without taking into account what type of certificate is used by the resources (e.g., scripts). Given the high cost of EV certificates, it is not unusual that complex sites often rely on DV certificates for the largely invisible subdomains.[55]

This means that a careful network attacker can use a DV certificate against an EV site, potentially without affecting the green security indicators. Zusman and Sotirov demonstrated several interesting attack vectors:[56]

**Resources delivered from other domain names**
In many cases, sites will use an EV certificate on the main domain name but retrieve resources from many other hostnames, all of which will typically use DV certificates. Browser connections for these other names can be intercepted with a fraudulent DV certificate, leading to malware injection.

**Cookie theft**
Because browsers do not enforce certificate continuity, it's possible to use a DV certificate to intercept a connection for the main domain name, steal existing or set new cookies, and redirect back to the real server. The attack happens quickly and won't be noticed by most users.

**Persistent malware injection**
If caching is enforced (the attacker can essentially say that a resource is never refreshed), injected malware can persist in the browser file cache and stay active for long periods of time, even on subsequent site visits.

# Certificate Revocation

When it comes to the certificate validity period, there is a tension between wanting to reduce administrative burden and needing to provide reasonably fresh information during verification. In theory, the idea is that every certificate should be checked for revocation before it is trusted. In practice, there are a number of issues that make revocation very difficult.

---

[55] Beware of Finer-Grained Origins [fsty.uk/b206] (Jackson and Barth, Web 2.0 Security and Privacy, 2008)

[56] Sub-Prime PKI: Attacking Extended Validation SSL [fsty.uk/b207] (Zusman and Sotirov, Black Hat USA, 2009)

# Inadequate Client-Side Support

Arguably the biggest problem with revocation checking is that client-side support is inadequate. Making things worse is the fact that revocation is something you never need—until you need it badly. As such, it's always something that can be dealt with "later."

It's genuinely quite difficult to understand what browsers do, when they do it, and how. Because there is no documentation, you have to rely on mining mailing lists, bug reports, and source code to understand what is happening. For example, there is anecdotal evidence that intermediate certificates are not checked. For a long time, it wasn't clear that CRLs are not used by many browsers. Support for new features, such as OCSP stapling, is slow to arrive. The topic is largely a black box. Testing can provide some answers, but only at a point in time; there are no guarantees that the next version will continue to behave in the same manner.

Outside the browser world, command-line tools still struggle with certificate validation, let alone revocation. And because most libraries do not use revocation checks by default, developers generally don't bother either.

The overall conclusion is that revocation does not work as designed, for one reason or another.

This became painfully clear during 2011, after several CAs had been compromised. In each case, the only way to reliably revoke fraudulent certificates was to use blacklisting, but not via CRL or OCSP. Instead, all vendors resorted to issuing patch releases, which contained hardcoded information about the fraudulent certificates. Chrome and Microsoft built special mechanisms to allow them to push new blacklisted certificates to their users without forcing software upgrade. Other browsers followed or are planning to follow.

# Key Issues with Revocation-Checking Standards

At a high level, there are some design flaws in both CRL and OCSP that limit their usefulness. There are three main problems:

**Disconnect between certificates and queries**
CRL and OCSP refer to certificates using their serial numbers, which are just arbitrary numbers assigned by CAs. This is unfortunate, because it's impossible to be completely certain that the certificate you have is the same one the CA is referring to. This fact could be exploited during a CA compromise by creating a forged certificate that reuses a serial number of an existing and valid certificate.

**Blacklisting instead of whitelisting**
CRL is, by definition, a blacklist, and cannot be anything else. OCSP suffered from coming after CRLs and was probably designed in a way that's easy to use on top of the existing CRL infrastructure. In the early days, OCSP responders operated largely by

feeding from the information available in CRLs. That was a missed opportunity to change from blacklisting to whitelisting to make it possible to check that a certificate is valid, not just that it has not been revoked.

The focus on blacklisting was amplified by the practice to treat the "good" OCSP response status as "not revoked," even when the server actually had no knowledge of the serial number in question. As of August 2013, the CA/Browser Forum forbids this practice.

It sounds like a small difference, but this design flaw came up as a real problem during the DigiNotar incident. Because this CA had been completely compromised, there was no record of what fraudulent certificates had been issued. As a result, they could not be revoked individually. Although DigiNotar's root certificates were eventually removed from all browsers, as a short-term measure their OCSP responders were configured to return "revoked" for all their certificates.

### Privacy

Both CRL and OCSP suffer from privacy issues: when you communicate with a CA to obtain revocation information, you disclose to it some information about your browsing habits. The leakage is smaller in the case of CRLs as they usually cover a large number of certificates.

With OCSP, the privacy issue is real, making many unhappy. If a powerful adversary wishes to monitor everyone's browsing habits, it's much easier to monitor the traffic flowing to a dozen or so major OCSP responders than to eavesdrop on the actual traffic of the entire world.

To address this problem, site operators should deploy *OCSP stapling*, which is a mechanism that allows them to deliver OCSP responses directly to their users along with their certificates. With this change, users no longer need to talk to CAs, and there is no information leakage.

# Certificate Revocation Lists

Initially, *Certificate Revocation Lists* (CRLs) were the only mechanism for revocation checking. The idea was that every CA would make a list of revoked certificates available for download at a location specified in all their certificates. Clients would consult the appropriate list before trusting a certificate. This approach proved difficult to scale, leading to the creation of OCSP for real-time checks.

## Issues with CRL Size

CRLs might have seemed like a good idea initially, when the number of revocations was small. But when the number of revocations exploded, so did the size of the CRLs. According to GoDaddy, their revocation information grew from 158 KB in 2007 to 41 MB in 2013.[57]

According to Netcraft, they track 220 public CRLs worldwide, and many of them are quite long.[58] At the top of the list is CAcert (a CA that is not trusted by most browsers) with a list that's about 6 MB. After it follow several larger lists, and those are followed by a long tail of CRLs of decreasing size. For illustration, you can see the top 10 in the following table.

Table 5.3. Top 10 CRLs by size [Source: Netcraft, 13 March 2014]

| CRL | Size (in KB) |
| --- | --- |
| CAcert | 6,219 |
| TrustCenter (Symantec) | 1,583 |
| Entrust | 1,460 |
| VeriSign 1 (Symantec) | 1,346 |
| VeriSign 2 (Symantec) | 744 |
| Comodo 1 | 450 |
| Comodo 2 | 366 |
| Thawte (Symantec) | 346 |
| GoDaddy | 320 |
| Comodo 3 | 314 |

GoDaddy might not feature on the list with a CRL of 41 MB, but they dominate the entire list with *many* smaller CRLs. Other large CAs also use multiple lists. This makes the CRL size problem less visible; if you're an active web user you are likely to need many of the CRLs, which means that you will have to download large quantities of data on an ongoing basis. It might not be an issue for desktop users, but it's definitely unacceptable for mobile users. Even if bandwidth consumption does not worry you, the CPU power required for processing such large files might be prohibitive.

### Note

The problem with CRL size could have been solved by using *delta CRLs*, which contain only the differences from a previously known full CRL. However, this feature, even though supported on all Windows platforms, has found little use in Internet PKI.

---

[57] NIST Workshop: Improving Trust in the Online Marketplace [fsty.uk/b208] (Ryan Koski, 10 April 2013)
[58] CRLs tracked by Netcraft [fsty.uk/b209] (Netcraft, retrieved 15 July 2014)

---

Chapter 5: HTTP and Browser Issues

## Client-Side Support for CRLs

CRLs have never been supported particularly well on the client side. Today, in particular, the situation is pretty dire.

- Chrome does not check CRLs by default, but will use them for EV certificates if CRLSets (their proprietary mechanism for revocation checking) and OCSP do not provide a satisfactory answer.

- Firefox never checked CRLs for non-EV certificates. It had a mechanism that allowed users to manually configure CRLs, after which they would be downloaded in regular time intervals. But that feature was effectively killed with Firefox 24.[59] As of version 28, Firefox does not check CRLs, even for EV certificates.[60]

- Internet Explorer (and all applications relying on Windows APIs) does everything correctly and downloads and checks CRL if no better revocation information is available.

- Safari will attempt to chase all available revocation possibilities these days, ignoring failures. On my OS X 10.9 laptop, both OCSP and CRL configuration is set to "Best attempt." There are many reports on the internet (mostly from 2011, around the Comodo and DigiNotar compromises) that suggest that these settings were previously at "Off" by default.

## CRL Freshness

CRL size is not the only problem. Long validity periods pose a significant problem and reduce CRL effectiveness. For example, in May 2013 Netcraft reported how a revoked intermediary certificate on a popular web site went unnoticed (until they reported on it).[61]

The certificate in question did not have any OCSP information, but the CRL was correct. What happened? A part of the explanation could be that no client used the CRL to check the intermediate certificates, which reflects the sad state of CRL support. However, even assuming that clients use CRLs correctly (e.g., Internet Explorer), the fact remains that the CA industry currently allows unreasonably long validity periods for intermediate certificates. Here's the relevant quote from Baseline Requirements[62] (emphasis mine):

> *The CA SHALL update and reissue CRLs at least (i) once every twelve months and (ii) within 24 hours after revoking a Subordinate CA Certificate, and **the value of the nextUpdate field MUST NOT be more than twelve months beyond the value of the thisUpdate field**; [...]*

---

[59] No CRL UI as of Firefox 24 [fsty.uk/b210] (Kathleen Wilson, August 2013)

[60] As of Firefox 28, Firefox will not fetch CRLs during EV certificate validation [fsty.uk/b211] (Brian Smith, 13 December 2013)

[61] How certificate revocation (doesn't) work in practice [fsty.uk/b212] (Netcraft, 13 May 2013)

[62] Baseline Requirements [fsty.uk/b64] (CA/Browser Forum, retrieved 13 July 2014)

---

Thus, a CRL for an intermediate certificate is going to be considered fresh for 12 months, whereas a critical revocation can be added at any day of the year. Allowing such a long period was probably partially motivated by the desire to cache the CRLs for as long as possible, because intermediate certificates are often used by millions of sites. In addition, CRLs are signed by roots keys, which are kept offline for safety; frequent issuance of CRLs would impact the security. Still, long freshness periods of CRLs negatively impact the effectiveness of revocation. This is especially true for intermediate certificates, which, if compromised, could be used to impersonate any web site. By comparison, CRLs for server certificates must be updated at most every 10 days.

# Online Certificate Status Protocol

*Online Certificate Status Protocol* (OCSP) came after CRL to provide real-time access to certificate revocation information. The idea was that without the burden of having to download a large CRL you can afford to use OCSP on every visit to a web site.

## OCSP Replay Attacks

In cryptography, a well-understood attack against secure communication is the *replay attack*, in which the attacker captures and reuses a genuine message, possibly in a different context. OCSP, as originally designed,[63] is not vulnerable to replay attacks; clients are invited to submit a one-time token (*nonce*) with every request, and servers are expected to include that same value in their signed response. The attacker cannot replay responses because the nonce is different every time.

This secure-by-default approach ended up being difficult to scale and, at some point, gave way to a lightweight approach that is less secure but easier to support in high-volume environments. The *Lightweight OCSP Profile*[64] introduced a series of recommendations designed to allow for batch generation of OCSP responses and their caching. In order to support the caching, the replay protection had to go. Without the nonce, an OCSP response is just a file that you can generate once, keep for a while, and deliver using a CDN.

As a result, clients generally don't even try to use nonces with OCSP requests. If they do (you can try it with the OpenSSL command-line client), servers usually ignore them. Thus, the only defense against replay attacks is the built-in time limit: attackers can reuse OCSP responses until they expire. That window of opportunity will depend on the CA in question and on the type of certificate (e.g., responses for EV certificates might have a short life, but those for DV certificates might have a much longer one), but it ranges from hours to days. Seeing OCSP responses that are valid for a week is not unusual.

---

[63] RFC 2560: X.509 Internet Public Key Infrastructure Online Certificate Status Protocol - OCSP [fsty.uk/b213] (Myers et al., June 1999)

[64] RFC 5019: The Lightweight OCSP Profile for High-Volume Environments [fsty.uk/b214] (A. Deacon and R. Hurst, September 2007)

As is the case with CRLs, Baseline Requirements allow OCSP responses that are valid for up to 10 days; up to 12 months for intermediate certificates.

## OCSP Response Suppression

The *OCSP response suppression* attack relies on the fact that most browsers that use OCSP ignore failures; they submit OCSP requests in good faith but carry on when things go wrong. Thus, an active attacker can suppress revocation checks by forcing all OCSP requests to fail. The easiest way to do this is to drop all connections to OCSP responders. It is also possible to impersonate the responders and return HTTP errors. Adam Langley did this once and concluded that "revocation doesn't work."[65]

Prior to Adam's experiment, in 2009 Moxie Marlinspike highlighted a flaw in the OCSP protocol that allows for suppression without network-level failures. In OCSP, successful responses are digitally signed, which means that even an active attacker cannot forge them. However, there are several unauthenticated response types dealing with failures. If all you need is to make a response fail, you simply return one of the unauthenticated error codes.[66]

## Client-Side OCSP Support

In many cases, there is no need to attack OCSP revocation because user agents ignore it completely. Older platforms and browsers do not use OCSP or do not use it by default. For example, Windows XP and OS X before 10.7 fall into this category.

More important, however, is the fact that some modern browsers choose not to use OCSP. For example, iOS uses OCSP (and, presumably, CRL) only for EV certificates.[67] Chrome largely stopped using OCSP in 2012,[68] replacing all standards-based revocation checks with a lightweight proprietary mechanism called CRLSets.[69] CRLSets improve revocation checking performance (all checks are local and thus fast) but decrease security because they cover only a subset of all revocations, mostly those related to CA certificates. Private CAs are especially vulnerable, because there is no way for them to be included in the CRLSets. In the most recent versions, OCSP revocation checking is attempted only for EV certificates and only if their CRLSets don't already cover the issuing CA.

Even when OCSP is used, virtually all browsers implement *soft-fail*. They attempt OCSP requests and react properly to successful OCSP responses but ignore all failures. In practice, this provides protection only in a small number of use cases. As you've seen in the previous

---

[65] Revocation doesn't work [fsty.uk/b215] (Adam Langley, 18 March 2011)

[66] Defeating OCSP With The Character '3' [fsty.uk/b216] (Moxie Marlinspike, 29 July 2009)

[67] CRL and OCSP behavior of iOS / Security.Framework? [fsty.uk/b217] (Stack Overflow, answered 2 March 2012)

[68] Revocation checking and Chrome's CRL [fsty.uk/b218] (Adam Langley, 05 February 2012)

[69] CRLSets [fsty.uk/b219] (Chromium Wiki, retrieved 15 July 2014)

section, soft-fail clearly does not work against an active attacker who can simply suppress all OCSP traffic.

Typically, the worst that can happen when revocation checking fails is that an EV site will lose its security status, leading to all EV indicators being stripped from the user interface. I am not sure we can expect anyone to actually notice such an event. And, if they do, how should they react to it?

## Responder Availability and Performance

From the beginning and to this day, OCSP has had a reputation for being unreliable. The problems in the early days caused browsers to adopt the inadequate soft-fail approach, and OCSP has never recovered. CAs are much better these days at making their responders available, but browser vendors still refuse to switch to hard-fail and put their reputation on the line.

> **Note**
>
> Thanks to Netcraft, we now have visibility into the performance of OCSP responders of various CAs.[70]

There are three separate issues to consider:

**Availability**

OCSP responder availability is the biggest issue. If you're running a secure web site and your CA's OCSP responder is down, your site will suffer. If browsers implemented hard-fail, then your site would be down, too.[71]

With soft-fail, it's likely that you will experience severe performance issues in the case of the OCSP responder downtime. User agents that use OCSP will attempt to check for revocation, and they all have a network timeout after which they give up. This timeout is typically set at several seconds. As an illustration, Firefox uses three seconds by default and 10 seconds when in hard-fail mode.

There is also an additional problem with the so-called *captive portals*, which arise when users don't have full access to the Internet (and thus to various OCSP responders) but still need to validate certificates in some way. In practice, this happens most often when you are required to authenticate on a Wi-Fi network. Although captive portals could take care to whitelist public OCSP responders, most don't do that.

**Performance**

By its nature, OCSP is slow. It requires user agents to first parse a certificate, then obtain the OCSP URL, open a separate TCP connection to the OCSP responder, wait

---

[70] OCSP Uptime [fsty.uk/b220] (Netcraft, retrieved 15 July 2014)

[71] Certificate revocation and the performance of OCSP [fsty.uk/b221] (Netcraft, 16 April 2013)

for a response, and only then proceed to the original web site. A slow OCSP responder will add hundreds of milliseconds of latency to the first connection to your web site.

OCSP responder performance is possibly the single biggest differentiator among CAs today. You basically want to select a CA that will provide minimal slowdown to your web site. For that, a fast and globally distributed OCSP responder network is required. Some CAs are using their own infrastructure, while others are opting for commercial CDNs, such as Akamai and CloudFlare.

Maintaining a robust OCSP responder is not a trivial task. VeriSign (now Symantec) is known for operating a highly available OCSP responder service. According to their report, during 2012 they were serving over 4.5 billion OCSP responses every day.[72] A more recent article mentions as many as 14 billion transactions per day in 2014.[73]

## Correctness

If an OCSP responder is available and fast, that does not mean that it is actually responding correctly. Some CAs do not synchronize their OCSP responders with changes in their main database. For example, some time ago I obtained a certificate from a public CA, installed it on my web site, and promptly discovered that all OCSP requests were failing.

After contacting the CA, I learned that they allow up to 40 minutes from the creation of a certificate until they update the OCSP responders. My suggestion to postpone certificate issuance until their entire infrastructure was ready was dismissed as "too complicated."

At this point, it's unlikely that OCSP revocation will ever be changed to a hard-fail system. CAs had a slow start initially, and when browsers adopted soft-fail they had little incentive to improve. Today, the likely scenario is that the availability and performance concerns will be addressed by a wider adoption of *OCSP stapling*, which allows servers to retrieve OCSP responses from the CAs once and deliver them directly to end users along with their certificates.

> ### Note
>
> For a period of several years, I had my Firefox browser configured to hard-fail (in about:config, set security.ocsp.require to true). In all of that time, I had OCSP responder availability issues only with one CA. Interestingly, it was the same CA that has the 40-minute delay on their OCSP responders.

---

[72] 2013 Internet Security Threat Report, Volume 18 [fsty.uk/b222] (Symantec, April 2013)

[73] Three years after Diginotar closed, hackers still trying to use its digital certificates [fsty.uk/b223] (CSO, 14 March 2014)

# 6 Implementation Issues

The software we write today is inherently insecure, for several reasons. First, the basic tools —programming languages and libraries—are not written with security in mind. Languages such as C and C++ allow us to write code that is fast but fragile. Often, a single coding mistake can crash the entire program. That is simply absurd. Libraries and APIs are virtually never designed to minimize errors and maximize security. Documentation and books are rife with code and designs that suffer from basic security issues. We don't have to go far to find a representative example: OpenSSL itself, the most widely used SSL/TLS library, is notorious for being poorly documented and difficult to use.

The second problem is much deeper and has to do with the economics of writing software. In today's world, emphasis is on getting work "done" by minimizing up-front costs (in both time and money), without caring about the long-term effects of insecure code. Security—or, more generally, code quality—is not valued by end users, which is why companies tend not to invest in it.

As a result, you will often hear that cryptography is bypassed, not broken. The major cryptographic primitives are well understood and, given choice, no one attacks them first. But the primitives are seldom useful by themselves; they need to be combined into schemes and protocols and then implemented in code. These additional steps then become the main point of failure, which is why you will also often hear that only a fool implements their own crypto.

The history is full of major cryptographic protocols with critical design flaws, but there are even more examples of various implementation problems in well-known projects. The situation gets much worse when you start looking at projects developed without the necessary expertise in cryptography.

This chapter reviews the major implementation issues, both historical and still relevant ones.

# Certificate Validation Flaws

For a TLS connection to be trusted, every client must perform two basic checks: determine that the certificate applies to the intended hostname and determine that the certificate is valid and can be trusted. Sounds simple, but the devil is in the details. When certificate-checking code is developed, developers will test with the certificate chains they find in real life, but those will never be malicious and designed to subvert security. As a result, it isn't uncommon that developers miss some critical checks.

For example, the following is a list of some (but not all!) of the things that need to be checked for each certificate chain.

1. The end entity (server) certificate is valid for the intended hostname.

2. All chain certificates (including the end-entity one) must be checked to see that:

   - They have not expired.

   - Their signatures are valid.

3. An intermediate certificate might need to satisfy further requirements:

   - Can be used to sign other certificates for the intended purpose (e.g., an intermediate certificate might be allowed to sign web server certificates, but cannot be used for code signing).

   - Can be used to sign other CA certificates.[1]

   - Can be used to sign the hostname in the leaf certificate.

In addition, a robust implementation will check a number of other things, for example, that all the keys are strong and that weak signatures (e.g., MD2, MD5, and (soon) SHA1) are not used.

# Library and Platform Validation Failures

Certificate validation flaws are not very common, but their impact is usually significant, because all code that relies on them inherits the problems. Well-known validation flaws include the following:

**Basic Constraints check failure in Microsoft CryptoAPI (2002)[2]**
This is an early example of validation failure in probably the most widely used code-base, which affected all Microsoft platforms as well as some products running on other operating systems. Because of this flaw, any valid server certificate could be used to

---

[1] For security reasons, the CA certificate that issues the end-entity certificate shouldn't be allowed to issue subordinate CA certificates. All other intermediate certificates in the chain must have this privilege.

[2] Certificate Validation Flaw Could Enable Identity Spoofing [fsty.uk/b224] (Microsoft Security Bulletin MS02-050, 4 September 2002)

sign a fraudulent certificate that would then be trusted. The fraudulent certificate could be then used in active MITM attacks. Konqueror (the default browser of the KDE desktop) was also found to suffer from the same problem. Further variations of the flaw were later discovered in Microsoft's code, including some that could be used for code signing on the Windows platform.

This problem was discovered by Moxie Marlinspike in August 2002.[3] Moxie went on to write sslsniff,[4] a MITM attack tool, for the sole purpose of demonstrating that this problem can be exploited. In 2009, Moxie also reported that OpenSSL (around version 0.9.6) had been vulnerable to the same problem, but no further details are available.

### Chain validation failure in GnuTLS (2008)[5]

A flaw in the certificate chain validation code allowed invalid chains to be recognized as valid by simply appending any trusted root certificate to the end of any nontrusted chain. The error was that the appended certificate, which caused the entire chain to be trusted, was removed prior to checking that all certificates are part of a single chain.

### DSA and ECDSA signature validation failures in OpenSSL (2009)[6]

In 2009, the Google Security Team discovered that, due to insufficient error checking in OpenSSL code, DSA and ECDSA signature failures could not be detected. The practical impact of this problem was that any MITM attacker could present a fraudulent certificate chain that would be seen as valid.

### Basic Constraints check failure in iOS (2011)[7]

Almost a decade later, Apple was discovered to have made the same mistake in the chain validation as Microsoft and others before. The iOS platforms before 4.2.10 and 4.3.5 were not checking if certificates are allowed to act as subordinate CAs, making it possible for any leaf certificate to sign any other certificate.

### Connection authentication failure in iOS and OS X (2014)

On 21 February 2014, Apple released updates for iOS 6.x and 7.x in order to fix a bug in TLS connection authentication.[8] Although Apple didn't provide any details (they never do), the description caught everyone's attention and sparked a large-scale hunt for the bug. It turned out that a devastating slip in the connection authentication code allowed any DHE and ECDHE connection to be silently hijacked by an active MITM.[9] The bug was also found to exist in the latest version of OS X (10.9), which

---

[3] Internet Explorer SSL Vulnerability [fsty.uk/b225] (Moxie Marlinspike, 8 August 2002)

[4] sslsniff [fsty.uk/b179] (Moxie Marlinspike, retrieved 20 February 2014)

[5] Analysis of vulnerability GNUTLS-SA-2008-3 CVE-2008-4989 [fsty.uk/b226] (Martin von Gagern, 10 November 2008)

[6] Incorrect checks for malformed signatures [fsty.uk/b227] (OpenSSL, 7 January 2009)

[7] TWSL2011-007: iOS SSL Implementation Does Not Validate Certificate Chain [fsty.uk/b228] (Trustwave SpiderLabs, 25 July 2011)

[8] About the security content of iOS 7.0.6 [fsty.uk/b229] (Apple, 21 February 2014)

had been released in October 2013. Unfortunately, a fix was not immediately available; it's not clear why Apple would choose not to synchronize releases for such a significant security issue. Possibly because of a strong backlash, the fix (OS X 10.9.2) came only a couple of days later, on February 25th.

In the context of TLS authentication, this bug is as bad as they get. The weakness is in a transient part of the handshake that is never logged. (If you were to attack certificate authentication, for example, you would need to provide a fraudulent certificate chain, which might be recorded and reported.) If proper care is taken to use it only against vulnerable clients (which should be possible, given that the TLS handshake exposes enough information to allow for pretty reliable fingerprinting), an attack could be reliable, silent, and effective without leaving any trace.

All applications running on the vulnerable operating systems were exposed to this problem. The only exceptions were cross-platform applications (for example, Chrome and Firefox) that rely on their own TLS stack.

### Chain validation failures in GnuTLS (2014)

In early 2014, GnuTLS disclosed two separate vulnerabilities related to certificate chain validation.[10] The first bug caused GnuTLS to treat any X.509 certificate in version 1 format as an intermediary CA certificate. If someone could obtain a valid server certificate in v1 format (not very likely, given that this is an obsolete format), they could use it to impersonate any server when GnuTLS is used for access. This vulnerability had been introduced in GnuTLS 2.11.5.

As for the second vulnerability, shortly after Apple's TLS authentication bug had been revealed GnuTLS disclosed a similar bug of their own: a malformed certificate could short-circuit the validation process and appear as valid.[11] It is probable that the maintainers, after learning about Apple's bug, decided to review their code in search for similar problems. Although GnuTLS isn't used by major browsers and isn't as popular as OpenSSL on the server side, it still has some major users. For example, many of the packages shipped by Debian use it. Thus, this vulnerability might have had a significant impact. This vulnerability had been present in the code for a very long time, possibly from the very first versions of GnuTLS.

### OpenSSL ChangeCipherSpec Injection (2014)

In June 2014, the OpenSSL project disclosed a long-standing vulnerability that allowed an active network attacker to inject ChangeCipherSpec messages into handshakes between two OpenSSL endpoints and force negotiation of a predictable master secret.[12] This problem existed in virtually every version of OpenSSL, but—as far as we

---

[9] Apple's SSL/TLS bug [fsty.uk/b230] (Adam Langley, 22 February 2014)

[10] Advisories [fsty.uk/b231] (GnuTLS, retrieved 17 July 2014)

[11] Dissecting the GnuTLS Bug [fsty.uk/b232] (Johanna, 5 March 2014)

know—it's not exploitable unless a vulnerable version from the OpenSSL 1.0.1 branch is running on the server. The root cause is that during a TLS handshake the ChangeCipherSpec message is used by each side to signal the end of negotiation and a switch to encryption, but this message is not authenticated because it's not part of the handshake protocol. If the attacker sends the message early (which OpenSSL should have caught), the vulnerable sides construct encryption keys too early and with the information the attacker knows.[13]

This vulnerability is quite serious and easy to exploit, but its impact is reduced, because OpenSSL is required on both sides of the communication, and yet OpenSSL is rarely used on the client side. The most prominent platform that uses OpenSSL in this way is Android 4.4 (KitKat), which was subsequently fixed. According to SSL Pulse, immediately after the vulnerability was released there were about 14% of servers running the exploitable versions of OpenSSL.

In 2014, a group of researchers published the results of comprehensive adversarial testing of certificate validation in several libraries.[14] They developed a concept of "mutated" certificates, or *frankencerts*, built from real certificates.[15] Although the widely used libraries and browsers passed the tests, the lesser-used libraries, such as PolarSSL, GnuTLS, CyaSSL, and MatrixSSL, were all found to have serious flaws.

## Application Validation Failures

If major platforms and libraries can have serious validation vulnerabilities, we can intuitively expect that other software will fare much worse. After all, for most developers security is something that stands in the way between them and shipping their project. There's been ample anecdotal evidence of certificate validation failures in end-user code, but the scale of the problem became more clear after a research paper on the topic was published in 2012.[16] From the abstract (emphasis mine):

> We demonstrate that SSL certificate validation is completely broken in many security-critical applications and libraries. Vulnerable software includes Amazon's EC2 Java library and all cloud clients based on it; Amazon's and PayPal's merchant SDKs responsible for transmitting payment details from e-commerce sites to payment gateways; integrated shopping carts such as osCommerce, ZenCart, Ubercart, and PrestaShop; AdMob code used by mobile web-

---

[12] OpenSSL Security Advisory CVE-2014-0224 [fsty.uk/b233] (OpenSSL, 5 June 2014)

[13] Early ChangeCipherSpec Attack [fsty.uk/b234] (Adam Langley, 5 June 2014)

[14] Using Frankencerts for Automated Adversarial Testing of Certificate Validation in SSL/TLS Implementations [fsty.uk/b235] (Brubaker et al., S&P, 2014)

[15] Frankencert [fsty.uk/b236] (sumanj, GitHub, retrieved 17 July 2014)

[16] The most dangerous code in the world: validating SSL certificates in non-browser software [fsty.uk/b237] (Georgiev et al., CCS, 2012)

*sites; Chase mobile banking and several other Android apps and libraries; Java Web-services middleware—including Apache Axis, Axis 2, Codehaus XFire, and Pusher library for Android—and all applications employing this middleware. **Any SSL connection from any of these programs is insecure against a man-in-the-middle attack.***

If this is not cause for alarm, then I don't know what is. Clearly, there are some major components of the Internet infrastructure mentioned in the report. According to the team behind the research, the root cause is the badly designed APIs. Not only are the libraries often insecure by default (no certificate validation at all), but they make it difficult to write code that is secure. Most libraries are simply too low level and expect too much from their users. For example, OpenSSL expects developers to provide their own code to perform hostname validation.

The report very accurately describes a major problem with our entire development stacks, affecting all code and security, not only SSL and TLS. Yes, there are libraries that are insecure and difficult to use, but the real problem is that we keep on using them. No wonder we keep on repeating the same mistakes.

To be -fair, there are some platforms that behave correctly. Java's SSL/TLS implementation (JSSE), for example, performs all necessary validation by default, much to the annoyance of many developers who don't want to bother to set up a trusted development infrastructure. Anecdotal evidence suggests that most developers, in development, disable all validation in their code. We can only wonder how often are checks re-enabled in production.

## Hostname Validation Issues

Speaking of hostname validation—how difficult can it be to verify if a certificate is valid for the intended hostname? As it turns out, the verification is often skipped, as several vulnerabilities show. At Black Hat USA in 2009, Dan Kaminsky[17] and Moxie Marlinspike[18] independently detailed how to perform MITM attacks entirely silently, without any warnings experienced by the victims.

Several flaws were needed to pull the attacks off, but in both cases the key was the NUL byte, which is used in C and C++ for string termination. In this context, the NUL byte is not part of the data but only indicates that the data is ending. This way of representing textual data is handy, because you only need to carry a pointer to your data. Then, as you're processing the text, whenever you see the NUL byte, you know that you've reached the end.

---

[17] PKI Layer Cake: New Collision Attacks Against the Global X.509 Infrastructure [fsty.uk/b238] (Kaminsky et al., Black Hat USA, 2009)

[18] More Tricks For Defeating SSL In Practice [fsty.uk/b239] (Moxie Marlinspike, Black Hat USA, 2009)

Figure 6.1. Representation of a C string in memory

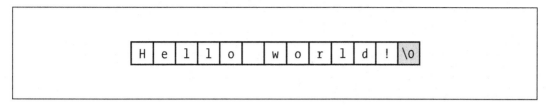

Certificate structures, which rely on the ASN.1 notation standard, use a different approach, in which all structures are stored with their length. Problems arise when these different approaches to handling strings meet: certificates are encoded in one way (ASN.1) but processed in another (C code).

The attack is this: construct a certificate that has a NUL byte in the hostname, and bet that (1) most clients will think that that's where the hostname ends and that (2) the NUL byte will thwart a CA's validation process.

Here's how Moxie executed the attack:

1. Construct a special hostname with a NUL byte in it. Moxie used the following: *www.paypal.com\0.thoughtcrime.org* (the NUL byte is indicated with \0, but is normally "invisible"). The rules are to:

   - Place the hostname you wish to impersonate before the NUL byte.

   - Put some domain name you control after the NUL byte.

2. For CAs, the NUL byte is nothing special.[19] They issue certificates based on the validation of the hostname suffix, which maps to some top-level domain name. In the previous attack example, the domain name is *thoughtcrime.org*, which belongs to Moxie. He will naturally approve the certificate request.

3. The resulting certificate can now be used against vulnerable clients with a modified version of `sslsniff`.

---

[19] Actually, that's not strictly true. Some CAs were found to incorrectly process the NUL byte and mistake it for a string terminator. These days, it's very likely that CAs perform all sorts of checks on the submitted hostnames.

Figure 6.2. The domain name used by Moxie Marlinspike in his proof-of-concept attack

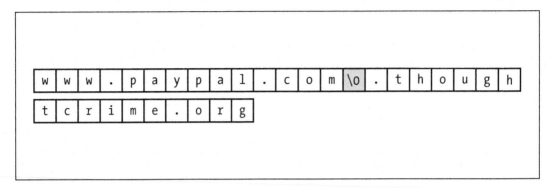

Microsoft's CryptoAPI, GnuTLS, and NSS libraries were all found to be vulnerable to the NUL byte attack, affecting Firefox, Internet Explorer, and many other user agents. And when you add to the mix the PKI feature that allows for wildcards in hostnames you may end up with a certificate issued to *\0thoughtcrime.org, which worked as a universal interception certificate.

## Random Number Generation

All cryptography relies on random number generation, making this functionality the essential building block of secure communication.[20] For example, you need random numbers whenever you are generating a new key. Keep in mind that key generation is not something you do only once in a while (e.g., if you're installing a new server) but something that protocols (e.g., TLS) do behind the scenes on every single connection.

With a good *random number generator* (RNG), for example, a 256-bit symmetric key will provide 256 bits of security (when used with a strong algorithm). But if the RNG is flawed, rather than having a random number from that large 256-bit space you may end up with one from a much smaller space, say, 32 bits. The smaller the effective space, the worse the security. If the effective size of the key is too small, even brute-force attacks against it may be possible.

## Netscape Navigator (1994)

One of the early examples of random number generation failure was in Netscape Navigator, the flagship product of the company that designed SSL itself. This browser used a simplistic

---

[20] True random number generation is not possible unless specialized hardware components are used. In practice, we rely on *pseudorandom number generators* (PRNGs). Most PRNGs use a small amount of entropy as a seed, after which they can produce a large quantity of pseudorandom numbers. In this section, I use RNG and PRNG interchangeably.

algorithm for random number generation that relied on the time since boot in microseconds and the IDs of the underlying operating system process and that of its parent. The problem was revealed in 1995, when two researchers reverse engineered the code of the RNG[21] and wrote a program that uncovers the master encryption key.[22]

In the best case for the attacker, having an account on the same Unix machine as the victim meant that he could determine the process and parent process IDs. The attacker would then determine the time in seconds from observing packets as they travel on the network, reducing the problem to guessing the microseconds value—which is only about 20 bits of security. To break through that required only 25 seconds on the hardware they had at hand.

In the more realistic case of an attacker with no knowledge of process IDs, the size of the problem would be reduced to 47 bits—still within reach of brute-force attacks, even at that time.

## Debian (2006)

In May 2008, Luciano Bello discovered[23] that a catastrophic programming error concerning the RNG used in the OpenSSL system libraries had been made by the Debian Project in September 2006 and that the bug consequently ended up in the project's stable release (Debian *etch*) in April 2007. Debian is not only a very popular Linux distribution but also a starting point from which many other distributions are built (most notably, Ubuntu), which meant that the problem affected a great number of servers in the world.

The programming error had been the accidental removal (commenting out) of a single line of code, which fed entropy to the random number generator. With that line removed, the only entropy left was some auxiliary input from the process ID, which meant that there were only 16 (!) bits of entropy for all cryptographic operations. With so few bits, all crypto on the affected installations was effectively nonexistent.

This was the affected fragment of the code:[24]

```
/*
 * Don't add uninitialised data.
        MD_Update(&m,buf,j);
 */
        MD_Update(&m,(unsigned char *)&(md_c[0]),sizeof(md_c));
        MD_Final(&m,local_md);
        md_c[1]++;
```

---

[21] Randomness and the Netscape Browser [fsty.uk/b240] (Ian Goldberg and David Wagner, January 1996)

[22] unssl.c [fsty.uk/b241] (Ian Goldberg and David Wagner, September 1995)

[23] DSA-1571-1: openssl — predictable random number generator [fsty.uk/b242] (Debian, 13 May 2008)

[24] Diff of /openssl/trunk/rand/md_rand.c r140:r141 [fsty.uk/b243] (Debian OpenSSL package, 2 May 2006)

---

The biggest practical problem was weak OpenSSH keys,[25] but that was largely mitigated by the fact that these keys are stored in well-known locations and could be easily checked. The Debian project built a black list of vulnerable keys as well as tools to look for them.

Replacing vulnerable TLS keys was more difficult, because the process could not be implemented as part of the automated patching process. Scripts were built to scan all files and detect weak keys. Because the problem can be detected from a server's public key, remote-testing tools were made available. (I, for example, added such a test to the SSL Labs code.) In addition, because most server certificates last only for a year or two, CAs were able to apply tests (against public keys, which are embedded in certificate signing requests) and refuse to issue certificates for vulnerable private keys. Overall, however, there was a great sense of confusion, and many people reported that the detection tools were not correctly flagging vulnerable keys even though they had been generated on vulnerable systems.

The discovery of the Debian RNG issue highlighted the fact that open source projects are often touched—for whatever reason—by those who are not very familiar with the code. There is often very little quality assurance even for critical system components such as OpenSSL. And yet millions rely on that code afterward.

Tension between project developers and packagers is a well-known problem in open source circles.[26] Distributions often fork open source projects and change their behavior in significant ways but keep the names the same. As a result, there is often confusion regarding which versions are affected by problems and who is responsible for fixing them. The underlying root cause is friction between developers and packages, which results from different development schedules and different priorities and development goals.[27]

> ### Note
>
> Debian is not the only operating system that has suffered problems with random number generation. In 2007, three researchers published a paper discussing RNG weaknesses in Windows 2000.[28] It was later discovered that Windows XP was also affected. Then, as recently as March 2013, the NetBSD project announced that NetBSD 6.0, first released in October 2012, had a bug in the kernel RNG that impacted security.[29]

## Insufficient Entropy on Embedded Devices

In February 2012, a group of researchers published the results of an extensive study of the quality of RSA and DSA keys found on the Internet.[30] The results indicated that at least

---

[25] Working exploit for Debian generated SSH Keys [fsty.uk/b244] (Markus Müller, 15 May 2008)

[26] Vendors Are Bad For Security [fsty.uk/b245] (Ben Laurie, 13 May 2008)

[27] Debian and OpenSSL: The Aftermath [fsty.uk/b246] (Ben Laurie, 14 May 2008)

[28] CryptGenRandom [fsty.uk/b247] (Wikipedia, retrieved 17 July 2014)

[29] RNG Bug May Result in Weak Cryptographic Keys [fsty.uk/b248] (NetBSD, 29 March 2013)

0.5% of the seen RSA keys (used for SSL/TLS) were insecure and could easily be compromised. The results for DSA (used for SSH) were worse, with 1.03% of the keys considered insecure.

The large majority of the discovered problems could be attributed to issues with random number generation. The study concluded:

> *Ultimately, the results of our study should serve as a wake-up call that secure random number generation continues to be an unsolved problem in important areas of practice.*

On the positive side, virtually all of the discovered problems were on headless and embedded devices, and the study concluded that nearly all keys used on nonembedded servers are secure. Just a fraction of the discovered certificates were signed by public CAs. The main problems identified were the following:

**Default keys**

Some manufacturers are shipping their products with default encryption keys. Clearly, this practice defeats the purpose, because all product users end up using the same keys and can compromise one another after extracting the private keys (from the hardware or software). Furthermore, those keys will inevitably be shared with the world.[31]

**Repeated keys due to low entropy**

Some devices generate keys on first boot, when there is little entropy available. Such keys are generally predictable. The paper describes the experiment of a simulated headless first boot running Linux, which clearly demonstrates the weaknesses of the Linux entropy-gathering code in the first seconds after first boot.

**Factorable keys**

Most interestingly, for RSA keys it was discovered that many share one of the two primes that make the modulus, a condition that allows the keys to be compromised. Given that the primes should be randomly generated, same primes should not occur. According to the research, the root cause is a particular pattern in the OpenSSL code that generates RSA keys coupled with low-entropy conditions.

The summary of the TLS-related findings can be seen in the following table.

---

[30] Widespread Weak Keys in Network Devices [fsty.uk/b249] (factorable.net, retrieved 17 July 2014)

[31] LittleBlackBox [fsty.uk/b250] (Database of private SSL/SSH keys of embedded devices, retrieved 17 July 2014)

Table 6.1. Summary of vulnerable private keys [Source: factorable.net]

| | | |
|---|---:|---:|
| Number of live hosts | 12,828,613 | (100.00%) |
| . . . using repeated keys | 7,770,232 | (60.50%) |
| . . . using vulnerable repeated keys | 714,243 | (5.57%) |
| . . . using default certificates or default keys | 670,391 | (5.23%) |
| . . . using low-entropy repeated keys | 43,852 | (0.34%) |
| . . . using RSA keys we could factor | 64,081 | (0.50%) |
| . . . using Debian weak keys | 4,147 | (0.03%) |
| . . . using 512-bit RSA keys | 123,038 | (0.96%) |
| . . . identified as a vulnerable device model | 985,031 | (7.68%) |
| . . . using low-entropy repeated keys | 314,640 | (2.45%) |

Clearly, there are failures at every level (e.g., manufacturers could have checked for these issues and worked around them), but ultimately the study uncovered what is really a usability problem: cryptographic applications rely on the underlying operating system to provide them with enough randomness, but that often does not happen. And when it does not, there is no way to detect failures directly (e.g., Linux will never block on /dev/urandom reads). Few applications use defense-in-depth measures and use statistical tests to verify that their random data is indeed random.

This inability to rely on system-provided randomness may force some developers to take matters into their own hands and use their own RNGs instead. This approach is unlikely to be successful, however, because random number generation is a difficult task that's easy to get wrong.

If you have an embedded device and wish to check the quality of its keys, the authors behind this study provide an online tool that can check any server on the Internet.[32]

# Heartbleed

*Heartbleed*,[33] a devastating vulnerability in OpenSSL, was disclosed to the public in April 2014. The attack exploits the implementation of the *Heartbeat* protocol, a little-used TLS protocol extension (more about it in the section called "Heartbeat" in Chapter 2).

Heartbleed is arguably the worst thing to happen to TLS, which is ironic, given that it's not a cryptographic failure. Rather, it's a testament to the poor state of software development and quality of open source in general.

In the fallout after Heartbleed, everyone's eyes were on OpenSSL. Although the lack of funding for the project and its poor code quality had been known for a very long time, it took a

---

[32] Check Your Key [fsty.uk/b251] (factorable.net, retrieved 17 July 2014)

[33] Heartbleed [fsty.uk/b252] (Wikipedia, retrieved 19 May 2014)

massive vulnerability for the community to take action. The results were good and bad, depending on your point of view. The Linux Foundation announced a three-year project called Core Infrastructure Initiative, which aims to distribute $3.9 million to underfunded open source projects,[34] OpenSSL published a roadmap to identify and fix the problems with the project,[35] and, in the meantime, the OpenBSD Project forked OpenSSL into a new project called LibreSSL and started to make rapid changes with a goal to improve the code quality.[36]

# Impact

Because of a missing check for the read length in the code, successful exploitation enables the remote attacker to retrieve up to 64 KB of server process memory in a single heartbeat request. By submitting multiple requests, the attacker can retrieve an unlimited number of memory snapshots. If there is any sensitive data in the server memory—and there always is —the attacker can probably retrieve it. Because OpenSSL deals with encryption, the most likely extraction target is the server's private key, but there are many other interesting assets: session ticket keys, TLS session keys, and passwords come to mind.

Heartbleed affects OpenSSL versions 1.0.1 through 1.0.1f. Versions from the earlier branches, 0.9.x and 1.0.0, are not vulnerable. Unsurprisingly, vast numbers of servers were impacted. Netcraft estimated that 17% of the servers (or about half a million) worldwide were susceptible.[37]

Remarkably, most of the servers have been patched already. The combination of the seriousness of the problem, freely available testing tools, and media attention resulted in the fastest patching rate TLS has ever seen. One Internet-wide scan suggests that about 1.36% of devices listening on port 443 remain vulnerable one month later.[38] At about the same time, the SSL Pulse dataset (popular web sites, according to the Alexa list) shows only 0.8% of sites vulnerable.

Immediately after the disclosure, most recommended changing private keys as a precaution, but it was felt that most believed that the keys could not be compromised. In reality, it's likely that everyone was initially too busy testing for the vulnerability and patching. Later, when the attention turned back to exploitation, retrieving server private keys turned out to be straightforward.[39] In some cases, the keys would fall after many requests—in others, after few. More advanced exploitation techniques were subsequently developed.[40]

---

[34] Tech giants, chastened by Heartbleed, finally agree to fund OpenSSL [fsty.uk/b253] (Jon Brodkin, Ars Technica, 24 April 2014)

[35] OpenSSL Project Roadmap [fsty.uk/b254] (OpenSSL, retrieved 17 July 2014)

[36] LibreSSL [fsty.uk/b255] (OpenBSD, retrieved 17 July 2014)

[37] Half a million widely trusted websites vulnerable to Heartbleed bug [fsty.uk/b256] (Netcraft, 8 April 2014)

[38] 300k servers vulnerable to Heartbleed one month later [fsty.uk/b257] (Robert Graham, 8 May 2014)

[39] The Results of the CloudFlare Challenge [fsty.uk/b258] (Nick Sullivan, 11 April 2014)

[40] Searching for The Prime Suspect: How Heartbleed Leaked Private Keys [fsty.uk/b259] (John Graham-Cumming, 28 April 2014)

---

In the days immediately after the disclosure, exploitation of vulnerable sites was rampant. Private keys were not the only target. For example, Mandiant reported detecting a successful attack on a VPN server that resulted in a bypass of multifactor authentication. It attacked extracted TLS session keys from server memory.[41]

Social insurance numbers were stolen from the Canadian tax authority and passwords extracted from the Mumsnet web site (a popular site for parents in the UK).[42]

Heartbleed was easy to exploit to begin with, but now, with so many tools publicly available, anyone can exploit a vulnerable server in minutes. Some tools are quite advanced and provide full automation of private key discovery.

> **Note**
>
> If you'd like to learn more about the bug itself and how to test for vulnerable servers, head to the section called "Testing for Heartbleed" in Chapter 12, *Testing with OpenSSL*.

## Mitigation

Patching is the best way to start to address Heartbleed. If you're relying on a system-provided version of OpenSSL, your vendor will have hopefully provided the patches by now. If you're compiling from source, use the most recent OpenSSL 1.0.1 version available. In that case, you can also configure OpenSSL to remove support for the Heartbeat protocol, using the OPENSSL_NO_HEARTBEATS flag. For example:

```
$ ./config -DOPENSSL_NO_HEARTBEATS
$ make
```

After this you'll probably need to recompile all other software packages that depend on your version of OpenSSL.

Many products (e.g., appliances) embed OpenSSL and might be vulnerable. Because they had no advanced warning about Heartbleed, none of them were ready with patches on the day of the disclosure. Vendors with many products probably struggled to issue patches for all of them.

After the vulnerability is fixed, turn your attention to the sensitive data that might have leaked from the server. At the very least, you'll need to replace the server private keys, obtain new certificates, and revoke the old certificates. According to Netcraft, which is monitoring the status of Heartbleed remediation activities worldwide, sites often omit performing one or more of these steps.[43]

---

[41] Attackers Exploit the Heartbleed OpenSSL Vulnerability to Circumvent Multi-factor Authentication on VPNs [fsty.uk/b260] (Christopher Glyer, 18 April 2014)

[42] Heartbleed hacks hit Mumsnet and Canada's tax agency [fsty.uk/b261] (BBC, 14 April 2014)

After the private keys and certificates are dealt with, focus on what else might have been in the server memory. Session ticket keys are the obvious next target. Replace them. After that, consider other secrets, for example, user passwords. Depending on your risk profile, it might be necessary to advise or ask your users to change their passwords, as some web sites have done.

Heartbleed could not be used to gain access to your data stores, at least not directly. Indirectly, it could have been possible to obtain some information that is as useful. For example, on a database-driven web site, the database password is used on every request and thus resides in memory. Replacing all internal passwords is the best way to remain safe.

Sites who had forward secrecy deployed before the attack are in the best situation: their past communication can't be decrypted following a compromise of the server private key. If you're in the other group, consider deploying forward secrecy now. This is exactly why this feature is so important.

> **Warning**
>
> Although we focus on servers, clients using vulnerable versions of OpenSSL are vulnerable too. Heartbeat is a two-way protocol. If a vulnerable client connects to a rogue server, the server can extract the client's process memory.[44]

# Protocol Downgrade Attacks

*Protocol downgrade attacks* occur when an active MITM attempts to interfere with the TLS handshake in order to influence connection parameters; the idea is that he might want to force an inferior protocol or a weak cipher suite. In SSL 2, such attacks are easy, because this protocol doesn't provide handshake integrity. Subsequent protocol versions do provide handshake integrity as well as additional mechanisms to detect similar attacks.

However, what the protocol designers failed to anticipate is interoperability issues related to protocol evolution. Browsers try very hard to communicate successfully with every server. Unfortunately, when it comes to TLS, such attempts often result in security compromises because browsers will voluntarily downgrade their security capabilities, thus sacrificing security for interoperability.

## Rollback Protection in SSL 3

In SSL 2, there was no mechanism to ensure the integrity of the handshake, thus making that protocol version vulnerable to downgrade attacks. As a result, a MITM could always

---

[43] Keys left unchanged in many Heartbleed replacement certificates! [fsty.uk/b262] (Netcraft, 9 May 2014)

[44] Pacemaker [fsty.uk/b263] (Heartbleed client exploit, retrieved 19 May 2014)

force a handshake to use the least secure parameters available. Handshake integrity validation was added in SSL 3, as part of a major protocol cleanup.

But in order to provide handshake integrity (as well as other improvements) SSL 3 had to change the format of the initial handshake request (ClientHello). Additionally, it was agreed that the servers that understood the new protocol would automatically upgrade to the new format with compatible clients. But several problems remained:

1. The SSL 3 handshake provides integrity protection, but you can't use that handshake format because most servers understand only SSL 2.

2. Even with an SSL 3 server, if there is an active MITM, he can always intercept the connection and pretend to be an SSL 2–only server that does not understand anything better.

3. If you subsequently attempt to use an SSL 2 handshake, there is no handshake integrity, and the MITM can interfere with the negotiation.

To address these loopholes, SSL 3 incorporates *protocol rollback protection*[45] that enables SSL 3–aware clients and servers to detect when they are under attack. When an SSL 3 client falls back to SSL 2 for compatibility reasons, it formats the PKCS#1 block of the RSA key exchange in a special way.[46] In SSL 2, the end of the block must contain at least eight bytes of random data; an SSL 3 client instead fills those eight bytes with 0x03. Thus, if an SSL 3 client is forced down to SSL 2 by a MITM attack, the SSL 3 server will notice the special formatting, detect the attack, and abort the handshake. A genuine SSL 2 server will not inspect the padding, and the handshake will proceed normally.

However, there is one loophole that can break the rollback protection.[47] In SSL 2, the length of the master key mirrors the length of the negotiated cipher suite; in the worst case, it's only 40 bits long. Furthermore, it's the client that selects the cipher suite from those supported by the server, generates the master key, and sends it to the server using public encryption. The server decrypts the message using its private RSA key, obtains the master key, and proves ownership to the client.

For a MITM, brute-forcing the RSA key might be too much work, but he can attack the weak master key. He could pose as a server and offer only one 40-bit suite, uncover the master key by brute force, and complete the handshake successfully. This attack is easy to carry out given the computational power available today. This attack vector is largely obsolete by now, given that few clients continue to support SSL 2. Still, the conclusion is that SSL 2 does not provide more than 40 bits of security. Attackers who can execute brute-force attacks of that strength in real time can consistently break all SSL 2 connections.

---

[45] RFC 6101: The SSL Protocol Version 3.0, Section E.2. [fsty.uk/b264] (Freier et al., August 2011)

[46] In SSL 2, RSA was the only authentication and key exchange mechanism. Thus, rollback protection implemented as a hack of this key exchange was sufficient to fully address the issue.

[47] *SSL and TLS: Designing and Building Secure Systems*, page 137 (Eric Rescorla, Addison-Wesley, October 2000)

# Interoperability Problems

With the release of the first follow-up version (SSL 3), interoperability problems started to appear. In this section, I will enumerate the most common problems.

## Version Intolerance

The first problem encountered was *version intolerance*. SSL 2 did not consider protocol evolution and didn't provide instructions for how to handle unknown protocol versions. This excerpt from Eric Rescorla's SSL book illustrates the situation:[47]

> *Unfortunately, the SSLv2 specification wasn't very clear on how servers should handle CLIENT-HELLO messages with version numbers higher than they support. This problem was made worse by the fact that Netscape's SSLREF reference implementation simply rejected connections with higher version numbers. Thus, it's not guaranteed that all SSLv2 servers will respond correctly to the backward-compatible handshake, although the vast majority will.*

SSL 3 did not greatly improve in this respect, mentioning client version handling only in one sentence of the specification:

> `server_version`: *This field will contain the lower of that suggested by the client in the client hello and the highest supported by the server.*

Starting with TLS 1.0, there is more text to handle backward compatibility, but only TLS 1.2 provides clear guidance:

> *A TLS 1.2 client who wishes to negotiate with such older servers will send a normal TLS 1.2 ClientHello, containing {3,3} (TLS 1.2) in ClientHello.client_version. If the server does not support this version, it will respond with a ServerHello containing an older version number. If the client agrees to use this version, the negotiation will proceed as appropriate for the negotiated protocol.*

As a result of these specification ambiguities, many servers refused handshakes if the offered protocol version was not to their liking. The result was a serious interoperability issue when browsers began to support TLS 1.2. For this reason, Internet Explorer, the first browser to implement TLS 1.2, launched with both TLS 1.1 and TLS 1.2 disabled by default.

The *Renegotiation Indication Extension* (which was released in 2010, two years after TLS 1.2) made an attempt to solve the problem, in the hope that developers will, while implementing the new renegotiation mechanism, also address version and extension intolerance. In Section 3.6., it says:

*TLS servers implementing this specification MUST ignore any unknown extensions offered by the client and they MUST accept version numbers higher than their highest version number and negotiate the highest common version. These two requirements reiterate preexisting requirements in RFC 5246 and are merely stated here in the interest of forward compatibility.*

## Extension Intolerance

Early versions of the protocol (SSL 3 and TLS 1.0) had no explicit mechanism for adding new functionality without introducing new protocol revisions. The only thing resembling forward compatibility is a provision that allows the ClientHello message to include extra data at the end. Implementations were instructed to ignore this extra data if they could not understand it. This vague extension mechanism was later replaced with *TLS Extensions*,[48] which added a generic extension mechanism to both ClientHello and ServerHello messages. In TLS 1.2, extensions were merged with the main protocol specification.

Given the vagueness of the early specifications, it's not surprising that a substantial number of SSL 3 and TLS 1.0 servers refuse handshakes with clients that specify extra data.

## Other Interoperability Problems

There are other interoperability problems, mostly arising due to a combination of specification vagueness and sloppy programming:

**Long handshake intolerance**

The size of the ClientHello message is not limited, but in the early days clients tended to support only a small number of cipher suites, which kept the length low. That changed with the OpenSSL 1.0.1 branch, which added support for a wide range of cipher suites. That, combined with the use of extensions to specify additional information (e.g., desired hostname and elliptic curve capabilities), caused the size of ClientHello to grow substantially. It then transpired that one product—F5's BIG IP load balancer—could not handle handshake messages over 255 bytes and under 512 bytes. Given the popularity of BIG IP (especially among some of the largest web sites), this issue had long been a showstopper.

**Arbitrary extension intolerance**

Sometimes servers that understand TLS extensions fail, for no apparent reason, to negotiate connections that include extensions unknown to them. This usually happens with the *Server Name Indication* and *Status Request* (OCSP stapling) extensions.

---

[48] RFC 3546: TLS Extensions [fsty.uk/b265] (Blake-Wilson et al., June 2003)

---

Chapter 6: Implementation Issues

**Failure to correctly handle fragmentation**

Historically, there were many issues related to message fragmentation. SSL and TLS protocols allow all higher-level messages to be fragmented and delivered via several (lower-level) record protocol messages. Most implementations handle fragmentation of application data messages (which are expected to be long) but fail when faced with fragmented messages of other types simply because such fragmentation almost never occurs in practice. Similarly, some products would fail when faced with zero-size records—which derailed initial attempts to mitigate the predictable IV problem in TLS 1.0 and earlier protocols. Early attempts to address the same problem using the 1/n-1 split (sending two records instead of just one, with the first record containing only one byte) were equally derailed, because some products could not handle an HTTP request split across two TLS messages.

# Voluntary Protocol Downgrade

When the interoperability issues started to appear, browsers responded by implementing *voluntary protocol downgrade*. The idea is that you first try your best version of TLS, with all options enabled, but if that fails you try again with fewer options and lower protocol versions; you continue in this manner until (hopefully) a connection is successful. When TLS 1.0 was the best supported protocol, voluntary protocol downgrade approach meant at least two connection attempts. Now that browsers support TLS 1.2, three and four attempts are the norm.

> **Note**
>
> Interoperability issues are not the only problem causing TLS handshakes to fail. There is ample anecdotal evidence that proxies, firewalls, and antivirus software often intercept and filter connections based on protocol version numbers and other handshake attributes.

To understand this behavior, I surveyed various versions of popular desktop browsers. I used a custom TCP proxy designed to allow only SSL 3 connections. Everything else was rejected with a `handshake_failure` TLS alert. You can see the results in the following table.

Table 6.2. Voluntary protocol downgrade behavior of modern browsers

| Browser | First attempt | Second attempt | Third attempt | Fourth attempt |
|---|---|---|---|---|
| Chrome 33 | TLS 1.2 | TLS 1.1 | TLS 1.0 | SSL 3 |
| Firefox 27 | TLS 1.2 | TLS 1.1 | TLS 1.0 | SSL 3 |
| IE 6 | SSL 3 | SSL 2 | | |
| IE 7 (Vista) | TLS 1.0 | SSL 3 | | |
| IE 8 (XP) | TLS 1.0 (no ext.) | SSL 3 | | |
| IE 8-10 (Win 7) | TLS 1.0 | SSL 3 | | |
| IE 11 | TLS 1.2 | TLS 1.0 | SSL 3 | |
| Safari 7 | TLS 1.2 | TLS 1.0 | SSL 3 | |

My test results show that you can downgrade all current browsers to SSL 3.[49] And in the case of Internet Explorer 6 you can actually go as low as SSL 2. Given that SSL 2 is vulnerable to brute-forcing of the master key, Internet Explorer 6 can expect a maximum 40 bits of security.

Going back to SSL 3, this old protocol version is significantly inferior to the latest TLS 1.2. Here are some major disadvantages:

- No support for the GCM, SHA256 and SHA384 suites.

- No elliptic curve cryptography. When it comes to forward secrecy, very few sites support ephemeral Diffie-Hellman (DH) key exchange to use in absence of EC. Without EC, those sites lose forward secrecy.

- SSL 3 is vulnerable to the BEAST attack, but modern browsers implement countermeasures for it. However, some sites prefer to use RC4 with TLS 1.0 and earlier protocols. For such sites, the attacker can force the inferior RC4.

- Microsoft's SSL 3 stack does not support AES, which means that IE will offer only RC4 and 3DES suites.

From this list, I'd say the biggest problem is the loss of forward secrecy. A serious attack could downgrade someone's connections to force a RSA key exchange and then later recover the server's private key to recover the encrypted conversation.

> **Note**
>
> Depending on the exact nature of the communication failure, the fallback mechanism can be triggered even with servers that are not intolerant. For example, there are reports that Firefox sometimes, over unreliable connections, falls back to SSL 3,

---

[49] Even Opera, which had previously implemented protocol downgrade protection, lost that capability when its team abandoned their own engine and switched to Chrome's Blink for version 15.

breaking sites that use virtual secure hosting. (That's because virtual secure hosting relies on TLS extensions, which are not supported in SSL 3.)[50]

# Rollback Protection in TLS 1.0 and Better

Because SSL 3 and newer protocol versions provide handshake integrity, rollback attacks against parties that support only SSL 3 and better do not work.[51]

In case you're wondering, brute-forcing the master key, which was possible against SSL 2, no longer works either, because the master key is now fixed at 384 bits.

TLS 1.0 (and all subsequent protocol revisions) also continued with the SSL 3 tradition and included rollback protection in the RSA key exchange, using an additional version number sent by the client and protected with the server's private key. From section 7.4.7.1 of the TLS 1.2 specification:

> The version number in the PreMasterSecret is the version offered by the client in the ClientHello.client_version, not the version negotiated for the connection. This feature is designed to prevent rollback attacks.

This protection mechanism can be used only if RSA is used for authentication and key exchange, but it doesn't apply to other key-exchange algorithms (even when RSA is used for authentication).

In addition, it appears that protocol implementers have struggled to use correct version numbers in the right places. Yngve Pettersen, who used to maintained the SSL/TLS stack for Opera (while they were using a separate stack), had this to say on the topic (emphasis mine):[52]

> Second, the RSA-based method for agreeing on the TLS encryption key is defined in such a way that the client also sends a copy of the version number it sent to the server and against which the server is then to check against the version number it received. This would protect the protocol version selection, even if the hash function security for a version is broken. **Unfortunately, a number of clients and servers have implemented this incorrectly, meaning that this method is not effective.**

There's a statement to the same effect in the TLS 1.2 specification:

---

[50] Bug #450280: PSM sometimes falls back from TLS to SSL3 when holding F5 (which causes SNI to be disabled) [fsty.uk/b266] (Bugzilla@Mozilla, , reported on 12 August 2008)

[51] The protection is provided by the Finished message, which is sent at the end of the handshake to verify its integrity. In SSL 3, this message is 388 bits long. Curiously, TLS 1.0 reduced the size of this message to only 96 bits. In TLS 1.2, the Finished message still uses only 96 bits by default, but the specification now allows cipher suites to increase its strength. Despite that, all cipher suites continue to use only 96 bits.

[52] Standards work update [fsty.uk/b267] (Yngve Nysæter Pettersen, 2 November 2012)

---

*Unfortunately, some old implementations use the negotiated version instead, and therefore checking the version number may lead to failure to interoperate with such incorrect client implementations.*

The same specification subsequently advises implementers to enforce rollback protection only with newer clients:

*If* `ClientHello.client_version` *is TLS 1.1 or higher, server implementations MUST check the version number as described in the note below.*

But despite having two defense mechanisms rollback attacks are still possible, because of the voluntary protocol downgrade behavior discussed earlier.

## Attacking Voluntary Protocol Downgrade

The built-in protocol defenses against rollback attacks are effective at preventing an attacker from interfering with a single connection. However, when voluntary protocol downgrade is taken into account, rollback attacks are still possible. This is because the MITM doesn't actually need to change any handshake data. Rather, he can block attempts to negotiate any protocol version greater than SSL 3, simply by closing such connections as they are attempted. To defend against this type of attack, a different defense is needed.

## Modern Rollback Defenses

Voluntary protocol downgrade behavior is a gaping hole in TLS security. Despite everyone's efforts to upgrade the infrastructure to TLS 1.2, an active attacker can still downgrade communication to TLS 1.0 or, sometimes, even SSL 3. This subject has been discussed on the TLS WG mailing list many times, but consensus has been difficult to achieve so far. I have collected a series of links and pointers to mailing discussions, which are of interest not only to see how the thoughts about this problem evolved but also to observe the complexities involved with the working group operation.

The topic was first brought up in 2011,[53] when Eric Rescorla proposed to use special *signaling cipher suite values* (or SCSVs) to enable clients to communicate their best supported protocol version even when trying to negotiate a lower version. A server that detects version number discrepancy is required to terminate the connection. The assumption is that a server that supports this defense also won't be prone to any of the intolerance issues. The SCSV approach was chosen because it had been successfully deployed to signal support for secure renegotiation in combination with SSL 3 protocol.[54]

In 2012, Adam Langley proposed a system also based on signaling suites and keeping the attack detection on the server side.[55]

---

[53] One approach to rollback protection [fsty.uk/b268] (Eric Rescorla, 26 September 2011)

Chapter 6: Implementation Issues

After the discussion that followed, Yngve Pettersen submitted a alternative proposal,[56] preferring to implement detection in the client.[57] (That would make deployment much easier; rather than upgrading lots of servers, which would inevitably take a very long time, only the handful of user agents need to be upgraded.) His proposal built on RFC 5746 (Renegotiation Indication Extension), which specifically forbids compliant servers to be intolerant to future protocol version numbers. According to Yngve's measurements, only 0.14% of the servers implementing RFC 5746 showed signs of intolerance. He subsequently implemented this rollback protection in Opera 10.50.[58]

Another discussion followed in April 2013.[59] Finally, in September 2013, Bodo Moeller submitted a draft[60] that was subsequently refined[61] and is currently being considered for the working group's acceptance.[62] Bodo's proposal is to use a single signaling suite to indicate voluntary fallback activity. A server that understands the signal and supports a newer protocol version than the one client is attempting to negotiate is required to abort the negotiation. Chrome 33 was the first browser to implement this feature.[63]

How can we explain the lack of interest in Yngve's proposal? Probably because no matter how rare, there are still servers that implement secure renegotiation but are intolerant to higher protocol version numbers. I think that browser vendors simply don't want to go into a direction that would inevitably result in a backlash against them. On the other hand, a SCSV solution would be enforced server-side and trigger only on genuine attacks.

The problem with the SCSV solution is that it will take many years to spread widely. The few sites that care about their security very much could deploy it quickly, but for the rest doing so would be too costly to justify.

# Truncation Attacks

In a *truncation attack*, an attacker is able to prematurely terminate a secure conversation, preventing one or more messages from being delivered. Normally, a secure protocol is ex-

---

[54] With modern protocol versions, clients can use TLS extensions to signal their capabilities. But because SSL 3 does not support extensions, another mechanism was needed. The solution was to use signaling suites, which cannot be negotiated but can be used to pass small bits of information from clients to servers.

[55] Cipher suite values to indicate TLS capability [fsty.uk/b269] (Adam Langley, 5 June 2012)

[56] Fwd: New Version Notification for draft-pettersen-tls-version-rollback-removal-00.txt [fsty.uk/b270] (Yngve Pettersen, 3 July 2012)

[57] Managing and removing automatic version rollback in TLS Clients [fsty.uk/b271] (Yngve Pettersen, February 2014)

[58] Starting with version 15, Opera switched to the Blink browser engine (Google's fork of WebKit), abandoning its own engine and the SSL/TLS stack. That probably meant also abandoning the rollback implementation as proposed by Yngve.

[59] SCSVs and SSLv3 fallback [fsty.uk/b272] (Trevor Perrin, 4 April 2013)

[60] TLS Fallback SCSV for Preventing Protocol Downgrade Attacks [fsty.uk/b273] (Bodo Moeller and Adam Langley, June 2014)

[61] An SCSV to stop TLS fallback. [fsty.uk/b274] (Adam Langley, 25 November 2013)

[62] Call for acceptance of draft-moeller-tls-downgrade-scsv [fsty.uk/b275] (Eric Rescorla, 23 January 2014)

[63] TLS Symmetric Crypto [fsty.uk/b276] (Adam Langley, 27 February 2014)

pected to detect such attacks. SSL 2 is vulnerable to truncation attacks, but SSL 3 addressed the issue with the addition of the `close_notify` message. Subsequent protocol revisions kept the protection. For example, the following text is included in TLS 1.2 (Section 7.2.1):

> *Unless some other fatal alert has been transmitted, each party is required to send a `close_notify` alert before closing the write side of the connection. The other party MUST respond with a `close_notify` alert of its own and close down the connection immediately, discarding any pending writes.*

This works because `close_notify` is authenticated. If any of the preceding messages are missing, the integrity verification mechanisms built into TLS detect the problem.

Unfortunately, connection closure violations have always been widespread. Many clients and servers abruptly close connections and omit the shutdown procedure mandated by the standard. Internet Explorer is one such client, but there are many more.

Drowning in bogus warning messages about truncation attacks, well-behaved applications started to ignore this problem, effectively opening themselves up to real attacks.

Actually, the standards themselves encouraged such behavior by not actually requiring reliable connection termination. The following text appears in the SSL 3 specification:

> *It is not required for the initiator of the close to wait for the responding `close_notify` alert before closing the read side of the connection.*

In other words, don't bother confirming that the other side received all of the sent data. TLS, in version 1.1, made things worse by relaxing the rules about session resumption. Before, errors of any kind required TLS sessions to be dropped. In practice, this meant that the client would have to perform a full (CPU-intensive) handshake on the following connection. But TLS 1.1 removed this requirement for incorrectly terminated connections. From Section 7.2.1 (emphasis mine):

> *Note that as of TLS 1.1, failure to properly close a connection no longer requires that a session not be resumed. **This is a change from TLS 1.0 to conform with widespread implementation practice.***

That's a shame, because the change removed the only real incentive to get the misbehaving user agents to improve. As a result, we are effectively without defense against truncation attacks.

# Truncation Attack History

The issue was first discussed in 2007,[64] when Berbecaru and Lioy demonstrated truncation attacks against a variety of browsers. They focused on truncating responses. For example, the browser would show only a partial page or image delivered over TLS without any indication that the documents were incomplete.

The topic was revisited in 2013,[65] this time in more detail. In particular, Smyth and Pironti were able to show several compelling attacks, ranging from attacks against electronic voting systems (Helios) to attacks against web-based email accounts (Microsoft and Google) in public computer environments. In all cases, the trick was to prevent the user from logging out without him noticing. To do this, they exploited applications that told their users that they had logged off before they actually did. By using TLS truncation against HTTP requests, the researchers were able to keep the users logged in. After that, if the attacker could access the same computer he could assume the victim's application session and thus the user's identity.

> **Note**
>
> It is particularly interesting that truncation attacks work against HTTP, even though HTTP messages tend to include length information. This is another example of cutting corners just to make the Web "work."

# Cookie Cutting

In 2014, new and more effective techniques to perform truncation attacks came to light.[66] Researchers applied the ideas from earlier attacks on TLS (such as the BEAST attack), in which the attacker is able to control TLS record length by injecting data of arbitrary length into HTTP requests and responses. If you control TLS record length, then you can control the point at which records are split (due to size limits and other constraints). Combined with a truncation attack, you can split HTTP request or response headers, which has some interesting consequences.

One application of HTTP response header truncation is now known as a *cookie cutter* attack; it can be used to downgrade secure cookies into plain, insecure ones. Let's examine a set of HTTP response headers in which secure cookies are used:

```
HTTP/1.1 302 Moved Temporarily
Date: Fri, 28 Mar 2014 10:49:56 GMT
```

---

[64] On the Robustness of Applications Based on the SSL and TLS Security Protocols (Diana Berbecaru and Antonio Lioy, *Public Key Infrastructure, Lecture Notes in Computer Science*, volume 4582, pages 248–264; 2007)

[65] Truncating TLS Connections to Violate Beliefs in Web Applications [fsty.uk/b277] (Ben Smyth and Alfredo Pironti, Black Hat USA, 2013)

[66] Triple Handshakes and Cookie Cutters [fsty.uk/b278] (Bhargavan et al., March 2014)

---

```
Server: Apache
Strict-Transport-Security: max-age=31536000; includeSubDomains
Cache-Control: no-cache, must-revalidate
Location: /account/login.html?redirected_from=/admin/
Content-Length: 0
Set-Cookie: JSESSIONID=9A83C2D6CCC2392D4C1A6C12FFFA4072; Path=/; Secure; HttpOnly
Keep-Alive: timeout=5, max=100
Connection: Keep-Alive
```

To make a cookie secure, you append the Secure attribute to the header line. But, because this attribute comes after the name and value, if you can truncate the HTTP response immediately after the Path attribute an insecure cookie will be created.

Clearly, if you truncate the response headers they become incomplete and thus invalid; the truncated header line will not be terminated with a newline (CRLF), and there won't be an empty line at the end. However, it turns out that some browsers ignore even such obviously malformed HTTP messages and process the headers anyway. Most browsers were vulnerable to one type of truncation attack or another, as the following table illustrates.

Table 6.3. TLS truncation in browsers [Source: Bhargavan et al.]

| | In-header truncation | Content-Length ignored | Missing terminating chunk ignored |
|---|---|---|---|
| Android browser 4.2.2 | Yes | Yes | Yes |
| Android Chrome 27 | Yes | Yes | Yes |
| Android Chrome 28 | No | No | Yes |
| Android Firefox 24 | No | Yes | Yes |
| Safari Mobile 7.0.2 | Yes | Yes | Yes |
| Opera Classic 12.1 | Yes | Yes | Yes |
| Internet Explorer 10 | No | Yes | Yes |

The attack is quite elaborate, but if automated it seems reasonably practical. Here's how to do it:

1. **Attack a user that does not yet have an established session with the target web site.** The web site will not set a new cookie if an old one exists. This can be achieved with some social engineering or, from an active network attacker perspective, by redirecting a plaintext request.

2. **Find an entry point that allows you to inject arbitrary data into the HTTP response.** This is key to the attack; it allows you to position the truncation location at the TLS record boundary. For example, on many web sites when you attempt to access a resource that requires authentication, the redirection includes the resource address. You can see this in the earlier example, which uses the redirected_from parameter for this purpose.

Redirection responses are the ideal entry point because they don't have any content (response body). If you attempt to truncate any other response, the absence of content might make the user suspicious.

3. **Submit padding that splits response headers into two TLS records.** Normally, the entire HTTP redirection response is small and fits in a single TLS record. Your goal is to split this record into two. Because TLS records are limited to 16,384 bytes, if you submit a very long payload and push the size past this limit, the TLS stack will split the response into two records.

4. **Close the secure connection after the first TLS record.** This part of the attack is straightforward: observe the TLS communication and drop the connection (e.g., by sending an RST signal) immediately after the first TLS record.

5. **Extract the insecure cookie.** At this point, the partial cookie will have been consumed and all that remains is to extract it from the user agent. This is a *cookie stealing* attack.

Another target for the cookie cutter attack is the `Strict-Transport-Security` response header. If you truncate the header immediately after the first digit of the `max-age` parameter, the HSTS entry will expire after nine seconds at most. Additionally, the `includeSubDomains` parameter, if present, will be neutralized, too. With HSTS out of the way, you can proceed with an *HTTPS stripping* attack or manipulate the cookies in some other way, as discussed in Chapter 5, *HTTP and Browser Issues*.

It is expected that the cookie cutting attack will be addressed by implementing stricter checks and parsers at the browser level. Some vendors have already implemented fixes, but for most the current status is unknown.

# Deployment Weaknesses

Sometimes, weakness arise in deployment, when commonly used practices lead to exploitable weaknesses. The problems described in this section arise from the secure protocols defined in abstract, without clear guidance as to how they should be implemented by servers. As a result, subtle problems arise.

## Virtual Host Confusion

Certificate sharing is generally not recommended, unless it's used by closely related web sites. At one level, there's the issue that all sites that share the certificate must also share the private key. The sharing weakens security and reduces it to the strength of the weakest link. Also, you don't want multiple independent teams to all have access to the same private key.

However, all sites that share a certificate are also bound at the application level; if one site is compromised or otherwise exploited in some way, other sites that share the same certificate can also be attacked if the circumstances are right. The other sites could be running on a different port or IP address and be located anywhere on the Internet.

For example, let's suppose that an attacker gains control of a weak site that uses a multidomain certificate. Operating from an active network attack perspective, she observes users connecting to other sites from the same certificate. (I'll call them secure sites.) She then hijacks a TLS connection intended for one such secure site and sends it to the weak site under her control. Because the certificate is the same, the victim's browser won't detect anything unusual and the HTTP request will be processed by the web server. Because the attacker controls that web server, she can record the cookies included in the hijacked connection and use them to hijack the victim's application session. She can also respond with arbitrary JavaScript code that will be executed in the context of the *secure* site.

There's a catch: the web server on the weak site must ignore the fact that the HTTP Host headers reference a site that isn't hosted there. Depending on the level of control, the attacker might be able to reconfigure the server to ensure that's the case. However, it's also common that servers ignore invalid host information and always respond with a default site.

Robert Hansen was the first to highlight this problem when he successfully transferred a XSS vulnerability from *mxr.mozilla.org* to *addons.mozilla.org* because both used the same certificate.[67] In 2014, Delignat-Lavaud and Bhargavan highlighted this problem in a research paper and gave it the name *virtual host confusion*.[68] They also showed how to exploit the problem in several real-life scenarios and even uncovered a long-standing problem that could have been used to impersonate some of the most popular web sites in the world.

> **Note**
>
> The same attack can be applied to other protocols. Take SMTP servers, for example. Using the same traffic redirection trick, the attacker can break into one weak SMTP server and later redirect TLS connections to it. If the certificate is shared, email for some other secure sites will be effectively delivered to the attacker.

## TLS Session Cache Sharing

Another problem highlighted by Delignat-Lavaud and Bhargavan is that TLS session cache sharing among unrelated servers and web sites, which is common, can be abused to bypass certificate authentication.[67] Once a TLS session is established, the client can resume it not only with the original server but also with any other server that shares the same session cache, even if it isn't intended to respond to the requested web site and doesn't have the correct certificate.

---

[67] MitM DNS Rebinding SSL/TLS Wildcards and XSS [fsty.uk/b279] (Robert Hansen, 22 August 2010)

[68] Sharing your Webserver with Mallory: (In-)Secure Multiplexing of HTTPs Traffic (Antoine Delignat-Lavaud and Karthikeyan Bhargavan, forthcoming)

This weakness effectively creates a bond among all sites that share the cache (either via server session caching or session tickets) and allows the attacker who compromises one site to escalate access to the other sites. Traffic redirection, the same trick as discussed in the previous section, is the primary attack technique.

For server-side session caching, the flaw is in server applications that don't check that a session is resumed with the same host with which it was originally established. It's a similar situation with session tickets. However, in the latter case there is usually a workaround, because servers allow per-host ticket key configuration. It's best practice to have each host use its own ticket key.

# 7 Protocol Attacks

Over the years, the security of SSL and TLS protocols has been going in and out of the focus of researchers. The early beginnings were very shaky. At Netscape, SSL version 1 was apparently considered to be so insecure that they scrapped it and released version 2 instead. That was in late 1994. That version did well enough to kick off the e-commerce boom, but it didn't do very well as far as security is concerned. The next version, SSL 3, had to be released in 1996 to address the many security problems.

A long, quiet period followed. In 1999, SSL 3 was standardized as TLS 1.0, with almost no changes. TLS 1.1 and TLS 1.2 were released in 2006 and 2008, respectively, but virtually everyone stayed with TLS 1.0. At some point around 2008, we started to focus on security again. Ever since, there's been a constant pressure on TLS, scrutinizing every little feature and use case.

In this chapter, I document the attacks that broke aspects of TLS in recent years; the focus is on the problems that you might encounter in practice. In chronological order, they are: insecure renegotiation in 2009, BEAST in 2011, CRIME in 2012, Lucky 13, RC4 biases, TIME, and BREACH in 2013 and Triple Handshake in 2014. I conclude the chapter with a brief discussion of the possibility that some of the standards and cryptographic algorithms have been subverted by government agencies.

## Insecure Renegotiation

*Insecure renegotiation* (also known as *TLS Authentication Gap*) is a protocol issue first discovered by Marsh Ray and Steve Dispensa in August 2009. After the discovery, they initiated an industry-wide effort to fix the protocol and coordinate public disclosure. Before the process was complete, the issue was independently discovered by Martin Rex (in November of the same year).[1] At that point, the information became public, prematurely.[2]

---

[1] MITM attack on delayed TLS-client auth through renegotiation [fsty.uk/b280] (Martin Rex, 4 November 2009)

[2] Renegotiating TLS [fsty.uk/b281] (Marsh Ray and Steve Dispensa, 4 November 2009)

# Why Was Renegotiation Insecure?

The renegotiation vulnerability existed because there was no continuity between the old and new TLS streams even though both take place over the same TCP connection. In other words, the server does not verify that the same party is behind both conversations. As far as integrity is concerned, it is entirely possible that after each renegotiation a different client is talking to the server.

Application code typically has little interaction with the encryption layer. For example, if renegotiation occurs in the middle of an HTTP request, the application is not notified. Furthermore, web servers will sometimes buffer data that was received prior to renegotiation and forward it to the application together with the data received after renegotiation. Connection parameters may also change; for example, a different client certificate might be used after renegotiation. The end result is that there is a mismatch between what is happening at the TLS layer and what applications see.

A *man-in-the-middle* (MITM) attacker can exploit this problem in three steps:

1. Intercept a TCP connection request from the victim (client) to the target server.

2. Open a new TLS connection to the server and send the attack payload.

3. From then on, continue to operate as a transparent proxy between the victim and the server. For the client, the connection has just begun; it will submit a new TLS handshake. The server, which has already seen a valid TLS connection (and the attack payload), will interpret the client's handshake as renegotiation. Once the renegotiation is complete, the client and the server will continue to exchange application data. The attacker's payload and the client's data will both be seen as part of the same data stream by the server, and the attack will have been successful.

Figure 7.1. Man-in-the-middle attack against insecure renegotiation

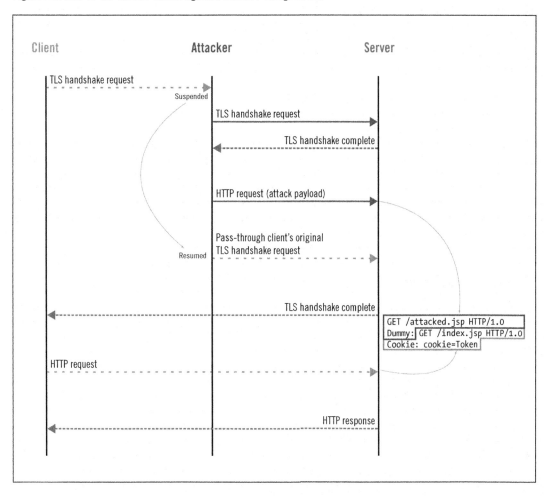

This scenario shows the attacker violating the integrity of application data, which TLS was designed to protect. The attacker was able to inject arbitrary plaintext into the beginning of the connection. The impact of the attack depends on the underlying protocol and server implementation and will be discussed in the following sections.

## Triggering the Weakness

Before he can exploit the insecure renegotiation vulnerability, the attacker needs to find a way to trigger renegotiation. Before this vulnerability was discovered, most servers were allowing client-initiated renegotiation, which meant that most were easy targets. A rare exception was Microsoft IIS, which, starting with version 6, would not accept client-initiated renegotiation at all.

But even without client-initiated renegotiation sites using client certificates or supporting SGC might be equally easy to exploit. The attacker just needs to examine the web site to determine under what conditions renegotiation is required. If such a condition is easily triggered, the attacker may use it for the attack. Depending on the exact configuration of the server, the resulting attack vector may be as useful as client-initiated renegotiation.

# Attacks against HTTP

When it comes to insecure renegotiation, attacks against HTTP are the best understood. Many variants exist, with their feasibility depending on the design of the target web site and on the technical prowess (and the browser used) by the victim. Initially, only one attack was discussed, but the security community collaborated to come up with other possibilities. Thierry Zoller, in particular, spent considerable effort tracking down and documenting the attack vectors as well as designing proof-of-concept attacks.[3]

## Execution of Arbitrary GET Requests

The easiest attack to carry out is to perform arbitrary GET requests using the credentials of the victim. The effective request consisting of the attack payload (in bold) and the victim's request might look something like this:

```
GET /path/to/resource.jsp HTTP/1.0
X-Ignore: GET /index.jsp HTTP/1.0
Cookie: JSESSIONID=B3DF4B07AE33CA7DF207651CDB42136A
```

We already know that the attacker can prepend arbitrary plaintext to the victim's request. The attacker's challenge is to use this ability to control the attack vector, neutralize the parts of the genuine request that would break the attack (that's the victim's request line), and use the parts that contain key information (e.g., session cookies or HTTP Basic Authentication) to successfully authenticate.

The attacker can do that by starting the attack payload with a complete HTTP request line—thereby choosing the entry point of the attack—and then following with a *partial header line*; this header, which is purposefully left incomplete (no newline at the end), will neutralize the first line of the victim's request. All subsequent request headers submitted by the victim will become part of the request.

So what do we get with this? The attacker can choose where the request goes, and the victim's credentials are used. But the attacker cannot actually retrieve the credentials, and the HTTP response will go back to the victim. It appears that the effect of this attack is similar to that of a *cross-site request forgery* (abbreviated to CSRF or, sometimes, XSRF). Most sites

---

[3] TLS/SSLv3 renegotiation vulnerability explained [fsty.uk/b282] (Thierry Zoller, 23 December 2011)

that care about security will have already addressed this well-known web application securi-ty problem. Those sites that did not address CSRF are probably easier to attack in other ways.

This was the attack vector that was initially presented and, because of the similarity to CSRF, caused many to dismiss the insecure vulnerability as unimportant.

## Credentials Theft

In the days following the public disclosure, improved attacks started to appear. Just a couple of days later, Anil Kurmus improved the attack to retrieve encrypted data.[4]

In researching the possible attack vectors, most focused on trying to use the credentials in-cluded with hijacked requests (i.e., session cookies or Basic Authentication credentials). Anil realized that although he was not able to retrieve any data directly he was still able to submit it to the web site using a *different* identity, one that was under his control. (Reverse session hijacking, if you will.) From there, the challenge was to get the data back from the web site somehow.

His proof-of-concept attack was against Twitter. He managed to post the victim's credentials (which were in the headers of the victim's HTTP request) as a tweet of his own. This was the request (the attacker's payload in bold):

```
POST /statuses/update.xml HTTP/1.0
Authorization: Basic [attacker's credentials]
Content-Type: application/x-www-form-urlencoded
Content-Length: [estimated body length]

status=POST /statuses/update.xml HTTP/1.1
Authorization: Basic [victim's credentials]
```

In the improved version of the attack, the entire victim's request is submitted in the request body as the contents of the `status` parameter. As a result, Twitter treats it as the text of a tweet and publishes it in the attacker's tweet stream. On other sites, the attacker might post a new message on the forum, send an email message to himself, and so forth.

The only challenge here is getting the `Content-Length` header right. The attacker does not know the size of the request in advance, which is why he cannot use the correct length. But to succeed with the attack he only needs to use a large enough value to cover the part of the victim's request that contains sensitive data. Once the web server hits the limit specified in the `Content-Length` header, it will consider the request complete and process it. The rest of the data will be treated as another HTTP request on the same connection (and probably ignored, given that it's unlikely that it would be well formed).

---

[4] TLS renegotiation vulnerability: definitely not a full blown MITM, yet more than just a simple CSRF [fsty.uk/b283] (Anil Kurmus, 11 November 2009)

## User Redirection

If the attacker can find a resource on the target web site that responds with a redirection, he might be able to perform one of the following attacks:

**Send the user to a malicious web site**

An open redirection point on the web site could be used to send the victim to the destination of the attacker's choice. This is ideal for phishing, because the attacker can build a replica of the target web site, possibly using a similar domain name to make the deception more effective. It's very easy to make up a name that feels related and "official" (e.g., *www.myfeistyduck.com*, when the real domain name is *www.feisty-duck.com*). To finalize the deception, the attacker can get a proper certificate for the malicious web site.

**Downgrade connection to plaintext HTTP**

If the attacker can find a redirection on the target web site that will send the user to (any) plaintext web site, then the TLS connection is effectively downgraded. From there, the attacker can use a tool such as `sslstrip` and establish full control over the victim's browsing.

**Capture credentials via redirected POST**

If the site contains a redirection that uses the 307 status code—which requires that the redirection is carried out without changing the original request method—it may be possible to redirect the entire request (`POST` body included) to the location of the attacker's choice. All browsers support this, although some require user confirmation. [5] This attack is quite dangerous, because it allows the attacker to retrieve encrypted data without having to rely on the site's own functionality. In other words, it may not be necessary to have an account on the target web site. This is a big deal, because the really juicy targets make that step difficult (think banks and similar financial institutions). On the positive side, the 307 status code is relatively new and rarely seen in practice.

A good discussion of the use of redirection to exploit insecure renegotiation is available in the research paper from Leviathan Security Group.[6]

---

[5] The last time I tested this feature, in July 2013, the latest versions of Chrome, Internet Explorer, and Safari were happy to redirect the request to an entirely different web site without any warning. Firefox and Opera asked for confirmation, but the prompts used by both could be improved. For example, Firefox provided no information about where the new request would be going. Opera provided the most information (the current address as well as the intended destination) along with options to cancel, proceed with the POST method, or convert to a GET method. Still, all that would probably be too confusing for the average user.

[6] Generalization of the TLS Renegotiation Flaw Using HTTP 300 Redirection to Effect Cryptographic Downgrade Attacks [fsty.uk/b284] (Frank Heidt and Mikhail Davidov, December 2009)

## Cross-Site Scripting

In some rare cases, the attacker might be able to inject HTML and JavaScript into the victim's browser and take full control of it via XSS. This could be done using the TRACE HTTP method, which requires servers to mirror the request in the response. Under attack, the reflected content would contain the attacker's payload.

This attack will not work against the major browsers, because TRACE requires that the response content type is set to message/http. But, according to Thierry Zoller[3], there are some less used Windows browsers that always handle responses as HTML; those are vulnerable. In addition, custom scripts rarely check response content types, and they might be vulnerable, too.

# Attacks against Other Protocols

Although HTTP received most of the attention, we should assume that all protocols (that rely on TLS) are vulnerable to insecure renegotiation unless the opposite can be proven. Any protocol that does not reset state between renegotiations will be vulnerable.

### SMTP

Wietse Venema, a member of the Postfix project, published an analysis of the insecure renegotiation impact on SMTP and the Postfix mail server.[7] According to the report, SMTP is vulnerable, but the exploitation might tricky, because, unlike HTTP, one SMTP transaction consists of many commands and responses. He concluded that Postfix was not vulnerable—but only by luck, because of certain implementation decisions. The report suggested several client- and server-side improvements to defend against this problem.

Insecure renegotiation did not pose a significant threat to SMTP because, unfortunately, most SMTP servers do not use valid certificates and (possibly as a result) most SMTP clients do not actually validate certificates. In other words, man-in-the-middle attacks against SMTP are already easy to execute; no further tricks are required.

### FTPS

Alun Jones, author of the WFTPD Server, published an analysis of the impact of the insecure renegotiation vulnerability on FTPS.[8] The main conclusion is that due to the way file transfer is implemented in some FTP servers a MITM attacker could use the renegotiation issue to tell the server to disable encryption of the command channel. As a result, the integrity of the transferred files could be compromised.

---

[7] Redirecting and modifying SMTP mail with TLS session renegotiation attacks [fsty.uk/b285] (Wietse Venema, 8 November 2009)

[8] My take on the SSL MITM Attacks – part 3 – the FTPS attacks [fsty.uk/b286] (Alun Jones, Tales from the Crypto, 18 November 2009)

---

## Insecure Renegotiation Issues Introduced by Architecture

System design and architecture decisions can sometimes introduce insecure renegotiation where it otherwise doesn't exist. Take *SSL offloading*, for example. This practice is often used to add encryption to services that otherwise do not support it or to improve the performance of a system by moving TLS handling away from the main service point. If insecure renegotiation is supported at the point of TLS termination, the system as a whole will be vulnerable even if the actual web servers are not.

## Impact

Insecure renegotiation is a serious vulnerability because it completely breaks the security guarantees promised by TLS. Not only is communication integrity compromised, but the attacker might also be able to retrieve the communicated data itself. There's a variety of attacks that can take place, ranging from CSRF to theft of credentials to sophisticated phishing. Because a good technical background and per-site research is required, this is a type of attack that requires good attacker motivation, likely against higher-value targets.

The ideal case for the attacker is one in which there are automated systems involved, because automated systems rarely scrutinize failures, have poor logging facilities, and retry requests indefinitely until they are successful. This scenario thus creates a large attack surface that is much easier to exploit than attacking end users (browsers) directly.

The attack against insecure renegotiation is well understood, and the tools needed to carry it out are widely available. The proof of concept for the Twitter attack can be found on the Internet, and only a slight modification to any of the widely available MITM tools would be needed to extend them to exploit the vulnerability.

The compromise of integrity has another side effect, which stems from the fact that the attacker can submit arbitrary requests under the identity of the victim. Even if the attacker is not able to retrieve any data or trick the victim, he can always forge his attack payloads to make it seem as if the victim was attacking the server. Because of inadequate logging facilities at most web sites, this type of attack (executed under the identity of the victim) would be extremely difficult to dispute, and yet it could have devastating consequences for the victim. For this reason alone, end users should configure their browsers to accept communication only with servers that support secure renegotiation.[9]

## Mitigation

There are several ways in which insecure renegotiation can be addressed, but some are better than others.

---

[9] For example, in Firefox, on the about:config page, change the security.ssl.require_safe_negotiation setting to true.

**Upgrade to support secure renegotiation**

In early 2010, the *Renegotiation Indication* extension was released to address the problem with renegotiation at the protocol level.[10] Today, several years later, you should expect that all products can be upgraded to support secure renegotiation. If you're dealing with products that cannot be upgraded, it's probably an opportunity to consider if they're still worth using.

**Disable renegotiation**

In the first several months after the discovery, disabling renegotiation was the only mitigation option.

This approach is inferior to supporting secure renegotiation. First, some deployments actually need renegotiation (typically when deploying client certificate authentication). Second, not supporting secure renegotiation promotes renegotiation uncertainty on the Web, effectively preventing users from protecting themselves.

---

### Disabling SSL Renegotiation Is a Crutch, Not a Fix

We should all make an effort to upgrade our systems to support secure renegotiation. If, in 2009 or 2010, you patched your systems to disable renegotiation, you might feel that you are safe and that no further action is required. From a very narrow perspective, you'd be right. However, not supporting secure renegotiation is actually holding the entire world back, because it's preventing browser vendors from adopting strict renegotiation policies.

Unlike servers, which either ask for renegotiation or receive unsolicited renegotiation requests, when under attack browsers can't tell that renegotiation is taking place. After all, they are not the ones renegotiating.

The only way for browsers to protect themselves is to refuse to connect to servers that do not support secure renegotiation. And therein lies the problem: there are still many such servers on the Web, and the browser vendors don't want to be the ones breaking web sites. A server that disables renegotiation might be safe to talk to, but it's prolonging the transition period by increasing the overall number of servers that are not verifiably secure.

---

## Discovery and Remediation Timeline

The insecure renegotiation issue gave us a rare opportunity to examine and assess our collective ability to fix a vulnerable protocol. Clearly, in an ecosystem as complex as TLS fixing any problem will require extensive collaboration and take years; but how many years, exactly? The following chart will give us a good idea.

---

[10] RFC 5746: TLS Renegotiation Indication Extension [fsty.uk/b287] (Rescorla et al., February 2010)

Figure 7.2. Insecure renegotiation remediation timeline

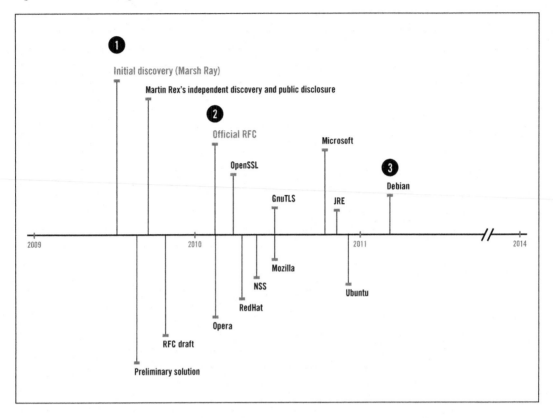

Roughly, what the timeline shows is that we need:

1. About six months to fix the protocol.

2. A further 12 months for libraries and operating systems to be fixed and patches issued.

3. A further 24 months for the majority to apply the patches (or recycle those old systems).

According to the measurements done by Opera, 50% of the servers they tracked had been patched to support secure renegotiation within one year of the official RFC release.[11]

The same data set, in February 2014, reported 83.3% patched servers.[12] The conclusion is that we need about four years to address flaws of this type.

As I am writing this, in July 2014, 88.4% of the servers in the SSL Pulse data set support secure renegotiation.[13] About 6.1% support insecure renegotiation, and 6.8% don't support

---

[11] Secure browsing like it's 1995 [fsty.uk/b288] (Audun Mathias Øygard, 17 March 2011)

[12] Re: Call for acceptance of draft-moeller-tls-downgrade-scsv [fsty.uk/b289] (Yngve N. Pettersen, 9 February 2014)

[13] SSL Pulse [fsty.uk/b70] (SSL Labs, retrieved 15 July 2014)

Chapter 7: Protocol Attacks

renegotiation at all. The numbers add up to more than 100%, because there's about 1.3% of servers that accept both secure and insecure renegotiation.

# BEAST

In the summer of 2011, Duong and Rizzo announced a new attack technique that could be used against TLS 1.0 and earlier protocols to extract small pieces of encrypted data.[14] Their work built on previously known weakness in the predictable *initialization vector* (IV) construction as used in TLS 1.0. The weakness, which was thought to be impractical to exploit, had been fixed in TLS 1.1, but at the time of discovery there was no browser support for newer TLS versions.

In many ways, the so-called BEAST attack was a wake-up call for the ecosystem. First, it emphasized (again) that attacks only get better. As you will learn later in this section, this was a weakness that had been known for almost a decade and dismissed, but all it took was two motivated researchers to make it practical. Duong and Rizzo showed that we must not ignore small problems, because they eventually grow big.

Second, the disclosure and the surrounding fuss made it painfully clear how little attention browser vendors paid to security. They, along with most of the software industry, became too focused on exploitability. They didn't take into account that protocol issues, and other problems that require interoperability of large numbers of clients and servers, take years to address. They are much different from buffer overflows and similar flaws, which can be fixed relatively quickly.

Thai gave a candid account of how BEAST came together in his blog post,[15] and you can almost feel his frustration when he realizes that he is losing the attention of browser vendors because, even though he can demonstrate the attack in a simulation, he is unable to demonstrate it in a practical environment. But they persisted, managed to build a working proof of concept, demonstrated it, and finally got the attention they deserved.

## How the Attack Works

The BEAST attack is an exploit targeted at the *Cipher Block Chaining* (CBC) encryption as implemented in TLS 1.0 and earlier protocol versions. As mentioned earlier, the issue is that IVs are predictable, which allows the attacker to effectively reduce the CBC mode to *Electronic Code Book* (ECB) mode, which is inherently insecure.

---

[14] Here come the ⊕ Ninjas [fsty.uk/b290] (Duong and Rizzo, incomplete version, 21 June 2011)
[15] BEAST [fsty.uk/b291] (Thai Duong, 5 September 2011)

## ECB Oracle

ECB is the simplest mode of operation: you split input data into blocks and encrypt each block individually. There are several security issues with this approach, but the one we're interested in here is that ECB does not hide the deterministic nature of block cipher encryption. What this means is that every time you encrypt the same piece of data the output is also the same. This is a very useful property for the attacker; if he is able to choose what is encrypted, he can also guess the plaintext. It goes like this:

1. Observe a block of encrypted data that contains some secret. The size of the block will depend on the encryption algorithm, for example, 16 bytes for AES-128.

2. Submit 16 bytes of plaintext for encryption. Because of how block ciphers work (one bit of difference anywhere in input affects all output bytes), the attacker is only able to guess the entire block at once.

3. Observe the encrypted block and compare it to the ciphertext observed in step 1. If they are the same, the guess is correct. If the guess is incorrect, go back to step 2.

Because the attacker can only guess the entire block at a time, this is not a great attack. To guess 16 bytes, the attacker would need to make $2^{128}$ guesses, or $2^{127}$ on average. But, as we shall see later, there are ways in which the attack can be improved.

## CBC with Predictable IV

The key difference between CBC and ECB is that CBC uses an IV to mask each message before encryption. The goal is to hide patterns in ciphertext. With proper masking in place, the ciphertext is always different even if the input is the same. As a result, CBC is not vulnerable to plaintext guessing in the way ECB is.

For the IV to be effective, it must be unpredictable for each message. One way to achieve this is to generate one block of random data for every block that we wish to encrypt. But that wouldn't be very practical, because it would double the size of output. In practice, CBC in SSL 3 and TLS 1.0 uses only one block of random data at the beginning. From there on, the encrypted version of the current block is used as the IV for the next block, hence the word *chaining* in the name.

The chaining approach is safe, but only if the attacker is not able to observe encrypted data and influence what will be encrypted in the immediately following block. Otherwise, simply by seeing one encrypted block he will know the IV used for the next. Unfortunately, TLS 1.0 and earlier treat the entire *connection* as a single message and use a random IV only for the first TLS record. All subsequent records use the last encryption block as their IV. Because the attacker can see all the encrypted data, he knows the IVs for all records from the second one onwards. TLS 1.1 and 1.2 use per-record IVs and thus don't have the same weakness.

This approach fails catastrophically when faced with an active attacker who can submit arbitrary plaintext for encryption, observe the corresponding ciphertexts, and adapt the attacks based on the observations. In other words, the protocol is vulnerable to a *blockwise chosen-plaintext* attack. When the IV is predictable, CBC effectively downgrades to ECB.

Figure 7.3, "BEAST attack against CBC with predictable IV" illustrates the attack against CBC with predictable IV showing three encryption blocks: two blocks sent by the browser and one block sent (via the browser) by the attacker. For simplicity, I made it so that each message consumes exactly one encryption block; I also removed padding, which TLS would normally use.

The attacker's goal is to reveal the contents of the second block. He can't target the first block, because its IV value is never seen on the network. But after seeing the first block he knows the IV of the second ($IV_2$), and after seeing the second block he knows the IV of the third block ($IV_3$). He also knows the encrypted version of the second block ($C_2$).

After seeing the first two blocks, the attacker takes over and instruments the victim's browser to submit plaintext for encryption. For every guess, he can observe the encrypted version on the wire. Because he knows all the IVs, he can craft his guesses in such a way that the effects of IV are eliminated. When a guess is successful, the encrypted version of the guess ($C_3$) will be the same as the encrypted version of the secret ($C_2$).

Figure 7.3. BEAST attack against CBC with predictable IV

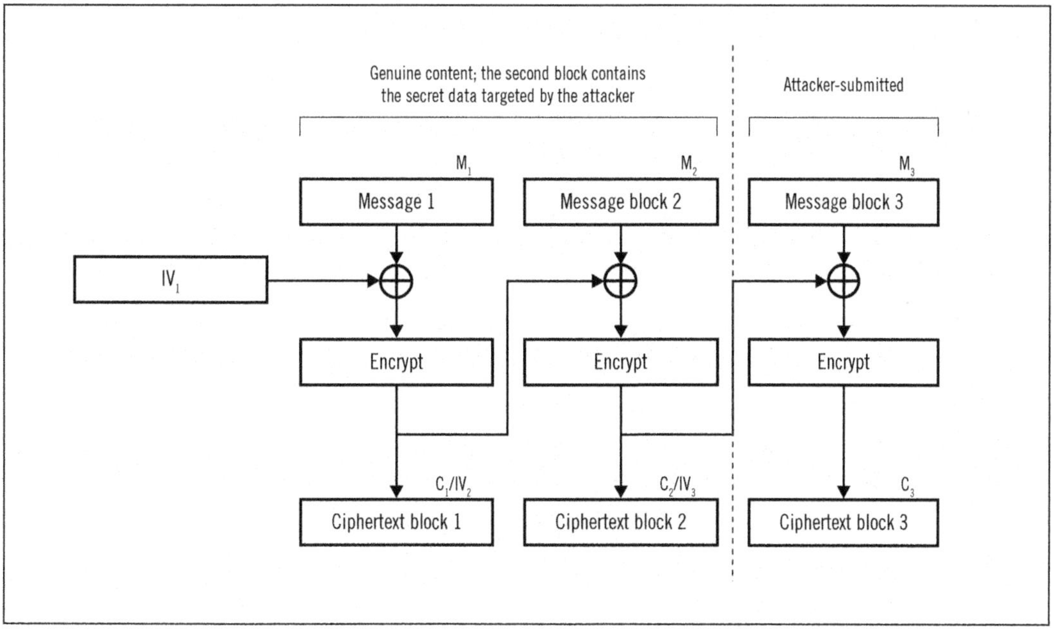

To understand how the IVs can be effectively eliminated, we have to look at some of the maths involved. Let's examine the encryption of $M_2$, which contains some secret, and $M_3$, which is controlled by the attacker:

$$C_2 = E(M_2 \oplus IV_2) = E(M_2 \oplus C_1)$$
$$C_3 = E(M_3 \oplus IV_3) = E(M_3 \oplus C_2)$$

Messages are first XORed with their IV, then encrypted. Because different IVs are used each time, even if $M_2$ is the same as $M_3$ the corresponding encryptions, $C_2$ and $C_3$, will be different. However, because we know both IVs ($C_1$ and $C_2$), we can craft $M_3$ in such a way as to neutralize the masking. Assuming $M_g$ is the guess we wish to make:

$$M_3 = M_g \oplus C_1 \oplus C_2$$

The encryption of $M_3$ will thus be:

$$C_3 = E(M_3 \oplus C_2) = E(M_g \oplus C_1 \oplus C_2 \oplus C_2) = E(M_g \oplus C_1)$$

And if our guess is correct ($M_g = M_2$), then the encryption of our block will be the same as the encryption of the second block:

$$C_3 = E(M_g \oplus C_1) = E(M_2 \oplus C_1) = C_2$$

## Practical Attack

We now understand the weakness of predictable IVs, but exploiting it is still difficult due to the fact that we have to guess the entire block (typically 16 bytes) at a time. However, when applied to HTTP, there are some optimizations we can make.

- HTTP messages often contain small fragments of sensitive data, for example, passwords and session tokens. Sometimes guessing only 16 bytes is all we need.

- The sensitive data typically uses a restricted character set; for example, session tokens are often encoded as hexadecimal digits, which can have only 16 different values.

- The structure of HTTP messages is very predictable, which means that our sensitive data will often be mixed with some other content we know. For example, the string Cookie: will always be placed before the name of the first cookie in a HTTP request.

When all these factors are taken into account, the required number of guesses can be much lower, although still not low enough for practical use.

BEAST became possible when Duong and Rizzo realized that modern browsers can be almost fully instrumented by a skilful attacker, giving him an unprecedented level of control. Crucially, the attacker needs to be able to (1) influence the position of the secret in the request and (2) have full control over what is being encrypted and when it is sent.

The first condition is not difficult to fulfill; for example, to push a cookie value around you only need to add extra characters to the request URI. The second condition is problematic; that level of control is not available from JavaScript. However, Duong and Rizzo determined that they could use Java applets. They also needed to exploit a separate bug in order to get Java to send traffic to arbitrary web sites.[16] They needed to do this to make BEAST universal and able to attack any web site. Exploitation of this additional problem in Java is not always necessary. Web sites that allow user-uploaded content can be tricked into accepting Java applets. They then run in the context of the target web site and can send traffic to it.[17]

There is another condition, mentioned earlier, and that is to be able to observe encrypted network traffic, which is necessary in order to determine the next IV values. Further, the IVs need to be communicated to the code running in the browsers.

In practice, BEAST is an active network attack. Although social engineering could be used to send the victim to the web site that contains the rogue JavaScript code, it's much simpler to inject the code into any plaintext web site visited by the victim at the time of attack.

If you can manage all of that, then implementing BEAST is easy. By changing the position of the secret within the HTTP request, you can align it with encryption blocks in such a way that a single block contains 15 bytes of known plaintext and only one byte of the secret. Guessing that one byte is much easier; you need $2^8$ (256) guesses in the worst case, and $2^7$ (128) guesses on average. Assuming low-entropy data (e.g., hexadecimal digits), you can get as low as eight (average) guesses per character. When time is of the essence, you can also submit multiple guesses in parallel.

---

### JavaScript Malware

*JavaScript Malware* is a generic term used for malicious code running in a victim's browser. Most malware is designed to attack the browser itself, impersonate the user, or attack other web sites, often without being noticed. BEAST was the first exploit to use JavaScript malware to break cryptography, but many others followed. You'll find their details later in the chapter.

The use of JavaScript malware is a good example of the changing threat model. When SSL was first designed in 1994, browsers were only simple tools designed for HTML rendering. Today, they are powerful application-delivery platforms.

---

## Client-Side Mitigation

BEAST is a client-side vulnerability and requires that countermeasures are deployed at the user-agent level. In 2004, when the problem was originally discovered, OpenSSL tried to address it by injecting an empty (no data) TLS record before each real TLS record. With this

---

[16] Without permission, Java applets can only communicate with their parent web site. This restriction is known as the *same-origin policy* (SOP). Duong and Rizzo discovered a way to bypass that restriction. It's not entirely clear if the Java SOP bypass remains: when I reviewed the updated Java release in 2013, it was possible to exploit it with additional effort.

[17] The pitfalls of allowing file uploads on your website [fsty.uk/b292] (Mathias Karlsson and Frans Rosén, 20 May 2014)

---

change, even though the attacker can predict the next IV, that value is used for the zero-length TLS record that has no value. The application data follows in the next record, but it uses an IV that the attacker does not know *in advance* (at the time the attack payload is constructed), which means that there is no opportunity to execute an attack.

Unfortunately, this approach did not work, because some TLS clients (most notably, Internet Explorer) were found to react badly to zero-sized TLS records. Given that at the time there was no practical attack to worry about, OpenSSL dropped the mitigation technique. As far as we know, no other library tried to address the issue.

In 2011, browsers mitigated BEAST by using a variation of the empty fragment technique. The so-called *1/n-1 split*, proposed by Xuelei Fan,[18] still sends two records instead of one but places one byte of application data in the first record and everything else in the second. This approach achieves an effectively random IV for the bulk of the data: whatever is in the second record is safe. One byte of the data is still exposed to the predictable IV, but because it sits in an encryption block with at least seven (more likely 15) other bytes that are effectively random and different for every record (the MAC) the attacker cannot guess that byte easily.

The 1/n-1 split fared much better than the original approach, but the adoption still did not go smoothly. Chrome enabled the countermeasures first but had to revert the change because too many (big) sites broke.[19] The Chrome developers persisted, and soon other browser vendors joined, making the change inevitable.

The cost of the 1/n-1 split is an additional 37 bytes that need to be sent with every burst of client application data.[20]

You can see the status of BEAST mitigations in the major platforms in the following table.

---

[18] Bug #665814, comment #59: Rizzo/Duong chosen plaintext attack (BEAST) on SSL/TLS 1.0 [fsty.uk/b293] (Xuelei Fan, 20 July 2011)

[19] BEAST followup [fsty.uk/b294] (Adam Langley, 15 January 2012)

[20] Some user agents (e.g., Java and OS X) do not use BEAST countermeasures for the first burst; they deploy it only from the second burst onwards. This saves on bandwidth but provides less security. Application data is probably still safe, because to make a guess you need to see something encrypted first. However, before any application data is sent, TLS uses encryption for its own needs. In most cases, this will be the Finished message, which is not very interesting because it changes on every connection. However, as TLS is evolving, other bits and pieces are being encrypted in the first message. In theory, a future change might make TLS vulnerable again. In practice, because BEAST was fixed in TLS 1.1 it's very unlikely that TLS 1.0 servers will support these new features.

In TLS 1.1, the cost is equal to the size of the encryption block, which is typically 16 bytes.

---

Table 7.1. BEAST mitigation status of major libraries, platforms, and browsers

| Product | Version (Date) | Comments |
|---|---|---|
| Apple | OS X v10.9 Mavericks (22 October 2013) and v10.8.5 Mountain Lion (25 February 2014) | The 1/n-1 split shipped in Mountain Lion (OS X v10.8), but it was disabled by default. The mitigation is supposed to be configurable, but there's a bug that prevents the defaults from being changed.[a] |
| Chrome | v16 (16 December 2011) | Initially enabled in v15, but backed off due to too many big sites not working. |
| Firefox | v10 (31 January 2012) | Almost made it to Firefox v9, but Mozilla changed their minds at the last moment to give the incompatible sites more time to upgrade.[b] |
| Microsoft | MS12-006[c] (10 January 2012) | The mitigation is enabled in Internet Explorer, but disabled by default for all other Schannel (Microsoft's TLS library) users. Microsoft recommended deployment of TLS 1.1 as a way of addressing BEAST for nonbrowser scenarios. The knowledge base article 2643584 discusses the various settings in detail.[d] |
| NSS | v3.13[e] (14 October 2011) | Enabled by default for all programs. |
| OpenSSL | Not mitigated yet | The issue is tracked under bug #2635[21]. |
| Opera | v11.60[f] (6 December 2011) | The comment "Fixed a low severity issue, as reported by Thai Duong and Juliano Rizzo; details will be disclosed at a later date" was in the release notes of v11.51 but was subsequently removed. |
| Oracle | JDK 6u28 and 7u1 (18 October 2011)[g] | |

[a] Apple enabled BEAST mitigations in OS X 10.9 Mavericks [fsty.uk/b295] (Ivan Ristić, 31 October 2013)

[b] Bug #702111: Servers intolerant to 1/n-1 record splitting. "The connection was reset" [fsty.uk/b296] (Bugzilla@Mozilla, 13 November 2011)

[c] Microsoft Security Bulletin MS12-006 [fsty.uk/b297] (10 January 2012)

[d] Microsoft Knowledge Base Article 2643584 [fsty.uk/b298] (10 January 2012)

[e] NSS 3.13 Release Notes [fsty.uk/b299] (14 October 2011)

[f] Opera 11.60 for Windows changelog [fsty.uk/b301] (6 December 2012)

[g] Oracle Java SE Critical Patch Update Advisory - October 2011 [fsty.uk/b302] (Oracle's web site)

Many client-side tools (e.g., libraries and command-line applications) continue to lack the 1/n-1 split and are thus technically vulnerable, but they are not likely to be exploitable. Without the ability to inject arbitrary plaintext into the communication, there is nothing the attacker can do to exploit the weakness.

## Server-Side Mitigation

Even though BEAST has been addressed client-side, we don't control the upgrade cycle of the millions of browsers that are out there. Things have gotten a lot better with the rise of Chrome and its automated updates. Firefox now uses the same approach, and it's possible that Microsoft will, too. Still, a potentially large number of users with vulnerable browsers remain.

---

[21] fsty.uk/b300

Up until 2013, the recommended approach for BEAST mitigation server-side was to ensure RC4 suites are used by default. With CBC suites out of the picture, there is nothing for BEAST to exploit. But in early 2013 we learned about two new attacks, one against RC4 and another against the CBC construction in TLS. (Both are discussed in detail later in this chapter.) The RC4 weaknesses broke the only server-side mitigation strategy available to us.

We are now forced to choose between having some of our users vulnerable to either the BEAST attack or the RC4 weaknesses. With neither attack particularly practical, the choice is somewhat difficult. In this situation, it is helpful to think not only about the impact of these attacks today but also the future trends. BEAST can be executed successfully *if* you can find a victim–site combination that satisfies the requirements. Making it work at scale is impossible. The technique might be useful for targeted attacks, provided the victim is using unpatched software and has Java enabled. But overall the chances of successful attacks are small. More importantly, the likelihood is going to continue to decrease over time.

## History

That predictable IV is insecure has been known since at least 1995, when Phil Rogaway published a critique of cryptographic constructions in the IPsec standard drafts.[22] He said that:

> [...] it is essential that the IV be unpredictable by the adversary.

Clearly, this problem had not been widely understood, because predictable IVs made it into SSL 3 (1996) and later TLS 1.0 (1999).

In 2002, the problem was rediscovered in the SSH protocol[23] and was also found to apply to TLS.[24] Some countermeasures (which I will discuss later in this section) were added to OpenSSL in May 2002 but were effectively turned off in July, because of interoperability issues; they broke Internet Explorer.[25]

Apparently no one thought this attack was worth pursuing further, and thus no one tried to find a mitigation technique that worked. It was a missed opportunity to address the problem almost a decade before the practical attack came to light. Still, two papers were published that year: one to discuss how to fix the SSH protocol[26] and the other to discuss blockwise-adaptive attacks against several encryption approaches, including CBC.[27]

---

[22] Problems with Proposed IP Cryptography [fsty.uk/b303] (Phil Rogaway, 3 April 1995)

[23] An Attack Against SSH2 Protocol [fsty.uk/b304] (Wei Dai, 6 February 2002)

[24] Re: an attack against SSH2 protocol [fsty.uk/b305] (Bodo Moeller, 8 February 2002)

[25] But even if the countermeasures stayed enabled they wouldn't have addressed the BEAST attack. TLS is a duplex protocol, with two separate streams of data, one sent by the client and the other sent by the server, each using separate IVs. An empty fragment mitigation technique implemented on the server wouldn't have fixed the same vulnerability in the client stream, which is where BEAST attacked. TLS stacks used by browsers (e.g, NSS and Schannel) had no countermeasures for predictable IVs.

---

In 2004, Gregory Bard showed how predictable IVs in TLS can be exploited to reveal fragments of sensitive information.[28] He spelled out the problem inherent in the CBC encryption as implemented in SSL 3.0 and TLS 1.0:

> We show that this introduces a vulnerability in SSL which (potentially) enables easy recovery of low-entropy strings such as passwords or PINs that have been encrypted. Moreover, we argue that the open nature of web browsers provides a feasible "point of entry" for this attack via a corrupted plug-in [...]

Bard didn't find a way to exploit the weakness, but later published another paper, this one describing a *blockwise-adaptive chosen-plaintext attack* on SSL, showing how the position of sensitive data within block boundaries significantly impacts the number of guesses required to recover it.[29]

The protocol weakness was finally resolved in TLS 1.1 (2006) by using a random IV for each TLS record. However, fixing the protocol didn't really achieve anything, because few browsers bothered to implement it. Only after BEAST made a big splash in 2011 did browser vendors start to think about supporting newer protocols.

In 2011, most libraries and browser vendors implemented the 1/n-1 split mitigation technique. After all the time spent researching the problem, the fix was almost trivial; for NSS, it took only about 30 lines of code.[30]

Apple waited until late 2013 to implement BEAST mitigations in their TLS stack (and thus Safari). As for protocol support, it took browser vendors more than two years to catch up and support TLS 1.2.

# Impact

If a BEAST attack is successful, the attacker will obtain the victim's session token, which will give him access to the entire web application session. He will be able to perform arbitrary actions on the web site, using the identity of the victim. Under the right conditions, BEAST is easy to execute; however, getting everything aligned (especially today) is difficult.

Because the vulnerability exploited by the BEAST attack is in the protocols, at the time of the announcement virtually all SSL and TLS clients were vulnerable. BEAST is a client-only vulnerability. TLS operates two data streams, one sent from the client to the server and the

---

[26] Breaking and Provably Repairing the SSH Authenticated Encryption Scheme: A Case Study of the Encode-then-Encrypt-and-MAC Paradigm [fsty.uk/b306] (Bellare, Kohno, and Namprempre, Ninth ACM Conference on Computer and Communication Security, 18 November 2002)

[27] Blockwise-Adaptive Attackers: Revisiting the (In)Security of Some Provably Secure Encryption Modes: CBC, GEM, IACBC [fsty.uk/b307] (Joux, Martinet, and Valette, pages 17–30, CRYPTO 2002)

[28] Vulnerability of SSL to Chosen-Plaintext Attack [fsty.uk/b308] (Gregory V. Bard, ESORICS, 2004)

[29] A Challenging but Feasible Blockwise-Adaptive Chosen-Plaintext Attack on SSL [fsty.uk/b309] (Gregory Bard, SECRYPT, 2006)

[30] cbcrandomiv.patch [fsty.uk/b310] (NSS 1/n-1 patch in Chromium, 18 August 2011)

---

other sent from the server to the client. The BEAST attack targets the client data stream and requires the attacker to be able to control exactly what is sent to the target web server. The interactivity is key; without it, the attack cannot succeed. Thus, even though the server data stream suffers from the same problem of predictable IVs it is impossible to exploit it in practice because the attacker cannot have sufficient control of the server-sent data.

In addition to the interactivity requirement, two further server-controlled conditions are required:

**CBC suites have priority**

> Because only CBC suites are vulnerable, those servers that prefer RC4 suites over CBC (or don't support CBC at all) are not vulnerable to the BEAST attack. Even if both sides support CBC suites, the attacker cannot influence the suite selection.

**TLS compression is disabled**

> TLS has the ability to compress content prior to encryption. Compression does not protect against the BEAST attack, but it does make it more difficult. Normally, the bytes sent by the attacker are encrypted and sent over the wire. With compression enabled, the bytes are first compressed, which means that the attacker no longer knows what exactly is encrypted. To make the attack work, the attacker would also have to guess the compressed bytes, which may be very difficult. For this reason, the original BEAST exploit implemented by Duong and Rizzo could not attack compressed TLS connections. In my estimates, compression was enabled on about half of all web servers at the time BEAST was announced. However, client-side support for compression was very weak then and is nonexistent today.

Going back to the interactivity, native browser capabilities were not sufficient to carry out the attack, which is why the authors resorted to using third-party plug-ins. The final exploit was implemented in Java and used a previously unknown weakness in the Java plug-in. This meant that the presence of Java was yet another requirement for a successful attack.

To sum up:

1. The attacker must be able to execute a MITM attack from a location close to the victim. For example, any Wi-Fi network or a LAN would probably do. Strong cryptography and programming skills are required to implement the exploit.

2. The victim must have the Java plug-in installed. Java was in those days virtually universally available (now not as much), so there wouldn't have been a shortage of candidates.

3. In addition to being authenticated to the target web site, the victim must also be browsing some other site controlled by the attacker. This could be achieved with social engineering, for example. Alternatively, the attacker can hijack any other plaintext HTTP web site. Because the majority of web sites are still not encrypted, this constraint was also easy to satisfy.

4. The server must use CBC suites by default and have compression disabled. Anecdotally, a large number of servers fit these criteria.

To conclude, at the time it was announced, the BEAST attack was relatively easy to carry out by a determined attacker despite the long list of constraints.

Today the situation is different, mostly because all modern browsers (as well as Java, which was used for the exploit) have implemented BEAST countermeasures. Furthermore, there has been a clampdown on the insecurity of in-browser Java, making it much more difficult to run applets. That's assuming your user base has been updating their software; some users running older software might still be vulnerable.

The ecosystem is slowly moving towards supporting TLS 1.2 throughout, although it's going to be some time before that happens. Still, the pool of users and servers susceptible to the BEAST attack is continuously getting smaller, and the risk is fairly low by now.

# Compression Side Channel Attacks

*Compression side channel attacks* are a special case of *message length side channel attacks*. Let's assume that you can observe someone's encrypted communication while they are using their online banking application. To obtain the current balance of a savings account, the application might invoke a particular API call. Just seeing the size of that one response might be sufficient to approximate the value: the balance of a particularly wealthy victim will have many digits, making the response longer.

It turns out that when you add compression to the mix, and the attacker is able to submit his own data for compression, a *compression oracle* is created. In this section, I discuss a series of compression-related attacks on TLS, including CRIME, TIME, and BREACH.

## How the Compression Oracle Works

Compression is very interesting in this context because it changes the size of data, and the differences depend on the nature of the data itself. If all you can do is observe compression ratios, your attacks might not amount to much; there is only so much you can deduce from knowing if something compresses well. At best, you might be able to distinguish one type of traffic from another. For example, text usually compresses very well, but images not so much.

This attack gets far more interesting if you are able to submit your own data for compression and mix it with some other secret data (that you don't know but want to recover) while observing the results. In this case, your data influences the compression process; by varying your data you discover things about what else is compressed at the same time.

To understand why this attack is so powerful, we need to look at how compression works. In essence, all lossless compression algorithms work by eliminating redundancy. If a series of characters is repeated two or more times in input, the output will contain only one copy of such data along with instructions for where to place copies. For example, consider how a very popular LZ77 algorithm would compress a piece of text (see the following figure).

Figure 7.4. Compression reduces data size by identifying and removing redundancies.

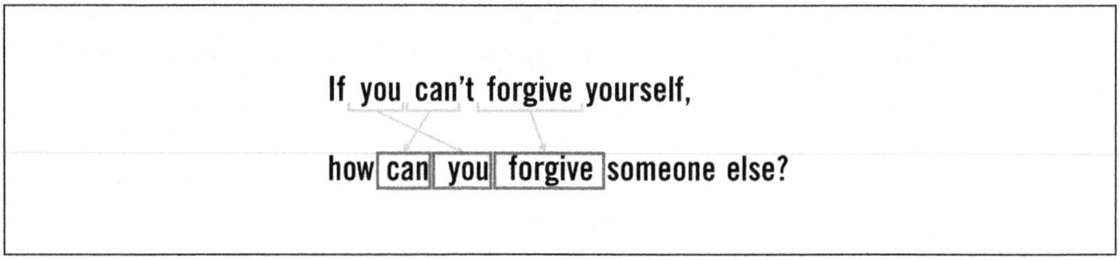

**If you can't forgive yourself,**

**how can you forgive someone else?**

An *oracle* is said to exist if you can have your arbitrary data (guesses) compressed in the same context as some secret. By observing the size of the compressed output, you are able to tell if your guesses are correct. How? If you guess correctly, compression kicks in and reduces the size of the output, and you know that you are right. If you submit random content, there's no compression, and the size increases.

Figure 7.5. Illustration of a compression oracle: one correct and one incorrect guess

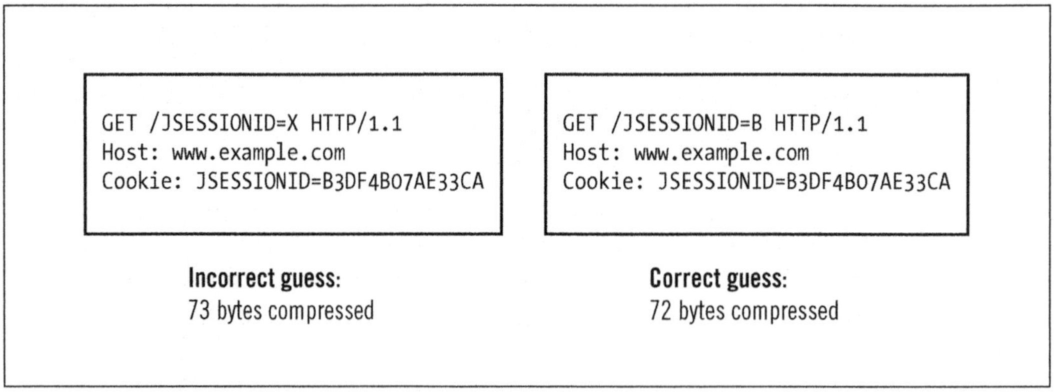

```
GET /JSESSIONID=X HTTP/1.1
Host: www.example.com
Cookie: JSESSIONID=B3DF4B07AE33CA
```

**Incorrect guess:**
73 bytes compressed

```
GET /JSESSIONID=B HTTP/1.1
Host: www.example.com
Cookie: JSESSIONID=B3DF4B07AE33CA
```

**Correct guess:**
72 bytes compressed

As you shall see in the following sections, there are many obstacles to deal with in order to make the attack practical, but conceptually it really is that simple.

## Is Information Leakage a Flaw in the TLS protocol?

Your expectations might be that information leakage is a flaw in the SSL and TLS protocols, but it's actually a documented limitation. Here's the relevant part of TLS 1.2 (Section 6):

> *Any protocol designed for use over TLS must be carefully designed to deal with all possible attacks against it. As a practical matter, this means that the protocol designer must be aware of what security properties TLS does and does not provide and cannot safely rely on the latter.*
>
> *Note in particular that type and length of a record are not protected by encryption. If this information is itself sensitive, application designers may wish to take steps (padding, cover traffic) to minimize information leakage.*

Some might say that the real flaw is the fact that browsers allow adversaries unprecedented level of control of their victims' browsers—and that might be true. Adaptive plaintext attacks are a big deal in cryptography, but here we have TLS, designed with one set of capabilities in mind and used in scenarios that were outside the scope of the original design.

All browser-based attacks against encryption rely on the fact that the attacker can submit requests in the context of a *genuine user session*, which results in attacker-supplied data transported in the same request as the victim's confidential data. Few will argue that this is natural. If we accept that a random web page should be allowed to submit requests to arbitrary web sites, we should at least ensure that they do so from their own separate environment (i.e., a sandbox).

Sadly, the Web has evolved in such a way that everything is entangled, which means that enforcing strict separation in this way would break far too many web sites. In time, the solution will probably come in the form of elective separation, which will allow a site to declare its own security space.

As for length hiding, even if such a feature is ever implemented, there is always the question of its effectiveness. It most certainly won't work in all situations. Some highly secure systems address this problem by always communicating at a constant rate, using the full bandwidth provided by the underlying channel. However, that approach is prohibitively expensive for most deployments.

# History of Attacks

Compression as a side channel mechanism was first introduced by John Kelsey. In his 2002 paper,[31] he presented a series of attack scenarios, each varying in effectiveness. Among them was the extraction of fragments of sensitive data, the attack that was later going to be improved in the browser context. The world was a much different place in 2002, and the best attack was difficult to utilize in real life. Hence, the author concluded that:

---

[31] Compression and Information Leakage of Plaintext [fsty.uk/b311] (John Kelsey, FSE, 2002)

*The string-extraction attacks are not likely to be practical against many systems, since they require such a specialized kind of partial chosen-plaintext access.*

Compression side channel attacks were again in the news a couple of years later, although not against TLS. In 2007, a team of researchers first developed algorithms to identify the spoken language of an encrypted internet call[32] and later managed to identify spoken English phrases with an average accuracy of 50%, rising to 90% for some phrases.[33]

In the following years, browsers continued to evolve, making adaptive chosen-plaintext attacks not only possible but also practical against virtually everyone. In 2011, the BEAST attack showed how the attacker can take control of a victim's browser in order to execute a blended attack against encryption.

In August 2011, privacy issues stemming from compression side channel attacks were discussed on the SPDY[34] development mailing list.[35] In particular, this quote from Adam Langley describes how a compression side channel attack might work against browsers:

*The attacker is running script in evil.com. Concurrently, the same client has a compressed connection open to victim.com and is logged in, with a secret cookie. evil.com can induce requests to victim.com by, say, adding <img> tags with a src pointing to victim.com. [...] The attacker can watch the wire and measure the size of the requests that are sent. By altering the URL, the attacker could attempt to minimise the request size: i.e. when the URL matches the cookie.*

*I've just tried this with an HTTP request for fun and it's pretty easy to get the first 5 characters in a base64 encoded cookie. [...] That's a practical attack and would make a great paper if someone has the time.*

# CRIME

A practical compression side channel exploit came in 2012, under the name CRIME, developed by Duong and Rizzo, the authors behind BEAST. CRIME exploits the TLS compression side channel by using JavaScript malware to extract client cookies in an active MITM attack. It was officially presented at the Ekoparty conference in September 2012.[36] Unoffi-

---

[32] Language identification of encrypted VoIP traffic: Alejandra y Roberto or Alice and Bob? [fsty.uk/b312] (Wright et al., USENIX Security, 2007)

[33] Uncovering Spoken Phrases in Encrypted Voice over IP Conversations [fsty.uk/b313] (Wright et al., ACM Transactions on Information and System Security, Vol. 13, No. 4, Article 35, December 2010)

[34] SPDY is a relatively new protocol designed by Google to speed up web browsing.

[35] Compression contexts and privacy considerations [fsty.uk/b314] (Adam Langley, 11 August 2011)

[36] The CRIME attack [fsty.uk/b315] (Duong and Rizzo, Ekoparty Security Conference 9° edición, 2012)

---

Chapter 7: Protocol Attacks

cially, early press briefings[37] leaked enough information to enable experts to correctly guess what the attack was about.[38]

A proof of concept, the collaboration of several speculators, was published.[39] With the cat out of the bag, further information and a video demonstration were revealed days before the conference.[40] The CRIME authors never released their code, but they claimed that their exploit was able to uncover one cookie character using only six requests.

The mechanics of the CRIME attack are the same as for BEAST: the attacker must instrument the victim's browser to submit many requests to the target server, while observing network packets as they travel on the wire. Each request is a guess, exactly as discussed in the earlier compression oracle section. Unlike BEAST, CRIME requires less control over request content and timing, making exploitation much easier and using only native browser functionality.

## TIME

After CRIME, we didn't have to wait long for the attacks to improve. In March 2013, Tal Be'ery presented TIME at Black Hat Europe 2013.[41] A significant constraint on CRIME is the fact that the attacker must have access to the local network in order to observe the network packets. Although TIME still uses compression as its principal weapon, the improved attack extends the JavaScript component to use I/O timing differences to measure the size of compressed records. The approach is straightforward, with <img> tags used to initiate requests from the victim's browser and onLoad and onReadyStateChange event handlers to take measurements. The entire attack takes place in the browser itself.

With this change, the attack can now be executed against anyone on the Internet, provided you can get them to run your JavaScript malware. In practice, this will require some form of social engineering.

One problem still remains, though. CRIME works by observing one-byte differences in compressed output; is it really possible to use timing to detect differences that small? As it turns out, it's possible, by playing tricks at the network layer.

In TCP, great care is taken not to overwhelm the other party by sending too much data. The problem is this: there's usually a significant distance between two sides engaged in a conversation. For example, it takes about 45 msec for a packet to travel between London and New York. If you send only one packet at a time and wait for a confirmation, you can send only one packet of data every 90 msec. To speed up the communication, TCP allows both sides

---

[37] New Attack Uses SSL/TLS Information Leak to Hijack HTTPS Sessions [fsty.uk/b316] (Threatpost, 5 September 2012)

[38] CRIME - How to beat the BEAST successor? [fsty.uk/b317] (Thomas Pornin, 8 September 2012)

[39] It's not a crime to build a CRIME [fsty.uk/b318] (Krzysztof Kotowicz, 11 September 2012)

[40] Crack in Internet's foundation of trust allows HTTPS session hijacking [fsty.uk/b319] (Ars Technica, 13 September 2012)

[41] A Perfect CRIME? TIME Will Tell [fsty.uk/b320] (Tal Be'ery and Amichai Shulman, March 2013)

---

to send many packets at once. However, to ensure that the other party is not overwhelmed, they have to stay within a prescribed limit, or the *congestion window*. The congestion window starts small and grows over time, an approach otherwise known as *slow start*.

Initial congestion window sizes vary. Older TCP stacks will use smaller windows of 5 to 6 KB, but there was recently a push to increase this to about 15 KB. The attack works equally well for all sizes. In the following example, I assume the client uses an initial congestion window of 5 KB (three packets).

Figure 7.6. Using the TCP initial congestion window size as a timing oracle

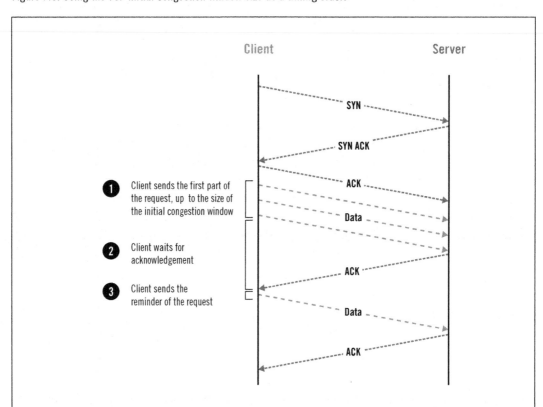

At the beginning of a connection, if the data you want to send fits into the congestion window, then you can send it all at once. But if you have too much data you will first have to send as much as you can, then wait for the server to confirm receipt, then send what you have remaining. That wait will add one *round-trip time* (RTT) to the operation. For the London–New York connection, that comes to about 90 ms of extra time. To use this behavior as a timing oracle, you increase the size of the data until you completely fill the initial congestion window. If you add just one more byte, the request will take one RTT longer, which is a delay you can measure from JavaScript. At this point you can start playing with compression; if you manipulate the data so that compression reduces the size by one byte, the request will take one RTT less. From here, exploitation continues as discussed in earlier sections.

Attacks against HTTP requests are easier because you have direct control over what is sent. They allow you to extract secrets that browsers have, for example, session cookies. If you want to extract secrets transported in HTTP responses, things get more complicated:

- Response compression takes place on the server, which means that you need to observe the server's initial congestion window, not the client's (as with HTTP requests).

- You must be able to inject your data into the page that contains the secret you wish to contain. In practice, this means that the application must mirror some data you send to it.

- When timing responses, you must take into account that both the client's and the server's windows are likely to overflow, making it more difficult to know what caused a delay.

On the other hand, unlike TLS compression, HTTP-level response compression is very common. Compression side channel attacks work equally well against both.

As far as we know, TIME has not progressed beyond a proof of concept. In practice, there might be many obstacles to overcome in order to make the attack work in real life. For example, the authors mention that due to network jitter they need to repeat the same request several times to reliably detect boundaries. Furthermore, the congestion window size grows over the time of the connection, which means that you need to take your measurements with a fresh connection every time. However, most servers use persistent connections for performance reasons, and you don't have control over this from JavaScript. As a result, the attack might need to operate slowly, using one connection, then waiting for the browser to close it, then trying again. Overall, it might take quite a while for successful extraction of, say, a 16-character secret.

## BREACH

Another compression side channel attack focused on HTTP responses, called BREACH, followed in August 2013.[42] The authors focused on demonstrating that CRIME works equally well on HTTP response compression. They used the same attack position—that of an active man in the middle—and developed a working exploit. Their main contribution is in the analysis and the practical demonstration. For example, they used their exploit to attack Outlook Web Access (OWA), showing that they can retrieve CSRF tokens with 95% reliability and often in under 30 seconds.[43]

---

[42] BREACH: Reviving the CRIME Attack [fsty.uk/b321] (Gluck et al., August 2013)

The BREACH authors put together a web site to publicize their work,[44] and the proof-of-concept source code is available at GitHub.[45]

## Attack Details

BREACH is conceptually identical to CRIME, requiring that the attacker has access to the victim's network traffic and ability to run JavaScript code in the victim's browser. The attack surface is different. HTTP response compression applies only to response bodies, which means that no secrets can be extracted from the response headers. However, response bodies often have interesting sensitive data. The authors focused on extracting CSRF tokens (their example is shown ahead), which would allow them to impersonate the victim in the attacked web application.

To bootstrap the attack, an injection point into the response body is needed. In OWA, the `id` parameter is reflected in output. Thus, if the attacker submits the following request with the attack payload:

```
GET /owa/?ae=Item&t=IPM.Note&a=New&id=INJECTED-VALUE
```

The response body will contain the injected value:

```
<span id=requestUrl>https://malbot.net:443/owa/forms/
basic/BasicEditMessage.aspx?ae=Item&amp;t=IPM.Note&
amp;a=New&amp;id=INJECTED-VALUE</span>
```

This is sufficient to begin to extract any secret placed elsewhere in the body, for example, a CSRF token:

```
<td nowrap id="tdErrLgf"><a href="logoff.owa?
canary=d634cda866f14c73ac135ae858c0d894">Log
Off</a></td>
```

To establish the baseline, the attacker submits `canary=` as the first payload. Because of the duplication, the compressed response body will be smaller, which can be detected on the network. From here, the attack continues as in CRIME.

Although the attack seems simple at first, in practice there are further issues that need to be dealt with:

**Huffman encoding**
> Most of the Internet runs on DEFLATE compression, which is actually a combination of two algorithms: LZ77 and Huffman encoding. The former is what we use for the

---

[43] The authors presented BREACH at Black Hat USA 2013, in a session titled "SSL, Gone in 30 seconds."

[44] BREACH web site [fsty.uk/b322] (retrieved 16 July 2014)

[45] BREACH repository [fsty.uk/b323] (Neal Harris, retrieved 16 July 2014)

attacks, but the latter actually makes us work harder. Huffman encoding is a variable-length encoding that exploits the fact that, usually, some characters appear more often than others. Normally, we always use one byte to represent one character. To save space, we can represent more frequent characters with shorter symbols (fewer bits than in a byte) and less frequent characters with longer symbols (more bits than in a byte).

Huffman encoding can skew the resulting lengths of both successful and unsuccessful guesses. To deal with this problem, it's necessary to double the number of requests, using two for each guess.

**Block ciphers**

The conceptual attack works great against encryption, but expects streaming ciphers, for which the size of data is directly reflected in ciphertext. When block ciphers are used, ciphertext grows only one block at a time, for example, 16 bytes for 128-bit AES. In such a case, further padding is needed to bring ciphertext to the edge of growing by another block. For this, several requests might be needed. Once you determine the size of the padding, you can make as many guesses as there are padding bytes. For every new guess, you remove one byte of the padding.

**Response content diversity**

For the attacks that work against HTTP responses (TIME and BREACH), the "diverse" nature of markup formatting, coding practices, and encodings tends to make the attacks more difficult. For example, the attacks require a known prefix to bootstrap the attack, but the secret values are sometimes prefixed with characters that cannot be injected (e.g., quotes). Or, there might be variations in response size (in absence of attacks), which make guessing more difficult.

The CRIME authors used an interesting technique variation when attacking TLS compression. TLS record sizes are limited to 16 KB (16,384 bytes), which also means that this is the largest block on which compression can operate. This is interesting because the attacker is able to fully control the first 16 KB. It goes something like this:

1. For a GET request, the first 5 bytes are always going to be the same: the request method (GET) followed by a space and the first character in the URL (/). If you then add 16,379 bytes of random data to the URL, you fill the entire TLS record. You can submit this request and observe its compressed size.

2. You can now start reducing the amount of random data in the URL, one byte at a time, allowing bytes from the request back in the block. Some of the bytes will be predictable (e.g., HTTP/1.1, the protocol information that always follows the URL), but at some point you will encounter the first unknown byte.

3. Now you have a block of 16,383 bytes you know and one byte you don't. You submit that as a request. Then, without making further requests, you build a list of candidates

for the unknown byte, simulate the first 16 KB as a request and compress it using the same compression method, and compare the compressed size to that of the size of the actual request. In the ideal case, there will be only one match, and it will disclose the unknown byte.

This technique is quite neat, because it requires a smaller number of requests. On the other hand, the compression library used by the attacker needs to produce the same output for the same input. In practice, different compression settings and different library versions might introduce variations.

## Impact against TLS Compression and SPDY

In this section, I discuss the various prerequisites necessary for a successful exploitation of a compression side channel attack against either TLS compression or SPDY. In both cases, CRIME attacks header compression, which makes session cookies the best target.

**Active MITM attack**

CRIME requires access to the victim's network traffic. It's a local attack, which can be performed with little effort against someone on the same LAN or Wi-Fi network. The attack can be either passive or active, but the latter gives the attacker more flexibility.

**Client-side control**

The attacker must also be able to assert enough control over the victim's browser to submit arbitrary requests to the target web site. You could do this with JavaScript malware, but it can be done much more simply with a series of <img> tags with specially crafted source URLs.

This could be achieved with social engineering or, more likely, by injecting HTML markup into any plaintext web site that the victim is interacting with at the time of attack.

**Vulnerable protocols**

As the authors of CRIME themselves said, compression is everywhere. They detailed attacks against TLS compression and the SPDY protocol. At the time of the announcement, I was able to use the SSL Pulse statistics and some of the other metrics obtained via the SSL Labs web site to estimate support for compression on both the client and server sides. For TLS compression, about 42% of the servers in the SSL Pulse data set supported it. Only about 2% of the servers supported SPDY, but those were some of the biggest sites (e.g., Google, Twitter, etc.).

That said, two sides are required to enable compression, and this is where the situation got better. Because TLS compression was never a high priority for browser vendors,[46] Chrome was the only browser that supported compression then. Firefox had compression implemented, but to my knowledge the code never went into a production release. Because both browser vendors had advance knowledge of the problem, they made sure that compression was disabled ahead of time. My measurements (from observing the visits to the SSL Labs web site) showed only 7% client-side support for compression.

In response to CRIME, most vendors patched their products and libraries to disable TLS compression altogether.

**Preparation**

This is not an attack that can be blindly executed against just any web site. For example, to start the attack it's necessary to use a known prefix as a starting point. Because these things differ from site to site, some amount of research is necessary, but it's not a lot of effort for the attack against TLS compression.

**Outcome**

In the best case, the attacker is able to obtain the password used for HTTP Basic Authentication. In practice, this authentication method is not often used, making session cookies the next best thing. A successful attack results in the attacker obtaining full control over the victim's session and everything that comes with it.

## Impact against HTTP Response Compression

Against HTTP compression, the impact of compression side channels is very different: (1) the attack surface is much larger and there is little chance that it will be reduced and (2) successful exploitation requires the attacker to do much more work upfront and their reward is smaller.

The prerequisites for attacks against HTTP compressions are the same as in the previous case; the attacker must be able to take control over the network communication and have limited control over the victim's browser. But there are differences when it comes to other factors:

**Attack surface**

HTTP compression is also vulnerable to compression side attacks. (The CRIME authors did not spend much time on it, but others have since worked in this area.) Unlike TLS compression, HTTP compression exposes a huge attack surface and cannot be simply turned off. Many sites depend on it so heavily that they might not be able to operate (cost efficiently) without it.

There is also an additional requirement that the attacker is able to inject arbitrary text into the HTTP response body at the desired attack point. In practice, this is almost always possible.

---

[46] Sites that care about performance will already compress HTTP responses, which is where the bulk of the bandwidth is. Trying to compress already compressed traffic increases CPU and RAM consumption but yields little improvement. It might be possible to move compression entirely to the TLS layer, but then it would try to compress images, which are not likely to compress well.

**Preparation**

On the other side, much more work is needed to exploit HTTP compression. In fact, you could say that an intimate understanding of the target web site is required. Session cookies are generally not available in HTTP response bodies, which means that the attackers must look for some other secret information. And that information might be much more difficult to find.

**Outcome**

The exact outcome will depend on the nature of the secret information. Any secret information can be extracted, provided the attacker knows it's there. For most applications, the most interesting target will be the CSRF protection tokens. If one such token is uncovered, the attacker might be able to carry out an arbitrary command on the target web site under the identity of the victim. There are some sites that use their session tokens for CSRF protection. In such cases, the outcome will be session hijacking.

## Mitigation of Attacks against TLS and SPDY

TLS compression is dead, and CRIME killed it. Before the disclosure a good chunk of the user base—all Chrome users—supported compression; it's difficult to say what Chrome's market share was in September 2012, but let's say it was about 30%.[47] Thanks to its autoupdate feature, however, once Chrome disabled compression the support quickly disappeared.

OpenSSL had support for compression, so it's possible to find old installations and user agents that still support it, but they are not likely to be attacked because they are not browsers (i.e., malware injection is not likely).

Still, it is prudent to disable compression on the server side. In most cases, just patching your servers should work. At the time of writing (July 2014), about 10% of the servers from the SSL Pulse data set still support compression. Given that Microsoft's TLS stack never supported compression and that Nginx disabled it a long time ago, most of those are probably older versions of Apache.

It's unlikely that compression will be making a comeback at the TLS layer. As I mentioned before, people didn't really use it much. (And if they did it was probably because it was enabled by default.) Even without compression as an oracle, the fact that data length is revealed in TLS is not a positive feature. There are currently efforts to implement a length-hiding extension.[48]

As for SPDY, header compression had been disabled in both Chrome and Firefox. Now that the problem is known, we can assume that the future versions of this protocol will not be vulnerable.

---

[47] Usage share of web browsers [fsty.uk/b324] (Wikipedia, retrieved 20 February 2014)

[48] Length Hiding Padding for the Transport Layer Security Protocol [fsty.uk/b325] (Pironti et al., September 2013)

---

# Mitigation of Attacks against HTTP Compression

Addressing the compression side channel inherent in HTTP compression is a much more difficult problem, even if the attack is not exactly easy to execute. The difficulty is twofold: (1) you probably can't afford to disable compression and (2) mitigation requires application changes, which are cost-prohibitive. Still, there are some hacks that just might work well enough. Here's a quick overview of the possibilities:

**Request rate control**

Both the authors of TIME and BREACH have commented on sometimes getting caught due to the excessive number of requests they had to submit. (The BREACH authors cited thousands of requests against OWA.) Enforcing a reasonable rate of requests for user sessions could detect similar attacks or, in the worst case, slow down the attacker significantly. This mitigation could be implemented at a web server, load-balancer, or web application firewall (WAF) layer, which means that it does not need to be very costly.

**Length hiding**

One possible defense measure is to hide the real response length. For example, we could deploy a response body filter to analyze HTML markup and inject random padding. Whitespace is largely ignored in HTML, yet variations in response size would make the attackers' job more difficult. According to the BREACH authors, random padding can be defeated using statistical analysis at the cost of a significant increase in the number of requests.

The best aspect of this approach is that it can be applied at the web server level, with no changes to deployed applications. For example, Paul Querna proposed to use variations in chunked HTTP encoding at a web server level for length hiding.[49] This approach does not change the markup at all, yet it changes the size of the packets on the wire.

**Token masking**

Threats against CRSF tokens can be mitigated by the use of *masking*, ensuring that the characters that appear in HTML markup are never the same. Here's how: (1) for every byte in the token, generate one random byte; (2) XOR the token byte with the random byte; and (3) include all the random bytes in the output. This process is reversible; by repeating the XOR operations on the server, you recover the original token value. This measure is ideally suited for implementation at framework level.

**Partial compression disabling**

When I first thought about attacks against HTTP response bodies, my thoughts were to focus on the fact that the Referer header will never contain the name of the target

---

[49] breach attack [fsty.uk/b326] (Paul Querna, 6 August 2013)

web site. (If the attacker can do that, then she already has enough access to the site via XSS.) Initially, I proposed to drop cookies on such requests. Without the cookies, there is no user session, and no attack surface. Someone from the community had a better idea: for requests with the incorrect referrer information, simply disable response compression.[50] There would be a small performance penalty but only for the small number of users who don't supply any referrer information. More importantly, there wouldn't be any breakage, unlike with the cookie approach.

# Padding Oracle Attacks

In February 2013, AlFardan and Paterson released a paper detailing a variety of attacks that can be used to recover small portions of plaintext provided that a CBC suite is used.[51] Their work is commonly known as the Lucky 13 attack. As with BEAST and CRIME, small portions of plaintext in the web context virtually always translate to browser cookies. Outside HTTP, any protocol that uses password authentication is probably vulnerable.

The root cause of the problem is in the fact that the padding, which is used in the CBC mode, is not protected by the integrity validation mechanisms of TLS. This allows the attacker to modify the padding in transit and observe how the server behaves. If the attacker is able to detect the server reacting to the padding issues, information leaks out and leads to plaintext discovery.

This is one of the best attacks against TLS we saw in recent years. Using JavaScript malware injected into a victim's browser, the attack needs about 8,192 HTTP requests to discover one byte of plaintext (e.g., from a cookie or password).

## What Is a Padding Oracle?

There is a special class of attack that can be mounted against the receiving party if the padding can be manipulated. This might be possible if the encryption scheme does not authenticate ciphertext; for example, TLS doesn't in CBC mode. The attacker can't manipulate the padding directly, because it's encrypted. But she can make arbitrary changes to the ciphertext, where she thinks the padding might be. An *oracle* is said to exist if the attacker is able to tell which manipulations result in a correct padding after decryption and which do not.

But how do you get from there to plaintext recovery? At the end of the day, encryption is all about hiding (masking) plaintext using some secret seemingly random data. If the attacker can reveal the mask, she can effectively reverse the encryption process and reveal the plaintext, too.

---

[50] BREACH mitigation [fsty.uk/b327] (manu, 14 October 2013)

[51] Lucky Thirteen: Breaking the TLS and DTLS Record Protocols [fsty.uk/b328] (AlFardan and Paterson, 4 February 2013)

Going back to the padding oracle, every time the attacker submits a guess that results in correct padding after decryption she discovers one byte of the mask that is used for decryption. She can now use that byte to decrypt one byte of plaintext. From here, she can continue to recover the next byte, and so on, until the entire plaintext is revealed.

The key to successful padding oracle exploitation is to (1) submit a lot of guesses and (2) find a way to determine if a guess was successful. A badly designed protocol might be explicit about bad padding. More likely, the attacker will need to deduce the outcome by observing server behavior. For example, timing oracles observe the response latency, watching for differences when padding is correct and when it is not.

If you care to learn about the details behind padding oracle attacks, you can head to one of the tutorials available online[52] or review an online simulation that shows the process in detail.[53]

Padding oracle issues are best avoided by verifying the integrity of data before any of it is processed. Such checks prevent ciphertext manipulation and preempt all padding oracle attacks.

## Attacks against TLS

The *padding oracle attack* (against TLS and other protocols) was first identified by Serge Vaudenay in 2001 (formally published in 2002).[54] TLS 1.0 uses the `decryption_failed` alert for padding errors and `bad_record_mac` for MAC failures. This design, although insecure, was not practically exploitable because alerts are encrypted and the network attacker can't differentiate between the two.

In 2003, Canvel et al.[55] improved the attack to use a timing padding oracle and demonstrated a successful attack against OpenSSL. They exploited the fact that OpenSSL skipped the MAC calculation and responded slightly faster when the padding was incorrect. The researcher's proof-of-concept attack was against an IMAP server; situated close to the target, they could obtain the IMAP password in about one hour.

Padding oracles are exploited by repeatedly making guesses about which combinations of bytes might decrypt to valid padding. The attacker starts with some intercepted ciphertext, modifies it, and submits it to the server. Most guesses will naturally be incorrect. In TLS, every failed guess terminates the entire TLS session, which means that the same encrypted block cannot be modified and attempted again. For her next guess, the attacker needs to in-

---

[52] Automated Padding Oracle Attacks with PadBuster [fsty.uk/b329] (Brian Holyfield, 14 September 2010)

[53] Padding oracle attack simulation [fsty.uk/b330] (Erlend Oftedal, retrieved 28 February 2014)

[54] Security Flaws Induced by CBC Padding - Applications to SSL, IPSEC, WTLS... [fsty.uk/b331] (Serge Vaudenay, pages 534–546, EUROCRYPT 2002)

[55] Password Interception in a SSL/TLS Channel [fsty.uk/b332] (Canvel et al., CRYPTO 2003)

tercept another valid encrypted block. That is why Canvel et al. attacked IMAP; automated services that automatically retry after failure are the ideal case for this attack.

In order to improve the security of CBC, OpenSSL (and other TLS implementations) modified its code to minimize the information leakage.[56] TLS 1.1 deprecated the `decryption_failed` alert and added the following warning (emphasis mine):

> *Canvel et al. [CBCTIME] have demonstrated a timing attack on CBC padding based on the time required to compute the MAC. In order to defend against this attack, implementations MUST ensure that record processing time is essentially the same whether or not the padding is correct. In general, the best way to do this is to compute the MAC even if the padding is incorrect, and only then reject the packet. For instance, if the pad appears to be incorrect, the implementation might assume a zero-length pad and then compute the MAC.* **This leaves a small timing channel, since MAC performance depends to some extent on the size of the data fragment, but it is not believed to be large enough to be exploitable, due to the large block size of existing MACs and the small size of the timing signal.**

In February 2013, AlFardan and Paterson demonstrated that the remaining side channel is, in fact, exploitable, using new techniques to realize Vaudenay's padding oracle. They named their new attack Lucky 13 and showed that CBC—as implemented in TLS and DTLS—is too fragile and that it should have been abandoned a long time ago. They also showed that small problems, left unattended, can escalate again if and when the technologies evolve in unpredictable ways.

## Impact

For the padding oracle to be exploited, the adversary must be able to mount an active attack, which means that he must be able to intercept and modify encrypted traffic. Additionally, because the timing differences are subtle the attacker must be very close to the target server in order to detect them. The researchers performed their experiments when the attacker and the server were both on the same local network. Remote attacks do not appear to be feasible for TLS, although they are for DTLS, when used with timing amplification techniques developed by AlFardan and Paterson in 2012.[57]

**Attacks against automated systems**
    The classic full plaintext recovery padding oracle attack is carried out against automated systems, which are likely to communicate with the server often and have built-in resiliency mechanisms that makes them try again on failed connections. Because the

---

[56] Security of CBC Ciphersuites in SSL/TLS: Problems and Countermeasures [fsty.uk/b333] (Moeller et al., last updated on 20 May 2004)

[57] Plaintext-Recovery Attacks Against Datagram TLS [fsty.uk/b334] (AlFardan and Paterson, NDSS, February 2012)

attack is spanning many connections, it works only with protocols that always place sensitive data (e.g., passwords) in the same location. IMAP is a good candidate. This attack requires roughly 8.4 million connections to recover 16 bytes of data. Because each incorrect guess results in a TLS error and because TLS is designed to destroy sessions in such situations, every new connection is forced to use a full handshake with the server. As an effect, this attack is slow. Still, it's not far from being feasible under certain circumstances if the attacker has months of time available and is able to influence the automated process to open connections at a faster rate.

**Attacks when some of the plaintext is known**

A partial plaintext recovery attack, which can be performed if one byte at one of the last two positions in a block is known, allows each of the remaining bytes to be recovered with roughly 65,536 attempts.

**Attacks against browsers using JavaScript malware**

AlFardan and Paterson's best attack uses JavaScript malware against the victim's browser, targeting HTTP cookies. Because the malware can influence the position of the cookie in a request, it is possible to arrange the encryption blocks in such a way that only one byte of the cookie is unknown. Because of the limited character range used by cookies, the researchers estimate that only 8,192 requests are needed to uncover one byte of plaintext. The best aspect of this attack is the fact that the malware is submitting all the requests and that, even though they all fail, all the connection failures are invisible to the victim. Furthermore, no special plug-ins or cross-origin privileges are required.

# Mitigation

AlFardan and Paterson identified problems in a number of implementations, reported the problems to the developers, and coordinated the disclosure so that all libraries were already fixed at the time of announcement. Thus, patching your libraries should be sufficient for the mitigation, at least in the first instance.

Given the fragility of the CBC implementation in TLS, it's best to avoid CBC suites whenever possible. But this is easier said than done; in many cases there are no safe alternatives. Streaming ciphers do not use padding, and so they are not vulnerable to this problem, but the only streaming cipher in TLS is RC4; it suffers from other problems (described in the next section) and should not be used. Other streaming ciphers will be added to TLS, but that will take time.[58] This leaves us only with authenticated GCM suites, which require TLS 1.2. In the future, TLS might be extended to authenticate encryption instead of plaintext, in which case CBC suites might become safe again.[59]

---

[58] ChaCha20 and Poly1305 based Cipher Suites for TLS [fsty.uk/b335] (Langley and Chang, November 2013)

# RC4 Weaknesses

RC4, designed by Ron Rivest in 1987, is one of the oldest ciphers still in use and, despite all its many flaws, still one of the most popular. Its popularity comes from the fact that it's been around for a very long time but also because it's simple to implement and runs very fast in software and hardware.

Today, we know that RC4 is broken, but attacks have not yet sufficiently improved to become practical. For this reason, and also for the fact that there are environments in which alternatives are even less desirable, RC4 is still being used. (Of course, a much bigger reason is inertia and the fact that most people don't know that they need to abandon RC4.)

If possible, it's best to avoid RC4 completely. For example, the TLS 1.2 environment offers safe alternatives, which means that RC4 should not be used. In practice, however, you might have good reasons to keep it around, as I will discuss in this section.

## Key Scheduling Weaknesses

For a very long time, the biggest known problem with RC4 was the weakness in the key scheduling algorithm, published in a paper by Fluhrer, Mantin, and Shamir in 2001.[60] The authors discovered that there are large classes of keys that have a weakness where a small part of the key determines a large number of initial outputs. In practice, this means that if even a part of a key is reused over a period of time the attacker could (1) uncover parts of the keystream (e.g., from known plaintext at certain locations) and then (2) uncover unknown plaintext bytes at those positions in all other streams. This discovery was used to break the WEP protocol.[61] The initial attack implemented against WEP required 10 million message for the key recovery. The technique was later improved to require only under 100,000 messages.

TLS is not vulnerable to this problem, because every connection uses a substantially different key. As a result, even though RC4 was known to have weaknesses it remained in wide use because there the issues didn't apply to the way it was used in TLS.[62] Despite its known flaws, RC4 remained the most popular cipher used with TLS. My 2010 large-scale survey of SSL usage found that RC4 was the preferred cipher[63] and supported by about 98% of sur-

[59] Encrypt-then-MAC for TLS and DTLS [fsty.uk/b37] (Peter Gutmann, June 2014)

[60] Weaknesses in the Key Scheduling Algorithm of RC4 [fsty.uk/b336] (Fluhrer, Mantin, and Shamir, 2001)

[61] WEP didn't quite reuse its keys but derived new keys from a master key using concatenation, a method that resulted in the session keys that are similar to the master key. TLS, for example, uses hashing, which means that connection keys cannot be traced back to the master key.

[62] RSA Security Response to Weaknesses in Key Scheduling Algorithm of RC4 [fsty.uk/b337] (RSA Laboratories Technical Note, 1 September 2001)

[63] Anecdotally, only about a half of TLS servers on the Internet enforce suite preference. The other half uses the first supported suite from the list submitted by browsers.

veyed servers.[64] People who understood the key scheduling weakness disliked RC4 because it was easy to misuse and, as a result, recommended against it for new systems.[65]

When the BEAST attack was announced in 2011, it instantly made all block cipher suites unsafe. (Even though BEAST works only against TLS 1.0 and earlier protocol versions, support for TLS 1.1 or better was nonexistent at the time.) Because RC4—a streaming cipher—is not vulnerable to BEAST, it suddenly became the only secure algorithm to use in TLS. In March 2013, when new devastating flaws in RC4 were announced, the ICSI Certificate Notary project showed RC4 usage at about 50% of all traffic. At the time of writing, in July 2014, the RC4 market share is about 26%.[66]

## Early Single-Byte Biases

*Encryption biases* were another reason cryptographers were worried about RC4. As early as 2001, it was known that some values appear in the keystream more often than others.[67] In particular, the second keystream byte was known to be biased toward zero with a probability of 1/128 (twice as much as the expected 1/256).

To understand how biases can lead to the compromise of plaintext, we need to go back to how RC4 works. This cipher operates in a streaming fashion; after the initial setup phase, it produces an endless stream of data. This data, which was supposed to be effectively random looking from the outside, is then mixed with the plaintext, using a XOR operation against one byte at a time. The XOR operation, when used with a sufficiently random data stream, changes plaintext into something that's effectively gibberish for everyone except those who know the RC4 key.

When we say that a bias exists, that means that some values appear more often than others. The worst case is the already mentioned bias toward zero. Why? Because a value XORed with a zero remains unchanged. Thus, because we know that the second byte of every RC4 data stream leans toward zero we also know that the second byte of encrypted output will lean to be the same as the original text!

To exploit this problem you need to obtain the same text encrypted with many different encryption keys. Against TLS, this means attacking many connections.[68] Then you look at all the bytes at position 2; the value that appears most often is most likely to be the same as in

---

[64] Internet SSL Survey 2010 is here! [fsty.uk/b83] (Ivan Ristić, 29 July 2010)

[65] What's the deal with RC4? [fsty.uk/b338] (Matthew Green, 15 December 2011)

[66] The ICSI Certificate Notary [fsty.uk/b339] (International Computer Science Institute, retrieved 16 July 2014)

[67] A Practical Attack on Broadcast RC4 [fsty.uk/b340] (Mantin and Shamir, 2011)

[68] In cryptography, this is known as a *multisession* attack. The name might be confusing in the context of TLS, because a *TLS session* is a set of cryptographic parameters that are used across multiple connections via the session reuse mechanism. Even with session reuse, TLS generates new encryption keys for every connection.

plaintext. Some amount of guessing is involved, but, the more different encryptions you obtain, the higher the chances that you will guess correctly.

Figure 7.7. The bias in the second byte of the RC4 keystream [Source: AlFardan et al., 2013]

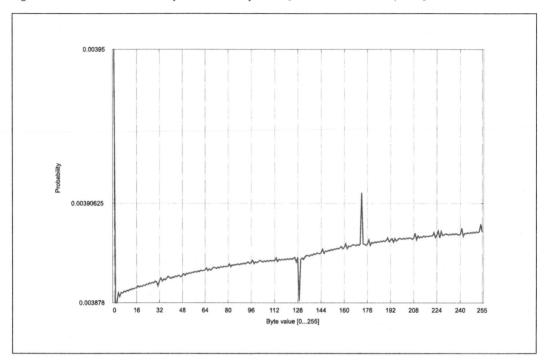

What can be achieved using these individual biases varies and depends on protocol design. The first requirement is that useful data actually exists at the given location. For example, in TLS the first 36 bytes are most commonly used by the Finished protocol message that changes with every connection and has no long-term value.[69] For TLS, the second-byte bias is not going to be useful.

The second requirement is to get the same application data in the same location every time across a great number of connections. For some protocols, this is not a problem. In HTTP, for example, cookies and passwords are in the same place on every request.

## Biases across the First 256 Bytes

In March 2013, AlFardan et al. published a paper describing newly discovered weaknesses in RC4 and two strong attacks against its use in TLS.[70]

---

[69] Some protocol extensions add additional messages that are also encrypted. For example, this is the case with the *Next Protocol Negotiation* (NPN) extension, which is used to negotiate SPDY. Unlike the Finished message, whose contents are effectively random, those other messages could be attacked using the RC4 biases.

---

One of the attacks was based on the fact that RC4 biases were not limited to a few bytes here and there. By producing and analyzing keystreams of $2^{44}$ different RC4 keys, the researchers uncovered multiple biases at every one of the first 256 positions. They further improved the recovery algorithms to deal with multiple biases at individual positions (e.g., a certain byte is more likely to have values 10 and 23, with all other values equally likely). The resulting attack requires $2^{32}$ data samples to recover all 256 bytes with a success rate close to 100%. With optimization that can be applied when the attacked data uses a reduced character set (e.g., passwords and HTTP cookies), the number of data samples can be reduced to about $2^{28}$. This is a far cry from the $2^{128}$ bits of security promised by RC4.

## Note

How is it possible that the full scope of the bias issues remained undiscovered for so long after so many early warning signs? One theory I heard was that most cryptographers thought that RC4 had already been demonstrated to be insecure and that no further work was needed. In fact, many cryptographers were very surprised to learn how popular it was. It's likely that the lack of a strong attack against RC4 as used in TLS contributed to its continued use.

Despite the seriousness of the attack, it remains largely theoretical due to many constraints:

**Number of connections**

In the best case, this attack requires $2^{28}$ samples of encrypted plaintext. Put another way, that's 268,435,456 connections. Clearly, obtaining all those samples is going to take a lot of time and potentially utilize a lot of network traffic. Under controlled conditions, with two sides designed to produce as many RC4 connections as possible, and with session resumption enabled, the authors cite an experiment of about 16 hours using over 500 connections per second for a total of $2^{25}$ connections.

In a scenario closer to real life, a purely passive attack would take much longer. For example, assuming one connection per second (86,400 connections per day), it would take over eight years to obtain all the required samples.

The connection rate might be increased by controlling a victim's browser (using injected JavaScript), forcing it to submit many connections at the same time. This is the same approach taken by the BEAST exploit. In this case, additional effort is needed to defeat persistent connections (keep-alives) and prevent multiple requests over the same connection (the attack can use only the first 256 bytes of each connection). To do this, the MITM could reset every connection at the TCP level after the first response is observed. Because TLS is designed to throw away sessions that encounter errors, in this scenario every connection would require a full handshake. That would make the attack much slower.[71]

---

[70] On the Security of RC4 in TLS and WPA [fsty.uk/b341] (AlFardan et al., 13 March 2013)

### Positioning

This is a man-in-the-middle attack. Per the previous discussion, a pure passive attack is very unlikely to produce results within a reasonable amount of time. An active attack would require a combination of JavaScript malware and MITM ability.

### Scope

This attack works only against the first 256 bytes of plaintext. Because such a large number of samples is required, it's unlikely that the same meaningful secret data will be present throughout. This restricts the attack to protocols that use password authentication or, for HTTP, cookies. As it turns out, the HTTP use case is not very likely because all major browsers place cookies past the 220-byte boundary. (If you recall, the first 36 bytes are of little interest because they are always used by the TLS protocol.) HTTP Basic Authentication is vulnerable in Chrome, which places the password at around the 100-byte mark. All other browsers place passwords out of the reach of this attack.

## Double-Byte Biases

In addition to having single-byte biases, RC4 was known to also have biases involving consecutive bytes. These do not exist at only one position in the encrypted stream but show up continuously in the output at regular intervals.[72]

In their second attack, AlFardan et al. showed how to use the double-byte biases for plaintext recovery. The double-byte attack has an advantage in that it does not require samples to be obtained using different RC4 keys. This makes the attack much more efficient, because multiple samples can be obtained over the same connection. On the other hand, because it's still the case that the same plaintext needs to be encrypted over and over, the attacker must have near-complete control over the traffic. Passive attacks are not possible.

The double-byte bias attack can recover 16 bytes of plaintext from $13 \times 2^{30}$ samples of encrypted plaintext. To collect one sample, a POST request of exactly 512 bytes is used. Assuming a response of similar size, the attack would consume about 3.25 TB of traffic in both directions. Under controlled conditions, that many samples would take about 2,000 hours (or 83 days) to collect at a speed of six million samples per hour.

Although much more practical than the first attack, this version is equally unlikely to be useful in practice.

---

[71] In theory. In practice, applications tend to be very tolerant of connections that are not properly shutdown, a fact that can be exploited for truncation attacks. You can find out more about this topic in the section called "Truncation Attacks" in Chapter 6.

[72] Statistical Analysis of the Alleged RC4 Keystream Generator [fsty.uk/b342] (Fluhrer and McGrew, 2001)

---

# Mitigation: RC4 versus BEAST and Lucky 13

The attacks against RC4 are serious and allow for plaintext recovery in controlled environments, but they are still not very practical for use against real systems. But given that the safety margin of RC4 has become very small the best approach is to stop using it as soon as possible.

The problem is that this might not be the best decision given that there are situations in which a secure alternative is not available. There are two aspects to consider:

**Interoperability**

RC4 has long been one of the most popular ciphers, "guaranteed" to always be there. As a result, there are some clients that do not support anything else. However, chances are that there is only a very small number of them. If you have a truly diverse client base and you think that RC4-only clients might cause substantial breakage, consider keeping RC4 around—but at the bottom of your list of prioritized suites. Because most clients will negotiate something else, you will have reduced your attack surface while minimizing disruption.

**Security**

If you disable RC4, then you might need to worry about using CBC suites in combination with TLS 1.0 or earlier protocol versions. In this case, the BEAST attack might apply. For one thing, your servers might still be at TLS 1.0. (If they are, you should stop worrying about RC4 and upgrade your infrastructure to TLS 1.2 as soon as possible.) If your servers are up to date, your user base might consist of clients that are not. Some of them might genuinely be vulnerable to the BEAST attack.

There is little real data from which to decide which of the two attacks (BEAST and RC4) is more likely. Both attacks are difficult to carry out. The RC4 attack is possible with any protocol version but requires a willing browser and a large amount of time and network traffic. BEAST, on the other hand, is difficult to exploit but can be done quickly when everything is just right. The biggest thing going against BEAST is that the major platforms have been patched, and the number of vulnerable users is falling all the time. The real question is this: are there any better attacks against these flaws that might currently be unknown to us? Many are asking this question—especially for RC4, which has always been excluded from the FIPS-approved algorithms. Could it be that the weaknesses have always been known to the NSA? What other problems do they know about?

Lucky 13 is also a concern. Even though the immediate dangers have been addressed with patches, the CBC construction in TLS is inherently unsafe. On the positive side, TLS 1.2 clients and servers tend to support authenticated GCM suites, which use neither RC4 nor CBC. They are currently the best way to avoid all known TLS cipher suite weaknesses.

We can't make decisions based on speculation and paranoia. Besides, there might not be any one correct decision anyway. Mitigating BEAST might be appropriate in some cases; removing RC4 might be best in others. In situations such as this, it's always helpful to see what others are doing; at the time of writing, Google still allows RC4 but uses it only with clients that do not support modern protocols (TLS 1.0 and earlier versions).

On the other hand, Microsoft boldly deprecated RC4 in Windows 8.1 and, in some cases, even Windows 7. Schannel will still use RC4 in client mode, but only if no other cipher suite is available on the server. Some would say that such a fallback is necessary, because there are still servers out there that support only RC4 cipher suites. There is also an Internet-Draft in progress that prohibits RC4 usage.[73]

# Triple Handshake Attack

In 2009, when the TLS renegotiation mechanism had been found to be insecure, the protocols were fixed by creating a new method for *secure renegotiation*. (If you haven't already, read about insecure renegotiation earlier in this chapter, in the section called "Insecure Renegotiation".) But that effort hadn't been quite successful. In 2014, a group of researchers showed their *Triple Handshake Attack*, which combines two separate TLS weaknesses to break renegotiation one more time.[74]

## The Attack

To understand how the attack works, you first need to know how renegotiation is secured. When renegotiation takes place, the server expects the client to supply its previous verify_data value (from the encrypted Finished message in the previous handshake). Because only the client can know that value, the server can be sure that it's the same client.

At first, that might seem like an impossible task given that this value is always encrypted. And yet it was possible to uncover the "secret" value and break renegotiation; the attack works in three steps and exploits two weaknesses in TLS.

### Step 1: Unknown Key-Share Weakness

The first exploited weakness is in the RSA key exchange. The generation of the master secret, which is the cornerstone of TLS session security, is chiefly driven by the client:

1. Client generates a premaster key and a random value and sends them to the server

---

[73] Prohibiting RC4 Cipher Suites [fsty.uk/b343] (Andrei Popov, 11 April 2014)

[74] Triple Handshakes Considered Harmful: Breaking and Fixing Authentication over TLS [fsty.uk/b278] (Bhargavan et al., March 2014)

2. Server generates its own random value and sends it to the client

3. Client and server calculate the master secret from these three values

Both random values are transported in the clear, but to prevent just anyone from performing MITM attacks on TLS the premaster secret is protected; the client encrypts it with the server's public key, which means that the attacker can't get to it. Unless she has access to the server's private key, that is; therein lies the first twist.

The triple handshake attack relies on a *malicious server*. In this variant, you somehow convince the victim to visit a seemingly innocent web site under your control. (The usual approach is to use social engineering.) On that web site, you have your own valid certificate.

This is where the fun begins. The client generates a premaster key and a random value and sends them to the malicious server.[75] The premaster secret is encrypted, but the malicious server is the intended recipient and has no trouble decrypting it. Before the handshake with the client is complete, the malicious server opens a separate connection to the target server and *mirrors* the premaster key and the client's random value. The malicious server then takes the target server's random value and forwards it to the client. When this exchange is complete, there are two separate TLS connections and three parties involved in the communication, but they all share the same connection parameters and thus also the same master key.

---

[75] Because the malicious server is in the middle, it can always force the use of a suite that relies on the RSA key exchange for as long as there is one such suite supported by both sides that are being attacked. In TLS, servers choose suites. When opening a handshake to the target server, the malicious server offers only suites that use the RSA key exchange.

---

Figure 7.8. Triple handshake: unknown key-share

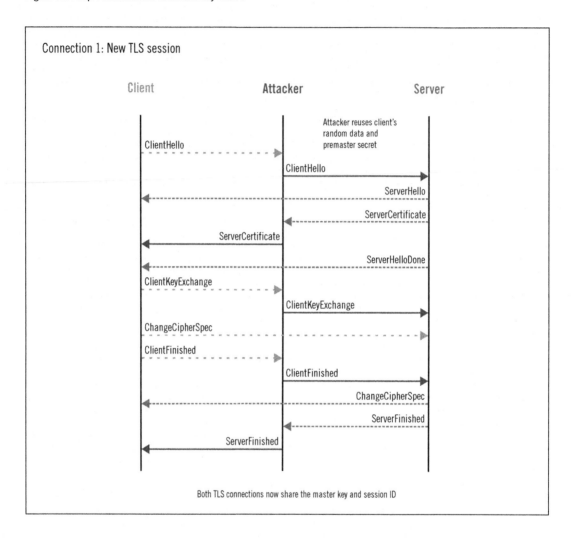

This weakness is called an *unknown key-share*,[76] and you can probably guess that it is not desirable. However, on its own it does not seem exploitable. The malicious server cannot really achieve anything sinister at this point. It has the same master key and can thus see all the communication, but it could do that anyway and without involving the other server. If the attacker attempted to do anything at this point, she would be performing a phishing attack; it's a real problem, but not one TLS can solve.

---

[76] Unknown key-share attacks on the station-to-station (STS) protocol [fsty.uk/b344] (S. Blake-Wilson and A. Menezes, pages 154–170, in *Public Key Cryptography*, 1999)

---

> **Note**
>
> The RSA key exchange is almost universally supported, but there is also an attack variant that works against the ephemeral Diffie-Hellman (DHE) key exchange. The researchers discovered that the mainstream TLS implementations accept insecure DH parameters that are not prime numbers. In the TLS protocol, it is the server that chooses DH parameters. Thus, a malicious server can choose them in such a way that the DHE key exchange can be easily broken. The ECDHE key exchange, an elliptic curve variant of DHE, cannot be broken because no TLS implementation supports arbitrary DH parameters (as is the case with DHE). Instead, ECDHE relies on *named curves*, which are known good sets of parameters.

## Step 2: Full Synchronization

The attacker can't attack renegotiation just yet because each connection has a different client verify_data value. Why? Because the server certificates differ: the first connection sees that attacking hostname's certificate, whereas the second connection sees the certificate of the target web server.

There's nothing the attacker can do for that first connection, but in the next step she can take advantage of the session resumption mechanism and its abbreviated handshake. When a session is resumed, there is no authentication; the assumption is that the knowledge of the master key is sufficient to authenticate the two parties.

But, when the session resumes, the only elements that were different in the first connection (the certificates) are not required any more. Thus, when the handshake completes, the Finished messages on both connections will be the same!

Figure 7.9. Triple handshake attack: full TLS connection synchronization

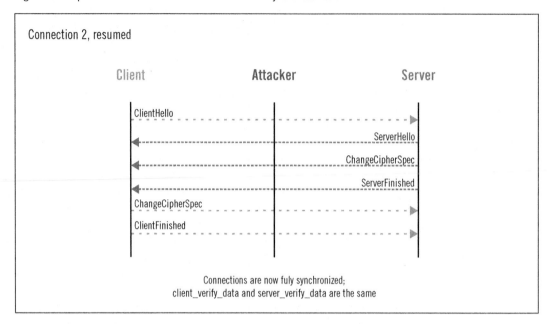

## Step 3: Impersonation

The attacker can now proceed to trigger renegotiation in order to force the use of the victim's client certificate, leading to impersonation. She is in full control of both connections and can send arbitrary application data either way. On the target web server, she navigates to a resource that requires authentication. In response, the target server requests renegotiation and a client certificate during the subsequent handshake. Because the security parameters are now identical on both connections, the attacker can just mirror the protocol messages, leaving the victim and the target server to negotiate new connection parameters. Except that this time the client will authenticate with a client certificate. At that point, the attack is successful.

Figure 7.10. Triple handshake: impersonation

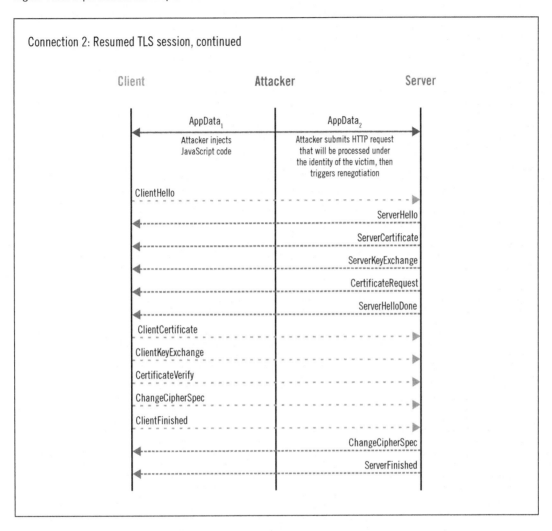

After renegotiation, the malicious server loses traffic visibility, although it still stays in the middle and continues to mirror encrypted data until either side terminates the connection.

## Impact

The triple handshake attack demonstrates how a supposedly secure TLS connection can be compromised. Application data sent to the target server before renegotiation comes from the attacker, the data sent after renegotiation comes from the authenticated user, and yet for the server there is no difference. The exploitation opportunities are similar to those of the original insecure renegotiation vulnerability (described at the beginning of this chapter in the section called "Insecure Renegotiation "). The easiest exploit is to execute a request on the target web server under the identity of the victim. Think money transfers, for example.

However, this attack vector is not very easy to use. First, the attacker has to find suitable entry points in the application and design specific payloads for each. Second, after renegotiation she loses traffic visibility and thus can't see the results of the attack or perform further attacks on the same connection. She can perform another attack, but doing so at the TLS level is going to be frustrating and slow.

There is another, potentially more dangerous, attack vector. Because the attacker can send arbitrary data to either connection before renegotiation, she has full control over the victim's browser. The victim is on *her web site*, after all. This allows the attacker to inject JavaScript malware into the browser. After renegotiation and authentication, the malware can submit unlimited background HTTP requests to the target server—all under the identity of the victim—and freely observe the responses.

Normally, browsers do not allow one web site to submit arbitrary requests to other sites. In this case, all communication is carried out in the context of the attacker's site. Behind the scenes they are routed to the target web site, but, as far as the browser is concerned, it's all one web site.

This second attack vector is effectively a form of phishing, with the triple handshake component required in order to subvert client certificate authentication. It's a much more powerful form of attack, limited only by the programming skills of the attacker and her ability to keep the victim on the web site for as long as possible.

## Prerequisites

The triple handshake attack is quite complex and works only under some very specific circumstances. Two aspects need to align before the weaknesses can be exploited.

The first is that it can be used only against sites that use client certificates. Take away that and there can be no impersonation. The second aspect is more intriguing. The attack is a form of phishing; the victims must be willing to use their client certificates on a site where they are not normally used. I would love to say that this is unlikely to happen, but the opposite is probably true.

When it comes to getting the victim to the rogue web server, it's always possible to use social engineering or email, like all other phishing attacks. Given the attacker's position (MITM), he can also redirect any plaintext HTTP request to the site. However, that might create suspicions from the user, who will unexpectedly arrive at an unknown web site.

Given that few sites use client certificates, the applicability of the triple handshake attack is not massive, unlike with the original insecure renegotiation problem. On the other hand, the sites that use client certificates are usually the more sensitive ones. This attack was never going to be used by petty criminals.

## Mitigation

The core vulnerabilities exploited by the triple handshake attack are in the protocol, and that makes TLS the best place to address the issue. Work is currently under way to tweak the protocol so that there is a stronger binding between a handshake and the master secret,[77] as well as a stronger binding on session resumption.[78]

In the short term, browser vendors reacted by tweaking their software to abort connections when they see a different certificate after renegotiation. Similarly, degenerate DH public keys are no longer accepted. Of course, these mitigations are generally available only in the more recent browser versions; older Internet Explorer versions should be safe too, because Microsoft patches the system-wide libraries, not just their browser.

Despite the browser improvements, there are several remaining attack vectors that are exploitable under specific circumstances (when certificates are not used): SASL, PEAP, and Channel ID. These can't be addressed in any other way except with protocol changes.

If possible, I recommend that you undertake some server-side measures to further minimize the risk. The most recent browsers might not be exploitable, but there's always a long tail of users running old software, which could be attacked. Consider the following measures:

**Require client certificates for all access**

If a client certificate is required for all TLS connections to a site, then the attacker will need a certificate of her own to carry out the first part of the attack. Depending on how easy it is to obtain a client certificate, this fact alone might be sufficient to reduce the risk of the attack.

**Disable renegotiation**

A strong constraint on the attack is the fact that it requires renegotiation. However, renegotiation is often used only in combination with client certificates. For example, a site might allow anyone access to the homepage but use renegotiation to request a client certificate in a subdirectory. If this arrangement is changed so that renegotiation never takes place, there can be no attack.

**Enable only ECDHE suites**

ECDHE suites are not vulnerable to this attack. Given that all modern browsers support ECDHE suites, if the user base is small and does not use very old browsers (chiefly Android 2.x and IE on Windows XP) disabling the vulnerable key exchange

---

[77] TLS Session Hash and Extended Master Secret Extension [fsty.uk/b345] (Bhargavan et al., April 2014)

[78] TLS Resumption Indication Extension [fsty.uk/b346] (Bhargavan et al., April 2014)

methods (DHE and RSA) might be another good defense method. But this approach won't work with a diverse user base.

# Bullrun

*Bullrun* (or *BULLRUN*) is the codename for a classified program run by the United States *National Security Agency* (NSA). Its purpose is to break encrypted communication by any means possible. Probably the most successful approach taken is, simply, computer hacking. If you can obtain a server's private key by hacking into it, there is no reason to attack encryption. More interesting for us, however, is that one of the means is weakening of products and security standards. This is a statement from a budget proposal from a leaked confidential document:[79]

> *Influence policies, standards and specification for commercial public key technologies.*

According to The New York Times, the NSA has about $250 million a year to spend on these activities. British GCHQ apparently has its own program for similar activities, codenamed *Edgehill.*[80]

TLS, one of the major security protocols, is an obvious target of this program. The public disclosure of Bullrun has caused many to view standards development in a completely different light. How can we trust the standards if we don't trust the people who design them?

## Dual Elliptic Curve Deterministic Random Bit Generator

*Dual Elliptic Curve Deterministic Random Bit Generator* (Dual EC DRBG) is a *pseudorandom number generator* (PRNG) algorithm standardized by the *International Organization for Standardization* (ISO) in ISO 18031 in 2005 and the United States *National Institute of Standards and Technology* (NIST) in 2006.[81]

In 2007, two researchers discussed a possible backdoor in this algorithm,[82] but their discovery received little attention.

When the Bullrun program came to light in September 2013, Dual EC DRBG was implicated as an NSA backdoor. In the same month, NIST issued a bulletin denouncing their own algorithm:[83]

---

[79] Secret Documents Reveal N.S.A. Campaign Against Encryption [fsty.uk/b347] (The New York Times, 5 September 2013)

[80] Revealed: how US and UK spy agencies defeat internet privacy and security [fsty.uk/b348] (The Guardian, 6 September 2013)

[81] Dual_EC_DRBG [fsty.uk/b349] (Wikipedia, retrieved 3 April 2014)

[82] On the Possibility of a Back Door in the NIST SP800-90 Dual Ec Prng [fsty.uk/b350] (Shumow and Ferguson, August 2007)

[83] SUPPLEMENTAL ITL BULLETIN FOR SEPTEMBER 2013 [fsty.uk/b351] (NIST, September 2013)

*NIST strongly recommends that, pending the resolution of the security concerns and the re-issuance of SP 800-90A, the Dual_EC_DRBG, as specified in the January 2012 version of SP 800-90A, no longer be used.*

In 2013, Reuters wrote about a $10 million payment from the NSA to RSA Security, Inc., leading to the RSA adopting Dual EC DRBG as the default PRNG in their TLS implementation, BSAFE.[84] Many other TLS implementations offered Dual EC DRBG as an option (most likely because it was required for the FIPS 140-2 validation), but as far as we know none used it by default. The implementation in OpenSSL was found to be faulty and thus unusable.[85]

How does this affect TLS, you may ask? In cryptography, all security depends on the quality of the data produced by the PRNG in use. Historically, we've seen many implementations fail at this point, as discussed in the section called "Random Number Generation" in Chapter 6. If you can break someone's PRNG, chances are you can break everything else. The TLS protocol requires client and server to send 28 bytes of random data each as part of the handshake; this data is used to generate the master secret, which is used to protect the entire TLS session. If you can backdoor the PRNG implementation, those 28 bytes might be enough to reveal the internal state of the generator and thus help substantially with breaking the TLS session.

In 2014, researchers demonstrated that Dual EC DRBG could, indeed, be backdoored,[86] although they couldn't offer proof that a backdoor existed. At the same time, they discovered that a nonstandard TLS extension, written at the request of the NSA, had been implemented in BSAFE to expose more data from the PRNG on a TLS connection.[87]

With more random data exposed to the attacker, it becomes up to 65,000 times easier to break TLS connections.

---

[84] Exclusive: Secret contract tied NSA and security industry pioneer [fsty.uk/b352] (Reuters, 20 December 2013)

[85] Flaw in Dual EC DRBG (no, not that one) (Steve Marquess, 19 December 2013)

[86] On the Practical Exploitability of Dual EC in TLS Implementations [fsty.uk/b353] (Checkoway et al., 2014)

[87] Extended Random [fsty.uk/b354] (projectbullrun.org, retrieved 16 July 2014)

# 8 Deployment

After several chapters of theory and background information, this chapter is where it all comes together; it gives you advice—everything you should know, at a high level—for deploying TLS servers securely. In many ways, this chapter is the map for the entire book. As you read through each section, refer to earlier chapters for more information on a particular topic. After you're satisfied that you have all the information you need, refer to the later chapters for practical configuration advice for your platform of choice.

This chapter is best read along with the next one about performance. Although the advice here takes performance into consideration, the next chapter provides a much greater level of detail, as well as further advice that could be used by those sites that want to be as fast as possible.

## Key

Private keys are the cornerstone of TLS security. With appropriately selected key algorithm and size, TLS will provide strong authentication over a period of many years. But, despite our focus on the numbers ("the bigger the better"), the weakest link is key management, or the job of keeping the private keys private.

### Key Algorithm

There are three key algorithms supported for use in TLS today, but only one of them—RSA —is practical. DSA has been long abandoned, and ECDSA is the algorithm that we will be deploying more widely in the following years.

**DSA**

DSA is easy to rule out: due to the fact that DSA keys are limited to 1,024 bits (Internet Explorer does not support anything stronger), they're impossible to deploy securely. On top of that, no one uses DSA keys for TLS anyway; going against everyone could potentially expose you to unforeseen interoperability issues.

### RSA

The easy choice is to use RSA keys because they are universally supported and currently used by virtually all TLS deployments. But, at 2,048 bits, which is the current minimum, RSA keys offer less security and worse performance than ECDSA keys. There is also the issue that RSA keys don't scale well with size increase. If you decide that 2,048-bit RSA keys are not sufficiently strong, moving to, say, 3,072-bit RSA keys would result in a substantial performance degradation.

### ECDSA

ECDSA is the algorithm of the future. A 256-bit ECDSA key provides 128 bits of security versus only 112 bits of a 2,048-bit RSA key. At these sizes, in addition to providing more security, ECDSA is also 2x faster. Compared at equivalent security, against a 3,072-bit RSA key, ECDSA is over 6x faster.

Because elliptic curve (EC) cryptography is a relatively recent addition to the TLS ecosystem, ECDSA is at a disadvantage because not all user agents support this algorithm. Modern browsers support it, but older user agents don't. You can work around this by deploying RSA and ECDSA keys simultaneously, except that not all server platforms support this option. Additionally, it's more work to maintain two sets of keys and certificates. For this reason, ECDSA keys are today best used if you want to squeeze the best possible performance out of your TLS servers. In the future, as we require more security, ECDSA will become more relevant.

## Key Size

When it comes to key size, most deployments will be satisfied with 2,048-bit RSA keys or 256-bit ECDSA keys. They provide security of 112 and 128 bits, respectively. That said, most deployments can afford to stay at the lower end of key sizes because even the weaker keys are sufficient for their needs.

If you require long-term protection, you should use keys that provide at least 128 bits of security. At that level, 256-bit ECDSA keys fit the bill and perform well. With RSA, you'd have to use 3,072-bit keys, which are much slower. If the performance degradation is not acceptable (e.g., you operate in a commercial environment), dual-key deployment might be a good compromise: use stronger ECDSA keys with modern browsers (and hopefully the majority of your user base) and weaker RSA keys with everyone else. Otherwise, accept the performance penalty.

> ### Warning
>
> If you are currently using keys that provide less than 112 bits of security (e.g. 1,024-bit RSA keys or weaker), replace them as a matter of urgency. They are insecure. This is especially true for 512- and 768-bit RSA keys, which can be broken with ac-

> cess to modest resources. It is estimated that breaking 1,024-bit RSA keys costs only $1m.

Consider the following when selecting key sizes: (1) is your choice secure today, (2) will it be secure when the key is retired, and (3) how long do you want your secrets to stay private after you retire the keys.

# Key Management

While we spend most time obsessing about key size, issues surrounding key management are more likely to have a real impact on your security. There is ample evidence to suggest that the most successful attacks bypass encryption rather than break it. If someone can break into your server and steal the private key, or otherwise compel you to disclose the key, why would they bother with brute-force attacks against cryptography?

**Keep your private keys private**
> Treat your private keys as an important asset, restricting access to the smallest possible group of employees while still keeping the arrangements practical. Some CAs offer to generate private keys for you, but they should know better. The hint is in the name—private keys should stay private, without exception.

**Think about random number generation**
> The security of encryption keys depends on the quality of the random number generator (RNG) of the computer on which the keys are generated. Keys are often created on servers right after installation and rebooting, but, at that point, the server might not have sufficient entropy to generate a strong key. It's better to generate all your keys in one (off-line) location, where you can ensure that a strong RNG is in place.

**Password-protect the keys**
> Your keys should have a passphrase on them from the moment they are created. This helps reduce the attack surface if your backup system is compromised. It also helps prevent leakage of the key material when copying keys from one computer to another (directly or using USB sticks); it's getting increasingly difficult to impossible to safely delete data from modern file systems.

**Don't share keys among unrelated servers**
> Sharing keys is dangerous; if one system is broken into, its compromised key could be used to attack other systems that use the same key, even if they use different certificates. Different keys allow you to establish strong internal access controls, giving access to the keys only to those who need them.

**Change keys frequently**
> Treat private keys as a liability. Keep track of when the keys were created to ensure they don't remain in use for too long. You must change them after a security incident

and when a key member of your staff leaves, and should change them when obtaining a new certificate. When you generate a new key, you wipe the slate clean. This is especially true for systems that do not use or support forward secrecy. In this case, your key can be used to decrypt all previous communication, if your adversary has it recorded. By deleting the key safely, you ensure that it can't be used against you. Your default should be to change keys yearly. Systems with valuable assets that do not use forward secrecy (which is not advisable) should have their keys changed more often, for example quarterly.

**Store keys safely**

Keep a copy of your keys in a safe location. Losing a server key is not a big deal because you can always generate a new one, but it's a different story altogether with keys used for intermediate and private CAs, and keys that are used for pinning.

Generating and keeping private keys in tamper-resistant hardware is the safest approach you can take, if you can afford it. Such devices are known as *Hardware Storage Modules*, or HSMs. If you use one of those, private keys never leave the HSM and, in fact, can't be removed from the device. These days, HSMs are even available as a service.[1] If you care about your security enough to think about an HSM, the idea of using one in the cloud might seem unusual. That said, given what we know about high-tech spying,[2] even when deploying in-house it might still be challenging to find a manufacturer whom you trust not to have created a backdoor into the device. After all, you don't want to spend a lot of money on a device and only later find out that the keys can be extracted from it.

# Certificate

In this section I discuss the topics surrounding certificate selection. There's a variety of decisions to make, starting with what type of certificate to use, over hostname selection, to the choice of certificate authority.

## Certificate Type

There are three types of certificates: *domain validated* (DV), *organization validated* (OV), and *extended validation* (EV). The issuance of DV certificates is automated, which is why they are cheap. They should be your default choice. OV certificates require validation of the organization behind the domain name and contain identifying information. Despite that, browsers don't actually treat OV certificates differently nor they show any of the information embedded in them.

---

[1] AWS CloudHSM [fsty.uk/b355] (Amazon Web Services, retrieved 16 May 2014)

[2] Photos of an NSA "upgrade" factory show Cisco router getting implant [fsty.uk/b21] (Ars Technica, 14 May 2014)

EV certificates differ from DV and OV certificates in several ways: (1) validation procedures are standardized by the CAB Forum; (2) identifying information is displayed in browser chrome and highlighted in green; and (3) they are more likely checked for revocation. The security benefits are slight, but they provide better assurance to some better-educated users. This might be valuable, depending on the nature of the business.

## Certificate Hostnames

The main purpose of a certificate is to establish trust for the appropriate hostnames, allowing users smooth secure access. On the Web, users are often confused by needless certificate name mismatch warnings. This problem usually arises from the use of certificates that are valid for only one of the two name variants; for example *www.example.com*, but not for *example.com*.

To avoid such issues follow this simple rule: if there is a DNS entry pointing to your TLS server, ensure that the certificate covers it. We can't control what others are typing in their browser URL bars, or how they link to our sites. The only way to be sure is to have certificates with appropriate name coverage. In my experience, some CAs automatically issue certificates that cover both variants, but there is still a number of CAs who don't.

> **Note**
>
> Another frequently seen problem comes from hosting plaintext web sites on the same IP address on which port 443 is used for some other secure web site. Someone who arrives at your plaintext web site using the https:// prefix will not only get a certificate warning due to the name mismatch, but will also be surprised to see some other content there. This problem is best avoided by closing the port 443 on the IP addresses used only for plaintext web sites.

## Certificate Sharing

There are two ways in which a certificate can be shared. First, you can get one that lists all desired hostnames (e.g., *www.example.com*, *example.com* and *blog.example.com*). Alternatively, you can get a wildcard certificate that's valid for any number of subdomains (e.g., by getting a certificate for the names *\*.example.com* and *example.com*).

Certificate sharing has the advantage of reducing maintenance costs and allowing you to use one IP address for multiple secure web sites. It's widely used by content delivery networks, who operate servers on behalf of others.

In principle, there is nothing wrong with this practice, but only if it doesn't reduce your security. However, that's usually the case. Speaking strictly about encryption, to share a certificate you also have to share the underlying private key. This means that certificate sharing is not appropriate for sites operated by multiple teams or unrelated web sites. If one of the sites is attacked, the compromised private key can be used to attack other sites from the group. Further, after a compromise, all servers from the group will have to be reconfigured to use the new key material.

More importantly, certificate sharing creates a bond at the application level; a vulnerability in one site can be exploited to attack all other sites from the same certificate. For this reason, this practice is best avoided. The same problem occurs if TLS session information is shared among unrelated servers. You'll find a more thorough discussion of this problem in the section called "Virtual Host Confusion" in Chapter 6.

## Signature Algorithm

To prove that a certificate is valid the issuing CA attaches a signature to it. Digital signatures typically depend on the security of two components: one is the size of the CA's private key; the other, the strength of the hashing function. Although the private keys used for certificate issuance tend to be sufficiently strong, the most commonly used hashing function—SHA1— is weak. Although it was designed to provide 80 bits of security, it's currently thought to offer only 61 bits.

After the debacle with MD5 certificate signatures, which were spectacularly broken in 2009, this time the industry appears to be moving away from SHA1 in a timely fashion. In 2013, Microsoft decreed that they will not accept SHA1 certificates after 2016 at the latest.[3] CAs are currently in the process of moving toward using SHA256 as their default hashing function for certificate signatures.

For your new certificates, you should aim to use SHA256. Because this is not something you can request via a CSR, you'll need to check with your CA in advance. Your existing SHA1 certificates can remain in use until they expire, unless the date is after 2016; in that case, you'll have to replace them sooner or later. At this time, it's better for interoperability to avoid SHA384 or stronger hashing functions; they might not be supported on all platforms.

> **Note**
>
> Whenever new cryptographic primitives are deployed, we have to deal with older platforms that do not support them. In the case of SHA256, the biggest problems seem to be with Windows XP users who have not yet upgraded to SP3.[4]

## Certificate Chain

Although we tend to talk about valid server certificates, in reality we configure TLS servers with *certificate chains*. A chain is an ordered list of certificates that lead to a trusted root. A

---

[3] SHA1 Deprecation Policy [fsty.uk/b356] (Windows PKI blog, 12 November 2013)

[4] SHA-256 certificates are coming [fsty.uk/b357] (Adam Langley, 14 May 2014)

common problem is to see servers whose chains are incomplete and thus invalid. According to SSL Pulse, there were 5.9% such servers in July 2014.[5]

Some user agents know how to reconstruct an incomplete chain. Two approaches are common: (1) all intermediate CA certificates are cached and (2) user agents retrieve the missing certificates following the parent certificate information that's usually embedded in every certificate. Neither of these approaches is reliable. The latter is also slow because the users have to wait until the missing certificates are retrieved from the CAs' web sites.

It's also common to see certificates delivered in incorrect order, which is technically invalid. In practice, almost all user agents know how to reorder certificates to fix the chain. For best results, ensure that your certificate chains are valid and that the order is correct.

Although intermediate certificates are usually valid for longer, they expire, too. If you're installing a new certificate it's recommended to replace all certificates, even if you're staying with the same CA. This practice will help you avoid problems with expired intermediate certificates.

For best performance, your chains should contain the right number of certificates; no more and no less. Extra certificates (e.g., the root, which is never needed) slow down the TLS handshake. However, there can be a question of *which* chain is correct. Multiple trust paths sometimes exist for historical reasons. For example, a new CA can get their root into modern browsers, but, to support older clients, they have their root key cross-signed by another (better-established) CA. In this case you don't want to "optimize" your chain to be the shortest possible. The shorter chain would work only in newer browsers, but fail in older devices.

# Revocation

A certificate can and should include two types of revocation information: CRL and OCSP. It's possible that a certificate does not include some of the required information, but it's rare. Nevertheless, you should still check.

It's more important that your CA provides a reliable and fast OCSP responder service. After all, every time your users connect to your web site, they'll be connecting to the CA's site as well. For best results and reliability, deploy OCSP stapling, which allows you to deliver OCSP responses directly from your own server, avoiding potential performance, availability, and privacy issues.

# Choosing the Right Certificate Authority

For a small site that needs only a simple DV certificate, virtually any CA will suffice. You can do what I do—just buy the cheapest certificate you can find. After all, any public CA can

---

[5] SSL Pulse [fsty.uk/b70] (SSL Labs, retrieved 17 July 2014)

issue a certificate for your web site without asking you; what's the point of paying more? But, if you need a certificate for something important, take your time and select carefully to ensure the CA meets your needs. With some advanced techniques such as pinning, by selecting a CA you are making a long-term commitment.

**Service**

At the end of the day, it's all about the service. The certificate business is getting more complicated by the day. If you don't have experts on your staff, perhaps you should work with a CA on which you can rely. Costs matter, but so do the management interfaces and the quality of the support.

**Reach**

If you have a large and diverse user base, you need a CA with widely trusted roots. The older CAs—who have had a lot of time to embed their roots in various trust stores—have a clear advantage here, but a young CA with a root cross-signed by a better-established CA could do just fine. It's best to check: (1) make a list of platforms that are important for you; (2) ask the candidate CAs to document their trust store placement; (3) ensure that the support is available where you need it. Finally, test some of those key platforms against a test certificate and see for yourself. Remember that it is not only important what platforms are supported today, but when exactly the support had been added. There are plenty of devices that do not update their trust stores.

**Quick adoption of new technologies**

Some CAs are in the business of shifting certificates; others shape and lead the industry. You should generally work with the CAs who are leading in adoption of new technologies and migration away from the weak old ones. Today, look for a CA who issues SHA256 certificates by default, provides good OCSP responder service, and has a plan to support pinning and *Certificate Transparency*.

**Security**

Clearly, a CA's ability to run their business securely is an important criterion. But how do you judge security? All CAs go through audits and are thus nominally equally secure, but we know from the past that they are not equal. The best approach is to look for evidence of good security posture.

## Self-Signed Certificates and Private CAs

Although this section assumes that you'll be getting a certificate from a publicly trusted CA, you can just as well decide to use a self-signed certificate. You could also create your own private CA and use it to issue certificates for all your servers. All three approaches have their place.

For public web sites, the only safe approach is to use certificates from a public CA.

Self-signed certificates are the least useful of the three. Firefox makes it easier to use them safely; you create an exception on the first visit, after which the self-signed certificate is treated as valid on subsequent connections. Other browsers make you click-through a certificate warning every time.[6] Unless you're actually checking the certificate fingerprint every time, it is not possible to make that self-signed certificate safe. Even with Firefox, it might be difficult to use self-signed certificates safely. Ask yourself this: what will the members of your group do if they encounter a certificate warning on a site where they previously accepted a self-signed certificate? Would they check with you to confirm that the certificate had been changed, or would they click through?

In virtually all cases, a much better approach is to use a private CA. It requires a little more work upfront, but once the infrastructure is in place and the root key is safely distributed to all users, such deployments are as secure as the rest of the PKI ecosystem.

# Protocol Configuration

When it comes to protocol configuration, your choices are likely to be influenced by a combination of security and interoperability requirements. In the ideal world, just on security alone, you would allow only TLS 1.2 and disable all other protocol versions. But such approach can work only for small groups and tightly-controlled environments—although modern browsers support TLS 1.2, many other products and tools don't.

A web site intended for public use needs to support TLS 1.0, TLS 1.1, and TLS 1.2. SSL 2 is obsolete and insecure. SSL 3 is obsolete and, although not obviously insecure, lacks support for many important features available only in newer protocol versions. Virtually all clients support at least TLS 1.0. I recommend that you disable SSL 3, unless you have a very good reason not to. If in doubt, record the connection parameters of your visitors to check. (Monitoring TLS operations is always a good idea.)

---

[6] That said, it's usually possible to bypass the browser user interface and import the self-signed certificate directly into the underlying trusted certificate store. With this, you achieve the same effect as with Firefox exceptions, except that more work is required and there's more room for mistakes.

**Note**

Older protocol versions are of concern because most browsers can be forced to downgrade to the oldest (and worst) protocol they support. By doing this, an active network attacker can disable advanced protocol features and indirectly influence cipher suite selection. I discuss this in the next section.

# Cipher Suite Configuration

In this section I discuss several aspects that influence cipher suite configuration: encryption strength, long-term security, performance and interoperability.

## Server cipher suite preference

Enforcing server cipher suite preference is vital to achieving best security with a variety of clients. Cipher suite selection takes place during the TLS handshake; because TLS enforces handshake integrity, there is no danger that an active network attacker can force some connections to use a weaker suite by attacking the protocol directly.

That doesn't mean that you should offer insecure suites, however. The same active network attacker could force a browser (but generally not other types of clients, for example command-line utilities) to voluntarily downgrade the protocol version. In most cases that means downgrading to SSL 3, which implies no authenticated suites, no EC cryptography, and sometimes not even AES.

## Cipher Strength

Use strong ciphers that provide 128 bits of security. Although AES and CAMELLIA both fit this description, AES has a strong advantage because it can be used with authenticated (GCM) suites that are supported by modern user agents. Authenticated suites are the best TLS can offer; using them you avoid the inherently unsafe (although not necessarily practically exploitable) CBC suites. For example, the NSA Suite B cryptography, which defines security policies for national security applications, recommends using only GCM suites with TLS.[7]

## Forward Secrecy

Do not use the RSA key exchange, which does not provide forward secrecy. Instead, look for the string ECDHE or DHE in the cipher suite name. Don't be confused by the fact that RSA can be used for key exchange and authentication; there is nothing wrong with the latter. For as

---

[7] RFC 6460: Suite B Profile for TLS [fsty.uk/b358] (M. Salter and R. Housley, January 2012)

long as you continue to use RSA keys, the string RSA will remain in the suite name. For performance reasons (more about that in the next chapter), prefer ECDHE suites over DHE.

With forward secrecy, every connection to your site is individually protected, using a different key. Without forward secrecy, the security of *all connections* effectively depends on the server's private key. If that key is ever broken or stolen, all previous communication can be decrypted. This is a huge liability that can be trivially fixed by adjusting configuration. In fact, this is so important that future TLS versions are expected to support only suites that provide forward secrecy.

For ECDHE, the secp256r1 curve will provide 128 bits of security for the key exchange. There is little choice at the moment when it comes to named curve selection. However, new curves are being added, along with mechanisms (e.g., in OpenSSL) to choose the best curve supported by the client. Once those become available, you should prefer the newer curves with clients that support them.

For DHE, most servers continue to use DH parameters of 1,024 bits, which provide about 80 bits of security. In general, given that with forward security each connection has its own key, 80 bits might be sufficient for sites that don't have security as a priority. Everyone else should generally use DH parameters that match the strength of the server private key. For most sites, that will be 2,048 bits. That said, if you prioritize ECDHE, which most modern clients support, the DHE key exchange will be used only with older clients.

When configuring DHE strength, you have the option to generate your own parameters of desired strength, but you can also use the standardized groups recommended by RFC 3526.[8]

# Performance

The good news is that GCM suites are also the fastest, which means that you don't have to choose between security and speed. Although AES and CAMELLIA are of similar speeds when implemented in software, AES again has an advantage because modern processors accelerate it with a special instruction set; it ends being much faster in practice. In addition, hardware-accelerate AES is though to be more resistant to cache timing attacks.

Avoid CBC suites that use SHA256 and SHA384 for integrity validation. They are much slower with no clear security benefits over SHA1. But don't be confused with the fact that GCM suites also have SHA256 and SHA384 in their names; authenticated suites work differently and aren't slow.

For the ECDHE key exchange, use the secp256r1 curve, which provides 128 bits of security and best performance. Always prefer ECDHE over DHE; the latter is slower even at the commonly-used and not very secure 1,024 bits. It's much slower at 2,048 bits.

---

[8] RFC 3526: More MODP Diffie-Hellman groups for IKE [fsty.uk/b359] (T. Kivinen and M. Kojo, May 2003)

## Interoperability

The key to interoperability is supporting a wide selection of suites. TLS clients come in all shapes and sizes and you don't want to needlessly refuse access to some of them. If you follow the recommendations here and enforce server cipher suite preference, you are going to negotiate your preferred suites with most clients. The remaining, less-wanted, suites will be used only by old clients that don't support anything better. Here are some examples:

- Some very old clients might support only 3DES and RC4.[9] The latter is insecure and shouldn't be used but 3DES, which provides 112 bits of security, is still acceptable for legacy applications.

- By default, Java clients do not support 256-bit suites.

- Java, before version 8, could not support DHE parameters over 1,024 bits. This should not be a problem for Java 7, because it supports ECDHE suites: by giving higher priority to ECDHE you can ensure that DHE is never attempted. If you need to support Java 6 clients, you must choose between no forward secrecy (using the RSA key exchange) and forward secrecy with DH parameters of 1,024 bits. The latter is preferable.

- For the ECDHE key exchange, only two named curves are widely supported: secp256r1 and secp384r1. If you use some other curves you might end up not negotiating any ECDHE suites with some clients (e.g., Internet Explorer).

# Server Configuration and Architecture

The only way to achieve strong overall security is to ensure that each individual system component is secure. Best practices such as disabling unnecessary services, regular patching, and strict access controls all apply. There is plenty of good literature on this subject. Complex architectures introduce their own challenges. Special care is needed—ideally during the design phase—to ensure that scaling up doesn't introduce new weaknesses.

## Shared Environments

Shared environments don't go well with security. Shared hosting, in particular, shouldn't be used by any business that operates encryption. There are many attack vectors via the filesystem or direct memory access that could result in private key compromise. Shared virtual servers might be similarly unacceptable, depending on your security requirements. Encryption is particularly tricky to get right when resources are shared among unrelated parties. Attacks sometimes depend on having very fast access to the target server (e.g., Lucky 13). In some cases (e.g., cache timing attacks), the prerequisite is access to the same CPU as the target server, which is possible in virtual environments.

---

[9] The Web is World-Wide, or who still needs RC4? [fsty.uk/b360] (John Graham-Cumming, 19 May 2014)

---

Infrastructure sharing is always a compromise between costs and convenience on one side and security on the other. I don't think you'll find it surprising that the best security requires exclusive hardware, strong physical security, and competent engineering and operational practices.

## Virtual Secure Hosting

Today, the widely accepted practice still is to use one IP address per secure server. The main reason for this is that virtual secure hosting (placing many unrelated secure servers on the same IP address) depends on a feature called *Server Name Indication* (SNI), which was added to TLS only in 2006. Because that was a rather late addition, many older products (e.g., early Android versions, older embedded devices, and Internet Explorer on Windows XP) don't support it. Sites that target a wide audience should therefore continue to use a separate IP address for each site.

That said, relying on SNI availability is on the verge of being practical. Sites that have a modern user base can already do it. I expect that, over the next several years, we'll see a rise in SNI-only sites. Support for Windows XP ended in 2014, and that's expected to encourage its users to migrate to more recent operating systems.

## Session Caching

Session caching is a performance optimization measure; client and server negotiate a master secret during their first connection and establish a session. Subsequent connections use the same master secret to reduce CPU costs and network latency. The increase of performance comes at the expense of reduced security: all connections that are part of the same session can be broken if the shared master secret is broken. However, because sessions typically last only for a limited time, the tradeoff is acceptable to most deployments.

I wouldn't advise disabling session caching, as that would seriously degrade server performance. For anything but the most secure sites, caching a session for up to a day is acceptable. On the other end, to maximize the benefits of forward secrecy, reduce the cache timeout to a shorter value, for example, one hour or less.

When session tickets are used, the security of all connections depends on the same ticket key. This is one area in which current server software doesn't provide adequate configuration controls. Most applications based on OpenSSL use implicit ticket keys that are created on server startup and never rotated. This could lead to the same key used for weeks and months, effectively disabling forward secrecy. Thus, if you're using session tickets, take care to regularly rotate ticket keys (e.g., daily). Twitter, for example, uses fresh keys every 12 hours and deletes old keys after 36 hours.[10]

# Complex Architectures

Usually, the most secure TLS deployment is that of a standalone server, which comes with well-defined security boundaries. Complex architectures, which involve many components and services spread among many servers, often introduce new weaknesses and attack points:

**Distributed session caching**

When a site is served by a cluster of servers, ensuring good performance through session caching is more difficult. There are typically two ways to address this problem: (1) use sticky load balancing, which ensures that the same client is always sent to the same cluster node,[11] or (2) share the TLS session cache among all the nodes in the cluster.

Session cache sharing has a security impact, because the attack surface is larger with the sessions stored on multiple machines. In addition, plaintext communication protocols are often used for backend session synchronization. This means that an attacker who infiltrates the backend network can easily record all master secrets.

**Session cache sharing**

Session cache sharing among unrelated applications increases the attack surface further; it creates a bond among the applications that can be exploited at the application level, in the same way that certificate sharing, discussed earlier, can. Your default approach should be to avoid session cache sharing unless it's necessary. This might not always be easy, as not all servers allow for strict cache separation. If using tickets, ensure that each server uses a different ticket key.

**SSL offloading and reverse proxies**

SSL offloading is a practice of terminating encryption at a separate architecture layer. This practice is dangerous, because, most often, the traffic from the proxy to the application is not encrypted. Although you might perceive that the internal network is secure, in practice this design decision creates a serious long-term attack vector that can be exploited by an attacker who infiltrates the network.

**Network traffic inspection**

The design of the RSA key exchange allows for network-level traffic inspection via private key sharing. It's typically done by intrusion detection and network monitoring tools that can passively decrypt encryption. In some environments, the ability to inspect all network traffic might be a high priority. However, this practice defeats for-

---

[10] Forward Secrecy at Twitter [fsty.uk/b361] (Jacob Hoffman-Andrews, 22 November 2013)

[11] This is usually done based on the source IP address. Some load balancers can also observe server-assigned session IDs and route based on their repeated use by clients.

---

ward secrecy, which potentially creates a much bigger long-term liability, because now the security of all traffic depends on the shared private key.

**Outsourced infrastructure**

Take special care when outsourcing critical components of your infrastructure to someone else. Cloud-based deployments are increasingly popular, but vendors often don't provide enough information about how their services are implemented. This could lead to unpleasant surprises. In 2014, a group of researchers analyzed the HTTPS implementations of content delivery networks and discovered that some failed to perform certificate validation.[12]

The best approach is to keep encryption under your complete control. For example, if using Amazon's Elastic Load Balancer to ensure high availability, configure it at the TCP level and terminate TLS at your nodes.

# Issue Mitigation

In recent years we saw a number of protocol attacks and other security issues that affect TLS. Some of those are easy to address, typically by patching. Others require a careful consideration of the involved risks so that an appropriate configuration can be deployed.

## Renegotiation

Insecure renegotiation is an old flaw from 2009 but a large number of systems still suffer from it. Patching should be sufficient to fix this problem. If you're not using client certificates, then disabling client-initiated renegotiation will make your systems safe. For the safety of others, you should support the new standard for secure renegotiation.

Servers that still support insecure renegotiation can be attacked with outcomes such as cross-site request forgery (user impersonation), information leakage, and cross-site scripting. Exploitation is easy, with tools readily available.

## BEAST (HTTP)

BEAST is a 2011 attack against CBC suites in TLS 1.0 and earlier protocol versions, which rely on predictable initialization vectors for block ciphers. This attack is a client-side issue that can be used only against browsers, but not against non-interactive tools. All modern browsers deploy mitigation measures, but users with older browsers (and older versions of Java, which are needed for the exploit to work) might still be vulnerable. Although newer

---

[12] When HTTPS Meets CDN: A Case of Authentication in Delegated Service [fsty.uk/b362] (Liang et al., IEEE Symposium on Security and Privacy, 2014)

protocols (TLS 1.1 onwards) are not vulnerable to BEAST, they are not supported by those older vulnerable browsers. BEAST is relatively easy to execute and can be used to retrieve fragments of sensitive information (e.g., session cookies).

## CRIME (HTTP)

CRIME is a 2012 attack that exploits information leakage inherent in compression as used in TLS and earlier versions of the SPDY protocol. Like BEAST, CRIME can be used against browsers, but not against non-interactive tools. Also like BEAST, CRIME targets fragments of sensitive information stored in request headers (e.g., session cookies and passwords). Although a large number of servers still support TLS compression, there is little client-side support and the attack surface is small. Still, TLS compression should be disabled, typically by patching.

## Lucky 13

Lucky 13 is a 2013 attack against CBC suites. It uses statistical analysis and other optimization techniques to exploit very small timing differences that occur during block cipher operation. A successful attack requires close proximity to the target web server. Lucky 13 typically targets fragments of sensitive information, for example passwords.

As far as we know, the attacks have been addressed by implementing constant-time decryption in popular TLS libraries; ensuring you're running the patched versions everywhere is necessary to be safe against this attack. Despite that, CBC suites remain inherently vulnerable (i.e., difficult to implement correctly) and the problem might return again in the future. For complete safety, deploy authenticated encryption using GCM suites, which are available in TLS 1.2.

## RC4

In 2013, RC4 was found to exhibit many weaknesses that can be used to recover sensitive information, but only if the same information occurs in the same place across a great number of connections. RC4 has been exploited under controlled conditions, but the attacks are not practical yet. There have been rumors that better attacks are available, but no evidence so far. For this reason, you should avoid using RC4 unless you *really* need it. In some environments, RC4 could be the lesser evil when compared to BEAST and Lucky 13 attacks.

There are several attacks against RC4. One of the attacks can retrieve the first 256 bytes on an encrypted connection. The second attack can retrieve fragments of sensitive information from anywhere in the data stream.

## RC4 versus BEAST and Lucky 13

BEAST and Lucky 13 can be addressed by avoiding to use CBC suites and using a streaming cipher instead. Unfortunately, RC4, the only streaming cipher available in TLS, is also known to contain weaknesses. So what to do?

BEAST requires a lot of effort to exploit. Still, the attack is practical, if only against users with old and vulnerable software. BEAST is thus of limited use and, because of the high effort required, suitable only for targeted attacks. RC4 weaknesses have so far been exploited only in controlled environments. However, there is an expectation that attacks against RC4 will get better, whereas the number of users vulnerable to BEAST is going to continue to decline.

For most sites, the best approach is to ensure that they are running a TLS stack not vulnerable to Lucky 13 (in other words, patch) and focus on the future: use TLS 1.2 with GCM suites, don't use RC4 and don't worry about BEAST.

High profile sites with large and potentially vulnerable user bases might consider using RC4 as a way to mitigate the attacks against CBC. They should still use TLS 1.2 and GCM suites with modern browsers, but rely on RC4 with TLS 1.0 and older protocols.

# TIME and BREACH (HTTP)

TIME and BREACH are 2013 attacks that extend CRIME to attack HTTP compression. Unlike TLS compression, which was never widely deployed, HTTP compression is very useful and popular, and can't be disabled without performance and financial penalties. TIME was largely a conceptual attack, without any tools published. BREACH authors released the source code for their proof-of-concept, which means that this attack is easier to carry out. Both attacks require a lot of work to execute, which suggests that they are more suitable for use against specific targets, but not at scale. BREACH can be used to retrieve small fragments of sensitive data that appear anywhere in an HTML page, if compression is used.

Addressing BREACH requires more effort because its attack surface is at the application layer. There are two practical mitigation techniques that you should consider:

**Masking of sensitive tokens**

For sensitive tokens such as those used for CSRF defense and session management, the best defense is to use masking. BREACH requires that the sensitive string appears in an HTML page across many requests. An effective mitigation technique is to mask the original value so that it appears different every time, provided the process can be reversed. This approach requires extensive changes to application source code and might not be suitable for legacy applications. However, it's ideal for implementation in frameworks and libraries.

**Disable compression when referrer information is incorrect or unavailable**

Disabling compression prevents the attack, but that's too costly. However, an attack always comes from elsewhere and not from your own web site. This means that you can examine the referrer information and disable compression only when the attack is possible—when you see a request arriving from some other web site. In practice, you also have to disable compression when the referrer information is not available, which can happen for privacy reasons or if the attacker uses tricks to hide it. This mitigation technique is easy to deploy at web server level and requires no changes to the source code. There's only a very small performance penalty involved because compression will be disabled only on requests that arrive from other sites.

# Triple Handshake Attack

Triple Handshake Attack is a high-effort attack revealed in 2014. It can be used only against environments that use client certificates for authentication. This attack has similar consequences to insecure renegotiation, with some variations that make exploitation easier. In the short-term, the best mitigation is to use the latest versions of modern browsers, which have incorporated counter-defenses. The TLS protocol is currently being extended to address the underlying core issue.

# Heartbleed

Heartbleed is a vulnerability in OpenSSL, a widely deployed cryptographic library. It was discovered in April 2014. Although not a cryptographic issue in itself, Heartbleed can be devastating for the vulnerable server. Since the vulnerability was announced, a number of advanced exploitation techniques have been developed. Attack tools are readily available and can be used to retrieve server private keys very quickly.

Addressing this problem requires several steps: (1) first, patch the affected systems so that the vulnerability is addressed; (2) generate new private keys, obtain new certificates, and revoke the old certificates; (3) if using session ticket, change the ticket keys; (4) consider if other sensitive data might have existed in server memory and determine if further actions are necessary (e.g., user passwords were commonly found present; some web sites advised their users to change their passwords).

> **Warning**
>
> It's common to see servers patched for Heartbleed and with new certificates installed, but still using the same private keys. Such servers are still vulnerable because the private keys compromised before the patching can still be used by the attacker.

# Pinning

Public trust depends on hundreds of CAs who issue certificates to prove server legitimacy. Although this approach works well for average web sites that are unlikely to be attacked via certificate forgery, high-profile sites are left exposed because any CA can issue a certificate for any domain name. This problem can be fixed using a technique called *public key pinning*, which allows you to specify exactly which CAs are allowed to issue certificates for your domain names.

Pinning greatly reduces the attack surface for certificate forgery attacks but comes at a cost: it requires an effort to design a pinning strategy and operational maturity to carry it out. At this time, pinning is possible only via the proprietary mechanism embedded in Chrome. Several standards are currently in various stages of development: DANE (based on DNSSEC), Public Key Pinning for HTTP, and TACK.

# HTTP

Although SSL and TLS were designed so that they can secure any connection-oriented protocol, the immediate need was to protect HTTP. To this day, web site encryption remains the most common TLS use case. Over the years, the Web evolved from a simple document distribution system into a complex application delivery platform. This complexity creates additional attack vectors and requires more effort to secure.

## Making Full Use of Encryption

In HTTP, encryption is optional. As a result, many sites fail to use it even though it is genuinely necessary. In some cases by design, in others by omission. Many don't use encryption because it requires additional effort and expertise. Some justify lack of encryption citing performance reasons and costs. Browsers make the situation difficult by allowing secure and insecure resources to be mixed within the same HTML page.

The truth is that if you have anything of value online, you need encryption. And you need full encryption across the entire site because partial encryption is practically impossible to use securely. There are issues with cookie scope and user transitions between insecure and secure areas that can't be implemented securely. Mixed content issues—when insecure resources are requested from an otherwise secure page—can be used to achieve a complete security compromise.

For all these reasons, the best approach is to enforce encryption on the entire domain name, across all the applications you might have installed on the subdomains.

## Cookie Security

HTTP cookies that have not been declared as secure (a frequent programming error) can be retrieved by an active network attacker even in the extreme case when the web site in question does not operate in plaintext at all. During the quality assurance (QA) phase, pay special attention to cookie generation.

Further, due to the lax cookie specification, it is very easy for attackers to inject cookies into unsuspecting applications. This can be typically achieved from other applications that operate from a related subdomain (e.g., from *blog.example.com* into *www.example.com*), or even from a non-existent subdomain in an active network attack. Although no information can leak this way, a skilled attacker could use this approach for privilege escalation. For best security, deploy a cookie encryption or an integrity validation scheme. The former is better, but the latter can be used in the cases when cookie read access is needed from JavaScript.

## Backend Certificate and Hostname Validation

Many applications use HTTP for backend communication; this practice is very common in native, web, and mobile applications alike. Unfortunately, they suffer from a common failure where they don't validate certificates correctly, leaving them wide open to active network attacks. Your QA processes should include tests that check for failures in this area.

In most cases, all that's needed is to enable certificate checking in the underlying TLS library. In others, developers rely on low-level APIs that implement some generic certificate checks, but not the protocol-specific functionality, such as hostname checking. As a rule of thumb, low-level APIs should be avoided if there are higher-level alternatives available.

For best security, you should consider using public key pinning in your applications. Unlike with browsers, where you must wait on pinning to be standardized, in your own applications you have full control over the code. Pinning is easy to implement and significantly reduces the attack surface.

## HTTP Strict Transport Security

*HTTP Strict Transport Security* (HSTS) is a standard that allows web sites to request strict handling of encryption. Web sites signal their policies via an HTTP response header for enforcement in compliant browsers. Once HSTS is deployed, compliant browsers will switch to always using TLS when communicating with the web site. This addresses a number of issues that are otherwise difficult to enforce: (1) users who have plaintext bookmarks and follow plaintext links; (2) insecure cookies; (3) HTTPS stripping attacks; (4) mixed-content issues within the same site.

In addition, and perhaps more importantly, HSTS fixes handling of invalid certificates. Without HSTS, when browsers encounter invalid certificates they allow their users to proceed to the site. Most users can't differentiate between attacks and configuration issues and decide to proceed, which makes them susceptible to active network attacks. With HSTS, certificate validation failures are final and can't be bypassed. That brings TLS back to how it should have been implemented in the first place.

For best results, HSTS should be activated for the entire namespace of a particular domain name (e.g. for *example.com* and all subdomains).

# Content Security Policy

*Content Security Policy* (CSP) is a mechanism that allows web sites to control how resources embedded in HTML pages are retrieved and over what protocols. As with HSTS, web sites signal their policies via an HTTP response header for enforcement in compliant browsers. Although CSP was originally primarily designed as a way of combating XSS, it has an important application to web site encryption: it can be used to prevent third-party mixed content by rejecting plaintext links that might be present in the page.

# Protocol Downgrade Protection

Although TLS has protocol downgrade protections built-in, browsers make them ineffective by voluntarily downgrading on negotiation failures. This is arguably the biggest practical protocol flaw we have at the moment.

After months of discussion, Google adopted a proposal around using a special *fallback signaling suite* to inform servers of potential downgrade attacks. It's currently implemented in Chrome. To be fully effective, the mechanism must also be supported server-side. When the feature is eventually incorporated into libraries it will work transparently. In the meantime, it is also possible to implement it externally, via a protocol-parsing intrusion detection system.

# 9 Performance Optimization

People sometimes care about security, but they *always* care about speed; no one ever wanted their web site to be slower. Some of the motivation for increasing performance comes from our fascination with being fast. For example, there is a lot of anecdotal evidence that programmers are obsessed with performance, often needlessly and at expense of code quality. On the other hand, it is well documented that speed improvements increase revenue. In 2006, Google said that adding 0.5 seconds to their search results caused a 20% drop in traffic.[1] And Amazon said that an increase of 100 ms in latency costs them 1% in revenue.[2]

There is no doubt that TLS has a reputation for being slow. Most of it comes from the early days, when CPUs were much slower and only a few big sites could afford encryption. Not so today; computing power is no longer a bottleneck for TLS. In 2010, after Google enabled encryption on their email service by default, they famously stated that SSL/TLS is not computationally expensive any more:[3]

> On our production frontend machines, SSL/TLS accounts for less than 1% of the CPU load, less than 10KB of memory per connection and less than 2% of network overhead. Many people believe that SSL takes a lot of CPU time and we hope the above numbers (public for the first time) will help to dispel that.

This chapter is all about getting as close as possible to Google's performance numbers. A large part of the discussion is about latency reduction. Most of the techniques apply to any protocol (even when encryption is not used) but are especially important for TLS because of its increased connection setup costs. The rest is about using the least amount of CPU power possible to achieve desired security and making sure that user agents need to do as little work as possible to validate your certificates.

---

[1] Marissa Mayer at Web 2.0 [fsty.uk/b363] (Greg Linden, 9 November 2006)

[2] Make Data Useful [fsty.uk/b364] (Greg Linden, 28 November 2006)

[3] Overclocking SSL [fsty.uk/b365] (Adam Langley, 25 Jun 2010)

> **Note**
>
> In this chapter I focus on the performance profile of TLS, but there are many other potential gains elsewhere in the application stack. For a wider look at the topic of performance of web applications, I recommend Ilya Grigorik's book *High Performance Browser Networking*, published by O'Reilly in 2013. This book is freely available online.[4]

# Latency and Connection Management

The speed of network communication is shaped by two main factors: bandwidth and latency.[5] Bandwidth is a measure of how much data you can send in a unit of time. Latency describes the delay from when a message is sent until it is received on the other end. Of the two, bandwidth is the less interesting factor because you can generally always buy more of it. Latency can't be avoided because it's imposed on us by the speed limits at which data travels over network connections.

Latency is a big limiting factor whenever an interactive exchange of messages is required. In a typical request-response protocol, it takes some time for the request to reach its destination, and for the response to travel back. This measure, known as one *round-trip*, is how we measure latency.

For example, every TCP connection begins a setup phase called the *three-way handshake*: (1) client sends a SYN message to request a new connection; (2) server accepts with SYN ACK; (3) client confirms with ACK and starts sending data. It takes 1.5 round-trips for this handshake to complete. In practice, with *client-speaks-first* protocols such as HTTP and TLS, the actual latency is one round-trip, because the client can start sending data immediately after the ACK signal.

Latency has a particularly large impact on TLS, because it has its own elaborate handshake that adds two further round-trips to connection setup.

---

[4] High Performance Browser Networking [fsty.uk/b366] (Ilya Grigorik, retrieved 17 July 2014)

[5] What is Network Latency and Why Does It Matter? [fsty.uk/b367] (O3b Networks, retrieved 11 May 2014)

---

Figure 9.1. TCP and TLS handshake latencies

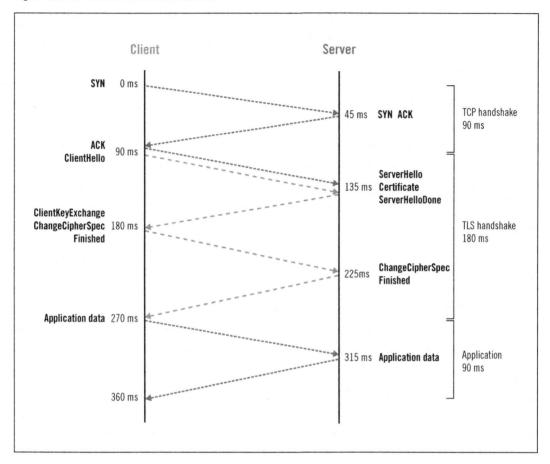

## TCP Optimization

Although a complete discussion of TCP optimization is out of the scope of this book, there are two tweaks that are so important and easy to use that everyone should know about them. Both are related to the *congestion control* mechanism built into TCP. At the beginning of a new connection, you don't know how fast the other side can go. If there is ample bandwidth, you can send data at the fastest possible rate, but what if you're dealing with a slow mobile connection? If you send too much data, you will overwhelm the link, leading to the connection breakdown. For this reason, a speed limit—known as a *congestion window*—is built into every TCP connection. This window is initially small, but grows over time with evidence of good performance. This mechanism is known as *slow start*.

This brings us to the ugly truth: all TCP connections start slow and increase speed over time until they reach their full potential. This is bad news for HTTP connections, which tend to be short; they almost always operate under suboptimal conditions.

The situation is even worse for TLS connections, which consume the precious initial connection bytes (when the congestion window is small) with TLS handshake messages. If the congestion window is big enough, then there will be no additional delay from slow start. If, however, it happens that there is a long handshake message that can't fit into the congestion window, the sender will have to split it into two chunks, send one chunk, wait for a response (one round-trip), increase the congestion window, and only then send the reminder. Later in this chapter, I will discuss several cases in which this situation can happen.

## Initial Congestion Window Tuning

The starting speed limit is known as the *initial congestion window* (initcwnd). If you are deploying on a modern platform, the limit will probably be already set at a high value. RFC 6928, which came out in April 2013,[6] recommended setting initcwnd to 10 network segments (about 15 KB) by default. The previous recommendation was to use two to four network segments as a starting point, which is 4.5 KB at best.

On older Linux platforms, you can change the initcwnd size for all your routes with:

```
# ip route | while read p; do ip route change $p initcwnd 10; done
```

## Preventing Slow Start When Idle

Another problem is that slow start can kick in on a connection that has not seen any traffic for some time, reducing its speed. And very quickly, too. The period of inactivity can be very small, for example, one second. This means that, by default, virtually every long-running connection (e.g., a HTTP connection that uses keep-alives) will be downgraded from fast to slow! For best results, this feature is best disabled.

On Linux, you can disable slow start due to inactivity with:

```
# sysctl -w net.ipv4.tcp_slow_start_after_idle=0
```

The setting can be made permanent by adding it to your /etc/sysctl.conf configuration.

# Connection Persistence

Most of the TLS performance impact is concentrated in the handshake, which takes place at the beginning of every connection. One important optimization technique is to reduce the number of connections used by keeping each connection open for as long as possible. With this, you minimize the TLS overhead and also improve the TCP performance. As we've seen in the previous section, the longer the TCP connection stays open, the faster it goes.

---

[6] RFC 6928: Increasing TCP's Initial Window [fsty.uk/b368] (Chu et al., April 2013)

In HTTP, most transactions tend to be very short, translating to short-lived connections. Although the standard originally didn't provide a way for a connection to stay open for a long time, *keep-alives* were added to HTTP/1.0 as an experimental feature and became enabled by default in HTTP/1.1.

Keeping many connections open for long periods of time can be challenging, because many web servers are not designed to handle this situation well. For example, Apache was initially developed to dedicate an entire *worker* (process or thread, depending on configuration) to one client. The problem with this approach is that slow clients can use up all the available workers and block the web server. Also, it's very easy for an attacker to open a large number of connections and send data very slowly, if at all.[7]

More recently, the trend has been to use event-driven web servers, which handle all communication by using a fixed thread pool (or even a single process), thus minimizing per-connection costs and reducing the chances of attack. Nginx is an example of a web server that was built from the start to operate in this way. Apache also started to use the event-driven model by default on platforms that support it.

The disadvantage of long-lived connections is that, after the last HTTP connection is complete, the server has to wait for a certain time (the *keep-alive timeout*) before the connection can be closed. Although any one connection won't consume too many resources, keeping connections open reduces the overall scalability of the server. The best case for keep-alives is with a client that sends a large number of requests in a burst. The worst case is when the client sends only one request and leaves the connection open but never submits another request.

### Warning

When deploying with long keep-alive timeouts, it's critical to limit the maximum number of concurrent connections so that the server is not overloaded. Tune the server by testing its operation at the edge of capacity. If TLS is handled by OpenSSL, make sure that the server is setting the SSL_MODE_RELEASE_BUFFERS flag correctly.[8]

It's difficult to recommend any one keep-alive timeout value, because different sites have different usage patterns. That said, 60 seconds is probably a good starting point. A better value can be selected on per-site basis by monitoring the user agent behavior.[9]

There is a limit to the maximum keep-alive timeout you can use, because user agents have their maximums, no matter what servers say. In my tests, Internet Explorer 11 on Windows

---

[7] Slowloris HTTP DoS [fsty.uk/b369] (RSnake et al., 17 June 2009)

[8] SSL_CTX_set_mode(3) [fsty.uk/b370] (OpenSSL, retrieved 6 July 2014)

[9] This can be done by recording the keep-alive status of each connection to the web server access log. The Apache and Nginx chapters both show how that can be done.

7 closed the connection after 30 seconds, Safari 7 after 60, and Chrome 35 after 300 seconds. As for Firefox 30, although the configuration states 115 seconds for the keep-alive timeout (the `network.http.keep-alive.timeout` in `about:config`), it seems that Firefox uses this value only with servers that don't explicitly state the desired timeout. With servers that do, Firefox is happy to stay connected until the server closes the connection.

## SPDY, HTTP 2.0, and Beyond

There is only so much we can achieve by tuning TCP and HTTP connection persistence alone. To go further, in 2009 Google started to experiment with a new protocol called SPDY. [10] The idea was to introduce a new protocol layer between TCP and HTTP to speed things up. Positioned in the middle, SPDY could improve HTTP connection management without actually making any changes to HTTP itself.

With SPDY, multiple HTTP requests and responses are multiplexed, which means that a browser only ever needs one connection per server. To achieve similar performance with HTTP alone, browsers have to use multiple connections in parallel. A single long-lived connection allows for much better TCP utilization and reduced server load.

SPDY was a great success, showing great performance improvements in a variety of situations. Perhaps most importantly, SPDY experiments led to an industry-wide effort to design HTTP 2.0[11] around the same concepts, waking up HTTP from deep sleep: the previous version, HTTP 1.1, was released in 1999.

Whereas HTTP 2.0 is still being developed, SPDY is practical to deploy. Client support is pretty good among modern browsers: Chrome and Firefox have supported it for a long time, Internet Explorer added support in 2013 (although only in version 11 running on Windows 8.1), and Apple announced that it will support SPDY in OS X Yosemite. On the server side, popular web serving platforms as Apache and Nginx either support or can be extended to support SPDY.

We should expect that SPDY and HTTP 2.0 will squeeze more performance out of TCP, but what next? One option is to try to improve the performance of TCP further. For example, TCP *Fast Open* is an optimization technique that removes one round-trip from the TCP handshake.[12] Alternatively, we can look at bypassing TCP altogether. Another experiment led by Google, called QUIC (*Quick UDP Internet Connections*),[13] is a new reliable connection protocol built on top of UDP that aims to improve both performance (with better connection management, congestion control, and packet loss handling) and security (by using

---

[10] SPDY [fsty.uk/b371] (The Chromium Projects, retrieved 27 June 2014)

[11] HTTP 2.0 [fsty.uk/b372] (Wikipedia, retrieved 27 June 2014)

[12] TCP Fast Open [fsty.uk/b373] (Wikipedia, retrieved 27 June 2014)

[13] QUIC [fsty.uk/b374] (Wikipedia, retrieved 27 June 2014)

encryption by default). QUIC is not yet production ready, but it's already supported by Chrome and Google's servers.

## Content Delivery Networks

If you maintain a web site that targets a global audience, you need to use a *content delivery network* (CDN) to achieve world-class performance. In a sentence, CDNs are geographically distributed servers that add value largely by offering edge caching and traffic optimization (often also called *WAN optimization*).

Most times, when you need to scale a web site, throwing money at the problem helps. If your database is dying under heavy load, you can buy a bigger server. If your site can't run on a single server, you can deploy a cluster. However, no amount of money can reduce network latency. The further away your users are from your servers, the slower your web site will be.

In such situations, connection setup is a big limiting factor. TCP connections start with a three-way handshake, which requires a round-trip to complete. Then there's the TLS handshake, which requires two additional round trips, bringing the total to three for HTTP.[14] That's about 90 ms for a nearby user who's about 30 ms away, but may be much more for someone who is on the other side of the world.

CDNs typically operate large numbers of geographically distributed servers, with the idea being to have servers as close to end users as possible. With that proximity, they typically reduce latency in two ways—edge caching and connection management.

**Edge caching**

Because CDNs place servers close to users, they can deliver your files to users as if your servers were right there. Some CDNs enable you to push your files to them; this approach offers the best control and performance, but it's more difficult to manage. Some other CDNs operate as reverse proxies (they retrieve files over HTTP when they need them and cache them locally for a period of time); they are not as optimized but are instead almost trivial to deploy.

**Connection management**

Caching is the best-case scenario for CDN deployment, but it's not suitable for all sites. If your content is dynamic and user specific, your servers will need to do the actual work. But a good CDN should be able to help, even without any caching, via connection management. This seems counterintuitive at first. How can traffic go faster through a CDN than it can if it goes directly to the origin server? The answer is

---

[14] The same latency applies to any client-speaks-first protocol. Latency for a *server-speaks-first* protocol is 2.5 round-trips, because the server can send application data immediately after its Finished message.

that a CDN can eliminate most of the connection setup cost by keeping connections open over long distances.

During connection setup, most of the time is spent waiting. You send a packet and wait for a response. When the other end is very far away, you wait for a long time. But when the other end is near, you get a quick response. To minimize the waiting, CDNs can route their traffic so that long distances are covered using their own servers. With full control over long network segments, their servers can keep connections open for a long time. If they use TCP, that means that there is no connection setup and that connections run at their maximum speed. But they can also use proprietary protocols and connection multiplexing for even better performance.

When a CDN is used, the user connects to the closest CDN node, which is only a short distance away. Because the distance is small, the TLS handshake will be fast—for example, 30 ms for a distance of 10 ms (one way). In the ideal case for a new TLS connection, the CDN can reuse existing connections that it keeps open, going from that node all the way to the final destination. That means that no further work is necessary; after the initial fast TLS handshake with the CDN, the user's connection with the server is effectively open and application data can begin to flow.

Of course, not all CDNs operate sophisticated internal networks that operate in this way; it's necessary to research the implementation details when deciding which CDN to use. Or, even better, test the actual performance.

Figure 9.2. TLS connection setup time comparison between direct traffic and a CDN with already open origin connections

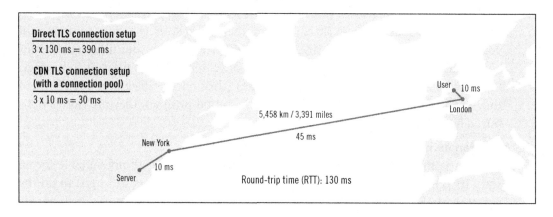

## Note

Not all CDNs are equal, especially when it comes to following best practices for TLS performance outlined in this chapter. Before you decide which CDN to use, make sure to check if they can serve TLS at the fastest possible speed. Ilya Grigorik maintains a handy chart on his web site dedicated to TLS performance. [15]

# TLS Protocol Optimization

With connection management out of the way, I'll now focus on the performance characteristics of TLS. The aim here is to understand how each aspect of TLS impacts performance, equipping you with the knowledge to tune the protocol for both security and speed.

## Key Exchange

After latency, the next biggest cost of using TLS comes from having to perform CPU-intensive cryptographic operations in order to securely agree on connection security parameters. This part of the communication is known as *key exchange*. Its cost is largely determined by the choice of server private key algorithm, key size, and the key exchange algorithm.

**Key size**

> To achieve security, cryptography relies on processes that are relatively fast with access to relevant keys but hugely expensive and time consuming otherwise. The effort required to break an encryption key depends on its size; the bigger the key, the better the protection. However, a bigger key also means longer encryption and decryption times. For best results, select a key size that provides the appropriate level of security but not anything over that.

**Key algorithm**

> There are two private key algorithms that you can use today: RSA and ECDSA.[16] RSA is still the dominating algorithm, largely because it was the only choice for a very long time. But RSA is starting to be too slow now that 2,048 bits is the minimum strength and many are considering deploying 3,072 bits of security in the near future. ECDSA is much faster and thus increasingly more attractive. At a modest size of 256 bits, ECDSA provides security equivalent to 3,072-bit RSA and better performance.

**Key exchange**

> In theory, you can choose from three key exchange algorithms: RSA, DHE, and ECDHE. But you don't want to use RSA because it does not provide forward secrecy. Of the remaining two, DHE is too slow; that leaves you with ECDHE.

> The performance of the DHE and ECDHE key exchanges depends on the strength of the configured negotiation parameters. For DHE, commonly seen parameter strengths are 1,024 and 2,048 bits, which provide 80 and 112 bits of security, respectively. As for ECDHE, the security and performance are influenced by the choice of named curve. The de facto standard `secp256r1` curve provides 128 bits of security.

---

[15] CDN & PaaS performance [fsty.uk/b375] (Is TLS Fast Yet?, retrieved 27 June 2014)

[16] Although the protocol includes many DSA (DSS) suites, there isn't wide support for using DSA keys at 2,048 and higher strengths. The maximum is 1,024 bits, which is insecure.

The only other practical choice is secp384r1, but this curve is about 30% slower server-side and doesn't provide a meaningful increase in security.

In practice, you can't freely combine key and key exchange algorithms. Instead, you can use the combinations specified by the protocol. There are four possibilities: RSA, DHE_RSA, ECDHE_RSA, and ECDHE_ECDSA. To understand the performance differences among these suites, I ran a test of all four choices using 2,048-bit RSA keys and 256-bit ECDSA keys. These key sizes are what you would expect to use for an average web site. The DHE key exchange was represented with two DH parameter strengths—1,024 and 2,048 bits. The ECDHE key exchange used the secp256r1 curve.

For the test, I used a dedicated Amazon EC2 m3.large instance, which has two Intel Xeon E5-2670 2.5 GHz processors. The test was run using a modification[17] of Vincent Bernat's tool for OpenSSL microbenchmarking.[18] I tested OpenSSL 1.0.1f that comes with Ubuntu 14.04 LTS. The tool runs on two threads (one for the client and another for the server), performs 1,000 TLS handshakes sequentially, and measures CPU consumption of each thread at the end. You can see the results in the following graph.

---

[17] ivanr / ssl-dos [fsty.uk/b376] (GitHub, retrieved 27 June 2014)
[18] SSL/TLS & Perfect Forward Secrecy [fsty.uk/b377] (Vincent Bernat, 28 November 2011)

---

Chapter 9: Performance Optimization

Figure 9.3. Performance comparison of TLS key exchange algorithms (lower is better)

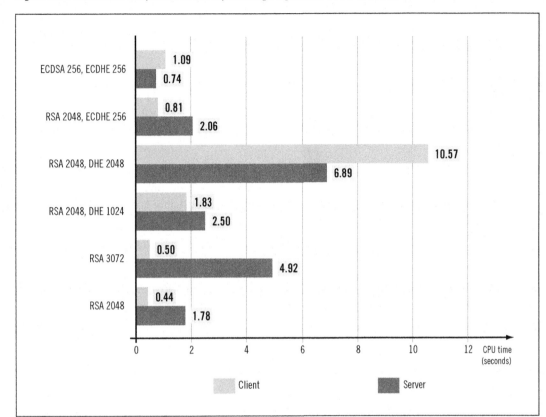

What can we conclude from the test results?

- The servers using RSA today could enable forward secrecy *and* improve their handshake performance by a factor of two by moving to the ECDHE key exchange and ECDSA keys.

- Enabling forward secrecy (using the ECDHE key exchange) while keeping RSA for authentication degrades the handshake performance slightly, but it's unlikely that there would be a measurable impact overall.

- The DHE key exchange is slower even with weak 1,024-bit parameters, but it's much slower when used with stronger 2,048-bit parameters. If you care about performance, DHE should be used only as a last resort. Because most modern clients support ECDHE, you can configure DHE suites with lower priority so that only old clients use them. Twitter reported that 75% of their clients use ECDHE,[19] which means that up to 25% might end up using the slower DHE.

---

[19] Forward Secrecy at Twitter [fsty.uk/b361] (Jacob Hoffman-Andrews, 22 November 2013)

Compared to ECDHE, the DHE key exchange also increases the size of the server side of the handshake by 320 to 450 bytes, depending on the strength of the parameters. This is because the ECDHE key exchange uses standardized parameters that are referenced by name, but the DHE key exchange requires the server to select the negotiation parameters and send them to the client every time.[20]

- Clients need to do more work when ECDHE and ECDSA are deployed, but that's not a problem, because they submit at most a few connections at any one time. Servers, on the other hand, have to handle hundreds and thousands of connections in parallel.

> **Note**
>
> The test results presented here should be used only as a guideline. They measure the performance of a particular version of OpenSSL that's used for both sides of the connection. In practice, TLS performance will vary across libraries, devices, and CPUs.

For a more detailed look at the key exchange performance, I recommend a study by Huang et al., who looked at the performance of forward secrecy deployments.[21] Another good source of information is Symantec's 2013 whitepaper that discusses the performance of EC cryptography.[22]

---

[20] I discuss the structure of the key exchange messages in the section called "Key Exchange " in Chapter 2.

[21] An Experimental Study of TLS Forward Secrecy Deployments [fsty.uk/b378] (Huang et al., 2014)

[22] Elliptic Curve Cryptography (ECC) Certificates Performance Analysis [fsty.uk/b379] (Kumar et al., 12 June 2013)

Chapter 9: Performance Optimization

# False Start

In 2010, Google proposed a modification to the TLS protocol with an aim to reduce the latency of the full handshake from two round-trips to only one round-trip.[23] Normally, a full TLS handshake requires two round-trips, consisting of four bursts of protocol messages (two for each client and server), and TLS allows sending of (encrypted) application data only after the handshake is fully complete. *False Start* proposes a tweak to the timing of protocol messages; rather than wait for the entire handshake to be complete, we can start sending application data earlier, *assuming* that the handshake will be successful.

With this change, it's possible to achieve much better performance. Google cited a 30% reduction in handshake latency, which is a really big deal.[24] The downside of this change is that if attacked the client will have sent some encrypted application data to the attacker, which normally doesn't happen. Furthermore, because the integrity of the handshake is validated only after it is fully completed, the parameters used for the encryption could have been influenced by the attacker.

To counter this attack vector, Google proposed to only ever use False Start with strong cryptography: sufficiently strong private keys, key exchanges that support forward secrecy, and 128-bit cipher suites.

Despite the performance improvements, Google declared False Start a failure in 2012—there were too many incompatible servers on the Internet.[25] But they didn't turn it off altogether; Chrome continued to use False Start with servers that implement the NPN extension (used to negotiate the SPDY protocol), which were deemed safe. Other browsers followed and adopted similar behaviors. Firefox supports False Start since version 28[26] and has the same requirements as Chrome. Apple added support in OS X 10.9, requiring strong cipher suites and Forward Security but not NPN.[27] Internet Explorer, starting with version 10, implements False Start as per the original proposal, but also uses a blacklist to disable this feature on sites that are known not to support it.[28]

False Start is a great incentive to support forward secrecy. Not only will your security be significantly better, but the performance will improve too.

---

[23] Transport Layer Security (TLS) False Start [fsty.uk/b380] (Langley et al., June 2010)

[24] SSL FalseStart Performance Results [fsty.uk/b381] (Mike Belshe, The Chromium Blog, 18 May 2011)

[25] False Start's Failure [fsty.uk/b382] (Adam Langley, 11 Apr 2012)

[26] Re-enable TLS False Start [fsty.uk/b383] (Bugzilla@Mozilla, bug #942729)

[27] sslTransport.c [fsty.uk/b384] (Apple Secure Transport source code, retrieved 5 May 2014)

[28] Networking Improvements in IE10 and Windows 8 [fsty.uk/b385] (Eric Lawrence, IEInternals, 1 August 2012)

# Certificates

During a full TLS handshake, the server presents its certificate chain for inspection by the client. The size of the certificate chain and its correctness can have an impact on handshake performance.

**Use as few certificates as possible**

Each certificate in the chain adds to the size of the handshake. Too many certificates in the chain may cause overflow of the initial congestion window, as discussed earlier. In the early days of SSL, there were CAs that issued server certificates directly from their roots, but this practice is dangerous (the roots should be kept offline) and is being deprecated. Today, having two certificates in the chain is the best you can have: one certificate for the server and the other for the issuing CA.

Size is not the only factor; each certificate in the chain must be validated by checking that the signature matches the public key in the issuing certificate. Depending on the user agent, the revocation status of each certificate might need to be checked, too.

Although I wouldn't recommend to choose your CA based on the size of its trust chain, you should check ahead of time that its chain is not too long.

**Include only necessary certificates**

It's a frequent error to include unnecessary certificates in the chain. Each such certificate typically adds 1–2 KB to the overall size of the handshake.

Often, the root certificate is included, even though it serves no purpose there. User agents will either trust the root certificate (and thus already have a copy) or they won't. Having the root in the chain makes no difference. This is a common problem because even some CAs include their root certificates in the installation instructions.

In other cases, unnecessary certificates in the chain are a result of the configuration error. For example, certificates from earlier chains are often seen along with, in rare cases, the entire collection of all trusted certificates—hundreds of them.

**Provide a complete chain**

For a TLS connection to be trusted, the server must provide a complete chain with certificates that lead a trusted root. Another common error is to provide an incomplete certificate chain. Although some user agents are able to obtain the missing certificates, doing that might involve looking for them over HTTP, which is an activity that might take many seconds. For best results, ensure that the chain is valid.

**Use EC certificate chains**

Because ECDSA keys use fewer bits, ECDSA certificates take less space. Huang et al. (2014) observed that a 256-bit ECDSA certificate chain is about 1 KB shorter than a 2,048-bit RSA chain.

### Be careful about using too many hostnames on the same certificate

Recently, it has become common practice to share one certificate among dozens and, in some cases, even hundreds of sites. This is done to allow many sites to share the same IP address, thus supporting clients that do not support virtual secure sites (via the *Server Name Extension*, or SNI). Each hostname added to the certificate increases its size. A few hostnames are not going to have any detectable effect, but hundreds might.

There's a trick you can use if you want to keep handshake size down to a minimum but still have to host multiple sites on the same IP address: (1) get a separate certificate for each hostname you wish to run and configure your web server to serve these certificates to the clients that support SNI; (2) get one fallback certificate that contains all the hostnames you have on the same IP address and configure your web server to serve it to the clients that do not support SNI. If you do this, your SNI clients (the majority) will get small certificates for the sites they wish to access, and everyone else (a small number of legacy clients) will get the single long certificate.

> ### Warning
>
> When client authentication is required, it's possible to configure your server to advertise which issuing CAs are acceptable for the client certificate. Each such CA is identified with its distinguished name. When there are too many CAs in the configuration, the size of the list can run into many kilobytes, which impedes performance. Because advertising acceptable CAs is optional, you can avoid it for performance reasons.

## Revocation Checking

Even though certificate revocation is in a state of flux and user agent behavior varies widely, the server operator's job is clear—deliver revocation information at the fastest speed possible. In practice, this translates to the following rules.

### Use certificates with OCSP information

OCSP is designed for real-time lookups, which allow user agents to request revocation information only for the web site they are visiting. As a result, lookups are short and quick (one HTTP request). CRL, by comparison, is a list of many revoked certificates. Some browsers download CRLs when OCSP information is not available, in which case the communication with your web site might be suspended until the download is complete. Delays of tens of seconds are not unusual, especially over slow internet connections (think mobile devices).

### Use CAs with fast and reliable OCSP responders

OCSP responder performance varies among CAs. This fact remained hidden for a long time, which is unusual given the potential for high performance degradation by slow and faulty OCSP responders. Before you commit to a CA, check their OCSP responder history. Refer to the section called "Responder Availability and Performance" in Chapter 5 for more information. As a rule of thumb, the best performance is going to be with CAs who have or use CDNs to distribute revocation information.

Another criteria for CA selection is how quickly they update their OCSP responders. To avoid site errors, you want your certificates to be known to the responder as soon as they are issued. Inexplicably, some CAs have long delays for new certificates, during which OCSP responders return errors.

### Deploy OCSP stapling

*OCSP stapling* is a protocol feature that allows revocation information (the entire OCSP response) to be included in the TLS handshake. With OCSP stapling enabled, user agents are given all the information they need to perform revocation checking, resulting in much better performance. At about 450 bytes, OCSP stapling increases the size of the handshake and slows it down a bit, but the savings come from user agents not having to look for revocation information on a separate connection to the CAs' OCSP responders.

OCSP responses vary in size, depending on the issuing CA's deployment practices. Short OCSP responses will be signed by the same certificate that issued the end-entity certificate (the one that is being checked for revocation). Because the user agent will already have the issuing certificate, the OCSP response can contain only the revocation status and a signature.

Some CAs prefer to use a different certificate to sign their OCSP responses. Because user agents don't know about that other certificate in advance, the CAs must include it with every OCSP response. This practice adds slightly over 1 KB to the size of the OCSP response.

> **Note**
>
> When browsers skip on revocation checking, they achieve better performance but security suffers. EV certificates are always checked for revocation and thus provide best security. DV certificates, which are not always checked, have a slight performance edge. This problem can be solved with the use of OCSP stapling, in which case the performance will be the same for both certificate types.

## Session Resumption

TLS understands two types of handshakes: full and abbreviated. In theory, the full handshake is performed only once, after which the client establishes a *TLS session* with the server. On subsequent connections, the two can use the faster abbreviated handshake and resume the previously negotiated session. The abbreviated handshake is faster because it doesn't require any costly cryptographic operations and uses one less round-trip. A good resumption rate reduces server load and improves latency for end users.

TLS session resumption is jointly controlled by both parties involved in the communication. On your side, you should aim to configure session caching so that individual sessions remain valid for about a day. After that, it will be up to clients to decide when to resume and when to start afresh. My personal experience and anecdotal evidence from others suggests that you can expect a 50% resumption rate on a properly configured server.[3]

# Transport Overhead

In TLS, the minimal transport unit is a TLS record, which can contain up to 16,384 bytes of data. Without encryption, TLS records don't do much and have only a small overhead; each record starts with five bytes of metadata: content type (one byte), protocol version (two bytes), and data length (two bytes).

Figure 9.4. TLS record overhead for streaming, block, and authenticated cipher suites

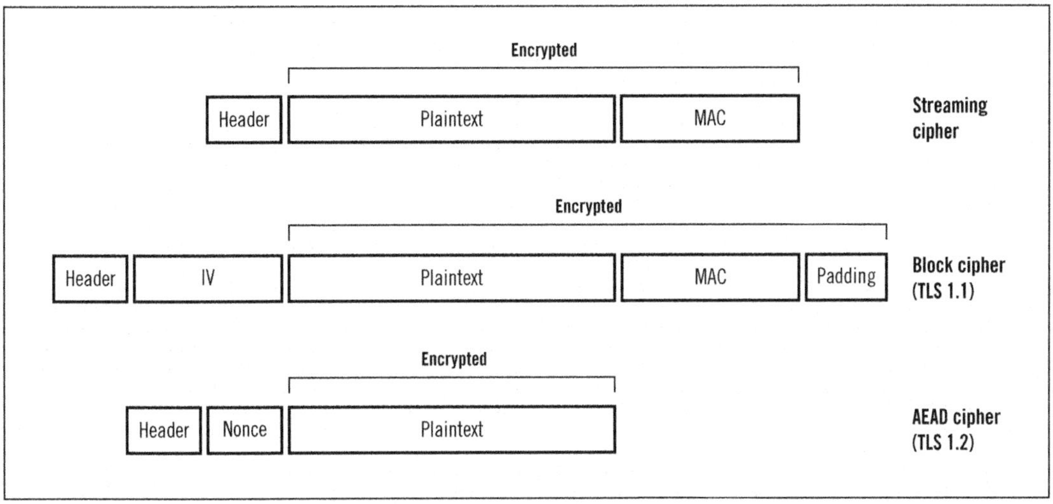

Encryption and data-integrity algorithms introduce additional overhead, which varies depending on the negotiated cipher suite. Streaming ciphers incur little overhead, because they produce one byte of output for every byte of input; overhead comes only from integrity validation.

Block ciphers incur more overhead, because each TLS record needs to include an explicit IV equal to the cipher block size as well as padding to force the length of plaintext to be a multiple of the block size. The length of the padding varies depending on the length of data, but it's going to be one half of the block size on average. Most secure ciphers currently in use are designed with a 16-byte block size.

Ciphers that provide integrated authentication (AEAD suites) are somewhere in the middle: they don't use padding, but they include an eight-byte nonce with every record.

The following table presents overhead calculations for the most commonly used suites.

Table 9.1. Transport overhead for each of the widely available ciphers

| Cipher | TLS Record | IV/Nonce | Padding (average/ worst) | HMAC/Tag | Total (average) |
|---|---|---|---|---|---|
| AES-128-CBC-SHA | 5 | 16 | 8 / 16 | 20 | 49 |
| AES-128-CBC-SHA256 | 5 | 16 | 8 / 16 | 32 | 61 |
| AES-128-GCM-SHA256 | 5 | 8 | - | 16 | 29 |
| AES-256-CBC-SHA | 5 | 16 | 8 / 16 | 20 | 49 |
| AES-256-CBC-SHA256 | 5 | 16 | 8 / 16 | 32 | 61 |
| AES-256-GCM-SHA384 | 5 | 8 | - | 16 | 29 |
| CAMELLIA-128-CBC | 5 | 16 | 8 / 16 | 20 | 49 |
| 3DES-EDE-CBC-SHA | 5 | 8 | 4 / 8 | 20 | 37 |
| RC4-128-SHA | 5 | - | - | 20 | 25 |
| SEED-CBC-SHA | 5 | 16 | 8 / 16 | 20 | 49 |

As you can see, the overhead varies a lot among cipher suites. In the worst case, suites that use AES and SHA256 add 61 bytes of overhead on average. In the best case, authenticated suites are quite slim at 29 bytes. This amount of overhead is not huge, especially when compared with the overhead of the next layer down; the overhead of TCP/IP is 52 bytes per packet for IPv4 and 72 bytes per packet for IPv6. Given that IP packets tend to be around 1,500 bytes but TLS records go as far as 16,384 bytes, it seems that TCP will incur much more overhead than TLS.

Either way, it's vital not to send small amounts of data if you can avoid it. Unless real-time delivery of short messages is required, some buffering of application data is necessary to ensure low network overhead. For example, when constructing an HTML page dynamically it's generally better to use a small output buffer of, say, 4 KB so that tiny writes are combined and sent in larger batches. I've seen some misconfigured applications in which every single data write (of only a few bytes) produced a TCP packet and resulted with a huge network overhead. This type of problem will be more common when working with sockets directly rather than in web applications.

If you're not sure what your application is doing (which is not uncommon, given how many abstraction layers we have in our software these days), capture the traffic at the network layer to observe the TCP packet and TLS record sizes.

# Symmetric Encryption

When it comes to CPU consumption, the worst is over once a TLS handshake completes. Still, cryptographic operations used for symmetric encryption have a noticeable CPU cost, which depends on the choice of cipher, cipher mode, and integrity validation functions.

To determine performance characteristics of various ciphers suites, I conducted further tests using the same environment that I used earlier in this chapter. I made sure to select a processor that supports the AES-NI instruction set, which provides hardware acceleration for the AES cipher.[29] I expect most performance-sensitive web sites to operate on similar hardware. Each test run consisted of two threads—one for the client and the other for the server—sending about 1 GB of data to the other side, 16 KB at time. I tested all practical and secure cipher suites available today as well as some legacy suites for comparison.

---

[29] If you're purchasing hardware, examine the CPU specifications to determine AES-NI support. In a cloud environment, you should be able to do the same by examining the vendor's documentation. On a server running Linux, look for the "aes" flag in /proc/cpuinfo.

Figure 9.5. Performance comparison of various cipher suites, relative to AES-128-CBC-SHA (lower is better)

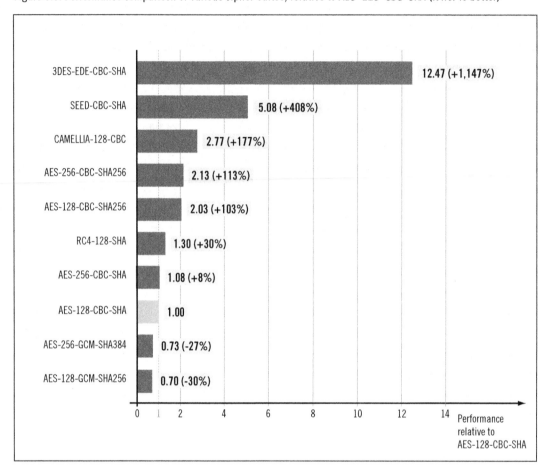

I decided on AES-128-CBC as the reference suite, because it's one of the most commonly used suites among the still-secure ones. The results tell us an interesting story:

- AES is a clear performance winner. Even without hardware acceleration, AES is fast—faster than all other ciphers except for RC4. With hardware acceleration, we see that AES-128-CBC is 2.77 times faster than CAMELLIA-128-CBC. Compared to the fastest AES result, AES-128-GCM-SHA256, CAMELLIA-128-CBC is four times slower.

- AES used with SHA256, as specified in TLS 1.2, is significantly slower. This is because SHA256 is much slower than SHA.

- AES-128 in authenticated (GCM) mode is 1.4 times faster than the reference AES suite. It's even faster than RC4-128-SHA, which was the previous speed champion. This is very encouraging, given that this suite is also one of the strongest currently available.

- The legacy 3DES and SEED suites are many times slower and should be avoided. The same goes for RC4, which, although pretty fast, is insecure.

Chapter 9: Performance Optimization

Although we tend to spend most of our time benchmarking servers, it's worth keeping an eye on client-side performance. Newer desktops and laptops might support hardware-accelerated AES, but there are large numbers of underpowered mobile devices that don't. For this reason, Google is currently experimenting with a new authenticated cipher suite called ChaCha20-Poly1305.[30] Although roughly half the speed of accelerated AES, the performance of this new suite is about three times better on mobile devices, with potential for further improvements. Google is already heavily using the new suite; the rest of us will have to wait for the standardization process to complete.[31]

## TLS Record Buffering Latency

If you recall from an earlier discussion, TLS records are the smallest unit of data TLS can send and receive. Because there is mismatch between the size of TLS records and the size of the underlying TCP packets, a full-sized TLS record of 16 KB needs to be chopped up into many smaller TCP packets, typically each under 1.5 KB.

Figure 9.6. Example fragmentation of 32 KB of application data for transport using TLS and TCP

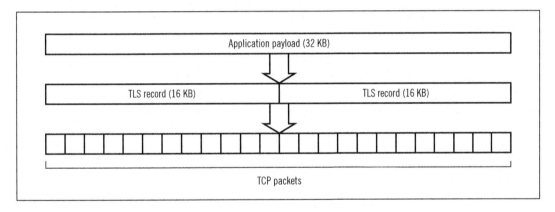

But there's a catch: even though some pieces of an entire record will arrive sooner and some later, no processing can be done until all of them are available. This is because a TLS record is also the smallest unit of data that can be encrypted and its integrity validated. This buffering effect can sometimes result in an increase in latency.

### Packet loss and delay

Although TCP can recover from lost and delayed packets, it does so at a cost of one round-trip. Each additional round-trip means a delay for the entire TLS record, not just the lock packet.

---

[30] TLS Symmetric Crypto [fsty.uk/b276] (Adam Langley, 27 Feb 2014)

[31] ChaCha20 and Poly1305 based Cipher Suites for TLS [fsty.uk/b386] (Langley and Wang, November 2013)

### Initial congestion window

Another way to trigger an additional round-trip delay is by sending large chunks of data early in a connection, overflowing the initial congestion window. Once the congestion window is full, the sender will need to wait for an acknowledgment (one round-trip) before it can grow the congestion window and send more data.

If your web server supports TLS record tuning, you should consider changing the default value—which is probably large, most likely 16 KB—to something more reasonable. Finding the best size requires some experimentation, because it depends on the deployed cipher suites and their transport overhead, as discussed in an earlier section.

If you don't want to spend much time on this task, consider using about 4 KB as a reasonable default. If you want to set the TLS record size to match the size of TCP packets exactly, start at about 1,400 bytes and tweak the exact size by observing the packets on the wire. For example, assuming that the IP *Maximum Transfer Unit* (MTU) is 1,500 bytes:

```
  1,500 bytes MTU
-    40 bytes IPv6 header
-    32 bytes TCP header
-    49 bytes TLS record
  ------------------------
= 1,378 bytes
```

There are several problems with using a static TLS record size, no matter what value is selected. First, MTU values vary. Although most clients inherit the Ethernet limit of 1,500 bytes, there are protocols that support larger sizes. For example, so-called *jumbo frames* allow for up to 9,000 bytes. Second, it's easy to miscalculate and specify an incorrect size. For example, the calculation is slightly different if you're using IPv4 (20 bytes in the header, rather than 40) or if your cipher suite configuration changes.

Another problem is that by reducing the size of the TLS record you increase the transport overhead. To transmit 16 KB of data using a large TLS record, you might incur an overhead of about 50 bytes (0.3%). But if you have to split that same record into, say, 10 records, the overhead will be 500 bytes (3%).

It's probably best to leave TLS record size tuning to web servers, for two reasons: (1) they can discover the MTU at the beginning of each connection and (2) they can vary the record size over the connection lifetime, using small values early on when the congestion window is small and switching to larger values as more data is transferred. HAProxy does exactly that.[32]

---

[32] OPTIM: ssl: implement dynamic record size adjustment [fsty.uk/b387] (Willy Tarreau, 2 February 2014)

# Interoperability

Interoperability issues can sometimes have a substantial negative performance impact, yet they can remain hidden unless you know exactly where to look. For example, if your server is intolerant to some of the newer protocol features (e.g., TLS 1.2), browsers might need to make several connection attempts to negotiate an encrypted connection.[33] However, unless you experience this problem yourself and notice the performance degradation, it's unlikely that you will know about it; servers can't detect it and browsers don't alert you about it.

The best way to ensure good TLS performance is to run an up-to-date TLS stack with support for the most recent protocol versions and extensions.

# Hardware Acceleration

In the early days of SSL, public cryptography was too slow for the then available hardware. As a result, the only way to achieve decent performance was by using hardware acceleration. Over time, as the speed of general-purpose CPUs increased, acceleration devices started to lose their market.[34]

Companies running the world's largest web sites are happy handling encryption in software. For example, Facebook had this to say on hardware acceleration:[35]

> *We have found that modern software-based TLS implementations running on commodity CPUs are fast enough to handle heavy HTTPS traffic load without needing to resort to dedicated cryptographic hardware. We serve all of our HTTPS traffic using software running on commodity hardware.*

Today, hardware cryptographic devices are purchased more for their ability to store private keys safely (this type of product is known as *Hardware Security Module*, or HSM) and less for their ability to accelerate public key cryptography. However, using an HSM could create a bottleneck in your architecture, because such devices are more difficult to scale.

Hardware acceleration could be the right thing to do depending on your circumstances. For example, if you have an existing system that is operating at the edge of capacity, installing an acceleration card might be the preferred option over other hardware and architectural changes.

---

[33] Multiple connection attempts are part of the voluntary protocol downgrade mechanism employed by modern browsers. I discuss it at length in the section called "Voluntary Protocol Downgrade" in Chapter 6.

[34] High Scalability for SSL and Apache [fsty.uk/b388] (Cox and Thorpe, July 2000)

[35] HTTP2 Expression of Interest [fsty.uk/b389] (Doug Beaver, on the HTTP Working Group mailing list, 15 July 2012)

---

# Denial of Service Attacks

Denial of Service (DoS) attacks—for fun or for profit—are common on the Internet. Attacking is easy and cheap. Defending, on the other hand, is costly and time consuming. Any small web site can be quickly overwhelmed by pretty much anyone who wants to try. As for bigger sites, if they stay up, it's only because they spent a lot of money on defense and the attacker hasn't tried hard enough.

The principal way of executing serious DoS attacks is using botnets, which are large networks of compromised computers. Servers are valued as botnet nodes because they tend to have access to ample bandwidth. Home computers are valued because there are so many of them; what they lack in power, they make up in numbers.

If someone is willing to use a botnet to attack you, chances are that your TLS configuration is not going to make a difference. With or without TLS, the attackers can continuously increase the size of the botnet until they succeed, at little cost to them. That said, there's currently an interesting experimental proposal to extend TLS to require proof of client work before spending server resources.[36] However, ultimately, defending against DoS attacks is usually done at the network level.

**Connection throttling**

This is an "entry-level" DoS defense measure, which you can deploy for an entire network using specialized devices or even on individual servers in kernel configuration.[37] With this approach, you should be able to defend against the simpler attacks—for example, those executed from a few IP addresses. Connection throttling is not going to be of much help with attackers that flood your internet connection with traffic from many individual hosts.

**Overprovisioning**

The more resources you have, the more difficult it will be for your attackers to succeed. Overprovisioning is expensive, but buying more servers and having a very large internet connection could be a viable approach if you're under frequent attacks.

**Third-party mitigation**

When all else fails, you can deal with the situation by employing one of the companies who specialize in mitigation of distributed DoS attacks. Their primary advantage is that they have ample resources at their disposal as well as the know-how.

All of this does not mean that you should give up on tuning TLS to minimize your exposure to DoS attacks. On the contrary, there are certain aspects of TLS that make DoS attacks easier; they require your attention.

---

[36] Using Client Puzzles to Protect TLS Servers From Denial of Service Attacks [fsty.uk/b390] (Y. Nir, 29 April 2014)

[37] SSL computational DoS mitigation [fsty.uk/b391] (Vincent Bernat, 1 November 2011)

---

# Key Exchange and Encryption CPU Costs

With plaintext protocols (e.g., HTTP), servers frequently spend most of their time sending files to their clients. This operation is so common that applications can ask the kernel to send a particular file to a socket without bothering with the details. With TLS, the same application has to read a file, encrypt it, and transmit it. That's always going to be slower.

But it's going to be slower for clients, too, because they have to perform those same operations, just in a different order. Where it gets messy is the handshake, which requires several CPU-intensive cryptographic operations. Clients and servers spend different amounts of time during a handshake, with a different performance profile for each key-exchange algorithm. If clients have to perform less work than servers, then we have a situation that can be used for DoS attacks.

This is exactly the case with RSA, which is used in a particular way (with short public exponents) that makes operations with public keys (which clients perform) faster than operations with private keys (which servers perform). In practice, with an average 2,048-bit RSA key, servers end up doing about four times more work. As a result, a client with a modest CPU can overpower a strong server by asking to perform many handshakes in parallel.

To confirm this, I ran a test with two identical servers, one running a web server with a 2,048-bit RSA key and the other attacking it. I was able to trivially overwhelm the CPU on the target server by using the popular ab benchmarking tool against it. In the meantime, the attacking server was running comfortably at slightly over 10% CPU consumption.

RSA is still the dominant authentication and key-exchange algorithm, but there's good news: it's on the way out. Its biggest problem is that it does not support forward secrecy. In the short term, people are turning to ECDHE_RSA, which keeps RSA for authentication but uses ECDHE for the key exchange. With ECDHE_RSA, clients still perform less work, but it's not as bad: only 2.5 times less. Further in the future is ECDHE_ECDSA, which turns things around—clients perform about 1.5 times more work!

> **Note**
>
> To benefit from these alternative algorithms, you'd have to remove support for the RSA key exchange from your configuration. Otherwise, the attacker could force the slowest suites during the attacks.

Encryption has its costs, too. You saw earlier in this chapter that the SEED cipher is 4x times slower and 3DES is 11x times slower than the most commonly used AES-128. Many servers keep 3DES in their configuration for older clients such as Internet Explorer 6. Although it's unlikely that the choice of cipher suite plays a major role in a TLS DoS attack, it certainly can make things worse.

## Client-Initiated Renegotiation

*Renegotiation* is a protocol feature that allows either side to request a new handshake to negotiate potentially different connection parameters. This feature is rarely needed; allowing clients to request renegotiation, in particular, has no practical purpose at present, but it does make DoS mitigation more difficult.

In a "standard" TLS computational DoS attack, there's one handshake per connection. If you have connection throttling in place, you know that one connection to your TLS server costs you some amount in CPU processing power. If client-initiated renegotiation is allowed, attackers can perform many handshakes on the same connection, bypassing the detection mechanisms.[38] This technique also reduces the number of concurrent connections needed and thus improves overall attack latency.

In October 2011, a German hacker group, "The Hacker's Choice," released a tool called thc-ssl-dos, which uses renegotiation to amplify computational DoS attacks against TLS.[39]

Not all servers support client-initiated renegotiation. IIS stopped supporting it with IIS 6, Nginx never supported it, and Apache stopped supporting it in 2.2.15. But there is still a number of vendors who are reluctant to remove this feature. Some vendors who are keeping client-initiated renegotiation are looking to limit the number of renegotiations that take place on the same connection. Ideally, you shouldn't allow client-initiated renegotiation at all.

## Optimized TLS Denial of Service Attacks

Renegotiation makes TLS computational DoS attacks more difficult to detect, but tools that use it are not fundamentally different; they're still essentially sending a large number of virtual clients to a web site. In both cases, the handshake CPU processing asymmetry is what makes the attack possible. As it turns out, it is possible to improve the approach so that no cryptographic operations are needed on the client.

When the thc-ssl-dos tool was announced, it received a fair amount of media interest. Eric Rescorla, one of the TLS protocol designers, followed up with an analysis of the use of renegotiation as a DoS amplification technique.[40] His conclusion was that there is an easier way to execute computational TLS DoS. In his approach, clients use hardcoded handshake messages that require no cryptographic operations. In addition, they avoid parsing or otherwise validating any of the messages received from the server. Because the messages are structur-

---

[38] It's still possible to detect the attacks, but that would typically require deep traffic inspection, ideally by parsing the protocol messages. This ability is not as common as straightforward connection counting.

[39] THC SSL DOS [fsty.uk/b392] (The Hacker's Choice, 24 October 2011)

[40] SSL/TLS and Computational DoS [fsty.uk/b393] (Eric Rescorla, 25 October 2011)

ally correct, they appear valid to the server until the very end of the handshake. By that point, it's too late, because all the expensive work had been done.

Using Eric's blueprint, Michal Trojnara subsequently wrote a proof-of-concept tool called sslsqueeze.[41]

When I tested sslsqueeze, I found that it performed much better than ab. I installed it on a single-CPU server running a 2.80 GHz Intel Xeon E5-2680, and the target was an eight-CPU server in the same data center. The tool consumed all CPU resources on the target server after only a few seconds in operation.

---

[41] Index of ftp://ftp.stunnel.org/sslsqueeze/ [fsty.uk/b394] (Michal Trojnara, 16 November 2011)

# 10 HSTS, CSP, and Pinning

This chapter discusses several technologies that can substantially improve the security of the SSL/TLS and PKI ecosystem. They fall into two groups. In the first group, we have *HTTP Strict Transport Security* (HSTS) and *Content Security Policy* (CSP), which are HTTP-specific and widely supported by browsers. They are not only practical today but also fundamental for the security of your web sites. I cover them in detail sufficient for deployment.

The second group of technologies implements *pinning*, which is a technique that makes TLS authentication more secure. Outside of native applications (where pinning is fully practical), pinning is still early in its lifecycle; there is currently no good support in browsers. Thus, this chapter presents the possible future directions, but we're yet to see which will gain wide adoption and become standards.

## HTTP Strict Transport Security

*HTTP Strict Transport Security* (HSTS), released in November 2012 as RFC 6797,[1] is a proposed standard that describes a strict approach to the handling of web site encryption. It is designed to mitigate several critical weaknesses in how TLS is implemented in today's browsers.

**No way of knowing if a site supports TLS**

HTTP does not specify a way for user agents to determine if web sites implement TLS.[2] Because of this, when given a hostname (but not the protocol), browsers default to a plaintext connection, which is vulnerable to interception.

**Tolerance of certificate problems**

Since the very beginning of the Web, browsers have been sidestepping the problem of TLS connection authenticity. Rather than abandon connections to sites with invalid certificates, browsers display warnings and allow their users to click through. Studies

---

[1] RFC 6797: HTTP Strict Transport Security (HSTS) [fsty.uk/b174] (Hodges and Jackson, November 2012)

[2] This could be implemented using DNS SRV records, which are designed to point to the exact hostname and port that provide a particular service. SRV records are specified in RFC 2782, which was published in February 2000.

have shown that a large percentage of users ignores the warnings and exposes itself to active attacks.

**Mixed content issues**

A frequent mistake when developing secure web sites is to use plaintext resources from an otherwise secure HTML page. All browsers allow such resources to a certain degree, and in many cases these plaintext connections can be used to compromise the entire user session. Another common problem is mixing plaintext and encrypted pages on the same domain name. This is very difficult to implement correctly and most commonly leads to vulnerabilities.

**Cookie security issues**

Another common implementation mistake is to forget to secure application cookies. Even when a web site is available only under TLS, an active network attacker can tease the cookies out from the victim's browser.

> **Note**
>
> For a complete discussion of all the problems listed here and different ways to attack them, head to Chapter 5, *HTTP and Browser Issues*.

When HSTS is deployed on a web site, it addresses all of these issues by using two mechanisms: (1) plaintext URLs are transparently rewritten to use encryption and (2) all certificate errors are treated as fatal (users are not allowed to click through). In this way, HSTS significantly reduces the attack surface and makes the job of secure web site deployment much easier. It is quite possibly the best thing to happen to TLS recently.

HSTS has its origins in the work of Jackson and Barth, who, in 2008, designed ForceHTTPS, [3] a cookie-based mechanism to allow "sophisticated users to transparently retrofit security onto some insecure sites that support HTTPS." Along with their paper, they provided a proof of concept in the form of a Firefox extension.

# Configuring HSTS

Web sites that wish to support HSTS do so by emitting the `Strict-Transport-Security` header on all of their *encrypted* HTTP responses, like so:

```
Strict-Transport-Security: max-age=31536000; includeSubDomains
```

Assuming that the TLS connection is error free, a compliant browser will activate HSTS for the duration of the retention period specified in the `max-age` parameter. The `includeSubDomains` parameter specifies that HSTS should be enabled on the host that emitted the header and also on all its subdomains.

---

[3] ForceHTTPS: Protecting High-Security Web Sites from Network Attacks [fsty.uk/b395] (Jackson and Barth, 2008)

---

**Warning**

Before deploying HSTS with `includeSubDomains` enabled, determine if forcing browsers to use encryption on the entire domain name space might have negative consequences on other sites in the neighborhood. At the very least, ensure that all your sites do support encryption and have valid certificates.

The specification requires user agents to ignore the HSTS header if it is seen on a plaintext connection or on a connection with certificate errors (this includes self-signed certificates). This behavior is intended to prevent *Denial of Service* (DoS) attacks against plaintext-only sites, which would otherwise be trivial to execute by an active network attacker. In addition, using HSTS on IP addresses is not permitted.

It is possible to revoke HSTS; to do so, set the `max-age` parameter to zero:

```
Strict-Transport-Security: max-age=0
```

However, the revocation happens only when a browser (one that previously enabled HSTS for the site) visits the site again and updates its configuration. Thus, the success of revocation (and policy adjustment, for that matter) will depend on the frequency of user visits.

In the best case, HSTS should be configured at the location that is closest to the user. For example, if you have many web servers and a reverse proxy (or web application firewall) in front of them, it makes sense to configure HSTS there, in a single location. Otherwise, configure your HSTS policies at the web-server level. If your web server does not explicitly support HSTS, it most likely has a mechanism that allows adding of arbitrary response headers. The latter approach can work equally well, but do read the fine print. In some cases, adding headers to error responses (e.g., 404 pages) either is impossible or requires special configuration.

If all else fails, you can also add HSTS at the application level. However, be aware that your application might not see all web site requests. For example, web servers typically deliver static resources directly and also handle some redirections themselves.

# Ensuring Hostname Coverage

By default, HSTS is enabled only on the hostname that emits the `Strict-Transport-Security` response header. Sites that are deployed across more than one hostname (e.g., *store.example.com* and *accounts.example.com*) should therefore take care to activate HSTS on all of them. Otherwise, it might happen that some users, who visit some hosts but not the ones with the HSTS instructions, are left unprotected.

Some applications use so-called *domain cookies*, which are set on the root domain name (e.g., *example.com*) and can be used by any subdomain. This technique is typically used with sites that are spread across multiple hostnames but require unified authentication and session management. In this case, it is even more important to enable HSTS on all deployed hostnames, including the root domain name. You don't want to leave a loophole that might be exploited for attacks.

Even sites that use only one hostname need to consider this problem, because it is very likely that their users will sometimes access the site without the prefix (e.g., *example.com*) and sometimes with (e.g., *www.example.com*). Because we don't control inbound links, we have to take extra care when configuring HSTS and enable it on all hostnames.

> ### Warning
>
> A common mistake is to forget to configure HSTS on redirections. For example, some of your users might arrive at your root domain name (e.g., *example.com*) first. If you don't have HSTS configured there, users who arrive that way might still be vulnerable to SSL stripping attacks, despite HSTS on the main domain name. For best results, enumerate all paths that lead to your web site, and add HSTS to all of them.

# Cookie Security

Because HSTS enforces encryption on all connections to a particular web site, you might think that even insecure cookies remain safe against an active network attacker. Unfortunately, the cookie specification is very permissive and creates opportunities for additional attack vectors, such as:

**Attacks via made-up hostnames**
Cookies are typically set for a particular hostname and all its subdomains. At the same time, an active network attacker can manipulate the DNS at will and create arbitrary hostnames under the same domain name as the target web site. Thus, if you set a cookie for *www.example.com*, the attacker can steal it by forcing and intercepting access to *madeup.www.example.com*. If the cookie is insecure, plaintext access will do. If the cookie is secure, the attacker can present a self-signed certificate and hope that the user will click through.

**Cookie injection**
The cookie specification doesn't use a separate namespace for secure cookies. What this means is that a cookie set from a plaintext connection can overwrite an existing secure cookie. In practice, this means that an active network attacker can inject arbitrary cookies into an otherwise secure application.

In the case of domain cookies, the attacker can inject a cookie from an existing sibling hostname (e.g., `blog.example.com`). Otherwise, an active network attacker can make up an arbitrary hostname and inject from it.

These problems can largely be addressed with the use of the `includeSubDomains` parameter, which activates HSTS on the main hostname and all its subdomains. When domain cookies are used, the only secure approach is to activate HSTS on the root domain name and thus on the entire domain namespace. I discuss cookie security issues at length in the section called "Cookie Manipulation" in Chapter 5.

# Attack Vectors

HSTS greatly improves our ability to secure web sites, but there are several edge cases that you need to be aware of. Consider the following situations.

**First access**

Because HSTS is activated via a HTTP response header, it does not provide security on the first access. However, once activated the protection will remain enabled until the retention period expires. The lack of security on the first access is mitigated by browsers embedding (or *preloading*) a list of sites that are known to support HSTS. This is possible only because the number of sites that support HSTS is still very small.

**Short retention duration**

HSTS works best when deployed with a long retention period (e.g., at least six months). That way, users are protected for the duration of their first session but also on their subsequent visits to the web site. If the retention period is short and the users don't visit again before it expires, their next access will not be protected.

**Clock attacks**

Users whose computers are configured to automatically update their clocks using *Network Time Protocol* (NTP) could be attacked by an active network attacker who can subvert the NTP messages. Setting the computer's clock to a time in the future will cause a site's HSTS policy to lapse, making the victim's following visit insecure. The danger of this attack vector depends on the NTP access frequency. This will typically be once or twice a day.

**Response header injection**

Response header injection is a web application vulnerability that enables the attacker to inject arbitrary response headers into the victim's traffic. If such a vulnerability is present in an application, an attacker can inject a forged `Strict-Transport-Security` header that disables HSTS. Against an application that does not use HSTS, this attack could be used to enable it and thus execute a DoS attack.

When this attack is delivered against an application that already uses HSTS, the outbound response headers will include two copies of the `Strict-Transport-Security` header, which is allowed by the specification. The attacker's header will be used if it ends up being first in the response.

---

**TLS truncation**

Although the TLS protocol is not vulnerable to truncation attacks, most browsers' implementations are. A skilled active network attacker can use a special technique to intercept a TLS connection and truncate it after the first digit of the max-age parameter. If successful, such an attack can reduce the HSTS duration to, at most, nine seconds. This is a so-called *cookie cutter attack*, which I discuss in the section called "Cookie Cutting" in Chapter 6.

**Mixed content issues**

The HSTS designers chose not to fully address mixed content issues, most likely because it's a hard problem and because browser vendors tend to have different ideas about dealing with it. As a result, HSTS includes only non-normative advice against allowing mixed content in Section 12.4 ("Disallow Mixed Security Context Loads").

Still, HSTS provides a partial solution because plaintext requests for the same hostname (where HSTS is active) are not allowed. To address third-party mixed content, deploy *Content Security Policy* (CSP), which can be used to allow only HTTPS requests from a given page.

**Hostname and port sharing**

HSTS is activated on an entire hostname and across all ports. This approach does not work very well in shared hosting situations in which multiple parties are able to control a site's response headers. In such situations, care should be taken to screen all responses to ensure that the correct HSTS header is sent (or that no HSTS header is sent at all).

## Robust Deployment Checklist

Even though HSTS is relatively simple, deploying it can be quite complicated if the environment in which you're operating is complex enough. For all but the simplest environments, I recommend deploying HSTS in two major steps: start with a test run that does everything right in terms of configuration but uses a very short duration value. Later, increase the duration to the desired long-term value.

Follow these steps for the test run:

1. Ensure that the Strict-Transport-Security header is emitted on all encrypted requests across all hostnames (e.g., *accounts.example.com* and *www.example.com*) and with includeSubDomains specified.

2. Enable HSTS on the root domain name (e.g., *example.com*), also with includeSubDomains specified.

3. Determine all paths that lead to your site, and double-check that all redirections emit HSTS policies.

4. Initially, start with a temporary short-term policy retention duration. This will allow you to relatively easily recover from forgetting that you have an important plaintext-only site in production.

5. Redirect all port 80 traffic to port 443. This will ensure that your users always receive the HSTS instructions on their first visits.

6. Modify your sites so that each hostname submits at least one request to the root domain name. This will ensure that HSTS is fully enabled on the entire domain name-space, even if your users do not visit the root domain name directly.

7. For extra points, if you have a reverse proxy in front of your web site(s), configure your HSTS policy centrally at the proxy level. To prevent header injection vulnerabilities from being used to bypass HSTS, delete any HSTS response headers set by the back-end web servers.

After a period of time, when you establish that your deployment is correct in all aspects, increase the policy retention duration. You can do this incrementally, or by immediately switching to a long-term value. Take the following steps:

1. Increase the policy retention duration to a long-term value, for example, 12 months. This will not only give you the best protection but also ensure that you are put on preload lists that have minimum duration requirements.

2. Notify preload list maintainers.

---

### What if You Can't Activate HSTS on the Entire Domain Name?

For best results, HSTS should be enabled on the entire domain name. Unfortunately, this might not always be possible. Especially if you're working with a large existing infrastructure, it might be some time until you are able to migrate all the services to HTTPS.

Even in this situation, you could still use `includeSubDomains` only on the main application hostname (e.g., *www.example.com*, but not on *example.com*). This will provide sufficient security, except in a case in which domain cookies are used. However, you need to do this carefully. Because HSTS policies do not include the names of the hostnames to which they apply, it's possible to inadvertently activate HSTS from the wrong place.

When deploying HSTS without any subdomain coverage, the risks described in the section called "Cookie Security" apply. Such risks can be mitigated by deploying a cryptographic security mechanism to guarantee cookie confidentiality and integrity.

---

## Browser Support

There is currently decent support for HSTS in desktop browsers thanks to early adoption by Chrome and Firefox, in 2010 and 2011, respectively. Of other major browsers, Safari added support in the OS X 10.9 release in late 2013. Internet Explorer does not currently implement HSTS, but the word from the development team is that they are working on it.[4]

Table 10.1. Browser support for HTTP Strict Transport Security

| Browser | HSTS Support | Since | Preloading |
| --- | --- | --- | --- |
| Chrome | Yes | v4.0.249.78;[a] January 2010 | Yes |
| Firefox | Yes | v4;[b] March 2011 | Yes (from v17) |
| Internet Explorer | No (in development) | - | - |
| Opera | Yes | v12 (Presto/2.10.239);[c] June 2012 | Yes (from v15) |
| Safari | Yes | v7 (OS X 10.9 Mavericks); October 2013 | Yes |

[a] Stable Channel Update [fsty.uk/b397] (Chrome Releases blog, 25 January 2010)

[b] Firefox 4 release notes [fsty.uk/b398] (Mozilla, 22 March 2011)

[c] Web specifications support in Opera Presto 2.10 [fsty.uk/b399] (Opera, retrieved 19 April 2014)

Most browsers ship preloaded with a list of sites that are known to support HSTS. However, it seems that at this point in time the lists are largely compiled manually. Some vendors (e.g., Mozilla) are talking about scanning the Web to generate a comprehensive list of sites that support HSTS, but the details are scarce.

**Chrome**

Chrome maintains a preload list for HSTS and public key pinning.[5] At the time of writing, the list contains about 500 sites. The list is updated manually.

**Firefox**

Mozilla seeded their HSTS list from Chrome in November 2012.[6] It's possible and likely that they have been synchronizing the list since. Mozilla's list is smaller than Google's, because they require a minimum max-age of 18 weeks in order to include a site.

**Opera**

Starting with version 15, the Opera browser uses the same engine as Chrome and thus inherits its HSTS preload list.

**Safari**

Safari on OS X preloads a number of HSTS-enabled hostnames. At the time of writing, I counted 179 entries on my computer (~/Library/Cookies/HSTS.plist). Apple never announced support for HSTS, and thus we know little about their plans for the list's maintenance.

---

[4] HTTP Strict Transport Security [fsty.uk/b396] (IE Platform Status, retrieved 29 June 2014)

[5] HTTP Strict Transport Security [fsty.uk/b400] (The Chromium Projects, retrieved 29 June 2014)

[6] Preloading HSTS [fsty.uk/b401] (Mozilla Security Blog, 1 November 2012)

## Privacy Implications

The nature of HSTS dictates that browsers use a persistent store to keep track of the HSTS sites they visit. When a user encounters an HSTS site for the first time, an entry is added to the browser's HSTS database. This fact makes it possible to test if someone has visited a particular site before—just ask them to follow a plaintext link to the site. If they visit the link, they had never been to that site before. However, if they had visited that site before, HSTS will kick in, rewrite the link, and visit the HTTPS variant instead.

In essence, a HSTS policy can be used to store one bit of information in a browser. One bit does not sound like much, but, when used with a wildcard certificate, an adversary could create as many different hostnames as they needed, each with a separate HSTS policy, and each carrying one bit of information.[7]

# Content Security Policy

*Content Security Policy* (CSP) is a declarative security mechanism that allows web site operators to control the behavior of compliant user agents (typically browsers). By controlling what features are enabled and where content is downloaded from, web sites can reduce their attack surface.

The main drive goal of CSP is defense against *cross-site scripting* (XSS) attacks. For example, CSP can be used to completely disable inline JavaScript and control where external code is loaded from. It can also disable dynamic code evaluation. With all of those attack vectors disabled, attacking with XSS becomes much more difficult.

CSP had been developed at Mozilla, who experimented with the concept over several years, first calling it *content restrictions*[8] and later Content Security Policy.[9] CSP 1.0 became a W3C Candidate Recommendation in November 2012;[10] work is currently in progress on CSP 1.1.[11]

A web site that wishes to enable CSP sets the desired policy by using the Content-Security-Policy response header.[12] To give you an idea of what policies look like, consider this example adapted from the specification:

---

[7] The Double-Edged Sword of HSTS Persistence and Privacy [fsty.uk/b402] (Leviathan Security Group, 4 April 2012)

[8] Content Restrictions [fsty.uk/b403] (Gervase Markham, last update 20 March 2007)

[9] Content Security Policy [fsty.uk/b404] (Mozilla's CSP Archive, last updated in 2011)

[10] Content Security Policy 1.0 [fsty.uk/b405] (W3C Candidate Recommendation, 15 November 2012)

[11] Content Security Policy 1.1 [fsty.uk/b406] (W3C Working Draft, retrieved 23 April 2014)

[12] You might see other header names mentioned in blog posts, for example, X-Content-Security-Policy and X-Webkit-CSP. Those headers were used in the early days of CSP, when the functionality was largely experimental. The only header name relevant today is the official one.

---

```
Content-Security-Policy: default-src 'self'; img-src *;
                         object-src *.cdn.example.com;
                         script-src scripts.example.com
```

This policy allows resources to be loaded only from its own origin by default, but allows images to be loaded from any URI, plugin content only from the specified CDN addresses, and external scripts only from *scripts.example.com*.

Unlike with HSTS, CSP policies are not persistent; they're used only on the pages that reference them and are then promptly forgotten. Thus, CSP is much less risky to use. If an error is made, the policy can be updated with immediate effect. There is also no danger of denial of service attacks stemming from injected response headers.

## Preventing Mixed Content Issues

Mixed content issues arise when a secure web page relies on resources (e.g., images and scripts) that are retrieved over plaintext connections. Browsers improved their handling of this problem in recent years, but their approach is generally still too lax. For example, all browsers allow so-called *passive mixed content*, typically images. Not unexpectedly, there are also differences in the handling among browsers. Safari, for example, does not currently impose any restrictions, not even on scripts. You'll find a detailed discussion of mixed content issues in the section called "Mixed Content" in Chapter 5.

Because CSP allows us to control where content comes from, we can use it to instruct compliant browsers to use only secure protocols. That's wss for the WebSocket protocol and https for everything else.

Thus, to address only mixed content issues without attempting to improve anything else, consider the following CSP policy as a starting point:

```
Content-Security-Policy: default-src https: 'unsafe-inline' 'unsafe-eval';
                         connect-src https: wss:
```

The policy includes three main elements:

- The default-src directive establishes that the page can load content from anywhere (any host and any port), provided it's done securely (https).
- The 'unsafe-inline' and 'unsafe-eval' expressions re-enable inline JavaScript and dynamic code evaluation, which are disabled by default by CSP. Ideally, you wouldn't want to have these expressions in a policy, but without them most existing applications break.
- The connect-src directive controls content locations used by server push notifications,[13] WebSocket protocol,[14] and XMLHttpRequest.[15]

Once you establish that this initial policy is working for you, consider tightening JavaScript execution (by removing the 'unsafe-inline' and 'unsafe-eval' expressions) and replacing generic source restrictions with more specific hosts (e.g., `https://cdn.example.com` instead of `https:`).

## Policy Testing

A nice thing about CSP is that it is able to enforce one policy while testing others in parallel. This means that you are even able to deploy testing policies in production, which tend to be much more complex than development environments.

The `Content-Security-Policy-Report-Only` response header is used to create a testing-only policy:

```
Content-Security-Policy-Report-Only: default-src 'self'
```

## Reporting

Another nice feature of CSP is that it supports reporting, which can be used to track policy violations. With this feature, development is much easier. It is also very comforting to know that the policy deployed in production is not breaking anything.

To enable reporting, use the `report-uri` directive:

```
Content-Security-Policy: default-src 'self';
                         report-uri http://example.org/csp-report.cgi
```

With that, CSP policy violations will be submitted to the specified URI, using the POST request method and the report data in the request body. For example:

```
{
  "csp-report": {
    "document-uri": "http://example.org/page.html",
    "referrer": "http://evil.example.com/haxor.html",
    "blocked-uri": "http://evil.example.com/image.png",
    "violated-directive": "default-src 'self'",
    "original-policy": "default-src 'self'; report-uri http://example.org↵
/csp-report.cgi"
  }
}
```

---

[13] Server-Sent Events [fsty.uk/b407] (W3C Editor's Draft, published 14 May 2014)

[14] RFC 6455: The WebSocket Protocol [fsty.uk/b408] (Fette and Melnikov, December 2011)

[15] XMLHttpRequest Level 1 [fsty.uk/b409] (W3C Working Draft, published 30 January 2014)

---

# Browser Support

CSP is well supported in current browsers. Chrome and Firefox have been experimenting with it for years, and it's recently started to arrive in other mainstream browsers. The only major desktop browser not to support CSP is Internet Explorer; their team lists this feature as *In Development*.[16]

Table 10.2. Browser support for Content Security Policy

| Browser | CSP Support | Since |
| --- | --- | --- |
| Android Browser | Yes | 4.4.x (October 2013).[a] |
| Chrome | Yes | v25 (February 2013).[b] Experimental support since June 2011.[c] |
| Firefox | Yes | v23 (August 2013).[d] Experimental support since June 2009, in Firefox v4.[e] |
| Internet Explorer | No (in development) | - |
| Opera | Yes | v15 (July 2013). |
| Safari | Yes | v7 (iOS 7 on September 2013 and OS X 10.9 on October 2013). Experimental support since v6 in Mountain Lion.[f] |

[a] Content Security Policy [fsty.uk/b411] (Can I use, retrieved 29 June 2014)

[b] Chrome 25 Beta: Content Security Policy and Shadow DOM [fsty.uk/b412] (The Chromium Blog, 14 January 2013)

[c] New Chromium security features, June 2011 [fsty.uk/b413] (The Chromium Blog, 14 June 2011)

[d] Content Security Policy 1.0 lands in Firefox Aurora [fsty.uk/b414] (Mozilla Hacks, 29 May 2013)

[e] Shutting Down XSS with Content Security Policy [fsty.uk/b415] (Brandon Sterne, Mozilla Security Blog, 19 June 2009)

[f] Safari 6 gets Content-Security-Policy right [fsty.uk/b416] (rachelbythebay, 29 July 2012)

# Pinning

*Pinning* is a security technique that can be used to associate a service with one or more cryptographic identities such as certificates and public keys. Depending on where and how it is used, pinning can achieve three main security improvements:

**Attack surface reduction**

> The dominant TLS authentication model in use today relies on public CAs. Their job is to issue certificates to domain name owners but not to other random people. In turn, user agents trust all CA-issued certificates unconditionally. This model suffers from an enormous flaw: a domain owner's authorization is not required for certificate issuance. As a consequence, any CA can issue a certificate for any domain name. Given that there are hundreds of CAs and possibly thousands of entities who influence certificate issuance in one way or another, the attack surface is huge.

---

[16] Content Security Policy [fsty.uk/b410] (IE Platform Status, retrieved 29 June 2014)

With pinning, owners can specify (pin) the CAs that are allowed to issue certificates for their domain names. They can look at the market, decide which one or two CAs are best for them, and configure the pins accordingly. After that, they no longer care that there are hundreds of public CAs because they are no longer a risk.

**Key continuity**

*Key continuity* is a variation on the previous use case, but it can be used without relying on public CAs. Let's assume that you somehow know that a particular key is valid for some web site. With that, whenever you visit the site you can compare their current key with your "correct" key; if the keys match, you know that you are not under attack.

Key continuity is commonly used with the SSH protocol. Keys are associated with servers when they are seen for the first time and checked on subsequent visits. This is also known as *trust on first use* (TOFU).

Firefox uses key continuity when it allows you to create an exception for a certificate it can't verify; the exception is valid only for that particular certificate. If you are later attacked with a different (MITM) certificate, Firefox will show a certificate warning again.

**Authentication**

Pinning can even be used for authentication, provided there is a reliable (secure) channel to communicate the required cryptographic identities to end users. For example, if we ever deployed a secure DNS that cannot be subverted by active network attacks, then we could use it to store the fingerprints of web site certificates. Those fingerprints could then be checked on every site visit.

# What to Pin?

Pinning can be used with several cryptographic elements; the usual candidates are certificates and public keys. For example, a possible approach is to have a copy of the certificate you expect to see for a particular site so that you can compare it with the certificate you actually get. There is little reason to keep the entire certificate; you can achieve the same effect by using its hash (e.g., SHA256), which is much shorter and easier to handle.

In practice, public key pinning is more practical, because certificates are sometimes reissued without changing the public key. It is also common to see several certificates for the same public key. Thus, if you pin the public key the pin will work across all certificates associated with it.

Protocols that do not rely on certificates could pin public keys directly, but for TLS the best element to pin is the SubjectPublicKeyInfo (SPKI) field of X.509 certificates.[17] This field contains the public key itself as well as additional metadata that's necessary for accurate identification:

```
SubjectPublicKeyInfo  ::=  SEQUENCE  {
    algorithm           AlgorithmIdentifier,
    subjectPublicKey    BIT STRING  }
```

If you want to examine the contents of the SPKI field for a given certificate, use this command:

```
$ openssl x509 -in server.crt -noout -text
[...]
Subject Public Key Info:
            Public Key Algorithm: rsaEncryption
                Public-Key: (2048 bit)
                Modulus:
                    00:b8:0e:05:25:f8:81:e9:e7:ba:21:40:5f:d7:d4:
                    09:5c:8c:d4:e9:44:e7:c0:04:5b:7f:6e:16:8a:01:
                    37:2b:b9:ed:b6:09:cd:1f:55:d5:b8:ee:79:13:ae:
                    e7:1d:6a:ec:01:7c:02:5a:10:af:f9:68:28:ff:d5:
                    61:b0:37:f8:a6:b2:87:42:90:3c:70:19:40:67:49:
                    99:1d:3c:44:3e:16:4e:9a:06:e4:06:66:36:2f:23:
                    39:16:91:cf:92:56:57:1d:30:db:71:5a:68:a2:c3:
                    d5:07:23:e4:90:8e:9e:fb:97:ad:89:d5:31:3f:c6:
                    32:d0:04:17:5c:80:9b:0c:6d:9b:2a:b2:f9:39:ac:
                    85:75:84:82:64:23:9a:7d:c4:96:57:1e:7b:bf:27:
                    2e:48:2d:9e:74:90:32:c1:d8:91:54:12:af:5a:bb:
                    01:20:15:0e:ff:7b:57:83:9d:c2:fe:59:ce:ea:22:
                    6b:77:75:27:01:25:17:e1:41:31:4c:7f:a8:eb:0e:
                    8c:b9:18:b2:9a:cc:74:5e:36:1f:8f:a1:f4:71:a9:
                    ff:72:e6:a0:91:f0:90:b2:5a:06:57:79:b6:1e:97:
                    98:6b:5c:3a:a9:6a:be:84:bc:86:75:cb:81:6d:28:
                    68:c0:e5:d5:3e:c5:f0:7d:85:27:ae:ce:7a:b7:41:
                    ce:f9
                Exponent: 65537 (0x10001)
```

To generate a SPKI hash, first extract the field from the certificate into its own file:

```
$ openssl x509 -in server.crt -noout -pubkey | \
  openssl asn1parse -inform PEM -noout -out server.spki
```

You can then, for example, calculate a SHA256 hash of it and encode it using Base64 encoding:

```
$ openssl dgst -sha256 -binary server.spki | base64
zB8EXAKscl3P+4a5lFszGaEniLrNswOQ1ZGwD+TzADg=
```

---

[17] More information on the structure of X.509 certificates is available in the section called "Certificates" in Chapter 3.

---

# Where to Pin?

When it comes to deciding where to pin, the answer is not as clear. The obvious choice is to pin the server's public key, but there are several downsides to this approach. One is that servers are naturally very exposed to attacks. If the server's private key is compromised and replaced, the old pin will no longer be valid. Even in absence of attack, server keys should be frequently rotated in order to minimize the amount of data protected with the same key. Finally, complex deployments often rely on multiple keys and certificates for the same site; maintaining pins for all of them would be difficult and time consuming.

For this reason, we can consider pinning elsewhere in the certificate chain. These days, most certificate chains start with the end-entity certificate, have one intermediate CA certificate, and finish with a root. If you pin to either of the latter two, you should be able to change the server identity, get a new certificate from the same CA, and continue to use the same pins.

This sounds ideal, but there are some complications. First, CAs usually have multiple roots. They also have multiple intermediate CAs, which they use for different classes of certificates, to minimize risk, change signature algorithms, and so on. Your next certificate from the same CA might not use exactly the same intermediate and root certificates.

In addition, CAs also rely on cross-certification with other, more established, roots from other CAs in order to support older clients. What this means is that there might be multiple valid trust paths for a given certificate. In practice, a user agent can decide to use a different trust path from the one you have in mind. If that happens, and if your pin is attached to an excluded trust path, the validation will fail.

With all of this in mind, the best candidate for pinning appears to be the second certificate in the chain, that of the issuing CA. Because its signature is on the end-entity certificate, the issuing CA's public key must always be in the chain. This approach ensures that a user agent won't bypass the pin, but it's still possible that the CA will issue a future certificate from a different intermediate CA. There is no clear solution to this, but there are steps you can take to mitigate the risks:

- Ask your CAs to support pinning and commit to practices that will ensure that your pins remain valid with future certificates.

- Always have a backup pin and a spare certificate from a different CA.

> **Note**
>
> The most reliable way to use pinning is with your own intermediary CA. This setup ensures that the pinned public key is always in the chain. It also gives you a degree of root agility; if you're not happy with your CA, you can get a different intermediate certificate (using the same private key) from someone else. Finally, because you're always pinning to the same public key, the pins can be shared among all your sites.

# Should You Use Pinning?

Pinning is a powerful technique for attack surface reduction, but it does not come for free. To deploy pinning, you need a good understanding of the tradeoffs and a mature organization that can deal with the operational challenges. The obvious problem is that pinning ensures that TLS connections are established only to the pinned identities. What happens if you lose those identities, for whatever reason?

The fear of the self-inflicted denial of service attack is possibly the reason that pinning has been slow to take off. Browser vendors understand this, and it's also evident from the pinning proposals. Unlike HSTS, where long policy-retention periods (e.g., one year) are common, pinning periods are usually measured in days. A maximum of 30 days is common. However, no matter how short the pinning period is, mistakes will always happen. I am curious to see if browser vendors will eventually implement a mechanism for pin breaking to use for emergencies.

In the remainder of this section, I describe several ways to deploy pinning, but only one of them (Chrome pinning) can be used straight away. The only exception is pinning for native applications, in which you control both sides of the communication. In this case, pinning is fully under your control and, with careful planning, can be very effective.

So, given that pinning for web sites is still an immature technology, there is generally no need to rush. If you're running a high-profile web site, consider using Chrome pinning now. Otherwise, you should first evaluate if pinning is for you. Evaluate your environment, try to prepare a deployment plan, and assess the challenges and costs. Then decide.

# Pinning in Native Applications

The most straightforward use of pinning is in native applications, in which you control both sides of the communication. This will be the case with desktop and mobile applications. In an increasingly connected world, most modern applications have a backend that they talk to, and many use HTTPS for that communication.

## Private Backends

There are two approaches you can take. The first applies when the backend is used only by your applications. In this case, you can generate your own root key and use it to issue your own certificates. By distributing the root's public key with your applications, you will be able to reliably verify certificate signatures.

On many platforms, this type of pinning is easy to do. For example, Java ships with a number of trust roots that are used by default. Whenever you open an HTTPS connection to a site, those trust roots are used to verify the authenticity of the connection. But, because you don't want to trust all those roots, you can create your own *trust store*, and then place only your own root in it. If whenever you open an HTTPS connection to *your* site you specify your own trust store, then you have pinning in action.

If you don't want to maintain your own root key, you can use SPKI pinning, as described earlier. If you're after some code, Moxie Marlinspike described both of these approaches in his article.[18]

Starting with version 4.2, Android has limited support for public key pinning.[19]

## Public Backends

In some cases, applications have backends that are also accessed by third parties (i.e., the public). Then, obtaining certificates from a public CA is the way to go. That way, others will be able to connect to the service and verify its authenticity. You won't be able to deploy pinning to secure their access, at least not until one of the pinning proposals becomes widely supported.

If you still want to protect access from your own applications, you can follow the advice from the previous section and pin to the public key. A possibly more secure approach is to create another private backend, in which case you can also use your own root key for the certificates.

# Chrome Public Key Pinning

Google started to experiment with public key pinning with Chrome 12,[20] when they shipped a user interface that allows for custom HSTS and pinning configuration.[21] Then, in Chrome 13, they added (preloaded) pins for most of their own web sites.[22]

Behind the scenes, the same mechanism is used for both HSTS preloading and pinning; the required information is hardcoded in the browser itself. Because Chrome is based on the open-source Chromium browser, the source file containing this information is available for us to view.[23]

There's only one policy file, and it contains a single JSON structure with two further lists: (1) web sites that support HSTS or pinning and (2) *pinsets* to define acceptable public keys for them.

Each web site entry carries information about its HSTS configuration and the desired pinset:

---

[18] Your app shouldn't suffer SSL's problems [fsty.uk/b417] (Moxie Marlinspike, 5 December 2011)

[19] Certificate pinning in Android 4.2 [fsty.uk/b418] (Nikolay Elenkov, 12 December 2012)

[20] New Chromium security features, June 2011 [fsty.uk/b413] (The Chromium Blog, 14 June 2011)

[21] The present versions of Chrome still include this user interface; it can be accessed via chrome://net-internals/#hsts.

[22] Public key pinning [fsty.uk/b419] (Adam Langley, 4 May 2011)

[23] transport_security_state_static.json [fsty.uk/b420] (Chromium source code, retrieved 29 June 2014)

---

```
{ "name": "encrypted.google.com",
  "include_subdomains": true,
  "mode": "force-https",
  "pins": "google"
}
```

A pinset is a collection of allowed SPKI hashes; it uses the names of certificates that are not in the file but are shipped with the browser:

```
{ "name": "google",
  "static_spki_hashes": [
      "GoogleBackup2048",
      "GoogleG2"
  ]
}
```

With the pinset approach, Chrome creates a whitelist of public keys that can be used in certificate chains for the pinned sites. The format also allows for public key blacklisting (via the `bad_static_spki_hashes` parameter), but no site appears to be using it at the moment. There is also a provision to disable pinning when SNI is not available, which is necessary for some sites that provide correct certificate chains only when SNI is enabled.[24]

As you can see, this all seems very straightforward. Because the Chrome developers have graciously allowed others to include their pinning information in their browsers, some high-profile sites and projects (e.g., Twitter and Tor) are also protected with pinning. Hundreds of sites have their HSTS information preloaded.

> ### Warning
>
> To allow users to MITM their own traffic, pinning is not enforced on manually added root certificates. On the one hand, this allows for local debugging (e.g., using local developer proxies) and content inspection by antivirus products; on the other, it also allows for transparent corporate traffic interception. It has been reported that some malware authors install custom certificates to perform MITM attacks; such certificates would also bypass pin validation.[25]

Chrome includes a reporting mechanism that is used to report pin validation failures to Google. (Anecdotally, for privacy reasons, the reporting is enabled only in Google's own properties.) We know this because Chrome's pinning detected several PKI incidents: Digi-Notar, TURKTRUST, and ANSSI. You can read about them in Chapter 4, *Attacks against PKI*.

---

[24] Chrome supports SNI, which is why this feature might seem illogical at first. However, there are still situations in which Chrome is ready to fall back all the way from TLS 1.2 to SSL 3, which doesn't support extensions (which means that Chrome can't send the SNI information).

[25] New Man-in-the-Middle attacks leveraging rogue DNS [fsty.uk/b421] (Don Jackson, PhishLabs, 26 March 2014)

# Microsoft Enhanced Mitigation Experience Toolkit

Microsoft does not currently support site-controlled pinning in Internet Explorer, but it provides an add-on called *Enhanced Mitigation Experience Toolkit* (EMET),[26] which can be used by end users to protect themselves individually. Although EMET is largely focused on buffer overflow and similar attacks, one of its features is certificate pinning. EMET 5, currently in beta, ships with pinning rules for several key Microsoft sites, Facebook, Twitter, and Yahoo. Users can add their own pins if they wish.[27]

# Public Key Pinning Extension for HTTP

*Public Key Pinning Extension for HTTP* (HPKP)[28] is a standard for public key pinning for HTTP user agents that's been in development since 2011. The work was initiated by Google, which, even though it had implemented pinning in Chrome, understood that manually maintaining a list of pinned sites can't scale. Although there are no firm statements from browsers vendors regarding support for this standard, Chrome and Firefox will probably support it after the design is complete. In the meantime, we can examine the features HPKP offers in its most recent development version.

Because there are many similarities between HPKP and HSTS, if you haven't already read the section on HSTS (earlier in this chapter), I propose that you do now. Here's a quick overview of the common features:

- HPKP is set at the HTTP level, using the `Public-Key-Pins` (PKP) response header.

- Policy retention period is set with the `max-age` parameter, which specifies duration in seconds.

- Pinning can be extended to subdomains if the `includeSubDomains` parameter is used.

- The PKP header can be used only over a secure encryption without any errors; if multiple headers are seen, only the first one is processed.

- When a new PKP header is received, the information in it overwrites previously stored pins and metadata.

Pins are created by specifying the hashing algorithm and an SPKI fingerprint computed using that algorithm. For example:

```
Public-Key-Pins: max-age=2592000;
    pin-sha256="E9CZ9INDbd+2eRQozYqqbQ2yXLVKB9+xcprMF+44U1g=";
    pin-sha256="LPJNul+wow4m6DsqxbninhsWHlwfpOJecwQzYpOLmCQ="
```

---

[26] Enhanced Mitigation Experience Toolkit 4.1 [fsty.uk/b422] (Microsoft, 12 February 2013)

[27] Announcing EMET 5.0 Technical Preview [fsty.uk/b423] (Microsoft Security Research and Defense Blog, 25 February 2014)

[28] Public Key Pinning Extension for HTTP [fsty.uk/b424] (Internet-Draft, Evans et al., 25 June 2014)

---

The only hashing algorithm supported at the moment is SHA256; the sha256 identifier is used when configuring the pins. The fingerprints are encoded using Base64 encoding.

To enable pinning, you must specify the policy retention period and provide at least two pins. One of the pins must be present in the chain used for the connection over which the pins were received. The other pin *must not* be present. Because pinning is a potentially dangerous operation (it's easy to make a mistake and perform a self-inflicted denial of service attack), the second pin is required as a backup. The recommended practice is to have a backup certificate from a different CA and to keep it offline. Further, it is recommended that the backup certificate is occasionally tested. You really don't want to need it and only then find that it is not working.

## Reporting

Unlike HSTS, but similarly to CSP, HPKP specifies a mechanism for user agents to report pin-validation failures. This feature is activated using the report-uri parameter, which should contain the endpoint to which the report will be submitted.

```
Public-Key-Pins: max-age=2592000;
        pin-sha256="E9CZ9INDbd+2eRQozYqqbQ2yXLVKB9+xcprMF+44U1g=";
        pin-sha256="LPJNul+wow4m6DsqxbninhsWHlwfpOJecwQzYpOLmCQ=";
        report-uri="http://example.com/pkp-report"
```

The report is submitted using a POST HTTP request, which includes a JSON structure in the request body. For example:

```
{
  "date-time": "2014-04-06T13:00:50Z",
  "hostname": "www.example.com",
  "port": 443,
  "effective-expiration-date": "2014-05-01T12:40:50Z"
  "include-subdomains": false,
  "served-certificate-chain": [
    "-----BEGIN CERTIFICATE-----\n
    MIIEBDCCAuygAwIBAgIDAjppMAOGCSqGSIb3DQEBBQUAMEIxCzAJBgNVBAYTAlVT\n
    ...
    HFa9llF7b1cq26KqltyMdMKVvvBulRP/F/A8rLIQjcxz++iPAsbw+zOzlTvjwsto\n
    WHPbqCRiOwY1nQ2pM714A5AuTHhdUDqB1O6gyHA43LL5Z/qHQF1hwFGPa4NrzQU6\n
    yuGnBXj8ytqUOCwIPX4WecigUCAkVDNx\n
    -----END CERTIFICATE-----",
    ...
  ],
  "validated-certificate-chain": [
    "-----BEGIN CERTIFICATE-----\n
    MIIEBDCCAuygAwIBAgIDAjppMAOGCSqGSIb3DQEBBQUAMEIxCzAJBgNVBAYTAlVT\n
    ...
```

```
        HFa9llF7b1cq26KqltyMdMKVvvBulRP/F/A8rLIQjcxz++iPAsbw+zOzlTvjwsto\n
        WHPbqCRiOwY1nQ2pM714A5AuTHhdUDqB1O6gyHA43LL5Z/qHQF1hwFGPa4NrzQU6\n
        yuGnBXj8ytqUOCwIPX4WecigUCAkVDNx\n
        -----END CERTIFICATE-----",
        ...
    ],
    "known-pins": [
      'pin-sha256="d6qzRu9zOECb9OUez27xWltNsjOe1Md7GkYYkVoZWmM="',
      "pin-sha256=\"E9CZ9INDbd+2eRQozYqqbQ2yXLVKB9+xcprMF+44U1g=\""
    ]
  }
```

## Deployment without Enforcement

Reports are especially useful when HPKP is deployed without enforcement. This can be achieved using the Public-Key-Pins-Report-Only response header. This approach allows organizations to deploy pinning without fear of failure, ensure that it is configured correctly, and only later move to enforcement. Depending on their risk profile, some organizations might choose to never enable enforcement; knowing that you are being attacked is often as useful as avoiding the attack.

# DNS-Based Authentication of Named Entities (DANE)

*DNS-Based Authentication of Named Entities* (DANE),[29] is a proposed standard designed to provide associations between domain names and one or more cryptographic identities. The idea is that domain name owners, who already have control over their DNS configuration, can use the DNS as a separate channel to distribute information needed for robust TLS authentication. DANE is straightforward and relatively easy to deploy, but does not provide any security by itself. Instead, it relies on the availability of *Domain Name System Security Extensions* (DNSSEC).[30]

DNSSEC is an attempt to extend the current DNS implementation, which does not provide any security, with a new architecture that supports authentication using digital signatures. With authentication, we should be able to cryptographically verify that the DNS information we obtain is correct. DNSSEC is quite controversial. It's been in development for more than a decade, and its deployment has been slow. Experts' opinions differ widely as to whether DNSSEC is an improvement over the current DNS system or alternative improvements should be sought.

At the time of writing, about 70% of all top level domain names are signed.[31] However, enabling the DNSSEC backend is the easier part; getting wide end-user system support is going

---

[29] RFC 6698: The DNS-Based Authentication of Named Entities (DANE) Transport Layer Security (TLS) Protocol: TLSA [fsty.uk/b425] (Hoffman and Schlyter, August 2012)

[30] Domain Name System Security Extensions [fsty.uk/b426] (Wikipedia, retrieved 29 June 2014)

to take some more time. Fedora, a major Linux distribution, is the first operating system to consider enabling DNSSEC by default, in version 21 planned for Q4 2014.[32]

## DANE Use Cases

In our current model for TLS authentication, we rely on a two-step approach: (1) first we have a group of certification authorities that we trust to issue certificates only to genuine domain name owners, then, whenever a site is accessed, (2) user agents (e.g., browsers) check that the certificates are correct for the intended names. This split model is required because authentication of distant parties (e.g., people who have never met) is very tricky to get right, especially at scale. The system is designed to work on the assumption that the information provided by DNS is not reliable (i.e., can be subverted by an active network attacker).

DNSSEC challenges the assumption about DNS reliability. When DNS supports authentication, we have a new reliable channel to communicate to domain name owners; this means that we don't necessarily need third parties (CAs) to vouch for them. This opens up several interesting use cases:

**Secure deployment of self-signed certificates**

Today, self-signed certificates are considered insecure because there is no way for average users to differentiate them from self-signed MITM certificates. In other words, all self-signed certificates look the same. But, we can use a secure DNS to pin the certificate, thus allowing our user agent to know that they are using the right one. MITM certificates are easily detected.

**Secure deployment of private roots**

If you can securely pin the server certificate, then you can just as well pin any other certificate in the chain. That means that you can create your own root certificate and make users agents trust it—but only for the sites you own. This is a variation of the previous use case and largely of interest to those who have many sites. Rather than pin individual certificates (of which there are many, and they need to be frequently rotated), you create one root and pin it only once on all sites.

**Certificate and public key pinning**

DANE is not necessarily about displacing the current trust architecture. You can as easily pin CA-issued certificates and public CA roots. By doing this, you will be reducing the attack surface and effectively deciding which CAs are allowed to issue certificates for your properties.

---

[31] TLD DNSSEC Report [fsty.uk/b427] (ICANN Research, retrieved 29 June 2014)

[32] Fedora 21 To Have DNSSEC Validation Enabled By Default [fsty.uk/b428] (Dan York, 2 May 2014)

# Implementation

DANE introduces a new DNS entry type, called *TLSA Resource Record* (TLSA RR, or just TLSA), which is used to carry certificate associations. TLSA consists of four fields: (1) *Certificate Usage* to specify which part of a certificate chain should be pinned and how the validation should be performed; (2) a *Selector* to specify what element is used for pinning; (3) a *Matching Type* to choose between an exact match or hashing; and (4) *Certificate Association Data*, which carries the actual raw data used for matching. Different combinations of these four fields are used to deploy different pinning types.

## Certificate Usage

The *Certificate Usage* field can have four different values. In the original RFC, the values are simply digits from 0 to 3. A subsequent RFC added acronyms to make it easier to remember the correct values.[33]

**CA constraint (0; PKIX-TA)**

Creates a pin for a CA, whose matching certificate must be found anywhere in the chain. PKIX validation is performed as usual, but the root must come from a trusted CA.

**Service certificate constraint (1; PKIX-EE)**

Creates an end-entity pin, whose certificate must be presented at the first position in the chain. PKIX validation is performed as usual, but the root must come from a trusted CA.

**Trust anchor assertion (2; DANE-TA)**

Creates a trust anchor pin for a CA certificate (root or intermediate) that must be present in the trust chain. PKIX validation is performed as usual, but user agents must trust the pinned CA certificate. This option allows for certificates that are not issued by public CAs.

**Domain-issued certificate (3; DANE-EE)**

Creates an end-entity pin, whose certificate must be presented at the first position in the chain. There is no PKIX validation, and the pinned certificate is assumed to be trusted.

## Selector

The *Selector* field specifies how the association is presented. This allows us to create an association with a certificate (0; Cert) or with the SubjectPublicKeyInfo field (1; SPKI).

---

[33] RFC 7218: Adding Acronyms to Simplify Conversations about DANE [fsty.uk/b429] (Gudmundsson, April 2014)

## Matching Type

The *Matching Type* field specifies if the matching is by direct comparison (0; Full) or via hashing (1 and 2, or SHA2-256 and SHA2-512, respectively). Support for SHA256 is required; support for SHA512 is recommended.

## Certificate Association Data

The *Certificate Association Data* field contains the raw data that is used for the association. Its contents are determined by the values of the other three fields in the TLSA record. The certificate, which is always the starting point of an association, is assumed to be in DER format.

# Deployment

Leaving DNSSEC configuration and signing aside (only because it is out of scope of this book), DANE is pretty easy to deploy. All you need to do is add a new TLSA record under the correct name. The name is not just the domain name you wish to secure; it's a combination of three segments separated by dots:

- The first segment is the port on which the service is running, prefixed with an underscore. For example, _443 for HTTPS and _25 for SMTP.
- The second segment is the protocol, also prefixed with an underscore. Three protocols are supported: UDP, TCP, and SCTP. For HTTPS, the segment will be _tcp.
- The third segment is the fully qualified domain name for which you wish to create an association. For example, www.example.com.

In the following example, an association is created between a domain name and the public key of a CA (Certificate Usage is 0) identified by the SubjectPublicKeyInfo field (Selector is 1) via its SHA256 hash (Matching Type is 1):

```
_443._tcp.www.example.com. IN TLSA (
    0 1 1 d2abde240d7cd3ee6b4b28c54df034b9
        7983a1d16e8a410e4561cb106618e971 )
```

DANE is activated by adding one or more TLSA records to the desired domain name. If at least one association is present, user agents are required to establish a match; otherwise they must abort the TLS handshake. If there are no associations, then the user agent can process the TLS connection as it would normally.

Because multiple associations (TLSA records) can be configured for a domain name, it's possible to have one or more backup associations. It's also possible to rotate associations without any downtime. Unlike HPKP, DANE does not specify a memory effect, but there is one built into DNS itself: the *time to live* (TTL) value, which is the duration for which a record can be cached. Still, the lack of explicit memory effect is DANE's strength; mistakes are easy to correct by reconfiguring DNS. When deploying, especially initially, it's best to use the shortest TTL possible.

A potential disadvantage is the fact that the DANE RFC does not mandate any user interaction when a matching association can't be found. For example, HPKP requires that the user is given the means to manually break the pins in case of failure. This is a double-edged sword: stubborn users might end up overriding the security mechanisms in the case of a genuine attack. On the other hand, with DANE, there is no recourse when configuration mistakes happen. Another problem is that DANE does not support reporting, making it difficult to find out about association matching failures as they occur.

## Application Support

DANE is currently not supported by any major browser. Adding support is difficult, because DANE builds on DNSSEC; until operating systems start supporting DNSSEC, browsers need to implement DNSSEC resolution themselves. Chrome experimented with DANE back in 2011 (in Chrome 14), but eventually removed support, citing lack of use.[34] Because of this, DANE is currently of interest only to enthusiasts and those who wish to learn where public TLS authentication might be heading.

Despite lack of support, you can play with DANE today thanks to the DNSSEC TLSA Validator add-on, which is available for all major browsers.[35] Their releases are not always up-to-date with the latest browser versions. When I tried it, the Firefox version wouldn't work with my installation. If you do successfully install the add-on, VeriSign operates a demonstration site that you can test with.[36]

Outside of browsers, applications are slowly adding support for DNSSEC. For example, Postfix did with version 2.11, which shipped in January 2014.[37]

## Trust Assertions for Certificate Keys (TACK)

*Trust Assertions for Certificate Keys* (TACK)[38] is a proposal for public key pinning that aims to be independent of both public CAs and the DNS. The idea is that site operators create and establish their own signing keys (known as *TACK Signing Keys*, or TSKs), to provide support for independence. Once a user agent recognizes a TSK for a particular site, that key can be used to revoke old server keys, issue new ones, and so on. In other words, a TSK is

---

[34] DNSSEC authenticated HTTPS in Chrome [fsty.uk/b430] (Adam Langley, 16 Jun 2011)

[35] DNSSEC/TLSA Validator add-on for Web Browsers [fsty.uk/b431] (CZ.NIC, retrieved 29 June 2014)

[36] Verisign Labs DANE Demonstration [fsty.uk/b432] (VeriSign, retrieved 29 June 2014)

[37] DANE TLS authentication [fsty.uk/b433] (Postfix TLS Support, retrieved 29 June 2014)

[38] Trust Assertions for Certificate Keys [fsty.uk/b434] (Marlinspike and Perrin, January 2013)

similar to a private CA. Although a per-site TSK is recommended, related sites could rely on the same signing key.

TACK is the most ambitious of all pinning proposals, and that also makes it the most complex. A compliant user agent expresses support for TACK by submitting en empty `tack` extension in its `ClientHello`. In response, a compliant server uses the same extension to send one or more *tacks*, which are pins of the server's public key signed with the site's TSK. Pins are noted on the first sighting, but are activated only when seen for the second time. There is no fixed policy retention duration. Instead, on every visit a user agent works out a new policy retention time by subtracting the timestamp of the first pin sighting from the current timestamp. There is also a maximum limit of 30 days.

TACK is interesting because it can be used with any protocol (unlike, say, HPKP, which works only for HTTP). On the other hand, the use of a separate signing key introduces more complexity. In addition, it requires changes to the TLS protocol. At this time, it isn't clear whether browser vendors are planning to provide support for it.

# Certification Authority Authorization

*Certification Authority Authorization* (CAA)[39] proposes a way for domain name owners to authorize CAs to issue certificates for their domain names. It is intended as a defense-in-depth measure against attacks on the validation process during certificate issuance; with CAA, CAs can satisfy themselves that they are communicating with the real domain name owner.

CAA relies on DNS for policy distribution; it recommends DNSSEC but doesn't require it. It extends DNS by adding the *CAA Resource Record* (CAA RR), which is used to create authorization entries.

CAA supports several *property tags*, which are instructions to CAs. For example, the `issue` tag can be used to allow a CA (identified by its domain name) to issue a certificate for a particular domain name:

```
certs.example.com      CAA 0 issue "ca.example.net"
```

The same tag can be used to forbid certificate issuance:

```
nocerts.example.com    CAA 0 issue ";"
```

Other tags include `issuewild`, which concerns itself with wildcard certificates, and `iodef`, which defines a communication channel (e.g., email address) for CAs to report invalid certificate issuance requests back to site owners.

---

[39] RFC 6944: DNS Certification Authority Authorization (CAA) Resource Record [fsty.uk/b435] (Hallam-Baker, January 2013)

True success of CAA requires wide adoption by CAs. Attackers can always target the non-compliant CAs and get fraudulent certificates from them. Of course, from the perspective of a compliant CA, this is not necessarily a failure; anything that reduces the likelihood of attacks will be seen as positive. However, if there isn't a sufficient number of CAs supporting this feature, site owners are unlikely to make the effort to configure authorizations for their properties.

Like DANE, CAA works best with DNSSEC. Without it, CAs must take special care not to expose themselves to DNS spoofing attacks.

# 11 OpenSSL Cookbook

OpenSSL is an open source project that consists of a cryptographic library and an SSL/TLS toolkit. From the project's web site:

> The OpenSSL Project is a collaborative effort to develop a robust, commercial-grade, full-featured, and Open Source toolkit implementing the Secure Sockets Layer (SSL) and Transport Layer Security (TLS) protocols as well as a full-strength general purpose cryptography library. The project is managed by a worldwide community of volunteers that use the Internet to communicate, plan, and develop the OpenSSL toolkit and its related documentation.

OpenSSL is a de facto standard in this space and comes with a long history. The code initially began its life in 1995 under the name SSLeay,[1] when it was developed by Eric A. Young and Tim J. Hudson. The OpenSSL project was born in the last days of 1998, when Eric and Tim stopped their work on SSLeay to work on a commercial SSL/TLS toolkit called BSAFE SSL-C at RSA Australia.

Today, OpenSSL is ubiquitous on the server side and in many client tools. The command-line tools are also the most common choice for key and certificate management as well as testing. Interestingly, browsers have historically used other libraries, but that might change soon, given that the Google Chrome team is planning a transition to OpenSSL on all platforms.[2] The command-line tools provided by OpenSSL are most commonly used to manage keys and certificates.

OpenSSL is dual-licensed under OpenSSL and SSLeay licenses. Both are BSD-like, with an advertising clause. The license has been a source of contention for a very long time, because neither of the licenses is considered compatible with the GPL family of licenses. For that reason, you will often find that GPL-licensed programs favor GnuTLS.

---

[1] The letters "eay" in the name SSLeay are Eric A. Young's initials.

[2] Chrome: From NSS to OpenSSL [fsty.uk/b436] (Chrome design document, retrieved 10 July 2014)

# Getting Started

If you're using one of the Unix platforms, getting started with OpenSSL is easy; you're virtually guaranteed to already have it on your system. The only problem that you might face is that you might not have the latest version. In this section, I assume that you're using a Unix platform, because that's the natural environment for OpenSSL.

Windows users tend to download binaries, which might complicate the situation slightly. In the simplest case, if you need OpenSSL only for its command-line utilities, the main OpenSSL web site links to Shining Light Productions[3] for the Windows binaries. In all other situations, you need to ensure that you're not mixing binaries compiled under different versions of OpenSSL. Otherwise, you might experience crashes that are difficult to troubleshoot. The best approach is to use a single bundle of programs that includes everything that you need. For example, if you want to run Apache on Windows, you can get your binaries from the Apache Lounge.[4]

## Determine OpenSSL Version and Configuration

Before you do any work, you should know which OpenSSL version you'll be using. For example, here's what I get for version information with openssl version on Ubuntu 12.04 LTS, which is the system that I'll be using for the examples in this chapter:

```
$ openssl version
OpenSSL 1.0.1 14 Mar 2012
```

At the time of this writing, a transition from OpenSSL 0.9.x to OpenSSL 1.0.x is in progress. The version 1.0.1 is especially significant because it is the first version to support TLS 1.1 and 1.2. The support for newer protocols is part of a global trend, so it's likely that we're going to experience a period during which interoperability issues are not uncommon.

> **Note**
>
> Various operating systems often modify the OpenSSL code, usually to fix known issues. However, the name of the project and the version number generally stay the same, and there is no indication that the code is actually a fork of the original project that will behave differently. For example, the version of OpenSSL used in Ubuntu 12.04 LTS[5] is based on OpenSSL 1.0.1c. At the time of this writing, the full name of the package is openssl 1.0.1-4ubuntu5.16, and it contains patches for the many issues that came to light over time.

---

[3] Win32 OpenSSL [fsty.uk/b437] (Shining Light Productions, retrieved 3 July 2014)

[4] Apache 2.4 VC11 Binaries and Modules Win32 and Win64 [fsty.uk/b438] (Apache Lounge, retrieved 3 July 2014)

[5] "openssl" source package in Precise [fsty.uk/b439] (Ubuntu, retrieved 3 July 2014)

To get complete version information, use the -a switch:

```
$ openssl version -a
OpenSSL 1.0.1 14 Mar 2012
built on: Fri Jun 20 18:54:15 UTC 2014
platform: debian-amd64
options:  bn(64,64) rc4(8x,int) des(idx,cisc,16,int) blowfish(idx)
compiler: cc -fPIC -DOPENSSL_PIC -DZLIB -DOPENSSL_THREADS -D_REENTRANT -DDSO_DLFCN ↵
-DHAVE_DLFCN_H -m64 -DL_ENDIAN -DTERMIO -g -O2 -fstack-protector ↵
--param=ssp-buffer-size=4 -Wformat -Wformat-security -Werror=format-security -D↵
_FORTIFY_SOURCE=2 -Wl,-Bsymbolic-functions -Wl,-z,relro -Wa,--noexecstack -Wall ↵
-DOPENSSL_NO_TLS1_2_CLIENT -DOPENSSL_MAX_TLS1_2_CIPHER_LENGTH=50 -DMD32_REG_T=int ↵
-DOPENSSL_IA32_SSE2 -DOPENSSL_BN_ASM_MONT -DOPENSSL_BN_ASM_MONT5 -DOPENSSL_BN_ASM↵
_GF2m -DSHA1_ASM -DSHA256_ASM -DSHA512_ASM -DMD5_ASM -DAES_ASM -DVPAES_ASM -DBSAES↵
_ASM -DWHIRLPOOL_ASM -DGHASH_ASM
OPENSSLDIR: "/usr/lib/ssl"
```

The last line in the output (/usr/lib/ssl) is especially interesting because it will tell you where OpenSSL will look for its configuration and certificates. On my system, that location is essentially an alias for /etc/ssl, where Ubuntu keeps TLS-related files:

```
lrwxrwxrwx  1 root root   14 Apr 19 09:28 certs -> /etc/ssl/certs
drwxr-xr-x  2 root root 4096 May 28 06:04 misc
lrwxrwxrwx  1 root root   20 May 22 17:07 openssl.cnf -> /etc/ssl/openssl.cnf
lrwxrwxrwx  1 root root   16 Apr 19 09:28 private -> /etc/ssl/private
```

The misc/ folder contains a few supplementary scripts, the most interesting of which are the scripts that allow you to implement a private *certification authority* (CA).

## Building OpenSSL

In most cases, you will be using the operating system–supplied version of OpenSSL, but sometimes there are good reasons to upgrade. For example, your current server platform may still be using OpenSSL 0.9.x, and you might want to support newer protocol versions (available only in OpenSSL 1.0.1). Further, the newer versions may not have all the features you need. For example, on Ubuntu 12.04 LTS, there's no support for SSL 2 in the s_client command. Although not supporting this version of SSL by default is the right decision, you'll need this feature if you're routinely testing other servers for SSL 2 support.

You can start by downloading the most recent version of OpenSSL (in my case, 1.0.1h):

```
$ wget http://www.openssl.org/source/openssl-1.0.1h.tar.gz
```

The next step is to configure OpenSSL before compilation. In most cases, you'll be leaving the system-provided version alone and installing OpenSSL in a different location. For example:

```
$ ./config \
--prefix=/opt/openssl \
--openssldir=/opt/openssl \
enable-ec_nistp_64_gcc_128
```

The enable-ec_nistp_64_gcc_128 parameter activates optimized versions of certain frequently used elliptic curves. This optimization depends on a compiler feature that can't be automatically detected, which is why it's disabled by default.

You can then follow with:

```
$ make
$ make depend
$ sudo make install
```

You'll get the following in /opt/openssl:

```
drwxr-xr-x 2 root root  4096 Jun  3 08:49 bin
drwxr-xr-x 2 root root  4096 Jun  3 08:49 certs
drwxr-xr-x 3 root root  4096 Jun  3 08:49 include
drwxr-xr-x 4 root root  4096 Jun  3 08:49 lib
drwxr-xr-x 6 root root  4096 Jun  3 08:48 man
drwxr-xr-x 2 root root  4096 Jun  3 08:49 misc
-rw-r--r-- 1 root root 10835 Jun  3 08:49 openssl.cnf
drwxr-xr-x 2 root root  4096 Jun  3 08:49 private
```

The private/ folder is empty, but that's normal; you do not yet have any private keys. On the other hand, you'll probably be surprised to learn that the certs/ folder is empty too. OpenSSL does not include any root certificates; maintaining a trust store is considered outside the scope of the project. Luckily, your operating system probably already comes with a trust store that you can use. You can also build your own with little effort, as you'll see in the next section.

> **Note**
>
> When compiling software, it's important to be familiar with the default configuration of your compiler. System-provided packages are usually compiled using all the available hardening options, but if you compile some software yourself there is no guarantee that the same options will be used.[6]

## Examine Available Commands

OpenSSL is a cryptographic toolkit that consists of many different utilities. I counted 46 in my version. If it were ever appropriate to use the phrase *Swiss Army knife of cryptography*,

---

[6] compiler hardening in Ubuntu and Debian [fsty.uk/b440] (Kees Cook, 3 February 2014)

this is it. Even though you'll use only a handful of the utilities, you should familiarize your-self with everything that's available, because you never know what you might need in the future.

There isn't a specific help keyword, but help text is displayed whenever you type something OpenSSL does not recognize:

```
$ openssl help
openssl:Error: 'help' is an invalid command.

Standard commands
asn1parse        ca               ciphers          cms
crl              crl2pkcs7        dgst             dh
dhparam          dsa              dsaparam         ec
ecparam          enc              engine           errstr
gendh            gendsa           genpkey          genrsa
nseq             ocsp             passwd           pkcs12
pkcs7            pkcs8            pkey             pkeyparam
pkeyutl          prime            rand             req
rsa              rsautl           s_client         s_server
s_time           sess_id          smime            speed
spkac            srp              ts               verify
version          x509
```

The first part of the help output lists all available utilities. To get more information about a particular utility, use the man command followed by the name of the utility. For example, man ciphers will give you detailed information on how cipher suites are configured.

Help output doesn't actually end there, but the rest is somewhat less interesting. In the second part, you get the list of message digest commands:

```
Message Digest commands (see the `dgst' command for more details)
md4              md5              rmd160           sha
sha1
```

And then, in the third part, you'll see the list of all cipher commands:

```
Cipher commands (see the `enc' command for more details)
aes-128-cbc      aes-128-ecb      aes-192-cbc      aes-192-ecb
aes-256-cbc      aes-256-ecb      base64           bf
bf-cbc           bf-cfb           bf-ecb           bf-ofb
camellia-128-cbc camellia-128-ecb camellia-192-cbc camellia-192-ecb
camellia-256-cbc camellia-256-ecb cast             cast-cbc
cast5-cbc        cast5-cfb        cast5-ecb        cast5-ofb
des              des-cbc          des-cfb          des-ecb
des-ede          des-ede-cbc      des-ede-cfb      des-ede-ofb
des-ede3         des-ede3-cbc     des-ede3-cfb     des-ede3-ofb
des-ofb          des3             desx             rc2
```

| | | | |
|---|---|---|---|
| rc2-40-cbc | rc2-64-cbc | rc2-cbc | rc2-cfb |
| rc2-ecb | rc2-ofb | rc4 | rc4-40 |
| seed | seed-cbc | seed-cfb | seed-ecb |
| seed-ofb | zlib | | |

# Building a Trust Store

OpenSSL does not come with any trusted root certificates (also known as a *trust store*), so if you're installing from scratch you'll have to find them somewhere else. One possibility is to use the trust store built into your operating system. This choice is usually fine, but default trust stores may not always be up to date. A better choice—but one that involves more work —is to turn to Mozilla, which is putting a lot of effort into maintaining a robust trust store. For example, this is what I did for my assessment tool on SSL Labs.

Because it's open source, Mozilla keeps the trust store in the source code repository:

```
https://hg.mozilla.org/mozilla-central/raw-file/tip/security/nss/lib/ckfw/builtins↵
/certdata.txt
```

Unfortunately, their certificate collection is in a proprietary format, which is not of much use to others as is. If you don't mind getting the collection via a third party, the Curl project provides a regularly-updated conversion in *Privacy-Enhanced Mail* (PEM) format, which you can use directly:

```
http://curl.haxx.se/docs/caextract.html
```

But you don't have to write a conversion script if you'd rather download directly from Mozilla. Conversion scripts are available in Perl or Go. I describe both in the following sections.

> **Note**
>
> If you do end up working on your own conversion script, note that Mozilla's root certificate file actually contains two types of certificates: those that are trusted and are part of the store and also those that are explicitly distrusted. They use this mechanism to ban compromised intermediate CA certificates (e.g., DigiNotar's old certificates). Both conversion tools described here are smart enough to exclude distrusted certificates during the conversion process.

## Conversion Using Perl

The Curl project makes available a Perl script written by Guenter Knauf that can be used to convert Mozilla's trust store:

```
https://raw.github.com/bagder/curl/master/lib/mk-ca-bundle.pl
```

After you download and run the script, it will fetch the certificate data from Mozilla and convert it to the PEM format:

```
$ ./mk-ca-bundle.pl
Downloading 'certdata.txt' ...
Processing  'certdata.txt' ...
Done (156 CA certs processed, 19 untrusted skipped).
```

If you keep previously downloaded certificate data around, the script will use it to determine what changed and process only the updates.

### Conversion Using Go

If you prefer the Go programming language, Adam Langley has a conversion tool in it that you can find on GitHub:

```
https://github.com/agl/extract-nss-root-certs
```

To kick off a conversion process, first download the tool itself:

```
$ wget https://raw.github.com/agl/extract-nss-root-certs/master/convert_mozilla↵
_certdata.go
```

Then download Mozilla's certificate data:

```
$ wget https://hg.mozilla.org/mozilla-central/raw-file/tip/security/nss/lib/ckfw↵
/builtins/certdata.txt --output-document certdata.txt
```

Finally, convert the file with the following command:

```
$ go run convert_mozilla_certdata.go > ca-certificates
2012/06/04 09:52:29 Failed to parse certificate starting on line 23068: negative ↵
serial number
```

In my case, there was one invalid certificate, but otherwise the conversion worked.

# Key and Certificate Management

Most users turn to OpenSSL because they wish to configure and run a web server that supports SSL. That process consists of three steps: (1) generate a strong private key, (2) create a *Certificate Signing Request* (CSR) and send it to a CA, and (3) install the CA-provided certificate in your web server. These steps (and a few others) are covered in this section.

# Key Generation

The first step in preparing for the use of public encryption is to generate a private key. Before you begin, you must make several decisions:

**Key algorithm**

OpenSSL supports RSA, DSA, and ECDSA keys, but not all types are practical for use in all scenarios. For example, for web server keys everyone uses RSA, because DSA keys are effectively limited to 1,024 bits (Internet Explorer doesn't support anything stronger) and ECDSA keys are yet to be widely supported by CAs. For SSH, DSA and RSA are widely used, whereas ECDSA might not be supported by all clients.

**Key size**

The default key sizes might not be secure, which is why you should always explicitly configure key size. For example, the default for RSA keys is only 512 bits, which is simply insecure. If you used a 512-bit key on your server today, an intruder could take your certificate and use brute force to recover your private key, after which he or she could impersonate your web site. Today, 2,048-bit RSA keys are considered secure, and that's what you should use. Aim also to use 2,048 bits for DSA keys and at least 256 bits for ECDSA.

**Passphrase**

Using a passphrase with a key is optional, but strongly recommended. Protected keys can be safely stored, transported, and backed up. On the other hand, such keys are inconvenient, because they can't be used without their passphrases. For example, you might be asked to enter the passphrase every time you wish to restart your web server. For most, this is either too inconvenient or has unacceptable availability implications. In addition, using protected keys in production does not actually increase the security much, if at all. This is because, once activated, private keys are kept unprotected in program memory; an attacker who can get to the server can get the keys from there with just a little more effort. Thus, passphrases should be viewed only as a mechanism for protecting private keys when they are not installed on production systems. In other words, it's all right to keep passphrases on production systems, next to the keys. This, although not ideal, is much better than using unprotected keys. If you need better security, you should invest in a hardware solution.[7]

To generate an RSA key, use the genrsa command:

```
$ openssl genrsa -aes128 -out fd.key 2048
Generating RSA private key, 2048 bit long modulus
```

---

[7] A small number of organizations will have very strict security requirements that require the private keys to be protected at any cost. For them, the solution is to invest in a *Hardware Security Module* (HSM), which is a type of product specifically designed to make key extraction impossible, even with physical access to the server. To make this work, HSMs not only generate and store keys, but also perform all necessary operations (e.g., signature generation). HSMs are typically very expensive.

---

```
....+++
.........................................................................⏎
+++
e is 65537 (0x10001)
Enter pass phrase for fd.key: ****************
Verifying - Enter pass phrase for fd.key: ****************
```

Here, I specified that the key be protected with AES-128. You can also use AES-192 or
AES-256 (switches -aes192 and -aes256, respectively), but it's best to stay away from the
other algorithms (DES, 3DES, and SEED).

> ## Warning
>
> The e value that you see in the output refers to the public exponent, which is set to
> 65,537 by default. This is what's known as a *short public exponent*, and it signifi-
> cantly improves the performance of RSA verification. Using the -3 switch, you can
> choose 3 as your public exponent and make verification even faster. However, there
> are some unpleasant historical weaknesses associated with the use of 3 as a public
> exponent, which is why generally everyone recommends that you stick with 65,537.
> The latter choice provides a safety margin that's been proven effective in the past.

Private keys are stored in the so-called PEM format, which is ASCII:

```
$ cat fd.key
-----BEGIN RSA PRIVATE KEY-----
Proc-Type: 4,ENCRYPTED
DEK-Info: AES-256-CBC,717D24945A0CA95E2800B026D9D431CC

vERmFJzsLeAEDqWdXX4rNwogJp+y95uTnw+bOjWRw1+O1qgGqxQXPtH3LWDUz1Ym
mkpxmIwlSidVSUuUrrUzIL+V21EJ1W9iQ71SJoPOyzX7dYX5GCAwQm9Tsb4OFhV/
[21 lines removed...]
4phGTprEnEwrffRnYrt7khQwrJhNsw6TTtthMhx/UCJdpQdaLW/TuylaJMWL1JRW
i321s5me5ej6Pr4fGccNOe7lZK+563d7v5znAx+Wo1C+F7YgF+g8LOQ8emC+6AVV
-----END RSA PRIVATE KEY-----
```

A private key isn't just a blob of random data, even though that's what it looks like at a
glance. You can see a key's structure using the following rsa command:

```
$ openssl rsa -text -in fd.key
Enter pass phrase for fd.key: ****************
Private-Key: (2048 bit)
modulus:
    00:9e:57:1c:c1:0f:45:47:22:58:1c:cf:2c:14:db:
    [...]
publicExponent: 65537 (0x10001)
privateExponent:
    1a:12:ee:41:3c:6a:84:14:3b:be:42:bf:57:8f:dc:
```

```
     [...]
prime1:
    00:c9:7e:82:e4:74:69:20:ab:80:15:99:7d:5e:49:
    [...]
prime2:
    00:c9:2c:30:95:3e:cc:a4:07:88:33:32:a5:b1:d7:
    [...]
exponent1:
    68:f4:5e:07:d3:df:42:a6:32:84:8d:bb:f0:d6:36:
    [...]
exponent2:
    5e:b8:00:b3:f4:9a:93:cc:bc:13:27:10:9e:f8:7e:
    [...]
coefficient:
    34:28:cf:72:e5:3f:52:b2:dd:44:56:84:ac:19:00:
    [...]
writing RSA key
-----BEGIN RSA PRIVATE KEY-----
[...]
-----END RSA PRIVATE KEY-----
```

If you need to generate the corresponding public key, you can do that with the following rsa command:

```
$ openssl rsa -in fd.key -pubout -out fd-public.key
Enter pass phrase for fd.key: ****************
```

The public key is much shorter than the private key:

```
$ cat fd-public.key
-----BEGIN PUBLIC KEY-----
MIIBIjANBgkqhkiG9w0BAQEFAAOCAQ8AMIIBCgKCAQEAnlccwQ9FRyJYHM8sFNsY
PUHJHJzhJdwcS7kBptutf/L6OvoEAzCVHi/m0qAA4QM5BziZgnvv+FNnE3sgE5pz
iovEHJ3C959mNQmpvnedXwfcOIlbrNqdISJiPOjs6mDCzYjSO1NCQoy3UpYwvwj7
0ryR1F+abARehlts/Xs/PtX3Vamrlji JN6JNgFICy3ZvEhLZEKxR7oob7TnyZDrj
IHxBbqPNzeiqLCFLFPGgJPaOcH8DdovBTesvu7wr/ecsf8CYyUCdEwGkZh9DKtdU
HFa9H8tWW2mX6uwYeHCnf2HTwOE8vjtOb8oYQxlQxtL7dpFyMgrpPOoOVkZZW/PO
NQIDAQAB
-----END PUBLIC KEY-----
```

It's good practice to verify that the output contains what you're expecting. For example, if you forget to include the -pubout switch on the command line, the output will contain your private key instead of the public key.

DSA key generation is a two-step process: DSA parameters are created in the first step and the key in the second. Rather than execute the steps one at a time, I tend to use the following two commands as one:

```
$ openssl dsaparam -genkey 2048 | openssl dsa -out dsa.key -aes128
Generating DSA parameters, 2048 bit long prime
This could take some time
[...]
read DSA key
writing DSA key
Enter PEM pass phrase: ***************
Verifying - Enter PEM pass phrase: ***************
```

This approach allows me to generate a password-protected key while avoiding leaving any temporary files (DSA parameters) and/or temporary keys on disk.

The process is similar for ECDSA keys, except that it isn't possible to create keys of arbitrary sizes. Instead, for each key you select a *named curve*, which controls key size, but it controls other EC parameters as well. The following example creates a 256-bit ECDSA key using the secp256r1 named curve:

```
$ openssl ecparam -genkey -name secp256r1 | openssl ec -out ec.key -aes128
using curve name prime256v1 instead of secp256r1
read EC key
writing EC key
Enter PEM pass phrase: ***************
Verifying - Enter PEM pass phrase: ***************
```

OpenSSL supports many named curves (you can get a full list with the -list_curves switch), but, for web server keys, you're limited to only two curves that are supported by all major browsers: secp256r1 (OpenSSL uses the name prime256v1) and secp384r1.

# Creating Certificate Signing Requests

Once you have a private key, you can proceed to create a *Certificate Signing Request* (CSR). This is a formal request asking a CA to sign a certificate, and it contains the public key of the entity requesting the certificate and some information about the entity. This data will all be part of the certificate.

CSR creation is usually an interactive process that takes the private server key as input. Read the instructions given by the openssl tool carefully; if you want a field to be empty, you must enter a single dot (.) on the line, rather than just hit Return. If you do the latter, OpenSSL will populate the corresponding CSR field with the default value. (This behavior doesn't make any sense when used with the default OpenSSL configuration, which is what virtually everyone does. It *does* make sense once you realize you can actually change the defaults, either by modifying the OpenSSL configuration or by providing your own configuration files.)

```
$ openssl req -new -key fd.key -out fd.csr
Enter pass phrase for fd.key: ***************
```

```
You are about to be asked to enter information that will be incorporated
into your certificate request.
What you are about to enter is what is called a Distinguished Name or a DN.
There are quite a few fields but you can leave some blank
For some fields there will be a default value,
If you enter '.', the field will be left blank.
-----
Country Name (2 letter code) [AU]:GB
State or Province Name (full name) [Some-State]:.
Locality Name (eg, city) []:London
Organization Name (eg, company) [Internet Widgits Pty Ltd]:Feisty Duck Ltd
Organizational Unit Name (eg, section) []:
Common Name (e.g. server FQDN or YOUR name) []:www.feistyduck.com
Email Address []:webmaster@feistyduck.com

Please enter the following 'extra' attributes
to be sent with your certificate request
A challenge password []:
An optional company name []:
```

> ## Note
>
> According to Section 5.4.1 of RFC 2985,[8] *challenge password* is an optional field
> that was intended for use during certificate revocation as a way of identifying the
> original entity that had requested the certificate. If entered, the password will be
> included verbatim in the CSR and communicated to the CA. It's actually quite rare
> to find a CA that relies on this field, however. All instructions I've seen recommend
> leaving it alone. Having a challenge password does not increase the security of the
> CSR in any way. Further, this field should not be confused with the key passphrase,
> which is a separate feature.

After a CSR is generated, use it to sign your own certificate and/or send it to a public CA
and ask him or her to sign the certificate. Both approaches are described in the following
sections. But before you do that, it's a good idea to double-check that the CSR is correct.
Here's how:

```
$ openssl req -text -in fd.csr -noout
Certificate Request:
    Data:
        Version: 0 (0x0)
        Subject: C=GB, L=London, O=Feisty Duck Ltd, CN=www.feistyduck.com↵
/emailAddress=webmaster@feistyduck.com
        Subject Public Key Info:
```

---

[8] RFC 2985: PKCS #9: Selected Object Classes and Attribute Types Version 2.0 [fsty.uk/b441] (M. Nystrom and B. Kaliski, November 2000)

```
        Public Key Algorithm: rsaEncryption
            Public-Key: (2048 bit)
            Modulus:
                00:b7:fc:ca:1c:a6:c8:56:bb:a3:26:d1:df:e4:e3:
                [16 more lines...]
                d1:57
            Exponent: 65537 (0x10001)
        Attributes:
            a0:00
    Signature Algorithm: sha1WithRSAEncryption
        a7:43:56:b2:cf:ed:c7:24:3e:36:0f:6b:88:e9:49:03:a6:91:
        [13 more lines...]
        47:8b:e3:28
```

# Creating CSRs from Existing Certificates

You can save yourself some typing if you're renewing a certificate and don't want to make any changes to the information presented in it. With the following command, you can create a brand-new CSR from an existing certificate:

```
$ openssl x509 -x509toreq -in fd.crt -out fd.csr -signkey fd.key
```

> **Note**
>
> Unless you're using some form of public key pinning and wish to continue using the existing key, it's best practice to generate a new key every time you apply for a new certificate. Key generation is quick and inexpensive and reduces your exposure.

# Unattended CSR Generation

CSR generation doesn't have to be interactive. Using a custom OpenSSL configuration file, you can both automate the process (as explained in this section) and do certain things that are not possible interactively (as discussed in subsequent sections).

For example, let's say that we want to automate the generation of a CSR for www.feistyduck.com. We would start by creating a file fd.cnf with the following contents:

```
[req]
prompt = no
distinguished_name = dn
req_extensions = ext

[dn]
CN = www.feistyduck.com
emailAddress = webmaster@feistyduck.com
```

```
O = Feisty Duck Ltd
L = London
C = GB

[ext]
subjectAltName = DNS:www.feistyduck.com,DNS:feistyduck.com
```

Now you can create the CSR directly from the command line:

```
$ openssl req -new -config fd.cnf -key fd.key -out fd.csr
Enter pass phrase for fd.key: ****************
```

You'll be asked for the passphrase only if you used one during key generation.

## Signing Your Own Certificates

If you're installing a TLS server for your own use, you probably don't want to go to a CA to get a publicly trusted certificate. It's much easier to sign your own. The fastest way to do this is to generate a self-signed certificate. If you're a Firefox user, on your first visit to the web site you can create a certificate exception, after which the site will be as secure as if it were protected with a publicly trusted certificate.

If you already have a CSR, create a certificate using the following command:

```
$ openssl x509 -req -days 365 -in fd.csr -signkey fd.key -out fd.crt
Signature ok
subject=/CN=www.feistyduck.com/emailAddress=webmaster@feistyduck.com/O=Feisty Duck ↵
Ltd/L=London/C=GB
Getting Private key
Enter pass phrase for fd.key: ****************
```

You don't actually have to create a CSR in a separate step. The following command creates a self-signed certificate starting with a key alone:

```
$ openssl req -new -x509 -days 365 -key fd.key -out fd.crt
```

If you don't wish to be asked any questions, use the -subj switch to provide the certificate subject information on the command line:

```
$ openssl req -new -x509 -days 365 -key fd.key -out fd.crt \
  -subj "/C=GB/L=London/O=Feisty Duck Ltd/CN=www.feistyduck.com"
```

## Creating Certificates Valid for Multiple Hostnames

By default, certificates produced by OpenSSL have only one common name and are valid for only one hostname. Because of this, even if you have related web sites, you are forced to use a separate certificate for each site. In this situation, using a single *multidomain* certificate makes much more sense. Further, even when you're running a single web site, you need to ensure that the certificate is valid for all possible paths that end users can take to reach it. In practice, this means using at least two names, one with the www prefix and one without (e.g., www.feistyduck.com and feistyduck.com).

There are two mechanisms for supporting multiple hostnames in a certificate. The first is to list all desired hostnames using an X.509 extension called *Subject Alternative Name* (SAN). The second is to use wildcards. You can also use a combination of the two approaches when it's more convenient. In practice, for most sites, you can specify a bare domain name and a wildcard to cover all the subdomains (e.g., feistyduck.com and *.feistyduck.com).

> **Warning**
>
> When a certificate contains alternative names, all common names are ignored. Newer certificates produced by CAs may not even include any common names. For that reason, include all desired hostnames on the alternative names list.

First, place the extension information in a separate text file. I'm going to call it fd.ext. In the file, specify the name of the extension (subjectAltName) and list the desired hostnames, as in the following example:

```
subjectAltName = DNS:*.feistyduck.com, DNS:feistyduck.com
```

Then, when using the x509 command to issue a certificate, refer to the file using the -extfile switch:

```
$ openssl x509 -req -days 365 \
-in fd.csr -signkey fd.key -out fd.crt \
-extfile fd.ext
```

The rest of the process is no different from before. But when you examine the generated certificate afterward, you'll find that it contains the SAN extension:

```
X509v3 extensions:
        X509v3 Subject Alternative Name:
            DNS:*.feistyduck.com, DNS:feistyduck.com
```

# Examining Certificates

Most of the time, certificates appear to use what are essentially random arrays of bytes. But they contain a great deal of information; you just need to know how to unpack it. The x509 command does just that, so let's look at our self-signed certificates.

In the following example, I use the -text switch to print certificate contents and -noout to reduce clutter by not printing the encoded certificate itself (which is the default behavior):

```
$ openssl x509 -text -in fd.crt -noout
Certificate:
    Data:
        Version: 1 (0x0)
        Serial Number: 13073330765974645413 (0xb56dcd10f11aaaa5)
    Signature Algorithm: sha1WithRSAEncryption
        Issuer: CN=www.feistyduck.com/emailAddress=webmaster@feistyduck.com, ↵
O=Feisty Duck Ltd, L=London, C=GB
        Validity
            Not Before: Jun  4 17:57:34 2012 GMT
            Not After : Jun  4 17:57:34 2013 GMT
        Subject: CN=www.feistyduck.com/emailAddress=webmaster@feistyduck.com, ↵
O=Feisty Duck Ltd, L=London, C=GB
        Subject Public Key Info:
            Public Key Algorithm: rsaEncryption
                Public-Key: (2048 bit)
                Modulus:
                    00:b7:fc:ca:1c:a6:c8:56:bb:a3:26:d1:df:e4:e3:
                    [16 more lines...]
                    d1:57
                Exponent: 65537 (0x10001)
    Signature Algorithm: sha1WithRSAEncryption
        49:70:70:41:6a:03:0f:88:1a:14:69:24:03:6a:49:10:83:20:
        [13 more lines...]
        74:a1:11:86
```

Self-signed certificates usually contain only the most basic certificate data, as seen in the previous example. By comparison, certificates issued by public CAs are much more interesting, as they contain a number of additional fields (via the X.509 extension mechanism). Let's go over them quickly.

The *Basic Constraints* extension is used to mark certificates as belonging to a CA, giving them the ability to sign other certificates. Non-CA certificates will either have this extension omitted or will have the value of CA set to FALSE. This extension is critical, which means that all software-consuming certificates must understand its meaning.

```
X509v3 Basic Constraints: critical
    CA:FALSE
```

The *Key Usage* (KU) and *Extended Key Usage* (EKU) extensions restrict what a certificate can be used for. If these extensions are present, then only the listed uses are allowed. If the extensions are not present, there are no use restrictions. What you see in this example is typical for a web server certificate, which, for example, does not allow for code signing:

```
X509v3 Key Usage: critical
    Digital Signature, Key Encipherment
```

```
X509v3 Extended Key Usage:
    TLS Web Server Authentication, TLS Web Client Authentication
```

The *CRL Distribution Points* extension lists the addresses where the CA's *Certificate Revocation List* (CRL) information can be found. This information is important in cases in which certificates need to be revoked. CRLs are CA-signed lists of revoked certificates, published at regular time intervals (e.g., seven days).

```
X509v3 CRL Distribution Points:
    Full Name:
     URI:http://crl.starfieldtech.com/sfs3-20.crl
```

> **Note**
>
> You might have noticed that the CRL location doesn't use a secure server, and you might be wondering if the link is thus insecure. It is not. Because each CRL is signed by the CA that issued it, browsers are able to verify its integrity. In fact, if CRLs were distributed over TLS, browsers might face a chicken-and-egg problem in which they want to verify the revocation status of the certificate used by the server delivering the CRL itself!

The *Certificate Policies* extension is used to indicate the policy under which the certificate was issued. For example, this is where *extended validation* (EV) indicators can be found (as in the example that follows). The indicators are in the form of unique object identifiers (OIDs), and they are unique to the issuing CA. In addition, this extension often contains one or more *Certificate Policy Statement* (CPS) points, which are usually web pages or PDF documents.

```
X509v3 Certificate Policies:
    Policy: 2.16.840.1.114414.1.7.23.3
    CPS: http://certificates.starfieldtech.com/repository/
```

The *Authority Information Access* (AIA) extension usually contains two important pieces of information. First, it lists the address of the CA's *Online Certificate Status Protocol* (OCSP) responder, which can be used to check for certificate revocation in real time. The extension may also contain a link to where the issuer's certificate (the next certificate in the chain) can be found. These days, server certificates are rarely signed directly by trusted root certificates, which means that users must include one or more intermediate certificates in their configuration. Mistakes are easy to make and will invalidate the certificates. Some clients (e.g., Internet Explorer) can use the information provided in this extension to fix an incomplete certificate chain, but many don't.

```
Authority Information Access:
    OCSP - URI:http://ocsp.starfieldtech.com/
    CA Issuers - URI:http://certificates.starfieldtech.com/repository/sf↵
_intermediate.crt
```

The *Subject Key Identifier* and *Authority Key Identifier* extensions establish unique subject and authority key identifiers, respectively. The value specified in the Authority Key Identifier extension of a certificate must match the value specified in the Subject Key Identifier extension in the issuing certificate. This information is very useful during the certification path-building process, in which a client is trying to find all possible paths from a leaf (server) certificate to a trusted root. Certification authorities will often use one private key with more than one certificate, and this field allows software to reliably identify which certificate can be matched to which key. In the real world, many certificate chains supplied by servers are invalid, but that fact often goes unnoticed because browsers are able to find alternative trust paths.

```
X509v3 Subject Key Identifier:
    4A:AB:1C:C3:D3:4E:F7:5B:2B:59:71:AA:20:63:D6:C9:40:FB:14:F1
X509v3 Authority Key Identifier:
    keyid:49:4B:52:27:D1:1B:BC:F2:A1:21:6A:62:7B:51:42:7A:8A:D7:D5:56
```

Finally, the *Subject Alternative Name* extension is used to list all the hostnames for which the certificate is valid. This extension is optional; if it isn't present, clients fall back to using the information provided in the *Common Name* (CN), which is part of the *Subject* field.

```
X509v3 Subject Alternative Name:
    DNS:www.feistyduck.com, DNS:feistyduck.com
```

## Key and Certificate Conversion

Private keys and certificates can be stored in a variety of formats, which means that you'll often need to convert them from one format to another. The most common formats are:

**Binary (DER) certificate**
Contains an X.509 certificate in its raw form, using DER ASN.1 encoding.

**ASCII (PEM) certificate(s)**
Contains a base64-encoded DER certificate, with `-----BEGIN CERTIFICATE-----` used as the header and `-----END CERTIFICATE-----` as the footer. Usually seen with only one certificate per file, although some programs allow more than one certificate depending on the context. For example, the Apache web server requires the server certificate to be alone in one file, with all intermediate certificates together in another.

**Binary (DER) key**
Contains a private key in its raw form, using DER ASN.1 encoding. OpenSSL creates keys in its own traditional (SSLeay) format. There's also an alternative format called PKCS#8 (defined in RFC 5208), but it's not widely used. OpenSSL can convert to and from PKCS#8 format using the pkcs8 command.

### ASCII (PEM) key

Contains a base64-encoded DER certificate with additional metadata (e.g., the algorithm used for password protection).

### PKCS#7 certificate(s)

A complex format designed for the transport of signed or encrypted data, defined in RFC 2315. It's usually seen with `.p7b` and `.p7c` extensions and can include the entire certificate chain as needed. This format is supported by Java's `keytool` utility.

### PKCS#12 (PFX) key and certificate(s)

A complex format that can store and protect a server key along with an entire certificate chain. It's commonly seen with `.p12` and `.pfx` extensions. This format is commonly used in Microsoft products, but is also used for client certificates. These days, the PFX name is used as a synonym for PKCS#12, even though PFX referred to a different format a long time ago (an early version of PKCS#12). It's unlikely that you'll encounter the old version anywhere.

## PEM and DER Conversion

Certificate conversion between PEM and DER formats is performed with the x509 tool. To convert a certificate from PEM to DER format:

```
$ openssl x509 -inform PEM -in fd.pem -outform DER -out fd.der
```

To convert a certificate from DER to PEM format:

```
$ openssl x509 -inform DER -in fd.der -outform PEM -out fd.pem
```

The syntax is identical if you need to convert private keys between DER and PEM formats, but different commands are used: rsa for RSA keys, and dsa for DSA keys.

## PKCS#12 (PFX) Conversion

One command is all that's needed to convert the key and certificates in PEM format to PKCS#12:

```
$ openssl pkcs12 -export \
    -name "My Certificate" \
    -out fd.p12 \
    -inkey fd.key \
    -in fd.crt \
    -certfile fd-chain.crt
Enter Export Password: ****************
Verifying - Enter Export Password: ****************
```

The reverse conversion isn't as straightforward. You can use a single command, but in that case you'll get the entire contents in a single file:

```
$ openssl pkcs12 -in fd.p12 -out fd.pem -nodes
```

Now, you must open the file fd.pem in your favorite editor and manually split it into individual key, certificate, and intermediate certificate files. While you're doing that, you'll notice additional content provided before each component. For example:

```
Bag Attributes
    localKeyID: E3 11 E4 F1 2C ED 11 66 41 1B B8 83 35 D2 DD 07 FC DE 28 76
subject=/1.3.6.1.4.1.311.60.2.1.3=GB/2.5.4.15=Private Organization⏎
/serialNumber=06694169/C=GB/ST=London/L=London/O=Feisty Duck Ltd⏎
/CN=www.feistyduck.com
issuer=/C=US/ST=Arizona/L=Scottsdale/O=Starfield Technologies, Inc./OU=http:/⏎
/certificates.starfieldtech.com/repository/CN=Starfield Secure Certification Autho
-----BEGIN CERTIFICATE-----
MIIF5zCCBM+gAwIBAgIHBG9JXlv9vTANBgkqhkiG9w0BAQUFADCB3DELMAkGA1UE
BhMCVVMxEDAOBgNVBAgTBOFyaXpvbmExEzARBgNVBAcTClNjb3R0c2RhbGUxJTAj
[...]
```

This additional metadata is very handy to quickly identify the certificates. Obviously, you should ensure that the main certificate file contains the leaf server certificate and not something else. Further, you should also ensure that the intermediate certificates are provided in the correct order, with the issuing certificate following the signed one. If you see a self-signed root certificate, feel free to delete it or store it elsewhere; it shouldn't go into the chain.

> ### Warning
>
> The final conversion output shouldn't contain anything apart from the encoded key and certificates. Although some tools are smart enough to ignore what isn't needed, other tools are not. Leaving extra data in PEM files might result in problems that are difficult to troubleshoot.

It's possible to get OpenSSL to split the components for you, but doing so requires multiple invocations of the pkcs12 command (including typing the bundle password each time):

```
$ openssl pkcs12 -in fd.p12 -nocerts -out fd.key -nodes
$ openssl pkcs12 -in fd.p12 -nokeys -clcerts -out fd.crt
$ openssl pkcs12 -in fd.p12 -nokeys -cacerts -out fd-chain.crt
```

This approach won't save you much work. You must still examine each file to ensure that it contains the correct contents and to remove the metadata.

## PKCS#7 Conversion

To convert from PEM to PKCS#7, use the crl2pkcs7 command:

```
$ openssl crl2pkcs7 -nocrl -out fd.p7b -certfile fd.crt -certfile fd-chain.crt
```

To convert from PKCS#7 to PEM, use the `pkcs7` command with the `-print_certs` switch:

```
openssl pkcs7 -in fd.p7b -print_certs -out fd.pem
```

Similar to the conversion from PKCS#12, you must now edit the `fd.pem` file to clean it up and split it into the desired components.

# Configuration

In this section, I discuss two topics relevant for TLS deployment. The first is cipher suite configuration, in which you specify which of the many suites available in TLS you wish to use for communication. This topic is important because virtually every program that uses OpenSSL reuses its suite configuration mechanism. That means that once you learn how to configure cipher suites for one program, you can reuse the same knowledge elsewhere. The second topic is the performance measurement of raw crypto operations.

## Cipher Suite Selection

A common task in TLS server configuration is selecting which cipher suites are going to be supported. Programs that rely on OpenSSL usually adopt the same approach to suite configuration as OpenSSL does, simply passing through the configuration options. For example, in Apache `httpd`, the cipher suite configuration may look like this:

```
SSLHonorCipherOrder On
SSLCipherSuite "HIGH:!aNULL:@STRENGTH"
```

The first line controls cipher suite prioritization (and configures `httpd` to actively select suites). The second line controls which suites will be supported.

Coming up with a good suite configuration can be pretty time consuming, and there are a lot of details to consider. The best approach is to use the OpenSSL `ciphers` command to determine which suites are enabled with a particular configuration string.

### Obtaining the List of Supported Suites

Before you do anything else, you should determine which suites are supported by your OpenSSL installation. To do this, invoke the `ciphers` command with the switch `-v` and the parameter `ALL:COMPLEMENTOFALL` (clearly, `ALL` does not actually mean "all"):

```
$ openssl ciphers -v 'ALL:COMPLEMENTOFALL'
ECDHE-RSA-AES256-GCM-SHA384    TLSv1.2 Kx=ECDH Au=RSA   Enc=AESGCM(256) Mac=AEAD
ECDHE-ECDSA-AES256-GCM-SHA384  TLSv1.2 Kx=ECDH Au=ECDSA Enc=AESGCM(256) Mac=AEAD
```

```
ECDHE-RSA-AES256-SHA384      TLSv1.2 Kx=ECDH Au=RSA    Enc=AES(256)    Mac=SHA384
ECDHE-ECDSA-AES256-SHA384    TLSv1.2 Kx=ECDH Au=ECDSA Enc=AES(256)    Mac=SHA384
ECDHE-RSA-AES256-SHA         SSLv3   Kx=ECDH Au=RSA    Enc=AES(256)    Mac=SHA1
[106 more lines...]
```

> **Tip**
>
> If you're using OpenSSL 1.0.0 or later, you can also use the uppercase -V switch to
> request extra-verbose output. In this mode, the output will also contain suite IDs,
> which are always handy to have. For example, OpenSSL does not always use the
> RFC names for the suites; in such cases, you must use the IDs to cross-check.

In my case, there were 111 suites in the output. Each line contains information on one suite
and the following bits:

1. Suite name

2. Required minimum protocol version

3. Key exchange algorithm

4. Authentication algorithm

5. Cipher algorithm and strength

6. MAC (integrity) algorithm

7. Export suite indicator

If you change the `ciphers` parameter to something other than `ALL:COMPLEMENTOFALL`,
OpenSSL will list only the suites that match that configuration. For example, you can ask it
to list only cipher suites that are based on RC4, as follows:

```
$ openssl ciphers -v 'RC4'
ECDHE-RSA-RC4-SHA      SSLv3 Kx=ECDH        Au=RSA   Enc=RC4(128) Mac=SHA1
ECDHE-ECDSA-RC4-SHA    SSLv3 Kx=ECDH        Au=ECDSA Enc=RC4(128) Mac=SHA1
AECDH-RC4-SHA          SSLv3 Kx=ECDH        Au=None  Enc=RC4(128) Mac=SHA1
ADH-RC4-MD5            SSLv3 Kx=DH          Au=None  Enc=RC4(128) Mac=MD5
ECDH-RSA-RC4-SHA       SSLv3 Kx=ECDH/RSA    Au=ECDH  Enc=RC4(128) Mac=SHA1
ECDH-ECDSA-RC4-SHA     SSLv3 Kx=ECDH/ECDSA Au=ECDH  Enc=RC4(128) Mac=SHA1
RC4-SHA                SSLv3 Kx=RSA         Au=RSA   Enc=RC4(128) Mac=SHA1
RC4-MD5                SSLv3 Kx=RSA         Au=RSA   Enc=RC4(128) Mac=MD5
PSK-RC4-SHA            SSLv3 Kx=PSK         Au=PSK   Enc=RC4(128) Mac=SHA1
EXP-ADH-RC4-MD5        SSLv3 Kx=DH(512)     Au=None  Enc=RC4(40)  Mac=MD5  export
EXP-RC4-MD5            SSLv3 Kx=RSA(512)    Au=RSA   Enc=RC4(40)  Mac=MD5  export
```

The output will contain all suites that match your requirements, even if they're insecure.
Clearly, you should choose your configuration strings carefully in order to activate only
what's secure. Further, the order in which suites appear in the output matters. When you
configure your TLS server to actively select the cipher suite that will be used for a connec-

tion (which is the best practice and should always be done), the suites listed first are given priority.

## Keywords

Cipher suite *keywords* are the basic building blocks of cipher suite configuration. Each suite name (e.g., RC4-SHA) is a keyword that selects exactly one suite. All other keywords select groups of suites according to some criteria. Normally, I might direct you to the OpenSSL documentation for a comprehensive list of keywords, but it turns out that the ciphers documentation is not up to date; it's missing some more recent additions. For that reason, I'll try to document all the keywords in this section.

Group keywords are shortcuts that select frequently used cipher suites. For example, HIGH will select only very strong cipher suites.

Table 11.1. Group keywords

| Keyword | Meaning |
|---------|---------|
| DEFAULT | The default cipher list. This is determined at compile time and, as of OpenSSL 1.0.0, is normally ALL:!aNULL:!eNULL. This must be the first cipher string specified. |
| COMPLEMENTOFDEFAULT | The ciphers included in ALL, but not enabled by default. Currently, this is ADH. Note that this rule does not cover eNULL, which is not included by ALL (use COMPLEMENTOFALL if necessary). |
| ALL | All cipher suites except the eNULL ciphers, which must be explicitly enabled. |
| COMPLEMENTOFALL | The cipher suites not enabled by ALL, currently eNULL. |
| HIGH | "High"-encryption cipher suites. This currently means those with key lengths larger than 128 bits, and some cipher suites with 128-bit keys. |
| MEDIUM | "Medium"-encryption cipher suites, currently some of those using 128-bit encryption. |
| LOW | "Low"-encryption cipher suites, currently those using 64- or 56-bit encryption algorithms, but excluding export cipher suites. **Insecure.** |
| EXP, EXPORT | Export encryption algorithms. Including 40- and 56-bit algorithms. **Insecure.** |
| EXPORT40 | 40-bit export encryption algorithms. **Insecure.** |
| EXPORT56 | 56-bit export encryption algorithms. **Insecure.** |
| TLSv1, SSLv3, SSLv2 | TLS 1.0, SSL 3, or SSL 2 cipher suites, respectively. |

Digest keywords select suites that use a particular digest algorithm. For example, MD5 selects all suites that rely on MD5 for integrity validation.

Table 11.2. Digest algorithm keywords

| Keyword | Meaning |
| --- | --- |
| MD5 | Cipher suites using MD5. **Obsolete and insecure.** |
| SHA, SHA1 | Cipher suites using SHA1 and SHA2 (v1.0+). |
| SHA256 (v1.0+) | Cipher suites using SHA256. |
| SHA384 (v1.0+) | Cipher suites using SHA384. |

> **Note**
>
> TLS 1.2 introduced support for authenticated encryption, which bundles encryption with integrity checks. When the so-called AEAD (Authenticated Encryption with Associated Data) suites are used, the protocol doesn't need to provide additional integrity verification. For this reason, you won't be able to use the digest algorithm keywords to select AEAD suites, even though their names include SHA256 and SHA384 suffixes.

Authentication keywords select suites based on the authentication method they use. Today, virtually all public certificates use RSA for authentication. In the future, we should see a very slow rise in the use of Elliptic Curve (ECDSA) certificates.

Table 11.3. Authentication keywords

| Keyword | Meaning |
| --- | --- |
| aDH | Cipher suites effectively using DH authentication, i.e., the certificates carry DH keys. **Not implemented.** |
| aDSS, DSS | Cipher suites using DSS authentication, i.e., the certificates carry DSS keys. |
| aECDH (v1.0+) | Cipher suites that use ECDH authentication. |
| aECDSA (v1.0+) | Cipher suites that use ECDSA authentication. |
| aNULL | Cipher suites offering no authentication. This is currently the anonymous DH algorithms. **Insecure.** |
| aRSA | Cipher suites using RSA authentication, i.e., the certificates carry RSA keys. |
| PSK | Cipher suites using PSK (Pre-Shared Key) authentication. |
| SRP | Cipher suites using SRP (Secure Remote Password) authentication. |

Key exchange keywords select suites based on the key exchange algorithm. When it comes to ephemeral Diffie-Hellman suites, OpenSSL is inconsistent in naming the suites and the keywords. In the suite names, ephemeral suites tend to have an E at the end of the key exchange algorithm (e.g., ECDHE-RSA-RC4-SHA and DHE-RSA-AES256-SHA), but in the keywords the E is at the beginning (e.g., EECDH and EDH). To make things worse, some older suites do have E at the beginning of the key exchange algorithm (e.g., EDH-RSA-DES-CBC-SHA).

Table 11.4. Key exchange keywords

| Keyword | Meaning |
|---|---|
| ADH | Anonymous DH cipher suites. **Insecure.** |
| AECDH (v1.0+) | Anonymous ECDH cipher suites. **Insecure.** |
| DH | Cipher suites using DH (includes ephemeral and anonymous DH). |
| ECDH (v1.0+) | Cipher suites using ECDH (includes ephemeral and anonymous ECDH). |
| EDH (v1.0+) | Cipher suites using ephemeral DH key agreement. |
| EECDH (v1.0+) | Cipher suites using ephemeral ECDH. |
| kECDH (v1.0+) | Cipher suites using ECDH key agreement. |
| kEDH | Cipher suites using ephemeral DH key agreements (includes anonymous DH). |
| kEECDH (v1.0+) | Cipher suites using ephemeral ECDH key agreement (includes anonymous ECDH). |
| kRSA, RSA | Cipher suites using RSA key exchange. |

Cipher keywords select suites based on the cipher they use.

Table 11.5. Cipher keywords

| Keyword | Meaning |
|---|---|
| 3DES | Cipher suites using triple DES. |
| AES | Cipher suites using AES. |
| AESGCM (v1.0+) | Cipher suites using AES GCM. |
| CAMELLIA | Cipher suites using Camellia. |
| DES | Cipher suites using single DES. **Obsolete and insecure.** |
| eNULL, NULL | Cipher suites that don't use encryption. **Insecure.** |
| IDEA | Cipher suites using IDEA. |
| RC2 | Cipher suites using RC2. **Obsolete and insecure.** |
| RC4 | Cipher suites using RC4. **Insecure.** |
| SEED | Cipher suites using SEED. |

What remains is a number of suites that do not fit into any other category. The bulk of them are related to the GOST standards, which are relevant for the countries that are part of the Commonwealth of Independent States, formed after the breakup of the Soviet Union.

Table 11.6. Miscellaneous keywords

| Keyword | Meaning |
|---|---|
| @STRENGTH | Sorts the current cipher suite list in order of encryption algorithm key length. |
| aGOST | Cipher suites using GOST R 34.10 (either 2001 or 94) for authentication. Requires a GOST-capable engine. |
| aGOST01 | Cipher suites using GOST R 34.10-2001 authentication. |
| aGOST94 | Cipher suites using GOST R 34.10-94 authentication. **Obsolete**. Use GOST R 34.10-2001 instead. |
| kGOST | Cipher suites using VKO 34.10 key exchange, specified in the RFC 4357. |
| GOST94 | Cipher suites using HMAC based on GOST R 34.11-94. |
| GOST89MAC | Cipher suites using GOST 28147-89 MAC instead of HMAC. |

## Combining Keywords

In most cases, you'll use keywords by themselves, but it's also possible to combine them to select only suites that meet several requirements, by connecting two or more keywords with the + character. In the following example, we select suites that use RC4 and SHA:

```
$ openssl ciphers -v 'RC4+SHA'
ECDHE-RSA-RC4-SHA    SSLv3 Kx=ECDH       Au=RSA   Enc=RC4(128) Mac=SHA1
ECDHE-ECDSA-RC4-SHA  SSLv3 Kx=ECDH       Au=ECDSA Enc=RC4(128) Mac=SHA1
AECDH-RC4-SHA        SSLv3 Kx=ECDH       Au=None  Enc=RC4(128) Mac=SHA1
ECDH-RSA-RC4-SHA     SSLv3 Kx=ECDH/RSA   Au=ECDH  Enc=RC4(128) Mac=SHA1
ECDH-ECDSA-RC4-SHA   SSLv3 Kx=ECDH/ECDSA Au=ECDH  Enc=RC4(128) Mac=SHA1
RC4-SHA              SSLv3 Kx=RSA        Au=RSA   Enc=RC4(128) Mac=SHA1
PSK-RC4-SHA          SSLv3 Kx=PSK        Au=PSK   Enc=RC4(128) Mac=SHA1
```

## Building Cipher Suite Lists

The key concept in building a cipher suite configuration is that of the *current suite list*. The list always starts empty, without any suites, but every keyword that you add to the configuration string will change the list in some way. By default, new suites are appended to the list. For example, to choose all suites that use RC4 and AES ciphers:

```
$ openssl ciphers -v 'RC4:AES'
```

The colon character is commonly used to separate keywords, but spaces and commas are equally acceptable. The following command produces the same output as the previous example:

```
$ openssl ciphers -v 'RC4 AES'
```

## Keyword Modifiers

Keyword modifiers are characters you can place at the beginning of each keyword in order to change the default action (adding to the list) to something else. The following actions are supported:

**Append**

Add suites to the end of the list. If any of the suites are already on the list, they will remain in their present position. This is the default action, which is invoked when there is no modifier in front of the keyword.

**Delete (-)**

Remove all matching suites from the list, potentially allowing some other keyword to reintroduce them later.

**Permanently delete (!)**

Remove all matching suites from the list and prevent them from being added later by another keyword. This modifier is useful to specify all the suites you never want to use, making further selection easier and preventing mistakes.

**Move to the end (+)**

Move all matching suites to the end of the list. Works only on existing suites; never adds new suites to the list. This modifier is useful if you want to keep some weaker suites enabled but prefer the stronger ones. For example, the string RC4:+MD5 enables all RC4 suites, but pushes the MD5-based ones to the end.

## Sorting

The @STRENGTH keyword is unlike other keywords (I assume that's why it has the @ in the name): It will not introduce or remove any suites, but it will sort them in order of descending cipher strength. Automatic sorting is an interesting idea, but it makes sense only in a perfect world in which cipher suites can actually be compared by cipher strength.

Take, for example, the following cipher suite configuration:

```
$ openssl ciphers -v 'DES-CBC-SHA:DES-CBC3-SHA:RC4-SHA:AES256-SHA:@STRENGTH'
AES256-SHA          SSLv3   Kx=RSA  Au=RSA  Enc=AES(256)    Mac=SHA1
DES-CBC3-SHA        SSLv3   Kx=RSA  Au=RSA  Enc=3DES(168)   Mac=SHA1
RC4-SHA             SSLv3   Kx=RSA  Au=RSA  Enc=RC4(128)    Mac=SHA1
DES-CBC-SHA         SSLv3   Kx=RSA  Au=RSA  Enc=DES(56)     Mac=SHA1
```

In theory, the output is sorted in order of strength. In practice, you'll often want better control of the suite order.

- For example, AES256-SHA (a CBC suite) is vulnerable to the BEAST attack when used with TLS 1.0 and earlier protocols. If you want to mitigate the BEAST attack server-side, you'll prefer to prioritize the RC4-SHA suite, which isn't vulnerable to this problem.

- 3DES is only nominally rated at 168 bits; a so-called *meet-in-the-middle* attack reduces its strength to 112 bits,[9] and further issues make the strength as low as 108 bits.[10] This fact makes DES-CBC3-SHA inferior to RC4-SHA and any other 128-bit cipher suite.

## Handling Errors

There are two types of errors you might experience while working on your configuration. The first is a result of a simple typo (remember that keywords are case sensitive) or an attempt to use a keyword that does not exist:

```
$ openssl ciphers -v 'HIGH:@STRENGTH'
Error in cipher list
140460843755168:error:140E6118:SSL routines:SSL_CIPHER_PROCESS_RULESTR:invalid ↵
command:ssl_ciph.c:1317:
```

The output is cryptic, but it does contain an error message.

Another possibility is that you end up with an empty list of cipher suites, in which case you might see something similar to the following:

```
$ openssl ciphers -v 'SHA512'
Error in cipher list
140202299557536:error:1410D0B9:SSL routines:SSL_CTX_set_cipher_list:no cipher ↵
match:ssl_lib.c:1312:
```

## Putting It All Together

To demonstrate how various cipher suite configuration features come together, I will present one complete real-life use case. Please bear in mind that what follows is just an example. Because there are usually many aspects to consider when deciding on the configuration, there isn't such a thing as a single perfect configuration.

For that reason, before you can start to work on your configuration, you should have a clear idea of what you wish to achieve. In my case, I wish to have a reasonably secure and efficient configuration, which I define to mean the following:

1. Use only strong ciphers of 128 effective bits and up (this excludes 3DES).
2. Use only suites that provide strong authentication (this excludes anonymous and export suites).
3. Do not use any suites that rely on weak primitives (e.g., MD5).
4. Implement robust support for forward secrecy, no matter what keys and protocols are used. With this requirement comes a slight performance penalty, because I won't be

---

[9] Cryptography/Meet In The Middle Attack [fsty.uk/b442] (Wikibooks, retrieved 31 March 2014)
[10] Attacking Triple Encryption [fsty.uk/b443] (Stefan Lucks, 1998)

able to use the fast RSA key exchange. I'll minimize the penalty by prioritizing ECDHE, which is substantially faster than DHE.

5. Prefer ECDSA over RSA. This requirement makes sense only in dual-key deployments, in which we want to use the faster ECDSA operations wherever possible, but fall back to RSA when talking to clients that do not yet support ECDSA.

6. With TLS 1.2 clients, prefer AES GCM suites, which provide the best security TLS can offer.

7. Because RC4 was recently found to be weaker than previously thought,[11] we want to push it to the end of the list. That's almost as good as disabling it. Although BEAST might still be a problem in some situations, I'll assume that it's been mitigated client-side.

Usually the best approach is to start by permanently eliminating all the components and suites that you don't wish to use; this reduces clutter and ensures that the undesired suites aren't introduced back into the configuration by mistake.

The weak suites can be identified with the following cipher strings:

- aNULL; no authentication

- eNULL; no encryption

- LOW; low-strength suites

- 3DES; effective strength of 108 bits

- MD5; suites that use MD5

- EXP; obsolete export suites

To reduce the number of suites displayed, I'm going to eliminate all DSA, PSK, SRP, and ECDH suites, because they're used only very rarely. I am also removing the IDEA and SEED ciphers, which are obsolete but might still be supported by OpenSSL. In my configuration, I won't use CAMELLIA either, because it's slower and not as well supported as AES (e.g., no GCM or ECDHE variants in practice).

```
!aNULL !eNULL !LOW !3DES !MD5 !EXP !DSS !PSK !SRP !kECDH !CAMELLIA !IDEA !SEED
```

Now we can focus on what we want to achieve. Because forward secrecy is our priority, we can start with the kEECDH and kEDH keywords:

```
kEECDH kEDH !aNULL !eNULL !LOW !3DES !MD5 !EXP !kEDH !PSK !SRP !kECDH !CAMELLIA ↵
!IDEA !SEED
```

If you test this configuration, you'll find that RSA suites are listed first, but I said I wanted ECDSA first:

---

[11] On the Security of RC4 in TLS and WPA [fsty.uk/b341] (AlFardan et al., 13 March 2013)

```
ECDHE-RSA-AES256-GCM-SHA384     TLSv1.2 Kx=ECDH Au=RSA    Enc=AESGCM(256) Mac=AEAD
ECDHE-ECDSA-AES256-GCM-SHA384   TLSv1.2 Kx=ECDH Au=ECDSA Enc=AESGCM(256) Mac=AEAD
ECDHE-RSA-AES256-SHA384         TLSv1.2 Kx=ECDH Au=RSA    Enc=AES(256)    Mac=SHA384
ECDHE-ECDSA-AES256-SHA384       TLSv1.2 Kx=ECDH Au=ECDSA Enc=AES(256)    Mac=SHA384
ECDHE-RSA-AES256-SHA            SSLv3   Kx=ECDH Au=RSA    Enc=AES(256)    Mac=SHA1
ECDHE-ECDSA-AES256-SHA          SSLv3   Kx=ECDH Au=ECDSA Enc=AES(256)    Mac=SHA1
ECDHE-RSA-AES128-GCM-SHA256     TLSv1.2 Kx=ECDH Au=RSA    Enc=AESGCM(128) Mac=AEAD
[...]
```

In order to fix this, I'll put ECDSA suites first, by placing kEECDH+ECDSA at the beginning of the configuration:

```
kEECDH+ECDSA kEECDH kEDH !aNULL !eNULL !LOW !3DES !MD5 !EXP !DSS !PSK !SRP !kECDH ↵
!CAMELLIA !IDEA !SEED
```

The next problem is that older suites (SSL 3) are mixed with newer suites (TLS 1.2). In order to maximize security, I want all TLS 1.2 clients to always negotiate TLS 1.2 suites. To push older suites to the end of the list, I'll use the +SHA keyword (TLS 1.2 suites are all using either SHA256 or SHA384, so they won't match):

```
kEECDH+ECDSA kEECDH kEDH +SHA !aNULL !eNULL !LOW !3DES !MD5 !EXP !DSS !PSK !SRP ↵
!kECDH !CAMELLIA !IDEA !SEED
```

At this point, I'm mostly done. I only need to add the remaining secure suites to the end of the list; the HIGH keyword will achieve this. In addition, I'm also going to make sure RC4 suites are last, using +RC4 (to push existing RC4 suites to the end of the list) and RC4 (to add to the list any remaining RC4 suites that are not already on it):

```
kEECDH+ECDSA kEECDH kEDH HIGH +SHA +RC4 RC4 !aNULL !eNULL !LOW !3DES !MD5 !EXP ↵
!DSS !PSK !SRP !kECDH !CAMELLIA !IDEA !SEED
```

Let's examine the entire final output, which consists of 28 suites. In the first group are the TLS 1.2 suites:

```
ECDHE-ECDSA-AES256-GCM-SHA384   TLSv1.2 Kx=ECDH Au=ECDSA Enc=AESGCM(256) Mac=AEAD
ECDHE-ECDSA-AES256-SHA384       TLSv1.2 Kx=ECDH Au=ECDSA Enc=AES(256)    Mac=SHA384
ECDHE-ECDSA-AES128-GCM-SHA256   TLSv1.2 Kx=ECDH Au=ECDSA Enc=AESGCM(128) Mac=AEAD
ECDHE-ECDSA-AES128-SHA256       TLSv1.2 Kx=ECDH Au=ECDSA Enc=AES(128)    Mac=SHA256
ECDHE-RSA-AES256-GCM-SHA384     TLSv1.2 Kx=ECDH Au=RSA    Enc=AESGCM(256) Mac=AEAD
ECDHE-RSA-AES256-SHA384         TLSv1.2 Kx=ECDH Au=RSA    Enc=AES(256)    Mac=SHA384
ECDHE-RSA-AES128-GCM-SHA256     TLSv1.2 Kx=ECDH Au=RSA    Enc=AESGCM(128) Mac=AEAD
ECDHE-RSA-AES128-SHA256         TLSv1.2 Kx=ECDH Au=RSA    Enc=AES(128)    Mac=SHA256
DHE-RSA-AES256-GCM-SHA384       TLSv1.2 Kx=DH   Au=RSA    Enc=AESGCM(256) Mac=AEAD
DHE-RSA-AES256-SHA256           TLSv1.2 Kx=DH   Au=RSA    Enc=AES(256)    Mac=SHA256
DHE-RSA-AES128-GCM-SHA256       TLSv1.2 Kx=DH   Au=RSA    Enc=AESGCM(128) Mac=AEAD
DHE-RSA-AES128-SHA256           TLSv1.2 Kx=DH   Au=RSA    Enc=AES(128)    Mac=SHA256
AES256-GCM-SHA384               TLSv1.2 Kx=RSA  Au=RSA    Enc=AESGCM(256) Mac=AEAD
```

| AES256-SHA256 | TLSv1.2 Kx=RSA | Au=RSA | Enc=AES(256) | Mac=SHA256 |
| AES128-GCM-SHA256 | TLSv1.2 Kx=RSA | Au=RSA | Enc=AESGCM(128) | Mac=AEAD |
| AES128-SHA256 | TLSv1.2 Kx=RSA | Au=RSA | Enc=AES(128) | Mac=SHA256 |

ECDHE suites are first, followed by DHE suites, followed by all other TLS 1.2 suites. Within each group, ECDSA and GCM have priority.

In the second group are the suites that are going to be used by TLS 1.0 clients, using similar priorities as in the first group:

| ECDHE-ECDSA-AES256-SHA | SSLv3 | Kx=ECDH | Au=ECDSA | Enc=AES(256) | Mac=SHA1 |
| ECDHE-ECDSA-AES128-SHA | SSLv3 | Kx=ECDH | Au=ECDSA | Enc=AES(128) | Mac=SHA1 |
| ECDHE-RSA-AES256-SHA | SSLv3 | Kx=ECDH | Au=RSA | Enc=AES(256) | Mac=SHA1 |
| ECDHE-RSA-AES128-SHA | SSLv3 | Kx=ECDH | Au=RSA | Enc=AES(128) | Mac=SHA1 |
| DHE-RSA-AES256-SHA | SSLv3 | Kx=DH | Au=RSA | Enc=AES(256) | Mac=SHA1 |
| DHE-RSA-AES128-SHA | SSLv3 | Kx=DH | Au=RSA | Enc=AES(128) | Mac=SHA1 |
| DHE-RSA-SEED-SHA | SSLv3 | Kx=DH | Au=RSA | Enc=SEED(128 ) | Mac=SHA1 |
| AES256-SHA | SSLv3 | Kx=RSA | Au=RSA | Enc=AES(256) | Mac=SHA1 |
| AES128-SHA | SSLv3 | Kx=RSA | Au=RSA | Enc=AES(128) | Mac=SHA1 |

Finally, the RC4 suites are at the end:

| ECDHE-ECDSA-RC4-SHA | SSLv3 | Kx=ECDH | Au=ECDSA | Enc=RC4(128) | Mac=SHA1 |
| ECDHE-RSA-RC4-SHA | SSLv3 | Kx=ECDH | Au=RSA | Enc=RC4(128) | Mac=SHA1 |
| RC4-SHA | SSLv3 | Kx=RSA | Au=RSA | Enc=RC4(128) | Mac=SHA1 |

## Recommended Configuration

The configuration in the previous section was designed to use as an example of cipher suite configuration using OpenSSL suite keywords, but it's not the best setup you could have. In fact, there isn't any one configuration that will satisfy everyone. In this section, I'll give you several configurations to choose from based on your preferences and risk assessment.

The design principles for all configurations here are essentially the same as those from the previous section, but I am going to make two changes to achieve better performance. First, I am going to put 128-bit suites on top of the list. Although 256-bit suites provide some increase in security, for most sites the increase is not meaningful and yet still comes with the performance penalty. Second, I am going to prefer HMAC-SHA over HMAC-SHA256 and HMAC-SHA384 suites. The latter two are much slower but also don't provide a meaningful increase of security.

In addition, I am going to change my approach from configuring suites using keywords to using suite names directly. I think that keywords, conceptually, are not a bad idea: you specify your security requirements and the library does the rest, without you having to know a lot about the suites that are going to be used. Unfortunately, this approach no longer works well in practice, as we've become quite picky about what suites we wish to have enabled and in what order.

Using suite names in a configuration is also easier: you just list the suites you want to use. And, when you're looking at someone's configuration, you now know exactly what suites are used without having to run the settings through OpenSSL.

The following is my default starting configuration, designed to offer strong security as well as good performance:

```
ECDHE-ECDSA-AES128-GCM-SHA256
ECDHE-ECDSA-AES256-GCM-SHA384
ECDHE-ECDSA-AES128-SHA
ECDHE-ECDSA-AES256-SHA
ECDHE-ECDSA-AES128-SHA256
ECDHE-ECDSA-AES256-SHA384
ECDHE-RSA-AES128-GCM-SHA256
ECDHE-RSA-AES256-GCM-SHA384
ECDHE-RSA-AES128-SHA
ECDHE-RSA-AES256-SHA
ECDHE-RSA-AES128-SHA256
ECDHE-RSA-AES256-SHA384
DHE-RSA-AES128-GCM-SHA256
DHE-RSA-AES256-GCM-SHA384
DHE-RSA-AES128-SHA
DHE-RSA-AES256-SHA
DHE-RSA-AES128-SHA256
DHE-RSA-AES256-SHA256
EDH-RSA-DES-CBC3-SHA
```

This configuration uses only suites that support forward secrecy and provide strong encryption. Most modern browsers and other clients will be able to connect, but some very old clients might not. As an example, older Internet Explorer versions running on Windows XP will fail.

If you really need to provide support for a very old range of clients—and only then—consider adding the following suites to the end of the list:

```
AES128-SHA
AES256-SHA
DES-CBC3-SHA
ECDHE-RSA-RC4-SHA
RC4-SHA
```

Most of these legacy suites use the RSA key exchange, which means that they don't provide forward secrecy. The AES cipher is preferred, but 3DES and (the insecure) RC4 are also supported for maximum compatibility with as many clients as possible. If the use of RC4 can't be avoided, the preference is to use the ECDHE suite that provides forward secrecy.

# Performance

As you're probably aware, computation speed is a significant limiting factor for any cryptographic operation. OpenSSL comes with a built-in benchmarking tool that you can use to get an idea about a system's capabilities and limits. You can invoke the benchmark using the speed command.

If you invoke speed without any parameters, OpenSSL produces a lot of output, little of which will be of interest. A better approach is to test only those algorithms that are directly relevant to you. For example, for usage in a secure web server, you might care about RC4, AES, RSA, ECDH, and SHA algorithms:

```
$ openssl speed rc4 aes rsa ecdh sha
```

There are three relevant parts to the output. The first part consists of the OpenSSL version number and compile-time configuration. This information is useful if you're testing several different versions of OpenSSL with varying compile-time options:

```
OpenSSL 0.9.8k 25 Mar 2009
built on: Wed May 23 00:02:00 UTC 2012
options:bn(64,64) md2(int) rc4(ptr,char) des(idx,cisc,16,int) aes(partial) ↵
blowfish(ptr2)
compiler: cc -fPIC -DOPENSSL_PIC -DZLIB -DOPENSSL_THREADS -D_REENTRANT -DDSO_DLFCN ↵
-DHAVE_DLFCN_H -m64 -DL_ENDIAN -DTERMIO -O3 -Wa,--noexecstack -g -Wall -DMD32_REG↵
_T=int -DOPENSSL_BN_ASM_MONT -DSHA1_ASM -DSHA256_ASM -DSHA512_ASM -DMD5_ASM -DAES↵
_ASM
available timing options: TIMES TIMEB HZ=100 [sysconf value]
timing function used: times
The 'numbers' are in 1000s of bytes per second processed.
```

The second part contains symmetric cryptography benchmarks (i.e., hash functions and private cryptography):

| type | 16 bytes | 64 bytes | 256 bytes | 1024 bytes | 8192 bytes |
|------|----------|----------|-----------|------------|------------|
| sha1 | 29275.44k | 85281.86k | 192290.28k | 280526.68k | 327553.12k |
| rc4 | 160087.81k | 172435.03k | 174264.75k | 176521.50k | 176700.62k |
| aes-128 cbc | 90345.06k | 140108.84k | 170027.92k | 179704.12k | 182388.44k |
| aes-192 cbc | 104770.95k | 134601.12k | 148900.05k | 152662.30k | 153941.11k |
| aes-256 cbc | 95868.62k | 116430.41k | 124498.19k | 127007.85k | 127430.81k |
| sha256 | 23354.37k | 54220.61k | 99784.35k | 126494.48k | 138266.71k |
| sha512 | 16022.98k | 64657.88k | 113304.06k | 178301.77k | 214539.99k |

Finally, the third part contains the asymmetric (public) cryptography benchmarks:

| | sign | verify | sign/s | verify/s |
|--|------|--------|--------|----------|
| rsa 512 bits | 0.000120s | 0.000011s | 8324.9 | 90730.0 |
| rsa 1024 bits | 0.000569s | 0.000031s | 1757.0 | 31897.1 |

```
rsa 2048 bits 0.003606s 0.000102s      277.3    9762.0
rsa 4096 bits 0.024072s 0.000376s       41.5    2657.4
                                  op      op/s
 160 bit ecdh (secp160r1)    0.0003s    2890.2
 192 bit ecdh (nistp192)     0.0006s    1702.9
 224 bit ecdh (nistp224)     0.0006s    1743.5
 256 bit ecdh (nistp256)     0.0007s    1513.3
 384 bit ecdh (nistp384)     0.0015s     689.6
 521 bit ecdh (nistp521)     0.0029s     340.3
 163 bit ecdh (nistk163)     0.0009s    1126.2
 233 bit ecdh (nistk233)     0.0012s     818.5
 283 bit ecdh (nistk283)     0.0028s     360.2
 409 bit ecdh (nistk409)     0.0060s     166.3
 571 bit ecdh (nistk571)     0.0130s      76.8
 163 bit ecdh (nistb163)     0.0009s    1061.3
 233 bit ecdh (nistb233)     0.0013s     755.2
 283 bit ecdh (nistb283)     0.0030s     329.4
 409 bit ecdh (nistb409)     0.0067s     149.7
 571 bit ecdh (nistb571)     0.0146s      68.4
```

What's this output useful for? You should be able to compare how compile-time options affect speed or how different versions of OpenSSL compare on the same platform. For example, the previous results are from a real-life server that's using the OpenSSL 0.9.8k (patched by the distribution vendor). I'm considering moving to OpenSSL 1.0.1h because I wish to support TLS 1.1 and TLS 1.2; will there be any performance impact? I've downloaded and compiled OpenSSL 1.0.1h for a test. Let's see:

```
$ ./openssl-1.0.1h speed rsa
[...]
OpenSSL 1.0.1h 5 Jun 2014
built on: Thu Jul  3 18:30:06 BST 2014
options:bn(64,64) rc4(8x,int) des(idx,cisc,16,int) aes(partial) idea(int) ↵
blowfish(idx)
compiler: gcc -DOPENSSL_THREADS -D_REENTRANT -DDSO_DLFCN -DHAVE_DLFCN_H ↵
-Wa,--noexecstack -m64 -DL_ENDIAN -DTERMIO -O3 -Wall -DOPENSSL_IA32_SSE2 -DOPENSSL↵
_BN_ASM_MONT -DOPENSSL_BN_ASM_MONT5 -DOPENSSL_BN_ASM_GF2m -DSHA1_ASM -DSHA256_ASM ↵
-DSHA512_ASM -DMD5_ASM -DAES_ASM -DVPAES_ASM -DBSAES_ASM -DWHIRLPOOL_ASM -DGHASH↵
_ASM
                 sign     verify    sign/s verify/s
rsa  512 bits 0.000102s 0.000008s   9818.0 133081.7
rsa 1024 bits 0.000326s 0.000020s   3067.2  50086.9
rsa 2048 bits 0.002209s 0.000068s    452.8  14693.6
rsa 4096 bits 0.015748s 0.000255s     63.5   3919.4
```

Apparently, OpenSSL 1.0.1h is almost twice as fast on this server for my use case (2,048-bit RSA key): The performance went from 277 signatures/s to 450 signatures/s. This means that I'll get better performance if I upgrade. Always good news!

Using the benchmark results to estimate deployment performance is not straightforward because of the great number of factors that influence performance in real life. Further, many of those factors lie outside TLS (e.g., HTTP keep alive settings, caching, etc.). At best, you can use these numbers only for a rough estimate.

But before you can do that, you need to consider something else. By default, the speed command will use only a single process. Most servers have multiple cores, so to find out how many TLS operations are supported by the entire server, you must instruct speed to use several instances in parallel. You can achieve this with the -multi switch. My server has four cores, so that's what I'm going to use:

```
$ openssl speed -multi 4 rsa
[...]
OpenSSL 0.9.8k 25 Mar 2009
built on: Wed May 23 00:02:00 UTC 2012
options:bn(64,64) md2(int) rc4(ptr,char) des(idx,cisc,16,int) aes(partial) ↵
blowfish(ptr2)
compiler: cc -fPIC -DOPENSSL_PIC -DZLIB -DOPENSSL_THREADS -D_REENTRANT -DDSO_DLFCN ↵
-DHAVE_DLFCN_H -m64 -DL_ENDIAN -DTERMIO -O3 -Wa,--noexecstack -g -Wall -DMD32_REG↵
_T=int -DOPENSSL_BN_ASM_MONT -DSHA1_ASM -DSHA256_ASM -DSHA512_ASM -DMD5_ASM -DAES↵
_ASM
available timing options: TIMES TIMEB HZ=100 [sysconf value]
timing function used:
                  sign     verify   sign/s verify/s
rsa  512 bits 0.000030s 0.000003s 33264.5 363636.4
rsa 1024 bits 0.000143s 0.000008s  6977.9 125000.0
rsa 2048 bits 0.000917s 0.000027s  1090.7  37068.1
rsa 4096 bits 0.006123s 0.000094s   163.3  10652.6
```

As expected, the performance is almost four times better than before. I'm again looking at how many RSA signatures can be executed per second, because this is the most CPU-intensive operation performed on a server and is thus always the first bottleneck. The example number of 1,090 signatures/second tells us that this server can handle about 1,000 brand-new TLS connections per second. In my case, that's sufficient—with a very healthy safety margin. Because I also have session resumption enabled on the server, I know that I can support many more than 1,000 TLS connections per second. I wish I had enough traffic on that server to worry about the performance of TLS.

Another reason why you shouldn't believe the output of the speed command too much is because it doesn't use the fastest available cipher implementations by default. In some ways, the default output is a lie. For example, on servers that support the AES-NI instruction set to hardware AES acceleration, this feature won't be used by default:

```
$ openssl speed aes-128-cbc
[...]
The 'numbers' are in 1000s of bytes per second processed.
```

```
type              16 bytes    64 bytes    256 bytes   1024 bytes   8192 bytes
aes-128 cbc       67546.70k   74183.00k   69278.82k   155942.87k   156486.38k
```

To activate hardware acceleration, you have to use the -evp switch on the command line:

```
$ openssl speed -evp aes-128-cbc
[..]
The 'numbers' are in 1000s of bytes per second processed.
type              16 bytes    64 bytes    256 bytes   1024 bytes   8192 bytes
aes-128-cbc       188523.36k  223595.37k  229763.58k  203658.58k   206452.14k
```

# Creating a Private Certification Authority

If you want to set up your own CA, everything you need is already included in OpenSSL. The user interface is purely command line–based and thus not very user friendly, but that's possibly for the better. Going through the process is very educational, because it forces you to think about every aspect, even the smallest details.

The educational aspect of setting a private CA is the main reason why I would recommend doing it, but there are others. An OpenSSL-based CA, crude as it might be, can well serve the needs of an individual or a small group. For example, it's much better to use a private CA in a development environment than to use self-signed certificates everywhere. Similarly, client certificates—which provide two-factor authentication—can significantly increase the security of your most sensitive web applications.

The biggest challenge in running a private CA is not setting everything up but keeping it secure. For example, the root key, which you need to distribute to every client application, must be kept offline. CRLs and OCSP responder certificates must be refreshed on a regular basis.

> **Note**
>
> Before you begin to properly read this section, I recommend first going through Chapter 3, *Public-Key Infrastructure*, which will give you a good background in certificate structure and the operation of certification authorities.

## Features and Limitations

In the rest of this section, we're going to create a private CA that's similar in structure to public CAs. There's going to be one root CA from which other subordinate CAs can be created. We'll provide revocation information via CRLs and OCSP responders. To keep the root CA offline, OCSP responders are going to have their own identities. This isn't the simplest private CA you could have, but it's one that can be secured properly. As a bonus, the subordinate CA will be *technically constrained*, which means that it will be allowed to issue certificates only for the allowed hostnames.

After the setup is complete, the root certificate will have to be securely distributed to all intended clients. Once the root is in place, you can begin issuing client and server certificates. The main limitation of this setup is that the OCSP responder is chiefly designed for testing and can be used only for lighter loads.

# Creating a Root CA

Creating a new CA involves several steps: configuration, creation of a directory structure and initialization of the key files, and finally generation of the root key and certificate. This section describes the process as well as the common CA operations.

## Root CA Configuration

Before we can actually create a CA, we need to prepare a configuration file that will tell OpenSSL exactly how we want things set up. Configuration files aren't needed most of the time, during normal usage, but they are essential when it comes to complex operations, such as root CA creation. OpenSSL configuration files are powerful; before you proceed I suggest that you familiarize yourself with their capabilities (man config on the command line).

The first part of the configuration file contains some basic CA information, such as the name and the base URL, and the components of the CA's distinguished name. Because the syntax is flexible, information needs to be provided only once:

```
[default]
name                    = root-ca
domain_suffix           = example.com
aia_url                 = http://$name.$domain_suffix/$name.crt
crl_url                 = http://$name.$domain_suffix/$name.crl
ocsp_url                = http://ocsp.$name.$domain_suffix:9080
default_ca              = ca_default
name_opt                = utf8,esc_ctrl,multiline,lname,align

[ca_dn]
countryName             = "GB"
organizationName        = "Example"
commonName              = "Root CA"
```

The second part directly controls the CA's operation. For full information on each setting, consult the documentation for the ca command (man ca on the command line). Most of the settings are self-explanatory; we mostly tell OpenSSL where we want to keep our files. Because this root CA is going to be used only for the issuance of subordinate CAs, I chose to have the certificates valid for 10 years. For the signature algorithm, the secure SHA256 is used by default.

The default policy (policy_c_o_match) is configured so that all certificates issued from this CA have the countryName and organizationName fields that match that of the CA. This wouldn't be normally done by a public CA, but it's appropriate for a private CA:

```
[ca_default]
home                    = .
database                = $home/db/index
serial                  = $home/db/serial
crlnumber               = $home/db/crlnumber
certificate             = $home/$name.crt
private_key             = $home/private/$name.key
RANDFILE                = $home/private/random
new_certs_dir           = $home/certs
unique_subject          = no
copy_extensions         = none
default_days            = 3650
default_crl_days        = 365
default_md              = sha256
policy                  = policy_c_o_match

[policy_c_o_match]
countryName             = match
stateOrProvinceName     = optional
organizationName        = match
organizationalUnitName  = optional
commonName              = supplied
emailAddress            = optional
```

The third part contains the configuration for the req command, which is going to be used only once, during the creation of the self-signed root certificate. The most important parts are in the extensions: the basicConstraint extension indicates that the certificate is a CA, and the keyUsage contains the appropriate settings for this scenario:

```
[req]
default_bits            = 4096
encrypt_key             = yes
default_md              = sha256
utf8                    = yes
string_mask             = utf8only
prompt                  = no
distinguished_name      = ca_dn
req_extensions          = ca_ext

[ca_ext]
basicConstraints        = critical,CA:true
keyUsage                = critical,keyCertSign,cRLSign
subjectKeyIdentifier    = hash
```

The fourth part of the configuration file contains information that will be used during the construction of certificates issued by the root CA. All certificates will be CAs, as indicated by the basicConstraints extension, but we set pathlen to zero, which means that further subordinate CAs are not allowed.

All subordinate CAs are going to be constrained, which means that the certificates they issue will be valid only for a subset of domain names and restricted uses. First, the extendedKeyUsage extension specifies only clientAuth and serverAuth, which is TLS client and server authentication. Second, the nameConstraints extension limits the allowed hostnames only to *example.com* and *example.org* domain names. In theory, this setup enables you to give control over the subordinate CAs to someone else but still be safe in knowing that they can't issue certificates for arbitrary hostnames. If you wanted, you could restrict each subordinate CA to a small domain namespace. The requirement to exclude the two IP address ranges comes from CA/Browser Forum's Baseline Requirements, which have a definition for technically constrained subordinate CAs.[12]

In practice, name constraints are not entirely practical, because some major platforms don't currently recognize the nameConstraints extension. If you mark this extension as critical, such platforms will reject your certificates. You won't have such problems if you don't mark it as critical (as in the example), but then some other platforms won't enforce it.

```
[sub_ca_ext]
authorityInfoAccess     = @issuer_info
authorityKeyIdentifier  = keyid:always
basicConstraints        = critical,CA:true,pathlen:0
crlDistributionPoints   = @crl_info
extendedKeyUsage        = clientAuth,serverAuth
keyUsage                = critical,keyCertSign,cRLSign
nameConstraints         = @name_constraints
subjectKeyIdentifier    = hash

[crl_info]
URI.0                   = $crl_url

[issuer_info]
caIssuers;URI.0         = $aia_url
OCSP;URI.0              = $ocsp_url

[name_constraints]
permitted;DNS.0=example.com
permitted;DNS.1=example.org
excluded;IP.0=0.0.0.0/0.0.0.0
excluded;IP.1=0:0:0:0:0:0:0:0/0:0:0:0:0:0:0:0
```

---

[12] Baseline Requirements [fsty.uk/b64] (CA/Browser Forum, retrieved 9 July 2014)

The fifth and final part of the configuration specifies the extensions to be used with the certificate for OCSP response signing. In order to be able to run an OCSP responder, we generate a special certificate and delegate the OCSP signing capability to it. This certificate is not a CA, which you can see from the extensions:

```
[ocsp_ext]
authorityKeyIdentifier   = keyid:always
basicConstraints         = critical,CA:false
extendedKeyUsage         = OCSPSigning
keyUsage                 = critical,digitalSignature
subjectKeyIdentifier     = hash
```

## Root CA Directory Structure

The next step is to create the directory structure specified in the previous section and initialize some of the files that will be used during the CA operation:

```
$ mkdir root-ca
$ cd root-ca
$ mkdir certs db private
$ chmod 700 private
$ touch db/index
$ echo 1001 > db/serial
$ echo 1001 > db/crlnumber
```

The following subdirectories are used:

**certs/**

Certificate storage; new certificates will be placed here as they are issued.

**db/**

This directory is used for the certificate database (index) and the files that hold the next certificate and CRL serial numbers. OpenSSL will create some additional files as needed.

**private/**

This directory will store the private keys, one for the CA and the other for the OCSP responder. It's important that no other user has access to it. (In fact, if you're going to be serious about the CA, the machine on which the root material is stored should have only a minimal number of user accounts.)

## Root CA Generation

We take two steps to create the root CA. First, we generate the key and the CSR. All the necessary information will be picked up from the configuration file when we use the -config switch:

```
$ openssl req -new \
    -config root-ca.conf \
    -out root-ca.csr \
    -keyout private/root-ca.key
```

In the second step, we create a self-signed certificate. The -extensions switch points to the ca_ext section in the configuration file, which activates the extensions that are appropriate for a root CA:

```
$ openssl ca -selfsign \
    -config root-ca.conf \
    -in root-ca.csr \
    -out root-ca.crt \
    -extensions ca_ext
```

## Structure of the Database File

The database in db/index is a plaintext file that contains certificate information, one certificate per line. Immediately after the root CA creation, it should contain only one line:

```
V    240706115345Z    1001    unknown    /C=GB/O=Example/CN=Root CA
```

Each line contains six values separated by tabs:

1. Status flag (V for valid, R for revoked, E for expired)
2. Expiration date (in YYMMDDHHMMSSZ format)
3. Revocation date or empty if not revoked
4. Serial number (hexadecimal)
5. File location or unknown if not known
6. Distinguished name

## Root CA Operations

To generate a CRL from the new CA, use the -gencrl switch of the ca command:

```
$ openssl ca -gencrl \
    -config root-ca.conf \
    -out root-ca.crl
```

To issue a certificate, invoke the ca command with the desired parameters. It's important that the -extensions switch points to the correct section in the configuration file (e.g., you don't want to create another root CA).

```
$ openssl ca \
    -config root-ca.conf \
```

```
    -in sub-ca.csr \
    -out sub-ca.crt \
    -extensions sub_ca_ext
```

To revoke a certificate, use the -revoke switch of the ca command; you'll need to have a copy of the certificate you wish to revoke. Because all certificates are stored in the certs/ directory, you only need to know the serial number. If you have a distinguished name, you can look for the serial number in the database.

Choose the correct reason for the value in the -crl_reason switch. The value can be one of the following: unspecified, keyCompromise, CACompromise, affiliationChanged, superseded, cessationOfOperation, certificateHold, and removeFromCRL.

```
$ openssl ca \
    -config root-ca.conf \
    -revoke certs/1002.pem \
    -crl_reason keyCompromise
```

## Create a Certificate for OCSP Signing

First, we create a key and CSR for the OCSP responder. These two operations are done as for any non-CA certificate, which is why we don't specify a configuration file:

```
$ openssl req -new \
    -newkey rsa:2048 \
    -subj "/C=GB/O=Example/CN=OCSP Root Responder" \
    -keyout private/root-ocsp.key \
    -out root-ocsp.csr
```

Second, use the root CA to issue a certificate. The value of the -extensions switch specifies ocsp_ext, which ensures that extensions appropriate for OCSP signing are set. I reduced the lifetime of the new certificate to 365 days (from the default of 3,650). Because these OCSP certificates don't contain revocation information, they can't be revoked. For that reason, you want to keep the lifetime as short as possible. A good choice is 30 days, provided you are prepared to generate a fresh certificate that often:

```
$ openssl ca \
    -config root-ca.conf \
    -in root-ocsp.csr \
    -out root-ocsp.crt \
    -extensions ocsp_ext \
    -days 365
```

Now you have everything ready to start the OCSP responder. For testing, you can do it from the same machine on which the root CA resides. However, for production you must move the OCSP responder key and certificate elsewhere:

```
$ openssl ocsp \
    -port 9080
    -index db/index \
    -rsigner root-ocsp.crt \
    -rkey private/root-ocsp.key \
    -CA root-ca.crt \
    -text
```

You can test the operation of the OCSP responder using the following command line:

```
$ openssl ocsp \
    -issuer root-ca.crt \
    -CAfile root-ca.crt \
    -cert root-ocsp.crt \
    -url http://127.0.0.1:9080
```

In the output, `verify OK` means that the signatures were correctly verified, and *good* means that the certificate hasn't been revoked.

```
Response verify OK
root-ocsp.crt: good
        This Update: Jul  9 18:45:34 2014 GMT
```

# Creating a Subordinate CA

The process of subordinate CA generation largely mirrors the root CA process. In this section, I will only highlight the differences where appropriate. For everything else, refer to the previous section.

## Subordinate CA Configuration

To generate a configuration file for the subordinate CA, start with the file we used for the root CA and make the changes listed here. We'll change the name to `sub-ca` and use a different distinguished name. We'll put the OCSP responder on a different port, but only because the `ocsp` command doesn't understand virtual hosts. If you used a proper web server for the OCSP responder, you could avoid using special ports altogether. The default lifetime of new certificates will be 365 days, and we'll generate a fresh CRL once every 30 days.

The change of `copy_extensions` to `copy` means that extensions from the CSR will be copied into the certificate, but only if they are not already set in our configuration. With this change, whoever is preparing the CSR can put the required alternative names in it, and the information from there will be picked up and placed in the certificate. I wouldn't recommend extension copying for large operations, but I think it's fine for smaller environments:

```
[default]
name                    = sub-ca
```

```
crl_url                   = http://$name.$domain_suffix:9081/$name.crl

[ca_dn]
countryName               = "GB"
organizationName          = "Example"
commonName                = "Sub CA"

[ca_default]
default_days              = 365
default_crl_days          = 30
copy_extensions           = copy
```

At the end of the configuration file, we'll add two new profiles, one each for client and server certificates. The only difference is in the keyUsage and extendedKeyUsage extensions. Note that we specify the basicConstraints extension but set it to false. We're doing this because we're copying extensions from the CSR. If we left this extension out, we might end up using one specified in the CSR:

```
[server_ext]
authorityInfoAccess       = @issuer_info
authorityKeyIdentifier    = keyid:always
basicConstraints          = critical,CA:false
crlDistributionPoints     = @crl_info
extendedKeyUsage          = clientAuth,serverAuth
keyUsage                  = critical,digitalSignature,keyEncipherment
subjectKeyIdentifier      = hash

[client_ext]
authorityInfoAccess       = @issuer_info
authorityKeyIdentifier    = keyid:always
basicConstraints          = critical,CA:false
crlDistributionPoints     = @crl_info
extendedKeyUsage          = clientAuth
keyUsage                  = critical,digitalSignature
subjectKeyIdentifier      = hash
```

After you're happy with the configuration file, create a directory structure following the same process as for the root CA. Just use a different directory name, for example, sub-ca.

## Subordinate CA Generation

As before, we take two steps to create the subordinate CA. First, we generate the key and the CSR. All the necessary information will be picked up from the configuration file when we use the -config switch.

```
$ openssl req -new \
    -config sub-ca.conf \
```

```
    -out sub-ca.csr \
    -keyout private/sub-ca.key
```

In the second step, we get the root CA to issue a certificate. The -extensions switch points to the sub_ext section in the configuration file, which activates the extensions that are appropriate for the subordinate CA.

```
$ openssl ca \
    -config root-ca.conf \
    -in sub-ca.csr \
    -out sub-ca.crt \
    -extensions sub_ca_ext
```

## Subordinate CA Operations

To issue a server certificate, process a CSR while specifying server_ext in the -extensions switch:

```
$ openssl ca \
    -config sub-ca.conf \
    -in server.csr \
    -out server.crt \
    -extensions server_ext
```

To issue a client certificate, process a CSR while specifying client_ext in the -extensions switch:

```
$ openssl ca \
    -config sub-ca.conf \
    -in client.csr \
    -out client.crt \
    -extensions client_ext
```

> ### Note
>
> When a new certificate is requested, all its information will be presented to you for verification before the operation is completed. You should always ensure that everything is in order, but especially if you're working with a CSR that someone else prepared. Pay special attention to the certificate distinguished name and the basicConstraints and subjectAlternativeName extensions.

CRL generation and certificate revocation are the same as for the root CA. The only thing different about the OCSP responder is the port; the subordinate CA should use 9,081 instead. It's recommended that the responder uses its own certificate, which avoids keeping the subordinate CA on a public server.

# 12 Testing with OpenSSL

Due to the large number of protocol features and implementation quirks, it's sometimes difficult to determine the exact configuration and features of secure servers. Although many tools exist for this purpose, their implementation details are typically unknown, and that sometimes makes it difficult to fully trust their results. Even though I have spent years testing secure servers and have access to good tools, when I really want to understand what is going on I resort to using OpenSSL and Wireshark. I am not saying that you should use OpenSSL for everyday testing; on the contrary, you should find a tool that you trust and use it by default. But at the end of the day, when you really need to be certain of something, the only way is to get your hands dirty with OpenSSL.

## Connecting to SSL Services

OpenSSL comes with a client tool that you can use to connect to a secure server. The tool is similar to `telnet` or `nc`, in the sense that it handles the SSL/TLS layer but allows you to fully control the layer that comes next.

To connect to a server, you need to supply a hostname and a port. For example:

```
$ openssl s_client -connect www.feistyduck.com:443
```

Once you type the command, you're going to see a lot of diagnostic output (more about that in a moment) followed by an opportunity to type whatever you want. Because we're talking to an HTTP server, the most sensible thing to do is to submit an HTTP request. In the following example, I use a `HEAD` request because it instructs the server not to send the response body:

```
HEAD / HTTP/1.0

HTTP/1.1 301 Moved Permanently
Date: Mon, 04 Jun 2012 18:47:41 GMT
Server: Apache/2.2.14 (Ubuntu)
Location: https://www.feistyduck.com/
```

```
Vary: Accept-Encoding
Connection: close
Content-Type: text/html; charset=iso-8859-1

closed
```

Now we know that the TLS communication layer is working: we got through to the HTTP server, submitted a request, and received a response back. Let's go back to the diagnostic output. The first couple of lines will show the information about the server certificate:

```
CONNECTED(00000003)
depth=3 L = ValiCert Validation Network, O = "ValiCert, Inc.", OU = ValiCert Class ↵
2 Policy Validation Authority, CN = http://www.valicert.com/, emailAddress = ↵
info@valicert.com
verify error:num=19:self signed certificate in certificate chain
verify return:0
```

On my system (and possibly on yours), s_client doesn't pick up the default trusted certificates; it complains that there is a self-signed certificate in the certificate chain. In most cases, you won't care about certificate validation; but if you do, you will need to point s_client to the trusted certificates, like this:

```
$ openssl s_client -connect www.feistyduck.com:443 -CAfile /etc/ssl/certs↵
/ca-certificates.crt
CONNECTED(00000003)
depth=3 L = ValiCert Validation Network, O = "ValiCert, Inc.", OU = ValiCert Class ↵
2 > Policy Validation Authority, CN = http://www.valicert.com/, emailAddress = ↵
info@valicert.com
verify return:1
depth=2 C = US, O = "Starfield Technologies, Inc.", OU = Starfield Class 2 ↵
Certification Authority
verify return:1
depth=1 C = US, ST = Arizona, L = Scottsdale, O = "Starfield Technologies, Inc.", ↵
OU = http://certificates.starfieldtech.com/repository, CN = Starfield Secure ↵
Certification Authority, serialNumber = 10688435
verify return:1
depth=0 1.3.6.1.4.1.311.60.2.1.3 = GB, businessCategory = Private Organization, ↵
serialNumber = 06694169, C = GB, ST = London, L = London, O = Feisty Duck Ltd, CN ↵
= www.feistyduck.com
verify return:1
```

Instead of s_client complaining, you now see it verifying each of the certificates from the chain. For the verification to work, you must have access to a good selection of CA certificates. The path I used in the example (/etc/ssl/certs/ca-certificates.crt) is valid on Ubuntu 12.04 LTS but might not be valid on your system. If you don't want to use the system-provided CA certificates for this purpose, you can rely on those provided by Mozilla, as discussed in the section called "Building a Trust Store" in Chapter 11 .

Chapter 12: Testing with OpenSSL

The next section in the output lists all the certificates presented by the server in the order in which they were delivered:

```
Certificate chain
 0 s:/1.3.6.1.4.1.311.60.2.1.3=GB/businessCategory=Private Organization↵
/serialNumber=06694169/C=GB/ST=London/L=London/O=Feisty Duck Ltd↵
/CN=www.feistyduck.com
   i:/C=US/ST=Arizona/L=Scottsdale/O=Starfield Technologies, Inc./OU=http:/↵
/certificates.starfieldtech.com/repository/CN=Starfield Secure Certification ↵
Authority/serialNumber=10688435
 1 s:/C=US/ST=Arizona/L=Scottsdale/O=Starfield Technologies, Inc./OU=http:/↵
/certificates.starfieldtech.com/repository/CN=Starfield Secure Certification ↵
Authority/serialNumber=10688435
   i:/C=US/O=Starfield Technologies, Inc./OU=Starfield Class 2 Certification ↵
Authority
 2 s:/C=US/O=Starfield Technologies, Inc./OU=Starfield Class 2 Certification ↵
Authority
   i:/L=ValiCert Validation Network/O=ValiCert, Inc./OU=ValiCert Class 2 Policy ↵
Validation Authority/CN=http://www.valicert.com//emailAddress=info@valicert.com
 3 s:/L=ValiCert Validation Network/O=ValiCert, Inc./OU=ValiCert Class 2 Policy ↵
Validation Authority/CN=http://www.valicert.com//emailAddress=info@valicert.com
   i:/L=ValiCert Validation Network/O=ValiCert, Inc./OU=ValiCert Class 2 Policy ↵
Validation Authority/CN=http://www.valicert.com//emailAddress=info@valicert.com
```

For each certificate, the first line shows the subject and the second line shows the issuer information.

This part is very useful when you need to see exactly what certificates are sent; browser certificate viewers typically display reconstructed certificate chains that can be almost completely different from the presented ones. To determine if the chain is nominally correct, you might wish to verify that the subjects and issuers match. You start with the leaf (web server) certificate at the top, and then you go down the list, matching the issuer of the current certificate to the subject of the next. The last issuer you see can point to some root certificate that is not in the chain, or—if the self-signed root is included—it can point to itself.

The next item in the output is the server certificate; it's a lot of text, but I'm going to remove most of it for brevity:

```
Server certificate
-----BEGIN CERTIFICATE-----
MIIF5zCCBM+gAwIBAgIHBG9JXlv9vTANBgkqhkiG9w0BAQUFADCB3DELMAkGA1UE
[30 lines removed...]
os5LW3PhHz8y9YFep2SV4c7+NrlZISHOZVzN
-----END CERTIFICATE-----
subject=/1.3.6.1.4.1.311.60.2.1.3=GB/businessCategory=Private Organization↵
/serialNumber=06694169/C=GB/ST=London/L=London/O=Feisty Duck Ltd↵
```

```
/CN=www.feistyduck.com
issuer=/C=US/ST=Arizona/L=Scottsdale/O=Starfield Technologies, Inc./OU=http:/↵
/certificates.starfieldtech.com/repository/CN=Starfield Secure Certification ↵
Authority/serialNumber=10688435
```

> **Note**
>
> Whenever you see a long string of numbers instead of a name in a subject, it means
> that OpenSSL does not know the *object identifier* (OID) in question. OIDs are
> globally unique and unambiguous identifiers that are used to refer to "things." For
> example, in the previous output, the OID 1.3.6.1.4.1.311.60.2.1.3 should have
> been replaced with jurisdictionOfIncorporationCountryName, which is used in
> *Extended Validation* (EV) certificates.

If you want to have a better look at the certificate, you'll first need to copy it from the output
and store it in a separate file. I'll discuss that in the next section.

The following is a lot of information about the TLS connection, most of which is self-explanatory:

```
---
No client certificate CA names sent
---
SSL handshake has read 3043 bytes and written 375 bytes
---
New, TLSv1/SSLv3, Cipher is ECDHE-RSA-AES256-SHA
Server public key is 2048 bit
Secure Renegotiation IS supported
Compression: NONE
Expansion: NONE
SSL-Session:
    Protocol  : TLSv1.1
    Cipher    : ECDHE-RSA-AES256-SHA
    Session-ID: 032554E059DB27BF8CD87EBC53E9FF29376265F0BBFDBBFB7773D2277E5559F5
    Session-ID-ctx:
    Master-Key: 1A55823368DB6EFC397DEE2DC3382B5BB416A061C19CEE162362158E90F1FB0846E↵
EFDB2CCF564A18764F1A98F79A768
    Key-Arg   : None
    PSK identity: None
    PSK identity hint: None
    SRP username: None
    TLS session ticket lifetime hint: 300 (seconds)
    TLS session ticket:
    0000 - 77 c3 47 09 c4 45 e4 65-90 25 8b fd 77 4c 12 da   w.G..E.e.%..wL..
    0010 - 38 f0 43 09 08 a1 ec f0-8d 86 f8 b1 f0 7e 4b a9   8.C..........~K.
    0020 - fe 9f 14 8e 66 d7 5a dc-0f d0 0c 25 fc 99 b8 aa   ....f.Z....%....
    0030 - 8f 93 56 5a ac cd f8 66-ac 94 00 8b d1 02 63 91   ..VZ...f......c.
```

```
0040 - 05 47 af 98 11 81 65 d9-48 5b 44 bb 41 d8 24 e8   .G....e.H[D.A.$.
0050 - 2e 08 2d bb 25 59 f0 8f-bf aa 5c b6 fa 9c 12 a6   ..-.%Y....\.....
0060 - a1 66 3f 84 2c f6 0f 06-51 c0 64 24 7a 9a 48 96   .f?.,...Q.d$z.H.
0070 - a7 f6 a9 6e 94 f2 71 10-ff 00 4d 7a 97 e3 f5 8b   ...n..q...Mz....
0080 - 2d 1a 19 9c 1a 8d e0 9c-e5 55 cd be d7 24 2e 24   -........U...$.$
0090 - fc 59 54 b0 f8 f1 0a 5f-03 08 52 0d 90 99 c4 78   .YT...._..R....x
00a0 - d2 93 61 d8 eb 76 15 27-03 5e a4 db 0c 05 bb 51   ..a..v.'.^.....Q
00b0 - 6c 65 76 9b 4e 6b 6c 19-69 33 2a bd 02 1f 71 14   lev.Nkl.i3*...q.

Start Time: 1390553737
Timeout   : 300 (sec)
Verify return code: 0 (ok)
---
```

The most important information here is the protocol version (TLS 1.1) and cipher suite used (ECDHE-RSA-AES256-SHA). You can also determine that the server has issued to you a session ID and a TLS session ticket (a way of resuming sessions without having the server maintain state) and that secure renegotiation is supported. Once you understand what all of this output contains, you will rarely look at it.

> **Warning**
>
> Operating system distributions often ship tools that are different from the stock versions. We have another example of that here: The previous command negotiated TLS 1.1, even though the server supports TLS 1.2. Why? As it turns out, OpenSSL shipped with Ubuntu 12.04 LTS disables TLS 1.2 for client connections in order to avoid certain interoperability issues. To avoid problems like these, I recommend that you always test with a version of OpenSSL that you configured and compiled.

# Testing Protocols that Upgrade to SSL

When used with HTTP, TLS wraps the entire plain-text communication channel to form HTTPS. Some other protocols start off as plaintext, but then they upgrade to encryption. If you want to test such a protocol, you'll have to tell OpenSSL which protocol it is so that it can upgrade on your behalf. Provide the protocol information using the -starttls switch. For example:

```
$ openssl s_client -connect gmail-smtp-in.l.google.com:25 -starttls smtp
```

At the time of writing, the supported protocols are smtp, pop3, imap, ftp, and xmpp.

# Using Different Handshake Formats

Sometimes, when you are trying to test a server using OpenSSL your attempts to communicate with the server may fail even though you know the server supports TLS (e.g., you can see that TLS is working when you attempt to use a browser). One possible reason this might occur is that the server does not support the older SSL 2 handshake.

Because OpenSSL attempts to negotiate all protocols it understands and because SSL 2 can be negotiated only using the old SSL 2 handshake, it uses this handshake as the default. Even though it is associated with a very old and insecure protocol version, the old handshake format is not technically insecure. It supports upgrades, which means that a better protocol can be negotiated. However, this handshake format does not support many connection negotiation features that were designed after SSL 2.

Therefore, if something is not working and you're not sure what it is exactly, you can try to force OpenSSL to use the newer handshake format. You can do that by disabling SSL 2:

```
$ openssl s_client -connect www.feistyduck.com:443 -no_ssl2
```

Another way to achieve the same effect is to specify the desired server name on the command line:

```
$ openssl s_client -connect www.feistyduck.com:443 -servername www.feistyduck.com
```

In order to specify the server name, OpenSSL needs to use a feature of the newer handshake format (the feature is called *Server Name Indication* [SNI]), and that will force it to abandon the old format.

## Extracting Remote Certificates

When you connect to a remote secure server using s_client, it will dump the server's PEM-encoded certificate to standard output. If you need the certificate for any reason, you can copy it from the scroll-back buffer. If you know in advance you only want to retrieve the certificate, you can use this command line as a shortcut:

```
$ echo | openssl s_client -connect www.feistyduck.com:443 2>&1 | sed --quiet '↵
/-BEGIN CERTIFICATE-/,/-END CERTIFICATE-/p' > www.feistyduck.com.crt
```

The purpose of the echo command at the beginning is to separate your shell from s_client. If you don't do that, s_client will wait for your input until the server times out (which may potentially take a very long time).

By default, s_client will print only the leaf certificate; if you want to print the entire chain, give it the -showcerts switch. With that switch enabled, the previous command line will place all the certificates in the same file.

# Testing Protocol Support

By default, s_client will try to use the best protocol to talk to the remote server and report the negotiated version in output.

```
Protocol  : TLSv1.1
```

If you need to test support for specific protocol versions, you have two options. You can explicitly choose one protocol to test by supplying one of the -ssl2, -ssl3, -tls1, -tls1_1, or -tls1_2 switches. Alternatively, you can choose which protocols you don't want to test by using one or many of the following: -no_ssl2, -no_ssl3, -no_tls1, -no_tls1_1, or -no_tls1_2.

> **Note**
>
> Not all versions of OpenSSL support all protocol versions. For example, the older versions of OpenSSL will not support TLS 1.1 and TLS 1.2, and the newer versions might not support older protocols, such as SSL 2.

For example, here's the output you might get when testing a server that doesn't support a certain protocol version:

```
$ openssl s_client -connect www.example.com:443 -tls1_2
CONNECTED(00000003)
140455015261856:error:1408F10B:SSL routines:SSL3_GET_RECORD:wrong version ↵
number:s3_pkt.c:340:
---
no peer certificate available
---
No client certificate CA names sent
---
SSL handshake has read 5 bytes and written 7 bytes
---
New, (NONE), Cipher is (NONE)
Secure Renegotiation IS NOT supported
Compression: NONE
Expansion: NONE
SSL-Session:
    Protocol  : TLSv1.2
    Cipher    : 0000
    Session-ID:
    Session-ID-ctx:
    Master-Key:
    Key-Arg   : None
    PSK identity: None
    PSK identity hint: None
    SRP username: None
    Start Time: 1339231204
```

```
    Timeout    : 7200 (sec)
    Verify return code: 0 (ok)
---
```

# Testing Cipher Suite Support

A little trick is required if you wish to use OpenSSL to determine if a remote server supports a particular cipher suite. The cipher configuration string is designed to select which suites you wish to use, but if you specify only one suite and you successfully handshake with a server, then you know that the server supports the suite. If the handshake fails, you know the support is not there.

As an example, to test if a server supports RC4-SHA, type:

```
$ openssl s_client -connect www.feistyduck.com:443 -cipher RC4-SHA
```

If you want to determine all suites supported by a particular server, start by invoking openssl ciphers ALL to obtain a list of all suites supported by your version of OpenSSL. Then submit them to the server one by one to test them individually. I am not suggesting that you do this manually; this is a situation in which a little automation goes a long way. In fact, this is a situation in which looking around for a good tool might be appropriate.

There is a disadvantage to testing this way, however. You can only test the suites that OpenSSL supports. This used to be a much bigger problem; before version 1.0, OpenSSL supported a much smaller number of suites (e.g., 32 on my server with version 0.9.8k). With a version from the 1.0.1 branch, you can test over 100 suites and probably most of the relevant ones.

No single SSL/TLS library supports all cipher suites, and that makes comprehensive testing difficult. In SSL Labs, I resorted to using partial handshakes for this purpose, with a custom client that pretends to support arbitrary suites. It actually can't negotiate even a single suite, but just proposing to negotiate is enough for servers to tell you if they support a suite or not. Not only can you test all the suites this way, but you can also do it very efficiently.

# Testing Servers that Require SNI

Initially, SSL and TLS were designed to support only one web site per IP address. SNI is a TLS extension that enables use of more than one certificate on the same IP address. TLS clients use the extension to send the desired name, and TLS servers use it to select the correct certificate to respond with. In a nutshell, SNI makes virtual secure hosting possible.

Because SNI is not yet very widely deployed, in most cases you won't specify it on the s_client command line. But when you encounter an SNI-enabled system, one of three things can happen:

---

- Most often, you will get the same certificate you would get as if SNI information had not been supplied.
- The server might respond with the certificate for some site other than the one you wish to test.
- Very rarely, the server might abort the handshake and refuse the connection.

You can enable SNI in s_client with the -servername switch:

```
$ openssl s_client -connect www.feistyduck.com:443 -servername www.feistyduck.com
```

You can determine if a site requires SNI by testing with and without the SNI switch and checking if the certificates are the same. If they are not, SNI is required.

Sometimes, if the requested server name is not available, the server says so with a TLS warning. Even though this warning is not fatal as far as the server is concerned, the client might decide to close the connection. For example, with an older OpenSSL version (i.e., before 1.0.0), you will get the following error message:

```
$ /opt/openssl-0.9.8k/bin/openssl s_client -connect www.feistyduck.com:443 ↵
-servername xyz.com
CONNECTED(00000003)
1255:error:14077458:SSL routines:SSL23_GET_SERVER_HELLO:reason(1112):s23↵
_clnt.c:596:
```

# Testing Session Reuse

When coupled with the -reconnect switch, the s_client command can be used to test session reuse. In this mode, s_client will connect to the target server six times; it will create a new session on the first connection, then try to reuse the same session in the subsequent five connections:

```
$ echo | openssl s_client -connect www.feistyduck.com:443 -reconnect
```

The previous command will produce a sea of output, most of which you won't care about. The key parts are the information about new and reused sessions. There should be only one new session at the beginning, indicated by the following line:

```
New, TLSv1/SSLv3, Cipher is RC4-SHA
```

This is followed by five session reuses, indicated by lines like this:

```
Reused, TLSv1/SSLv3, Cipher is RC4-SHA
```

Most of the time, you don't want to look at all that output and want an answer quickly. You can get it using the following command line:

```
$ echo | openssl s_client -connect www.feistyduck.com:443 -reconnect -no_ssl2 2> ↵
/dev/null | grep 'New\|Reuse'
New, TLSv1/SSLv3, Cipher is ECDHE-RSA-AES256-GCM-SHA384
Reused, TLSv1/SSLv3, Cipher is ECDHE-RSA-AES256-GCM-SHA384
Reused, TLSv1/SSLv3, Cipher is ECDHE-RSA-AES256-GCM-SHA384
Reused, TLSv1/SSLv3, Cipher is ECDHE-RSA-AES256-GCM-SHA384
Reused, TLSv1/SSLv3, Cipher is ECDHE-RSA-AES256-GCM-SHA384
Reused, TLSv1/SSLv3, Cipher is ECDHE-RSA-AES256-GCM-SHA384
```

Here's what the command does:

- The -reconnect switch activates the session reuse mode.

- The -no_ssl2 switch indicates that we do not wish to attempt an SSL 2 connection, which changes the handshake of the first connection to that of SSL 3 and better. The older, SSL 2 handshake format handshake doesn't support TLS extensions and interferes with the session-reuse mechanism on servers that support session tickets.

- The 2> /dev/null part hides stderr output, which you don't care about.

- Finally, the piped grep command filters out the rest of the fluff and lets through only the lines that you care about.

> **Note**
>
> If you don't want to include session tickets in the test—for example, because not all clients support this feature yet—you can disable it with the -no_ticket switch.

# Checking OCSP Revocation

If an OCSP responder is malfunctioning, sometimes it's difficult to understand exactly why. Checking certificate revocation status from the command line is possible, but it's not quite straightforward. You need to perform the following steps:

1. Obtain the certificate that you wish to check for revocation.

2. Obtain the issuing certificate.

3. Determine the URL of the OCSP responder.

4. Submit an OCSP request and observe the response.

For the first two steps, connect to the server with the -showcerts switch specified:

```
$ openssl s_client -connect www.feistyduck.com:443 -showcerts
```

The first certificate in the output will be the one belonging to the server. If the certificate chain is properly configured, the second certificate will be that of the issuer. To confirm, check that the issuer of the first certificate and the subject of the second match:

---

```
---
Certificate chain
 0 s:/1.3.6.1.4.1.311.60.2.1.3=GB/businessCategory=Private Organization↵
/serialNumber=06694169/C=GB/ST=London/L=London/O=Feisty Duck Ltd↵
/CN=www.feistyduck.com
   i:/C=US/ST=Arizona/L=Scottsdale/O=Starfield Technologies, Inc./OU=http:/↵
/certificates.starfieldtech.com/repository/CN=Starfield Secure Certification ↵
Authority/serialNumber=10688435
-----BEGIN CERTIFICATE-----
MIIF5zCCBM+gAwIBAgIHBG9JXlv9vTANBgkqhkiG9w0BAQUFADCB3DELMAkGA1UE
[30 lines of text removed]
os5LW3PhHz8y9YFep2SV4c7+NrlZISHOZVzN
-----END CERTIFICATE-----
 1 s:/C=US/ST=Arizona/L=Scottsdale/O=Starfield Technologies, Inc./OU=http:/↵
/certificates.starfieldtech.com/repository/CN=Starfield Secure Certification ↵
Authority/serialNumber=10688435
   i:/C=US/O=Starfield Technologies, Inc./OU=Starfield Class 2 Certification ↵
Authority
-----BEGIN CERTIFICATE-----
MIIFBzCCA++gAwIBAgICAgEwDQYJKoZIhvcNAQEFBQAwaDELMAkGA1UEBhMCVVMx
[...]
```

If the second certificate isn't the right one, check the rest of the chain; some servers don't serve the chain in the correct order. If you can't find the issuer certificate in the chain, you'll have to find it somewhere else. One way to do that is to look for the *Authority Information Access* extension in the leaf certificate:

```
$ openssl x509 -in fd.crt -noout -text
[...]
    Authority Information Access:
        OCSP - URI:http://ocsp.starfieldtech.com/
        CA Issuers - URI:http://certificates.starfieldtech.com/repository/sf↵
_intermediate.crt
[...]
```

If the *CA Issuers* information is present, it should contain the URL of the issuer certificate. If the issuer certificate information isn't available, you can try to open the site in a browser, let it reconstruct the chain, and download the issuing certificate from its certificate viewer. If all that fails, you can look for the certificate in your trust store or visit the CA's web site.

If you already have the certificates and just need to know the address of the OCSP responder, use the -ocsp_uri switch with the x509 command as a shortcut:

```
$ openssl x509 -in fd.crt -noout -ocsp_uri
http://ocsp.starfieldtech.com/
```

Now you can submit the OCSP request:

---

```
$ openssl ocsp -issuer issuer.crt -cert fd.crt -url http://ocsp.starfieldtech.com/ ↵
-CAfile issuer.crt
WARNING: no nonce in response
Response verify OK
fd.crt: good
        This Update: Feb 18 17:59:10 2013 GMT
        Next Update: Feb 18 23:59:10 2013 GMT
```

You want to look for two things in the response. First, check that the response itself is valid (Response verify OK in the previous example), and second, check what the response said. When you see good as the status, that means that the certificate hasn't been revoked. The status will be revoked for revoked certificates.

> **Note**
>
> The warning message about the missing nonce is telling you that OpenSSL wanted to use a nonce as a protection against replay attacks, but the server in question did not reply with one. This generally happens because CAs want to improve the performance of their OCSP responders. When they disable the nonce protection (the standard allows it), OCSP responses can be produced (usually in batch), cached, and reused for a period of time.

You may encounter OCSP responders that do not respond successfully to the previous command line. The following suggestions may help in such situations.

**Do not request a nonce**

Some servers cannot handle nonce requests and respond with errors. OpenSSL will request a nonce by default. To disable nonces, use the -no_nonce command-line switch.

**Supply a Host request header**

Although most OCSP servers occupy an entire IP address and respond to HTTP requests no matter the hostname, some don't. If you encounter an error message that includes an HTTP error code (e.g., 404), you should try supplying the correct hostname in your OCSP request. You can do this if you are using OpenSSL 1.0.0 or later by using the undocumented -header switch.

With the previous two points in mind, the final command to use is the following:

```
$ openssl ocsp -issuer issuer.crt -cert fd.crt -url http://ocsp.starfieldtech.com/ ↵
-CAfile issuer.crt -no_nonce -header Host ocsp.starfieldtech.com
```

# Testing OCSP Stapling

OCSP stapling is an optional feature that allows a server certificate to be accompanied by an OCSP response that proves its validity. Because the OCSP response is delivered over an already existing connection, the client does not have to fetch it separately.

OCSP stapling is used only if requested by a client, which submits the status_request extension in the handshake request. A server that supports OCSP stapling will respond by including an OCSP response as part of the handshake.

When using the s_client tool, OCSP stapling is requested with the -status switch:

```
$ echo | openssl s_client -connect www.feistyduck.com:443 -status
```

The OCSP-related information will be displayed at the very beginning of the connection output. For example, with a server that does not support stapling you will see this line near the top of the output:

```
CONNECTED(00000003)
OCSP response: no response sent
```

With a server that does support stapling, you will see the entire OCSP response in the output:

```
OCSP Response Data:
    OCSP Response Status: successful (0x0)
    Response Type: Basic OCSP Response
    Version: 1 (0x0)
    Responder Id: C = US, O = "GeoTrust, Inc.", CN = RapidSSL OCSP-TGV Responder
    Produced At: Jan 22 17:48:55 2014 GMT
    Responses:
    Certificate ID:
      Hash Algorithm: sha1
      Issuer Name Hash: 834F7C75EAC6542FED58B2BD2B15802865301E0E
      Issuer Key Hash: 6B693D6A18424ADD8F026539FD35248678911630
      Serial Number: 0FE760
    Cert Status: good
    This Update: Jan 22 17:48:55 2014 GMT
    Next Update: Jan 29 17:48:55 2014 GMT
 [...]
```

The certificate status good means that the certificate has not been revoked.

# Checking CRL Revocation

Checking certificate verification with a *Certificate Revocation List* (CRL) is even more involved than doing the same via OCSP. The process is as follows:

1. Obtain the certificate you wish to check for revocation.

2. Obtain the issuing certificate.

3. Download and verify the CRL.

4. Look for the certificate serial number in the CRL.

The first steps overlap with OCSP checking; to complete them follow the instructions in the section called "Checking OCSP Revocation".

The location of the CRL is encoded in the server certificate; you can extract it with the following command:

```
$ openssl x509 -in fd.crt -noout -text | grep crl
                URI:http://rapidssl-crl.geotrust.com/crls/rapidssl.crl
```

Then fetch the CRL from the CA:

```
$ wget http://rapidssl-crl.geotrust.com/crls/rapidssl.crl
```

Verify that the CRL is valid (i.e., signed by the issuer certificate):

```
$ openssl crl -in rapidssl.crl -inform DER -CAfile issuer.crt -noout
verify OK
```

Now, determine the serial number of the certificate you wish to check:

```
$ openssl x509 -in fd.crt -noout -serial
serial=0FE760
```

At this point, you can convert the CRL into a human-readable format and inspect it manually:

```
$ openssl crl -in rapidssl.crl -inform DER -text -noout
Certificate Revocation List (CRL):
        Version 2 (0x1)
    Signature Algorithm: sha1WithRSAEncryption
        Issuer: /C=US/O=GeoTrust, Inc./CN=RapidSSL CA
        Last Update: Jan 25 11:03:00 2014 GMT
        Next Update: Feb  4 11:03:00 2014 GMT
        CRL extensions:
            X509v3 Authority Key Identifier:
                keyid:6B:69:3D:6A:18:42:4A:DD:8F:02:65:39:FD:35:24:86:78:91:16:30

            X509v3 CRL Number:
                92103
Revoked Certificates:
    Serial Number: 0F38D7
        Revocation Date: Nov 26 20:07:51 2013 GMT
    Serial Number: 6F29
```

```
                Revocation Date: Aug 15 20:48:57 2011 GMT
    [...]
        Serial Number: 0C184E
                Revocation Date: Jun 13 23:00:12 2013 GMT
        Signature Algorithm: sha1WithRSAEncryption
            95:df:e5:59:bc:95:e8:2f:bb:0a:4f:20:ad:ca:8f:78:16:54:
            35:32:55:b0:c9:be:5b:89:da:ba:ae:67:19:6e:07:23:4d:5f:
            16:18:5c:f3:91:15:da:9e:68:b0:81:da:68:26:a0:33:9d:34:
            2d:5c:84:4b:70:fa:76:27:3a:fc:15:27:e8:4b:3a:6e:2e:1c:
            2c:71:58:15:8e:c2:7a:ac:9f:04:c0:f6:3c:f5:ee:e5:77:10:
            e7:88:83:00:44:c4:75:c4:2b:d3:09:55:b9:46:bf:fd:09:22:
            de:ab:07:64:3b:82:c0:4c:2e:10:9b:ab:dd:d2:cb:0c:a9:b0:
            51:7b:46:98:15:83:97:e5:ed:3d:ea:b9:65:d4:10:05:10:66:
            09:5c:c9:d3:88:c6:fb:28:0e:92:1e:35:b0:e0:25:35:65:b9:
            98:92:c7:fd:e2:c7:cc:e3:b5:48:08:27:1c:e5:fc:7f:31:8f:
            0a:be:b2:62:dd:45:3b:fb:4f:25:62:66:45:34:eb:63:44:43:
            cb:3b:40:77:b3:7f:6c:83:5c:99:4b:93:d9:39:62:48:5d:8c:
            63:e2:a8:26:64:5d:08:e5:c3:08:e2:09:b0:d1:44:7b:92:96:
            aa:45:9f:ed:36:f8:62:60:66:42:1c:ea:e9:9a:06:25:c4:85:
            fc:77:f2:71
```

The CRL starts with some metadata, which is followed by a list of revoked certificates, and it ends with a signature (which we verified in the previous step). If the serial number of the server certificate is on the list, that means it had been revoked.

If you don't want to look for the serial number visually (some CRLs can be quite long), grep for it, but be careful that your formatting is correct (e.g., if necessary, remove the 0x prefix, omit any leading zeros, and convert all letters to uppercase). For example:

```
$ openssl crl -in rapidssl.crl -inform DER -text -noout | grep FE760
```

# Testing Renegotiation

The s_client tool has a couple of features that can assist you with manual testing of renegotiation. First of all, when you connect, the tool will report if the remote server supports secure renegotiation. This is because a server that supports secure renegotiation indicates its support for it via a special TLS extension that is exchanged during the handshake phase. When support is available, the output may look like this (emphasis mine):

```
New, TLSv1/SSLv3, Cipher is AES256-SHA
Server public key is 2048 bit
Secure Renegotiation IS supported
Compression: NONE
Expansion: NONE
SSL-Session:
    [...]
```

If secure renegotiation is not supported, the output will be slightly different:

```
Secure Renegotiation IS NOT supported
```

Even if the server indicates support for secure renegotiation, you may wish to test whether it also allows clients to initiate renegotiation. *Client-initiated renegotiation* is a protocol feature that is not needed in practice (because the server can always initiate renegotiation when it is needed) and makes the server more susceptible to denial of service attacks.

To initiate renegotiation, you type an R character on a line by itself. For example, assuming we're talking to an HTTP server, you can type the first line of a request, initiate renegotiation, and then finish the request. Here's what that looks like when talking to a web server that supports client-initiated renegotiation:

```
HEAD / HTTP/1.0
R
RENEGOTIATING
depth=3 C = US, O = "VeriSign, Inc.", OU = Class 3 Public Primary Certification ↵
Authority
verify return:1
depth=2 C = US, O = "VeriSign, Inc.", OU = VeriSign Trust Network, OU = "(c) 2006 ↵
VeriSign, Inc. - For authorized use only", CN = VeriSign Class 3 Public Primary ↵
Certification Authority - G5
verify return:1
depth=1 C = US, O = "VeriSign, Inc.", OU = VeriSign Trust Network, OU = Terms of ↵
use at https://www.verisign.com/rpa (c)06, CN = VeriSign Class 3 Extended ↵
Validation SSL CA
verify return:1
depth=0 1.3.6.1.4.1.311.60.2.1.3 = US, 1.3.6.1.4.1.311.60.2.1.2 = California, ↵
businessCategory = Private Organization, serialNumber = C2759208, C = US, ST = ↵
California, L = Mountain View, O = Mozilla Corporation, OU = Terms of use at ↵
www.verisign.com/rpa (c)05, OU = Terms of use at www.verisign.com/rpa (c)05, CN = ↵
addons.mozilla.org
verify return:1
Host: addons.mozilla.org

HTTP/1.1 301 MOVED PERMANENTLY
Content-Type: text/html; charset=utf-8
Date: Tue, 05 Jun 2012 16:42:51 GMT
Location: https://www.example.com/go/somewhere/else/
Keep-Alive: timeout=5, max=998
Transfer-Encoding: chunked
Connection: close

read:errno=0
```

When renegotiation is taking place, the server will send its certificates to the client again. You can see the verification of the certificate chain in the output. The next line after that continues with the Host request header. Seeing the web server's response is the proof that renegotiation is supported. Because of the various ways the renegotiation issue was addressed in various versions of SSL/TLS libraries, servers that do not support renegotiation may break the connection or may keep it open but refuse to continue to talk over it (which usually results in a timeout).

A server that does not support renegotiation will flatly refuse the second handshake on the connection:

```
HEAD / HTTP/1.0
R
RENEGOTIATING
140003560109728:error:1409E0E5:SSL routines:SSL3_WRITE_BYTES:ssl handshake ↵
failure:s3_pkt.c:592:
```

To test for insecure renegotiation, use the -legacy_renegotiation switch on the s_client command line. After that, the process is the same as when you're testing secure renegotiation.

> **Note**
>
> When you're testing a server for renegotiation, I suggest that you test for legacy renegotiation support even when the server indicates support for secure renegotiation. There is a small number of misconfigured servers that will support both!

# Testing for the BEAST Vulnerability

The BEAST attack exploits a weakness that exists in all versions of SSL, and TLS protocols before TLS 1.1. The weakness affects all CBC suites and both client and server data streams; however, the BEAST attack works only against the client side. Most modern browsers deployed workarounds to fight this flaw (the so-called 1/n-1 split), but some servers might continue to offer server-side mitigations still, especially if they have a user base that relies on older (and unpatched) browsers.

The ideal mitigation approach is to rely only on TLS 1.1 and better, but these newer protocols are not yet widely supported. The situation is more complicated by the fact that RC4 itself is now considered insecure. Thus, the practical approach to mitigation is to deploy TLS 1.1 and better to use with clients that support them (and avoid RC4), but force RC4 with all other clients.

RC4 is the second most popular cipher today, after 3DES. As such, virtually all clients support it. Consequently, there are two approaches for mitigation.

---

### Strict mitigation

Do not support any CBC suites when protocols TLS 1.0 and earlier are used, leaving only RC4 suites enabled. Clients that don't support RC4 won't be able to negotiate a secure connection. This mode excludes some potential web site users, but it's required by some PCI assessors.

### RC4 prioritization

Because there is only a very small number of clients that do not support RC4, the second approach is to leave CBC suites enabled, but enforce RC4 with all clients that support it. This approach provides protection to all but a very small number of visitors.

How you are going to test depends on what behavior you expect of the server. With both approaches, we want to ensure that only insecure protocols are used by using the -no_ssl2, -no_tls_1_1, and -no_tls_1_2 switches.

To test for strict mitigation, attempt to connect while disabling all RC4 suites on your end:

```
$ echo | openssl s_client -connect www.feistyduck.com:443 \
-cipher 'ALL:!RC4' -no_ssl2 -no_tls1_1 -no_tls1_2
```

If the connection is successful (which is possible only if a vulnerable CBC suite is used), you know that strict mitigation is not in place.

To test for RC4 prioritization, attempt to connect with all RC4 suites moved to the end of the cipher suite list:

```
$ echo | openssl s_client -connect www.feistyduck.com:443 \
-cipher 'ALL:+RC4' -no_ssl2 -no_tls1_1 -no_tls1_2
```

A server that prioritizes RC4 will choose one of RC4 suites for the connection, ignoring all the CBC suites that were also offered. If you see anything else, you know that the server does not have any BEAST mitigations in place.

# Testing for Heartbleed

You can test for Heartbleed manually or by using one of the available tools. (There are many tools, because Heartbleed is very easy to exploit.) But, as usual with such tools, there is a question of their accuracy. There is evidence that some tools fail to detect vulnerable servers.[1] Given the seriousness of Heartbleed, it's best to either test manually or by using a tool that gives you full visibility of the process. I am going to describe an approach you can use with only a modified version of OpenSSL.

Some parts of the test don't require modifications to OpenSSL, assuming you have a version that supports the Heartbeat protocol (version 1.0.1 and newer). For example, to determine if

---

[1] Bugs in Heartbleed detection scripts [fsty.uk/b444] (Shannon Simpson and Adrian Hayter, 14 April 2014)

the remote server supports the Heartbeat protocol, use the `-tlsextdebug` switch to display server extensions when connecting:

```
$ openssl s_client -connect www.feistyduck.com:443 -tlsextdebug
CONNECTED(00000003)
TLS server extension "renegotiation info" (id=65281), len=1
0001 - <SPACES/NULS>
TLS server extension "EC point formats" (id=11), len=4
0000 - 03 00 01 02                                       ....
TLS server extension "session ticket" (id=35), len=0
TLS server extension "heartbeat" (id=15), len=1
0000 - 01
[...]
```

A server that does not return the heartbeat extension is not vulnerable to Heartbleed. To test if a server responds to heartbeat requests, use the `-msg` switch to request that protocol messages are shown, then connect to the server, type B and press return:

```
$ openssl s_client -connect www.feistyduck.com:443 -tlsextdebug -msg
[...]
---
B
HEARTBEATING
>>> TLS 1.2  [length 0025], HeartbeatRequest
    01 00 12 00 00 3c 83 1a 9f 1a 5c 84 aa 86 9e 20
    c7 a2 ac d7 6f f0 c9 63 9b d5 85 bf 9a 47 61 27
    d5 22 4c 70 75
<<< TLS 1.2  [length 0025], HeartbeatResponse
    02 00 12 00 00 3c 83 1a 9f 1a 5c 84 aa 86 9e 20
    c7 a2 ac d7 6f 52 4c ee b3 d8 a1 75 9a 6b bd 74
    f8 60 32 99 1c
read R BLOCK
```

This output shows a complete heartbeat request and response pair. The second and third bytes in both heartbeat messages specify payload length. We submitted a payload of 18 bytes (12 hexadecimal) and the server responded with a payload of the same size. In both cases there were also additional 16 bytes of padding. The first two bytes in the payload make the sequence number, which OpenSSL uses to match responses to requests. The remaining payload bytes and the padding are just random data.

To detect a vulnerable server, you'll have to prepare a special version of OpenSSL that sends incorrect payload length. Vulnerable servers take the declared payload length and respond with that many bytes irrespective of the length of the actual payload provided.

At this point, you have to decide if you want to build an invasive test (which exploits the server by retrieving some data from the process) or a noninvasive test. This will depend on your circumstances. If you have permission for your testing activities, use the invasive test.

With it, you'll be able to see exactly what is returned, and there won't be room for errors. For example, some versions of GnuTLS support Heartbeat and will respond to requests with incorrect payload length, but they will not actually return server data. A noninvasive test can't reliably diagnose that situation.

The following patch against OpenSSL 1.0.1h creates a noninvasive version of the test:

```
--- t1_lib.c.original    2014-07-04 17:29:35.092000000 +0100
+++ t1_lib.c      2014-07-04 17:31:44.528000000 +0100
@@ -2583,6 +2583,7 @@
 #endif

 #ifndef OPENSSL_NO_HEARTBEATS
+#define PAYLOAD_EXTRA 16
 int
 tls1_process_heartbeat(SSL *s)
        {
@@ -2646,7 +2647,7 @@
                * sequence number */
               n2s(pl, seq);

-              if (payload == 18 && seq == s->tlsext_hb_seq)
+              if ((payload == (18 + PAYLOAD_EXTRA)) && seq == s->tlsext_hb_seq)
                      {
                      s->tlsext_hb_seq++;
                      s->tlsext_hb_pending = 0;
@@ -2705,7 +2706,7 @@
       /* Message Type */
       *p++ = TLS1_HB_REQUEST;
       /* Payload length (18 bytes here) */
-      s2n(payload, p);
+      s2n(payload + PAYLOAD_EXTRA, p);
       /* Sequence number */
       s2n(s->tlsext_hb_seq, p);
       /* 16 random bytes */
```

To build a noninvasive test, increase payload length by up to 16 bytes, or the length of the padding. When a vulnerable server responds to such a request, it will return the padding but nothing else. To build an invasive test, increase the payload length by, say, 32 bytes. A vulnerable server will respond with a payload of 50 bytes (18 bytes sent by OpenSSL by default, plus your 32 bytes) and send further 16 bytes of padding. By increasing the declared length of the payload in this way, a vulnerable server will return up to 64 KB of data. A server not vulnerable to Heartbleed will not respond.

To produce your own Heartbleed testing tool, unpack a fresh copy of OpenSSL source code, edit ssl/t1_lib.c to make the change as in the patch, compile as usual, but don't install. The resulting openssl binary will be placed in the apps/ subdirectory. Because it is statically compiled, you can rename it to something like `openssl-heartbleed` and move it to its permanent location.

Here's an example of the output you'd get with a vulnerable server that returns 16 bytes of server data (in bold):

```
B
HEARTBEATING
>>> TLS 1.2  [length 0025], HeartbeatRequest
    01 00 32 00 00 7c e8 f5 62 35 03 bb 00 34 19 4d
    57 7e f1 e5 90 6e 71 a9 26 85 96 1c c4 2b eb d5
    93 e2 d7 bb 5f
<<< TLS 1.2  [length 0045], HeartbeatResponse
    02 00 32 00 00 7c e8 f5 62 35 03 bb 00 34 19 4d
    57 7e f1 e5 90 6e 71 a9 26 85 96 1c c4 2b eb d5
    93 e2 d7 bb 5f 6f 81 0f aa dc e0 47 62 3f 7e dc
    60 95 c6 ba df c9 f6 9d 2b c8 66 f8 a5 45 64 0b
    d2 f5 3d a9 ad
read R BLOCK
```

If you want to see more data retrieved in a single response, increase the payload length, recompile, and test again. Alternatively, to retrieve another batch of the same size enter the B command again.

# 13 Configuring Apache

Apache httpd is a popular web server that has powered large parts of the Web since its early beginnings. Apache is a mature product and has superb TLS support in the 2.4.x branch, especially in the most recent releases (significant improvements were made in version 2.4.7). If you're compiling Apache from source code, you can take advantage of all the available features.

In practice, most people have access to some version from the 2.2.x branch, because that's what the previous generations of the popular server distributions (e.g., Debian, Ubuntu, Red Hat Enterprise Linux, etc.) used to ship. The current generations either ship or will ship Apache 2.4.x, which means that this newer version will slowly start to gain in popularity.

The following table shows the major differences between the 2.2.x and 2.4.x branches.

Table 13.1. Apache httpd TLS features across the most recent stable branches

|  | Apache 2.2.x | Apache 2.4.x |
| --- | --- | --- |
| Strong default DH parameters | Barely; fixed at 1,024 bits | 2,048 bits and stronger (2.4.7+) |
| Configurable DH and ECDH parameters | - | Yes (2.4.7+) |
| Elliptic curve support | Yes (2.2.26)[a] | Yes |
| OCSP stapling | - | Yes |
| Distributed TLS session caching | - | Yes |
| Configurable session ticket keys | - | Yes |
| Disable session tickets | - | - |

[a] Earlier versions can support ECDHE key exchange with a third-party utility called *TLS Interposer* (described later in this chapter).

> ## Note
>
> Most operating system distributions ship with software packages that carry the same (or similar) version numbers but differ in functionality from the stock releases made by the developers. The changes are most often only security fixes, but they could be features, too. You should review the package documentation and the

> source code (packages typically contain the original source code and the patches) to understand if the differences are important.

The biggest practical problem with the 2.2.x branch is lack of support for *elliptic curve* (EC) cryptography. Although Apache added EC support in 2.2.26 (released in November 2013), most distributions ship versions based on some earlier release. Without EC crypto, you cannot deploy the ECDHE key exchange, which means that you can't have fast and robust support for forward secrecy. Some distributions backport important features; check yours for this possibility.

The lack of other features is tolerable. OCSP stapling is nice to have (it improves site performance) but not critical for most people. If it's something you find important, you'll probably want to install Apache 2.4.x from source code.

In addition to the big and obvious differences, the 2.4.x branch contains a large number of small improvements that are not obvious at first but might be significant because they add up. As one example, Apache 2.4.x probably consumes much less memory because it uses the reduced memory consumption mode in OpenSSL (the `SSL_MODE_RELEASE_BUFFERS` option). This OpenSSL feature was not enabled in the latest 2.2.x version when I checked.

This chapter is designed to cover the most important and interesting aspects of Apache's TLS configuration, but it's not a reference guide. For the finer details, please refer to the official documentation.

## Installing Apache with Static OpenSSL

Back in 2004, when I was working on my first book, *Apache Security*, it was quite common to install Apache from source code, and I spent a lot of time documenting the process. As the technology stabilized, most people stopped bothering with the source code and relied on the binaries provided by the operating system.

Today, we're back to the beginning; to use the best TLS features many of us have to roll up our sleeves and do everything the old-fashioned way. For example, I have a couple of servers running Ubuntu 10.04 LTS; the OpenSSL version installed does not support TLS 1.2, and its Apache 2.2.x does not support the ECDHE suites. Luckily, Apache 2.4.x is available by default in modern distributions.

If you're running one of the older distributions, the easiest way to run Apache with a recent version of OpenSSL is to compile the crypto code statically and install everything into a separate location. That way, you achieve the goal, but you don't mess with the rest of the operating system.

First, get the most recent stable version of OpenSSL and install it at a location in which it will not interfere with your system version. Follow the instructions in the section called "Building OpenSSL" in Chapter 11 .

Then, get the latest versions of Apache and the APR and APR-Util libraries. Unpack all three packages into the same source tree, with the latter two in the location in which Apache expects them:

```
$ tar zxvf httpd-2.4.10.tar.gz
$ cd httpd-2.4.10/srclib/
$ tar zxvf ../../apr-1.5.1.tar.gz
$ ln -s apr-1.5.1/ apr
$ tar zxvf ../../apr-util-1.5.3.tar.gz
$ ln -s apr-util-1.5.3/ apr-util
```

You are now ready to configure and install Apache. The mod_ssl module will be compiled statically; all other modules will be compiled dynamically.

```
$ ./configure \
    --prefix=/opt/httpd \
    --with-included-apr \
    --enable-ssl \
    --with-ssl=/opt/openssl-1.0.1h \
    --enable-ssl-staticlib-deps \
    --enable-mods-static=ssl
$ make
$ sudo make install
```

From here, you can proceed to tweak the configuration. All modules will be compiled by default, but only some of them will be enabled in the configuration.

# Enabling TLS

If you are deploying a web site on the default HTTPS port (443), Apache will automatically enable the TLS protocol on the IP address in question. The only time you will need to explicitly enable TLS is when you're using a nonstandard port. For example:

```
# TLS is enabled by default on port 443
Listen 192.168.0.1:443

# But explicit configuration is required on all other ports
Listen 192.168.0.1:8443 https
```

You might also find many configurations that do not configure the protocol using the Listen directive; they instead enable TLS in the site configuration using the SSLEngine directive:

```
<VirtualHost 192.168.0.1:443>
    # Site hostname.
    ServerName site1.example.com
```

```
        # Enable front-end TLS in this virtual host.
        SSLEngine on

        # Other configuration directives.
        ...
    </VirtualHost>
```

This approach is popular with those who started with Apache 2.0.x, because the `Listen` directive in those versions had no support for protocol configuration.

> **Note**
>
> Apache implements a web server and a proxy server. Consequently, there are configuration directives that control TLS operation in both of these roles. Most proxy directives begin with `SSLProxy`; you should ignore them when you're configuring the web server side of things.

# Configuring TLS Protocol

To configure frontend TLS in Apache, you need three directives. The first is `SSLProtocol`, which specifies which protocols should be enabled:

```
# Enable all protocols except SSL 2 and
# SSL 3, which are obsolete and insecure.
SSLProtocol all -SSLv2 -SSLv3
```

The common approach is to enable all available protocols with `all`, then disable the ones you do not wish to deploy. The second directive is `SSLHonorCipherOrder`, which instructs Apache to select the best possible suite during TLS handshake (instead of leaving it to the client to make that choice):

```
# The server selects the cipher suite, not the clients.
SSLHonorCipherOrder on
```

Finally, `SSLCipherSuite` takes an OpenSSL suite-configuration string and configures which suites are going to be enabled and in which order:

```
# This cipher suite configuration uses only suites that provide
# forward security, in the order that provides the best performance.
SSLCipherSuite "ECDHE-ECDSA-AES128-GCM-SHA256 \
ECDHE-ECDSA-AES256-GCM-SHA384 \
ECDHE-ECDSA-AES128-SHA \
ECDHE-ECDSA-AES256-SHA \
ECDHE-ECDSA-AES128-SHA256 \
ECDHE-ECDSA-AES256-SHA384 \
```

```
ECDHE-RSA-AES128-GCM-SHA256 \
ECDHE-RSA-AES256-GCM-SHA384 \
ECDHE-RSA-AES128-SHA \
ECDHE-RSA-AES256-SHA \
ECDHE-RSA-AES128-SHA256 \
ECDHE-RSA-AES256-SHA384 \
DHE-RSA-AES128-GCM-SHA256 \
DHE-RSA-AES256-GCM-SHA384 \
DHE-RSA-AES128-SHA \
DHE-RSA-AES256-SHA \
DHE-RSA-AES128-SHA256 \
DHE-RSA-AES256-SHA256 \
EDH-RSA-DES-CBC3-SHA"
```

### Note

The cipher suite configuration from this example is secure, but, depending on your preferences and risk profile, you might prefer something slightly different. You'll find a thorough discussion of TLS server configuration in Chapter 8, *Deployment* and examples for OpenSSL in the section called "Recommended Configuration" in Chapter 11.

The previous example was primarily designed for newer Apache versions, which have elliptic crypto support, but will fall back gracefully on older installations.

### Tip

TLS protocol configuration is best placed in the main server scope, where it applies to all sites hosted on the server. Tune it on a per-site basis only if necessary.

# Configuring Keys and Certificates

In addition to configuring the TLS protocol, a secure web site also requires a private key and a certificate chain. For this, you typically require three directives, as in the following example:

```
# Configure the server private key.
SSLCertificateKeyFile conf/server.key

# Configure the server certificate.
SSLCertificateFile conf/server.crt

# Configure intermediate chain certificates supplied
# by the CA. This directive is not needed when the server
# certificate is self-signed.
SSLCertificateChainFile conf/chain.pem
```

> **Note**
>
> Starting with version 2.4.8, the `SSLCertificateChainFile` directive is deprecated. Instead, you are requested to provide all certificates in the file pointed to by the `SSLCertificateFile` directive. This change was probably driven by the fact that more sites want to use multikey deployments (e.g., RSA and ECDSA at the same time) and that each key might require a different certificate chain.

Not configuring the entire certificate chain correctly is a frequent mistake that results in unnecessary client certificate warnings. To avoid this problem, always follow the instructions provided by your CA. When renewing a certificate, make sure you use the new intermediate certificates provided; the old ones might no longer be appropriate.

> **Note**
>
> The example in this section assumes that your private key is not protected with a passphrase. I recommend that keys are created and backed up with a passphrase but deployed without a passphrase on the server. If you want to use protected keys, you will have to use the `SSLPassPhaseDialog` directive to interface Apache with an external program that will provide the passphrase every time it is needed.

# Configuring Multiple Keys

It's not widely known that Apache allows secure sites to use more than one type of TLS key. This facility, which had originally been designed to allow sites to deploy RSA and DSA keys in parallel, is virtually unused because DSA faded into obscurity for web server keys.

These days, there is a lot of discussion about deploying ECDSA keys in order to improve handshake performance. In parallel, there is a desire to migrate certificate signatures to SHA2, because the currently widely used SHA1 is nearing the end of its useful life. The problem is that older clients might not support ECDSA keys and SHA2 signatures. One solution is to deploy with two sets of keys and certificates: RSA and SHA1 for older clients and ECDSA and SHA2 for newer clients.

Deploying a site with multiple keys is straightforward: simply specify multiple keys and certificates, one set after another. For example:

```
# RSA key.
SSLCertificateKeyFile conf/server-rsa.key
SSLCertificateFile conf/server-rsa.crt

# DSA key.
SSLCertificateKeyFile conf/server-dsa.key
SSLCertificateFile conf/server-dsa.crt

# ECDSA key.
```

```
SSLCertificateKeyFile conf/server-ecdsa.key
SSLCertificateFile conf/server-ecdsa.crt

# Intermediate certificates; must work
# with all three server certificates.
SSLCertificateChainFile conf/chain.pem
```

The only catch is that the `SSLCertificateChainFile` directive can be used only once per server, which means that the intermediate certificates must be identical for all three certificates. There are early indications that the CAs who are starting to offer ECDSA keys are set up this way.

It's possible to use different certificate hierarchies, but then you must avoid `SSLCertificateChainFile` altogether. Instead, concatenate all the necessary intermediate certificates (for all the keys) into a single file, and point to it using the `SSLCACertificateFile` directive. There might be a slight performance penalty with this approach because, on every new connection, OpenSSL now needs to examine the available CA certificates in order to construct the certificate chain. This has probably been fixed as of 2.4.8, which deprecated the `SSLCertificateChainFile` directive.

> **Note**
>
> To ensure that all deployed keys are actually used, make sure you also enable the corresponding cipher suites in the configuration. ECDSA suites have the word "ECDSA" in the name; DSA suites have the word "DSS" in the name; all other authenticated suites are designed to work with RSA keys.

# Wildcard and Multisite Certificates

If you have two or more sites that share a certificate, it is possible to deploy them on the same IP address, despite the fact that virtual secure hosting is not yet feasible for public web sites. No special configuration is required; simply associate all such sites with the same IP address and ensure that they are all using the same certificate.[1]

This works because TLS termination and HTTP host selection are two separate steps. When terminating TLS, in the absence of SNI information (see the next section for more information) Apache serves the certificate of the default site for that IP address, which is the site that appears first in the configuration. In the second step, Apache looks at the Host request header provided and serves the correct site at the HTTP level. If the requested hostname is not configured on the IP address, the default web site will be served.

---

[1] Technically, the restrictions are per IP address and port combination (a TCP/IP endpoint). You could, for example, host one secure site on 192.168.0.1:443 and another on 192.168.0.1:8443. In practice, public sites can be hosted only on port 443, so the restrictions are effectively per IP address.

With this type of deployment, you might get a warning similar to this one:

```
[Mon Dec 30 11:26:04.058505 2013] [ssl:warn] [pid 31136:tid 140679275079488] AH0229↵
2: Init: Name-based SSL virtual hosts only work for clients with TLS server name ↵
indication support (RFC 4366)
```

This is because Apache notices that you have multiple secure sites on the same endpoint but does not check to see that the default certificate is valid for all sites. From version 2.4.10 onwards, the warning doesn't show.

# Virtual Secure Hosting

Unlike the setup discussed in the previous section, true virtual secure hosting takes place when a number of unrelated web sites, each with its own certificate, shares one IP address. Because this feature is not supported by SSL and the early versions of TLS, there are still many clients that do not have it. For this reason, it is not yet feasible to use virtual secure hosting for public web sites aimed at a wide audience, but it could possibly be used for sites with a modern user base.

Apache supports virtual secure hosting and uses it automatically when needed. The only question is: what happens if you do rely on virtual secure hosting but receive a client that does not support it? Normally, in situations like that Apache serves the certificate belonging to the default site associated with the requested IP address. Because that certificate is unlikely to match the desired hostname, the user ends up with a certificate warning. However, if they are able to bypass the warning, they will get through to the site they wanted to see.[2]

You can't avoid certificate warnings in situations like this, but it's best practice not to serve any content from sites that rely on virtual secure hosting to clients that don't understand SNI. This is what the SSLStrictSNIVHostCheck directive does, and there are two ways to use it.

The first way is to enforce strict virtual secure hosting on the entire IP address. To do that, you place the directive in the default virtual host. For example:

```
# Apache 2.2.x requires the following directive to support
# name-based virtual hosting. Apache 2.4.x and better do not.
NameVirtualHost 192.168.0.1:443

<VirtualHost 192.168.0.1:443>
    ServerName does-not-exist.example.com

    # Do not serve any content to the clients that
    # do not support virtual secure hosting (via SNI).
```

---

[2] Assuming, of course, that the requested hostname is configured on the server; if it isn't, they will get the default web site again.

```
        SSLStrictSNIVHostCheck On

        ...
    </VirtualHost>

    <VirtualHost 192.168.0.1:443>
        ServerName site1.example.com
        ...
    </VirtualHost>

    <VirtualHost 192.168.0.1:443>
        ServerName site2.example.com

        ...
    </VirtualHost>
```

Alternatively, you can enforce strict virtual secure hosting only for some sites, with relaxed configuration for others. In the following example, site1.example.com will not be served to clients that do not support SNI, but other sites will be:

```
    <VirtualHost 192.168.0.1:443>
        ServerName default.example.com

        ...
    </VirtualHost>

    <VirtualHost 192.168.0.1:443>
        ServerName site1.example.com

        # Do not serve this site to clients that
        # do not support virtual secure hosting (via SNI).
        SSLStrictSNIVHostCheck On

        ...
    </VirtualHost>

    <VirtualHost 192.168.0.1:443>
        ServerName site2.example.com
        ...
    </VirtualHost>
```

Whenever an error occurs due to a strict SNI check, Apache will force the request to fail with status 403 and no indication of the root cause. If the information provided in the Host header is correct, the ErrorDocument directive of the matching host will be consulted. If it specifies a redirection or a message, that message will be sent back to the client. If ErrorDocument specifies a file or a script, its processing will fail.

If you want to deliver a custom error message for this case, it's possible to do so by disabling the built-in strict SNI checking and implementing a custom check instead. The SSL_TLS_SNI

Apache variable contains the client-provided SNI information; if this variable is empty, that means that the client doesn't support SNI. The following mod_rewrite configuration (placed in a virtual host section) worked for me:

```
RewriteEngine On
RewriteCond %{SSL:SSL_TLS_SNI} =""
RewriteRule ^ /errors/no-sni.html
```

> **Note**
>
> The behavior described here is implemented in versions up until 2.4.9. From 2.4.10 onwards, Apache behaves differently: (1) the stock 403 response page includes the reason for the rejection and (2) the ErrorDocument directive can invoke a script. These changes make it possible to configure a script to handle 403 errors, detect the mention of SNI in the error note (the REDIRECT_ERROR_NOTES variable), and provide different messages depending on the exact context.

# Reserving Default Sites for Error Messages

It is never a good idea to deliver actual web site content in response to an incorrectly specified request. For example, you don't want a search engine to index a web site under arbitrary hostnames. Whatever content you deliver will be seen by the browser as belonging to the site that it requested; a mismatch can sometimes be used to exploit vulnerability from one site as if it existed on another. To avoid this, I suggest that you reserve default sites on each IP address and port combination for the delivery of error messages.

Here's an example configuration you could use:

```
# We're using this default web site to explain
# host mismatch and SNI issues to our users.
<VirtualHost 192.168.0.1:443>
    # The hostname used here should never match.
    ServerName does-not-exist.example.com
    DocumentRoot /var/www/does-not-exist

    # Require SNI support for all sites on this IP address and port.
    SSLStrictSNIVHostCheck on

    # Force all requests to this site to fail with a 404 status code.
    RewriteEngine On
    RewriteRule ^ - [L,R=404]

    # Error message for the clients that request
    # a hostname that is not configured on this server.
    ErrorDocument 404 "<h1>No such site</h1><p>The site you requested does not ↵
exist.</p>"
```

```
    # Other configuration directives as desired.
    # Enable TLS as usual and use a self-signed certificate.
    ...
</VirtualHost>
```

# Forward Secrecy

If you are deploying Apache from the 2.4.x branch and compiling everything from source code, you have at your disposal DHE and ECDHE suites, which allow you to support robust forward secrecy. Otherwise, when relying on the system-provided packages, they sometimes don't support EC cryptography, for several reasons:

**EC cryptography is not supported by older Apache 2.2.x versions**

Many Apache 2.2.x versions found in popular distributions do not support EC cryptography, even when coupled with an OpenSSL version that does. This is largely because when OpenSSL decided to add support for EC, it left it disabled by default. If you are in this situation but don't want to install Apache from source code, there's a workaround that might be sufficient, which I explain later in this section.

**Older OpenSSL version**

If the underlying OpenSSL installation does not support newer features (such as EC crypto), then it does not matter if Apache does. Older versions of OpenSSL are still prevalent on older installations, and even some newer operating system releases use it. For example, OS X Mavericks, released in November 2013, ships with OpenSSL 0.9.8y (that's the most recent version from the old 0.9.x branch).

A good OpenSSL version to use today is the most recent one from the 1.0.1 branch or newer. Luckily, Apache can be built with a statically compiled OpenSSL version, which means that you can upgrade just the web server without messing with a core operating system package.

**OpenSSL version without EC support**

For a long time, operating systems built by Red Hat used to ship without any support for EC cryptography, because their lawyers wanted to play it safe when it came to certain EC patents. This made it very difficult for anyone using Fedora and Red Hat Enterprise Linux distributions (and the open source derivatives, such as CentOS) to deploy forward secrecy well.[3] The only way to do it well was to recompile the key system packages.

This changed in October 2013, when Fedora 18 and later versions were updated with OpenSSL versions that have EC crypto enabled.[4]

---

[3] ECDHE is important, because the only alternative, DHE suites, can't be used to achieve forward secrecy with Internet Explorer. On top of that, DHE is much slower than the RSA and ECDHE key exchanges, which is why most sites don't want to use it.

Starting with version 6.5, which shipped in November 2013, all Red Hat Enterprise Linux versions support EC cryptography.[5]

---

### Enabling ECDHE Suites in Apache 2.2.x without Patching

TLS Interposer[6] is a Linux tool that can be used to improve how programs use OpenSSL without having to recompile them or change them in any other way. It works by intercepting calls to certain OpenSSL functions and overriding their behaviors.

By default, TLS Interposer will:

- Disable SSL 2 and SSL 3 protocols
- Enable support for ECDHE cipher suites
- Enforce its own cipher suite configuration, which is strong by default

A great use case for TLS Interposer is enabling ECDHE cipher suites on Apache 2.2.x. This tool can't add all EC features to Apache, but the addition of ECDHE suites enables you to support robust forward secrecy, which is the most common requirement.

---

# OCSP Stapling

*Online Certificate Status Protocol* (OCSP) is the protocol that's used to obtain certificate revocation information on demand. Most certificates include OCSP information, which allows TLS clients to talk directly to the issuing CA to confirm that the certificate has not been revoked. OCSP stapling allows the web server to obtain a fresh OCSP response from the CA, cache it locally, and submit it to the client along with the certificate. In this case, the client does not need to contact the CA, which saves time and improves performance but also results in better privacy. Apache supports OCSP stapling starting with the 2.4.x branch.

## Configuring OCSP Stapling

Although Apache has many directives for OCSP stapling, most of them are needed only for fine-tuning. You need only two directives to enable stapling initially:

```
# Configure a cache of 128 KB for OCSP responses. Tune the
# cache size based on the number of certificates in use on
# the server.
SSLStaplingCache shmcb:/opt/httpd/logs/stapling_cache(128000)
```

---

[4] Bug #319901: missing ec and ecparam commands in openssl package [fsty.uk/b445] (Red Hat Bugzilla, closed 22 October 2013)

[5] Red Hat Enterprise Linux 6.5 Release Notes [fsty.uk/b446] (Red Hat, 21 November 2013)

[6] TLS Interposer [fsty.uk/b447] (Marcel Waldvogel, retrieved 12 July 2014)

```
# Enable OCSP stapling by default for all sites on this server.
SSLUseStapling on
```

In this example, I configured a server-wide cache for OCSP responses and then enabled stapling by default for all sites. You can also use the SSLUseStapling directive elsewhere to enable or disable stapling for individual sites.

By default, successful OCSP responses will be cached for 3,600 seconds, but you can change this timeout using the SSLStaplingStandardCacheTimeout directive.

> **Note**
>
> OCSP requests are submitted over HTTP, which means that your web server needs to be allowed to make outbound requests to various OCSP responders across the Internet. If you're operating an outbound firewall, ensure that there are exceptions to allow this traffic.

Configuring OCSP stapling can fail if your site does not have a properly configured certificate chain. In order for Apache to verify OCSP responses (which it always does), it needs the CA certificate that issued the server certificate. Without it, stapling won't be possible and Apache will complain about the problem:

```
[Thu Jan 23 16:26:58.547877 2014] [ssl:error] [pid 1333:tid 140576489142080] AH0221⏎
7: ssl_stapling_init_cert: Can't retrieve issuer certificate!
[Thu Jan 23 16:26:58.547900 2014] [ssl:error] [pid 1333:tid 140576489142080] AH0223⏎
5: Unable to configure server certificate for stapling
```

If for some reason you are not using SSLCertificateChainFile to configure the chain, you can provide the required CA certificate in the SSLCACertificateFile configuration. In fact, the best practice is to always have the root certificate there.

To use OpenSSL to see if OCSP stapling is configured correctly, follow the instructions from the section called "Testing OCSP Stapling" in Chapter 12.

# Handling Errors

Apache caches both successful and failed OCSP responses. In theory, there is no harm in this, because your clients are expected to obtain the same result by talking to the CA directly. In practice, it depends. For example, because even failed responses are cached (600 seconds by default; change the value with SSLStaplingErrorCacheTimeout), a one-off problem might end up being propagated to all your users.

Given that there is a lot of anecdotal evidence that OCSP responders can be flaky, I think you should exercise caution and not return responder errors:

```
SSLStaplingReturnResponderErrors off
```

If you do choose to propagate the errors, remember that Apache by default generates fake OCSP tryLater responses in the cases in which the real OCSP responder is unresponsive. I think it's safer to disable this functionality, too:

```
SSLStaplingFakeTryLater off
```

As an example of when this might be an issue, consider someone reconfiguring the outbound firewall around your web server and inadvertently preventing Apache from reaching the OCSP responders. If you disable fake responses, your clients will still be able to communicate with the responders directly.

## Using a Custom OCSP Responder

Normally, OCSP requests are submitted to the OCSP responder, whose address is encoded in the certificate. But there are two cases in which you might want to use a different OCSP responder:

- Some certificates might not actually contain OCSP responder information, even though the CA operates a responder. In this case, you can provide the OCSP responder address manually.

- In heavily locked-down environments, outbound traffic from the web server might be forbidden. In this case, if you want to use OCSP stapling, you need to configure a HTTP proxy for OCSP requests.

You can override the OCSP responder information globally or on a per-site basis, using the SSLStaplingForceURL directive:

```
SSLStaplingForceURL http://ocsp.example.com
```

## Configuring Ephemeral DH Key Exchange

Traditionally, Apache has left OpenSSL to configure the default strength of the *Diffie-Hellman* (DH) key exchange. That worked for a long time, but the OpenSSL default strength of 1,024 bits is no longer considered adequate. Compare this strength to the current best practice that all server keys have at least 2,048 bits.

For a very long time, the only way to increase the strength of DH key exchange had been to change the source code, using a patch that was available only for the 2.4.x branch.[7] But this is no more. Starting with version 2.4.7, Apache will automatically tune the strength of the DH key exchange to match the strength of the corresponding private key.

---

[7] Increasing DHE strength on Apache 2.4.x [fsty.uk/b448] (Ivan Ristić, 15 August 2013)

> **Note**
>
> Given that 1,024-bit DH parameters are considered weak but not entirely insecure, most sites will probably be just fine even if they are stuck with an earlier version of Apache. Further, if your server supports ECDHE suites for forward secrecy (which you can achieve even with older Apache versions), the DH key exchange will be used only with older clients.

# TLS Session Management

Apache supports both mechanisms for session management: server-side state caching and session tickets. Apache 2.2.x has sufficient features for standalone deployments, but Apache 2.4.x adds features necessary for distributed operation.

## Standalone Session Cache

For individual web servers, there is only one practical option for TLS session caching: shared memory. It's also possible to cache the sessions in DBM files, but this approach is known to be unreliable under heavy load (per Apache documentation).

For caching using shared memory, you need to have the mod_socache_shmcb module enabled first. After that, specify the following two directives in the server scope:

```
# Specify session cache type, path, and size (1 MB).
SSLSessionCache shmcb:/path/to/logs/ssl_scache(1024000)

# Specify maximum session cache duration of one hour.
SSLSessionCacheTimeout 86400
```

By default, the timeout is set to five minutes, which is very conservative. There is little reason for new sessions to be renegotiated that often; I chose 24 hours instead. The default cache size is 512 KB, but I increased that to 1 MB. Both values would probably work for smaller web sites. Popular web sites will need to understand their usage patterns and set the cache size to the appropriate value. In my tests with Apache 2.4.x, you should expect to store roughly 4,000 sessions using a cache of 1 MB.

> **Note**
>
> Restarting Apache (even using the graceful option that keeps the master process around) clears the session cache. Thus, each restart comes with a small CPU penalty for the server and latency penalty for the users. In general, it's not something you should be worried about unless you're restarting *very* frequently.

Depending on the Apache version, for TLS session caching you might need to also configure the mutex that is used to synchronize access to the cache. Apache 2.4.x uses a mutex by

---

default, but the configuration can be tweaked using the `Mutex` directive. Inexplicably, stock Apache 2.2.x does not use a mutex by default, which means that its cache can get easily corrupted under heavy load.

To configure a mutex on Apache 2.2.x, use the `SSLMutex` directive:

```
# Configure the mutex for TLS session cache access synchronization.
SSLMutex file:/var/run/apache2/ssl_mutex
```

On Unix platforms, reliable automated mutex selection has traditionally been difficult, because it is generally not possible to select any one mutex type that performs and works well across all systems. For this reason, you'll find that programs tend to use file-based mutexes by default; they are the most reliable but not the fastest.

> ### Note
>
> Apache uses the same TLS session cache for the entire server, but sharing the session cache among unrelated applications can be dangerous. Session resumption uses an abbreviated TLS handshake that skips certificate validation. A network attacker who can redirect traffic from one port to another can potentially bypass certificate validation and force request processing by an incorrect application. This attack could, for example, lead to information leakage.

## Standalone Session Tickets

By default, the session ticket implementation is provided by OpenSSL. For standalone servers, this approach "just works," although there are some aspects that you should be aware of:

- Session tickets are protected using 128-bit AES encryption. A throwaway key is generated when the web server is initially started. It's possible that multiple keys will be used, depending on the configuration.

- The key size is fixed, but 128 bits is sufficiently strong for most use cases.

- When the server is restarted, new ticket keys are generated. This means that all connections that arrive after the restart will need to negotiate new TLS sessions.

- The same AES key is used for as long the server remains active. To minimize the impact of session tickets on forward secrecy, you should ensure that you regularly restart the web server. Daily is best.

## Distributed Session Caching

If you operate more than one server for the same web site but you're not terminating TLS centrally (e.g., on a load balancer) and not using sticky sessions (clients are always sent to the same node), you will need distributed TLS session caching—a mechanism to exchange session information among the cluster nodes.

Apache 2.4.x supports distributed TLS session caching out of the box, using the popular network caching program memcached. To use it, deploy an instance of memcached for the cache, and then connect all your web servers to it.

First, ensure you have the mod_socache_memcache module installed and activated:

```
LoadModule socache_memcache_module modules/mod_socache_memcache.so
```

Then, configure the TLS session caching, like so:

```
# Use memcached for the TLS session cache.
SSLSessionCache memcache:memcache.example.com:11211

# Specify maximum session cache duration of one hour.
SSLSessionCacheTimeout 3600
```

As for the memcached size, consider these important points:

- As with a standalone server, allocate enough RAM to ensure that the session data is cached for the entire duration of the session (the -m parameter).
- Lock the cache memory (the -k option) to improve performance and prevent the sensitive TLS session data from being written to swap.
- Ensure that the maximum number of connections allowed is sufficient to cover the maximum number of concurrent connections supported by the entire cluster (the -c option).

You can use the following configuration file as a starting point for customization:

```
# Run as daemon.
-d

# Run as user memcache.
-u memcache

# Run on port 11211.
-p 11211

# Log to this log file.
logfile /var/log/memcached.log

# Allocate a 10 MB cache.
-m 10

# Allow up to 10240 connections.
-c 10240
```

```
# Lock all memory to improve performance and (more importantly)
# to prevent sensitive TLS session data from being written to swap.
-k
```

At a glance, running a distributed TLS session cache appears to be straightforward. In practice, it depends on the details, and there are many additional issues that you need to consider, including the following.

**Availability**

Web server nodes no longer keep any TLS session information locally, instead relying on the configured memcache to provide the data. This means that the memcache is now a point of failure for your cluster. How are you going to handle the memcache misbehaving?

**Performance**

With TLS session data now hosted remotely, memcache lookups on resumed TLS connections will add to the latency. If the network is fast and reliable, that cost will be fixed and probably small. The only reliable way to tell is to measure the cost, by comparing the performance of a single server against that of the entire cluster. Just make sure you disable session tickets in the client; otherwise you'll be potentially measuring the wrong resumption mechanism.

**Security**

Communication with the memcache is not encrypted, which means that the sensitive TLS session data will be exposed as it travels over the network. This is not ideal, because a compromise of any server on the same network also results with the compromise of all your TLS sessions. This issue can be solved by communicating with the memcache over a special encrypted network segment.

> **Note**
>
> Because TLS session cache sharing can result in security weaknesses, it's best practice to never share a cache among unrelated applications. This is particularly true for distributed caching, for which it's more likely that servers powering multiple applications will use the same cache. For best security, run separate memcache sections, one for each application.

## Distributed Session Tickets

If you are deploying a web server cluster in which each node is expected to terminate TLS, then session tickets introduce an additional management challenge. In order to decrypt session data reliably, all the cluster nodes must share the same key; this means that you can no longer rely on the per-server keys generated by OpenSSL.

---

Apache 2.2.x does not support configurable ticket keys, which means that your only option is to disable session tickets, as explained in the previous section. Apache 2.4.x supports manually configured session ticket keys via the SSLSessionTicketKeyFile directive. With it, you can manually generate a ticket key file and push it to all your cluster nodes, using the same mechanism you use to manage other configuration data.

A session ticket key file consists of 48 bytes of cryptographically random data. The data is used for three 16-byte (128-bit) fragments, one each for key name, HMAC secret, and AES key.

Using OpenSSL, you can generate a ticket key file like this:

```
$ openssl rand -out ticket.key 48
```

After that, you only need to tell Apache where the key file is:

```
SSLSessionTicketKeyFile /path/to/ticket.key
```

> **Warning**
>
> The session ticket key file must be protected in the same way as all other private keys. Although it is not necessary to back it up, you must ensure that only the root user can access the file. Also, always use a different session ticket key for different applications. That will ensure that a session from one site can't be resumed on another.

As with standalone servers, to minimize the impact of session tickets on forward secrecy you have to rotate the session ticket key regularly—for example, once a day.

## Disabling Session Tickets

Apache doesn't currently have an option to disable session tickets, which is a problem if you want to deploy a cluster of Apache web servers but don't want to configure distributed ticket sharing. The only solution available right now is to patch the Apache source code.

To disable session tickets in Apache 2.2.x (tested against v2.2.27), apply the following patch:

```
--- ./modules/ssl/ssl_engine_init.c.orig    2014-07-16 10:53:06.000000000 +0100
+++ ./modules/ssl/ssl_engine_init.c    2014-07-16 10:53:44.000000000 +0100
@@ -615,6 +615,11 @@
     */
    SSL_CTX_set_options(ctx, SSL_OP_NO_SESSION_RESUMPTION_ON_RENEGOTIATION);
 #endif
+
+#ifdef SSL_OP_NO_TICKET
+    /* Disable session tickets. */
+    SSL_CTX_set_options(ctx, SSL_OP_NO_TICKET);
```

```
+#endif
 }
```

To disable session tickets in Apache 2.4.x (tested against v2.4.10), apply the following patch:

```
--- ./modules/ssl/ssl_engine_init.c.orig 2014-07-14 05:29:22.000000000 -0700
+++ ./modules/ssl/ssl_engine_init.c 2014-07-21 08:07:17.584482127 -0700
@@ -583,6 +583,11 @@
        SSL_CTX_set_mode(ctx, SSL_MODE_RELEASE_BUFFERS);
 #endif

+#ifdef SSL_OP_NO_TICKET
+ /* Disable session tickets. */
+ SSL_CTX_set_options(ctx, SSL_OP_NO_TICKET);
+#endif
+
     return APR_SUCCESS;
 }
```

# Client Authentication

As far as the configuration is concerned, using client authentication is straightforward: you enable it, provide all the necessary CA certificates to form a full chain for validation, and provide revocation information:

```
# Require client authentication.
SSLVerifyClient require

# Specify the maximum depth of the certification path,
# from the client certificate to a trusted root.
SSLVerifyDepth 2

# Allowed CAs that issue client certificates. The
# distinguished names of these certificates will be sent
# to each user to assist with client certificate selection.
SSLCACertificateFile conf/trusted-certificates.pem
```

The traditional way to check client certificates for revocation is to use a local CRL list. This option provides the best performance, because all operations are done locally. A script is usually configured to run periodically to retrieve fresh CRLs and reload the web server:

```
# Enable client certificate revocation checking.
SSLCARevocationCheck chain

# The list of revoked certificates. A reload is required
# every time this list is changed.
SSLCARevocationFile conf/revoked-certificates.crl
```

Starting with Apache 2.4.x, you can also use OCSP revocation checking. This option provides real-time revocation information at the cost of reduced performance:

```
# Use OCSP to check client certificates for revocation.
SSLOCSPEnable On
```

If client authentication is required but the client doesn't provide one, mod_ssl will reject the TLS handshake with a fatal alert. For end users, this means that they get a cryptic error message. It's possible to handle this situation more gracefully by using different values for the SSLVerifyClient directive:

optional

> Requests a client certificate during TLS handshake, but doesn't require it. The status of the validation is stored in the SSL_CLIENT_VERIFY variable: NONE for no certificate, SUCCESS for a valid certificate, and FAILED: followed by an error message for a certificate that failed validation. This feature is useful if you want to provide a custom response to those users who fail client certificate validation.

optional_no_ca

> Requests a client certificate during TLS handshake, but doesn't attempt validation. Instead, it's expected that an external service will validate the certificate (which is available in the SSL_CLIENT_ family of variables).

> **Note**
>
> Using optional client authentication can be problematic, because some browsers don't prompt the user or otherwise select a client certificate if this option is configured. There are also issues with some other browsers that won't proceed to the site if they can't provide a certificate. Before you seriously consider optional client authentication for deployment, test with the browsers you have in your environment.

For performance reasons, mod_ssl doesn't export its variables by default. If you need them, enable the export by configuring the required variables using the SSLOptions directive:

```
# Export standard mod_ssl variables as well
# as certificate data to the environment.
SSLOptions +StdEnvVars +ExportCertData
```

# Mitigating Protocol Issues

Apache developers have generally been quick to address TLS protocol–related issues. In practice, because most deployments are based on Apache versions included with various operating systems, it's up to the vendors to keep their packages secure.

## Insecure Renegotiation

Insecure renegotiation is a protocol flaw discovered in 2009 and largely mitigated during 2010. Before this issue was discovered, Apache 2.2.x used to support client-initiated renegotiation. Version 2.2.15, released in March 2010, not only disabled client-initiated renegotiation but also provided support for secure renegotiation (RFC 5746). Apache 2.4.x was first released in early 2012, which means that it was never vulnerable.

> ### Warning
>
> Disabling client-initiated renegotiation does not fully address this vulnerability if server-initiated renegotiation is used and if you are accepting clients that do not support RFC 5746. This is because the attacker can connect to the server, submit a request that initiates server-initiated renegotiation, then exploit the victim (client). For best security, inspect the SSL_SECURE_RENEG variable to confirm that the client supports secure renegotiation.

## BEAST

Technically, the predictable IV vulnerability in TLS 1.0 and earlier protocols—better known as the BEAST attack—affects both client and server sides of the communication. In practice, only browsers are vulnerable, because exploitation requires that the attacker is able to control what data is sent (and subsequently encrypted). For this reason, BEAST cannot be addressed with a server-side patch.

## CRIME

The 2012 CRIME attack exploits compression at the TLS protocol level. The issue has not been fixed in the protocol, which is why everyone resorted to disabling compression. Unrelated to the CRIME attack, Apache added the SSLCompression directive to versions 2.2.24 (February 2013) and 2.4.3 (August 2012), but compression stayed enabled by default.[8] Compression was disabled by default in versions 2.2.26 (November 2013) and 2.4.4 (February 2013).

When it comes to distribution-specific Apache versions, chances are that most vendors have provided security patches by now. For example, Debian fixed their version of Apache in November 2012[9] and Ubuntu in July 2013.[10] On Red Hat and derived distributions, for a period of time it was necessary to disable compression by manipulating environment variables,[11] but Red Hat eventually disabled compression by default in March 2013.[12]

---

[8] Bug #53219: mod_ssl should allow to disable ssl compression [fsty.uk/b449] (ASF Bugzilla, closed 3 March 2013)

[9] DSA-2579-1 apache 2 — Multiple issues [fsty.uk/b449] (Debian, 30 November 2012)

[10] USN-1898-1: OpenSSL vulnerability [fsty.uk/b450] (Ubuntu Security Notice, 3 July 2013)

If your version of Apache supports TLS compression, it's best to explicitly disable it with:

```
SSLCompression off
```

> **Warning**
>
> Disabling compression depends on the functionality that is available in OpenSSL 1.0.0 and later (the SSL_OP_NO_COMPRESSION configuration option). Older OpenSSL versions might not actually be able to disable compression.

# Deploying HTTP Strict Transport Security

Because *HTTP Strict Transport Security* (HSTS) is activated via a response header, configuring it on a site is generally easy. However, there are certain traps you can fall into, which is why I recommend that you read the section called "HTTP Strict Transport Security " in Chapter 10 before you make any decisions.

HSTS is enabled using the Header directive. It's best to use the always condition to ensure that the response header is set on all responses, including errors:

```
# Enable HTTP Strict Transport Security.
Header always set Strict-Transport-Security "max-age=31536000; includeSubDomains"
```

According to the RFC, the HSTS policy can be set only on HTTP responses delivered over an encrypted channel. The same site on port 80 doesn't need any HSTS configuration, but, for best results, it does need a redirection to port 443. This will ensure that all site visitors reach HTTPS as soon as possible:

```
<VirtualHost *:80>
    ServerName www.example.com
    ServerAlias example.com
    ...
    # Redirect all visitors to the encrypted portion of the site.
    RedirectPermanent / https://www.example.com.com/
</VirtualHost>
```

# Monitoring Session Cache Status

It's a little known fact that Apache exposes the status of the TLS session cache via the mod_status module. To enable this feature, first request that additional status information is recorded (in the main configuration context):

---

[11] Bug #857051: SSL/TLS CRIME attack against HTTPS, comment #5 [fsty.uk/b451] (Red Hat Bugzilla, closed 19 April 2013)
[12] RHSA-2013:0587-1 [fsty.uk/b452] (Red Hat, 4 March 2013)

---

```
# Request tracking of extended status information. This directive
# is only necessary with Apache 2.2.x. Apache 2.4.x should automatically
# enable it when mod_status is loaded.
ExtendedStatus On
```

Then configure mod_status output in the desired location:

```
<Location /status>
    SetHandler server-status

    # Restrict access to the following IP addresses. We don't
    # want the world to see our sensitive status information.
    Require ip 192.168.0.1
</Location>
```

> ### Warning
>
> The output of mod_status contains sensitive data, which is why you must always restrict access to it. The best way is via HTTP Basic Authentication, but then you'll have yet another password to remember. Network range restrictions, as in my example, are almost as useful.

When you open the status page, at the bottom you will see output similar to this (emphasis mine):

```
cache type: SHMCB, shared memory: 512000 bytes, current entries: 781
subcaches: 32, indexes per subcache: 88
time left on oldest entries' objects: avg: 486 seconds, (range: 0...2505)
index usage: 27%, cache usage: 33%
total entries stored since starting: 12623
total entries replaced since starting: 0
total entries expired since starting: 11688
total (pre-expiry) entries scrolled out of the cache: 148
total retrieves since starting: 6579 hit, 3353 miss
total removes since starting: 0 hit, 0 miss
```

# Logging Negotiated TLS Parameters

Default web server logging mechanisms care only about HTTP requests and errors; they won't tell you much about your TLS usage. There are two main reasons why you might want to keep an eye on your TLS operations:

**Performance**

Incorrectly configured TLS session resumption can incur a substantial performance penalty, which is why you will want to keep an eye on the session resumption hit ratio. Having a log file for this purpose is useful to ensure that your server does resume

TLS sessions and also to assist you with the tuning of the cache. Only Apache 2.4.x allows you to do this, via the SSL_SESSION_RESUMED environment variable.

**Protocol and cipher suite usage**

Knowing which protocol versions and cipher suites are actually used by your user base is important when the time to disable the weak, old versions comes. For example, SSL 2 remained widely supported over many years because people were afraid to turn it off. We are now facing similar problems with the SSL 3 protocol and the RC4 and 3DES ciphers.

Assuming that you're using Apache 2.4.x, use the following directives to monitor TLS connections:

```
# Make TLS variables available to the logging module.
SSLOptions +StdEnvVars

# Record per-request TLS information to a separate log file.
CustomLog /path/to/ssl.log "%t %h %k %X %{SSL_PROTOCOL}e\
 %{SSL_CIPHER}e %{SSL_SESSION_ID}e %{SSL_SESSION_RESUMED}e"
```

Please note the following:

- The session ID will be logged only when a session is resumed, not during the initial request.

- The value of the SSL_SESSION_RESUMED variable will be Initial for new sessions and Resumed for resumed sessions.

- The %k variable keeps track of how many requests there have been on the same connection. If you see a zero in a log entry, you'll know it's the first request. That's the one that counts.

- The %X variable records connection status at the end of the request. A dash means that the connection will be closed, whereas a plus sign means that the connection will stay open.

There's a slight mismatch between Apache's logging facilities and our need to track TLS processing in detail. TLS connection parameters are generally decided once at the beginning of a connection and don't change unless renegotiation occurs. Apache's CustomLog directive handles requests, which means that you will get multiple nearly identical log entries for long connections with many HTTP transactions. The %k variable is useful to keep track of this. On one hand, this will make the log grow more quickly. On the other, logging every transaction will help you determine the frequency of connection reuse, which is the most efficient mode of operation (for both HTTP and TLS).

> **Note**
>
> There is currently no way to log connections with successful TLS handshakes but without any requests. Similarly, it is not possible to log TLS handshake failures.

## Advanced Logging with mod_sslhaf

Apache's logging facilities allow you to determine which TLS parameters were used on a connection, but they don't give you any information beyond that. For example, you don't know the highest protocol version and cipher suites that were offered by each client. With that information, you could, for example, determine your users' capabilities and arrive at the optimal TLS configuration without having to go through a potentially painful process of trial and error.

To answer these and similar questions, I built an Apache module called mod_sslhaf. This module does not hook into Apache; instead, it passively observes and parses all TLS connections to extract client capabilities. It can be used to provide the following interesting information:

- Highest protocol version supported
- List of offered cipher suites
- List of used TLS extensions—in particular:
  - Availability of the SNI extension
  - Support for session tickets
  - Support for OCSP stapling

In addition to the above, mod_sslhaf can also log the entire raw ClientHello, which is very useful if you want to perform custom handshake analysis. There is also a special variable called SSLHAF_LOG, which is set only on the first request on a connection. This variable is designed to work with Apache's conditional logging feature, and it allows you to record only one log entry per connection (which saves a lot of disk space).

Installing mod_sslhaf is straightforward. There are no formal releases, so you'll have to use git to clone the source code repository:

```
$ git clone https://github.com/ssllabs/sslhaf.git
```

Because the module is small (only about 1,000 lines of code), the documentation is included with the source code itself, in the file mod_sslhaf.c. To compile the module, execute:

```
$ apxs -cia mod_sslhaf.c
```

The command line switches c, i, and a stand for *compile*, *install*, and *activate*. Depending on your configuration file, activation can sometimes fail. In that case, activate the module manually by adding the following line to your configuration (use the path that is correct on your system, of course):

```
LoadModule sslhaf_module /path/to/modules/mod_sslhaf.so
```

The following configuration uses all mod_sslhaf features and records the most important data points, but only once per connection:

```
# Make TLS variables available to the logging module.
SSLOptions +StdEnvVars

# Record per-request TLS information to a separate log file.
CustomLog /path/to/ssl.log "%t %h %k %X %{SSL_PROTOCOL}e\
  %{SSL_CIPHER}e %{SSL_SESSION_ID}e %{SSL_SESSION_RESUMED}e |\
  %{SSLHAF_HANDSHAKE}e %{SSLHAF_PROTOCOL}e %{SSLHAF_SUITES}e\
  %{SSLHAF_EXTENSIONS_LEN}e %{SSLHAF_EXTENSIONS}e \"%{User-Agent}i\""\
  env=SSLHAF_LOG
```

The first half of this log format is identical to the format used in the previous section; the additional mod_sslhaf information is provided after the pipe character.

> **Tip**
>
> Most people will never consider analyzing raw ClientHello records, which is why I have not included them in the log format. After all, they do take a lot of space and impact logging performance. If you do want to track this data, the variable that holds it is called SSLHAF_RAW.

# 14 Configuring Java and Tomcat

This chapter focuses on the TLS capabilities of the Java platform, covering the evolution of features across many releases, but focusing mostly on Java 7 and Java 8. I start the chapter with a discussion of the cryptographic features available in the platform itself, and then move on to cover both client and server deployments and configurations. Finally, I discuss Tomcat, one of the most popular Java web servers.

## Java Cryptography Components

In Java, there are several components that work together to provide a complete implementation of the SSL and TLS protocols and the surrounding functionality. They are:

**Java Cryptography Architecture (JCA)**
JCA provides a unified architecture for everything related to cryptography. Conceptually, JCA consists of only a set of abstract APIs and no actual code. The key aspect of JCA is that it allows an arbitrary number of *providers*, which compete to provide the specified functionality.

**Java Certification Path API**
The *Java Certification Path* API (or *CertPath*, as it is commonly referred to throughout the Java reference documentation) deals with everything related to certificates and certification paths. For SSL/TLS specifically, CertPath provides APIs that deal with X.509 certification paths, as specified by the PKIX standards. Most SSL and TLS deployments rely on PKIX to establish trust.

**Java Secure Socket Extension (JSSE)**
JSSE is the component that deals with the SSL and TLS protocols, building on the cryptographic algorithms and other APIs provided by JCA packages. JSSE is implemented as a set of APIs with support for interchangeable implementations.

**JCA Providers**
Java comes with a number of providers that implement various cryptographic algorithms and makes it easy to install new providers as desired. The default configura-

tion will satisfy the needs of most installations. Sometimes, when you wish to enable specific functionality or improve performance, you might decide to explicitly configure which providers are used and how.

**Keytool**

Java does not keep keys and certificates as individual files; rather it bundles them all in a single storage facility called a *keystore*. In order to manipulate the contents of a keystore, you will need to use `keytool`, which is included with every *Java Development Kit* (JDK).

**Java Root Certificate Store**

A TLS library is not very useful on the public Internet without a collection of trusted certificates, which are known as *roots* or *root certificates*. A collection of root certificates is also called a *truststore*. JVM vendors typically maintain their own truststores and ship them with their products.[1]

In this section, I aim to provide you all of the SSL/TLS-related information you will need. However, if you want to go deeper, it is recommended that you visit the Java 7[2] and Java 8[3] reference documentation.

## Strong and Unlimited Encryption

Java cryptography operates in one of two modes of strength. In both cases, the code base is exactly the same, but some limits are imposed by the configuration. By default, each installation operates in *strong mode*, which is somewhat restricted to comply with the US export restrictions for cryptography. In this mode, for example, the AES cipher is limited to 128 bits. The other mode is called *unlimited strength* and does not have any artificial restrictions. The default mode is strong enough for most use cases, but the use of unlimited-strength encryption is recommended to reduce potential interoperability issues in edge cases. (I will discuss these issues further later in this chapter.)

If you do want to enable the unlimited mode (e.g., it's very useful if you want to write an SSL assessment tool, in which case you want to have access to as many cipher suites as possible), you'll need to download special policy files from Oracle's web site[4] and put them in the correct location on the disk, per the installation instructions.

> **Note**
>
> On some systems, there will be more than one Java installation available. Make sure you patch the correct one or all of them. Even when there is only one version

---

[1] Including Certificate Authority Root Certificates in Java [fsty.uk/b453] (Oracle, retrieved 1 July 2014)

[2] Java SE 7 Security [fsty.uk/b454] Documentation (Oracle, retrieved 2 July 2014)

[3] Java SE 8 Security Documentation [fsty.uk/b455] (Oracle, retrieved 2 July 2014)

[4] JCE Unlimited Strength Jurisdiction Policy Files for Java 7 [fsty.uk/b456] and Java 8 [fsty.uk/b457] (Oracle, retrieved 2 July 2014)

installed, the JDK and JRE usually go into separate directories and might need to be patched separately.[5]

# Provider Configuration

Java ships with many providers; some are generic, and some are platform specific. Oracle's SSL/TLS implementation (SunJSSE) is a good example of a generic provider, because the same code is used on all platforms. On the other end of the spectrum, the SunMSCAPI provider is a special component that interfaces with cryptographic features of Windows operating systems.

You will generally not need to deal with provider configuration except in a few cases, such as when you desire specific functionality or if you are looking to improve performance. In the following cases, for example:

**Performance tuning**

Java-provided crypto is not inherently slower,[6] but in practice Java might not be the fastest platform. There is certainly some evidence that shows that crypto performance can be improved using OpenSSL and NSS. As an illustration, an Intel use case claims up to 38% performance improvement when Java is coupled with NSS libraries.[7]

**FIPS mode**

Java supports FIPS, but only if coupled with an external FIPS-certified provider. One such provider is Mozilla's NSS.

The ability to exchange one provider for another is also very useful if you come across bugs or implementation limitations. In theory, you should be able to overcome those by using another provider. Of course, in practice you might replace one set of bugs and limitations with another.

# Features Overview

Java's SSL/TLS implementation has traditionally been conservative and late to implement key protocol features. In that sense, Java's library has been quite similar to others (except Microsoft's). For example, client-side support for virtual secure hosting was added in Java 7, but for server-side support we had to wait until Java 8. Similarly, although TLS 1.2 support was added in Java 7, it was enabled by default only in Java 8.

---

[5] Patch-in-Place and Static JRE Installation [fsty.uk/b458] (Java Platform Standard Edition 7 Documentation; retrieved 2 July 2014)

[6] Best performance is usually achieved using assembly and optimization by hand. There is a lot of native and assembly code included with the Java platform, and some of it is used for cryptographic operations. For example, we know that Java 8 added assembly code to use the hardware-accelerated AES operations on Intel and AMD processors.

[7] Improved AES Crypto performance on Java with NSS using Intel® AES-NI Instructions [fsty.uk/b459] (Intel whitepaper; 6 April 2012)

---

Table 14.1. Evolution of SSL/TLS protocol features in JSSE

| | Java 5 (May 2004–October 2009) | Java 6 (December 2006–February 2013) | Java 7 (July 2011–) | Java 8 (March 2014–) |
|---|---|---|---|---|
| Elliptic Curve crypto | No[a] | Yes[b] | Yes[c] | Yes |
| Client-side SNI | - | - | Yes | Yes |
| Server-side SNI | - | - | - | Yes |
| TLS 1.1 and 1.2 | - | - | Yes[d] | Yes |
| AEAD GCM suites | - | - | - | Yes |
| SHA256 and SHA384 suites | | | Yes | Yes |
| DH over 1,024 bits (client) | - | - | - | Yes |
| DH over 768 bits (server) | - | - | - | Yes[e] |
| Secure renegotiation | u26+ | u22+ | Yes | Yes |
| BEAST mitigation (1/n-1 split) | - | u29+ | u1+ | Yes |
| OCSP stapling | - | - | - | - |
| Server cipher suite preference | - | - | - | Yes |
| Disable client-initiated renegotiation | - | - | - | Yes |
| Hardware-accelerated AES | - | - | - | Yes[f] |
| Default client handshake format | v2 | v2 | v3 | v3 |

[a] In Java 5, JCA provided only EC APIs, but no implementation.

[b] In Java 6, JSSE added support for EC suites, but the JDK itself didn't implement any EC algorithms. The only platform that supported EC suites by default was Solaris, which had native EC functionality and integrated with Java using PKCS#11.

[c] Official Java 7 implements EC algorithms via the SunEC provider. However, this component is not included in OpenJDK. To add EC support, look for third-party libraries such as BouncyCastle, or integrate with a native implementation using PKCS#11.

[d] Disabled by default in client mode. Enabled by default in server mode.

[e] Only 1,024 bits by default, but can be increased to 2,048 bits.

[f] JEP 164: Leverage CPU Instructions for AES Cryptography [fsty.uk/b460] (OpenJDK web site)

# Protocol Vulnerabilities

The most recent versions of Java do not suffer from any of the known SSL/TLS vulnerabilities, because most Java security issues apply to client-side usage and server installations tend to run older versions. However, occasionally a server-side bug is fixed. For example, the patch release in April 2014 fixed a serious problem in JSSE.[8]

Another reason to upgrade server installations is to refresh the truststores. This might be relevant for web applications that communicate with external systems.

---

[8] Easter Hack: Even More Critical Bugs in SSL/TLS Implementations [fsty.uk/b461] (Chris Meyer, 16 April 2014)

### Insecure renegotiation

Oracle initially addressed insecure renegotiation on 30 March 2010 with an interim patch that disabled renegotiation.[9] Secure renegotiation was implemented on 12 October 2010 in Java 5u26 and Java 6u22. Java 7 and later supported secure renegotiation from the first release.

Like most other client-side software, Java clients will connect to servers that do not implement secure renegotiation. This is dangerous, because clients have no way of detecting attacks against insecure renegotiation even if they themselves *do* support secure renegotiation. The alternative is to allow clients to connect only to servers that can demonstrate secure renegotiation, but in that case you will have to accept that connections with insecure servers will fail.[10]

### BEAST

To address the BEAST attack, Java implements the 1/n-1 split starting with Java 6u29 and Java 7u1.

### CRIME

The CRIME attack exploits information leakage inherent in compression. Java never supported compression at the TLS level, which means that no Java client was ever vulnerable to CRIME. Java web applications might still be vulnerable to the CRIME variants TIME and BREACH, which attack HTTP response body compression.

## Interoperability Issues

With Java in server mode, you are not very likely to experience interoperability issues; Java supports a variety of protocols and suites, which means that you will be able to communicate with virtually any client.

It's a different situation in client mode, for which there is a number of potential problems you need to be aware of:

### Missing root certificates

The root certificate store shipped with the JRE enables Java clients to communicate with previously unseen web sites. Over time, old roots are retired and new ones are added. If a web site is relying on a root certificate that is not in your store, connections to the site will fail. If you're not updating your JRE regularly, then the root store might become stale, causing connectivity failures. Old root stores might also contain roots that shouldn't be trusted any more. In some cases, it may be that the official root store does not contain a root you'd wish to trust. If that happens, you will need to manually add such roots.

---

[9] Transport Layer Security (TLS) Renegotiation Issue Readme [fsty.uk/b462] (Oracle, retrieved 2 July 2014)

[10] According to the SSL Pulse results from July 2014, about 11.6% of the monitored servers do not support secure renegotiation.

**Servers with only 256-bit suites enabled**

There's a very small number of sites that are configured with only 256-bit cipher suites. If your JRE hasn't been upgraded to the unlimited mode (it's capable only of 128-bit AES), you might not be able to communicate with such sites.

**DH parameters over 1,024 bits**

All versions prior to Java 8 are limited to supporting client-side Diffie-Hellman (DH) parameters of only up to 1,024 bits. Although few servers use anything stronger at the moment, 1,024-bit DH parameters are considered weak, and there is a trend to deploy stronger parameters.

**RSA keys under 1,024 bits**

Starting with 7u40, Java refuses to connect to servers that use insecure RSA keys that offer less than 1,024 bits of security. It is possible to bypass this restriction by changing the jdk.certpath.disabledAlgorithms property, but that's generally not a good idea.

**MD2 root certificates**

Also from 7u40, Java versions will not accept certificates with MD2 signatures. A small number of servers contain such certificates in their chains, and they will cause TLS connections to fail. Although it is possible to override the rejection of MD2, you should consider it only as a last resort.

---

### Stricter Algorithm Restrictions

Java's default algorithm restrictions for certification path building could be improved for better security, disabling all insecure algorithms and key sizes. Consider the following setting for the jdk.certpath.disabledAlgorithms security property:

```
MD2, MD5, RSA keySize < 2048, DSA keySize < 2048, ECDSA keySize < 256
```

These restrictions don't necessarily affect the root certificates in your truststores. For best results, you should also inspect all the root certificates and remove the weak ones (use the above criteria).

---

# Tuning via Properties

Java exposes a number of system and security properties that can be used to change the default cryptography settings. In this section, I am including a selection of the most useful settings. You can find the full list in the JSSE documentation.[11]

---

[11] Customizable Items in JSSE [fsty.uk/b463] (JSSE 8 Reference Guide, retrieved 2 July 2014)

Table 14.2. Most useful system and security properties for SSL/TLS and PKI tuning

| Purpose | Property name | Description |
| --- | --- | --- |
| Default client protocols for HttpsUrlConnection | `https.protocols` | Provide a comma-separated list of desired protocols. For example: `TLSv1,TLSv1.1,TLSv1.2`. Starting with Java 8, you can use `jdk.tls.client.protocols` to affect all SunJSSE clients. |
| Default client cipher suites for HttpsUrlConnection | `https.cipherSuites` | Comma-separated list of desired cipher suites to be used by `HttpsUrlConnection`. |
| Use Server Name Indication (SNI) | `jsse.enableSNIExtension` | Enabled by default in Java 7 and later. Should not be disabled unless you encounter incompatible servers. |
| Allow insecure renegotiation | `sun.security.ssl.allowUnsafeRenegotiation` | Disabled by default and should stay that way. |
| Allow insecure renegotiation clients | `sun.security.ssl.allowLegacyHelloMessages` | Enabled by default in order to allow not-yet-patched TLS clients. Ideally, it should be disabled, but that may cause interoperability problems. |
| Disabled suite algorithms | `jdk.tls.disabledAlgorithms` | A handy setting to use to disable certain algorithms without changing application source code. **Security property.** |
| Disabled certificate algorithms | `jdk.certpath.disabledAlgorithms` | Algorithm restrictions for certification path processing. Contains `MD2, RSA keySize < 1,024` in 7u40 and newer. The documentation for this parameter is in the `java.security`. **Security property.** |
| Reconstruct incomplete certificate chains | `com.sun.security.enableAIAcaIssuers` | If enabled, Java clients will follow AIA information when available and attempt to reconstruct incomplete certificate chains. Disabled by default. |
| Enable revocation checking | `com.sun.net.ssl.checkRevocation` | Disabled by default. If enabled, requires that either CRL or OCSP revocation methods are enabled. |
| Enable OCSP revocation checking | `ocsp.enable` | When enabled, Java clients will check certificates for revocation via OCSP. Disabled by default. **Security property.** |
| Enable CRL revocation checking | `com.sun.security.enableCRLDP` | When enabled, Java clients will check certificates for revocation via CRL. Disabled by default. If OCSP checking is enabled, it will be attempted first. |

In Java 8, several new properties are available:

Table 14.3. New configuration system properties available in Java 8

| Purpose | Property name | Description |
| --- | --- | --- |
| Disable client-initiated renegotiation | jdk.tls. rejectClientInitiatedRenego tiation | Set to true to disable client-initiated renegotiation. Not documented at the time of writing. |
| Configure server Diffie-Hellman strength | jdk.tls.ephemeralDHKeySize | Leave undefined for 1,024 bits. Set to legacy for the weak Java 7 behavior, matched to match key size, and a number from 1,024 to 2,048 for a fixed value. |
| Default SunJSSE client protocols | jdk.tls.client.protocols | Similar to https.protocols, but affects all SunJSSE clients, not just HttpsUrlConnection. |

System and security properties are similar, but they are configured differently. You can set a *system property* in one of two ways. First is via the -D switch on the JVM command line. For example:

```
$ java -Dhttps.protocols=TLSv1 myMainClass
```

Alternatively, at runtime you can use the System.setProperty() method:

```
System.setProperty("https.protocols", "TLSv1");
```

*Security properties*, on the other hand, are chiefly configured by editing the $JAVA_HOME/lib/security/java.security file. If you want to override the settings from the command line, you can, but under two conditions:

1. The security.overridePropertiesFile setting in the main configuration file must be set to true (the default).

2. You can't specify individual properties on the command line; instead, you have to create a property file with all of your property overrides in it.

If these two conditions are met, you can override the default security properties, like so:

```
$ java -Djava.security.properties=/path/to/my/java.security-overrides
```

There is also an undocumented feature that allows you to specify an entirely different security configuration (not just override the defaults) by using two equals signs:

```
$ java -Djava.security.properties==/path/to/my/java.security
```

At runtime, you can set a security property using the Security.setProperty() method. For example, to improve the default policy on algorithm strength you could do this:

```
Security.setProperty("jdk.certpath.disabledAlgorithms",
    "MD2, MD5, RSA keySize < 2048, DSA keySize < 2048, ECDSA keySize < 256");
```

> **Warning**
>
> Setting properties at runtime might not always be reliable. Some classes might look up the property values only once at startup, which might lead them to miss the changed properties. For best results, configure properties in the configuration files or by using command-line switches.

# Common Error Messages

When something unexpected happens, JSSE will throw an exception, but the language used in the error messages tends to be very technical and often does not provide enough clues to help resolve the problem. This section contains a collection of commonly observed JSSE error messages and options to deal with them.

## Certificate Chain Issues

Sometimes, a Java client attempting to connect to a server might not be able to validate the certificate. When that happens, the following exceptions are thrown:

```
javax.net.ssl.SSLHandshakeException: sun.security.validator.ValidatorException: ↵
PKIX path building failed: sun.security.provider.certpath.SunCertPathBuilderExcepti↵
on: unable to find valid certification path to requested target
```

As for the root cause behind the problem, it can be one of the following issues:

**Unknown certification authority**

The server's certificate is signed by a CA unknown to your Java client. This might happen if your keystore configuration is too old and does not contain the new CA or if the server is using a custom CA (which will never be recognized by the public). If you are certain that the CA is genuine, you can solve this problem by adding the missing certificate to your truststore. Other than that, trusting arbitrary root certificates is not recommended; once added, a root certificate can impersonate any web site in the world.

**Incomplete chain**

Although we spend most of our time discussing server certificates, in reality servers need to configure chains of certificates. If a server's chain is incomplete, clients won't be able to find a path to a trusted root. The solution is to reconfigure the server with the correct certificate chain.

Sometimes, incomplete chains can be reconstructed with the help of the *Authority Information Access* (AIA) extension, which contains a URL which you can use to download the next certificate in the chain. Java does not follow AIA information by default. To enable this feature, set the `com.sun.security.enableAIAcaIssuers` property to true.

### Self-signed certificate

Many servers run with only self-signed certificates. If they are delivering services intended for public consumption, that's unacceptable. If not, it might be all right, and you should be able to deal with the problem by creating an exception and trusting that certificate.

> **Warning**
>
> Contrary to many "solutions" you can find on the Internet, you should never attempt to solve the self-signed certificate problem by disabling validation in your code. If you do that, your programs will fail miserably when under a *man-in-the-middle* (MITM) attack. Basically, anyone would be able to present any certificate to your code and impersonate the server you're connecting to.

## Server Hostname Mismatch

When connecting to a remote web server over TLS, the expectation is that the hostname from the URL will match one of the hostnames specified in the certificate. If that's not the case, the following exception will occur:

```
javax.net.ssl.SSLHandshakeException: java.security.cert.CertificateException: No ↵
name matching beta.feistyduck.com found
```

The solution simply is to install a correct certificate, which includes the missing hostname.

## Client Diffie-Hellman Limitations

All versions prior to Java 8 support Diffie-Hellman (DH) parameters of only up to 1,024 bits. When a Java client running on one of those platforms encounters a server that wishes to use a suite with DH parameters over 1,024 bits (almost always 2,048 bits), you will see the following exceptions:

```
javax.net.ssl.SSLException: java.lang.RuntimeException: Could not generate DH ↵
keypair
...
Caused by: java.lang.RuntimeException: Could not generate DH keypair
...
Caused by: java.security.InvalidAlgorithmParameterException: Prime size must be ↵
multiple of 64, and can only range from 512 to 1024 (inclusive)
```

If you have control over the server in question, it is easy to make this problem go away, by doing one of the following:

- Enable and prioritize ECDHE suites on the server. Java 6 and 7 clients support these, and will happily use them. (But do note that with Java 6 you must switch to using the v3 handshake in order to utilize the ECDHE suites at the client level.)

- If the server does not support ECDHE suites, you can prioritize RSA suites on the server, but you will lose forward secrecy with your Java clients.

- As a last resort, you can downgrade DH parameters to 1,024 bits. This, of course, also downgrades the security of all DH suites.

If you'd rather make changes to the client configuration, you can try replacing Oracle's JCE component (where the limitation lives) with that developed by the Bouncy Castle project.[12] I've had mixed results with this approach. Sometimes it works, but the addition of a provider might produce other exceptions that can't be easily explained.

## Server Name Indication Intolerance

A small number of servers are intolerant to the *Server Name Indication* (SNI) extension, which is used by default by clients starting with Java 7. More commonly, servers that do support SNI send a TLS warning when the SNI information couldn't be matched to any virtual host on the server. Although TLS warnings are not fatal and can be ignored, Java clients react to them by aborting the connection. You will know you have this problem if you upgrade your JVM and start seeing the following exception:

```
javax.net.ssl.SSLProtocolException: handshake alert: unrecognized_name
```

## Strict Secure Renegotiation Failures

When the JVM is in the strict secure renegotiation mode, the requirement for every TLS handshake will be that both sides implement secure renegotiation. If that's not the case, you will get the following exception:

```
javax.net.ssl.SSLHandshakeException: Failed to negotiate the use of secure ↵
renegotiation
```

You will not get this exception unless you've explicitly enabled the strict secure renegotiation mode by setting sun.security.ssl.allowLegacyHelloMessages to false. If you experience this problem in a Java client, the best way to deal with it is to upgrade the server. If that's not possible, your only other option is to revert back to the default (and unsafe) mode.

## Protocol Negotiation Failure

SSL 3 is an older, obsolete protocol version that shouldn't be used. Virtually all servers on the Internet support at least TLS 1.0 and you're not likely to experience interoperability issues, but you might encounter an odd SSL 3-only server. If you disable SSL 3, you might encounter the following exception with such servers:

---

[12] Provider Installation [fsty.uk/b464] (Bouncy Castle, retrieved 2 July 2014)

```
javax.net.ssl.SSLHandshakeException: Server chose SSLv3, but that protocol version ↵
is not enabled or not supported by the client.
```

To resolve this problem, you either need to get the server to upgrade or downgrade the client.

On the other end of the spectrum, if you don't enable newer protocols, you might encounter a server that does not support TLS 1.0 and earlier. This, too, is rare, but if you come across it, the message will be:

```
javax.net.ssl.SSLException: Received fatal alert: protocol_version
```

### Handshake Format Incompatibility

Java 6 and older versions use the SSL 2 handshake format by default, but not all servers do. If you come across a server that does not, you will see the following message:

```
javax.net.ssl.SSLHandshakeException: Remote host closed connection during handshake
```

You can fix this problem by reconfiguring the client to use the SSL 3 handshake format, as described in the section called "Using Strong Protocols on the Client Side".

## Securing Java Web Applications

In this section, I discuss several topics related to secure use of encryption in either Java clients or web applications. These topics aren't very complicated, but the correct information is often difficult to find in the sea of documents available on the Web. Please note that I don't discuss here anything outside encryption. For example, cookie security and session management security are complex topics and there is a lot to be said, but those topics are outside the scope of this book.

### Enforcing Encryption

You can write a web application that wants to be secure (i.e., deployed under TLS), but you can't actually enforce that. Due to an operator mistake or configuration error, your application might be available under plain-text HTTP.

My advice is to always check programmatically if the application is accessed securely by invoking the isSecure() method on the HttpServletRequest instance supplied by the Servlet container. For existing applications in which you don't have control over the source code, checks can be added in a servlet filter.

> **Note**
>
> This programmatic check will catch the obvious configuration errors, but it is not foolproof. Some systems terminate TLS at earlier architectural layers (e.g., load bal-

ancers and proxies) but use web server configuration settings to convince applications that encryption is in place.

## Securing Web Application Cookies

The following code snippet creates a cookie with both httpOnly and secure flags set and adds it to the response (via the HttpServletResponse instance supplied by the Servlet container):

```
Cookie cookie = new Cookie(cookieName, cookieValue);
cookie.setMaxAge(cookieLifeInDays * 24 * 3600);
cookie.setHttpOnly(true);
cookie.setSecure(true);
response.addCookie(cookie);
```

Clearly, if you have an existing application that does not use cookies properly, you will need to examine the source code to find where the cookies are created, and make them all secure. If you don't want to make changes to the source code (or don't have access to it), try writing a servlet filter[13] that intercepts cookies as they are being created and forcefully makes them secure.

## Securing Web Session Cookies

Java applications almost universally rely on the underlying servlet containers to manage sessions for them. In practice, this means that configuration changes need to be made in order to secure session cookies.

This is easy to do for applications that rely on the Servlet 3 specification or newer,[14] which introduced configuration settings for securing session cookies. To do this, add the following snippet to the application's web.xml file:[15]

```
<session-config>
    <cookie-config>
        <secure>true</secure>
        <http-only>true</http-only>
    </cookie-config>
<session-config>
```

For applications using earlier Servlet specification, the exact behavior depends on the container. Some products automatically create secure cookies when encryption is used. The

---

[13] The Essentials of Filters [fsty.uk/b465] (Oracle, retrieved 2 July 2014)

[14] JSR-000315 Java™ Servlet 3.0 [fsty.uk/b466] (Java Community Process, December 2009)

[15] It is possible to achieve the same effect programmatically by configuring the SessionCookieConfig instance obtained from the current ServletContext, which is best done just after the context has been created from a ServletContextListener.

---

sane behavior is to make session cookies secure on all secure sites. That's what's been reported for Tomcat, for example.

## Deploying HTTP Strict Transport Security

*HTTP Strict Transport Security* (HSTS) is a new technology that enables strict handling of encryption by web applications that don't wish to receive any plaintext traffic. I cover HSTS in detail in Chapter 10, *HSTS, CSP, and Pinning*. To deploy it, you need to set a single response header in your application. Only one method invocation is needed for this:

```
response.setHeader("Strict-Transport-Security", "max-age=31536000; ↵
includeSubDomains");
```

However, configuring security policies is generally better done at the web server level. Java applications can also use servlet filters. Rather than writing your own, consider using one of the available open source projects, for example, HeadLines.[16]

## Using Strong Protocols on the Client Side

For client applications, Java's default protocol configuration has traditionally been focused on interoperability at the cost of security. Java 6, for example, uses the old SSL 2 handshake format, which is necessary only if you are actually willing to use SSL 2, but Java never supported this version of the protocol. Java 7 doesn't use the SSL 2 handshake format, but still doesn't use TLS 1.1 and 1.2 for clients by default, despite supporting these newer protocol versions. (They are enabled by default for servers.) Java 8 enables TLS 1.1 and 1.2 for clients and servers alike.

If all you need is HttpsURLConnection, then the simplest way to change the default behavior is via the https.protocols system property I discussed earlier, in the section called "Tuning via Properties". This will change the default protocol configuration for this class. Starting with Java 8, the jdk.tls.client.protocols system property does the same, but for all code that relies on SunJSSE.

If you're an application developer and don't control the environment in which your application runs, changing system properties is not appropriate; it's better to programmatically ensure your application uses the desired protocols. This task is straightforward if you're handling synchronous sockets directly; you can use SSLSocket.setSSLParameters() to deploy your own configuration.

But for many common tasks, sockets are too low level, which is why you'll often find yourself using the higher-level HttpsURLConnection class. Unfortunately, to change the protocols

---

[16] HeadLines [fsty.uk/b467] (SourceClear, retrieved 1 July 2014)

used by this class is more difficult; you will need to create a custom SSLSocketFactory and make sure it is always used.

Below is my custom factory, which enables all supported protocols (it's future compatible because protocol versions are not hardcoded) but disables the SSL 2 handshake format and the SSL 3 protocol:

```java
import java.io.IOException;
import java.net.InetAddress;
import java.net.Socket;
import java.net.UnknownHostException;
import java.util.ArrayList;
import java.util.List;

import javax.net.ssl.SSLSocket;
import javax.net.ssl.SSLSocketFactory;

public class MySSLSocketFactory extends SSLSocketFactory {

    private String enabledProtocols[] = null;

    private String enabledCipherSuites[];

    private SSLSocketFactory sslSocketFactory;

    public MySSLSocketFactory() {
        sslSocketFactory = (SSLSocketFactory) SSLSocketFactory.getDefault();
        enabledCipherSuites = sslSocketFactory.getDefaultCipherSuites();
    }

    private Socket reconfigureSocket(Socket socket) {
        SSLSocket sslSocket = (SSLSocket) socket;

        if (enabledProtocols != null) {
            sslSocket.setEnabledProtocols(enabledProtocols);
        } else {
            List<String> myProtocols = new ArrayList<String>();

            for (String p : sslSocket.getSupportedProtocols()) {
                if (p.equalsIgnoreCase("SSLv2Hello")
                        || (p.equalsIgnoreCase("SSLv3"))) {
                    continue;
                }

                myProtocols.add(p);
            }
```

```
        sslSocket.setEnabledProtocols(myProtocols
                .toArray(new String[myProtocols.size()]));
    }

    sslSocket.setEnabledCipherSuites(enabledCipherSuites);

    return socket;
}

public void setEnabledProtocols(String[] newEnabledProtocols) {
    enabledProtocols = newEnabledProtocols;
}

public void setEnabledCipherSuites(String[] newEnabledCipherSuites) {
    enabledCipherSuites = newEnabledCipherSuites;
}

@Override
public Socket createSocket(Socket s, String host, int port,
        boolean autoClose) throws IOException {
    return reconfigureSocket(sslSocketFactory.createSocket(s, host, port,
            autoClose));
}

@Override
public String[] getDefaultCipherSuites() {
    return enabledCipherSuites;
}

@Override
public String[] getSupportedCipherSuites() {
    return sslSocketFactory.getSupportedCipherSuites();
}

@Override
public Socket createSocket(String host, int port) throws IOException,
        UnknownHostException {
    return reconfigureSocket(sslSocketFactory.createSocket(host, port));
}

@Override
public Socket createSocket(InetAddress host, int port) throws IOException {
    return reconfigureSocket(sslSocketFactory.createSocket(host, port));
}

@Override
public Socket createSocket(String host, int port, InetAddress localHost,
```

```
            int localPort) throws IOException, UnknownHostException {
        return reconfigureSocket(sslSocketFactory.createSocket(host, port,
                localHost, localPort));
    }

    @Override
    public Socket createSocket(InetAddress address, int port,
            InetAddress localAddress, int localPort) throws IOException {
        return reconfigureSocket(sslSocketFactory.createSocket(address, port,
                localAddress, localPort));
    }
}
```

Then, whenever you create an instance of `HttpsUrlConnection`, assign it a custom factory:

```
URL u = new URL("https://www.feistyduck.com");
HttpsURLConnection uc = (HttpsURLConnection) u.openConnection();
uc.setSSLSocketFactory(new MySSLSocketFactory());
```

## Revocation Checking

By default, Java will not perform any revocation checks on the certificates it encounters. This is potentially insecure. You should enable both CRL and OCSP revocation checking for maximum security by setting `com.sun.net. ssl. checkRevocation`, `ocsp.enable`, and `com.sun.security.enableCRLDP` to true.

In addition, you should also consider allowing Java to attempt to reconstruct incomplete certificate chains, via the `com.sun.security.enableAIAcaIssuers` property. Incomplete certificate chains can't be validated, which means that communication with such servers will fail.

# Common Keystore Operations

In this section, I cover the most common tasks related to key and certificate management. The `keytool` utility will help you with many of these tasks, but you might need to resort to using OpenSSL for some, particularly for key and certificate import.

> ### Note
>
> If you don't enjoy spending time on the command line, consider using a tool called
> *KeyStore Explorer*,[17] which provides a friendly user interface for common keytool
> operations.

---

[17] KeyStore Explorer [fsty.uk/b468] (retrieved 1 July 2014)

## Keystore Layout

Although it might not be obvious at first, Java will allow you to use any number of keystores. For client-side activity, you most likely won't need to do much, because the system-provided root keystore will be sufficient. You might need to update this keystore from time to time, but you're unlikely to use more than one.

It's different for server operation. Here, not only are multiple keystores possible, they are actively recommended. Unless you have a very good reason to do otherwise, you should always use one keystore per web site. The advantages of this approach are that (1) you can secure web site keys individually, using different passphrases, and (2) migration of sites from one server to another is easy.

Within a keystore, each certificate chain is required to have a unique alias. If you adopt my recommendation about server keystore usage, you will not need to think about these aliases much, because there will always be only one certificate chain in the entire keystore. In the rest of this chapter, I will assume this is the case, and I will always use the alias "server."

## Creating a Key and a Self-Signed Certificate

To create a private key with a self-signed certificate, use the -genkeypair command:[18]

```
$ keytool -genkeypair \
    -keystore feistyduck.jks \
    -alias server \
    -keyalg RSA \
    -keysize 3072 \
    -validity 365 \
    -ext SAN="DNS:www.feistyduck.com,DNS:feistyduck.com"
Enter keystore password: ****************
Re-enter new password: ****************
```

In this example, I use a keytool feature that allows creation of certificates valid for multiple hostnames (the -ext switch). This feature is not available in Java 6 and earlier versions.

> **Warning**
>
> The keytool utility is able to accept the keystore password on the command line via the -storepass switch. However, I prefer not to use it, because if you do the password is recorded in your command-line history and might be seen on the process list.

---

[18] Before Java 7, this command was called -genkey.

After you provide the password, you will be asked for the information that will go into the certificate. The first question is misleading; you shouldn't respond with your name, but with the desired hostname (e.g., www.feistyduck.com):

```
What is your first and last name?
  [Unknown]:  www.feistyduck.com
What is the name of your organizational unit?
  [Unknown]:  Engineering
What is the name of your organization?
  [Unknown]:  Feisty Duck Limited
What is the name of your City or Locality?
  [Unknown]:  London
What is the name of your State or Province?
  [Unknown]:  England
What is the two-letter country code for this unit?
  [Unknown]:  GB
Is CN=www.feistyduck.com, OU=Engineering, O=Feisty Duck Limited, L=London, ↵
ST=England, C=GB correct?
  [no]:  yes

Enter key password for <server>
        (RETURN if same as keystore password):
```

You can now check the resulting keystore to see what your key and certificate look like:

```
$ keytool -keystore feistyduck.jks -list -v
Enter keystore password: ***************
[...]
Alias name: server
Creation date: 01-Jul-2014
Entry type: PrivateKeyEntry
Certificate chain length: 1
Certificate[1]:
Owner: CN=www.feistyduck.com, OU=Engineering, O=Feisty Duck Limited, L=London, ↵
ST=England, C=GB
Issuer: CN=www.feistyduck.com, OU=Engineering, O=Feisty Duck Limited, L=London, ↵
ST=England, C=GB
Serial number: 4f3326e0
Valid from: Tue Jul 01 17:10:31 BST 2014 until: Wed Jul 01 17:10:31 BST 2015
Certificate fingerprints:
        MD5:   55:63:0B:F5:F5:45:67:62:2D:85:FE:5C:D2:8E:1E:27
        SHA1: A4:AD:C6:1E:F6:1F:73:B0:BD:C6:2F:83:F5:B1:67:82:61:94:89:CE
        SHA256: FD:0A:BE:5B:9F:93:9D:BA:DF:FD:54:8B:37:0A:A4:7C:92:1F:03:25:8C:01:↵
ED:92:9B:BE:AA:19:68:27:B9:4D
        Signature algorithm name: SHA256withRSA
        Version: 3

Extensions:
```

```
#1: ObjectId: 2.5.29.17 Criticality=false
SubjectAlternativeName [
  DNSName: www.feistyduck.com
  DNSName: feistyduck.com
]

#2: ObjectId: 2.5.29.14 Criticality=false
SubjectKeyIdentifier [
KeyIdentifier [
0000: 02 14 B4 49 F6 15 F0 77   FE 9A C8 86 2A 02 10 95  ...I...w....*...
0010: 9A 46 FD EB                                        .F..
]
]
```

## Creating a Certificate Signing Request

After you create a key and a self-signed certificate, creating a *Certificate Signing Request* (CSR) requires little effort:

```
$ keytool -certreq \
    -keystore feistyduck.jks \
    -alias server \
    -file fd.csr
Enter keystore password: ***************
```

Now you can submit the file fd.csr to your CA to obtain a certificate.

## Importing Certificates

When you receive the server certificate back from your CA, you will need to import it into the keystore along with all other certificates that are necessary to construct the entire chain.

First, import the root certificate:

```
$ keytool -import \
    -keystore feistyduck.jks \
    -trustcacerts \
    -alias root \
    -file root.crt
```

Then, using the same command (but with a different alias each time), import the intermediate certificates:

```
$ keytool -import \
    -keystore feistyduck.jks \
    -trustcacerts \
```

```
-alias intermediate1 \
-file intermediate1.crt
```

Finally, import the server certificate:

```
$ keytool -import \
    -keystore feistyduck.jks \
    -alias server \
    -file fd.crt
```

> **Note**
>
> The great thing about keytool is that it checks that the imported certificate matches
> the key and that the certificate chain is valid. According to my research, about 6%
> of all servers have incorrect certificate chains. This behavior of keytool ensures that
> such mistakes do not happen.

## Converting Existing Certificates

If you are migrating an existing server from, say, Apache, you will need to merge several key
and certificate files into a single keystore. The keytool utility can't do this, but it's easy using
OpenSSL.

The following command will take existing keys and certificates and convert them into a new
keystore in pkcs12 format:

```
$ openssl pkcs12 -export \
    -out feistyduck.p12 \
    -inkey fd.key \
    -in fd.crt \
    -certfile fd-intermediates.crt \
    -name server
Enter Export Password: ***************
Verifying - Enter Export Password: ***************
```

If you have more than one intermediate certificate, put them all into a single file (fd-
intermediates.crt in the previous example).

You can use this new keystore directly, but because it's not in Java's native format you might
need to specify the type in the configuration. For example, in Tomcat you do that with the
keystoreType parameter set to pkcs12.

Alternatively, if you like everything neat and tidy, you can use keytool to convert the keystore into the native (JKS) format:

```
$ keytool -importkeystore \
    -srckeystore feistyduck.p12 \
    -srcstoretype pkcs12 \
```

```
    -destkeystore feistyduck.jks
Enter destination keystore password: ***************
Re-enter new password: ***************
Enter source keystore password: ***************
Entry for alias server successfully imported.
Import command completed:  1 entries successfully imported, 0 entries failed or ↵
cancelled
```

## Importing Client Root Certificates

From time to time, you might encounter a situation in which your Java clients can't connect to a server even though the certificate was issued by a public CA. In such cases, you will need to add the missing root certificate to your keystore.

The first step is to obtain the missing root certificate. This is generally easy, because these days every browser has a certificate viewer. Simply navigate to the web site in question, choose the certificate viewer option, and export the root certificate to a file. There is no need to export the intermediate certificates.

Then issue the following command:

```
$ keytool -import \
    -keystore /path/to/keystore.jks \
    -trustcacerts \
    -file /path/to/root.crt \
    -alias UNIQUE_ROOT_ALIAS
```

> **Note**
>
> If you're creating a custom keystore for explicit use by an application, you can choose an arbitrary password for it. The password is of little importance if you're only keeping root certificates in the keystore. If you intend to replace Java's default keystore, however, use "changeit" for the password, to match the one used by default.

I recommend that you maintain your master keystore in a separate location and distribute it as needed. To change the default Java keystore, simply copy yours to the correct location; in most cases that's $JAVA_HOME/jre/lib/security/cacerts.

# Tomcat

If you are looking to run a web server on the Java platform, chances are you will rely on Tomcat or one of the many products derived from it. Using TLS with Tomcat can be confusing, because there are several ways to do it:

## No TLS at Tomcat level

Historically, quite a few Tomcat deployments are placed behind Apache reverse proxies. Apache is not only popular but also robust, and it has a wide range of modules that support every feature imaginable; it makes sense to have it as a separate architecture layer to handle all HTTP-related functionality, leaving Tomcat to focus on Java-specific bits. This approach is so popular that Apache comes standard with a special proxy module, mod_proxy_ajp[19], which interfaces directly with Tomcat by using a custom protocol called AJP.

In this mode, everything related to TLS is configured at the Apache level. This approach will appeal to those who already have experience using Apache but also to those who wish to avoid Java's and Tomcat's TLS limitations.

## Using JSSE

If you do want to terminate TLS at the Tomcat level, the default choice is to use JSSE. This approach is straightforward, because every Java installation supports it out of the box without any tuning. Easy as it is, this choice also means accepting all the limitations of JSSE. However, many improvements in Java 8 mean that JSSE is now a viable platform for strong secure servers.

## Using APR and OpenSSL

In order to make Tomcat perform better, its developers have come up with a special native library called *Tomcat Native*.[20] This library wraps two other mature native libraries: APR (the core of the Apache web server) and OpenSSL. If Tomcat Native is discovered by Tomcat at startup, it's automatically picked up. There is some anecdotal evidence that the performance with Tomcat Native will be better, but because this library also takes over socket handling and other I/O operations it's difficult to say which performance improvements are from better I/O and which come from OpenSSL. At startup, Tomcat itself will tell you that using Tomcat Native improves performance.

A major downside of Tomcat Native is that it complicates deployment; it's another component that needs to be installed and maintained. Tomcat Native binds to the specific JDK, which means that you might need to recompile it whenever you change Java versions.

For Windows, binaries are provided. Some platforms—for example, Ubuntu—include Tomcat Native as an optional package (on Ubuntu the name is libtcnative-1), but that version might be too old for use with recent Tomcat versions. Furthermore, newer Tomcat Native versions include important improvements.

---

[19] fsty.uk/b469

[20] Tomcat Native [fsty.uk/b470] (Apache Software Foundation, retrieved 1 July 2014)

---

When you do decide to use OpenSSL, Java's cryptography features and performance no longer matter; it only matters what versions of Tomcat Native and OpenSSL you're using and what features they support.

To make things more confusing, Tomcat with JSSE supports two connectors (server components that handle incoming connections): the older BIO (blocking) and the newer NIO (nonblocking).[21] If you want to use OpenSSL, there is only one connector that supports a mix of blocking and nonblocking operations.

The following table, copied from Tomcat documentation, shows a comparison of the different options.

Table 14.4. Comparison of performance features of various Tomcat connectors

| | Java BIO | Java NIO | Java NIO2 | Tomcat Native |
|---|---|---|---|---|
| Class name | Http11Protocol | Http11NioProtocol | Http11Nio2Protocol | Http11AprProtocol |
| Tomcat version | 3.x onwards | 6.x onwards | 8.x onwards | 5.5.x onwards |
| Supports polling | No | Yes | Yes | Yes |
| Polling size | N/A | maxConnections | maxConnections | maxConnections |
| Read HTTP request | Blocking | Nonblocking | Nonblocking | Blocking |
| Read HTTP body | Blocking | Sim-blocking[a] | Blocking | Blocking |
| Write HTTP response | Blocking | Sim-blocking | Blocking | Blocking |
| Wait for next request | Blocking | Nonblocking | Nonblocking | Nonblocking |
| SSL implementation | Java (JSSE) | Java (JSSE) | Java (JSSE) | OpenSSL |
| SSL handshake | Blocking | Nonblocking | Nonblocking | Blocking |
| Max connections | maxConnections | maxConnections | maxConnections | maxConnections |

[a] Although the connector is nonblocking, traditionally the Servlet specification requires blocking I/O for request and response bodies. Thus, the nonblocking connector is simulating blocking I/O. The Servlet 3.1 specification (which is supported in Tomcat 8) introduces nonblocking I/O.

This complicated choice is perhaps why many decide to put a reverse proxy in front of Tomcat, thus avoiding a difficult decision. The main problem is that there are no clear guidelines to help us determine which approach might be best and when. However, performance is only one aspect of the decision. When it comes to TLS, the actual features are perhaps more important. The following table summarizes the differences between using JSSE with Java 7 and Java 8, Tomcat Native, and terminating TLS in an Apache reverse proxy before Tomcat.

---

[21] The blocking/nonblocking monikers are used to explain how TCP connections are handled. A blocking connector will dedicate a separate thread to each TCP client. A nonblocking connector might handle all TCP clients using only one or a small number of threads. Blocking connectors tend to perform better with fast clients, whereas nonblocking connectors better handle a large number of slower clients. Tomcat 7.x uses the BIO connector by default, whereas Tomcat 8.x uses NIO.

Table 14.5. Comparison of TLS features of the available options for TLS termination

| | Tomcat (Java 7) | Tomcat (Java 8) | Tomcat Native | Apache 2.4.x |
|---|---|---|---|---|
| Strong DH parameters | No (768 bits) | Borderline (1,024 bits) | Borderline (1,024 bits) | Yes (2.4.7) |
| Configure stronger DH parameters | - | Yes | - | Yes (2.4.7) |
| Elliptic Curve support | Yes | Yes | Yes (1.1.30) | Yes |
| Configure EC parameters | - | - | - | Yes (2.4.7) |
| Cipher suite preference | - | Not yet[a] | Yes | Yes |
| Virtual secure hosting | - | Not yet[a] | - | Yes |
| Disable client-initiated renegotiation | - | Yes | Yes | Yes |
| TLS session caching control | Yes | Yes | - | Yes |
| TLS session cache clustering | - | - | - | Yes |
| Session ticket support | - | - | Yes | Yes |
| Disable session tickets | - | - | - | No |
| Explicit session ticket configuration | - | - | - | Yes |
| OCSP stapling | - | - | - | Yes |
| Multikey support[b] | - | - | - | Yes |

[a] Although supported by JSSE in Java 8, this feature requires explicit support in the Tomcat code. It's not available at the time of writing.

[b] The underlying JSSE engine supports multikey operation starting with Java 7, but this feature is not used by Tomcat.

Some of the features listed in the previous table are of an advanced nature and will affect only demanding users. But some are quite basic and significantly limit JSSE in Java 7 and earlier releases:

**Insecure DHE suites**

In Java 8, server ephemeral Diffie-Hellman (DH) suites use 1,024 bits of security by default, which is a good choice for interoperability but not a great one for security. The strength can be increased to 2,048 bits by using the jdk.tls.ephemeralDHKeySize system property.

In Java 7 and earlier, server ephemeral DH is limited to 768 bits. For this reason, you should not use any ephemeral DH suites with JSSE unless you upgrade to Java 8.

**Cipher suite preference**

In versions before Java 8, JSSE does not allow servers to control cipher suite order. This means that the first supported suite from the list offered by the client will be used. In practice, this limits your ability to enforce secure configuration. For example, it's not possible to have RC4 in your configuration but use it only with clients that don't support anything better. Similarly, it's not possible to prefer suites that provide forward secrecy over the ones that don't.

Starting with Java 8, server preference is supported by JSSE, but each server application will probably need to be updated to support this feature. Tomcat doesn't support it yet, but a patch is available to enable it.[22]

**Disable client-initiated renegotiation**

Client-initiated renegotiation is a protocol feature that is not used for anything useful, but what it does do is create an opportunity for an attacker to execute a DoS attack by forcing the server to continuously renegotiate, consuming significant CPU resources. The weakness here is not that renegotiation itself consumes CPU; SSL is designed in such way that servers always consume more CPU on every handshake, and that can't be avoided. The weaknesses is that with renegotiation multiple handshakes are taking place on the same TCP connection. Because most DoS detection techniques operate by observing connection rates, this type of attack is difficult to mitigate.

Starting with Java 8, it is possible to disable client-initiated renegotiation by using the undocumented `jdk.tls.rejectClientInitiatedRenegotiation` system property.

In the light of these problems, until Java web servers are updated to support server cipher suite preference, I recommend using either Tomcat Native (version 1.1.30 or newer) or an Apache httpd reverse proxy for TLS termination.

> **Note**
>
> The TLS implementation (JSSE) included with Java 8 has been significantly improved, addressing all the major shortcomings from Java 7. If you're running TLS servers using Java, you should upgrade to version 8 as soon as the new runtime stabilizes and the new features are supported by server software.

# Configuring TLS Handling

To configure TLS,[23] you need to set a number of attributes on the Connector element of the Tomcat configuration. The protocol attribute determines which of the three supported connectors will be used. The default value ("HTTP/1.1") will have Tomcat first attempt to use the APR connector. If the APR connector is not available, Tomcat 7 and earlier will fall back to the BIO connector, whereas Tomcat 8 will use the NIO connector.

You shouldn't rely on this auto-configuration behavior in production; instead, explicitly configure the desired connector by entering its name into the protocol attribute, as described in the following sections.

To use JSSE with a blocking connector (BIO):

---

[22] Bug #55988: Add parameter useCipherSuitesOrder to JSSE (BIO and NIO) connectors [fsty.uk/b471] (ASF Bugzilla, retrieved 26 June 2014)

[23] SSL Support [fsty.uk/b472] (Apache Tomcat 8 Documentation, retrieved 2 July 2014)

---

```
<Connector
    protocol = "org.apache.coyote.http11.Http11Protocol"
    port = "443"
    ...
/>
```

To use JSSE with a nonblocking connector (NIO):

```
<Connector
    protocol = "org.apache.coyote.http11.Http11NioProtocol"
    port = "443"
    ...
/>
```

By default, Tomcat will look for Tomcat Native and enable it. This is implemented in the AprLifecycleListener class, whose parameters are described in a later section. If you don't want to use Tomcat Native, you can simply disable the class. Or if you only want to disable the OpenSSL bits, set the SSLEngine parameter to off:

```
<Listener
    className = "org.apache.catalina.core.AprLifecycleListener"
    SSLEngine = "off"
/>
```

If, on the other hand, you leave Tomcat Native in and wish to use OpenSSL, specify the Http11AprProtocol class in the protocol attribute:

```
<Connector
    protocol = "org.apache.coyote.http11.Http11AprProtocol"
    port = "443"
    ...
/>
```

## External TLS Termination

Some TLS configuration is necessary even if you are not terminating TLS at the Tomcat level. In this situation, the deployment is secure, but Tomcat is not aware of it, and the applications running on it won't be aware, either. This might lead to subtle problems and security issues. For example, session cookies might not be marked as secure, exposing sessions to the possibility of hijacking.

If you are deploying Tomcat behind Apache using mod_jk or mod_proxy_ajp, both of which implement the AJP communication protocol, there is actually nothing for you to do. This protocol will transparently communicate the TLS information from Apache to Tomcat.

In all other cases, you will have to invest more effort into configuration and information exchange. For example, to tell Tomcat that TLS is handled externally, configure the scheme and secure fields only:

```
<Connector
    scheme = "https"
    secure = "true"
    ...
>
```

For the information exchange, you can use Tomcat's SSL Valve,[24] which can extract information from request headers (placed there by the proxy terminating TLS) and use it to populate the relevant Tomcat structures.

If none of these solutions work for your case, it's easy to write a custom extension to do the same work as the AJP protocol, transparently setting the secure flag, the correct remote port, protocol scheme, and so on.[25]

## JSSE Configuration

The following configuration snippet enables TLS on port 443 and explicitly configures all parameters except client certificate authentication (which is only very rarely used):

```
<Connector
    protocol = "org.apache.coyote.http11.Http11Protocol"
    port = "443"

    SSLEnabled = "true"
    scheme = "https"
    secure = "true"

    clientAuth = "false"

    sslProtocol = "TLS"
    sslEnabledProtocols = "TLSv1, TLSv1.1, TLSv1.2"
    ciphers = "... omitted for clarity; see below"

    keystoreFile = "${catalina.home}/conf/feistyduck.jks"
    keystorePass = "YOUR_PASSWORD"
    keyAlias = "server"

    sessionTimeout = "86400"
    sessionCacheSize = "10000"
/>
```

---

[24] SSL Valve [fsty.uk/b473] (Tomcat 8 documentation, retrieved 26 June 2014)
[25] Tomcat and SSL Accelerators [fsty.uk/b474] (Paul Lindner's blog, 9 April 2009)

Most of the parameters are self-explanatory, but please note the following:

- You should never need to change the SSLEnabled, scheme, secure, and sslProtocol parameters.

- Use the sslEnabledProtocols parameter to control protocol selection. (Ignore sslProtocol, which interfaces with an internal detail of JSSE and does not let you do anything useful.) My example does not enable SSLv2Hello and SSLv3, which I think is reasonable given that these are needed only for very old clients, such as Internet Explorer 6 on Windows XP before Service Pack 3.

- I recommend that you always include the keystore along with the web server configuration. The ${catalina.home} variable is handy to avoid using absolute paths.

- The keyAlias parameter selects the correct key and certificate chain from the desired keystore.

- By default, Tomcat does not limit the number of cached TLS sessions, which could open you up to a DoS attack. The best approach is to set a fixed amount of RAM for the TLS session cache and configure this parameter accordingly.

Omitted from the configuration example are the cipher suites. I recommend the following default configuration:

```
TLS_ECDHE_ECDSA_WITH_AES_128_CBC_SHA
TLS_ECDHE_ECDSA_WITH_AES_256_CBC_SHA
TLS_ECDHE_ECDSA_WITH_AES_128_CBC_SHA256
TLS_ECDHE_ECDSA_WITH_AES_256_CBC_SHA384
TLS_ECDHE_RSA_WITH_AES_128_CBC_SHA
TLS_ECDHE_RSA_WITH_AES_256_CBC_SHA
TLS_ECDHE_RSA_WITH_AES_128_CBC_SHA256
TLS_ECDHE_RSA_WITH_AES_256_CBC_SHA384
```

I've made the following assumptions and choices:

- You are using Java 7, which means that you have access to EC suites.

- You are not using a DSA key (which is effectively limited to 1,024 bits and thus weak).

- You don't want to use insecure DHE suites that are limited to insecure 768-bit DH parameters.

- I've included suites that work with both ECDSA and RSA keys, which means that the same configuration will work no matter what keys you have.

This configuration uses only suites that support forward secrecy and provide strong encryption. Most modern browsers and other clients will be able to connect, but some very old clients might not. As an example, older Internet Explorer versions running on Windows XP will fail.

If you really need to provide support for a very old range of clients—and only then—consider adding the following suites to the end of the list:

```
TLS_RSA_WITH_AES_128_CBC_SHA
TLS_RSA_WITH_AES_256_CBC_SHA
SSL_RSA_WITH_3DES_EDE_CBC_SHA
TLS_ECDHE_RSA_WITH_RC4_128_SHA
SSL_RSA_WITH_RC4_128_SHA
```

> **Note**
>
> The complete list of supported cipher suites is available as part of the SunJSSE provider documentation.[26]

## Forward Secrecy

My recommended suite configuration allows for only spotty forward secrecy support. There are two reasons for that, and both stem from the limitations imposed by JSSE.

- JSSE does not allow explicit selection of cipher suite order. At the moment, most clients prefer ECDHE suites (that provide forward secrecy), but some don't. Crucially, Internet Explorer in all versions prefers vanilla RSA suites over ECDHE.

- ECDHE suites are the preferred way to enable forward secrecy, because they're fast. Unfortunately, older clients do not support them, and enabling DHE suites is necessary for robust forward secrecy configuration. In JSSE, all DHE suites are limited to 768 bits, which is insecure; for this reason you can't have any DHE suites in the configuration, which means no forward secrecy with older clients.

## Configuration with Java 8

If you are deploying with Java 8, some of the new features will be available to you automatically:

- Stronger (1,024-bit) DH parameters will be used by default, and you can configure the JVM to increase the strength to 2,048 bits to make it more secure.

- You can configure the JVM to reject client-initiated renegotiation.

- Deployments that rely on default cipher suite configuration will automatically start offering the new GCM cipher suites.

For everything else, we will have to wait a little while longer until the remaining new JSSE features are utilized by web servers. The two most important features are:

---

[26] JDK 8: The SunJSSE Provider [fsty.uk/b475] (Oracle, retrieved 17 July 2014)

- Respecting server-side cipher suite order.
- Support for virtual secure hosting.

The recommended cipher suite configuration for Java 8 deployments is as follows:

```
TLS_ECDHE_ECDSA_WITH_AES_128_GCM_SHA256
TLS_ECDHE_ECDSA_WITH_AES_256_GCM_SHA384
TLS_ECDHE_ECDSA_WITH_AES_128_CBC_SHA
TLS_ECDHE_ECDSA_WITH_AES_256_CBC_SHA
TLS_ECDHE_ECDSA_WITH_AES_128_CBC_SHA256
TLS_ECDHE_ECDSA_WITH_AES_256_CBC_SHA384
TLS_ECDHE_RSA_WITH_AES_128_GCM_SHA256
TLS_ECDHE_RSA_WITH_AES_256_GCM_SHA384
TLS_ECDHE_RSA_WITH_AES_128_CBC_SHA
TLS_ECDHE_RSA_WITH_AES_256_CBC_SHA
TLS_ECDHE_RSA_WITH_AES_128_CBC_SHA256
TLS_ECDHE_RSA_WITH_AES_256_CBC_SHA384
TLS_DHE_RSA_WITH_AES_128_GCM_SHA256
TLS_DHE_RSA_WITH_AES_256_GCM_SHA384
TLS_DHE_RSA_WITH_AES_128_CBC_SHA
TLS_DHE_RSA_WITH_AES_256_CBC_SHA
TLS_DHE_RSA_WITH_AES_128_CBC_SHA256
SSL_DHE_RSA_WITH_3DES_EDE_CBC_SHA
```

The list of recommended suites is now longer, not only because of the new GCM suites but also because I added back the DHE suites, which are secure when used with Java 8.

If you really need to provide support for a very old range of clients—and only then (see the discussion in the previous section)—consider adding the following suites to the end of the list:

```
TLS_RSA_WITH_AES_128_CBC_SHA
TLS_RSA_WITH_AES_256_CBC_SHA
SSL_RSA_WITH_3DES_EDE_CBC_SHA
SSL_RSA_WITH_RC4_128_SHA
```

## APR and OpenSSL Configuration

To use the APR and OpenSSL combination to handle TLS, use the following configuration snippet:

```
<Connector
    protocol = "org.apache.coyote.http11.Http11AprProtocol"
    port = "443"

    SSLEnabled = "true"
    scheme = "https"
```

```
        secure = "true"

        SSLVerifyClient = "none"

        SSLProtocol = "All"
        SSLCipherSuite = "... omitted for clarity; see below"
        SSLHonorCipherOrder = "true"

        SSLCertificateFile = "${catalina.home}/conf/fd.crt"
        SSLCertificateKeyFile = "${catalina.home}/conf/fd.key"
        SSLCertificateChainFile = "${catalina.home}/conf/fd-intermediates.crt"
        SSLPassword = "KEY_PASSWORD"

        SSLDisableCompression = "true"
    />
```

Compared to the JSSE equivalent, there are many similarities but also some differences:

- Protocol selection is broken. In the version I tested (7.0.40), Tomcat doesn't know that TLS 1.1 and TLS 1.2 exist, which means that the only practically useful value for the SSLProtocol parameter is All, which enables all protocols from SSL 3 onwards. All my attempts to disable SSL 3 failed. When Tomcat is updated, the configuration string TLSv1+TLSv1.1+TLSv1.2 should do the trick.

- Unlike with JSSE, it is not possible to control SSL 2 handshake format compatibility; this format is always supported.

- You can enforce cipher suite order using SSLHonorCipherOrder.

- There is no keystore; keys and certificates are stored as files.

- There is a configuration parameter to disable compression, which is necessary because, unlike JSSE, OpenSSL does support compression. (But you want it disabled nevertheless, because otherwise you'd be exposing yourself to the CRIME attack.)

- There appears to be no way to control TLS session caching, which is potentially worrying.

For the recommended cipher suite configuration, please refer to the section called "Recommended Configuration" in Chapter 11, *OpenSSL Cookbook*. However, do note that ECDSA keys are not supported by Tomcat Native at this time.

## Global OpenSSL Configuration

Some OpenSSL features are configured globally and controlled from the AprLifecycleListener configuration. For example:

```
<Listener
    className = "org.apache.catalina.core.AprLifecycleListener"
```

```
    SSLEngine = "on"
    SSLRandomSeed = "builtin"
    FIPSMode = "off"
/>
```

There are two situations in which you will want to make some changes:

- If your OpenSSL installation supports multiple engines (e.g., hardware acceleration), you can put the desired engine name in the SSLEngine parameter.
- If your OpenSSL installation is FIPS compliant and you wish to enable FIPS mode, set the FIPSMode parameter to on.

# 15 Configuring Microsoft Windows and IIS

Microsoft is one of the key players in the SSL/TLS and PKI ecosystem. Their client operating systems are everywhere, on the desktop and on mobile devices. Their server and cloud platforms power a large number of critical systems. Their development environments are a popular choice for building web sites.

In the light of Microsoft's very long history and the longevity of their platforms, it's not surprising that the biggest issues I encountered were complexity and lack of good documentation. The complexity comes from the fact that the software codebase is very old, with features added over a long period of time. Documentation often does not exist. When it does, finding it is not always easy; you will often run into older, now inaccurate articles online. That said, their cryptographic libraries provide good support for the important features, with only a few peculiarities here and there.

## Schannel

Microsoft *Secure Channel*[1] (or *Schannel*, as it's better known) is a cryptographic component that implements a set of protocols designed to enable secure communication. Schannel is the official SSL/TLS library on all Windows platforms, which means that most Windows programs rely on it, especially those developed by Microsoft.

## Features Overview

Schannel has generally always offered good coverage of SSL and TLS protocol features. Microsoft was the first to support TLS 1.2 when it introduced Windows 7 in 2009. For comparison, OpenSSL added support for TLS 1.2 in 2012; most other major desktop browsers started supporting it only in 2013. But even though TLS 1.2 had been implemented, it was left disabled by default. Ironically, Microsoft was subsequently late in enabling TLS 1.2 by default and did so only with Internet Explorer 11 in November 2013.

---

[1] Secure Channel [fsty.uk/b476] (Microsoft Windows Dev Center)

The biggest problem with Microsoft's SSL/TLS implementation is the fact that Windows XP does not support virtual secure hosting (via the *Server Name Indication* extension, or SNI). We can't blame Microsoft for not supporting SNI at the initial launch of Windows XP in 2001, because SNI did not exist until 2003. But, for one reason or another, Microsoft decided not to add SNI support in the following three service packs even though it was clear that this operating system was going to be supported for a very long time. Because Windows XP is still used by a substantial number of users, the lack of SNI makes it very complicated and costly to deploy web site encryption at scale. That said, the support for Windows XP Service Pack 3 ended in April 2014; there's hope that users will now start to migrate to other operating systems.

> ### Note
>
> This section describes the capabilities of Schannel, Microsoft's SSL/TLS library. Because Windows incorporates multiple layers of cryptographic functionality, it can sometimes be difficult to pinpoint where exactly limitations are coming from. Schannel inherits all limitations of the underlying lower-level libraries and then adds some of its own. For example, even though Windows 8 is documented to support DSA keys of up to 3,072 bits[2] (earlier versions supported DSA keys of only up to 1,024 bits), Internet Explorer still refuses to connect to servers that use such stronger keys. The limitation is probably in Schannel.

---

[2] BCryptGenerateKeyPair function [fsty.uk/b477] (Cryptography API: Next Generation documentation, retrieved 4 February 2014)

Table 15.1. Evolution of SSL/TLS protocol features in Schannel

| | Windows XP, Server 2003 / IIS 6 | Windows Vista, Server 2008 / IIS 7 | Windows 7, Server 2008 R2 / IIS 7.5 | Windows 8, Server 2012 / IIS 8 | Windows 8.1, Server 2012 R2 / IIS 8 |
|---|---|---|---|---|---|
| Elliptic curve cryptography | - | Yes | Yes | Yes | Yes |
| Client-side SNI | - | Yes | Yes | Yes | Yes |
| Server-side SNI | - | - | - | Yes | Yes |
| TLS 1.0 | Optional | Yes | Yes | Yes | Yes |
| TLS 1.1, TLS 1.2[a] | - | - | Yes (IE 11)[b] | Yes (IE 11)[b] | Yes |
| AES suites | -[c] | Yes | Yes | Yes | Yes |
| AES GCM suites | - | - | Yes[d] | Yes[d] | Yes[e] |
| DH parameters > 1,024 bits | - | - | Yes (IE 11) | Yes (IE 11) | Yes[f] |
| Ephemeral DH with RSA | - | - | - | - | - |
| DSA keys > 1,024 bits | - | - | - | - | - |
| Session tickets | - | - | - | Yes (client) | Yes |
| Secure renegotiation | MS10-049 | MS10-049 | MS10-049 | Yes | Yes |
| ALPN | - | - | - | - | Yes (client) |
| BEAST mitigation | MS12-006 | MS12-006 | MS12-006 | Yes | Yes |
| OCSP stapling | - | - | Yes | Yes | Yes |
| Default client handshake format[g] | v2 | v3 | v3 | v3 | v3 |

[a] This row describes the default settings of Internet Explorer. Other application might have different defaults depending on whether they explicitly configure SSL and exactly which underlying library they're using.

[b] Windows 7 added support for TLS 1.1 and 1.2, but kept them disabled by default until Internet Explorer 11.

[c] Windows Server 2003 can be updated with KB 948963 (released in 2008) to add support for some AES cipher suites.

[d] Only in combination with ECDSA keys, which are still a novelty.

[e] As of April 2014, four additional GCM suites are supported; they can be used with RSA keys.

[f] Starting with Windows 8, DH parameters up to 4,096 bits are supported.

[g] There are two client handshake formats: the old one used by SSL 2 and the new one introduced with SSL 3. Not all servers support the old format, meaning the connections from very old clients will fail.

# Protocol Vulnerabilities

Despite their very large user base (even small changes can have a large impact with such a large pool of users and require extensive testing), Microsoft has a very good record of addressing protocol issues as they arise.

### Insecure renegotiation

Like most other vendors, Microsoft initially addressed insecure renegotiation with a workaround that disables renegotiation; the patch was released as KB 977377 on 9

February 2010.[3] Secure renegotiation (RFC 5746) was implemented later, in MS10-049, which was released for all platforms on 10 August 2010.[4]

## BEAST

The BEAST vulnerability was fixed across all platforms in MS12-006, which was released on 10 January 2012. The fix implements the 1/n-1 split when protocols TLS 1.0 and earlier are used.

## CRIME

Microsoft never supported TLS compression in their SSL/TLS stack, which meant that it was never vulnerable to the CRIME attack.

# Interoperability Issues

Schannel does not suffer from many practical interoperability issues. Those aspects that you will need to be aware of are mainly related to the deprecation of weak and obsolete cryptographic primitives.

## DSA

Schannel does not support DSA keys stronger than 1,024 bits and never did. Given the size of the Microsoft's user base, this makes DSA practically dead. The strength of DSA keys is roughly equivalent to the strength of RSA keys, which means that 1,024 bits is too weak according to current standards. In practice, this is not an issue, because there are virtually no servers with DSA keys on the public Internet (and there never were).

## DH parameters over 1,024 bits

Another problem is that before version 11 Internet Explorer did not support DH parameters stronger than 1,024 bits. But this is a problem only in theory, because the only practical way to use such parameters is with a DHE and RSA suite combination (DHE_RSA), which IE also didn't support until April 2014.

## RSA keys under 1,024 bits

RSA keys and certificates weaker than 1,024 bits were initially deprecated with an optional update on 14 August 2012, which then became mandatory on 9 October 2012.[5] This update applies to certificates issued by both public and private CAs.

## MD5

On 13 August 2013, Microsoft deprecated MD5 signatures in the Microsoft Root Certificate Program with the release of KB 2862973.[6] The update applies to Windows

---

[3] Vulnerability in TLS/SSL could allow spoofing [fsty.uk/b478] (Microsoft Security Advisory 977377, 9 February 2010)

[4] Vulnerabilities in SChannel could allow remote code execution [fsty.uk/b479] (Microsoft Security Bulletin MS10-049, 10 August 2010)

[5] Update For Minimum Certificate Key Length [fsty.uk/b480] (KB 2661254, 14 August 2012)

---

Vista, Server 2008 and other older platforms but not to the newer Windows 8.1, RT 8.1, and Server 2012 R2, which rejected MD5 signatures from the start.

Because this update affects only the certificates issued under the root certificate program, MD5 certificates issued by private CAs are not expected. Deprecating all MD5 certificates can be done manually, after installing KB 2862966.[7]

## RC4

Microsoft was the first vendor to deprecate RC4. Starting with Windows 8.1, this cipher is not enabled by default. On 13 November 2013, Microsoft released KB 2868725 for Windows 8 and earlier platforms,[8] making it possible for applications to disable RC4 by requesting strong crypto and for users to completely disable RC4 by making registry tweaks.

Internet Explorer 11 is hyped as the first browser to not offer RC4 by default,[9] but although that's true on Windows 8.1, on my Windows 7 desktop (after the KB 2869725 update) RC4 is still present.

Removing support for RC4 leads to potential interoperability issues for those upgrading to IE 11 and Windows 8.1. According to Microsoft's research, about 3.9% of the SSL sites they sampled supported only RC4 in November 2013. SSL Pulse measurements indicate 1.8% in July 2014. When connecting to such sites, IE 11 will fail on the first attempt. It will then voluntarily downgrade the connection twice, first to TLS 1.0 (still without RC4 and failing again) and then to SSL 3, this time with RC4 added. Thus, for a site that offers only RC4 cipher suites, one of the following two situations can occur: (1) if the site supports SSL 3, IE 11 will use this protocol version after some delay while it determines how to successfully connect; (2) if the site doesn't support SSL 3, IE 11 won't be able to connect at all.

Microsoft should not be blamed for this problem. Being the first to disable a major cipher with such a large user base is a bold move. On the positive side, the introduction of a small penalty when connecting to RC4-only sites creates a small incentive for site operators to improve their configuration.

## SHA1

On November 12th, 2013, Microsoft announced their plans to deprecate SHA1 signatures by the end of 2016.[10] At the same time, they started to require that new roots

---

[6] Update for Deprecation of MD5 Hashing Algorithm for Microsoft Root Certificate Program [fsty.uk/b481] (KB 2862973, 13 August 2013)

[7] An update is available that improves management of weak certificate cryptographic algorithms in Windows [fsty.uk/b482] (KB 2862966, 13 August 2013)

[8] Update for Disabling RC4 [fsty.uk/b483] (KB 2868725, 13 November 2013)

[9] IE11 Automatically Makes Over 40% of the Web More Secure While Making Sure Sites Continue to Work [fsty.uk/b484] (IEBlog, 12 November 2013)

[10] SHA1 Deprecation Policy [fsty.uk/b485] (Windows PKI blog, 12 November 2013)

accepted to their Root Certificate Program must use SHA2 and RSA keys of at least 4,096 bits. Microsoft was famously bitten when the Flame malware attacked MD5 used past its due date. This time, they are not taking any chances.

Apart from the potential issues listed here, the main interoperability worry you will have related to Schannel is supporting very old clients—for example, Internet Explorer 6—running on old operating systems such as Windows XP before Service Pack 3.

# Microsoft Root Certificate Program

The *Microsoft Root Certificate Program*[11] maintains a collection of certificates trusted in Windows operating systems. Windows Vista and newer platforms ship only with a small number of trusted certificates that are required by the operating system. All other root certificates are securely retrieved from Microsoft the first time they are encountered (e.g., while browsing the Web). Because of this auto-update mechanism, Microsoft users are guaranteed to always have the latest trusted certificates.

Windows XP doesn't fully support the auto-update mechanism; updating the trusted roots requires a manual download and an update from the Microsoft Update Catalog.[12]

## Managing System Trust Stores

If you are running a modern Windows version, you should very rarely need to manually configure the trust stores; the auto-update processes will take care of everything for you. The list of trusted certificates is updated once a week, new roots are downloaded on demand, and blacklisted certificates are downloaded daily.[13]

> **Note**
>
> Windows operates multiple certificate repositories. There is the main one associated with the computer, but there are also separate stores for each service and user account. As a rule of thumb, it's best to work with the computer certificate repository.

To view and change the system trust stores, use Microsoft Management Console (MMC), as explained later in this chapter in the section called "Creating a Custom IIS Management Console". The main trust store is called *Trusted Root Certification Authorities;* it contains the roots from the Microsoft Root Program. By default, this store contains only a small number

---

[11] Introduction to The Microsoft Root Certificate Program [fsty.uk/b73] (Microsoft TechNet Wiki, retrieved 3 July 2014)

[12] How to get a Root Certificate update for Windows [fsty.uk/b486] (Microsoft, retrieved 2 July 2014)

[13] Announcing the automated updater of untrustworthy certificates and keys [fsty.uk/b487] (Windows PKI blog, 11 June 2012)

---

of certificates, but the number grows with usage. For example, after several years of usage my Windows desktop trusts 49 root certificates.

If you're administering a Windows domain, you can manage the entire domain's trust stores via Group Policy Management.[14]

## Importing a Trusted Certificate

Adding a new trusted CA is easy. Once you obtain the correct certificate, you need to follow the *Certificate Import* wizard. To start the process, simply double-click the certificate (the extension should be `.cer`) and then press the *Import Certificate* button.

> ### Warning
>
> The decision to trust a new CA should be made only after carefully considering the potential security impact. Once you trust a CA, you trust that it will issue only genuine certificates and that their security practices are strong. Remember, any CA can issue a certificate for any web site in the world.[15]

## Blacklisting Trusted Certificates

Because of the auto-update system, if you wish to revoke trust in a particular CA it is not sufficient to delete their certificates from the *Trusted Root Certification Authorities* store. If you do, your system will simply download the missing certificates the next time they are needed.

To ensure that a certificate is permanently blacklisted, place it into the *Untrusted Certificates* store. The next time you visit a web site that depends on the root certificate in question, Internet Explorer (and other programs that depend on the Windows trust stores) will refuse to connect.

## Disabling the Auto-Update of Root Certificates

If you don't like the auto-update mechanism for root certificates, you can disable it by following these steps:[16]

1. Open the Local Group Policy Editor by running `gpedit.msc`.

2. In the left pane, navigate to *Computer Configuration > Administrative Templates > System > Internet Communication Management > Internet Communication settings*.

---

[14] Manage Trusted Root Certificates [fsty.uk/b488] (Windows Server 2012 documentation, retrieved 3 July 2014)

[15] There is a feature called *Name Constraints*, that allows CAs to be restricted to issue certificates for only certain name hierarchies, but this feature is not widely used.

[16] Certificate Support and Resulting Internet Communication in Windows Vista [fsty.uk/b489] (Microsoft TechNet, retrieved 3 July 2014)

3. In the right pane, find and double-click on *Turn off Automatic Root Certificates Update.*

4. To disable automatic updates, change the setting to *Enabled.*

From this moment on, you will need to manually maintain your root certificates.

# Configuration

Interestingly for an operating system that is inherently GUI-oriented, Windows doesn't have tools for SSL/TLS protocol, suite, and cryptographic algorithm configuration. The Internet Information Server (IIS) comes with a basic user interface for key and certificate manipulation, but other than that configuration changes are made by changing the registry directly.

> **Note**
>
> The instructions in this section apply to the operating system and programs that use system libraries. Programs that use their own SSL/TLS and PKI libraries won't be affected unless they make an effort to respect Schannel configuration. For example, Firefox uses its own libraries and root certificates. Chrome also relies on its own libraries, but it uses system root certificates.

## Schannel Configuration

Schannel configuration can be tuned to decide what protocols and cipher suites should be used. For protocols, there are separate controls for client and server applications. For everything else, there is one set of registry keys that apply to all application types.

All Schannel configuration options are nested under the following root key:

```
HKEY_LOCAL_MACHINE\SYSTEM\CurrentControlSet\Control\SecurityProviders\Schannel
```

## Protocol Configuration

Protocols are configured using a number of registry keys nested under the Protocols subkey. Each protocol gets its own key, and there are two further subkeys to allow for separate configuration for client and server applications. Starting with Windows Server 2008 R2 and Windows 7, all major protocols are supported, starting with SSL 2.0 and ending with TLS 1.2. This is what the entire structure looks like:[17]

```
Protocols\SSL 2.0
Protocols\SSL 2.0\Client
```

---

[17] For brevity, I omitted several subkeys from the list. They are: Multi-Protocol Unified Hello, PCT 1.0, and DTLS 1.0. They refer to obsolete or rarely used protocols.

```
Protocols\SSL 2.0\Server
Protocols\SSL 3.0
Protocols\SSL 3.0\Client
Protocols\SSL 3.0\Server
Protocols\TLS 1.0
Protocols\TLS 1.0\Client
Protocols\TLS 1.0\Server
Protocols\TLS 1.1
Protocols\TLS 1.1\Client
Protocols\TLS 1.1\Server
Protocols\TLS 1.2
Protocols\TLS 1.2\Client
Protocols\TLS 1.2\Server
```

Each leaf key can contain one or both of the following DWORD entries:

**DisabledByDefault**

> This setting is for applications that do not explicitly configure enabled protocols but use system defaults. If the entry is not present or if the value is 0, the protocol is enabled by default. If the value is 1, the protocol is disabled by default. Normally, Windows will disable SSL 2 and leave all other protocols enabled.

**Enabled**

> This entry allows you to disable certain protocol versions for all applications, even those that explicitly enable them. To disable a protocol, set the Enabled entry to 0. If the entry is not configured or if its value is anything except zero (the documentation recommends 0xffffffff), the protocol will be enabled.

After you make a change to the protocol configuration, you will need to restart any active programs for the changes to take effect.

## Cipher Suite Algorithm Selection

Two configuration methods are available for cipher suite configuration. Cryptographic algorithms that make up suites can be configured individually. Then, if a particular algorithm is disabled all the suites that use it will also be disabled. This mechanism ensures that weak algorithms are not used anywhere, even if configuration elsewhere suggests to do so.

The following subkeys are available, one per algorithm:[18]

```
Ciphers\AES 128
Ciphers\AES 256
Ciphers\DES 56
Ciphers\NULL
Ciphers\RC4 40/128
```

---

[18] Older Windows versions also supported RC2 40/128, RC2 56/128, and RC2 128/128.

```
Ciphers\RC4 56/128
Ciphers\RC4 64/128
Ciphers\RC4 128/128
Ciphers\Triple DES 168
Hashes\MD5
Hashes\SHA
Hashes\SHA256
Hashes\SHA384
KeyExchangeAlgorithms\Diffie-Hellman
KeyExchangeAlgorithms\ECDH
KeyExchangeAlgorithms\PKCS
```

> **Note**
>
> The PKCS key refers to the use of RSA for key exchange only. The use of RSA for authentication is not affected (e.g., TLS_RSA_* suites will be disabled, but TLS_ECDHE_RSA_* will not).

To disable an algorithm, create a DWORD entry called Enabled under the correct key and set its value to 0. To reenable the algorithm, delete the entry or set its value to 0xffffffff. Changes sometimes take effect immediately, but you should always restart your programs to reliably change the settings.

> **Note**
>
> The restrictions on hashes apply only to cipher suites, not to certificate signatures. To disable, for example, MD5 for certificate signatures, follow the instructions later in this chapter.

## Cipher Suite Configuration

Disabling individual algorithms is useful, but in most cases what you really want to do is specify exactly which suites are enabled and in which order. Schannel on Vista and newer systems allows suites to be configured in this way, with the changes affecting client and server applications equally.

Cipher suite configuration is the only Schannel setting that can be configured via a graphical user interface:

1.  First, start the Local Group Policy Editor by running gpedit.msc.[19]

2.  In the left pane, navigate to *Computer Configuration > Administrative Templates > Network > SSL Configuration Settings*.

---

[19] Not all Windows operating systems ship with this tool. For example, Windows 7 Professional has it, but Windows 7 Home Premium doesn't. If you don't have it, you'll have to resort to editing the registry directly, which I discuss later in this section.

3. Then, in the right pane double-click on *SSL Cipher Suite Order* and edit away.

> **Warning**
>
> When editing cipher suite configuration via the policy editor, pay close attention to
> the size of the resulting suite string. The editor will accept only up to 1,023 bytes
> and will silently cut off any extra data you put in.

The list of cipher suites supported by Schannel can be found on Microsoft's web site.[20] I recommend the following cipher suite configuration, designed for security and speed:

```
TLS_ECDHE_ECDSA_WITH_AES_128_GCM_SHA256_P256
TLS_ECDHE_ECDSA_WITH_AES_256_GCM_SHA384_P384
TLS_ECDHE_ECDSA_WITH_AES_128_CBC_SHA_P256
TLS_ECDHE_ECDSA_WITH_AES_256_CBC_SHA_P256
TLS_ECDHE_ECDSA_WITH_AES_128_CBC_SHA256_P256
TLS_ECDHE_ECDSA_WITH_AES_256_CBC_SHA384_P384
TLS_ECDHE_RSA_WITH_AES_128_CBC_SHA_P256
TLS_ECDHE_RSA_WITH_AES_256_CBC_SHA_P256
TLS_ECDHE_RSA_WITH_AES_128_CBC_SHA256_P256
TLS_DHE_RSA_WITH_AES_128_GCM_SHA256
TLS_DHE_RSA_WITH_AES_256_GCM_SHA384
```

I made the following assumptions:

- Use only suites that provide forward secrecy.

- Provide support for RSA and ECDSA server keys in the configuration. At the moment,
  RSA keys are dominant by far, which means that ECDSA suites will remain unused in
  most cases. But if you do decide to switch, you won't have to change your suite configuration.

- The last two suites were added only to Windows 8.1 and Server 2012 R2 in April
  2014.[21] It's not clear if these suites will be used in practice because the clients that
  might support them already support the faster ECDHE suites.

This configuration uses only suites that support forward secrecy and provide strong encryption. Most modern browsers and other clients will be able to connect, but some very old
clients might not. As an example, older Internet Explorer versions running on Windows XP
will fail.

If you really need to provide support for a very old range of clients—and only then—consider adding the following suites to the end of the list:

---

[20] Cipher Suites in Schannel [fsty.uk/b490] (Microsoft, retrieved 17 July 2014)

[21] KB 2929781: Update adds new TLS cipher suites and changes cipher suite priorities in Windows 8.1 and Windows Server 2012 R2 [fsty.uk/
b491] (Microsoft, 8 April 2014)

---

```
TLS_RSA_WITH_AES_128_CBC_SHA
TLS_RSA_WITH_AES_256_CBC_SHA
TLS_RSA_WITH_3DES_EDE_CBC_SHA
TLS_RSA_WITH_RC4_128_SHA
```

> ### Note
>
> If you look carefully at the suite names, you will notice that Microsoft uses extended cipher suite name syntax, constructed by combining the official name (e.g., `TLS_ECDHE_ECDSA_WITH_AES_128_GCM_SHA256`) with a P256 or P384 suffix. These suffixes refer to the elliptic curves that can be used for the ECDHE key exchange, the NIST curves secp256r1 and secp384r1, respectively. Although the underlying suite is the same no matter which suffix is used, this naming approach enables you to have control over exactly which elliptic curve is preferred.

If you want to configure suites by manipulating the registry directly, the key that controls cipher suite configuration is:[22]

```
HKEY_LOCAL_MACHINE\SOFTWARE\Policies\Microsoft\Cryptography\Configuration\SSL\00010↵
002
```

If the key is empty, create a new entry: `Functions` of type `MULTI_SZ` (a list of strings). The value must contain the list of cipher suites enabled by default in the order of preference. Changing this entry is easy using the registry editor. When editing from a command line or via a registry file, put all suites on a single line separated with commas. Do not use any spaces. When you're done, a reboot is required for the changes to take effect.

## Key and Signature Restrictions

Microsoft relatively recently added the ability to restrict the usage of weak cryptographic algorithms during certificate chain validation. This capability is available by default on Windows 8.1 and Windows Server 2012 R2 as well as on other Microsoft platforms that have KB 2862966 applied.[7]

The policy framework is quite extensive and supports a wide range of useful functionality:

- Disable weak cryptographic algorithms

- For key algorithms, enforce minimum key length

- Apply policy depending on certificate type (e.g., different policies for server authentication and code signing)

---

[22] It seems that there are multiple keys that influence cipher suite configuration. Some sources recommend using `HKEY_LOCAL_MACHINE`
`\SYSTEM\CurrentControlSet\Control\Cryptography\Configuration\Local\SSL\00010002` for this purpose, but this key appears to have lesser priority and will not be used if other keys exist. It is generally best to avoid changing the registry directly, if you can.

- Specify policy that applies to all certificates or only to public CAs
- Apply policy only to certificates issued after a certain date (e.g., keep legacy certificates in use, but do not allow any new certificates with weak algorithms)
- Log policy violations
- Log violations but do not enforce the policy otherwise
- Create per-certificate exceptions

The recommended approach is to start with a logging-only policy that enables you to monitor the violations but avoids potential disruption due to the mismatch between what is ideally desired and what is used in real life. After policy tuning and further monitoring, it will be possible to switch to enforcement safely. Once a policy is tested on a single workstation, it can be pushed to other users via Group Policy Objects.

At the time of writing, it is possible to restrict the usage of the MD5 and SHA1 signatures and DSA, ECDSA, and RSA keys. Restrictions are created by manipulating the registry keys under the following root key:

```
HKEY_LOCAL_MACHINE\SOFTWARE\Microsoft\Cryptography\OID\EncodingType ↵
0\CertDllCreateCertificateChainEngine\Config
```

Because the policies can be elaborate, a special approach to key name construction is used to express the logic in a way that can be stored in the registry. Each key name must be in the following format:

Weak*<CryptoAlg><ConfigType><ValueType>*

To construct a key name, replace each option name with one of the possible values, as documented in the following table.

Table 15.2. Option values used for registry key name construction

| Option | Value | Description |
|---|---|---|
| CryptoAlg | Md5 | Specifies the name of the algorithm to which the policy applies. |
| | Sha1 | |
| | Dsa | |
| | Ecdsa | |
| | Rsa | |
| ConfigType | ThirdParty | Applies only to the roots in the Microsoft root program (public CAs). |
| | All | Applies to all certificate roots (public and private CAs). Because ThirdParty is a subset of All, the following also applies:<br><br>• Most flags set on All will also be set on ThirdParty; logging flags will not be affected.<br><br>• The earliest AfterTime will apply.<br><br>• The largest MinBitLength will apply. |
| ValueType | Flags | List of flags that are used to select which certificate types are restricted and how; see ahead for more information (REG_DWORD). |
| | MinBitLength | Specifies the minimum public key length in bits; applies only to key algorithms (REG_DWORD). |
| | AfterTime | Apply policy only to signatures generated after a certain time; does not apply to certificate chains used for timestamping (REG_BINARY with an 8-byte FILENAME). |
| | Sha256Allow | List of explicitly allowed weak certificates, specified using their hex-encoded SHA256 thumbprints (REG_SZ or REG_MULTI_SZ). |

The purpose of key flags is twofold. First, they are used to enable a rule and control if it is enforced (see following table).

Table 15.3. Flags that control rule activation and enforcement

| Flag | Description |
|---|---|
| CERT_CHAIN_ENABLE_WEAK_SETTINGS_FLAG (0x80000000) | This flag is required in order for a policy to be activated. If the flag is disabled, then all other settings (for the same combination of CryptoAlg and ConfigType) will be ignored. |
| CERT_CHAIN_ENABLE_WEAK_LOGGING_FLAG (0x00000004) | Enables logging of certificate chains that violate policy. |
| CERT_CHAIN_ENABLE_ONLY_WEAK_LOGGING_FLAG (0x00000008) | Policy violations are recorded, but weak certificate chains are not rejected. This setting is very useful to test policies before hard activation. |

Additionally, multiple flags are used to control which certificate types the rule applies to, as documented in the following table.

Table 15.4. Flags that select certificate types on which rules operate

| Flag | Description |
|---|---|
| CERT_CHAIN_DISABLE_ALL_EKU_WEAK_FLAG (0x00010000) | Applies policy to all certificates. |
| CERT_CHAIN_DISABLE_SERVER_AUTH_WEAK_FLAG (0x00100000) | Applies policy to certificates used for server authentication. |
| CERT_CHAIN_DISABLE_CODE_SIGNING_WEAK_FLAG (0x00400000) | Applies policy to certificates used for code signing. |
| CERT_CHAIN_DISABLE_MOTW_CODE_SIGNING_WEAK_FLAG (0x00800000) | Applies policy to certificates used for code signing, provided they originated from the Web. |
| CERT_CHAIN_DISABLE_TIMESTAMP_WEAK_FLAG (0x04000000) | Applies policy to certificates used for timestamping. |
| CERT_CHAIN_DISABLE_MOTW_TIMESTAMP_WEAK_FLAG (0x08000000) | Applies policy to certificates used for timestamping, provided they originated from the Web. |

> **Note**
>
> To specify a weak signature, all you need to do is enable CERT_CHAIN_ENABLE_WEAK_SETTINGS_FLAG on the appropriate registry key (e.g., WeakMd5AllFlags for weak MD5 on all certificates). To specify a weak key algorithm, you need to specify the flag as well as set the minimum key length (e.g., set WeakRsaAllMinBitLength to 1,024 for weak RSA below 1,024 bits on all certificates).

## Using CertUtil to Manipulate Cryptographic Policy

Manipulating the registry directly can sometimes be tricky, and it definitely is in this case because policies can get quite complex. Another way to work with policies is by using the CertUtil tool, which allows you to display, create and change, and delete policy registry keys. This tool also allows individual manipulation of flags, times, and string lists:

```
$ CertUtil -setreg -?
Usage:
  CertUtil [Options] -setreg [{ca|restore|policy|exit|template|enroll|chain|PolicyS↵
ervers}\[ProgId\]]RegistryValueName Value
  Set registry value
    ca -- Use CA's registry key
    restore -- Use CA's restore registry key
    policy -- Use policy module's registry key
    exit -- Use first exit module's registry key
    template -- Use template registry key (use -user for user templates)
    enroll -- Use enrollment registry key (use -user for user context)
    chain -- Use chain configuration registry key
    PolicyServers -- Use Policy Servers registry key
    ProgId -- Use policy or exit module's ProgId (registry subkey name)
```

```
RegistryValueName -- registry value name (use "Name*" to prefix match)
Value -- new numeric, string or date registry value or filename.
    If a numeric value starts with "+" or "-", the bits specified
    in the new value are set or cleared in the existing registry value.

    If a string value starts with "+" or "-", and the existing value
    is a REG_MULTI_SZ value, the string is added to or removed from
    the existing registry value.
    To force creation of a REG_MULTI_SZ value, add a "\n" to the end
    of the string value.

    If the value starts with "@", the rest of the value is the name
    of the file containing the hexadecimal text representation
    of a binary value.
    If it does not refer to a valid file, it is instead parsed as
    [Date][+|-][dd:hh] -- an optional date plus or minus optional
    days and hours.
    If both are specified, use a plus sign (+) or minus sign (-) separator.
    Use "now+dd:hh" for a date relative to the current time.

  Use "chain\ChainCacheResyncFiletime @now" to effectively flush cached CRLs.

Options:
  -f                    -- Force overwrite
  -user                 -- Use HKEY_CURRENT_USER keys or certificate store
  -GroupPolicy          -- Use Group Policy certificate store
  -gmt                  -- Display times as GMT
  -seconds              -- Display times with seconds and milliseconds
  -v                    -- Verbose operation
  -privatekey           -- Display password and private key data
  -config Machine\CAName    -- CA and Machine name string

CertUtil -?             -- Display a verb list (command list)
CertUtil -setreg -?     -- Display help text for the "setreg" verb
CertUtil -v -?          -- Display all help text for all verbs
```

> **Warning**
>
> Changes to cryptographic policy take effect immediately if you're changing the registry directly or using the CertUtil tool. As always, it is recommended that you make a backup of your registry before you begin.

## Recording Weak Certificate Chains

Weak certificate chains can be recorded for later analysis. To activate this feature, first configure the WeakSignatureLogDir key with the desired storage location:

```
$ CertUtil -setreg chain\WeakSignatureLogDir C:\Log\WeakCertificateChains
```

Then, when creating individual policies ensure that `CERT_CHAIN_ENABLE_WEAK_LOGGING_FLAG` is set. Alternatively, to record certificate chains without enforcing policy set `CERT_CHAIN_ENABLE_ONLY_WEAK_LOGGING_FLAG` instead.

## Complete Policy Example

To illustrate, I will put together a simple policy that enforces the following restrictions, with logging, on all certificate chains:

- MD5 signatures
- RSA keys below 1,024 bits
- DSA keys below 1,024 bits
- ECDSA keys below 160 bits

The initial policy will assume logging without enforcement:

```
$ CertUtil -setreg chain\WeakSignatureLogDir C:\Log\WeakCertificateChains
$ CertUtil -setreg chain\WeakMd5AllFlags 0x80010008
$ CertUtil -setreg chain\WeakRsaAllFlags 0x80010008
$ CertUtil -setreg chain\WeakRsaAllMinBitLength 1024
$ CertUtil -setreg chain\WeakDsaAllFlags 0x80010008
$ CertUtil -setreg chain\WeakDsaAllMinBitLength 1024
$ CertUtil -setreg chain\WeakEcdsaAllFlags 0x80010008
$ CertUtil -setreg chain\WeakEcdsaAllMinBitLength 160
```

The 0x80010008 value is made of the following three flags:

- `CERT_CHAIN_ENABLE_WEAK_SETTINGS_FLAG` (0x80000000)
- `CERT_CHAIN_DISABLE_ALL_EKU_WEAK_FLAG` (0x000010000)
- `CERT_CHAIN_ENABLE_ONLY_WEAK_LOGGING_FLAG` (0x000000008)

The equivalent registry file is:

```
Windows Registry Editor Version 5.00
[HKEY_LOCAL_MACHINE\SOFTWARE\Microsoft\Cryptography\OID\EncodingType ↵
0\CertDllCreateCertificateChainEngine\Config]
"WeakSignatureLogDir"="C:\\Log\\WeakCertificateChains"
"WeakMd5AllFlags"=dword:80010008
"WeakRsaAllFlags"=dword:80010008
"WeakRsaAllMinBitLength"=dword:00000400
"WeakDsaAllFlags"=dword:80010008
"WeakDsaAllMinBitLength"=dword:00000400
"WeakEcdsaAllFlags"=dword:80010008
"WeakEcdsaAllMinBitLength"=dword:000000a0
```

To change from logging only to enforcement, you can re-set the configuration later on, changing 0x80010008 to 0x80010004 (replacing CERT_CHAIN_ENABLE_ONLY_WEAK_LOGGING_FLAG with CERT_CHAIN_ENABLE_WEAK_LOGGING_FLAG). Alternatively, you can change individual flags as you see fit:

```
$ CertUtil -setreq chain\WeakMd5Flags -0x00000008
$ CertUtil -setreq chain\WeakMd5Flags +0x00000004
```

## Configuring Renegotiation

There are two or three aspects of renegotiation that you might want to configure on your Windows systems. The most important one is adding support for secure renegotiation, which is something you will want to do for all your servers and workstations alike. On all platforms before Windows 8, patching with MS10-049 is required.

However, adding support for secure renegotiation doesn't fully resolve the root issue. For compatibility reasons, most servers are configured to accept clients that do not support secure renegotiation; MS10-049 calls it *Compatible Renegotiation*. In this mode, when either a client or the server requests renegotiation Schannel will not refuse it, even if it can't be performed securely.

If you don't need server-initiated renegotiation, the issue is easy to fix. Before the secure renegotiation feature, Microsoft released a workaround in KB 977377 that added the ability to disable renegotiation. When you fully disable renegotiation in a server, even clients that do not support secure renegotiation can't be exploited. To do this, set the following key to any nonzero value:

```
HKEY_LOCAL_MACHINE\System\CurrentControlSet\Control\SecurityProviders\SCHANNEL\Disa↵
bleRenegoOnServer
```

> **Note**
>
> Early versions of IIS had allowed client-initiated renegotiation, but all versions from IIS 6 onwards don't. Strictly speaking, this means that if your server never initiates renegotiation (e.g., if you are not requiring client certificates), then it won't be possible to exploit insecure renegotiation. Still, I recommend that you take the extra step and explicitly disable renegotiation; other programs might be vulnerable. For example, Microsoft's Forefront Threat Management Gateway (TMG) is known to allow client-initiated renegotiation.

If, on the other hand, you do need server-initiated renegotiation, your only choice is to switch to *Strict Renegotiation*. In this mode, your servers will accept secure connections only from clients that implement secure renegotiation. This too adds security, but at the expense of rejecting unpatched browsers.

To enable the strict mode, set the value of the following key to zero:

```
HKEY_LOCAL_MACHINE\System\CurrentControlSet\Control\SecurityProviders\SCHANNEL\Allo↵
wInsecureRenegoClients
```

In my tests, changes take effect immediately without even requiring a program restart.

The final decision to make is whether to allow your clients (e.g., browsers) to connect to servers that do not support secure renegotiation. This is the default, but it can be dangerous because such servers can be attacked, and yet clients have no way of detecting the attacks. The tradeoff is the same as for the servers: after enabling strict mode you won't be able to connect to a potentially sizable portion of the Web. According to the SSL Pulse results from July 2014, about 11.6% of the monitored servers do not support secure renegotiation.

If you decide to change your clients to the strict mode, change the value of the following key to zero:

```
HKEY_LOCAL_MACHINE\System\CurrentControlSet\Control\SecurityProviders\SCHANNEL\Allo↵
wInsecureRenegoServers
```

> **Note**
>
> The workaround from KB 977377 also makes it possible to completely disable renegotiation in clients, but doing so doesn't improve their security. Insecure renegotiation is exploited by tricking servers to accept renegotiation, not clients.

# Configuring Session Caching

SSL and TLS use session caching to avoid repeating slow cryptographic operations on every connection. Schannel maintains a server-wide memory store of session information. Different default settings are used on different platforms, which is why explicitly configuring the values on all servers is the best approach.[23]

All session caching parameters reside in the main Schannel registry key:

```
HKEY_LOCAL_MACHINE\SYSTEM\CurrentControlSet\Control\SecurityProviders\Schannel
```

- To configure the server session retention period, set the ServerCacheTime entry to the desired duration in milliseconds.

- You are unlikely to ever need to change the retention period for client applications, but if you do, then use the ClientCacheTime entry. The value is also in milliseconds.

- To change the maximum number of stored sessions, create or change the MaximumCacheSize value. If you use a zero, session caching will be disabled.

As a rule of thumb, you should allocate as much RAM as you can for the session cache. Under ideal conditions, you want each session to stay in the cache until it expires (and not be

---

[23] How to configure Secure Sockets Layer server and Client cache elements [fsty.uk/b492] (Microsoft Support web site, 7 July 2008)

evicted due to RAM shortage). Each session consumes 2 to 4 KB of RAM. Thus, to arrive at the maximum number of stored sessions you can support, divide the amount of RAM reserved for this purpose by 4 KB.

However, the problem with this approach is that Schannel's session caching is implemented in a way that allows it to grow *over* the specified memory limit. This is because new sessions are created as needed, but old sessions are deleted only periodically (at intervals that match ServerCacheTime), even when the cache is at maximum capacity. With normal traffic, even with spikes, such behavior is unlikely to be a problem; however, it does create a new DoS attack vector. For example, an attacker could start creating a very high number of SSL sessions per second. They will all remain in memory (each consuming about 4 KB) until the cache is pruned.

Normally, I would recommend that you set the session retention period to 24 hours. In the light of Schannel's session cache behavior, it's prudent to reduce this value to something much lower: for example, one hour. And you should possibly allocate more memory to the cache to serve as a buffer.

> **Note**
>
> Starting with Windows 8.1, Schannel supports server *session tickets*, which are a stateless session resumption mechanism. However, at the time of writing, this feature is not yet documented. Some hints are available in the PowerShell documentation.[24]

## Monitoring Session Caching

Schannel exposes several performance counters that you can use to monitor the session cache as well as the session resumption success rate. On older platforms, the resumption rate will be influenced only by the server-side session cache. Presumably, session tickets will contribute to the success rate on systems that support this feature.

The performance counters (see the following table) are in the *Security System-Wide Statistics* category; you can view them by using the Performance Monitor tool (run perfmon on the command line).

---

[24] Transport Layer Security Cmdlets in Windows PowerShell [fsty.uk/b493] (Microsoft TechNet, 17 October 2013)

Table 15.5. Schannel performance counters

| Performance counter | Description |
| --- | --- |
| Active Schannel Session Cache Entries | This counter tracks the number of Secure Sockets Layer (SSL) entries that are currently stored in the secure channel (Schannel) session cache and that are currently in use. The Schannel session cache stores information about successfully established sessions, such as SSL session IDs. Clients can use this information to reconnect to a server without performing a full SSL handshake. |
| Schannel Session Cache Entries | This counter tracks the number of SSL entries that are currently stored in the Schannel session cache. The Schannel session cache stores information about successfully established sessions, such as SSL session IDs. Clients can use this information to reconnect to a server without performing a full SSL handshake. |
| SSL Client-Side Full Handshakes | This counter tracks the number of SSL full client-side handshakes that are being processed per second. During a handshake, signals are exchanged to acknowledge that communication can occur between computers or other devices. |
| SSL Client-Side Reconnect Handshakes | This counter tracks the number of SSL client-side reconnect handshakes that are being processed per second. Reconnect handshakes allow session keys from previous SSL sessions to be used to resume a client/server connection, and they require less memory to process than full handshakes. |
| SSL Server-Side Full Handshakes | This counter tracks the number of SSL full server-side handshakes that are being processed per second. During a handshake, signals are exchanged to acknowledge that communication can occur between computers or other devices. |
| SSL Server-Side Reconnect Handshakes | This counter tracks the number of SSL server-side reconnect handshakes that are being processed per second. Reconnect handshakes allow session keys from previous SSL sessions to be used to resume a client/server connection, and they require less memory to process than full handshakes. |

# FIPS 140-2

The *Federal Information Processing Standards* (FIPS) is a group of standards developed by the United States *National Institute of Standards and Technology* (NIST) for use in nonmilitary government systems. There's a variety of standards, and not all are focused on security. Among the security ones, FIPS 140-2 is of special interest to us because it defines the guidelines for the use of cryptography. For simplicity, I will refer to FIPS 140-2 simply as FIPS.

Any system designed for US government use must comply with FIPS. In general, ensuring compliance is quite complicated. First, you must ensure that the systems are running only validated cryptographic components. Then, for every deployed application you must also ensure that its use of cryptography complies with the standard.

Microsoft makes this process easier because it maintains compliance for the core libraries and components. Most difficulties lie in ensuring compliance of third-party applications and software developed in house.

On all Windows platforms, FIPS is effectively implemented in five layers:

**Low-level libraries**

Microsoft actively maintains FIPS 140 certifications for their two core cryptographic libraries: *Cryptographic API* (CAPI) and *Cryptographic API: Next Generation* (CNG). These libraries are not necessarily FIPS aware; they provide support for approved and unapproved algorithms alike. It is the responsibility of upper layers to comply with standards when needed.

**FIPS registry indicator**

There is a single registry key that is used to indicate that a particular system is required to comply with FIPS. All deployed applications must ultimately adjust their behavior to comply with this setting.

**Higher-level libraries**

Some higher-level cryptographic libraries are FIPS aware. They read the FIPS registry key and adjust their behavior accordingly. In particular, Schannel and Microsoft .NET Framework will comply with the FIPS setting.

**Operating system components**

Key operating system components are declared to rely on and respect FIPS. This makes FIPS deployments much easier. For example, the *Remote Desktop Protocol* (RDP), filesystem encryption (EFS, BitLocker), and IPSec are on the compliant list.

**Applications**

Applications are the actual consumers of cryptographic algorithms and have the ultimate responsibility to comply with FIPS. Applications that work with low-level libraries (CAPI and CNG) have the tedious job of ensuring that those components are used in a compliant fashion. On the other hand, applications that rely exclusively on higher-level libraries are compliant by default.

## Configuring FIPS

The easiest way to enable FIPS is by making changes using the Local Security Policy management console:

1. From the command prompt or the Run menu, invoke `secpol.msc`.

2. In the left pane, navigate to *Local Policies > Security Options*.

3. In the right pane, find and double-click the *System cryptography: Use FIPS compliant algorithms for encryption, hashing, and signing* entry.

4. A property window will appear; choose *Enabled* or *Disabled*, and press *Apply* (see the following figure).

> **Note**
>
> You should reboot after making any changes that might affect the FIPS status.

---

Chapter 15: Configuring Microsoft Windows and IIS

Figure 15.1. Configuring FIPS using the Local Security Policy management console

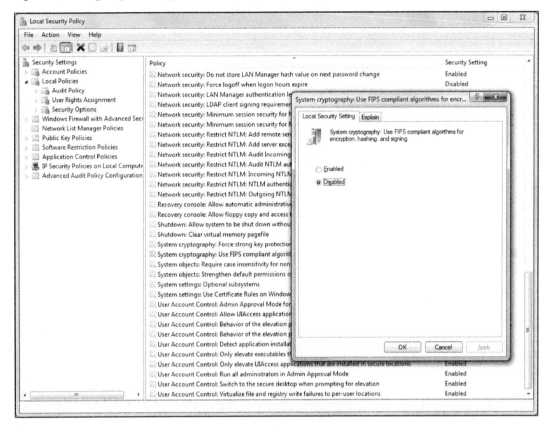

If you prefer to work with the registry directly, you need to set the value of the FIPS registry key to 1 for enabled or 0 for disabled. The location of the key differs depending on the operating system. On Windows Vista and later platforms, the key is at:

```
HKEY_LOCAL_MACHINE\System\CurrentControlSet\Control\Lsa\FIPSAlgorithmPolicy\Enabled
```

On Windows XP and Windows Server 2003, the key is at:

```
HKEY_LOCAL_MACHINE\System\CurrentControlSet\Control\Lsa\FIPSAlgorithmPolicy
```

## Third-Party Utilities

You might know all the Schannel registry keys, but that does not mean that you want to work directly with the registry every time. Nartac Software's *IIS Crypto* (shown in the following figure) is an IIS configuration utility that allows you to configure enabled cipher suites and their order. It comes with predefined templates and also has a handy link to the SSL Labs web site that allows you to test your new configuration.

Figure 15.2. Nartac Software's IIS Crypto configuration tool

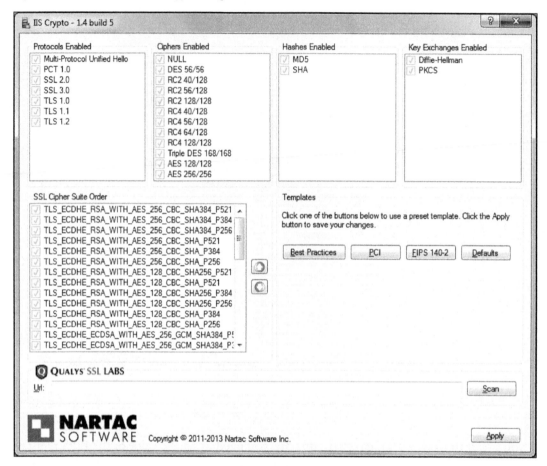

## Securing ASP.NET Web Applications

In this section, I discuss several topics related to the secure deployment of ASP.NET web applications. These topics cover several ways in which applications can subvert encryption, for example, by allowing plaintext access or using insecure cookies.

### Enforcing SSL Usage

To prevent misconfiguration, applications that expect to be run under TLS should actively check for its presence on every request. The check can be made in the code, like so:

```
if (Request.Url.Scheme.Equals("https") == false) {
    // Error, access without SSL.
}
```

However, it is generally not advisable for each execution unit (script) to check for SSL individually. A better approach is to write the code once and invoke it whenever necessary. ASP.NET supports authorization filters, which is a way of executing a common chunk of code on every request. This filter is the ideal location for your TLS checks.

## Securing Cookies

Every cookie you use in your application should be separately secured. All you need to do is set the Secure property to true. If the cookie is not intended to be accessed from JavaScript, also set the HttpOnly property to true:

```
// Create a new cookie and initialize it.
HttpCookie cookie = new HttpCookie();
cookie.Name = "CookieName";
cookie.Value = "CookieValue";
cookie.Expires = DateTime.Now.AddMinutes(10d);

// Secure the cookie.
cookie.HttpOnly = true;
cookie.Secure = true;

// Add the cookie to the response.
Response.Cookies.Add(cookie);
```

## Securing Session Cookies and Forms Authentication

In the ASP.NET configuration file, the <httpCookies> element[25] controls how the session cookies are secured. For example, to configure the session cookies to use the httpOnly flag (prevents access to the session cookie value from JavaScript) and the secure flag (ensures the cookies are sent only over SSL), do the following:

```
<configuration>
    <!-- other configuration options -->

    <system.web>
        <httpCookies
            domain = "www.example.com"
            httpOnlyCookies = "true"
            requireSSL = "true"
            lockItem = "true"
        />
    </system.web>
</configuration>
```

---

[25] httpCookies Element [fsty.uk/b494] (.NET Framework 4 documentation, retrieved 3 July 2014)

---

The purpose of the lockItem attribute is to prevent other parts of the configuration from overriding the values configured here. Despite that, there is still a catch. If your configuration also contains the <forms> element (in other words, you are using forms authentication), you will need to ensure that the requireSSL attribute on <forms> is also set to true:

```
<forms
    requireSSL = "true"
    cookieless = "UseCookies"
    <!-- Your other attributes here. -->
/>
```

You will notice that I also configured the cookieless attribute to UseCookies. Forms authentication supports two modes of session token transport: the main approach is to use cookies, but there is also the URI-based method, which embeds session tokens in the page links. The URI-based method is interesting because it allows your application to work even for those users that do not support cookies. However, it comes with a significant security problem: because browsers embed URIs in the Referer request header as they follow links to external sites the session tokens may be exposed in other sites' logs. If an attacker can trick one of your users into following a link to a web site under the attacker's control, he will be able to hijack that user's session.

# Deploying HTTP Strict Transport Security

*HTTP Strict Transport Security* (HSTS) is a recent standard that allows web applications to request that browsers use only encrypted access for them. This fact alone makes HSTS work as a defense-in-depth measure, even in the face of application design errors (e.g., insecure session cookies). In addition, the handling of invalid certificates is improved so that end users can no longer override warning messages. Deploying HSTS is easy, but before you do it make sure to fully understand its advantages and disadvantages.

The following code example enables HSTS with a long-term maximum age of about one year (specified in seconds), active on the main hostname as well as all subdomains:

```
Response.AppendHeader(
    "Strict-Transport-Security",
    "max-age=31536000; includeSubDomains"
);
```

Alternatively, you could configure the header in configuration, using the following snippet:

```
<configuration>
    <!-- other configuration options -->

    <system.webServer>
        <httpProtocol>
```

```
            <customHeaders>
                <add name="Strict-Transport-Security"
                    value="max-age=31536000; includeSubDomains" />
            </customHeaders>
        </httpProtocol>
    </system.webServer>
</configuration>
```

The IIS Manager GUI also supports custom response headers. However, using any of these methods can be tricky, because the HSTS specification doesn't allow for sending the Strict-Transport-Security header on plaintext responses. The easiest and cleanest approach is to use a third-party module that will take care of all the details for you.[26]

# Internet Information Server

Internet Information Server (IIS) is the main web server used on Windows operating systems. It comes in several flavors (e.g., desktop and server versions), but the underlying code is usually the same in all cases. And of course, all flavors ultimately rely on Schannel for their SSL/TLS needs.

Because Schannel is a reasonably well-rounded TLS library, IIS also provides decent features in this area. The biggest practical problem comes from the fact that the IIS exposes no user interfaces to configure TLS but relies on the underlying Schannel configuration. Schannel, in turn, can be configured only by working with the registry directly, which can be difficult.

In the rest of this section, I will highlight some of the issues with running secure sites on the Internet Information Server.

**Forward secrecy**

With the IIS, you will be unable to provide robust support for forward secrecy, because Schannel doesn't support ephemeral Diffie-Hellman (DHE) key exchange in combination with RSA keys. The majority of clients support the faster ECDHE key exchange, but, according to Twitter, about 25% don't.[27]

In April 2014, Microsoft released an update that added two new DHE_RSA suites (used with 1,024-bit DH parameters) to Windows 8.1 and Server 2012 R2. However, these suites won't provide better support for forward secrecy, because they use GCM authenticated encryption that's not supported by older clients.

**GCM suites**

At the time of writing, authenticated GCM suites are the only suites thought to be completely secure. Even though the issues in other suites are largely mitigated, if you're keen to have the best possible security, GCM suites should be your priority.

---

[26] HTTP Strict Transport Security IIS Module [fsty.uk/b495] (CodePlex, retrieved 2 July 2014)
[27] Forward Secrecy at Twitter [fsty.uk/b496] (Twitter's Engineering Blog, 22 November 2013)

---

Schannel does support GCM suites, but largely in combination with ECDSA keys. At this point, virtually all sites use RSA keys, and only the adventurous experiment with ECDSA.

### OCSP stapling

Starting with Windows 2008, the IIS enables OCSP stapling by default. Because most other web servers require manual configuration, 96% of all stapled responses are currently served by Microsoft.[28] The only catch is that your IIS server needs to be able to communicate with the CAs that issued the certificates in order to obtain OCSP responses and cache them locally. If you have a very restrictive outbound traffic policy (firewall), such traffic might be blocked. To deal with this, you can either relax your firewall policy or use a forward proxy for the OCSP traffic.[29]

### Lack of per-site configuration

The IIS allows for only partial SSL/TLS configuration on per-site basis, which means that for things such as protocol support and cipher suite order you will be forced to find one configuration that suits all your sites. It shouldn't be a problem in practice, but it might prove to be constraining if you're hosting sites with special needs (e.g., FIPS).

# Managing Keys and Certificates

The IIS Manager comes with a GUI that supports basic key and certificate operations. It's sometimes unintuitive, but it gets the job done. My instructions and examples here will be for Windows Server 2012 and IIS 8, but the workflow with the earlier (IIS 7 and 7.5) and later (IIS 8.5) versions should be the same.

> **Note**
>
> The language used in the IIS user interface is not accurate. Most labels and action names refer to *certificates*, whereas you will almost always be managing *keys and certificates* at the same time. For simplicity, in this section I will use the IIS terminology.

## Creating a Custom IIS Management Console

Before you start to do any actual certificate work, I recommend that you create a custom Microsoft Management Console (MMC).

1. On the *Run* menu, type mmc to create an empty console.

---

[28] Microsoft Achieves World Domination (in OCSP Stapling) [fsty.uk/b497] (Netcraft's blog, 19 July 2013)

[29] OCSP Stapling in IIS [fsty.uk/b498] (Ryan Hurst's blog, 12 June 2012)

2. From the *File* menu, select *Add/Remove Snap-in*. A new window will appear; the left pane will contain the list of available snap-ins.

3. Add the *Certificates* snap-in. On the first screen, select *Computer account*; on the second, select *Local computer*.

4. Add the *Internet Information Server* snap-in.

5. Again from the *File* menu, select *Save* to save this console for later. If you save it to the desktop, your custom console will be only a double-click away when you need it.

Now you have a custom console that gives you access to the web site certificates as well as the IIS manager.

## IIS Certificate Management

To start managing IIS certificates, open the IIS Management Console and click on the server name. A new pane will open with many configuration options; one will be *Server Certificates*.

Figure 15.3. Server certificates in the IIS Management Console

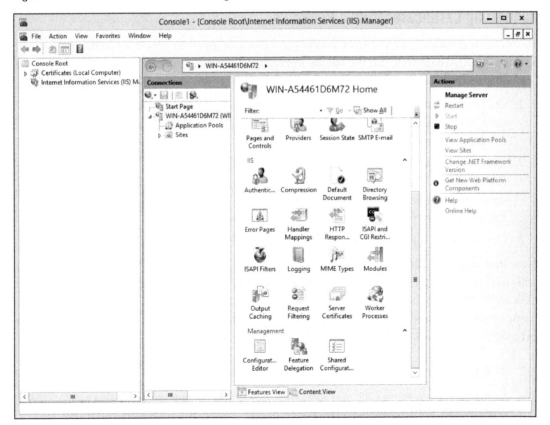

## Creating a Self-Signed Certificate

Creating self-signed certificates is trivial: simply select the *Create Self-Signed Certificate...* action from the right pane and provide a friendly name for it. You also have the ability to choose where the new certificate will go, to the *Personal* store or to the *Web Hosting* one. It's not clear what the difference is between the two, but I tend to choose the latter.

## Importing a Certificate

If you already have a certificate, you can import it using the *Import* action. The only supported format is PKCS#12, or PFX. If you are transitioning from a web server that uses different formats, you can use OpenSSL to convert the keys and certificates, as explained in the section called "Key and Certificate Conversion" in Chapter 11.

> ### Warning
> When you're importing the certificate, it's best to disable the *Allow this certificate to be exported* option. Doing that makes it more difficult to extract the key from the server. Of course, if you disable, make sure to have a backup of the key elsewhere.

## Requesting Certificates from a Public CA

To obtain a certificate signed by a public CA, you first need to create a *Certificate Signing Request* (CSR). To do this, use the *Create Certificate Request* action, which activates a wizard that consists of three steps:

1. On the first page, enter your information. Ensure that the information about your organization is accurate. You should use your web site's primary domain name for the *Common name* field.
2. On the second page, choose key type and strength. For the type, the default (*Microsoft RSA SChannel Cryptographic Provider*) is the only practical choice at the moment and needs no changing. For the strength, select 2,048 bits. (In my case, the default was 1,024, but that's weak and bordering on insecure.)
3. On the third page, specify the location of the CSR file.

Now that you have the CSR, you need to submit it to your selected CA. In most cases, you will need to open up the CSR file in a text editor and copy the contents into the form on the CA's web site. Once the CA verifies your right to hold a certificate in the requested domain name (a short and automated process for domain-validated certificates but a long one when extended validation is used), your certificate will be issued.

> ### Warning
> When you generate a CSR, you also create a private key that is stored on that computer and nowhere else. Because your certificate is not useful without the matching

key, you should ensure that both are safely kept in backup. It's best to create your keys and CSRs on the server on which they will be used, and export them for backup using the *Export* action.

## Completing Certificate Signing Requests

More often than not, your CA will send you several certificates, all of which are needed. The main one will be your site's certificate, but you will often need one or more intermediate certificates and, in some cases, even the root. If you get the certificates as a single file, importing will be easier. If you have them as separate files, you will need them to import them one by one, usually like this:

1. If the CA's root certificate is not already in your main trust store (called *Trusted Root Certification Authorities*), import it.

2. Import all the intermediary certificates to the *Intermediate Certification Authorities* store.

At this point, you can finally use the *Complete Certificate Request* action to import the site certificate and match it to the private key that's stored on your computer. If you've correctly configured the CA's root and intermediate certificates, this step will complete without a warning. Otherwise, the IIS will complain that it is unable to construct a complete trusted certificate chain.

> **Note**
>
> Completing CSRs sometimes fails with *Failed to Remove Certificate* or *Access Denied* error messages. When this happened to me, I discovered that the process actually completed successfully and that I was able to use my certificates despite the error messages.

## Configuring SSL Sites

Assuming you already have a certificate, to enable TLS on a web site you need to add *SSL bindings* to it. This translates to configuring the following:

- Protocol; always https
- IP address and port
- Hostname
- The correct setting for the *Require Server Name Indication* option (more about this in a minute)
- The desired SSL certificate

There are three ways in which you can configure secure web sites:

**One SSL site per IP address and port combination**

Traditionally, secure sites require a unique IP address and port combination. Because specifying ports is not practical for public services, this really means a unique IP address. This approach is straightforward for small hosting operations, but it requires that you procure a sufficient number of IP addresses.

**Certificate sharing**

Even though virtual secure hosting is not yet practical, it is possible to host more than one site on the same IP address, but only if you don't mind all of them using the same certificate. You can do this by obtaining a certificate that lists all the site names or by obtaining a wildcard certificate that supports an unlimited number of subdomains. (Or both, for that matter.) This option is fully supported in IIS 8; when configuring SSL bindings for a site, select the desired IP address and certificate and enter the correct hostname. You can repeat the process on as many web sites as you want. The SNI option should remain disabled.

Before version 8, the IIS user interface allowed only one secure site to be configured on the same IP address and port combination. However, it is still possible to achieve the same effect by making configuration changes directly from the command line and by using an asterisk as the first character in the certificate's friendly name.[30]

**Virtual secure hosting**

Because the support for virtual secure hosting was not available in TLS from the start, some older platforms still don't support it. And because one such older platform—Windows XP—remains quite popular, we must still continue to bind secure sites to IP addresses. Virtual secure hosting is supported by the IIS starting with version 8; you enable it by checking the *Require Server Name Indication* option. However, if you do, some of your users who are still using Internet Explorer on Windows XP might not be able to connect to your web site securely. If you are sure that you have no such users, SNI is safe to deploy today.

## Advanced Options

The instructions in this section are generally adequate for small deployments, such as when you have servers that are serving only a few sites, but they get increasingly difficult when you have to deal with complex architectures. If you fall into this category, there are some advanced options that you might want to consider:

**Centralized SSL certificates for web server clusters**

Starting with IIS 8.0, web server cluster management is much easier because it is possible to store keys and certificates in a single location on a file share.[31]

---

[30] SSL Host Headers in IIS 7 [fsty.uk/b499] (SSL Shopper, 26 February 2009)

**Active Directory integration with a public CA**

Public CAs have recently developed products that simulate a private CA but fulfill requests using their own (public) infrastructure. With this approach, many tasks (e.g., certificate renewal) are simplified and automated. The advantage of this approach is that you control certificate issuance via Active Directory policies, yet they are still backed up with a public CA.

---

31 IIS 8.0 Centralized SSL Certificate Support: SSL Scalability and Manageability [fsty.uk/b500] (IIS.Net, 29 February 2012)

# 16 Configuring Nginx

Nginx is a web server and reverse proxy that's become very popular because of its efficiency and frugal use of system resources. Nginx generally has good TLS support in the current stable branch (1.6.x), which means that you shouldn't experience any problems in this area. Because Nginx is a relatively young project, features are added at a fast pace. If you're an advanced user, I recommend that you keep an eye on the improvements in the development branch.

Table 16.1. Nginx TLS features across recent stable and development versions

| Feature | 1.4.x | 1.6.x | 1.7.x (development) |
| --- | --- | --- | --- |
| Strong default DH parameters | Barely; 1,024 bits | Barely; 1,024 bits | Barely; 1,024 bits |
| Configurable DH and ECDH parameters | Yes | Yes | Yes |
| Elliptic curve (EC) support | Yes | Yes | Yes |
| OCSP stapling | Yes | Yes | Yes |
| Distributed TLS session caching | - | - | - |
| Configurable session ticket keys | - | Yes | Yes |
| Disable session ticket keys | - | Yes | Yes |
| Backend certificate validation | - | - | Yes |

The stable version provides everything you need to deploy a well-configured standalone TLS server. The strength of ephemeral DH parameters (1,024 bits) is perhaps weaker than it should be, but that can be addressed in the configuration. One thing to watch is that this version doesn't perform backend certificate validation when Nginx operates as a reverse proxy. This might not be a problem when the backend is local (e.g., on the same network), but it's definitely insecure with backend servers that are reached over public networks.

This chapter is designed to cover the most important and interesting aspects of Nginx's TLS configuration, but it's not a reference guide. For other information, please refer to the official documentation.

# Installing Nginx with Static OpenSSL

Unless told differently, Nginx will detect and use system OpenSSL libraries during installation, linking to them dynamically. Sometimes you don't want to use the system libraries, however. For example, they could be an older version and missing some essential features.

It's possible to compile Nginx statically against any compatible OpenSSL version. To do this, when configuring Nginx for compilation, use the `--with-openssl` parameter to point to the OpenSSL *source code*:

```
$ ./configure \
--prefix=/opt/nginx \
--with-openssl=../openssl-1.0.1h \
--with-openssl-opt="enable-ec_nistp_64_gcc_128" \
--with-http_ssl_module
```

Unlike some other programs, which compile against an OpenSSL installation, Nginx wants access to the source code so that it can configure and compile OpenSSL itself. This creates a level of indirection, because you don't configure OpenSSL yourself. If you do need to pass a configuration parameter to OpenSSL, use the `--with-openssl-opt` Nginx parameter (as in my example, in which I activated EC optimizations that are disabled by default).

# Enabling TLS

To enable TLS, you need to tell Nginx that you want to use a different protocol on the desired port. You do this with the `ssl` parameter to the `listen` directive:

```
server {
    listen 192.168.0.1:443 ssl;
    server_name www.example.com;
    ...
}
```

Another parameter that you might want to use here is spdy, which enables the SPDY protocol.[1] To enable TLS and SPDY at the same time, do something like this:

```
server {
    listen 192.168.0.1:443 ssl spdy;
    server_name www.example.com;
    ...
}
```

---

[1] SPDY is not compiled-in by default. You have to use the `--with-http_spdy_module` configuration parameter to enable it.

---

Chapter 16: Configuring Nginx

# Configuring TLS Protocol

Once you enable TLS, you need to tweak the protocol configuration. I don't believe in using default settings; they change over time and you end up not knowing exactly what your servers are doing. For protocol configuration, there are three directives that you should use. The first is ssl_protocols, which specifies which protocols should be enabled:

```
# Enable all protocols except SSL 2 and
# SSL 3, which are obsolete and insecure.
ssl_protocols TLSv1 TLSv1.1 TLSv1.2;
```

The second is ssl_prefer_server_ciphers, which tells Nginx that we want the server to select the best cipher suite during TLS handshake instead of letting clients do it:

```
# Have the server decide what suites to use.
ssl_prefer_server_ciphers on;
```

Finally, ssl_ciphers controls which suites are going to be enabled and in which order; it takes an OpenSSL suite-configuration string. For example:

```
# This cipher suite configuration uses only suites that provide
# forward security, in the order that provides the best performance.
ssl_ciphers "ECDHE-ECDSA-AES128-GCM-SHA256 ECDHE-ECDSA-AES256-GCM-SHA384 ↵
ECDHE-ECDSA-AES128-SHA ECDHE-ECDSA-AES256-SHA ECDHE-ECDSA-AES128-SHA256 ↵
ECDHE-ECDSA-AES256-SHA384 ECDHE-RSA-AES128-GCM-SHA256 ECDHE-RSA-AES256-GCM-SHA384 ↵
ECDHE-RSA-AES128-SHA ECDHE-RSA-AES256-SHA ECDHE-RSA-AES128-SHA256 ↵
ECDHE-RSA-AES256-SHA384 DHE-RSA-AES128-GCM-SHA256 DHE-RSA-AES256-GCM-SHA384 ↵
DHE-RSA-AES128-SHA DHE-RSA-AES256-SHA DHE-RSA-AES128-SHA256 DHE-RSA-AES256-SHA256 ↵
EDH-RSA-DES-CBC3-SHA";
```

> ### Note
>
> The cipher suite configuration from this example is secure, but depending on your preferences and risk profile you might prefer something slightly different. You'll find a thorough discussion of TLS server configuration in Chapter 8, *Deployment* and examples for OpenSSL in the section called "Recommended Configuration" in Chapter 11.

# Configuring Keys and Certificates

The final step in configuring a secure server is to specify the desired private key and certificates, for which you need two directives:

```
# Server private key.
ssl_certificate_key server.key;
```

```
# Certificates; server certificate first, followed by all
# required intermediate certificates, but excluding the root.
ssl_certificate server.crt;
```

Nginx uses one directive for certificate configuration. If you have the server certificate and the intermediate certificates as separate files, you'll need to make a single file out of them. Just make sure you put the server certificate first; otherwise you will get a configuration error. Of course, you also need to ensure that all intermediate certificates are correctly ordered; not doing so might lead to subtle interoperability issues that are difficult to troubleshoot.[2]

> **Note**
>
> Although Nginx supports password-protected private keys, the only input mechanism it supports is interactive, on server startup. For this reason, the only practical approach in production is to configure a private key without a passphrase, which is not ideal. However, version 1.7.3 (in the development branch at the time of writing) added a new directive, ssl_password_file, which can be used to supply the password for encrypted keys.

## Configuring Multiple Keys

Nginx does not currently allow sites to have more than one private key. There had been some work done on this feature in November 2013, so we might see it in a future release.[3]

## Wildcard and Multisite Certificates

If you have two or more sites that share a certificate, it is possible to deploy them on the same IP address despite the fact that virtual secure hosting is not yet feasible for public web sites. No special configuration is required; just associate all such sites with the same IP address and ensure that they are all using the same certificate.[4]

This works because TLS termination and HTTP host selection are two separate processing steps. When terminating TLS, Nginx serves the certificate of the default server (the server that appears first in the configuration) for that IP address. When processing HTTP, Nginx examines the Host request header and looks for the correct site based on the server_name configuration. If the requested hostname cannot be found, the default web site is used.

---

[2] The ssl_certificate directive also allows the server private key to be included in the same file. However, storing private and public data in the same file is dangerous because it could lead to accidental disclosures of the keys.

[3] [PATCH] RSA+DSA+ECC bundles [fsty.uk/b501] (Rob Stradling, 17 October 2013)

[4] Technically, the restrictions are per IP address and port combination (a TCP/IP endpoint). You could, for example, host one secure site on 192.168.0.1:443 and another on 192.168.0.1:8443. In practice, public sites can be hosted only on port 443, so the restrictions are effectively per IP address.

The best approach when reusing certificates is to place them in the `http` scope so that the configuration is inherited by the servers that follow:

```
# Configure one key and certificates for all subsequent servers.
ssl_certificate     server.crt;
ssl_certificate_key server.key;

# site1.example.com
server {
    listen          443 ssl;
    server_name     site1.example.com;
    ...
}

# site2.example.com
server {
    listen          443 ssl;
    server_name     site2.example.org;
    ...
}
```

This approach simplifies maintenance and keeps only one copy of the certificate and key information in memory.

## Virtual Secure Hosting

Unlike the setup discussed in the previous section, true virtual secure hosting takes place when multiple unrelated web sites, each with its own certificate, share one IP address. Because this feature was not in the SSL and TLS protocols at the beginning, there are still many older clients that do not support it. For this reason, it is not yet feasible to use virtual secure hosting for public web sites that are targeted at a wide general audience, but it could possibly be used for sites whose users have access to modern browsers.

Nginx supports virtual secure hosting and uses it automatically when needed. The only question is: what happens if you *do* deploy with virtual secure hosting but then encounter a client that does not support this feature? Normally, Nginx will serve the certificate belonging to the default site associated with the requested IP address. Because that certificate is unlikely to match the desired hostname, the user will receive a certificate warning. However, if they are able to bypass the warning, they will get through to the site they wanted to see.[5]

---

[5] Assuming, of course, that the requested hostname exists as a virtual site at the HTTP level. If it doesn't, they will get the default web site.

# Reserving Default Sites for Error Messages

It is never a good idea to deliver web site content in response to an incorrectly specified request. For example, you don't want a search engine to index a web site under an incorrect hostname. More importantly, lax checking of hostnames can lead to security issues from one site being transferred to other sites. To avoid this, I suggest that you always deploy default sites to deliver error messages and nothing else.

Here's an example configuration you could use:

```
# This default web site will be used to deliver error
# messages to those clients that request a hostname
# we don't have a site for.
server {
    listen 443 ssl default_server;

    # There is no need to specify server_name, because we
    # never actually want it to match. We want this site
    # to be delivered when the correct site cannot be found.
    # server_name "";

    root /path/to/site/root;

    location / {
        return 404;
    }

    location /404.html {
        internal;
    }

    error_page 404 /404.html;
}
```

With this configuration, users who request a hostname that isn't configured on your server will see the contents of 404.html. In most cases, they will need to click through a certificate warning first, although it's possible that a server has a valid certificate for a name but doesn't have a virtual host for it. This is a potential issue with wildcard certificates, for example.

At the time of writing, Nginx doesn't support strict SNI checking that could detect a user that doesn't support SNI and refuse to serve the host specified at the HTTP level, even if the hostname is correct. Because all non-SNI users have to click through certificate warnings, this feature would be very useful to inform such users why they're experiencing problems.[6]

---

# Forward Secrecy

You won't have any trouble configuring robust forward secrecy with Nginx, given that it has had full support for the necessary key exchanges (DHE and ECDHE) since version 1.1.0, which was released in August 2011. The only thing to watch for is the support for EC cryptography in OpenSSL; not all versions have it, for two reasons:

**Older OpenSSL version**

If the underlying OpenSSL installation does not support newer features (such as EC crypto), then it does not matter that Nginx does. Older versions of OpenSSL are still prevalent on older installations, and even some newer operating system releases use it. For example, OS X Mavericks, released in November 2013, ships with OpenSSL 0.9.8y (that's the most recent version from the old 0.9.x branch). For EC cryptography you need version 1.0.1 or newer.

**OpenSSL version without EC support**

For a long time, operating systems built by Red Hat used to ship without support for EC cryptography, because their lawyers wanted to play it safe when it came to certain EC patents. This made it very difficult for anyone using Fedora and Red Hat Enterprise Linux distributions (and the derivatives) to deploy forward secrecy. The only way to do it well had been to recompile OpenSSL and all the packages that depend on it.

This changed in October 2013, when Fedora 18 and later versions were updated with OpenSSL packages that do have EC crypto enabled.[7] In November 2013, Red Hat Enterprise Linux 6.5 shipped with EC crypto enabled.[8]

# OCSP Stapling

Nginx supports OCSP stapling starting with the 1.4.x branch. At this time, Nginx treats this feature as an optimization, and this approach is reflected in the implementation. For example, Nginx does not prefetch OCSP responses on startup. Instead, it waits for the first connection and only then initiates its own OCSP request. As a result, the first connection is never going to have an OCSP response stapled. Further, OCSP responses are not shared among all worker processes, which means that each worker needs to obtain an OCSP response before the entire server is fully primed.

---

[6] That said, version 1.7.0 introduced a new variable called $ssl_server_name, which contains the SNI hostname when one is provided. This variable would be empty for a user that doesn't support SNI. You can detect this in the virtual host configuration and respond with a different error message. The only catch is that you'd have to include the check in the configuration of each virtual host.

[7] Bug #319901: missing ec and ecparam commands in openssl package [fsty.uk/b445] (Red Hat Bugzilla, closed 22 October 2013)

[8] Red Hat Enterprise Linux 6.5 Release Notes [fsty.uk/b446] (Red Hat, 21 November 2013)

---

In practice, because obtaining OCSP responses from the responders takes some time it is reasonable to assume that there will be a period immediately after server startup during which OCSP stapling will not be fully operational. The busier your server, the shorter this period will be.

The delay will not create problems in practice, because OCSP stapling is not mandatory; browsers will use a stapled response when one is provided, but will obtain their own otherwise. If you really want OCSP responses to be used on every connection, it is possible to provide them to Nginx manually. I discuss this feature later in this section.

> ### Warning
>
> Due to a bug,[9] Nginx might sometimes send expired OCSP responses. It appears that the OCSP response refresh process is triggered only by the internal response timeout (one hour), but not by the cached response's expiration time (set by the CA). Thus, if the server ever receives an OCSP response that expires in less than one hour, there will potentially be a period during which invalid responses will be served.

## Configuring OCSP Stapling

To use OCSP stapling, you just need to tell Nginx that you want to use it:

```
# Enable OCSP stapling.
ssl_stapling on;

# Configure a DNS resolver so that Nginx can convert
# domain names into IP addresses.
resolver 127.0.0.1;
```

> ### Note
>
> OCSP requests are submitted over HTTP, which means that your web server needs to be able to make outbound requests to various OCSP responders across the Internet. If you're operating an outbound firewall, ensure that there are exceptions to allow this type of traffic.

I recommend that you also enable OCSP response verification, which is disabled by default. This requires a bit more work to configure trusted certificates, but you can then be sure that only valid responses are served to your users:

```
# Verify responses before consdering them for stapling.
ssl_stapling_verify on;
```

---

[9] ocsp stapling may send expired response [fsty.uk/b502] (Nginx bug #425, retrieved 10 July 2014)

---

```
# OCSP response validation requires that the complete
# certificate chain is available. Provide here all intermediate
# certificates including the root, which is normally not
# included when configuring server certificates.
ssl_trusted_certificate trusted-for-ocsp.pem;
```

Notably absent from the OCSP stapling configuration are directives for cache configuration and various timeouts. The cache does not need to be configured because OCSP responses are not shared among workers; every worker has its own memory cache that grows as needed. As for timeouts, Nginx relies on hardcoded values: valid responses are cached for one hour, and errors are cached for five minutes. Networking timeouts are set to 60 seconds.[10]

## Using a Custom OCSP Responder

Normally, OCSP requests are submitted to the OCSP responder hardcoded in each certificate. However, there are two cases in which you might want to use a different responder:

- In a heavily locked-down environment, direct outbound traffic from the web server might not be allowed at all. In this case, if you want to support OCSP stapling, you will need to configure a forward proxy for OCSP requests.

- Some certificates might not actually contain OCSP responder information even though the issuing CA operates one. In this case, you can provide the OCSP responder URI manually.

You can override the OCSP responder information globally or on per-site basis, using the ssl_stapling_responder directive:

```
# Use a forward proxy for OCSP requests originating from this server.
ssl_stapling_responder http://ocsp.example.com;
```

> **Note**
>
> Nginx supports only plain-text HTTP OCSP responders at this time. Large parts of OCSP provide integrity protection, and most CAs seem to run their OCSP responders without encryption. I have seen CAs use TLS for their responders, however. It's best to check with your CA before you request a certificate from them.

## Manual Configuration of OCSP Responses

If you want reliable and consistent OCSP stapling for all secure connections, you'll have to manually handle OCSP response fetching and refreshing, leaving Nginx only to deliver them to clients.

---

[10] OCSP stapling patches [fsty.uk/b503] (Maxim Dounin, 5 September 2012)

---

For the Nginx part of the setup, use the `ssl_stapling_file` directive to specify a file that contains an OCSP response in DER format:

```
# Tell Nginx that it should not try to fetch
# OCSP responses; we will handle that ourselves.
ssl_stapling_file ocsp-response_www.example.com.der;
```

The simplest way to obtain an OCSP response is to use the OpenSSL command-line tools. Before you begin, you will need both the server certificate and the issuing CA's certificate. The issuing certificate should be among your intermediate certificates. It is also possible that the issuing certificate is a root (but that's getting increasingly rare these days), in which case you should obtain it directly from the CA.

Your next task will be to find the address of the OCSP responder. You can do this by examining the *Authority Information Access* (AIA) extension in the server certificate. For example:

```
$ openssl x509 -in server.crt -noout -ocsp_uri
http://rapidssl-ocsp.geotrust.com
```

With the URL and the two certificates, you can submit an OCSP request to the responder:

```
$ openssl ocsp -issuer issuer.crt -cert server.crt -url http://rapidssl-ocsp.geotru↩
st.com -noverify -respout ocsp-response_www.example.com.der
server.crt: good
    This Update: Jan 10 08:15:33 2014 GMT
    Next Update: Jan 17 08:15:33 2014 GMT
```

> **Note**
>
> Obtaining OCSP responses manually works without problems most of the time, but it can sometimes get messy because of edge cases. You will find more information about the possible issues in the section called "Checking OCSP Revocation" in Chapter 12.

You should now have a valid OCSP response in the designated file. Although this approach is good enough for a proof of concept, for deployment in production you will need to handle error cases and run continuously in order to keep all OCSP responses fresh. Reload Nginx whenever one of the files changes.

## Configuring Ephemeral DH Key Exchange

When it comes to the strength of the *Diffie-Hellman* (DH) key exchange, Nginx normally delegates all the work to OpenSSL. That will give you 1,024 bits of security, which is on the weak side, but not yet critically weak.

Fortunately, it's easy to tune the strength of the DH key exchange. Just use the `ssl_dhparam` directive and provide the name of the file containing stronger parameters:

```
# Use stronger DH parameters rather than the default 1024 bits.
ssl_dhparam dh-2048.pem;
```

Use the following OpenSSL command to generate the parameter file:

```
$ openssl dhparam -out dh-2048.pem 2048
```

Increasing DH parameter strength might negatively reflect on interoperability with some clients. For example, Java 6 and Java 7 don't support DH parameters stronger than 1,024 bits. Anything over that means that they might not be able to connect. In practice, Java 7 clients should be able to connect if you ensure that you always offer ECDHE suites first. For Java 6 clients, there is no workaround.

> **Tip**
>
> From the security point of view, you should choose the strength of DH parameters to match the strength of the private key used by the server. In practice, most sites use 2,048-bit private keys, which means that a 2,048-bit DH key exchange is going to be adequate for virtually everyone. Using stronger DH parameters is not recommended, as they significantly slow down the TLS handshake.

# Configuring Ephemeral ECDH Key Exchange

The default strength of the ephemeral ECDHE key exchange is 256 EC bits, using the `secp256r1` curve (OpenSSL prefers to call it `prime256v1`). That is sufficiently strong (equivalent to a 3,072-bit RSA key), and you probably won't need to change it. If you do want to change it, use the `ssl_ecdh_curve` directive:

```
# Use a stronger curve to give us 192 bits of
# security (equivalent to a 7680-bit RSA key).
ssl_ecdh_curve secp384r1;
```

At this time, there is little choice when it comes to curve selection. Even though OpenSSL and some other platforms might support a number of curves (for OpenSSL, you can obtain the complete list with `openssl ecparam -list_curves`), only `secp256r1` and `secp384r1` are widely supported by browsers at this time. You should know that `secp256r1` is currently optimized to run fast in OpenSSL, whereas `secp384r1` isn't.

# TLS Session Management

Nginx provides good support for TLS session resumption on standalone servers, supporting both server-side state caching and session tickets. But although there is support for distributed session tickets, distributed server session caching isn't supported.

## Standalone Session Cache

For standalone server deployments (which typically operate multiple workers), you should configure a shared memory cache so that TLS session information is shared among all the processes. The default for Nginx is to operate without a TLS session cache, which results in less than optimal performance.

To configure a cache, you need to allocate a certain amount of RAM to it and specify the maximum duration of a single session:

```
# Configure a shared memory cache of 1 MB.
ssl_session_cache shared:ssl_session_cache:1M;

# Expire individual sessions after 24 hours.
ssl_session_timeout 1440m;
```

It's difficult to recommend one default configuration that will work for everyone, but the values I used in this example will satisfy most sites. The 1 MB of RAM should accommodate about 4,000 sessions.

The default session timeout is only five minutes, which is too short. I used 24 hours instead. There is generally little reason to limit the session timeout, because you want to ensure that your cache runs at maximum capacity. If it runs out of space, the oldest session will be evicted to make room for a new one. That said, values over 24 hours are not recommended for security reasons.

Nginx provides a lot of flexibility for the cache configuration. For example, it's possible to have a hierarchy of caches within the same site. It's also possible to have many sites use the same cache. For best security, each site should be configured with its own session cache. Session cache sharing is safe only among sites that are logically part of the same application and share the certificate.

## Standalone Session Tickets

By default, session tickets are handled by OpenSSL, and no Nginx configuration is necessary. For standalone servers, this approach tends to "just work," although there are some aspects of it that you should be aware of:

- Session tickets are protected using 128-bit AES encryption. A throwaway key is generated when the web server is initially started. Depending on the server configuration, multiple ticket keys might be in use.

- The key size is fixed, but 128 bits is sufficiently strong for most use cases.

- A new private key is generated every time the server is restarted. This means that all connections that arrive after the restart will have to negotiate new TLS sessions. There will be a performance penalty, but it's unlikely to be noticeable.

- There is no key rotation between restarts, which means that you can potentially have the same AES key in use for a very long time. This is not recommended,[11] which is why you should ensure that your servers are regularly restarted: for example, daily.

When it comes to session ticket security, for best results allocate a different ticket key to each site.

## Distributed Session Cache

Distributed session caching is currently not supported. In 2011, a patch for Nginx 0.8.x was released to add this functionality,[12] but there are no patches for modern versions. Furthermore, according to one of the Nginx developers,[13] the patch operates in blocking mode, which breaks the event-based model on which Nginx is built. In practice, this means that a lookup in the network cache can suspend all processing of an entire Nginx process (affecting all ongoing requests), which translates to a serious performance penalty.

Because Nginx does not support distributed session caching, your cluster design options are limited; you cannot deploy a cluster in which new connections are freely distributed among the nodes. Instead, you have to design a sticky mode in which clients are always forwarded to the same node.[14] Then, on that node you can operate a standalone, shared memory cache.

## Distributed Session Tickets

Starting with version 1.5.7, Nginx supports manually configured session ticket keys. With this feature, you can implement your own rotation scheme on a single server or, more interestingly, share the same ticket in a web server cluster.

---

[11] With session tickets, the AES key is used to encrypt all session data (which includes the master secret, which can be used to decrypt all communication), after which that information is sent over the network to the client. This approach makes the AES key a new attack point. It also defeats forward secrecy, if the AES key is compromised.

[12] SSL Session Caching (in nginx) [fsty.uk/b504] (Matt Palmer, 28 June 2011)

[13] Re: Distributed SSL session cache [fsty.uk/b505] (Maxim Dounin, 16 September 2013)

[14] This is typically done by a load balancer, which remembers the origin of each session ID and directs subsequent visits belonging to the same ID to the same web server node.

The relevant directive is ssl_session_ticket_key, which you use to specify the ticket key:

```
# Explicit configuration of the session ticket key.
ssl_session_ticket_key ticket.key;
```

A session ticket key file consists of 48 bytes of cryptographically random data. The data is used for three 16-byte (128-bit) fragments, one each for key name, HMAC secret, and AES key. This isn't the same format as used by OpenSSL, which means that the keys probably can't be shared with other web servers.[15]

Use the following OpenSSL command to generate a new key file:

```
$ openssl rand -out ticket.key 48
```

In practice, you will need at least two keys in your configuration: your main key to generate new tickets and the previous key, kept around to use for decryption only:

```
# Specify the active session ticket key, which will
# be used for both encryption and decryption.
ssl_session_ticket_key current-ticket.key;

# Keep the previous key around so that we can
# resume the sessions protected by it.
ssl_session_ticket_key previous-ticket.key;
```

With the two-key setup, no tickets will be dropped because of key rotation.

Rotating session ticket keys in a cluster can be difficult to do reliably, because it requires that a new key is introduced simultaneously to all nodes. If one node uses a new key before others, other nodes will not be able to decrypt its tickets, forcing a full handshake. But this is probably not going to be an issue, unless you're reloading your keys *very* frequently. Furthermore, many clusters are configured to send the same client to the same node, which means that this scenario is unlikely to happen.

Still, if you want to implement session ticket keys rotation absolutely right and don't mind reconfiguring the cluster two times, here's what you can do:

1. Generate a new session ticket key.

2. Introduce the new key to the configuration as a decryption-only key and reconfigure the cluster. With this step, you've prepared all your nodes for decryption.

3. Change the configuration another time, promoting the key from the previous step to be your active key. Move the previously active key to be your decryption key. Then reconfigure the cluster again. Because all nodes have the new active key in the previous configuration, session resumption will work irrespective of any timing issues.

---

[15] NGINX SSL Session Ticket Key [fsty.uk/b506] (ZNV, 25 February 2014)

## Disabling Session Tickets

Starting with version 1.5.9, Nginx allows session tickets to be disabled. This could be useful if you're running a cluster of servers but don't want to set up a distributed ticket key:

```
# Disable session tickets.
ssl_session_tickets off;
```

If you're running an earlier Nginx version, a patch for this feature can be obtained from the development list archives.[16]

# Client Authentication

Using client authentication requires enabling it in configuration, providing all the CA certificates needed to form a complete certification path, and pointing Nginx to a certificate revocation list. Here's a complete example:

```
# Require client authentication.
ssl_verify_client on;

# Specify the maximum depth of the certification path,
# from the client certificate to a trusted root.
ssl_verify_depth 2;

# Allowed CAs that issue client certificates. The
# distinguished names of these certificates will be sent
# to each user to assist with client certificate selection.
ssl_client_certificate sub-ca.crt;

# Additional CA certificates that are needed to
# build a complete certification path.
ssl_trusted_certificate root-ca.crt;

# The list of revoked certificates. A reload is required
# every time this list is changed.
ssl_crl revoked-certificates.crl
```

With these changes, Nginx will accept only requests accompanied by a valid client certificate. If a certificate is not provided or if the validation fails, it will send with a 400 response instead.

In addition to enabling strict client authentication, there are also two further settings for ssl_verify_client that are useful in some situations:

---

[16] [PATCH] SSL: ssl_session_tickets directive [fsty.uk/b507] (Dirkjan Bussink, 10 January 2014)

---

**optional**

> Requests a client certificate during TLS handshake but doesn't require it. The status of the validation is stored in the $ssl_client_verify variable: NONE for no certificate, FAILED for a certificate that failed validation, and SUCCESS for a valid certificate. This feature is useful if you want to provide a custom response to those users who fail client certificate validation.

**optional_no_ca**

> Requests a client certificate during TLS handshake but doesn't attempt validation. Instead, it's expected that an external service will validate the certificate (which is available in the $ssl_client_cert variable).

> **Note**
>
> Using optional client authentication can be problematic, because some browsers don't prompt the user or otherwise select a client certificate if this option is configured. There are also issues with some browsers that won't proceed to the site if they can't provide a certificate. Before you seriously consider optional client authentication for deployment, test with the browsers you have in your environment.

# Mitigating Protocol Issues

Nginx users have little to worry about when it comes to SSL and TLS protocol issues. They have been as quickly addressed as they have arisen, in one case even before the public announcement.

## Insecure Renegotiation

Insecure renegotiation is a protocol flaw discovered in November 2009 and largely mitigated during 2010. Nginx addressed this issue in version 0.8.23, which was released within a week of discovery. Since then, client-initiated renegotiation is not accepted.

Additionally, Nginx does not use server-initiated renegotiation. This feature is typically used when the same site operates multiple security context. For example, you might allow anyone to visit the home page of your web site but require client certificates at a deeper level. Nginx supports client certificates, but only at the server level (no subfolder configuration), which means that renegotiation is unnecessary. Technically, Nginx supports secure renegotiation when compiled against a capable version of OpenSSL, but renegotiation will never take place.

## BEAST

Technically, the predictable IV vulnerability in TLS 1.0 and earlier protocols affects both client and server sides of the communication. In practice, only browsers are vulnerable (the so-called BEAST attack), because exploitation requires that the attacker is able to control what data is sent (and subsequently encrypted) by the victim. For this reason, there is nothing for server code to do about it.

## CRIME

The 2012 CRIME attack exploits information leakage that occurs when compression is used at the TLS protocol level.[17] No work has been done to address this issue and keep compression in the protocol. Instead, the advice is to disable compression altogether. For performance reasons, Nginx developers started to disable compression in 2011, but the initial changes (in versions 1.0.9 and 1.1.6) covered only OpenSSL 1.0.0 and better. Nginx disabled compression with all OpenSSL versions during 2012, in versions 1.2.2 and 1.3.2.[18]

# Deploying HTTP Strict Transport Security

Because *HTTP Strict Transport Security* (HSTS) is activated via a response header, configuring it on a site is generally easy. However, there are certain traps you can fall into, which is why I recommend that you read the section called "HTTP Strict Transport Security " in Chapter 10 before you make any decisions.

Once HSTS is deployed on a web site, your users will arrive on port 443 on their subsequent visits. But you still have to ensure that those who arrive on port 80 get redirected to the right place. For that redirection, and because the HSTS response header is not allowed on plaintext sites,[19] you should have two different servers in the configuration. For example:

```
server {
    listen 192.168.0.1:80;
    server_name www.example.com;

    return 301 https://www.example.com$request_uri;

    ...
}

server {
    listen 192.168.0.1:443 ssl;
    server_name www.example.com;

    add_header Strict-Transport-Security "max-age=31536000; includeSubDomains";
```

---

[17] TLS is not the only affected protocol; information leakage depends on how compression is implemented and might exist at other networking layers. For example, HTTP response compression using the gzip algorithm is also vulnerable.

[18] crime tls attack [fsty.uk/b508] (Igor Sysoev, 26 September 2012)

[19] If this were allowed, a man-in-the-middle attacker could inject HSTS information into plaintext-only sites and perform a DoS attack.

```
    ...
}
```

There are two Nginx add_header behaviors that you need to watch for. First, headers are added only to responses with non-error-status codes (e.g., from the 2xx and 3xx range). This shouldn't be a problem for HSTS, because most of your responses should be in the correct range. Second, the configuration directive inheritance behavior is sometimes surprising: if a child configuration block specifies add_header, then no directives of this type are inherited from the parent block. In other words, if you need to add a header in a child block, make sure to explicitly copy all add_header directives from the parent block.

## Tuning TLS Buffers

Starting with version 1.5.9, Nginx allows you to configure the size of the TLS buffer using the ssl_buffer_size directive. The default value for the buffer is 16 KB, but that might not be optimal if you want to deliver the first content byte as fast as possible. Using a value of 1,400 bytes is reported to substantially reduce the latency.[20]

```
# Reduce the size of the TLS buffer, which will result
# in substantially reduced time to first byte.
ssl_buffer_size 1400;
```

You should be aware, however, that reducing the size of TLS records might reduce the connection throughput, especially if you're transmitting large amounts of data.[21]

## Logging

Default web server logging mechanisms care only about errors and what content is being accessed and thus don't tell you much about your TLS usage. There are two main reasons why you might want to keep an eye on your TLS operations:

**Performance**

Incorrectly configured TLS session resumption can incur a substantial performance penalty, which is why you will want to keep an eye on the session-resumption hit ratio. Having a log file for this purpose is useful to ensure that your server does resume TLS sessions and also to assist you with the tuning of the cache.

Starting with version 1.5.10, Nginx supports the $ssl_session_reused variable, which allows you to track session reuse directly. If you are using an earlier version, you'll have to rely on log postprocessing to count the number of times the same session ID

---

[20] Optimizing NGINX TLS Time To First Byte (TTTFB) [fsty.uk/b509] (Ilya Grigorik, 16 December 2013)

[21] Optimizing NGINX TLS Time To First Byte (TTTFB) [fsty.uk/b510] (Discussion on the Nginx development list, 16 December 2013)

appears in the logs. From that, you can get a decent idea about the performance of your TLS session cache.

**Protocol and cipher suite usage**

Knowing what protocol versions and cipher suites are actually used by your user base is important, for two reasons: (1) you want to be sure that your assumptions about your configuration are correct and (2) you need to know if some older features are still required. For example, SSL 2 remained widely supported over many years because people were afraid to turn it off. We are now facing similar problems with the SSL 3 protocol and the RC4 and 3DES ciphers.

It is best to use a separate log file for TLS connection information. In Nginx, this means using two directives, one to define a new log format and another to generate the log files:

```
# Create a new log format for TLS-specific logging. The variable
# $ssl_session_reused is available only from v1.5.10 onwards.
log_format ssl "$time_local $server_name $remote_addr $connection $connection↵
_requests $ssl_protocol $ssl_cipher $ssl_session_id $ssl_session_reused";

# Log TLS connection information.
access_log /path/to/ssl.log ssl;
```

> **Warning**
>
> Due to a bug in Nginx versions before versions 1.4.5 and 1.5.9, the $ssl_session_id variable did not contain TLS session IDs. If you want to deploy this type of TLS logging, you'll need to upgrade to a newer release.

This type of log will create one entry for every HTTP transaction processed. In a sense, it's wasteful because the TLS parameters are determined only once, at the beginning of a connection (Nginx does not allow renegotiation, which would potentially change the parameters). On the other hand, connection reuse is the most efficient mode of operation, and you should be able to track it in the logs. For this reason, I added $connection and $connection_requests variables to the log format.

> **Note**
>
> There is currently no way to log connections with successful TLS handshakes but without any requests. Similarly, it is not possible to log TLS handshake failures.

# 17 Summary

Congratulations on making it all the way through this book! I hope you've had as much fun reading it as I did writing it. But with so many pages dedicated to the security of TLS, where are we now? Is TLS secure? Or is it irreparably broken and doomed?

As with many other questions, the answer is that it depends on what you expect. It's easy to poke holes in TLS by comparing it with an imaginary alternative that doesn't exist; and it's true, TLS has had many holes, which we've been repairing over the years. However, the success of a security protocol is measured not only in pure technical and security terms but also by its practical success and usefulness in real life. So, although it's certainly not perfect, TLS has been a great success for the billions of people who use it every day. If anything, the biggest problems in the TLS ecosystem come from the fact that we're not using enough encryption and that, when we do, we haven't quite made up our minds if we really want proper security. (Think about certificate warnings.) The weaknesses in TLS are not our biggest problem.

Therefore, we're discussing the security of TLS because it's been so successful. Otherwise, we would have long ago replaced it with something better. However, chances are that even if we replaced TLS with something else, years of steady use would have led us to the same situation we have now. I've come to realize that you can't have perfect security at world scale. The world, with its diversity, moves slowly and prefers avoiding breakage to enhanced security. And you know what? That's fine. It's the cost of participating in a global computer network.

The good news is that TLS is improving at a good pace. At some point a couple of years ago, we started to care about security, especially encryption. This process accelerated during 2013, when we started to accept the harsh realities of mass surveillance. The TLS working group is busy working on the next protocol version; it's not going to be fundamentally different, because it doesn't have to be—but it will take our security to the next level. I'll write about it in a future edition of this book.

# Index

## Symbols

0/n split, 195
1/n-1 split, 195
3DES, 246

## A

Abstract Syntax Notation One (see ASN.1)
Active network attack (see MITM)
Advanced Encryption Standard, 9
AEAD (see Authenticated encryption)
AES, 276 (see Advanced Encryption Standard)
AIA (see Authority Information Access)
Alert protocol, 47
Alice and Bob, 5
ALPN, **53**, 57
ANSSI, 110
Apache httpd, 381-407
Apple, 153
application_layer_protocol_negotiation extension, 53
Application data protocol, 47
Application Layer Protocol Negotiation (see ALPN)
ARP spoofing, 19
ASN.1, **67**, 157
ASP.NET, 466
Asymmetric encryption, 12
Authenticated encryption, 44
Authority Information Access, 351
Authority Information Access certificate extension, **70**, 76
Authority Key Identifier certificate extension, 70

## B

Baseline Requirements, 66
Basic Constraints, **69**, 94, 152, 153, 350
    Certificate extension, 69

Basic Encoding Rules (see BER)
BEAST, **191-201**, 249
    Testing, 375
    Versus Lucky 13 and RC4, 223
BER, 67
BGP route hijacking, 20
Bit (see Cryptography strength)
BlackSheep tool, 113
Black Tulip, 99
Block ciphers, 8
    In TLS, 43
    Modes of operation, 11
Brainpool elliptic curves, 54
BREACH, **207**, 251
Bullrun, 232

## C

CA (see Certification authority)
CA/Browser Forum, 66
CAA (see Certification Authority Authorization)
Captive portals, 148
CBC, 11
    (see also Block ciphers)
    In TLS, 43
    Padding attacks, 215
    Predictable IV, 192
CCM, 44
Certificate, 66-72
    Chains, 71
    Conversion, 330
    Exceptions, 130
    Extensions, 68
    Fields, 67
    Intermediary certificates, 71
    Lifecycle, 74
    Multiple hostnames, 239
    Optimization, 270
    Revocation, **141-149**, 76, 78
    Self-signed, 243

CPSIA information can be obtained at www.ICGtesting.com
Printed in the USA
BVOW08s1344140615

404093BV00005B/32/P